KING
IN EXILE

JAMES II: WARRIOR, KING
AND SAINT, 1689–1701

John Callow

SUTTON PUBLISHING

First published in the United Kingdom in 2004 by
Sutton Publishing Limited · Phoenix Mill
Thrupp · Stroud · Gloucestershire · GL5 2BU

British Library Cataloguing in Publication Data
A catalogue record for this book is available from the British Library.

ISBN 0-7509-3082-9

Typeset in 10/12 pt Baskerville.
Typesetting and origination by
Sutton Publishing Limited.
Printed and bound in England by
J.H. Haynes & Co. Ltd, Sparkford.

Contents

List of Illustrations

MAPS

These have been drawn by Derek Stone.

Acknowledgements

Books simply do not happen by themselves. Indeed, they are every bit as much the product of the interest, advice, and material assistance of others, as they are the sum of the inspiration and hard work of their authors. Consequently, my heartfelt thanks are extended to Professor Eric Evans, my mentor at Lancaster University, whose keen interest, sharp intellect and unfailing good counsel has acted as a constant point of reference, and as a beacon to guide all of my researches. Similarly, my thanks go out to Professor Michael Mullett – a fellow biographer of that most difficult and obstinate of kings – whose warmth and generosity of spirit provided the basis for many wonderful conversations about the character and convictions of James II, and who shared my excitement in exploring the forgotten landscape of Recusant and Jacobite Lancashire. To Professor Ronald Hutton, of the University of Bristol – the most original, exacting, and inspirational of scholars of seventeenth-century politics and popular culture – go my profound respects and deep gratitude for all of his interest, enthusiasm, and help. I would also like to thank Dr David Margolies, my friend and colleague at Goldsmiths College, University of London, who embodies all that is best in that institution, and Professor John Miller, of Queen Mary's College, University of London, who provided the initial encouragement over coffee at the Institute of Historical Research some three years ago.

I owe an enormous debt of gratitude to the understanding, patience, and perceptive comments of Christopher Feeney, Senior Commissioning Editor at Sutton Publishing, who believed in this book and made its realisation possible. I am likewise grateful for the help of Jane Entrican, Assistant Editor, and all of the production staff at Sutton.

To Derek Stone, who drew the wonderful maps, at short notice but with great care, thought, and diligence, I offer both my appreciation and thanks. With regard to the other illustrations, I have made every effort to trace the copyright holders. In a few cases this has not been possible, and for this I apologise.

My research was made possible by the help of the staff at the following archives: the British Library, London; the Bodleian Library, Oxford; Trinity College Dublin, the Royal Archives at Windsor Castle; and the National Archives at Kew. Particular thanks are due to David Knight, Archivist, and to Richard Dean, Historic Buildings Representative, the National Trust, at Sizergh Castle, Cumbria.

viii ACKNOWLEDGEMENTS

On a more personal level, thanks are also due to Tish, Mary and Tina who helped more than they knew, at just the right moment, and to Sheelagh MacDonald, who I hope will like this book and will find in it the fulfilment of a long-held ambition. To Harvey Osborne and Debbie Hodson, who accompanied me on the long road from undergraduate to postgraduate studies; I consider myself extremely fortunate to have such splendid, faithful and thoroughly supportive friends. Last, but far from least, come Mum and Dad who could not possibly have shown me any more love, or done any more to sustain me: Si monumentum requiris circumspice.

John Callow

A Note on Dating

Although many European nations had adopted the Gregorian Calendar over the course of the seventeenth century, the British and Irish remained stubbornly loyal to the Julian Calendar until 1752. The result was that their calendars lagged some ten days behind that which was generally used on the Continent: and by 1700 this difference had further increased to eleven days.

To add to this confusion, however, the days of the week on either side of the Channel were reckoned to be exactly the same. Understandably, this presents some particular difficulties for the historian, especially as it renders certain key dates in the calendar – Christmas, Easter and saints' days – of great significance for their celebration on one side of the Channel, but of absolutely no account on the other. In this manner it might be possible for a writer to describe Christmas Day 1688 as having actually been celebrated in the British Isles on 5 January 1689, if only the New Style – European – Calendar was employed throughout the text!

Consequently, the dating given relates to the setting of the events described with a single date given to denote action in the British Isles or Ireland, while both dates – or a simple abbreviation denoting the New Style dating – are provided for occurrences in Western Europe. As in modern usage, the new year is taken as beginning on 1 January and not 25 March.

Abbreviations

Ailesbury	T. Bruce, Earl of Ailesbury, *Memoirs of Thomas, Earl of Ailesbury*, 2 vols (Westminster, 1890)
Berwick	J. Fitzjames, Duke of Berwick, *Memoirs of the Marshal Duke of Berwick. Written by himself*, ed. C.L. Montesquieu, 2 vols (London, 1779)
Burnet	G. Burnet, *History of His Own Time*, ed. M.J. Routh, 2nd edition, 6 vols (Oxford, 1833)
CSPD	*Calendar of States Papers Domestic*
Dangeau	J. Davenport (ed. & trans.), *Memoirs of the Court of France . . . From the Diary of the Marquis de Dangeau*, 2 vols (London, 1825)
Devotions	G. Davies (ed.), *Papers of Devotion of James II* (Oxford, 1925)
DNB	*Dictionary of National Biography*
Evelyn's Diary	W. Bray (ed.), *Diary and Correspondence of John Evelyn*, 4 vols (London, 1850–2)
Hyde Correspondence	S. Weller Singer (ed.), *The Correspondence of Henry Hyde, Earl of Clarendon and of his Brother Lawrence Hyde, Earl of Rochester*, 2 vols (London, 1828)
JSAHR	*Journal of the Society for Army Historical Research*
Letters of Madame	G.S. Stevenson (ed. & trans.), *The Letters of Madame. The Correspondence of Elizabeth-Charlotte of Bavaria, Princess Palatine, Duchess of Orléans*, 2 vols (London, 1924)
Life	J.S. Clarke (ed.), *The Life of James the Second, King of England, Memoirs Collected out of Writ of his Own Hand, together with the King's Advice to his Son, and His Majesty's Will*, 2 vols (London, 1816)
Marchioness de Sévigné	A.M.F. Duclaux (ed. & trans.), *Letters of the Marchioness de Sévigné*, 10 vols (London, 1927)

CHAPTER ONE

Revolution

They came by night. The rain did little to muffle the sound of massed drums as the Dutch Guards bore down upon Whitehall. They hardly broke step as they crossed Hyde Park, colours unfurled, their progress now revealed to anxious civilians only by the hundreds of bright burning sparks thrown upwards from the tips of slow-matches lit in readiness for battle. From his window, the Imperial Ambassador Philip Hoffman watched their coming and made note of it for his master, while at St James's Palace the alarm was sounded and English soldiers were called out to bar the way. The elderly Earl of Craven, veteran of a hundred different fights from the Low Countries to Germany and England's own civil wars, barked out words of stern command and hurriedly dressed the ranks of his Coldstreamers, reinforcing the guard posts and strongpoints that linked together the royal palaces, even as the Dutch troops cleared the tree-line and advanced to within fifteen paces of his own men. Yet, as anxious soldiers took aim and prepared for the shock of action, the Dutch suddenly stopped short and the voice of their commander, Hendrik, Count Solms rang out demanding immediate admittance to Whitehall Palace and an audience with the King who sheltered within.[1]

During the past weeks, there could have been few emotions that James Stuart, King 'by Grace of God' of England, Scotland and Ireland, had not come to experience. Confronted by an invading army led by his own son-in-law, William, Prince of Orange; deserted by a great swathe of his general officers and by many of those councillors whom he felt had owed him the most; he had chosen, on 10 December 1688, to surrender his army and flee into exile rather than to attempt to shore up his tottering regime. As risings flared up against his rule in the north and in the Midlands, he had burned the writs for a general election before escaping across the Thames and casting the Great Seal into the waves. If these moves had been calculated to utterly disable the executive, to prevent the calling of a fresh parliament in his absence and to reduce the administration of the three kingdoms to a state of utter ruin in his wake, then they failed, through a combination of misjudgement and sheer bad luck, in all but the creation of chaos upon the streets and a palpable sense of fear which pervaded every corner of his lands. James had not counted on either the willingness of his opponents to ignore the extent of the royal prerogative, as he himself had conceived of it, or on the persistence and potency of their calls for the convening of a new and 'free parliament'. Moreover, he had reckoned without the vigilance of a gang of Kentish fishermen who mistook him for a fleeing priest and seized him near the coast at Faversham, abruptly ending his plans for a quick and easy flight from the impending collapse of governance that he had helped to precipitate. Writing later, Bishop Burnet would emphasise the importance of this particular incident for James's subsequent career and would lament sadly that: 'if he had got clear away, by all that could be judged, he would not have had a party left: all would have agreed, that here was a desertion . . . But what followed upon this gave them [i.e. his supporters] a colour to say, that he was forced away, driven out . . . [and] from this incident a party grew up, that has been long very active for his interests'.[2] Herein would lie the genesis of Jacobitism, but for the moment, however, the King had the indignity of being roundly cursed by his captors, of having his pockets rifled, his money stolen and his treasured piece of the 'true cross' prised out of his ornate crucifix and thrown away.[3] While rumours reached the French court that James had disappeared, been seized by the Prince of Orange, or been drowned out at sea, he was sent back to London to experience at first hand the breakdown of law, order and authority for which he himself in large measure had been responsible.

In the absence of the King, the capital had been convulsed by two nights of rioting and looting. Roman Catholic chapels and the houses of known 'papists' and foreign ambassadors had been targeted by the mob, and the King's printing press had been smashed and burnt. Lord Chancellor Jeffreys, abandoned by his sovereign lord and unable to secure a passage to Hamburg aboard a collier's brig, had been taken in the upstairs room of a tavern at Wapping, and though his face had been blackened with soot and his distinctive eyebrows shaved in an attempt at disguise, he had still been recognised. It was only with some difficulty that he was saved by soldiers from a lynching, before being safely conveyed to the Tower, with the crowds crying out behind him that as he had shown no mercy to those who had come before him at the Western Assizes, so now he should expect none for himself.[4] More serious still, the order to disband the royal army at Uxbridge had left some 4,000 confused and leaderless, but heavily armed, men to seek whatever sustenance they could from scouring the surrounding countryside. While some units retained their coherence and marched off to swell the ranks of William's advancing army, many of the soldiers suddenly found themselves bound together only by the bonds of religion and nation, now that their oath of loyalty to their King had effectively been absolved. Militant Protestants headed for London and joined with the apprentice boys in the search for Jesuits and in the firing of 'popish' chapels, while hundreds of Irish

Catholic soldiers – who just the day before had been numbered among their comrades, if not perhaps their friends – were left stranded far from home, the objects of almost universal suspicion and hatred. Reports on the movements of this latter group (who were desperate to secure a safe passage home), combined with fears of a general rising in Ireland, led to rumours that multiplied like wildfire of King James's unleashing of a vengeful Irish army upon his English subjects, and of outrages committed by them as far apart as Wigan, Birmingham, and Halifax. The Common Council in London hastily called out the militia and sanctioned the deployment of artillery at key points throughout the city and Westminster, while throughout the long 'Irish night' of 12 December, frightened citizens barred their doors and stockpiled arms in full expectation that a new St Bartholomew's Day Massacre was about to be visited upon them. Though the dawn came without any serious incident, and the majority of the Irish soldiers had by now split up into small groups hurrying as best they could along back roads towards the relative safety of north-western ports, the council still thought fit, on 14 December, to promise to pay them in full the wages owing them 'till they are employed or provided for', on the condition that they would promise to behave 'peaceably' and safely deliver up all of their weapons to the Tower of London. If not, they were warned in no uncertain terms that they were liable to be apprehended and dealt with by the local authorities, under common law and the vagrancy acts, as though they were no more than roving bands of cutpurses, paupers and vagabonds.[5]

Thus, although it was with some trepidation that King James began his journey back to his capital on 15 December, there was considerable relief in the minds of many of the populace at the thought of his coming. After days of fear, arbitrary violence and barely contained mob rule, the return of the King seemed to hold out the promise of a swift accommodation with the lords and with the Prince of Orange, and of a resumption of public order and political legitimacy without recourse to a bloody and protracted civil war. Consequently, even though James had slipped away from his capital barely four nights before like a thief in the night, his return now took on something of the aspect of a triumphal progress. Country gentlemen began to attach themselves to his escort on the road from Kent, and at Dartford, on the morning of Sunday 16 December, as his original detachment of Life Guards was replaced by fresh troopers, he was acclaimed and cheered on by the men with wild expressions of joy. At Blackheath, it seemed for a moment as though the city itself was emptying in order to welcome him home. Londoners thronged the road and jostled for position behind his official retinue. Bonfires were lit and bells sounded as the crowds pressed so tight that the cavalcade could scarcely pass, and two prominent merchants made so bold as to thrust their heads into the royal coach in order to counsel a sudden change of plan. Barges already waited for the King at Lambeth, to carry him straight back to Whitehall, but it was now argued that it would be more fitting if he were to drive back through the city and show himself to his expectant subjects, who – in their eagerness to catch the least glimpse of their sovereign – hung from every available window and balcony, and lined the route from Southwark through Fleet Street and the Strand up to the very gates of his palace. Yet if James expressed himself 'hugely surprised with the unexpected testimonys of the peoples affection to him', he chose only to remember that up until that moment the capital, once the bastion of the Exclusionists who had attempted to block his path to the throne, had never shown him any lasting or particular affection.[6] He did not now seek to recreate the scenes that had greeted the return of his brother in May 1660, or to play upon the potent and extremely popular mythologies that had grown up around the Restoration in the intervening years. Lacking the common touch, he made little attempt to capitalise on the spontaneous outpourings of loyalist sentiment that greeted him, did not think to abandon his coach in favour of horseback and chose neither to address his subjects nor to grasp at the hands that waved with such persistence at his window as he passed them by. Indeed, it was fear and the need to ensure his personal security, rather than the desire to seize control of the situation and re-establish his connection with the groundswell of Tory England, that now came to dominate his thoughts. News had already reached him that the companies of the First Foot Guards stationed at Whitehall had declared their allegiance to the Prince of Orange, and it was this knowledge that finally prompted him to give his grudging consent to the change in his proposed route. James flatly refused to be separated from his loyal escort, and realised that the cover afforded by the city crowds would render it difficult, if not impossible, to divorce him from his protective phalanx of Life Guards and Horse Grenadiers without the risk of serious disorder and bloodshed. Moreover, the Earl of Craven, who had devoted both his life and his considerable fortune to the support of the Stuart cause, was still quartered at the Royal Mews with several companies of his own Coldstream Guards. It mattered little now that in the first flush of his kingship, James had tried to wrest the Earl's commission away from him in order to bestow it upon one of his favourites. There had never been any doubt as to where Craven's loyalties lay, and as the King drew near to Whitehall, the pickets stationed there melted away and were replaced by the Coldstreamers who cleared a path for the easy passage of his coach through the still-swirling crowds, who cheered James back into his palace and on 'even to his Bed Chamber door'.[7]

Word that the King had returned to his capital amid scenes of genuine popular acclaim was brought to the Prince of Orange at Windsor Castle that evening, and could not have been more unwelcome. Since the mass defections which had swept the royal army on Salisbury Plain in late November, turning his opportunistic raid into a serious bid for lasting control of English foreign policy, he had enjoyed an unbroken run of successes. He had continually consolidated his position, conducting a stately progress through the West Country before thrusting out with a cavalry screen down the length of the Thames Valley in preparation for a final victorious drive on the capital. This was now threatened, as the self-appointed band of peers who had sat at the Guildhall since James's flight – and who had been negotiating terms with William for the summoning of a 'free parliament' and the quartering of his troops in London – were now found to be responsible for dispatching the Earl of Ailesbury to treat with the King, and for countenancing the despatch of Feversham and the Life Guards to secure his person and bring him back from the coast. It was imperative, therefore, that James did not regain his capital and, if he was not to be permitted to escape immediately into exile, then at least he should be safely contained in the south, within convenient reach of the shores of France.

However, in the meantime, Feversham had roused himself from the lethargy that had so often served to cloud his military career in the past, rendezvoused with his beleaguered sovereign and set off on the return journey, riding hard for Windsor with neither 'Trumpet or passeport' and carrying a letter that had the power to frustrate all of the Prince of Orange's carefully laid plans.[8] This unexpected and wholly unwelcome communication, received by William on 16 December, now came to represent the most formidable obstacle to a smooth and almost seamless transition of power. James had written that he wished to meet face-to-face with his son-in-law at Whitehall, permitted him to bring as many troops as he felt fit for a bodyguard with him to the capital, and offered to put St James's Palace at his complete disposal for the duration of the talks. Faced with the prospect of James simply re-assuming his mantle of kingship, the confident talk among the Prince's Whig partisans of an already-effected 'abdication', and William's own hopes of securing the throne with the clear blessing of a majority of the English people, were suddenly put in jeopardy and appeared to be premature in the extreme. However, though a negotiated settlement might well have been acceptable to the Prince a month before, and certainly would have done much to dispel the fears of many Anglicans about the future of their Church, by the middle of December the stakes had been raised significantly. Having risked everything and come so close to a spectacular success, William was in no mood to compromise and return home, however favourable the terms might be, if his father-in-law were to retain the faintest hint of autonomy. Similarly, there was little appetite among any of the lords who sat as a shadow government at the Guildhall, or among the radicalised tradesmen who had taken control of

Newcastle, Nottingham, York and Bristol, and the common soldiery who
had grounded their weapons after the debacle on Salisbury Plain and
readily taken up the boisterous refrain of 'Lilliburlero', to have to face
the rejuvenated power of their monarch or possible charges of high
treason. These very different and shifting constituencies now looked to
the Prince of Orange for a lead. A lesser politician might well have
hesitated, but William's statecraft – his consummate ability to sense
exactly when to shift from tact and diplomacy to a sudden devastating
show of force – now asserted itself. Having heard Feversham out, and
read the King's letter, he gave no reply but ensured that the luckless
peer was forced to surrender his sword and placed under arrest the very
moment that he left his presence. Without waiting for further word
from the Guildhall, William prepared his forces for a push on to
London and dispatched one of his most trusted emissaries, Willem
Zuylestein, to seek out James in order to advise him to come no closer
to the capital than Rochester.[9] For once, however, it was James's luck
that held good and Zuylestein, advised only of the King's original
schedule, spent a wasted afternoon at Lambeth waiting patiently for the
arrival of the royal party beside the empty barges, completely unaware
of the intervention of the two London merchants and the resulting
change of itinerary.

Thus, while William's message went undelivered, James's servants
began to sweep out the grates in his palace and light the fires in order to
take the edge off winter's chill. After experiencing such turmoil,
profound personal danger and so many bitter reverses, it is unsurprising
that the King should have been weary that night, or that he slept soundly
with the dust of the city still on his clothes. What is remarkable is that,
after he had so unexpectedly regained control of the capital, he should
have spent the afternoon and evening following his return in an attempt
to resume his office as though nothing at all out of the ordinary had
occurred since his hurried departure the previous Monday night.
Protocol had to be observed, as evidenced by his interruption of his
journey at Somerset House to pay his respects to Catherine of Braganza,
the dowager Queen, or when, with some understandable embarrassment,
Lord Chamberlain Mulgrave resumed his duties at the head of the royal
household despite having broken his wand of office, to signify the end of
the reign, not six nights before. There was simply no discernible sense of
pressing haste in either the King's movements or his judgements once he
had finally managed to alight from his coach at the Banqueting House.
What did appear to matter to James, however, was maintaining the
practice and dignity of his God-given office as King. Craven's men, having
secured the palace, were set to work vetting a representative sample of
the city's poor and sick before they were ushered in to be touched by
James for the 'King's Evil'.

In the meantime, a handful of courtiers had returned to their master's side, enabling James to reconvene the sitting of the Privy Council. Though the French Ambassador thought that the King still longed to be gone, there was certainly an attempt by all present to maintain the fiction that all was well and to underscore both the permanence of the body's existence and the seriousness of its deliberations. The meeting was formally minuted, as James had a proclamation drafted forbidding rioting and looting, and appealed to the local authorities to restore order. He also consciously reached out to those of his servants who had never failed him, and directed Samuel Pepys to do all he could to open up the traffic through the seaports and to reinvigorate the flow of foreign trade, which had dried to all but a trickle amid the fears of invasion and war. Yet if Pepys remained at his desk in the Navy Office and loyalists such as Craven still held their lord lieutenancies in the counties, they were increasingly isolated figures, who held the form of title without possessing the power or wherewithal to effectively carry out their duties. At the beginning of the month it had still been possible for Pepys to authorise the dispatch of one of the royal yachts to spirit away the Queen and the Prince of Wales to France. Now, with the navy almost entirely defected to the Prince of Orange, many of his staff absenting themselves from work, and the great ports in the hands of the insurgents, the command to restore the entire trade of the nation carried authority scarcely further than the threshold of his office door. Similarly, though Craven still theoretically commanded the militia in Middlesex, his three thin companies of the Coldstream Guards, spread out across the two royal palaces and the length of the Mall, could just be said to be in control of Westminster, but not of the city, and still less the outlying royal dockyards. The Tower of London, where an ailing Jeffreys still anxiously awaited his fate, was in rebel hands, while the docks and Tilbury Fort were firmly under the control of William's men. Consequently, when Zuylestein finally arrived at Whitehall and presented his redundant order to James, not to venture back to a capital that he had already occupied, the Dutchman found himself in a stronger and more useful position than might otherwise have been the case. It was his own master who was making all the demands, urging the King of England to be gone and to no longer risk fresh disturbances of the peace, while James had slipped all too easily into the role of the supplicant, pleading for an audience with William, almost at the latter's own convenience. Moreover, Zuylestein had had the wit, and sense of theatre, to turn a mission apparently rendered pointless by unexpected events to good, and possibly even devastating, account. He said nothing in his interview with the King about the arrest of Lord Feversham, but allowed that shocking intelligence to be delivered to James a few minutes after his withdrawal. The seizure of his messenger might well have called for a retaliatory

action against William's own man, but James thought fit to permit
Zuylestein to return unmolested through his lines, bearing only a
reiteration of the King's earlier offer for peace talks at St James's. That
William's treatment of his servant, or his profound silence on the subject
of a negotiated settlement, already appeared to be answer enough, did
not seem to have occurred to James as he arranged for Zuylestein's safe
conduct back to Windsor. Relieved of the threat to his person, the
courier made use of the time remaining to him at Whitehall, in the
manner of any good officer of dragoons, by taking careful note of
the strength and dispositions of the royal guards, and left James to
absorb, in private, the full force of the threat signalled by Feversham's
seemingly arbitrary imprisonment.[10]

Despite the Irish scare, it was the city's small but influential Roman
Catholic minority that had suffered the worst from the King's absence.
On the approach of invasion, many members of the religious orders had
begun to change out of their habits and to slip from public sight, while
James's former confessor and member of the Privy Council, Father Petre,
wasted little time in finding a pretext to attach himself to the embassy
sent out to Paris at the close of November. However, for those lay
members of the faith who had not the opportunity, the means or the
inclination to flee from their homeland, the nights of 10–11 December
must have been nothing short of terrifying, as bands of their fellow
citizens – often every bit as frightened and jumpy as they – swept through
the streets on the look-out for 'papists' and Jesuit priests, manhandling
suspects, forcing their way into homes and administering their own
brand of random, and inevitably rough, justice. While the spines of
books culled from the Spanish Ambassador's sumptuous library crackled
and spat in fires by the roadside, families of distraught English Catholics
were observed bundling up their possessions and wheeling them from
house to house, calling to friends for succour, and praying that the
Prince of Orange might come to save their property and restore some
semblance of order to their shattered lives. The reappearance of James
in the capital on the evening of 16 December unsurprisingly aroused
exactly the same sort of hopes and expectations, and many ordinary
Catholics, together with those priests, monks and nuns who had spent
many of the last weeks in hiding, understandably gravitated towards
Whitehall in search of much-needed aid and protection. Unfortunately,
such scenes merely served to confirm the worst nightmares of their
Protestant neighbours, of a priest-ridden court and of a King who was
merely the servant of the Pope, utterly enthralled and corrupted by the
agents of foreign powers. Sadly, James's own conduct did little to help
matters. With some difficulty, his Privy Council – now numbering a mere
eight members, all of whom were Protestants – prevailed upon him not
to provoke matters any further with his rebellious subjects by ordering

the jails to be opened and all those Catholics arrested since Monday to be released. At dinner, it was noted that he was accompanied to the table by Dominican monks, while a Jesuit said grace, and at midnight he celebrated a private Mass, with only his Household priests in attendance. News of his particular devotions spread rapidly, as did many other scurrilous stories about the conduct of the Jesuits and Irishmen who had flocked to his side. Lord Mulgrave was supposedly shocked by the confidence, and utter extravagance, of one priest who asked him to buy in a completely new set of furniture for his rooms, as he intended to continue in them for a long while to come.[11] As a consequence, James's hurried promises to the four Anglican bishops who had rejected overtures from the peers lodged at the Guildhall in order to visit him, that he would undertake never again to employ Catholic advisors, rang more than a little hollow. Of more immediate concern to the King, however, was his inability to pay his followers. Although the Treasury Office would begin its business afresh on the following morning, there was little or no ready money to hand at Whitehall on his return. Consequently, James spent much of Sunday afternoon and evening attempting to extract loans from those courtiers who had ventured back to him. Despite the applause of the crowds outside, the lords and ladies present generally concluded that the King was a bad investment, and were not prepared to risk their fortunes in so foolhardy a service. Tellingly, this was also true of those like the aged Lord Belasyse, who had survived the worst of Oates's slanders during the Popish Plot and who had latterly served as a faithful councillor to, and moderating influence upon, his impetuous and headstrong sovereign. A request for £3,000 now appeared too much to ask even from this wealthy stalwart. Moreover, the King's demands for money may well have deterred many other nobles from attending court the next day, when the palace appeared to be far more sparsely populated than had been the case before.

On the morning of Monday 17 December, the Earl of Balcarres and John Graham of Claverhouse, fresh from Scotland, accompanied James on his regular constitutional walk down the Mall. Schooled in the hard fratricidal struggle against the Covenanters, both men argued that the King should now be preparing for the immediate outbreak of civil war, and that he should be out rallying his disbanded soldiers back to the colours, in anticipation of a pre-emptive strike. Caught up in the emotion of the moment, they promised far more from James's northern kingdom, and from his geographically dispersed and politically fragmented army, than they could ever have hoped to deliver. They would come back to him, they said, with thousands of loyal troops if only he would give the word for the full-scale resumption of hostilities. Yet James neither forbade them to raise his standard in the north, nor commanded them to take decisive action against his foes. Instead he thanked them for their faithfulness and sent them on their way with ambiguous commissions to watch over his civil and military affairs respectively in Scotland.[12] Otherwise, the talk at Whitehall that day was dry, and it was later claimed that following the desertion of his family and army command, James now 'suspected an enemy or a betrayer, and from every look he gathered reasons for confirming the suspicions he had formed. Distance or approach were equally uneasy to him, for he imputed the one to a consciousness of guilt, and the other to a desire for concealing it'. Yet this mattered little, as none of the great magnates at the Guildhall broke ranks and sought an accommodation with the King, and he, for his part, made no move against them.

As the hours ticked by, the initiative slipped slowly but surely from James's hands. The memory and the emotion generated by his return had begun to fade, and it was realised that the enthusiasm of the crowds for the spectacle of monarchy could not easily be turned into a solid or reliable political constituency. As no more shocking news filtered through to his command post, and as the streets of London were reported quiet, William's supporters began to recover their nerve, and the Prince detached three battalions of his crack Household troops under the command of Count Solms for a final surgical strike against the centre of English government. A pretext had already been found in an incident that had occurred several days before, as William's troops had marched through the capital en route for Tilbury, with the young Duke of Grafton, a prominent defector from James's regime and an illegitimate son of the last King, Charles II, at their head. On the Strand, a drunken Irish soldier – no one could agree, or remember afterwards, if he was an officer or one of the discharged soldiers – rode up to him, presented his pistol and gave fire. Though the bullet missed its mark, and the reckless Irishman was instantly shot down from his saddle by the men of the First Foot Guards, the notion that the assassination attempt had been born out of a deliberate plot rather than out of the sudden rage and murderous folly of one individual gained wide currency, and it was used by the Prince of Orange to justify both his refusal to go to St James's and his rejection of a meeting with the King in person. His safety could not be ensured, it was argued, until James's own guards were dismissed and the nest of 'Irish Papists, Priests and Jesuits' that had surrounded him at Whitehall were cleared out by force.[13]

Thus, at eleven o'clock at night, the heavy tramp of soldiers' feet was heard in Whitehall and the Dutch Blue Guards faced off against the men of the Coldstream regiment. James had already retired to his private chambers, but though Lord Ailesbury, who had been sent to fetch him, knew him still to be up and about, it was some time before the King responded to the polite tappings and scrapings at his closet door and came to the threshold, bidding his servant to enter. At this desperate moment, James remained calm, clinging to the belief that there had been a misunderstanding and that Solms's men were merely William's escort come to prepare the way for his arrival at St James's for talks. Outside, however, the Earl of Craven and his men were under no such illusions, as the Dutch prepared for the assault and as Count Solms lost his temper, cursing all and sundry and threatening to begin to storm at once if he were not shown into the King's presence. After anxious minutes of delay that saw young men on both sides shifting uneasily and cupping their hands over their firing pans in an attempt to keep the rain out of their powder, Ailesbury returned with orders for both commanders to accompany him back to the privy chamber. There, James was surprised to learn that Count Solms was under orders from the Prince of Orange to take possession not only of St James's Palace, but also of Somerset House, home of the dowager Queen, and of the whole complex of royal apartments that spread across Whitehall. The King's men were to surrender their posts and leave the capital, while James was instructed to place himself under the protective watch of the Dutch Guards. Such a sweeping ultimatum did little to overawe Craven, who declared that he knew the temper of his men and that all of them would fight to the end, if called upon, in order to preserve something of the honour of British arms. Indeed, as James began to waver, the Earl dropped to his knees and begged the King to allow him to make even the most token show of resistance. Such actions, as all who were present knew, were doomed to end in failure. The English were hopelessly outnumbered and, though they had a better knowledge of the terrain and the palace's labyrinthine corridors, Whitehall's rambling and predominantly medieval structures had never been designed for defence. Probably only the two gatehouses would have been able to withstand an attack for any length of time, as the old wooden galleries were particularly susceptible to fire, and the open courts and gardens offered many points for entry, but few natural choke points at which to concentrate effective resistance. Yet if Craven was prepared to countenance the spilling of his men's blood, and possibly his own, then there was more than simple pride and the hunger for glory behind his thinking. The outbreak of hostilities over control of the King's person would strike an entirely different and far more dramatic chord with his subjects than news of the scrappy and inconclusive skirmishes at Wincanton and Reading had ever done. A show of resistance still offered the opportunity to recast William's forces as foreign invaders, and to rally the sympathies of the nation behind a monarch whose life had been threatened as a direct result of the ambition of the Prince of Orange. Moreover, if the need arose, gun smoke in Whitehall might serve to mask another sudden precipitate royal flight. However, such considerations failed to move James. The laudable desire to preserve the lives of his soldiers may be thought, considering his later comments, to have weighed less heavily on his mind than his utter failure to comprehend all that was happening about him and to recognise the grim resolve of his rival to remove him from the sinews of power once and for all. He repeated again his offer of talks at St James's and then asked that he might be permitted to keep his soldiers for just one more night. However, when faced with Solms's blunt ultimatum to surrender, he ignored Craven's increasingly desperate pleas and capitulated, without ever attempting to secure terms either for himself or for his men, and glumly commanded the Dutchman to 'do your office'.[14] While the King remained in his rooms, declining to show himself to his men for one last time or to give them a parting word of cheer, it was left to Craven to relay the unwelcome news and to stand down the royal guards. Solms, having performed his duty, would – though pressed – say nothing more to the King and his servants about his master's future intentions, and busied himself with supervising the dispositions of his own troops. James tried to shrug off suggestions that he was in danger from his new guards, declaring that given the desertions from his regular army, and the refusal of the militia to come out and fight, he 'knew not whether those or his own [soldiers] were wors[e]'.[15] To the huddles of damp, frightened guardsmen and their little General, who only minutes before had been prepared to lay down their lives for their King, this might have seemed small reward indeed for such selfless devotion. Yet there was nothing more that they could do. By midnight the Dutch were in complete control of Whitehall, taking over all the guard posts from the English soldiers, whom they disarmed and 'treated like a pack of rogues', while to the horror of courtiers, double sentries were placed at the bottom of the monarch's private staircase.[16]

   A King now in nought but name, James II returned to the comfort of his four-poster and gave himself completely up to sleep, while the Earl of Ailesbury fretted fitfully beneath the covers on a little trestle bed at his feet. It was not long, however, before James's slumbers and Ailesbury's peace of mind were both further disturbed, by the unexpected appearance of the King's Secretary of State, the Earl of Middleton, in the early hours of the morning. By torchlight, James was awakened and told that three rebel lords, who had followed in the wake of Solms's troops, were asking for an urgent audience with him. Having duly given his consent, James propped himself up on his pillows and listened as Halifax, Shrewsbury and Delamere delivered, albeit in respectful tones, an apology for coming at such an 'unseasonable' hour that was closely followed by a fresh ultimatum. James was to leave London for Ham House, near Richmond in Surrey, and was to be packed and gone by nine o'clock the next morning, as the Prince of Orange desired to be in the capital by twelve. The King accepted without argument, but after they had gone, suddenly changed his mind and had the lords recalled, objecting to their choice of his destination. In winter, he said, Ham was a cold and damp place, and moreover, it was unfurnished now that its owner, the Duchess of Lauderdale, was in Scotland. As the alternative, he suggested that he should take up residence in Rochester, and was pleased when the lords seemed to acquiesce in this idea all too readily, promising to relay it to their master for final confirmation.[17] It is not hard to see why they acted as they did, as for once James's desires neatly mirrored William's own plans for him, as confided to Zuylestein. More than twice the distance from London as Ham, and situated far to the east near the mouth of the River Medway, Rochester offered the immediate prospect of isolating the King from the political nation, and the medium to long-term opportunity for James to make use of its ideal location to effect his escape to France with as little noise and difficulty as possible.

Consequently, William's permission for the move was not slow in coming, and by eight o'clock in the morning his messenger had urged his horse back through Whitehall's Great Gate, to deliver the orders for James's removal to Rochester, as requested. This time, however, the King was not, under any circumstances, to be permitted the luxury of riding out through the city and of possibly reawakening the powerful sympathies of his subjects at his sorry plight. The Prince of Orange had made it clear that there was to be no repeat of Sunday's popular acclamation, and no opportunity was to be afforded for riots to break out in support of the fallen King. However, these pre-conditions, and James's own tardiness in leaving Whitehall Palace on time, were to combine to provide the surest, yet least predictable, threat to the King's life that he was to experience during the entire course of the Revolution. In staying to say a protracted goodbye to his courtiers and the foreign ambassadors, he missed the turn of the tide, and at London Bridge his barge was forced to shoot the rapids, risking all on board in the desperate attempt to have him out of both reach and mind before the Prince arrived to finally take possession of St James's. While Ailesbury clung to the sides of the barge and prayed hard for deliverance, a dozen oarsmen fought against the torrents that grabbed at them and threatened to submerge their craft underneath the piers of the bridge, before at last thankfully pulling clear into the calmer waters of the Upper Pool. Whether the result of an impressive display of regal self-control, or as the manifestation of that particular brand of paralysis which had all too often overcome him at particular moments of crisis in the past, James remained impassive throughout, saying and doing nothing as the royal barge pitched and rolled under the pounding of the waves. Drenched and thoroughly exhausted, his party limped down the Thames, surrounded by boatloads of Dutch soldiers, and presenting but 'a sad sight' to the handful of spectators who had turned out in the drizzle and high winds to watch the passing of their now captive King.[18]

Heartened by the skills of his cook and accompanied by the grumblings of John Adams, his coachman, who issued 'bloody oaths' against Fr Petre, without whom he felt 'we had not been here', James at last reached Rochester, after spending the night at Gravesend. He took up residence in the High Street, at the house of Sir Richard Head, the city's former Mayor and MP.[19] He was to spend six days there, at the heart of the town and in the shadow of the cathedral, but although he continued to receive visitors and packets of mail from his supporters, his thoughts turned once more to flight. There can be no doubt that he was in terror for his life. Revolution for him spelled the rule of fanatics, sectarians and king-killers, who would stop at nothing to dissolve the bonds of civil society and bring the land to irreligion, disorder and ruin. On the road from Faversham to London, he had already talked excitedly about his belief that the Prince of Orange would have him tried and executed, and was quick to repeat these fears to Fr Rizzini, whom he met at Gravesend, concluding that it 'was a weak and Childish immagination to think that he, who was so ready to usurpe upon the rights of an Uncle, Brother, Father, and Wife' could ever again be trusted.[20] Certainly, the demands for a parliamentary enquiry into the circumstances of his son's birth, with a view to barring him from the throne, and the raking over of every aspect of the King and Queen's private lives for public consumption, had sent out a clear signal to James that he would be held accountable by his subjects for his past actions, and found wanting. If the Prince of Wales was to be judged a suppositious royal infant, the son of a miller who had been foisted, cuckoo-like, upon the English people with the connivance of the Queen, Fr Petre and the Jesuit Order, then it was but a small step to dispensing with the royal prerogative altogether, reducing the King to a cipher and figure of fun at best, and at worst condemning him to the ignominy of the short journey through Traitor's Gate to the scaffold. 'I shall certainly be sent to the Tower', he told Ailesbury, 'and no King ever went out of that place but to his grave'.[21] William allowed a letter from the Queen to reach him, which begged him to keep his parting promise to hurry to join her and their baby son at the first available opportunity, and which seems to have confirmed James in his resolve to mount a fresh escape attempt. With a view to flying to France, he had left instructions to members of his Household to remove his valuables from Whitehall, and to secure his share portfolios, so that eventually they might be sent on to him at his chosen place of exile.[22]

Such barely disguised schemes, however, struck many of his followers as a supreme folly that threatened to ruin them all. Francis Turner, Bishop of Ely and Henry Hyde, the 2nd Earl of Clarendon both sent envoys to the King to beg him to reconsider his plans. Indeed, Hyde had duly noted that 'the manner of his being driven . . . from Whitehall, with such circumstances, moved compassion even in those who were not very fond of him' and that 'Several of the English army, both officers and soldiers, began to murmur' at his treatment.[23] If James were to remain in the country, then both William of Orange and his wife, Mary, would be placed in an embarrassing and possibly untenable position in the long term. The idea that a daughter might act as gaoler to her father, or that a foreign prince might continue to humble the King of England, was deeply disturbing to a society rooted in patriarchy and steeped in the patriotic myths of nationhood. Moreover, William's own polyglot army could not be maintained permanently as a garrison in the British Isles, and while he would continue as the Prince of Orange, or at best accept a 'Protectorship' from parliament as a form of regency over his disabled father-in-law, James would remain for the foreseeable future as the anointed King. The spectre of a show trial might well have haunted James's every waking moment, as he paced about his cramped lodgings at Rochester, but it was not an expedient that William could ever have seriously countenanced without shattering his alliances with the Catholic crowned heads of Europe, and exposing himself – and more significantly his wife – to general odium as patricides, pseudo-republicans and the destroyers of the fabric of civil society. If he had come to England in order to bolster his war effort against Louis XIV's France, and to preserve both his wife's claim to the succession and the established network of alliances between the Anglican Church and State, then the destruction of the hereditary principle and the royal prerogative would hardly have been the best way to go about achieving these aims. Similarly, given that every 30 January the Church of England held, by law, services of national atonement for the death of the 'martyr' King, Charles I, the last thing that William now wanted was the blood of James II dripping from his hands. The problem of what to do with the captive sovereign was something that had already provoked much argument and discord among those lords who had gathered about him at Windsor and Sion. An appeal by Clarendon to permit James to return to Hampton Court had been shouted down, while there was strong support for a proposal to whisk the King away to a prison cell in the fortress of Breda, until such time as a definitive settlement could be reached with an English parliament. William, however, had little appetite for holding James as a Dutch hostage, and preferred to make flight as easy and as attractive an option as possible. To this end, he filtered the royal correspondence of those enjoinders to stay and fight for the throne, while allowing any letter that smacked of defeat and dismay to reach the attention of the King.[24] The guard placed about James at Rochester, in large measure drawn purposely from among the Roman Catholic soldiers in the Dutch army, was ordered to show the prisoner every courtesy and to make no more than the merest pretence of keeping a watch over him. To make matters easier, William even went so far as to issue blank passports enabling the holders to leave England at will, with few questions asked, and ensured that they found their way swiftly to James and his attendants, via the capable hands of the King's natural son, the Duke of Berwick.

The return of the King, and his enduring presence at Rochester, threatened to thoroughly destabilise any attempt at a constitutional settlement. The sudden and unpredictable alliances forged between Whig and Tory, and Low and High churchmen, in order to bring about the total collapse of his regime now appeared to be fragile and already strained, as the peers assembled at the Guildhall attempted to explain away their decision to assume power in the realm, and to justify their claims that they had done no more than articulate the true desires of the English people and enter into negotiations on their behalf. Such claims to political legitimacy had seemed well-founded just a few days before, given the void left by the King's flight from London. However, with James under house arrest at Rochester, it was going to be increasingly difficult to maintain the fiction that he had voluntarily renounced his kingship and all his public offices. As a hard frost gripped the land, one Lancastrian gentleman confided to his diary that now 'its doubted whether the king will leave the Kingdome', while loyalists, who had been overwhelmed by recent events, began to rally and to take heart.[25] The local gentry had turned out to welcome James back through Rochester's crumbling walls, and close behind came word that William Sancroft, the Archbishop of Canterbury, had ignored the Prince's overtures of friendship and refused to wait upon him at St James's Palace. While James remained King and supreme governor of the Church of England, Anglican clergymen across the land were still compelled to pray for, and preach loyalty to, his person. Indeed, Sancroft and several of the bishops appealed to him 'not to go out of England but keep himSelf private in the Town or Country' until such time as the opposition exhausted itself, and those disparate groups of Whigs and Tories who had embraced William's cause fractured the revolutionary consensus, and lapsed once more into mutual recrimination, rivalry and factional fighting.[26] To outside observers, it seemed that James was in a relatively strong negotiating position and that time was most definitely on his side. The French army would not remain inactive forever on the banks of the Rhine, and the advent of a new campaigning season would surely necessitate William's departure from England during the spring months, in order to help defend the United Provinces from attack. With reliable intelligence reports arriving daily of 'how matters went in Town' and with many among the Anglican hierarchy threatening to fight a protracted rearguard action against any attempt to impose constraints upon the King or to alter the succession, James was by no means in the helpless position that he claimed.[27] Barrillon, the French Ambassador, had attempted to coordinate – with some success – the embryonic resistance to William in the capital, until he was expelled by the order of the Prince; and the arrival of Peter Mew, the indomitable Bishop of Winchester, had served to harden the resolve of many of the King's followers against another attempted escape. Only three years before, it had been the Bishop who had used his own coach-horses to drag the royal artillery through the mud to firing positions at the battle of Sedgemoor; now he counselled calm and thoughtful measures in order to salvage all that they could from among the wreckage of James II's personal monarchy. While Secretary Middleton told the King in no uncertain terms, 'that if his Majesty went out of the Kingdom, the door would immediately be shut upon him', the Bishop and Dr Brady, James's own physician, 'press'd him to stay . . . with Hopes that a Party would appear for him, good Terms be got, and things be brought to a reasonable Agreement'.[28] Yet James's overriding preoccupation with his own personal safety led him to make unrealistic demands upon his supporters, in the form of binding pre-conditions that they could never have possibly fulfilled, or even agreed to, with anything approaching a clear conscience. Thus, the King said that he would only endeavour to stay in England if Bishop Mew and those loyalists who still sat on the corporation of London would promise to personally guarantee his survival against the threat of assassination, and also against possible charges of treason. Once they had declined, on the grounds that they clearly lacked the ability to throw a ring of steel about his person, or to rescue him from his Dutch guards, James felt vindicated both in his fears and in his decision to flee the country. Matters were now out of his hands, he claimed. It was not he who had taken the decision to escape, but rather he had had flight forced upon him, by the abject failure of the Bishop and the city merchants to fully guarantee his safety. Having abnegated responsibility for his subsequent actions, James proceeded to arrange his escape, while still urging Middleton and Sancroft to press his case, with the utmost vigour, at a meeting of the peers which had been scheduled for Christmas Eve.

Though the themes were to be worked upon and refined over subsequent years, it is clear that even as the vessel was being chartered for the voyage to France, James had already done much to lay the foundations for Jacobitism, the ultra-royalist movement that was to bear his name, and to define the nature of his future role and persona within it. He was to stand for the dignity of monarchy in times of the greatest peril, and to cast himself as a man of sufferings, betrayed and vilified for his beliefs. Yet his part was also curiously passive and reflexive. The King stood above events, refusing to either shape or to be moulded by them, until finally forced to react to unfolding disaster with the sudden awareness of both the tragedy of his own position relative to it, and a deep, almost crippling, sense of resignation to forces that he felt – often wrongly – were far beyond his personal control and understanding. His fall from power also served to throw his own concept of authority, and his reaction to the operation of it, into particularly stark relief. From those under him, James continued to demand respect and total obedience, saving his particular scorn for those rebellious subjects who had, to his mind, inexplicably sought to overturn the natural, God-given order of society. Thus, he objected to the presence in his escort of Cornet Sayer, an Englishman whose family Charles II 'had raised . . . out of the kitchen' only for them to have 'turned ungrateful to the last degree', while welcoming the presence of professional soldiers who obeyed without question the Prince who paid their wages. Similarly, during his journey to Rochester he was moved to publicly rebuke the Earl of Arran for snapping at his Dutch guards, while repeatedly deferring to them himself.[29] In grave trouble, and without an immediate figure of authority to turn to – provided in the past by the presence of the 1st Earl of Clarendon or by his elder brother, Charles II – James was unprepared, or simply unable, to provide effective resistance to the demands levied upon him by William of Orange. Wrong-footed and undermined at almost every turn, he had chosen to capitulate each time rather than to stand firm when confronted by a seemingly superior force. Yet if the outer world was perilous and threatening, James preferred the safety of an inner world, whose strict discipline was guided by the authority of the Church of Rome. This knowledge was precisely what the King's former brother-in-law Henry Hyde feared the most, and in his desperate struggle to persuade his master to remain in England, he urged that 'some honest Roman Catholic' such as Mr Belson, 'a discreet . . . man, and one who never approved the foolish management of Father Peters [i.e. Petre]' might be sent, alongside the Anglican, Keightley, to wrest James from the gloomy influence of his would-be confessors.[30]

By the time these messengers reached Rochester, James's sprawling retinue had begun to take on something of the aspect of a little court. Correspondence from France, Spain and Italy was sorted, and promptly replied to, while stray notes and bills from merchants were re-sealed and forwarded on. It was noted that James slept and ate well, and that he delighted in the arrival of a sizeable number of his guards, each morning, to celebrate Mass alongside him. However, appearances were deceptive; the King had already resolved to flee and had contacted the Spanish Ambassador, Don Pedro Ronquillo, with a view to seeking refuge in Brussels. He knew the city well, having stayed there during his previous exiles in the 1650s and in 1679, and he appears to have considered it an ideal location from which to regain his crown. Unfortunately, this time the King of Spain expressed a marked reluctance to have him as one more unwelcome and impecunious guest drawing on his treasury and doing little more than stir up trouble in return. In an attempt to lessen the force of the blow, Ronquillo tactfully pointed out to James that with the war between France and Holland threatening to spill over its borders, the government of the Spanish Netherlands was simply unable, at the present, to fully guarantee his protection. If James could, therefore, expect nothing from Spain in the immediate future, then France continued to hold out the prospect of both a warm welcome and the sustained, forceful propagation of his cause. Furthermore, even though the King's demands for money had been largely ignored by the Treasury, which might have been forgiven for wondering just what he was planning to do with the £1,500 he had requested while at Rochester, the loans already secured before his expulsion from Whitehall had ensured that he could comfortably provide for his dependants and also advance the necessary monies needed in order to secure his passage to France.

Belson and Keightley thus found him at the Mayor's 'indifferent good house', surrounded by his papers and courtiers, in surprisingly high spirits and about to go in to supper. Though they pressed upon him that they brought important news from 'several of his old friends', James told them that he had letters to write that evening, but that he would make sure to see them, first thing, the very next morning. However, once he had retired into the tenuous privacy of his chamber, and the candles had been lit, James began work on a very different document from that envisaged by these expectant envoys. Word had already reached him that captains Trevanion and Macdonald had brought their sloop down into the river estuary, and hidden it among the other fishing boats gathered there, in expectation of nightfall. With everything set for his departure a little after midnight, he thought fit to provide those followers he left behind him with an alibi, in case they were held culpable by a new and possibly vengeful government. Ailesbury was dismissed from his customary post at his side and Lord Dumbarton was told to maintain the highly improbable fiction that he had spent the whole night sleeping fast in the King's chamber but 'wak'd not till after he was gone'.[31] As a reward for loyalty and good service, James slipped an emerald ring from his finger and palmed it to Sir Richard Head, rejecting a final plea to stay from Ailesbury, and asking him what he would have him do, seeing that 'My children hath abandoned me, my army hath deserted me, those that I raised from nothing hath done the same, what can I expect from those I have done little or nothing for?'.[32] A similar sense of the hopelessness of his situation pervaded the short paper that he had written, explaining his decision to go into exile, and which he left in a prominent position on his table as he hastily pulled his stockings back on and prepared for flight.

James had always had faith in his own literary skills, and intended his declaration to elicit support for his predicament and to lay the groundwork for his swift return. However, misreading the concerns of his subjects, and the ways in which his words might be variously used against him, he was to be proved spectacularly wrong in his presumptions. Reprising all the indignities that he had suffered since William's landing, and rejecting any claim that the Prince of Wales was not his son, James stressed his – primarily economic and nationalistic – commitment to religious toleration, while descending into self-pity when it came to an examination of his present circumstances and the fate that he thought would surely befall him, were he to remain in England. The Prince of Orange had, he declared, 'taken such pains, to make me apear as black as Hell to my own people, as well as to all the world besides', even though 'I have venter'd my life very frankly on severall occasions for the good and honour of my Country'. If James chose to recall the gun smoke of past battles at this moment, then he sincerely believed that he would rather brave the whistle of chain-shot once more than the deathly quiet of the prison cell, for 'I was born free and desire to continue so . . . [as] I think it not convenient to expose myself to be secur'd'. Significantly, James, at only 55 years of age, already chose to consider himself as an 'old' man, who could only 'withdraw . . . so as to be within call when the Nation's eyes shall be opened . . . [when] it will pleas God to touch their hearts out of his infinite mercy, and to make Sencible of the ill condition they are in'.[33] Although the paper had been written to be published, its themes seemed, if anything, to reinforce Williamite propaganda and polemic. The King, by his own admission, appeared to be leaving the country of his own free will and casting aside responsibility for both Crown and people, until such unspecified time as the Almighty might choose once more to favour him. Furthermore, by reiterating his commitment to toleration for Roman Catholics, James did little to distance himself from the policies of the last eighteen months of his reign. These had driven a fatal wedge between the King and his Anglican supporters, and were held to be thoroughly discredited by a clear majority of the political nation. Amid the suspicion, loathing and fear that coalesced under the broad banner of anti-popery and threatened to reduce the streets of London to a state of near anarchy at little more than a moment's notice, any allusion to the promotion of Catholicism as a social or political force, or even a veiled reference to advancing 'those of [the king's] own perswasion', was regarded as a dangerous and provocative admission of intent.[34] James's dramatic expansion of the army, combined with the breakneck speed at which Roman Catholics had been given commissions, appointed to the municipalities, and foisted upon the universities, had only served to bolster the impression among his Protestant subjects that he was the servant of aggressive foreign powers – namely the papacy and the kingdom of France – and was prepared to undermine the liberties of his people, and to countenance the extirpation of their faith by the very same methods of dragonnade, gallows and gun, that had proved so effective across the Channel. Viewed against the background of the Revocation of the Edict of Nantes, toleration appeared to many (if not most) as a Trojan Horse; not as an encouragement to fairness before the law and as a concession to rationality, but as a plain invitation to massacre and treachery.

More damaging still was the slight note that the King had chosen to enclose along with his declaration, expressing his thanks to those among his guards who had shown him kindness and sympathy during his stay at Rochester, and requesting that they be given bequests of between 80 and 100 guineas each for their trouble. Taken together with the gift of his ring to his host, these presents could appear to represent a form of will, to be set alongside the coda of the declaration, his last political testament. Though this was clearly not James's intention when he attempted to set his affairs in order on the night of 22 December 1688, it was certainly the interpretation placed forcefully upon these documents once they entered the public domain in the New Year. They seemed to provide compelling evidence that the King, in fleeing from Rochester, was actively choosing to remove himself from the world of politics, and that he freely desired to renounce his offices, give away his property, and pass on the succession to his legal heir or heirs, as though he were already dead before the eyes of the law. This convenient fiction – for fiction it certainly was – will be returned to again, but for now it is enough to signify that James's own words would be used to promote the idea that he had voluntarily abdicated the throne, rather than being driven from it through the unlikely but potent combination of foreign intervention and an indigenous revolutionary movement, which ultimately found expression in each of his three kingdoms, and drew upon extremely heterogeneous yet overwhelmingly strong levels of spontaneous popular support. If it suited William and Mary to stress the constitutional legality of their seizure of power, or generations of Whig historians to exorcise all notion of revolutionary intent from their sweeping canvases, then we can clearly see it was primarily James's own actions and public pronouncements of late December 1688 which permitted them to build their tenuous, if compelling, mythologies in such a convincing manner.

Having left behind his papers as hostages to fortune, James, accompanied only by his son Berwick and two gentlemen of his Household, descended via the back stairs, lifted the latch to an unbolted and unguarded door, and headed out into the winter night. The garden at the rear of the house was secluded, heavily planted with trees, and sloped straight down to the wasteland and marshes that bordered the river. While the Dutch sentries made a show of patrolling the High Street, Captain Macdonald emerged from the shadows to hurry the little party over a low wall and through the reeds to where Trevanion anxiously awaited them with the boat. Though it was later felt that the soldiers

would hardly have been moved to stop him had he marched boldly out of
the front door before their very eyes, the fear of discovery, of a second
ignominious capture, or of death upon the seas, naturally filled the
thoughts of the King as his rowing boat slipped past Rochester bridge
and began to perilously edge its way down the Medway. Unfortunately,
the weather and bad timing now conspired to undo his plans. With both
the wind and the tide against them, the oarsmen could make little
headway and were unable to cover the ten-mile journey to Sheerness,
where the fishing smack waited to carry them to France, before the break
of day. Forced to take shelter from the elements in the mouth of the
Swale, on the south side of the Isle of Sheppey, James and his
companions waited for the tide to turn and debated what their next
course of action should be. The Swale was crowded with traffic, and
Trevanion asked if he could take his hungry and tired sailors aboard a
merchantman, come from Hamburg, so that they might buy provisions
and refresh themselves. James prudently forbade such foolhardiness, but
thought that they might transfer to Trevanion's own battleship, the
Harwich, a 3rd rate, which lay at anchor close by. The Captain, however,
was in no doubt that while some of his officers would surely welcome the
King's appearance, the 400-strong crew would have no qualms about
arresting him and handing him back to the authorities. A compromise
was finally reached, by which the King and his party went aboard the
Eagle, a fireship, whose commander James knew to be loyal from past
experience. There they wrung out their damp clothes and, as dawn broke
and the morning wore on, they at last spied the twin masts of the fishing
vessel that they had charted, and prepared to transfer themselves to it.
Despite the gale that was now blowing up about them, James would brook
no delay and urged his oarsmen on through the churning waves to the
deck-side. Once on board, the King was relieved to find a large quantity
of swords, pistols and hand grenades stashed below decks, more than
enough, he felt, to frighten or fight off any customs-man or interloper
who might pry into the business of the smack and the rowing boat that it
now towed along behind it, as they picked their way with some
uncertainty back along the Essex coast towards the buoy of the Nore,
after having been blown far off course to the north-east. The wind
continued to drive hard against them, and for the remainder of the day
the vessels made little headway, being forced to seek refuge in the mouth
of the Thames, 'under the Lee of the Sand in smooth water till the next
tyde flood should be done'.[35]

Had James had either the time, or a propensity, for introspection, then
he might well have recalled that it was exactly a week since the crowds
had thronged his coach, cried out 'God save the King!', and put up
illuminations in their windows to welcome him back into his capital. As it
was, he found himself virtually stranded, at the mercy of the tides and the

winds, as at first vital minutes, and then hours, ticked slowly by. In his
own words, James was now experiencing 'continual apprehensions of
being attacked and Seized . . . by his Rebellious Subjects' and 'all those
hardships which are the never failing attendants of such hasty and
hidden expeditions'.[36] Yet the day passed without event: no sail of pursuit
appeared on the horizon, and no alarm appeared to disturb the peace of
the coastline as, at last, they were compelled to drop anchor and once
more furl their sails. This strange scene was repeated the following day, as
'they Saw not any Ship nor Vessel under Sail, and only Seaven at anchor
in the Downs'.[37] Fortunately, however, as the sun began to dip once more,
the winds abruptly changed and drove the two little boats on at last,
towards the darkened and foreboding mass of the French coast. For three
days James had only rarely, and with a marked sense of reluctance,
ventured far from the safety of the cramped cabin that he shared with the
Duke of Berwick. Unable to stand properly, or to stretch his legs, he had
sat all the while opposite his son, tensed and brooding upon his fate, as
his vessel struggled against contrary winds and strong gales. Now, as word
reached him that France had been sighted, the tension broke, his spirits
improved, and he called out for food and drink, joking freely with his
companions as Captain Trevanion attempted to improvise a meal. The
smell of frying bacon soon filled the cabin, spluttering and spitting about
the hole that had been newly discovered in the bottom of the pan, which
was quickly plugged by the ingenious sea captain with a rag soaked in
pitch. Amid the martial bonhomie of his friends, James felt able to set
aside formality and to acknowledge, for once, all that was incongruous
and even slightly ridiculous about his situation and the greatly reduced
circumstances in which he now found himself. As his drink spilled out
from the sides of the 'old furr'd Can' from which he was compelled to
sip, he felt nothing but an overwhelming sense of relief that his troubles
seemed about to end, and boisterously declared that he had never eaten
or drunk 'more heartily in his life'.[38]

Ordinarily, the village of Ambleteuse might not have presented a
welcoming prospect to the King of England. A later visitor found it a
'desolate, dull and melancholy spot' and even by the late seventeenth
century, the sands were already beginning to encroach upon the mouth
of its little harbour, threatening to silt it up entirely.[39] Vauban, Louis
XIV's great military engineer, had once planned to transform the area
into a major naval base, complete with state-of-the-art fortifications and
an enormous lighthouse, but the funds had not been forthcoming and
only a small coastal fort had eventually been built, jutting far out into the
sea. It was from this promontory that sentries spotted the fishing boat
carrying James, as it dropped its anchor beside a French man-of-war out
in the roadstead. Having been unable to make the safety of Calais, his
boats had been blown further westwards, through the night, past the Bay

of Wissant and the treacherous cliffs of Cap Gris-Nez, till they had come upon the safety of the anchorage off Ambleteuse, and as a consequence there could scarcely have been a sweeter sight to him than the fortress walls and mean cluster of houses that marked journey's end. By the English calendar, which still lagged a full ten days behind that used on the Continent, it was reckoned to be Christmas Day when the King and his tired and dishevelled party of fugitives were finally rowed ashore by lantern-light. As James was greeted by his new protectors, he appeared to be remarkably cheerful, and well-pleased with both the manner of his escape and the prospect of the fresh political crises that he felt sure would engulf his kingdoms once the news of his departure was made general. He had known exile before, but confident of God's providence, the friendship of the King of France, and the awesome power of combined Anglican and Tory sentiment, he had good reason to expect that his absence would only be of a short duration. However, the events of the next twelve years were to prove him gravely mistaken, as misfortune piled upon misfortune, and as his carefully crafted reputations as soldier and sovereign were systematically laid low by the evidence of his failures, and by the assaults of his foes. It was indeed fortunate that, as he shook the seasonable snows from his boots and prepared to put his case for assistance before the French King, he had no reason to suspect that he would never set foot in England again.

CHAPTER TWO

The Empty Throne

I

When Dr Truislen attempted, in the eighteenth century, to differentiate between the involuntary nature of abdication and the voluntary resignation of power, he had little hesitation in using the plight of James II to make his point: 'to resign an office', he declared, is 'noble, when generously given up in favour of another', but to 'abdicate a crown, is ever looked upon as disgraceful'.[1] Certainly the manner of James's departure gave rise to the impression, hotly denied by his supporters, that the King 'stole away to France' like a thief in the night, having renounced in perpetuity all right to rule in his three kingdoms. To the faithful, his leaving was disastrous and galling in equal measure. Keightley and Belson had awoken, on the morning of 23 December 1688, fully expecting to see their master after breakfast, and to press upon him the utter necessity of his remaining in England. All they had found, however, was the Household in confusion, the King gone, and his parting letter left on an upstairs table for Lord Middleton's attention. For those who had sent them, the Earl of Clarendon and Bishop Turner, James's flight came as nothing short of 'an earthquake' to destroy their hopefully laid plans. All chance of a peacefully negotiated settlement with William and the House of Lords was now lost, the political landscape was changed irrevocably and the alliance between Crown and Church, conceivably James's strongest remaining card, was thrown into jeopardy and doubt. Without a king to obey, the question of where political authority and legitimacy now rested became both of prime importance and of unique opaqueness, in the affairs of courtiers and subjects alike. Clarendon best summed up the feelings of many of James's friends when he admitted to being overcome with 'astonishment, as every body was, at the King's being again withdrawn', and terror for 'what will become of this poor, distracted and distempered nation . . . [after] this unhappy year, fatal, I fear to England'.[2]

If bewilderment was the key emotion experienced by the followers of the fallen King, left leaderless and explicitly forbidden from forming a party by James's repeated injunctions for them to sit tight and to wait upon events, then Prince William and his Whig allies might have been forgiven for exuding a quiet sense of triumph as they prepared to step into, and to fill, the political vacuum left by the King's sudden and fortuitous second flight. His departure immediately appeared to confirm the authority of the lords who sat in the Guildhall to act as if they were the *de facto* government, and to justify their attempts to negotiate a hasty redrawing of the constitution with William. In the absence of James, it was far easier to countenance the view that the 'Stupendous Revolution' that had struck at his person and policies had, in fact, been nothing of the sort and that the King had openly acknowledged his incapacity for office by his desertion of his crown and lands. Herein lay both the formula that allowed different and frequently conflicting interest groups to coalesce in the achievement of a truly revolutionary constitutional settlement, while maintaining – with a fairly good conscience – that it was nothing of the kind, and the germ of the idea which has become popular in recent years, that the King had been pushed out of England by unrepresentative conservative forces within the political establishment, and by the decisive use of foreign arms.[3] In this version of events, James may be turned into a thoroughly modern figure: the patriot, warrior and forward-thinking champion of religious and cultural plurality. It is a vision every bit as attuned to the concerns and paradigms of our own uncertain times, as was the mid-nineteenth century image of James in exile, as the unheeded prophet of empire, the embodiment of gentlemanly virtues and of the revivalist brand of Christian charity, that so captured one significant corner of the Victorian imagination.[4] However, it is no less flawed for all that, and is rooted not in the tumults of 1688–9 or in the refashioning of James's political legacy during the years of his final exile, but in the collapse of the monumental edifice that was the Whig school of history and, in much recent scholarship, in the reduction of the events following from his fall from power to a sad and tarnished spectacle of a revolution that never really was.[5]

The grand sweeps of historical narrative pioneered by Macaulay and Trevelyan, gripping, incisive and opinionated in tone, and brilliantly compelling in their style and scope, held but few doubts as to either the beneficial effects of James II's removal from the throne or his harsh temperament and narrow, destructive brand of bigotry. For them, the Glorious Revolution had led naturally and necessarily to the sovereignty of Parliament, the establishment of the Bank of England, to an aggressive colonial policy and to the intellectual syntheses of John Locke and Sir Isaac Newton. The Industrial Revolution and the supremacy of the British Empire could be seen to have grown inevitably from the freedoms won in 1688–9, and consolidated in the years immediately following, while James might be cast as an effective foil for William of Orange. Where William was brave, rational and thoroughly capable of adapting to events, James could be seen as a cowardly, illogical and curiously rigid figure, who had fortunately disappeared from the political stage into a long and disagreeable final exile, before he could do too much damage to both people and State.

Yet for Britons grappling their way through the uncertain political terrain of the early twenty-first century, such supreme confidence in economic, social and scientific progress, or in the perfection of a constitution that remains largely unwritten, might appear to be hopeful at best and, at worst, the very stuff of an irrelevant and dated Whig mythology, bearing little scrutiny or relation to the prevailing conditions governing contemporary life. The upheavals of 1688–9 can no longer be seen to provide the decisive point in a continuing ascent to commercial prosperity and political dominance. Britannia clearly no longer rules the waves, the bonds of the nation state have creaked under devolution, and the parliament at Westminster, sidelined by a more presidential style of government, can no longer be perceived to be the model for an effective administration that might be made general and applied throughout an envious world. The last flickering of the Whig tradition could be discerned in the decidedly lacklustre tercentenary celebrations held in 1988, at the Banqueting Hall in Whitehall, to mark 'the moment when the balance of power finally shifted from the Crown to Parliament'.[6] In contrast to the large and genuinely popular celebrations held in Holland and the USA, the talking mannequins of William and Mary which were installed in Whitehall at enormous cost apparently inspired little interest among London's tourists. Meanwhile, thick rolling fog conspired to thoroughly obscure the visit of Queen Elizabeth II and the Duke of Edinburgh to Brixham harbour on board the royal yacht.[7] Although the members of the Tercentenary Trust, the government quango charged with organising the commemorations, had correctly defined the period as representing something of a 'black hole in the school curriculum', they did little to remedy matters in the classroom. Worse still, they were singularly unwilling to address the central problem threatening the celebrations: that of the appropriation of William of Orange's image as a Protestant champion by hard-line Ulster Unionist politicians. Elsewhere in the United Kingdom, save for on a handful of football grounds, confessional conflict had retreated to the far-flung fringes of society, while the religious passions that had cost James II his throne appeared wholly strange and inexplicable to the vast majority of the inhabitants of these increasingly secular and materialistic isles. However, in Northern Ireland, where troops still patrolled the streets and Unionist and Republican paramilitaries drilled and clashed by night, and where slight variations in accent marked the sharp demarcation lines between Protestant and Catholic communities, the language and controversies of the seventeenth century were still very much live issues. Anything that might echo the themes of Unionist triumphalism was to be avoided at all costs in a bitterly divided and still contested land. This understandable concern not to be seen as condoning the later establishment of the Protestant ascendancy and the operation of the Penal Laws, carried ironically against the will of King William, undoubtedly served, in part, to explain the willingness of members of the Old Left to unite with the torchbearers of the New Right in a visceral attack on the supposed aims and objectives of the Revolution and all that it stood for.[8] Yet it was the protracted failure of the Left to examine the events of 1688–9 for what they were, rather than for what they wished them to be, that permitted this unedifying alliance and allowed the gradual resurgence of a potent Tory historiography which threatened first to divorce the 'Glory' from the Revolution, and then to deny the existence of any sort of revolution at all.

There was palpable disappointment in the lament of Christopher Hill that 'James II ran away too easily in 1688' to ignite a truly popular revolution, or to fan the embers of a new and radicalising civil war.[9] However, for the most part, those Marxist historians who chose to follow in his mighty shadow preferred to focus both scholarly and popular attention on the English Revolution of 1640–9, while downplaying the significance of the Glorious Revolution and relegating it to the outer realms of a rather dour form of economic determinism. This had not always been the case, for at the high-water mark of socialist self-confidence following the Second World War, the Revolution of 1688–9 took its place alongside those of France and Russia, celebrated as a major landmark in the ongoing struggle for freedom in a proud pageant of working-class history which was held at the Royal Albert Hall.[10] However, all of this had changed by the late 1980s, as Lawrence and Wishart sponsored a conference whose less than inspiring title of 'Back to the Future' reflected the fundamental malaise and crisis of identity that had begun to grip significant sections of the Left. Despite coinciding with the official commemorations organised by the Tercentenary Committee, the conference virtually ignored the themes surrounding the Glorious Revolution and invited Jonathan Clark, one of the most impressive of the rising generation of right-wing, revisionist scholars, to give a keynote address. Clark had already rejected the 'precarious' notion of the significance of James II's fall, citing the persistence of Jacobite agitation throughout the eighteenth century, and arguing that the sea change in favour of bourgeois power was only effected in the 1830s.[11] It was left to only a handful of slender pamphlets to keep the Marxist flame alive. A.L. Morton emphasised the role of an oligarchic conspiracy in the toppling of James II, and Willie Thompson stressed the essential 'Compromise of 1688' between the nobility and elements of the nascent bourgeoisie. However, Thompson went further and struck a note of pathos by contrasting the loyalty shown to the fallen King by the clans of the Great Glen with the bankruptcy, bloodshed and famine visited upon them by William III's agents. In this particular and surprising scheme of things, it was possible to detect a greater degree of sympathy for James's proto-absolutist vision of Scotland than for the new mercantile and artisan classes who had begun to erode the basis of the clan system, and who had clamoured so fervently to invest in the doomed Darien project.[12] It was left to James Stewart to strike a sounder note in the tercentenary year, by mounting an effective attack primarily on the Orangist tradition but also on some elements of the Nationalist myths surrounding the Williamite war in Ireland, in an attempt to restore the primacy of class to the argument.[13]

Given that the Left had confined itself largely to polemic rather than to sustained analysis, and ceded the field to the revisionist right mainly by default, it is notable that discussion of James II's fall and subsequent exile, while benefiting from the explosion in cultural history in the 1990s, remained untouched by the worst ravages of postmodernist critique and by the encroaching teleology of the free market. Dependent on primary source work and the careful checking of manuscript archives and empirical data, and lacking a fully developed Marxist interpretation that could be virulently attacked and hopefully debunked, the career of the exiled King had little of value to offer either of these fashionable schools of *fin de siècle* thought. This profound absence of effective debate made it possible for a body of socially conservative, traditionalist and antiquarian writers to advance an engaging and passionate critique of the Whig tradition, and to fundamentally recast our vision of the British Isles during the 1680s and 90s in the mould of an avowedly Jacobite political discourse. At its worst this approach brings to mind, with its utter rejection of the modern world, a form of romantic wish-fulfilment that has more in common with the characters of Compton MacKenzie, staring out towards the horizon in expectation of the Young Pretender's imminent return, or with the world of Willoughby Chase where English wolves still prowl the countryside and 'King James III' sits securely on his throne, than with any recognisable source of historical controversy.[14] However, in the hands of skilled researchers, such as Eveline Cruickshanks and Edward Corp, familiar with a wide range of continental archives and well attuned to the cultural sensibilities of the times, the result was some of the most provocative, erudite, and influential work published on the subject during the last twenty years. Concentrating on the question of James II's commitment to religious toleration, the structure and etiquette of his Household, and his patronage of the arts, these researchers slowly began to roll back the familiar stereotypes of St Germain as a gloomy and priest-ridden place, before attempting to make their detailed findings general.[15]

Yet it was one thing to fully recognise that John Macky's much-quoted account of 'A View of the Court of St. Germain from the Year 1690 to 95' was clearly a Williamite propaganda piece, and quite another to extrapolate from that fact that James II was a figure much traduced by his enemies; that he was, in reality, a remarkable forerunner of the policies and thought of the European Enlightenment, whose exile had deprived the British Isles of the creation of a sumptuous court culture which, in time, might have rivalled even that of Versailles.[16] However, if the whole experience of the Revolution of 1688–9 was now to be reduced to a mere palace coup, a conflict of dynastic personalities or – at the most banal populist level – the result of the shocking ingratitude of James II's daughters, then the decision of the King to flee to the safety of France might indeed appear to be the crowning tragedy of a shameful, and indecisive, episode in constitutional history.[17]

Nevertheless there remained discordant voices within the academic community who begged to differ. For Stuart E. Prall, an American scholar, the roots of the Revolution of 1688 lay clearly in the turbulence of the 1640s, while Lawrence Stone saw the second Royalist defeat of 1688–9 as final, decisively shifting the axis mundi and making possible 'the seizure of power by landed, mercantile and banking élites'.[18] However, the most powerful contribution to the debate came from the pen of Angus McInnes, who presented a convincing case for a solution to the problem surrounding the nature of an 'English Revolution' that lay squarely within the events of 1688–9, and the 'dozen or so years of the Dutch King's rule [which] saw a whole panoply of constitutional changes'. With none of his father's intrinsic trust in the goodness inherent in his subjects, James – whose character had been forged in the heat of revolution and civil war – was, according to McInnes, determined never to concede an inch to his political opponents. Neither was he overburdened by any sense of 'undue moderation' in his dealings with the political nation.[19] Although McInnes's article had appeared to be an authoritative and potentially decisive intervention in an argument that had divided the scholarly community since the end of the Second World War, his thesis surprisingly prompted no major reappraisal of either revolutionary period. With the academic profession compartmentalised into 'early' and 'late' Stuart specialists, and careers (and sometimes whole departments) committed to maintaining one or the other orthodoxy, such a radical synthesis was too disconcerting and challenging to make much headway. It was as though a gemstone had been thrown down the shaft of a particularly deep well, sparkled for a moment, and was then smothered by darkness and silence.

Even though the term 'Glorious Revolution' was not coined until November 1689, and would not become common for another hundred years, such a response by modern historians might have appeared strange to either the seventy-three lords who met on Christmas Eve 1688 to anxiously debate the future of their absentee King, or to the hapless companies of Guardsmen who, after their humiliation at Whitehall, had been sent to Rochester, only to discover that their sovereign had already fled.[20] Resigned to the cold, to a wasted march, and to an uncertain future, their sense of loss and confusion was mirrored by loyalists like Sir John Bramston, a lawyer and former MP, who thundered against the 'havock [James] was making in the Church and Universities, the nurseries of our religion . . . to settle Poperie, and the meanes and ways he tooke to make his power and rule absolute', while holding that 'as to those that invited the Prince in, they must answer for themselves; but I hold it was in them perfect rebellion'. For Bramston, as for many other Tory squires, James's actions were distasteful, but they had been 'established by laws, and could not be destroyed but by the same power that made them, that is, by a law' that had come down from the hand of the legitimate King himself.[21] However, James's flight had made it extremely difficult for his supporters among the lords to defend his use of the prerogative during his reign, and his continuing right to rule during his absence from his lands. Just hours after the King's departure, Francis Gwyn, a Tory MP, had complained to George Legge, the Earl of Dartmouth, that their master had chosen 'as ill a time now [to leave], as he did before, for tomorrow [i.e. 24 December 1688] the Lords are to meet concerning a Parliament, and I wish he had stayed to hear what their method had been'.[22] While James's craft had been floundering off the coast, and Londoners were coming to terms with the strange new army – including green-coated Danes, Finnish cavalry in blackened armour and bearskins and some 200 Africans in 'white furs and plumes of feathers' – that had been quartered among them, the lords were confronted with the unenviable task of settling a government and explaining away a clear transference of power from one sovereign to another to the distracted and fractious people.[23] William had wasted little time in consolidating his position in the capital, reconstituting the House of Lords at Westminster and summoning those members who had sat in Charles II's parliaments – but pointedly not those elected under James II – to meet him in order to discuss the holding of fresh elections. However, while he had taken upon himself both the aspect and many of the powers of a king, he lacked any formal title or status in law that might serve to make his control of events permanent, or to justify his already sweeping actions. Nevertheless, the uncomfortable reality that no recognisable form of central government now existed in the realm had effectively concentrated the minds of the assembled lords, causing them to vote down loyalist counter-measures that aimed to stall proceedings, and to abandon their long, rancorous and thoroughly inconclusive debate as to whether James might now be considered safely dead in the eyes of the law. Even James's final letter, penned at Rochester and faithfully presented by Middleton in an act of considerable personal bravery and bravura, was rejected out of hand and deemed to be unworthy of their attention. Significantly, it was Godolphin, a fellow Tory who still hoped to

come to terms with the King, who had moved decisively against the
calling of Middleton to the House. Having judged the mood of the
assembled peers, he had concluded that the Prince of Orange would
have to be dealt with, in the short term at least. Thus, on Christmas Day,
the Lords presented William with two addresses asking him to take on the
civil administration of the three kingdoms, and to expedite the calling of
the promised parliament.[24] However, they were taken aback by the
Prince's coolness towards them and his refusal to immediately accept
their proposals. Keen to construct the broadest possible platform of
support for the transference of power, and to emphasise the unanimity of
agreement regarding the rejection of James II's policies and person,
William was reluctant to rely on any single vested interest, and told the
Lords that he would wait upon the advice of the representatives of the
Lower House before coming to a final decision.

In the meantime, the shape that the future settlement was to take was
slowly beginning to emerge. Lord Danby, who had invited William into
England and who had led the rising of the gentry in Yorkshire, arrived in
London fully expecting to find a place at the Prince's side. Yet he found
himself already supplanted in William's trust and affection by the
Marquess of Halifax, and his plans for the establishment of a regency –
which would have guaranteed the primacy of a stridently Anglican House
of Lords over the Crown, and made it considerably more difficult for
William to tax and to wage war – withered and dying on the vine.
Similarly, blueprints for a parliament elected along restricted
Cromwellian lines were soon discarded, and replaced by precedents
drawn firmly from the experience of the orderly and genuinely popular
Restoration of 1660 and its creation of a Convention parliament to
decide on changes to the constitution. From the fastness and security of
his Swiss exile, Edmund Ludlow, the last surviving regicide, looked
hopefully on developments in England. He was eager to return to serve
William, the 'new Gideon', in ushering in the millennium and the rule of
God, but his republican vision was to go sadly unfulfilled, and his
presence would be judged unwelcome by all but the handful of young
radicals who gathered at his house in London in the summer of 1689.[25]
King-killing sat all too uneasily with the essential pragmatism espoused by
the nation's new masters, and too many Tory MPs had either profited
from the seizure of Ludlow's estates in the past, or harboured the desire
for a score-settling in the present, to make his stay either a long or a
rewarding experience. By the winter he was on his travels again, laden
down with his memories of past struggles and his dreams of a brand of
popular democracy that were not to be realised by the beneficiaries of
the events of 1688–9. Yet the fact remains that Ludlow was forewarned by
William of the moves to impeach him, and was permitted by the
authorities to make his escape in good time. If the Revolution was not

nearly so radical as either the elderly General or many modern historians might have wished, then it was neither a petty nor a vindictive affair, for its architects and the Prince of Orange, in particular, had no desire to re-open old controversies, or to create new martyrs who might linger in the popular consciousness for years to come.

The theme of the sovereignty of the people was not, however, to be entirely forgotten, as those MPs summoned by William were supplemented by representatives of the city and by the Lord Mayor, and an attempt by the Prince to segregate their meetings was greeted with the bold rebuff that the crisis required private citizens to assume the role of public magistrates.[26] With an eye to being returned to the forthcoming Convention parliament, the MPs mirrored the appeals already delivered to William by the Lords, but added their own proviso, that the circular letters authorising the election should not be delivered to the county sheriffs – held to be tainted by James's undue influence – but to the coroners, who had been locally elected rather than directly appointed by the Crown. The news of James's second flight, when compared to the turmoil and excitement generated by his first abortive escape attempt, had appeared as something of an anticlimax and had generated surprisingly little in the way of comment or fresh passion. As Dalrymple had it, his removal had 'produced a calm, and a relief from anxiety, not pity for him, not indignation against him; the weakness of his behaviour having stifled those passions equally in the breasts of his friends and of his foes'.[27] This wholly false impression of a return to normality was fostered by William's commands to existing office holders to return to their posts and resume their business pending the results of the election, and by his decision to confine his own troops to barracks, while ordering units of the English army to keep their distance from the capital. Despite the background of invasion, rebellion and military collapse, William intended at all costs to ensure that the forthcoming election would not be seen as having been conducted under the barrel of a gun. Partly as a result of this concern, and with time at a premium, local conditions and pre-existing networks of patronage now took on prime importance. The confusion created by the issue, and then by the belated recall, of James II's writs for a new election had already focused and in many cases resolved the question of candidacy for the forthcoming contests. The result was that a majority of seats for the new Convention were now left uncontested, with a single well-backed representative of the local community being virtually already in place. Moreover, despite the collapse of the executive's ability to direct and mobilise its support, the success of James's election agents in enfranchising Dissenting communities during the previous year now ironically acted to strengthen the hand of avowedly Williamite candidates across England and Wales. Those incumbents who had been too closely associated with the former regime experienced severe reverses at the polls. Samuel Pepys, who had once seamlessly shifted his loyalty from Commonwealth to King, was now unable – or simply unwilling – to abandon James II, and fell to vitriolic cries of 'No Tower Men!' amid the 'pride, heat, and faction' generated by the hustings at Harwich. Accused of graft, and of being a secret papist, he sought only to blame the establishment of a local Conventicle for all his troubles and for the loss of his previously safe constituency.[28]

With James a discredited and uniquely unpopular figure, and the Tories torn by schisms between those who heartily wished their King gone, and those who hoped for his speedy return, with or without preconditions, the Williamite party, comprising Whigs, neutrals and pro-Orangist Tories, gained a clear majority of some ninety seats over the loyalist opposition in the election of January 1689. However, the inbuilt Tory majority in the Lords, due in part to the presence of the Anglican bishops, threatened not only to provide a check to the Convention's more radical measures, but also to derail the settlement entirely. Unencumbered by the need to please an electorate or to return to constituencies, most of the peers had chosen to remain in London throughout January and had had the time and opportunity to forge or reconstruct alliances, and to adopt prepared positions for the coming debates. Richard Graham, Viscount Preston, had accompanied James to Rochester and had desired to follow his master into exile, but had been urged by the King that he might be of far better service watching and reporting on the disputes at Westminster, as opposition to William crystallised around the Hyde brothers and Bishop Lloyd of Asaph.

While the nation looked on, four major options presented themselves to the MPs returned to the parliament that opened, with little in the way of either fanfare or ceremony, on 22 January 1689. It was conceivable that James might have been asked to return immediately, but the events of December and the warm welcome accorded to the King on his arrival in France had served to harden attitudes, and to render this course of action largely unacceptable to the vast number of those assembled at Westminster. Though few were prepared to state matters so bluntly, or honestly, Robert Ferguson declared that the sole objective of the Convention was 'to bolt the door after [the King] and so foreclose his return', while Thomas Wharton proudly owned his part in 'driving King James out' and thought that he 'would do it again' if the King was ever allowed back in order to repossess his throne.[29] If there was no real appetite for James's unconditional return, then loyalists in both Houses could unite in seeking to establish the regency of either William or Mary, or possibly both, according to personal preference. This might preserve the hereditary principle intact, and permit the Prince of Orange to direct matters of foreign policy while enabling the King to retain his crown. According to this scheme, the succession would eventually devolve upon the Prince of Wales, and this knowledge, it was felt, would have done much to keep James II's critics wary of overstepping the mark of *lèse-majesté* and risking the future wrath of his son. For Halifax and the majority of Whigs, and indeed for William himself, such proposals were anathema, as they threatened to abandon their hard-won political initiative. Consequently, they continued to hold that it was imperative that James should be formally deposed as quickly as possible, so that the Prince could be declared king. However, this raised the spectacle of setting aside the succession and of acknowledging, as some braver and more foolhardy souls had hoped he would, William's right to rule by conquest alone. The final proposal also advocated the setting aside of the King, but aimed instead to preserve both the strict line of succession – for almost all had by now chosen to factor the Prince of Wales out of the equation, as either illegitimate or irrelevant – and English sensibilities by crowning Princess Mary as the sole sovereign, in place of her father.

The treatment afforded to Lord Middleton by the peers, and their refusal to discuss the contents of James's last letter, might have served warning upon the King that his pronouncements no longer carried the force to command, and that a change of strategy was now necessary. However, although he had little time or sympathy for those of his subjects who had 'run in, to pay their venerations to the new erected Idol' of the Convention, he still cherished hopes that he could shape events through the control of the Privy Council. He was still King and, though it had not sat since the 'hurrying of us under a Guard from our City of London', it followed, in theory at least, that it was still in existence and might be legally empowered to act in the absence of the sovereign as the executive. Though this sat uneasily with James's promise of a parliament capable of voicing popular grievances, and of arbitrating a settlement to the crisis – and entirely ignored the reality that the council was dissolved and that William was the decisive power in the land – the King still clung to this fiction and accordingly acted upon it. Within a few days of establishing himself at St Germain, he dictated a fresh letter to the members of the Privy Council and, more generally, to the Lords, reprising his charges that his life had been threatened, and stressing the 'high and Royal Station in which God Almighty by Right of Succession has placed us', for 'neither the Provocation or Ingratitude of our own Subjects, nor any other Consideration whatsoever shall ever prevail with us to make the least step contrary to the true Interest of the English nation'. If James's right to the throne was thus divinely ordained, and therefore unchallengeable by man, then the individuals who had sat in his Privy Council were obligated to restore order to the land and 'to send us your Advice, what is fit to be done by us towards our returning'.[30]

Unhappily for the royal exile, the lessons of 1660 did not hold good for 1689, and the political nation was not straining its gaze across the

Channel with the same intensity of hope and expectation with which James attempted to focus his gaze and peer back into the complexities of Westminster's politics. Accordingly, the ever-loyal Preston (who had retained his seals of office and still considered himself to be Secretary of State) attempted to mobilise the King's friends by publicising the letter and bringing it to the attention of the House, only to have the Lords merely rule it out of order, as before. Though James was loathe to recognise it, the situation had moved on, a parliament now existed and, while his promises to hold elections might have diffused tensions six or even three months earlier, they now appeared wholly redundant and as concessions given reluctantly, only after the point had been generally conceded.

Worse was to come. Following a noisy and acrimonious debate on 28 January 1689, when the loyalists failed to mount any sustained or even barely cohesive challenge to the chorus of Whig charges relating to James's abject misgovernment, the Commons passed a damning indictment of both the King and his reign, without even the need for a division. Sir George Treby spoke for many MPs when he held that, through his actions, James had proven himself unable – or worse, unwilling – to govern, and had given his people a 'manifest declaration of his will, no longer to retain the exercise of his kingly office' by his pre-emptive flight to France. As a result, the King might be judged before the law as if he were but a child or a madman, who could not be trusted to speak or act in his own best interests. It was, therefore, the unavoidable duty of the nation, as represented by the twin Houses of Parliament, to fill the void left by his departure as best, and as quickly, as they possibly could. Thus, the Commons chose to resolve: 'That King James the Second, having Endeavoured to Subvert the Constitution of the Kingdom, by Breaking the Original Contract between King and People; and by the Advice of Jesuits, and other Wicked Persons, having Violated the Fundamental Laws, and With-drawn himself out of the Kingdom, hath Abdicated the Government, and that the Throne is thereby Vacant'.[31] However, the Lords, far less united and vociferous in their condemnation of the King, regarded the motion with deep mistrust and sought to have it amended, replacing 'Abdicated' with 'Deserted' and deleting the declaration 'that the Throne is thereby Vacant' in its entirety. With the Commons holding firm in maintaining that James's government had permanently ceased, and the Lords recording large margins in favour of loyalist counter-motions, stating that according to common law 'Abdication is a Voluntary Express Act of Renuntiation, which is not in this Case', an impasse was reached. In an attempt to reach an accord, both Houses agreed to send representatives to meet in Westminster's Painted Chamber. The abiding fear of many MPs was that what 'is called Desertion . . . is Temporary and Relievable' and that James might legally return to exercise power and call to account all those who had risen in arms against him.[32] Yet the loyalists among the lords should have taken significant heart. They had inflicted bruising defeats on the Commons' motion, which in the case of the final vote on 31 January had reunited Danby with the King's partisans, and preserved the notion that James was still the reigning monarch, even if he was no longer in power.

Unfortunately, they had no hope of their allies in the Commons overturning the Whig majority, and lacked an able figurehead, adept at the management of parliamentary procedure, around whom the protesting voices might permanently coalesce. Archbishop Sancroft had refused to give a clear political lead since the royal government had collapsed, and had done little more than to register a series of weak and distinctly half-hearted complaints at the subsequent erosion of the King's vestigial authority. More damagingly, holding the Convention to be without any legal foundation, he had boycotted the proceedings entirely, and allowed conflicting Anglican opinions to be registered by his default. Clarendon, though active, lacked both the adroitness and the steady resolve needed to command a large following with precision and regularity, while Danby was now prepared to abandon the idea of a regency and was keen to negotiate directly with Princess Mary, so that she might ascend to the throne in her own right. What perhaps served to tie the hands of them all was the abiding, and understandable, fear that the conflict between the two Houses might spill over into the country at large and fan the embers of revolt into a full-scale civil war. This was certainly the thinking that prompted Huntingdon and Mulgrave to refrain from attending the House, while Churchill, with a view to future office, sought to account for his absence by claiming that he waited only upon the advice that Princess Anne was expecting daily from her sister. However, aside from the vote on the crucial wording of the Commons' declaration, the Lords had capitulated, with scarcely more than a murmur, on a series of seemingly minor but psychologically telling points. The House ordered a day of thanksgiving for the delivery of the nation from 'popery and arbitrary power' and resolved to suspend the customary saying of prayers for the life and soul of James II before their debates.[33] Moreover, they had decided that the annual day of celebration commemorating his accession to the throne, due to fall on 6 February at the height of their deliberations, was no longer to be observed. If they had already acknowledged that they were unwilling to be ruled by a 'popish' King and had sought to exorcise any mention of his sovereignty from their proceedings, then it was but a small step to acknowledge that James really was gone for good.

However, it was popular pressure and the intervention of William of Orange that finally decided matters. Alarmed by the failure of the Houses to reach a satisfactory agreement, and by the apparent obstinacy of the

Lords, a petition calling for the dual investiture of William and Mary was presented at Westminster, and was forcefully backed up on the streets by the presence of large crowds who, on occasion, pressed right up to the very doors of parliament. Unsurprisingly, William had watched these events unfold with a mounting sense of dismay. Having taken steps to prohibit the gatherings of the populace about Westminster, now that they had served their purpose, he turned his full attention to curtailing a potentially destructive cycle of parliamentary debate that increasingly appeared to be generating, rather than resolving, questions of profound constitutional ambiguity. Even though both the Lords and the Commons had seemed to agree that James had excluded himself from ruling on the grounds of his religion, they had reached an impasse over the status of the throne itself. While the Lower House held it to be empty, the Upper had repeatedly resolved that it was still occupied by King James, even though he was no longer physically present in his realms. As the behind-the-scenes negotiations conducted by William's chief of staff, Hans van Bentinck, faltered and failed to produce the necessary support in the Lords for the proclamation of his master as king, it appeared that the fragile series of alliances that had made the Revolution possible might be on the point of completely unravelling. With parallel political settlements seemingly about to founder, as we shall see, in Scotland and Ireland, and with worrying news emerging of French military successes along the Rhine, William could no longer afford to become embroiled in a protracted and unrewarding constitutional crisis in England, while Holland lay comparatively open, denuded of both troops and the watchful presence of its Commander-in-Chief.[34] However, fortunately for the Prince of Orange, Danby's rather clumsy machinations in the Lords and his attempts to drive a wedge between William and his wife were fully exposed and quickly rejected. Princess Mary, who might have become a rallying point for much of Tory England, had remained all the while at The Hague, and was possessed of enough wit and loyalty to decline Danby's offer, and to send his letter, together with a copy of her own damning reply, straight back to her husband. With no intention of relinquishing either his direct control over the English army, or of being reduced to the status of a consort – acting, as he scathingly put it, as no more than the mere 'gentleman usher' to his wife – William now effectively sought to call the bluff of the English nobility.

Having summoned several of the leading peers, including Danby, Shrewsbury and Halifax, to his side, he informed them in no uncertain terms, that if it was only a regent that they desired, then they should not look to him to perform that function, but should find another, while he, in turn, would be obliged to return home together with his army and to leave them henceforth to look to their own defences. Furthermore, he also refused to accept the offer of the crown, if it was to be conditional only upon the survival of Mary, and to be relinquished by him upon the very moment of her death. If the Lords wished him to rule England, then he held that he must also be permitted to reign over it, in his own right, thereby definitively re-ordering the succession and ruling out any possibility that King James and his son might ever be allowed to return to power. It was a truly devastating ultimatum, which cut the ground from underneath the positions carefully prepared by the adherents of Clarendon and Danby respectively, yet it also offered scraps of comfort to the Tory lords, conceding that the monarchy would not become elective and that the hereditary principle would be preserved, at least in part. William had been careful to acknowledge that Princess Anne and her progeny should rule after him if Mary failed to give birth to an heir, and that they should succeed in preference to any children that he might conceivably have by any subsequent spouse. Thus he had effectively reassured a heavily pregnant Anne – and her dour husband, Prince George of Denmark – that their rights, and those of their children, would be guaranteed, while sowing further division among those loyalist peers who had set their face against any settlement that barred James from the throne, but yet looked to his daughters to preserve both the Stuart line and the Church of England. For if both of King James's daughters and a substantial number of the bishops now acquiesced fully in stripping him of the crown, and in granting it to William, then the Tories were forced to make an uncomfortable decision about where, and in whom, their allegiances actually lay. With a Roman Catholic King opposed by each of his immediate Protestant heirs, and the established Church apparently on the point of schism, it was increasingly difficult to preserve the old fiction that only an unquestioning loyalty to the person and position of the sovereign could hope to preserve the Anglican faith intact. The simple truth was that, by the beginning of February 1689, few Tory lords were prepared to defend James's continuing right to wear the crown, at the risk of civil war, the destruction of property, and the thorough and possibly final dismemberment of their Church, when it had been the King himself who had seemingly been the first to abandon the struggle for his own prerogatives and his possession of the throne. As the Marquess of Halifax was later to muse, 'a people may let a King fall, yet still remain a people; but if a King let his people slip from him, he is no longer King'. Through his absence, James had permitted the bonds between himself and his subjects to be challenged and subjected to an unprecedented degree of public scrutiny. This had culminated in the conscious and gradual disengagement of large numbers of his natural allies among the Anglican gentry from a full-blooded commitment to his partisanship and a defence of his own Divinely-ordained right to rule. Whether through the need for self-preservation, the maintenance of social order, or as the result of disenchantment with their sovereign, increasing numbers of lords who had been previously unwilling to countenance the notion of the crown passing out of the King's grasp now began to seek a reconciliation with the Prince of Orange and James's sworn foes. What was needed, however, was agreement on the form of words that would both account for the King's flight and mark the point at which loyalty to his person might effectively be exorcised from their hearts, thus bringing down a curtain with satisfying finality upon the unhappy and divisive memory of his reign.

Crowded into the Painted Chamber, and jostled on all sides by anxious and curious spectators, the conference between the members of the two Houses began inauspiciously on the morning of 6 February 1689 amid scenes of confusion and high passion. However, as the corridors were slowly cleared by the Sergeant at Arms, the discussion took form, shaped on the one hand by the interventions of John Somers, MP for the city of Worcester, and Sir George Treby, MP for Plympton – who harnessed a welter of legalistic arguments, rooted in historical precedent, for the 'vacancy' of the throne – and on the other, by the earls of Nottingham, Clarendon and Rochester, who were at pains to establish that the monarchy should always be a hereditary matter, and not one of parliamentary election.[35] However, none of the loyalist lords were willing to break ranks and raise the political temperature by moving unilaterally that the Princess Mary should be crowned queen. While Somers hammered home the point that: 'The word Abdication doth naturally and properly signify Entirely to Renounce, Throw off, Disown, [and] Relinquish any thing or Person, so as to have no further to doe with it . . . whether it be done by Express Words, or in Writing', Rochester could do no more than to weakly concur that the Lords might 'be induced to agree, that the King hath abdicated, that is, renounced the government for himself', if not, perhaps, for his son.[36] Unwilling to persist in an argument that he believed to be deeply divisive to the existing social order, and already largely lost, the Earl of Nottingham advised his circle of friends and supporters to stay away from the crucial vote, to be held later in the afternoon. Godolphin, sensing that resistance was now at an end, chose to absent himself from the proceedings, pleading somewhat unconvincingly that prior business at the Treasury kept him away, while Nathaniel Crewe, the Bishop of Durham, abandoned all thought of flight to the Continent and attempted to rehabilitate himself in the eyes of the new administration by conspicuously voting alongside the Prince's friends. Such prominent defections and abstentions enabled the Commons' motion to be finally ratified by a majority of twenty votes, as the evening shadows drew in about the Upper Chamber. Having found James to have both 'abdicated' the crown and to have left the throne 'vacant', the Lords then pressed on with a new-found sense of urgency, to decide on the succession. With Halifax's motion for William to be proclaimed as sole monarch barely seconded, the Marquess of Winchester captured both the moment and the spirit of the time by proposing the novel – though already much touted – expedient that the crown should be conferred jointly upon the Prince and Princess of Orange. This compromise measure, the only practical one left open after all else had been considered and rejected, was carried by the Lords without even the calling of a division. Though the Commons would be allowed to ratify their decision only after the Upper House had given consideration to the framing of new oaths of allegiance, the die had essentially been cast and word of the settlement served to break the stifling tension, and to resolve the terrible uncertainties that had afflicted Londoners since the King had first fled from his capital almost two months before. While a ring of celebratory fires spread out from Westminster and the city limits to illuminate the streets of surrounding villages, English men and women attempted to make sense of the day's events and the sudden concord that had been achieved between the same assembly of Lords and Commons, who only that morning had threatened to plunge the nation into civil war through their rivalries and open discords. Some citizens attempted to rationalise their profoundly unsettling experiences, citing the workings of God's Providence in human affairs, and pointing to predictions in the almanacs of 1687 and 1688 that had discussed the possibility of a change of ruler, and which now seemed curiously accurate and prescient. Others sought to invest with meaning the momentary tottering of the crown upon the King's brow at his coronation, or else observed the curious symmetry inherent in the fact that the day on which James was officially deprived of his royal title and the right to rule also happened to be the fourth anniversary of his accession to the throne.[37]

While storms ravaged the coast of Holland and prevented Princess Mary from joining her husband, Somers was charged with hastily re-drafting the list of pre-conditions to be placed before the royal couple for their assent, prior to the formal offer of the crown. Though these guidelines were originally conceived as a wide-ranging blueprint for future government, 'for the better securing of our religion, laws, and liberties', their scope was soon rationalised to embrace only practical measures, rather than abstract theoretical principles, and reflected what parliamentarians were not prepared to accept, rather than that which they truly desired from their rulers. As a consequence, it was the catalogue of James's misdeeds as King – based in part upon the charges levied against him from the floor of the Convention Parliament – that formed the centrepiece of the first section of the document which subsequently became known as the 'Declaration of Rights'. Prohibitive clauses mirrored the indictments against the former regime, and attempted to ensure that a future monarch could not wield the prerogative with such surety and devastating effect as had James. Thus, the maintenance of a standing army in peacetime was held to be illegal, as was the prosecution of subjects for petitioning their king, and the activities of the much-reviled ecclesiastical commission. However, while the Declaration attempted to ensure that MPs should not, in future, be impeached as a result of their participation in controversial debates, promising to safeguard their 'freedom of speech', other clauses which stipulated that fines should not be 'excessive' and that judicial punishments could be neither 'cruel' nor 'unusual' were vague and open to a wide variety of interpretations. Furthermore, the commitment to limiting the dispensing power of the sovereign was only to extend as far as it had been 'assumed and exercised of late'.[38] It would, therefore, be wrong to view the Declaration (as many eighteenth-century Whigs and nineteenth-century liberals were minded to) as a binding contractual agreement between monarch and people, which represented the apotheosis of the English Constitution and a decisive break with the past subordination of Parliament to the wishes of the Crown. Rather than pointing towards the future, the text of the Declaration expressed a stubborn determination not to permit a repeat of the mistakes of the past, or to allow James to effect a return in the present. The fear of a vengeful Roman Catholic sovereign and the continuation of a 'popish' dynasty was what had motivated its conception, but – despite William's marked reluctance to allow any of its provisions to actually pass onto the statute books – it soon assumed a stature and symbolism out of all proportion to its original significance and intent. As a precedent, it came to be appealed to again and again by subjects concerned to tie their kings to the rule of law, as they themselves had conceived of it. Moreover, it served to legitimate the act of the Revolution, confirming and consolidating the idea that James was a man for arbitrary power, a ruthless, criminal King who strove only to 'extirpate the Protestant religion and the laws and liberties' of the land.[39] He was now the reviled and fallen monarch against whose actions all other misdeeds by the future rulers of England might be weighed, and accurately judged wanting.

Such considerations might not, however, have been immediately apparent to William as he struggled to adjust to the throng of place-seekers who gathered each day at the doors of his antechamber, and to the invidious combination of fumes, damp and stale air that seeped into his apartments at St James's and rendered his life scarcely worth living. Dust from the coal fires that heated London's homes, and polluted and choked up the skies, had settled upon his lungs, aggravated his asthma, and wracked his frail constitution. Upon her arrival, Princess Mary had been horrified to discover her husband 'in a very ill condition as to his health . . . [with] a violent cough upon him and . . . grown extreamly lean'.[40] Yet matters of state dictated that there was neither time for reflection, nor for the Prince's thorough recuperation, as the very next morning, Ash Wednesday, had been designated by Parliament for making the formal offer of the crown to William and Mary. While the rain drummed incessantly against the windowpanes and roof slates across Whitehall, the couple took their seats in the Banqueting House, to hear the Declaration of Rights read out, the throne declared officially vacant, and Halifax – who officiated in the absence of a Lord Chancellor – present them with the crown on behalf of both Houses, acting as 'the Representative of the Nation'. Observers noted that William was neither called upon to give, nor attempted to make, any explicit reference to the text of the Declaration in his terse acceptance speech, and that, while the Commons was well represented, many of the lords had chosen to stay away. Even though they might have acquiesced in the transfer of power from their anointed sovereign to the new dual monarchs, a substantial minority of the members of the Upper Chamber were determined to prove that they neither approved of nor wished to be associated with its taking effect. Yet this mattered comparatively little to those outside the confines of the palace, who had flocked to the scene, despite the appalling weather, in order to cheer on the heralds and trumpeters as they swept past, proclaiming the start of a new reign. The political volatility of the past weeks had repeatedly brought Londoners out onto the streets as a result of protest, curiosity and fear. Now they came only to celebrate, and – though there were undoubtedly those present who yelled as enthusiastically for William and Mary, as they had for James the previous December – the promise of a bloodless, constitutional solution to their problems, combined with the vision of domestic and political concordance enshrined by the King and Queen's acceptance of the crown hand-in-hand, did much to recommend the settlement to the ranks of bedraggled, yet cheerful, well-wishers who packed the roadside from Whitehall to the Temple in hopes of catching a glimpse of yet another royal procession. William's promise to continue to preserve the nation's 'Religion, Laws, and Liberties . . . and to do all that is in My power to advance the welfare and glory of the nation' was admittedly vague, yet touched upon the very concerns of Protestant England that had appeared to be under such a sustained and inexorable attack from the policies of James II.[41] The desire for a respite from the constant legislative innovations of the former reign might indeed have precipitated the King's fall and necessitated the forging of a fresh political consensus based upon compromise, but only radical and bold changes to the very structure of government and finance would enable the framers and beneficiaries of the Revolution to hold on to power, in the face of the sustained attempts of James and his French allies to wrest it back from them. For James was dead only according to the letter of the law, and since his landing on the French coast he had been far from inactive in seeking to reassert his rights as King. He would not, and could not, accept the verdict of the Convention Parliament regarding his loss of sovereignty and, having watched the political resistance mounted by his followers fail amid disunity and indecision, his mind – that of a man who above all else had always prided himself as a soldier – turned swiftly and firmly towards a military solution to his troubles. If the forfeiture of his throne had been confirmed in Parliament only through the loss of sleep, tempers and much spilled ink, then James was determined that his own struggle to regain it would now be costed thoroughly, over the following years, in terms of treasuries stripped, towns burned, and lives lost on the battlefields of Europe.

II

Upon landing at Ambleteuse, James had knelt on the shore and offered up his thanks to God for a deliverance from his foes that he believed to have been nothing short of miraculous. Having arranged for word of his arrival to be sent on to his wife, he took lodgings in a nearby cottage, and commanded those clergymen who had turned out to welcome him at such short notice and at such an early hour to pray for his soul, as he had sworn 'to defend the cause of Jesus Christ' with his life, adding rather mournfully that he now trusted that God would not forsake him in the midst of all his troubles. Then, having exhausted himself in recounting the tale of his escape over again to his hosts, he at last fell fast asleep and did not stir again until well past daybreak. A carriage and horses were already speeding their way to him and, upon their arrival, he set off immediately for Paris, stopping briefly at Boulogne in order to write to Colonel Preston, urging him to send all of his money over to him at the first available opportunity and begging to 'know a little newse' of how affairs were unfolding in England without him. It would seem, therefore, that James had already resigned himself to a lengthy stay in France, and that had the Convention called him back on anything but his own terms, he would almost certainly have declined.[42] A King by Divine Right, James had no stomach for a regency that would have entailed a compromise with the son-in-law he hated and feared in equal measure, and with a fractious and disloyal parliament whose authority he steadfastly refused even to recognise. Halting for the night when he reached the River Somme at Abbeville, he showed himself to the country people so that he might make himself 'publickly known' to them and later dined with the local nobility, before picking up post-horses and swinging westwards into Normandy, bound for Breteuil.[43] James had hoped to drive on for Versailles, to make his first call of state on Louis XIV and to appeal for the help of a fellow prince in offering him immediate sanctuary, and future support in the regaining of his throne. However, as his carriage approached the 'Sun King's' sprawling palace, he was informed that Louis had already left so that he might welcome Mary of Modena and her son into the old château of St-Germain-en-Laye. He had left instructions that James should follow him there and thus be reunited, through the auspices of the King of France, with his wife and child.

Since leaving England, Mary of Modena had been in a state of constant and dreadful apprehension about the fate of her husband. She had waited on the coast of Normandy, hoping for some word, until the weather closed in about her, the ports became choked by ice, and the mail pacquets stopped arriving. She refused to abandon the black silk gown of a widow, in which she had escaped from London, and raised concern among the French authorities by her resolve, were James to be arrested, 'to pass over again into England to suffer martyrdom with him'.[44] Moreover, while the little Prince of Wales seemed wholly unaffected by his voyage across the Channel, and indeed was thriving in his new home, freed from the attentions of over-zealous physicians at St James's and – blissfully unaware of the cataclysmic events unfolding about him – growing plump in his crib, his mother had fallen ill, with sharp stabbing pains that presaged an attack of lumbago. Louvois, at the war ministry, was apprised of Mary's 'pitiable state of grief' and issued hasty orders to have the former Queen conducted to the château of Vincennes, which had already been designated as her future home, if she showed any signs of preparing a passage back to England for herself and the child.[45] An escort of dragoons was promptly detailed to bring her closer to Paris, and King Louis ordered his garrison troops to clear the roads of snow drifts and of other travellers, so that her journey might be that much faster and more agreeable. She had reached Beaumont, making but slow work of her ride back through the province, and was deep in prayer when word of her husband's successful escape finally reached her. Now hurrying eastwards, she met Louis XIV the next day, on the roadside at Chatou. The whole court had left Versailles to greet her and their enormous convoy, more than a hundred coaches long, stretched far into the distance as the French King and his brother and son made their compliments to the Queen and pledged their support and assistance in the hour of her need. Lady Strickland passed the Prince of Wales out of his mother's carriage, and King Louis – his breath hanging in the frozen air – addressed a formal oration welcoming the infant to France, implicitly letting it be known that he was in no doubt as to either the child's legitimacy or right to the English throne. All talk of Queen Mary going to Vincennes was quickly forgotten, as it was decided that the grander residence of the King at St-Germain-en-Laye should be put at the indefinite disposal of her and her husband. The short ceremony had passed off to the satisfaction of all present, save for monsieur, the duc d'Orléans, whose pride had been hurt by Mary's forgetfulness and failure to observe the correct court etiquette, by pecking him only on one cheek, instead of on both as convention required. However, such oversights did nothing to blemish the overwhelmingly favourable impression created upon her hosts by the strikingly dignified Queen, still youthful at thirty, and retaining an element of chaste Mediterranean beauty – a vision of ivory and black – despite all her misfortunes. With Mary installed at St Germain, and an unfortunate tapestry depicting the family of the vanquished King Darius throwing themselves upon the mercy of Alexander the Great tactfully removed from her apartments, the stage was set for King Louis to enact a further piece of political theatre that would underscore not only his enormous generosity to the royal fugitives, but also their abject dependence on him.

James had rather enjoyed his journey from the coast, inveighing against his rebellious subjects, targeting John Churchill – who he believed had plotted to have him kidnapped on Salisbury Plain, and delivered captive to the Prince of Orange – for particular censure, and proudly revealing to his new travelling companions his cunning and presence of mind in escaping from England with rows of flawless diamonds sown onto the buckles of his shoes. That he had been permitted to go did not appear to trouble him at all, or diminish the compelling power with which, he believed, his stories of a fresh Stuart escape were invested. If the image of Captain Trevanion's herring boat lacked the potency and symbolism of the Royal Oak at Boscobel, then James certainly had not given up the hope of ever retelling his tales beside his own hearth at Whitehall. The only problem, which filled the exile with gloom and trepidation, was just how to effect his return with a degree of permanence, and with the minimum amount of effort, dislocation and danger to his person. After the shocks and betrayals of the past weeks, James still had the appetite and desire for kingship, but lacked the will and direction to achieve his stated aim. As his coach swung into the courtyard of the château of St-Germain-en-Laye, just as the sun was setting on the evening of 27 December 1688/7 January 1689, it was apparent that it would fall to King Louis XIV to provide both of these latter qualities for him.

Indeed it was the French King who hastened to James and made to embrace him as he reached the top of the palace stairs and crossed the threshold into the guard-chamber, now made claustrophobic by the presence of so many courtiers, soldiers and Princes of the Blood. Overcome by the warmth of his reception, James attempted to show his gratitude; he bowed low and then – in a movement that surprised and shocked those present – appeared to be on the point of throwing himself to the floor, in an act of complete supplication to his brother monarch. Louis, with the remarkable forethought that characterised each and every one of his movements as King, caught him and pulled him back up to his feet, hugging him tightly. Returning the embrace, James regained his composure and, straightening slightly, presented his compliments to the King before being conducted through a series of state apartments into the Queen's room. There, Louis formally reunited the exiled royal family, informing Mary of Modena, with elegant understatement, that he had brought her 'a man who you will be very happy to see' and confiding to James that he had taken good care of his son during his absence. Several courtiers noted that husband and wife 'remained a long time' in each others' arms, while Louis withdrew to a discreet distance and informed his courtiers that the King of England really was among the best of fellows.

Indeed, there appeared to be no end to Louis's munificence, as he told James that he should 'let me know all that you want', for 'You are the master of my kingdom'.[46] Unfortunately, this appeared to embarrass his guest further, for James did not how to respond properly, stammered awkwardly, and forgot much of his French vocabulary as he was introduced to the dauphin, monsieur's young son – the duc de Chartres – and the other Princes of the Blood. The verdict on him, already shaped by the jealousy of favour seekers displaced by his unexpected arrival, was consequently far from favourable. James was said to look 'old and much fatigued', and though this was hardly surprisingly given the collapse in his fortunes, it served to reinforce the impression that had been created at court by the poor quality of his conversation; that here was a prematurely aged, disagreeable and somewhat foolish man, who would be a great and potentially limitless drain upon the royal finances, while providing little in the way of either entertainment or gossip for the idle rich. The marquise de Sévigné conceded that 'he has much courage', but found his stories dull and thought that he had 'but a common mind', while madame de Lafayette believed him to be shockingly inarticulate, venturing only in his defence the English inability to master foreign tongues and the fact 'that so great a misfortune as that which has befallen him' would have diminished 'a much more perfect eloquence than his'.[47] More damaging was the perception – common to both the diarists of Versailles and the Williamite polemicists hard at work in London and The Hague – that James had deferred entirely to the King of France, and would henceforth be little more than a pawn in his hands. The truth of the matter was far more complicated than this; James, as we shall see, was on occasion willing to take action that was unilateral and wholly independent of his new-found patron. However, his excited acclamation of Louis XIV, on their meeting at St Germain, as 'the greatest king of kings in the word' did reveal a willingness to acknowledge the seniority of the French King and to accept his judgements with the same sense of respect and duty as he had once regarded the pronouncements of Marshal Turenne and King Charles II. Since ascending to the throne, James had had no other authority to turn to than God, but now he was able, and more than willing, to accept his place in a new hierarchy, this time of continental Roman Catholic monarchy with Louis XIV at its head.

It was to this European order, and to the Vatican as the ultimate source of God's authority on earth, that James now looked for assistance. On a superficial level at least, the signs were encouraging. Public prayers had been ordered to be said for James in all the churches of Rome at the height of the crisis, while a papal brief, issued at the beginning of February 1689 (New Style), offered comfort to the royal exiles and was quickly followed by a consistory in which the question of their fate loomed large. Innocent XI had sought to condemn the theft of James's crown by the Protestants and urged his cardinals to pray to God for the swift restoration of the King. He had devoted his efforts as pontiff to restoring peace to Christendom and to the creation of a holy league that was capable of driving the Turks out of Europe, and James reasoned with fairly good cause that Innocent would now be prepared to forge similar alliances in order to furnish the military and financial resources needed for the successful reconquest of England. When Leopold I had been faced with ruin six years before, and the Ottoman armies had swept on to the very gates of Vienna, it had been the influence of the papacy that had secured him the vital Polish and Venetian allies who had turned the tide of battle, saving both his throne and the territorial integrity of the Habsburg Empire. Thus James felt 'no small hope that divine Providence will shortly restore our fortunes' but that this 'assuredly can come to pass only by a well arranged and established peace among all the Princes of Catholic name'.[48] A flurry of letters in February, from James and Mary of Modena to the pontiff, prominent cardinals and the General of the Jesuit Order, served to reinforce this point and to promote the idea of a new confessional conflict, which might in time assume the aspect of a crusade against the northern Protestant powers. If James still paid lip service to religious toleration, then he was quite prepared to brand his former Protestant subjects before the Pope as 'the heretic sort', dedicated to spreading their 'abominable' creed 'throughout Christendom', while his wife showed but few reservations over the desirability of a military alliance 'by which we can hope that the Catholic faith and our Royal House should again set foot in England' in order to fight 'the insults of heresy, which is now triumphant'.[49] Yet, as the couple were forced to acknowledge, the fear of France weighed far more heavily in the minds of these princes than any overriding zeal for the promotion and security of their common faith. There were few illusions held in the courts of Europe about the long-term desire of Louis XIV to settle his clients on the throne of Spain and the chair of St Peter, or his ambition to establish himself as a second Charlemagne, breaking the hold of the Habsburg dynasty and refashioning the Holy Roman Empire as part of his own patrimony. Thus the Spanish Ambassador at The Hague had ordered public Masses to be held at his chapel for the success of the Prince of Orange's expedition, and Leopold I looked anxiously to Holland and England for allies to anchor his flanks and contain the pretensions of his bellicose western neighbour. Moreover, Innocent XI lacked any semblance of an army with which to transform his spiritual and moral authority into temporal power. The Papal States were largely dependent on foreign protection and Rome itself was perilously vulnerable to attack. With French troops already occupying Avignon and Venaissin, and the Gallican Church openly flouting papal authority, Innocent XI – whose own dreams of military glory had been denied to him as a young man – was fully aware of the dangers inherent in ceding command of a mighty Roman Catholic league to a sovereign who bore him precious little love or respect.

As a consequence, James was forced to struggle hard to reconcile the Pope to the King of France. He had earned the gratitude and thanks of Innocent XI, exactly one year before, through his willingness to act as a mediator between the two powers and by his firmness in warning the French Ambassador against contemplating any military strike against Rome. However, he was now no longer a powerful King, capable of ameliorating the threat posed by Louis XIV, but a fugitive entirely reliant on French charity for his subsistence and his ability to mount a challenge to regain his throne. With little but his past services and his undoubted devotion to the Church to recommend him to the pontiff and the Curia, James chose to despatch one of his Gentlemen of the Bedchamber, Colonel James Porter, to the Vatican on a mission to deliver his communiqués in person. However, even though Porter was received by the Pope within hours of his arrival in Rome, the audience quickly assumed a terse and strained aspect that threatened to turn at any moment into an open and acrimonious dispute. This was due in part to the uncompromising nature of James's instructions, which demanded that Innocent should immediately seek to reconcile himself with Louis, as a pre-condition to the signing of any alliance, and that a large subsidy should be settled forthwith upon the exiled English King and his followers. More damaging to the outcome of the mission was James's failure to accurately gauge the levels of hostility and deep suspicion with which the French were held throughout the Papal States. Even as Porter was delivering his credentials to the Curia, the Roman authorities were preparing to contain fresh outbreaks of anti-French rioting, and Louis XIV's Ambassador, Lavardin, was busy fortifying his home, protected by a phalanx of armed men and cheerfully continuing to defy the Pope, despite his recent excommunication. Consequently, James's evocation of 'the kingdom of France [as being] where now the main strength of the Catholic party lies' was but coolly received, while his report of the destruction wrought upon 'English ground . . . [with] churches plundered and demolished, the very houses of the Ambassadors of Catholic Princes pillaged, and almost all the orthodox [i.e. native Roman Catholics], whether laymen or bishops and priests, thrown into prison, with the spoiling of their goods' not only sat uneasily with the facts as reported by the most recent intelligence received by the Vatican, but also brought to mind more readily the depredations of Louis XIV's armies rather than the remarkably orderly descent upon England made by the forces of the Prince of Orange.[50] Innocent XI was yet to forgive the French for threatening his greatest triumph by sending their troops into the Rhineland during the last campaigning season, and thus relieving the pressure upon the Ottoman Turks, who had at last been brought to the negotiating table. Moreover, if there were few popes more thoroughly steeped in the asceticism of the Counter-Reformation than the tall and spare frame of Innocent XI, then there were also few who held the dignity and responsibility of office as pontiff in such high and precious regard, as the most sacred of all trusts. Even if James's strident vision of the establishment of a Roman Catholic league struck an emotional chord within him, he would not be the one to fatally compromise the authority of the papacy by acknowledging the right of the Gallican Church to near autonomy, in pursuit of what amounted to little more than a bloody and ill-conceived military adventure. He knew enough of the English Church, from his contacts with Cardinal Howard and the missionary priests, to tell that there was little appetite among the small and beleaguered Catholic minority to embark on a confessional conflict against their neighbours, who regarded them in the main, if not with friendship, then with mistrust rather than with murderous intent.

It was ever James's misfortune to choose his servants without sufficient regard to their fitness for the task at hand, and though there may have been something of resignation, as well as back-handed praise, in his rationale for entrusting the mission to Porter – 'since I have not anyone about me more capable of doing it' – the devout Irish soldier had simply not the aptitude, the independence, or the tact essential for effectively communicating such a difficult proposition. He had been instructed to act in close concert with the French Ambassador, a fact that was not lost on the Pope's servants, and he sought to bully and bluster at Innocent when his interview appeared to be on the verge of going badly wrong. He informed the Pope – hinting that he had heard the rumours about the Vatican's tacit support of William's invasion – that if he were now to refuse to come to the aid of King James, the world, and Roman Catholics in particular, would be forced to conclude that he was rejecting a holy alliance in favour of giving succour to the Protestant cause. At this, Innocent terminated the audience and dismissed James's emissary, whose credit and usefulness had all but evaporated in a matter of minutes. The fallen King of England would not now be riding to war with the benefit of a papal blessing, and the subsequent requests of Mary of Modena's uncle, Rinaldo, Cardinal d'Este for the grant of a subsidy to James fell upon markedly stony ground. Innocent told him that he could not help him until France ceased to threaten the invasion of his remaining territories. Furthermore, he was in no mind to refrain from informing the Cardinal that he would not hear of James being portrayed as a martyr to the faith, or be criticised on account of his reluctance to sanction a religious war, when the reality of the coming hostilities signified nothing of the kind. The King had fallen, he suggested, not because of his Catholicism, but because of his close alliance with Louis XIV and his thoroughly misplaced desire to emulate him.[51]

Without the support of the papacy, James's attempts to stitch together a complex series of alliances, based on religion rather than on national interest, appeared severely, if not fatally, compromised. While Roman Catholic princes such as Louis I of Monaco, and a handful of Italian potentates – including Francesco II of Modena, his brother-in-law – might sympathise with his plight and offer their heartfelt condolences for the loss of his crown, the truth was that they could do no more than chorus their disapproval of James's treatment. They had not the faintest hope, or any real inclination, to redress the military balance in his favour. Having firmly rejected the idea of being granted asylum in the territories of the Spanish Empire, James appears to have lacked faith in the willingness of the Count of Oropesa and the other policy-makers lodged at the Alcazar to further his cause, or to grant him a share of the treasures of the Americas. Still less was to be expected from the invalid King Carlos II, whose terrible afflictions were blamed on the weaving of dark enchantments, or on the failure of the Habsburg bloodline after repeated intermarriages, depending on the individual perspective – or relative credulity – of the courtiers and priests who populated the cloistered precincts of his magnificent palace-cum-monastery. Yet Carlos's reasoning was not so clouded as to make him entirely unaware of the covetous eyes that regarded his throne from Lisbon, Paris and Vienna, and he had wit enough to grimly apologise to the crowned heads of Europe for taking such an unpardonably long time to die. If Spain could do no more than look forward to a period of marked uncertainty, following the eventual extirpation of its ruling house, then only the Holy Roman Empire could offer sufficient might and political will to supplement that of France, in the quest to restore the erstwhile King of England to his throne. It was upon this possibility that James appears to have set his heart.

He was wise enough to recognise that Leopold I had provided valuable support to the Prince of Orange in his struggle against France, but he remained convinced that the Emperor might now be persuaded by his conscience, as a Roman Catholic, to realign himself according to his religion. This explains the veiled criticism running through his letters and those of his wife in February 1689, lamenting the inability of 'Catholic Princes' to make peace among themselves and attacking those among their number who had taken a share in Prince William's heretical 'crimes'.[52] Confident that the Pope would bring pressure to bear upon Leopold, James opened up a parallel line of communication with the Emperor, urging him in a lengthy and highly formal Latin address to reconsider the nature of his diplomacy and hoping 'that when his Imperial Ma[jes]ty saw the Prince of Orange make use of his friendship and assistance, to pursue his own unnatural ambition and dethrone a Catholick King, he might relent in some measure on account of Religion at least, and be inclined to redress so crying an unjustice . . . beyond what tis probable his intention was in the beginning'.[53] However, even though James's appeal certainly shook Leopold's resolve, a reply was not immediately forthcoming, as the Emperor sought to clarify the moral grounds on which his alliance with the Calvinist 'usurper' was based. He had no desire to be seen, either by his own people or by his fellow monarchs, as unilaterally breaking the political and spiritual consensus of Catholic Europe, yet he could not countenance diverting resources from his own campaigns in the east, or the ceding of the long-term political initiative to Louis XIV in the west. Thus he temporised and sought to shift the responsibility for the decision to a panel of Roman Catholic scholars resident in Vienna. After much deliberation, they decided by a narrow vote of four to three that his refusal to come to James's aid was more than justified by the threat presented by France, and by the need to achieve the 'greater good' in the attempt to preserve the whole of Christian Europe from invasion by the proselytising Muslim armies of the Ottoman Turks. Even then, Leopold still resisted replying to James's letter until he had declared war upon France at the start of April 1689 (New Style).[54]

As a result, James was forced to begin his plans for a forthcoming military campaign with no real inkling of the Emperor's attitude towards his cause. However, it would seem from his shocked response to Leopold's decision that he had harboured great hopes for the establishment of a lasting military pact between France and the Empire. Upon his belated receipt of Leopold's letter – which had arrived at St Germain after he had set out for Ireland – James could scarcely restrain his incredulity and rage at the Emperor's contention that he was the author of his own misfortunes through his willingness to countenance blindly the aggressions of France. Had James listened to the advice of the Imperial Foreign Minister, Dominic, Count of Kaunitz and backed an initiative to join England, Spain, the Papal States and the Empire in a single defensive coalition against Louis XIV's aggressions, or 'thought fit to use your power and authority, as Arbiter of the peace of Nimeghen [i.e. Nijmegen], to put an end to . . . continual breaches of faith and agreements' by the French then, it was argued, he would have remained secure on his throne. Instead, he had harkened 'to the fraudulent suggestions of France' and by so doing allowed Louis XIV to actively foment the 'division betwixt your Serenity and your people' that had served to topple him. Moreover, it was not the Holy Roman Emperor, but the King of France who had wrought 'unspeakable damage' to 'the whole Christian world' by allying himself with the Turks, 'the sworn enemys of the holy Cross'. All that Leopold would, or realistically could, offer to James in these circumstances was his hope that God's serenity might comfort him in the midst of his afflictions. Unsurprisingly, neither these words nor the Emperor's promise of 'lasting, tender and brotherly affection' did anything to appease James, who was not accustomed to being lectured, and who was devastated by the letter's 'harsh . . . and very unreasonable . . . way of arguing'.[55] Indeed, until his final illness, James would neither forgive nor forget the harm that he believed had been done to his cause by the Emperor's actions, and would henceforth number him alongside the Prince of Orange as the greatest of his enemies.

After the initial relief experienced at his reunion with his wife and son, a gradual sense of foreboding, and a realisation of the difficulties that lay ahead if he were ever to reassert himself on his throne, began to impinge upon James's thoughts. As the Convention moved to install William and Mary in his place, and his supporters in parliament appeared to lack both direction and leadership, he reconsidered the hasty manner of his departure from Rochester, and sought to justify his behaviour to the nuns at Chaillot, telling them 'that he was taken by surprise; that if the thing were to be done over again, he would act differently; and . . . if he had had time to collect himself, he would have taken other measures'.[56] Mary of Modena echoed his thoughts to the Cardinal de Bouillon, considering that having been overcome by the storm of revolution 'everything had to be thrown overboard to save our persons'.[57] However, signs of genuine hope were at hand. Real, as opposed to figurative, tempests had done little to deter the fresh boatloads of fugitives who arrived at Dunkirk with almost every tide, half-dazed as a result of the speed with which their fortunes had collapsed, yet pledging their continued devotion to their fallen King. Little more than a month after his arrival, James was in a position to dispense with those French servants whom Louis XIV had appointed to him, and to fully repopulate his Household with those of his former subjects who had chosen to follow him into exile across the

Channel. English agents were already busily compiling lists of those noblemen who had reappeared at James's side, noting the value of their estates and the fact that the great majority of them, such as lords Castlemaine, Powis and Stafford, were having their rents and fees sent on to them in France. The embryonic court was as yet a heterogeneous and ill-defined organism, which could encompass representatives of the northern Roman Catholic gentry alongside the King's natural daughter Henrietta Waldegrave and her husband, and religious Dissenters such as Dr Bromfield, a Quaker, who feared that without a second restoration any hopes for religious toleration would be irrevocably lost.[58]

Few among their number had experienced such perilous escapes as the abbé Rizzini, who had nearly been lynched at Sittingbourne, but had bribed his way out of trouble, or John Warner, the King's confessor, who had been imprisoned at Gravesend but had fled to France on forged papers. For the most part, as he increased his control of the levers of State, William of Orange had been keen to let them go, opening up the prisons and providing passports to carry the most obdurate of James's friends into exile with as little in the way of comment or of dramatic excitement as was possible. In this manner, Charles Skelton, a future Lieutenant General in the service of France, James's niece Anne Palmer, the Countess of Sussex, Sir Thomas Strickland and, shortly afterwards, his children, were all permitted to pass over to the Continent, while even Elizabeth Cellier, the Catholic midwife who had allegedly brought both babe and warming pan into the Queen's presence, was able to find her way safely to the gates of St-Germain-en-Laye. Tellingly, however, once it became clear that her co-religionists were not to be subject to new persecutions in the wake of the Revolution, she chose to slip back into England, returning to the quiet obscurity from which she had originally come. This yawning gap between the expectation of brutal score settling and the reality of moderation, which sought to pass over recent conflicts rather than to reawaken them – and which found its most telling expression in a new Act of Indemnity and Oblivion, passed by the Convention Parliament in the summer of 1689 – also struck James, who permitted himself to savour the discomfort and humiliation suffered by his former friend and counsellor, Robert Spencer, Earl of Sunderland. A Catholic by ambition rather than by principle, Sunderland had fled to Rotterdam in terror for his life, disguised, as James later sneered, in women's clothes, only to divest himself of both his new-found religion and past alliances in a desperate and protracted attempt to engineer his return home.[59]

In the lull between conflicts, the courtesies of princes were still to be observed and, missing his favourite possessions, James wrote to ask if William would see to it that all his coaches and horses were safely returned to him, while despatching one of his equerries, Ralph Sheldon, to expedite matters and bring back his clothes, plate and 'the best of [his] guns and pistols' from England. His requests were granted and passes were quickly issued so that all of his servants and huntsmen could join him, if they so wished, together with '45 couple of hounds'. Such requests, which seemed to suggest that James was preparing to make his stay in France permanent and wished only to maintain himself in state and to pursue his overwhelming private passion of hunting, were welcomed by William and his advisors, hoping against hope that the exiled King might have resigned himself to his condition and forsaken any desire to overturn the settlement imposed upon him by the Revolution. The news of his preparations for a war in Ireland, however, soon shattered these illusions and prevented him from receiving all that he had asked for. William authorised his 'King's Messengers' to swoop on the house of Thomas Heywood, who had been the keeper of James's closet, in a pre-emptive strike to seize all the 'books and papers belonging to the late King James' that he had amassed and was preparing to transfer over to France.[60] Though keen to prevent state papers from reaching St Germain, or the inquisitive eyes of officials at the French Ministry of War, William was still prepared to make a distinction between the goods belonging to the former King and Queen, and declared that while the former were now to be impounded, the latter were to be 'allowed to pass' over the Channel without any further hindrance. In this manner, Wat Dormer, Mary of Modena's coachman, was permitted to accompany his mistress' horses, carriages and domestic pets aboard the *Penelope*, a ketch bound for France, while Sheldon, who had arrived far too late to spirit away any of the King's goods, was forced to begin the long journey back to St Germain with nothing more to show for his endeavours than one of James's drivers, who had taken advantage of his presence to beg permission to resume his former employment.[61]

If James was not destined to be reunited with his possessions, then at least significant numbers of his soldiers were beginning to follow him into France, and the nucleus of a royalist army in exile was beginning to form. A letter to the Tuscan Secretary of State noted, at the beginning of February 1689 (New Style), that 'a Captain of Dragoons [had] succeeded in bringing his company and all their horses across the water' and claimed that there were now over 4,000 British soldiers – described as 'splendid' and well-equipped men – in James's service.[62] Furthermore, there was much to be hoped for from the junior officers, and from large swathes of the rank and file of the King's former regiments that were now fanned out across the English countryside. In January, John Churchill and the Duke of Grafton had been entrusted with the task of purging officers and men who had been too closely associated with the former regime, and with re-establishing an English army capable of following the Prince of Orange into a major European conflict. Whole units were disbanded, morale was low and desertion was rife. Cashiered officers sought to rejoin their King in France, took to plotting against William's life in ale and coffee houses with greater or lesser degrees of seriousness and caution, or adapted to a new life of violent crime on the highways and byways of England, furnishing generations of writers from Defoe to Farquhar and from Fielding to Scott with a ready-made cast of disaffected Jacobite highwaymen with which to populate the pages of their novels and plays. Then in March 1689, the regular army was convulsed by a series of mutinies as whole regiments, bound for transports to the United Provinces, refused to march any further. Complaining bitterly over the appointment of Dutch officers and of being forced to serve abroad for less pay, while foreign troops garrisoned their home towns, they went into revolt. The grenadier company of Prince George's Foot refused to leave its quarters at Brentford, while at Croydon, men from the other companies intermingled with mutineers from the Royal Scottish Horse, and departed with them at first light. More serious still, the foot companies of the Royal Scots – whose Roman Catholic Colonel, George Douglas, Earl of Dumbarton, had already fled into France – disarmed their officers at Ipswich, seized the regimental pay chest, powder carts and artillery, and began the march back to their homeland, vowing to fight for King James every step of the way.

It seemed to many members of the Convention Parliament that the outbreak was a prelude to a major rising, well planned and executed by those of the former King's adherents who still remained within the military establishment. The men of the Royal Scots, as they elected new officers to lead them on their march through Lincolnshire, certainly believed that this was the case, and buoyed themselves up with hopes that the Royal Fusiliers – until recently commanded by James's old friend, the Earl of Dartmouth – would follow them into full-scale rebellion. On the floor of the Commons, John Howe, the MP for Cirencester and a man of strong and occasionally violent passions, urged that the harshest measures should be taken against the mutineers, and that only Dutch troops should be used to break them, for the British regiments were unreliable and he knew 'not which else to trust'. Accordingly, General Ginkel was despatched up the Great North Road with three cavalry regiments, to 'fall upon them' and crush the embers of the revolt before they could be fanned into full flame.[63] It took Ginkel six days to bring his quarry to ground. He overtook them near Sleaford, swinging his dragoons round their flanks to cut off their escape, as they fanned out across Swanton Common and prepared for battle, attempting desperately to re-deploy their cannon in order to meet the unexpected new threat. Tired, greatly outnumbered and now completely surrounded, their leaders attempted to parley and 'yielded themselves to the King's mercy' after Ginkel promised to personally intercede with William on their behalf.[64] Thoroughly humbled, the mutineers, whose numbers had dwindled through desertion to little more than 500 during their march north, were escorted back to London under heavy guard, before being committed, a batch at a time, to the Gatehouse at Whitehall and to gaols at Bridewell, Clerkenwell and Newgate. As Parliament uttered a collective sigh of relief, a Mutiny Bill, removing the implementation of military justice from commanders and according it parliamentary sanction and supervision, was rushed through both Houses and received royal assent in early April, just three weeks after being tabled. Yet although the provisions of this emergency act, destined to be extended throughout the reign of William III and beyond, were intended to be draconian, they were primarily framed in order to act as a deterrent. Thus, as the affected units were brought to heel, and the Royal Scottish Horse and Prince George's Foot disbanded, the mutineers themselves were treated with a remarkable degree of leniency. Within six months the great majority of them had been released without trial, having given their word that they would never again take service with the army, and though seven officers and men of the Royal Scots Foot were tried at the assizes at Bury St Edmunds, and found guilty of treason, sentence was never carried out and they were allowed to leave the kingdom in January 1692.[65]

However, it was not to England, but to Ireland, that James's attention was now drawn, as a theatre of operations where his authority and titles were still respected, and as a convenient springboard for the launching of a possible future invasion of Scotland. For the time being, however, much hung upon the ability and preparedness of the Viceroy, Richard Talbot, Earl of Tyrconnel to prevent widespread civil disorder and to hold together in James's name a culturally disparate and politically divided nation. Since January 1687, Tyrconnel had single-mindedly pursued a high-risk strategy, commended and endorsed by the King, which had sought to thoroughly refashion Irish society, enfranchising the Gaelic and the 'old English' majorities, while avoiding a final breach with the economically powerful (if numerically small) community of Protestant Anglo-Scottish settlers that might have tipped them over into a fatal and blood-soaked rebellion. Even though a plan to co-opt Roman Catholic bishops onto the Irish Privy Council had been defeated, and the basic question of inequality in landownership had not even been addressed, the substitution of Catholics for Protestants in the judiciary and local government had already fundamentally shifted the balance of political power in their favour. At the same time, the return of the religious orders had brought about a popular spiritual revival that, together with the news that all government-controlled teaching posts that fell vacant were to be filled solely by members of the Jesuit Order, seemed to sound the death knell for the future of the Protestant ascendancy in Ireland. However, more challenging, provocative, and immediately significant, was the comprehensive remodelling of the Irish army by Tyrconnel's own hand. Although there was an unremarkable increase in numbers from approximately 7,500 men in 1685, to just under 9,000 men in the winter of 1688, the personnel had been subject to a dramatic and fundamental change, with units dismissed en masse in a single day, and recruiting parties sent out to fairs and holy springs to make good their numbers, seemingly without difficulty, from among the native Gaelic population. The officer corps was systematically purged of its Protestant members, who were replaced by a large number of raw Roman Catholic gentlemen, often of quite humble means and origins. They were reinforced by only a thin sliver of professionals, of the calibre of Patrick Sarsfield, Justin Macarty, and Richard and Anthony Hamilton, who shared their religion and would be invaluable in the training of large numbers of recruits during wargames held at the Curragh.[66]

With both the civil and military arms of the government loyal to his regime, and largely divested of their Protestant membership, Tyrconnel, and by extension the wider Gaelic community and their allies among the 'old English', had much to hope for from a promised Irish Parliament. They sought to confirm the transfer of power to their possession and to redress historic and economic grievances which had grown out of the Plantation, the Cromwellian conquest and the abject failure of the Restoration settlement. However, the collapse of James II's government and the loss of almost half the Irish army in England threatened to destroy all of Tyrconnel's work and prompted him to seek an accommodation with the new authorities in London. Despite rumours that had been circulating since the beginning of December 1688, that there was to be a general massacre of Protestants, and the continual presence of Anglo-Irish petitioners at Whitehall, demanding that their estates should be secured and that strong action be taken against the administration in Dublin Castle, William was prepared to open negotiations with Tyrconnel on the most fundamental of issues. In return for being acknowledged as King, and receiving the Viceroy's submission, William was willing – despite the clamour of the established Church and of the London merchants who had underwritten the creation of great estates from the virgin Gaeltacht – to offer complete toleration for the Roman Catholics in Ireland. Richard Hamilton, a Roman Catholic closely associated with both the English court and with Tyrconnel's immediate family circle, was despatched to negotiate terms and shuttled between the two capitals on his mission during January 1689. Unfortunately the talks stalled, for reasons which are now far from clear, and whether as the result of the intransigence of the City of London and the Anglo-Irish lobby, or through gradual realisation of the weakness of William's true position, Hamilton, who had given his parole to the Dutch Prince, broke it and remained in Ireland urging defiance, while Tyrconnel tentatively opened up communications with James and appealed for substantial French military assistance. Thus a chance to reach an equitable settlement over Ireland was lost and William, without an effective navy or an English army that he could fully trust, was reluctantly forced to acknowledge that he might have to fight a costly side-show of a war in order to secure his flanks, before returning to the European arena that he believed would prove decisive in his life-or-death struggle against Louis XIV's France.

Having secured himself a modest breathing space, Tyrconnel next disposed of Lord Mountjoy, the army commander around whom Protestant resistance might have coalesced, by sending him into France. Believing that he was being despatched in order to gain James's permission for the conclusion of a lasting peace treaty with William, the hapless Lord was quite unaware that his travelling companions carried with them instructions for his immediate arrest by the French authorities. Indeed, it was only as the gates of the Bastille closed tight behind him that Mountjoy finally realised the extent of Tyrconnel's betrayal and of James's complicity in his sorry plight. With no domestic rival to challenge the Viceroy's position, many of the Protestant homes in and about Dublin were successfully raided for caches of arms, while Justin Macarty proved himself singularly adept at both bringing to heel the rebellious districts of Munster and in breaking the will of the newly created Protestant 'defence associations'. Tyrconnel was able to receive a French officer, the sieur de Pointis, whose mission was to assess the feasibility of holding Ireland against Williamite invasion, and of mounting successful attacks upon England from its shores.[67] There was no doubt in de Pointis's mind, as he watched the eagerness and enthusiasm with which recruits received their orders from the drill instructors on St Stephen's Green, as to the courage and dedication of the Irish army, or to the ease with which a ready supply of volunteers could be called on to swell their ranks in the event of the outbreak of hostilities. However, money, time and equipment were all in short supply. The destruction of the old officer corps had created problems of discipline, as inexperienced commanders attempted to win the respect of their men or drove themselves close to bankruptcy in order to see them paid, while the arsenal at Dublin Castle could not keep pace with the extraordinary demands for weapons made by some 40,000 anxious and determined new soldiers. With Irish trade paralysed by domestic uncertainty, events in England, and by the perilous nature that routine sea-crossings had now assumed, Tyrconnel appealed directly to James to use his influence to prevail upon the King of France to send him ready money, the 500,000 crowns that he believed would be enough to fund his war effort for the coming year. He offered to dismember the country, ceding either Waterford or Galway to the French Crown, as a powerful incentive for their further involvement.[68] James had already promised that he would attempt to have '7 or 8,000 muskets' shipped over, as soon as he had word from his own envoy, Captain Roth, but had also cautioned his old comrade-in-arms that Louis XIV would not be 'willing to venture more armes or any men, till he knows the condition you are in'.[69]

The truth of the matter, as Tyrconnel detected straight away, was that the government of France was becoming war-weary. As the victories of the last three decades faded into memory and the Treasury prepared to haemorrhage even more of its riches on a fresh European campaign, the King and his council were divided over the wisdom of opening up a new front, and uncertain as to how best to proceed in achieving the restoration of King James to his throne. Turenne and Condé had been consigned to their lonely and dusty tombs, while that able soldier the duc de Luxembourg was still in disgrace, the result of a combination of court scandal, persistent rumours that he had once willingly dabbled in the making of potions and in the black arts, and, more significantly, due to his misfortune in having incurred the lasting enmity of the war minister, the marquis de Louvois. His replacement, the duc de Humieres, was widely said by courtiers and ministers alike to be a mediocrity, though none of them would make bold enough to communicate their profound misgivings about his appointment to their King. However, the power of Louvois, once unassailable in the planning and prosecution of war, was in turn beginning to be eclipsed through age and ill health, and by the marked hatred that madame de Maintenon, then the King's mistress, bore him. In Louvois's judgement, an expedition to Ireland was but a rash adventure, excessively prone to danger, and offering few obvious benefits. If James were to be restored, it was argued that he might all too easily forget his debt to France and seek a compromise with his English subjects, reasserting his independence and breaking those promises already given. Far more seriously, Louvois knew that the previous year's campaign along the Rhine had neither been so clinical nor so decisive as had been expected. Pushed back towards their fortress line, the French army had both experienced and committed many atrocities, and had found itself confronted at the beginning of 1689 by unexpected German resistance, with the princes of Brandenburg-Prussia, Bavaria, Saxony, Hesse-Kassel and Hanover all choosing to make common cause with Holland and the Empire in their bid for survival. As a consequence, Louvois had much to hope – and to fear – from the new campaigning season in Germany, and did not wish to see valuable effort and scarce resources diverted in a purely opportunistic and ill-conceived attempt to fulfil Louis XIV's debt to a brother monarch. However, he was vehemently opposed in this by Colbert's son, the marquis de Seignelay, the Minister of the Marine, and a particular favourite of madame de Maintenon. With his own star in the ascendant, Seignelay was keen to increase both the prestige and the operational effectiveness of the French navy, and saw the advantage of blockading Anglo-Irish trade and presiding over a major combined expedition, the success of which could only be guaranteed through dominance of the sea-lanes, facilitating the necessary and continual re-supply of the army once it had been landed successfully on the coast of Ireland. Confronted by a divided council, and by a military command lacking both the ready assurance and the clarity of decision inspired in the past by an unbroken string of successes, the fate of the projected Irish campaign now resided squarely with the King of France. Objectively, Louis might have been inclined to accept the advice of his war minister, and he seems to have shown little interest in the future of Ireland, save for its value as a base from which James might consolidate his position, drawing off William's troops from Flanders as a prelude to his possible return to power as a French client. Thus, it was the consideration of his princely duty to James, rather than an evaluation of the long-term viability of Tyrconnel's regime or of the prospects of French victory in Europe, that predisposed Louis towards the favourable reports filed from Ireland by Seignelay's protégé, the navy officer de Pointis.

From the time of his first arrival at St-Germain-en-Laye, the French King had been careful to keep James fully appraised of diplomatic and military developments, and had often closeted himself with his royal guest in order to sound out his attitudes and to proffer him advice. However, as Louis knew, and Tyrconnel feared, James was by no means fully committed as yet to leading the struggle to regain his throne in person. There is no evidence to support the King's later contention that he 'immediately resolved to pass over into Ireland himself, and to do it with so much expedition, as to give a fresh encouragement to his friends and be a surprize upon his Ennemys'.[70] Commentators at the French court thought that he had settled rather too easily into his comfortable new existence, and that he showed precious little interest in initiating any activity that would contribute to the furthering of his own cause. Indeed, at the end of January 1689 (New Style) the marquise de Sévigné was confiding to her diary that she thought that, cushioned by a monthly allowance of some 50,000 livres (approximately £3,000) from the French Crown, the inheritance of the salt rent on the Ile de Rhe, and the fortuitous smuggling over by their followers of some £23,000 from England, the royal couple were pursuing 'a plan of life likely to continue'.[71] For his part, Tyrconnel appeared surprised that his master had not been more disturbed by his pledge to hold Ireland only until the summer, if aid was not immediately available. Attempting to rekindle James's sense of pride, he enquired 'whether you can with honour continue where you are when you may possess a kingdom of your own' and promised that if 'your majesty will in person come hither and bring with you those succours to support the country . . . I will be responsible to you that you shall be entirely the master of this kingdom and of everything in it'. However, even this spirited and direct appeal failed to produce any tangible awakening of James's interest, and his Viceroy was forced to try a more conciliatory, if not desperate, line of persuasion in his next communication, promising that if the King would but show himself in Ireland for a season 'to arrange our affairs, [then] you could again return afterwards if you found it necessary'.[72] Yet by this time, the French King and his government had begun to swing round to the view that a descent upon Ireland would be extremely desirable, if conducted with speed and secrecy, and if it was led by James in person. As Vauban, the great military engineer, informed Louvois: 'I have an idea that when a man plays his last stake he ought to play it himself or to be on the spot. The King of England seems to be in this condition. His last stake is Ireland; it appears to me that he ought to go there, where with the help which . . . King [Louis] may give him he can get on his legs again and be supported by those of his subjects who remain loyal to him'.[73] The French appear to have been particularly aware of the propaganda value that could be gained, on his arrival, by the King's presence in Ireland rather than in France, and that he could then be portrayed to his erstwhile English subjects as a legitimate sovereign, rather than simply as the willing instrument of King Louis's foreign policy. Furthermore, they understood all too clearly, from the meticulous intelligence reports drawn up by de Pointis, the enormous boost to morale that James's mere appearance in Ireland would convey to his supporters there. Thus it would appear beyond all reasonable measure of doubt that French pressure was decisive in persuading James to commit himself to the scheme, and that Louis XIV had personally done much to awaken his interest in participating in a new military campaign.

It was scarcely a wonder, therefore, that there were those at the court of Versailles who scratched their heads in wonderment at the gulf between James's reputation as an active young soldier, which thanks to the Bouillon family had gained much credence throughout France, and the rather sorry reality of a monarch who appeared to be thoroughly unwilling to draw his sword in defence of his own rights, while perfectly content to let others – and the French and Irish in particular – fight and die for him.

This comparison leads us inevitably to a consideration of the state of the King's mental and physical health, and the lasting impact that the loss of his crown had wrought upon him. Traditionally, James's latter years have been dealt with in the briefest and most cursory of manners, with his seminal modern biographer, F.C. Turner, going so far as to declare that: 'From Christmas Day 1688 . . . until his death on September 16 1701, the life of James II has very little . . . interest'.[74] This interpretation is only possible because of the belief that a sudden and cataclysmic tide of hopelessness had engulfed the King upon Salisbury Plain, resulting in some form of stroke, brain tumour or complete nervous breakdown, from which he never fully recovered and which subsequently rendered him a broken man and a mere shadow of his former self.[75] The alleged irrationality of the King's actions, whether through his failure to recover his crown or through exaggerated displays of personal piety, can then be stressed without the need to acknowledge or to understand his success, during his final exile, in refashioning his reputation as warrior, king, and religious visionary. However, this approach entirely ignores James's ability to pursue each of these strands, relatively consistently, and for entirely rational ends, in the years from 1689 to 1701. Though they did not result in the successes envisaged at the time, they nevertheless offered the promise of great political rewards and genuinely popular acclaim. It is, therefore, not enough to view James's last years as marking nothing more than a 'retreat from reality' after he had lost his senses amid the wreckage of his regime.[76] Charles II suffered from profuse nosebleeds when subjected to extraordinary levels of stress when he was a hunted man after the battle of Worcester, yet it has never been suggested that royal policy was similarly misdirected, after his restoration, by his labouring under a brain tumour which proved debilitating, yet similarly inefficient at actually killing him. While James's failure to provide effective leadership in the winter of 1688 was certainly dramatic, and undoubtedly fatal to the maintenance of his personal monarchy, it is the theme of this study – and of its companion piece – that his failings, brought into the starkest of relief at times of political and military crisis, were both signalled and repeated throughout his earlier and subsequent careers, and that they were located primarily in the nature and expression of his aggressively authoritarian personality.

Consequently, it was not as a psychologically sick man, limping towards syphilis-fuelled degeneration and a premature state of senility, that James arrived in France. Though certainly stunned by events, the magnitude and implications of which his fundamentally unimaginative and blinkered mind could not fully and easily comprehend, James was still quick to regain his spirits, primarily as the result of the kindness and sensitivity with which the French King had chosen to approach his predicament. Through treating James, despite his objections, as an equal, and rounding upon those of his own suite who did not accord the royal exiles and their court sufficient respect, Louis was able – whether as the result of luck or good judgement – to establish himself in the eyes of the fallen King as a selfless benefactor, and a senior partner in any project that aimed at the restoration of his crown. As a result, James soon resumed his composure, regained his appetite 'as if there were no such man as the Prince of Orange in the world', and rediscovered his love of

the chase and the hunt, tearing through the countryside about
St Germain in the company of the dauphin 'as a man of twenty years
might have done'.[77] By the end of February 1689, as the frosts which had
glazed the Seine and the Rhone began to retreat, and transports began to
gather off the coast at Brest, it was already an open secret at the court of
Versailles that James was preparing to leave for Ireland. The idea, put to
him by Louis XIV and constantly reinforced thereafter, had taken hold of
him and he threw himself into preparations for the coming expedition.
Accordingly, the scale of the operation grew apace, with the original
commitment to sending little more than a reconnaissance force across to
safeguard the arms shipment promised to Tyrconnel expanding to fulfil a
much larger and more significant political and military remit: that of
providing for a new royal government in Ireland, and of comprehensively
training and re-equipping the existing Irish army. With this aim, a fleet of
thirteen warships, six frigates and three fireships assembled to protect the
transports sheltering under the guns of Brest. They were now loaded with
enough arms, powder and equipment to service some 20,000 men.[78] In
addition, a large number of French military specialists – among whom
were six general officers, twenty captains, thirty lieutenants, forty cadets
and a nucleus of engineers and artillery officers – had volunteered for
service, enticed by promises of rapid promotion, and intended to provide
the necessary expertise to wage siege warfare and to transform
Tyrconnel's untried recruits into the staple of a regular field army.

However, while 4,500 French and Anglo-Irish soldiers were mustering
and preparing for the march to the coast, James was voicing his own ideas
about who exactly should lead them. As a man who had always looked for,
expected and rewarded loyalty, his recent experiences had served quite
naturally to sharpen these proclivities, and to draw the comte de Lauzun
inexorably to him. Possessing daring, insolence and ambition in equal
measure, Lauzun had forfeited royal favour and been consigned to the
cells of the Bastille and the dungeons of Pignerol, but had emerged in
time to spirit Mary of Modena and her son out of England at the
Revolution, earning James's lasting gratitude through his quick-thinking
and nerve in conveying both wife and child to the safety of Calais. This
remarkably charmless individual appears henceforth to have captivated
the awkward and reserved James, who echoed the gratitude he had
already shown to Louis XIV by styling Lauzun as his 'governor' and
seeking to co-opt him into his Household. Unfortunately, the King of
France was not prepared to overlook past slights or to suspend his
judgement about the nobleman's conspicuous lack of military talent, and
refused Lauzun's appointment as Captain-General outright. With the
command conferred on two professional soldiers – Lieutenant-General
Rosen, an irascible Livonian who had fought his way up through the
ranks during long campaigns in Flanders, and his deputy, the competent

if unremarkable former Guards officer, Major-General Maumont – James could only signal his displeasure by creating Lauzun a Garter Knight after a service at Notre Dame de Paris, and by publicly bestowing on him a diamond-star badge of the order that had once been worn by his father, Charles I. This calculated snub did little, however, to cloud the affection and regard that Louis XIV had for his guest and, on hearing James miserably recall that his own weapons had been impounded in England, he took the opportunity to repair the damage done by the appointments of Rosen and Maumont, and offered him his own armour and 'the pistols that he carried on his saddle-bow', requesting that the returning King might make use of them.[79] The stage was thus set for their leave-taking, a ceremony that was purposely intended to mirror the arrival of the English King at St Germain and to bring full-circle the story of James's residence in France. As Louis embraced his cousin once more, he wished him every success in his great venture and, although it grieved him to see his friend go, said that he hoped that he would never see him again. Some at court believed, as James's carriage rattled out of Paris two days later on the road bound for Brittany, that his destiny offered him 'no other alternative than conquest or death', while others thought that the King had prolonged his leave-taking for rather too long and that he might soon be ready to return.[80] The events of the next sixteen months would determine which of these visions had the more veracity, and which way the fates and the gods of war would decide.

CHAPTER THREE

When the King Enjoys his Own Again

I

If James had been guilty of an exaggerated leave-taking, then there was no trace of reluctance in the speed and determination with which he pressed on to his rendezvous with the waiting fleet at Brest. He soon tired of, and outstripped, the slow and unwieldy cavalcade that had set out to accompany him – the Earl of Melfort had insisted upon taking no less than four carriages with him, just to accommodate his wife and her ladies – and 'leaveing his people to follow as fast as they could', James took off travelling with only his closest companions and a small escort of French cavalry.[1] However, his impatience cost him dear, as his carriage cast a wheel at Orléans and was subsequently dashed against the pier of a bridge, prior to being loaded aboard ship at Brest. Worse still, the barge carrying his new set of plate and part of his wardrobe sank on its way up the Loire, drowning a trusted and faithful servant in the process. Yet while the weather closed in about him at the harbour, and prevented his sailing for two further days, the King sought to establish his independence and authority by seeing to it that his own standard flew from the stern of the *St Michel*, and that English flags were raised throughout the fleet. His excitement about embarking on the campaign may have been welcomed by his junior officers, and by his two young sons, the Duke of Berwick and the Lord Grand Prior, but it neither communicated nor commended itself easily to the comte d'Avaux, the taciturn French diplomat who had been newly appointed as his political advisor and as Louis XIV's Ambassador Extraordinaire to Ireland. With secrecy at a premium, d'Avaux was horrified to discover the utter indiscretion with which: 'His Britannic Majesty speaks of everything before all the world'. He soon began the first of his despatches back to the French King, chronicling with an ever increasing sense of pessimism the mismanagement which he believed to be at the very heart of James II's affairs.[2]

However, despite his misgivings – and a further avoidable accident, when the *St Michel* collided with another vessel and had to return to port for repairs – the voyage to Ireland was remarkably uneventful. Without the available forces, or possibly even the will, to secure its own waters, the English navy was nowhere to be seen and only one merchantman was spotted, scurrying across the horizon, as the French fleet sailed across suddenly becalmed seas and anchored off the Irish coast at Kinsale. Having ordered, if not actually overseen, the unloading of the supplies, James hurried on to Cork, where he was met by Tyrconnel (whom he created a duke), and by a deputation of clergymen from the Church of Ireland, led by Edward Wetenhall, the local Protestant bishop. Though he had been censured for his willingness to take a large party of Jesuit priests with him on the expedition, James had also been careful to include the Anglican Bishop of Chester, the Bishop of Galway and the Dean of Glasgow in his party. The formal introduction, by James, of these Protestant divines to the Bishop of Cork and his clergy was aimed at – and partly succeeded in – allaying fears that the King was come to preside over the destruction of the Church of Ireland and the forced re-Catholicisation of both people and polity. Having played his part with some skill, James sought to underline the favourable first impressions gained, by pardoning a little group of Protestant rebels from Bandon, who ironically had been the first to raise a standard with the now ubiquitous 'No Surrender' motto embroidered upon its folds. They had been captured due to the prompt action of Justin Macarty, who with the 'bare reputation of an Army' had impressed upon them the futility of further resistance and promised them, to Tyrconnel's evident fury, generous and humane terms. It was his sense of military honour that now stood between the prisoners and the end of a rope, and which finally convinced James of the need for magnanimity and to declare, with more than a hint of regal condescension, that: 'You may now see [that] you have a gracious king'.[3] He might well have felt that such generosity was in order, as the intelligence that Tyrconnel presented before him at the council table was nothing if not positively encouraging.

The Protestant opposition had been caught completely unawares by James II's flight from England in December 1688, with the Revd Andrew Hamilton declaring that initially neither he, nor any of his neighbours, knew what had befallen their King. Some said that he had retired 'to a monastery, some to Rome, and some [said he was] dead, as every man's fancy led him'.[4] Fearing a rising of the Gaelic population and a repeat of the massacres of 1641 – which had irrevocably scarred the consciousness of the settler communities – Irish Protestants in Sligo and Ulster had banded together in armed associations, while boatloads of refugees had chosen flight over fight and, in full expectation of future outrages, set out to gain the safety of Scotland, England and the Isle of Man. Yet even though arms and supplies were gathered in abundance, due to extensive and active kinship networks across the Irish Sea, and a 'supreme council' had been established at Hillsborough under Lord Mount-Alexander, in

order to open up negotiations with William about the future sovereignty
of the kingdom, by March 1689 Protestant resistance appeared to be on
the verge of collapse. A brief skirmish just outside Hillsborough had
resulted in the undignified rout of their forces just a few days before
James's arrival, and, believing that all was lost, Mount-Alexander had
sought to desert his followers and taken ship for the Isle of Man. With
one of their natural leaders in exile and the other still languishing in a
French prison, the rebels were now experiencing a marked crisis of
confidence. They had lost the greater part of the territory that they had
seized over the winter and only the walled towns of Derry and
Enniskillen, which had refused to admit Catholic garrisons in December
1688, continued to offer any significant and organised resistance to
Tyrconnel's gathering forces. Given such circumstances, there were many
Irish Protestants who looked favourably upon James's initial overtures to
their community, and began to think seriously about the wisdom of
coming to terms with an administration which, if not quickly defeated by
external arms, possessed every indication that it might grow into a strong
and independently viable political entity.

Unfortunately, it was this very question of the shape which a Jacobite
Ireland might assume in the prosecution of a general war against William
of Orange that held the power to destroy the apparent unity of James's
council. Both the King and the Earl of Melfort, his new Secretary of State,
were alive to the possibility that their stay in a predominantly Roman
Catholic country, which had traditionally been the object of the fear and
scorn of their English and Scottish subjects, might gift an enormous
propaganda coup to their opponents. Indeed it would not be long before
Dutch print-makers would be re-cutting their plates, exorcising the more
obvious visual references to the previous year's depredations of the
French army along the Rhine and filling them instead with images of a
priest-ridden James presiding over the slaughter of innocents and the
creation of hanging trees, the boughs of which were laden down with a
grim – and by implication exclusively Protestant – human fruit. Yet the
contradictions facing the King ran far deeper than the production of
hostile imagery. In coming to Ireland, he wished for the mastery of a
loyal and docile population, who would re-stock his Treasury and march
to the sound of his drums, but not seek to fundamentally renegotiate the
terms on which their nation was bound to the British Isles. He had
neither use, nor desire, to be a king in Dublin if it meant renouncing
forever his dreams of returning in triumph to Whitehall. Central to his
concept of his own kingship was his coronation oath, made on behalf of
all his peoples to God Almighty, to protect his patrimonies as a sacred
trust and not to allow their dismemberment, or any change in the
manner of their governance. James saw himself as the sovereign of Great
Britain and Ireland, and not as merely the ruler of one of the constituent

parts over and above the rest. His legitimacy rested in his ability to govern in each and every one of his three kingdoms, and if one – or heaven forbid, two – of his titles were stripped away from him, then his right to rule in his other possessions would be seriously, if not fatally, compromised. Thus any talk of the redistribution of land, or of an assault upon the rights and privileges enjoyed by the Church of Ireland, was to be strongly and consistently opposed by James at every turn. Moreover, in his eyes, and also, significantly, in those of Melfort, Ireland was merely a convenient stepping-stone, from which to launch a landing in Scotland and an eventual victorious drive back into England that would place the Imperial crown of Great Britain squarely back upon James's head.

In their desire to retain the fabric of the state and its links with Whitehall, as they had existed from 1660–88, they were broadly supported by elements within the 'old English' aristocracy, among families such as the Dillons and the Plunketts, and by Tyrconnnel himself. Yet this influential grouping sought to stabilise Irish politics first, before embarking upon overseas campaigns, and desired both the full restoration of their lost lands and an unshakeable commitment to the open practice and furtherance of the Roman Catholic faith. Numerically the strongest and most zealous component within this alliance, the Gaelic Irish similarly wished for the return of their religious and political rights, and for the decisive breaking of the English and Protestant ascendancy, but they had no wish to maintain ties with the British Isles, or to be led off to fight and die in struggles to control and preserve the component parts of a unitary state in which they neither believed nor desired to continue in its present form. They had welcomed James because they believed him capable of granting Ireland political independence and a lasting autonomy over its religious and economic affairs, but they still lacked an effective voice within the King's aristocratically dominated councils to make their views accurately felt. Finally, there was the French interest, represented by d'Avaux, to be countenanced, and not easily denied. D'Avaux's clearly stated brief was to advance the power of the French Crown and to avoid becoming overly embroiled in James's private affairs. Accordingly, Ireland was to be refashioned as a French satellite, holding Britain in permanent threat of invasion, even though an immediate expedition from its shores was to be discouraged as being far too hazardous and a waste of the Sun King's precious resources.

It was not surprising therefore, that James acknowledged 'a great deal of goodwill in the Kingdom, but little means to execute it' and felt almost at a loss as how best to prosecute the coming war in a manner which would satisfy each disparate section of his followers.[5] Somewhat less forgivable is the sense of confusion and the profound lack of confidence that marred his councils, which led d'Avaux to wonder at the constant debilitating retreats from decisions already taken and the time

JACOBITE
IRELAND
1689~1691
→ Route of Williamite Advance - 1690
⇢ Route of Williamite Advance - 1691

Lough Swilly
Lough Foyle
R. Bann
DERRY 1689
ULSTER
CARRICKFERGUS 1689
Lough Neagh
BELFAST
Lower Lough Erne
BALLYSHANNON
DUNGANNON
CHARLEMONT FORT
R. Blackwater
ENNISKILLEN
ARMAGH
Mts. of Mourne
SLIGO
Moyry Pass
Upper Lough Erne
NEWTOWNBUTLER
NEWRY
DUNDALK
CONNAUGHT
R. Blackwater
DROGHEDA
R. Boyne
Boyne 1690
Aughrim 1691
ATHLONE 1690, 1691
R. Boyne
DUBLIN
R. Liffey
GALWAY
R. Shannon
Wicklow Mts.
LEINSTER
KILKENNY
R. Slaney
R. Barrow
LIMERICK 1690
R. Nore
MUNSTER
R. Suir
WEXFORD
WATERFORD
DUNCANNON FORT
CORK 1690
KINSALE 1690
James lands - 12 March 1689
James leaves - 4 July 1690

·miles·
0   25   50   75

wasted in meetings where 'we deliberate but nothing is decided'.[6] However, such tensions and failings were by no means apparent as James left Cork for Dublin, accompanied by more than two hundred mounted gentlemen, including the formidable and ruthless Lord Galmoy, who swelled his retinue en route. Tyrconnel, with an eye to his own continuing good fortune, made sure that he shared both d'Avaux's coach and counsels during the journey, while James appears quite literally to have been overwhelmed by the tumultuous displays of affection that marked his passing, and had to be saved from the unwelcome attentions of the country women at Carlow, who smothered him, despite all his increasingly shrill protests, with flurries of kisses and the most tender of hugs.

Thankfully, however, Dublin accorded him a far more dignified reception and, on Palm Sunday, 24 March 1689, he rode into the city dressed in a 'plain cinnamon-coloured cloth suit', over newly levelled streets that had been strewn in his honour with thousands of the choicest flower-petals, blossoms, and green shoots. Ahead of him Tyrconnel bore his Sword of State, while Berwick and Melfort rode at his side, and a host of ermine-clad peers followed behind in procession, as pipers struck up the refrain from Martin Parker's royalist anthem, which proclaimed to the crowds who hung from every available vantage post, that: 'the times they will mend . . . and the wars they will end . . . when the king enjoys his own again'.[7] It certainly seemed as if that prediction was about to be realised with the coming of the court to Dublin Castle. By nightfall, James had received the freedom of the city, been blessed by the Roman Catholic Primate of Ireland, and heard another favourable military report, this time from the turncoat Richard Hamilton. He had given a forceful display of the power and majesty inherent in his monarchy, and provided his Roman Catholic subjects with an appealing vision of an Ireland where their traditional hierarchies were both highly prized and restored to prominence in the affairs of the nation. Moreover, as even hostile pamphleteers were compelled to admit, he had shown great consideration to all of those who had turned out to greet him, and – while Williamites might choose to sneer at the emotion which overcame him as he gazed upon the elevation of the Host at the castle gates – he had done everything and more that had been required of him by an anxious people, caught between hopes of future freedoms and fears of the consequences of war and rebellion in their land.[8] If he had been an unknown quantity in the business of governing Ireland before his entry into Dublin – a figure upon whom the most unrealistic of Gaelic dreams and the wildest of Protestant nightmares might have been safely fastened – then he had done much to commend himself to his Roman Catholic subjects through his appearance that day upon the streets. However, his desire not to alienate his English and Scottish subjects irrevocably, or to be seen as ruling simply in the name of the majority in Ireland, moved him to attempt to placate the Reformed community by offering a forty-day amnesty, during which any of his Irish subjects who had fled abroad might return without charge upon their persons or property. Moreover, he published, within twenty-four hours of his arrival at the castle, a fresh declaration for the establishment of religious toleration, which was aimed at raising Catholic expectations of change, while simultaneously reassuring Protestants that his rule would not be one characterised by dragonnades, forced conversions and wholesale expropriation. Unfortunately, it failed to satisfy all of the former (or d'Avaux, who had counselled a policy of confiscation in order to pay for Tyrconnel's army), while doing nothing to allay the deep-rooted fears of the latter, who still prized the protection the statutes had afforded them against being swamped by greater numbers and potentially greater resources in the struggle for souls. For those who had not been subject to the full operation of the Test Acts, the promise of toleration for the majority, as well as for the minority, seemed to be nothing more than a cunning ruse designed to empower their foes till such a time as they could sweep away the last vestiges of Protestantism with impunity. The fact that soldiers would continue to raid Protestant homes in Dublin, as the result of James's marked fear of the possibility of a rising in his new capital, did little to help matters, but it is extremely doubtful if any seventeenth-century statesmen could have truly ruled without partiality in such volatile circumstances, and successfully bridged the confessional gap by the issue of a single decree.

However, for the time being, the single greatest problem facing James's administration was financial. The nation, as Sir William Petty had pointed out two years previously, was seriously under-capitalised, with coin in short supply and much of the available wealth and foreign trade concentrated in the hands of the Protestants. Though sheep and cattle remained plentiful and profitable commodities, restrictive legislation passed in Westminster had prevented their export to the Continent and to England respectively. Moreover, while land prices had been rising since mid-century, and were only now beginning to tail off, rents had also sharply increased, leading to a widening gulf between tenant and landlord, and reinforcing the sense of profound bitterness and loss experienced by those whose estates had been confiscated in the late 1640s and 1650s. The dependency on imported finished goods and even on basic commodities, which English merchants had sought to foster in Ireland, now threatened to cripple James's war effort before it was even properly underway, as his quartermasters discovered that although meat was cheap, bread, wine, oats and hay were all in short supply and consequently were very expensive. To make matters worse, recruitment for the new Jacobite army had successfully swept the countryside of manpower, with many labourers, who earned on average roughly half the wage of their English counterparts, preferring to opt for a life of supposed glamour, excitement and rapid advancement, over one of back-breaking, unmitigated and thankless toil. With fields left untended and unsown, and the generous French subsidy that he had brought over with him swallowed almost immediately in order to pay the arrears owing to his soldiers, James turned to a series of expedients which he hoped would stabilise the finances of Ireland, in the short term at least. Writs were sent out, calling for a parliament to meet in Dublin on 7 May 1689, in the hope that the legitimacy of the regime might be more fully established and that substantial revenue grants might be levied by it for the King's support. At the same time, letters were despatched to St Germain and Versailles, appealing for additional funds, for, as Tyrconnel later informed Mary of Modena, 'There is not a farthing of silver or gold to be seen in the whole nation'. Meanwhile, the small mint in Dublin Castle was radically overhauled as a prelude to the entire refashioning of the coinage.[9]

After landing James, his attendants, and supplies at Cork, the French fleet had returned to port at Brest and taken aboard those Anglo-Irish and French troops for whom there had simply not been space aboard ship on the first outward journey. Unfortunately, high winds and stormy seas had ensured that five weeks were to pass before they could set sail for Ireland once more. Taking advantage of this interval, Admiral Herbert had scoured the coast of County Cork with an English fleet, determined to attempt to locate the French convoy and to prevent a second landing of men and munitions. Blown far to the east of Kinsale, the French Admiral Château-Renault avoided contact with the enemy frigates who now prowled the entrance to the harbour and, abandoning his original instructions, decided to preserve the order of his fleet by running into the fog-shrouded expanse of Bantry Bay to effect a landing before the English scout ships – seen flying back to the west – could return with the rest of Herbert's fleet. Over the course of five anxious hours some 1,500 English, Scottish and Irish soldiers, together with the balance of the French regulars, were rowed ashore from the frigates and fireships, while anxious lookouts spotted the topsails of twenty-seven enemy vessels heading in towards the mouth of the bay. As drums beat out the alarm and decks were cleared for action, the last soldiers were hurriedly set down, cold and dispirited, among the nearest rocks and left to follow on the advance guard, who had already reached the town of Bantry, as best they could.

In the early hours of the following morning, 1 May 1689, Herbert's fleet, after tacking sail repeatedly in the face of a fresh gale, finally succeeded in gaining the bay and in forcing Château-Renault to abandon his anchorage. Shepherding his supply vessels and the fireships to the rear, the French Admiral turned into the protective narrows just to the south-west of the town, and swung his men-of-war into 'a very orderly line'.[10] Herbert believed that he might have attempted to turn the column of French ships and so gain the weather gauge, but this was soon denied to him, as the two lines converged upon each other, and as the French opened up at near point-blank range with their guns, small-arms and musketry. As hot lead tore across the decks, and sharpshooters picked off members of the English gun crews with alarming accuracy, several gun-ports were observed being closed in order to prevent further casualties, and ships of both sides began to drift dangerously towards the coast, before turning sharply from the western shore. For almost six hours broadside answered broadside as the fleets swept back out to sea, continuing to pound each other until darkness fell and, at last, Herbert gave the order to break off the engagement. Though a lucky shot had smashed into the poop-deck of *Le Diamant*, a 4th rate, causing a magazine to explode and the ship to be engulfed in fire, the French guns had at last begun to out-range those of the English, and had wrought a terrible havoc among the rigging of their foes. Château-Renault jubilantly reported that he had brought the mainsail of Herbert's flagship the *Elizabeth* crashing down, while five more English men-of-war had had, in the words of one midshipman, their topmasts and booms 'damnified' by the constant peppering of enemy shot. Though no vessel was lost in the engagement, French casualties – almost all of which had occurred when *Le Diamant* was hit – were less than half those of the English, who lost ninety-six killed and 250 wounded in the engagement. Moreover, Herbert had failed to press home his advantage against a foe who had been bottled up in the bay, and had not, by his own admission, 'been able to hinder them from landing whatever they brought' in terms of men and supplies. Yet while the French and Irish proclaimed the battle a great victory, and the English court sought to salve the feelings of their naval officers by lavishing knighthoods and titles for competent, if not remarkable, service, both commanders felt cheated of their triumph and badly let down by the conduct of several of their subordinates. As his captains made hasty running repairs to their vessels and his fleet limped back towards the Scillies, Herbert declared that 'I can trewly say it [i.e. the defeat] has not been my fault' and blamed the slight numerical advantage of the French, which he now chose to exaggerate, and the reluctance of some of his officers at the rear of his line to engage with the enemy closely enough. For his part, Château-Renault – who wrote his despatches that night with six feet of water in the hold of his flagship and spoiled powder barrels patching the gaping holes punched in its side by English shot – was even more forthright about the behaviour of the captains of both his van- and rear-guards, who, he charged, were more concerned with pursuing their private vendettas against him than with setting the seal upon a famous victory. Insult was added to his injury when the English Jacobites, whom he had protected and safely put ashore, refused to offer him their congratulations on his victory. A similar snub was delivered by James himself, who authorised the singing of a *Te Deum* and the lighting of fireworks to mark his success, but was overcome by feelings of deep melancholy at the losses suffered by the Royal Navy. With that particular brand of pride and egotism that characterised so many of his opinions, he still chose to own the English navy as his particular and personal creation, sniffing that if it had really been defeated by the French, then it was for 'the first time'.[11] The only explanation he could offer for Herbert's failure – which had, after all, saved his expedition from disaster and temporarily handed him control of the Irish Sea – was the love and devotion that the English sailors held for their true king, which had led them not to seriously press the fight. He would have cause to reprise a version of these sentiments, amid very different circumstances but to the same incredulous response from his French backers, some three years later. Yet for the moment, as rockets scribed their brightly coloured trails over the rooftops of Dublin, James was prepared to put such gloomy thoughts on hold, and to quickly grasp the potential significance that this victory might hold for him.

With a French fleet at his command, James might yet have made good his promise to land an army of 10,000 men in Scotland before July was out. His plan, communicated to d'Avaux on 6 May, envisaged a landing at Troon, a quick descent on Glasgow, and a rendezvous with the Highland clans at Stirling, where the castle might be prevailed upon to surrender and its arsenal distributed among the waiting clansmen. From there, James believed that he could be in Edinburgh within three days, and that William of Orange might be drawn out to meet him. He counted on a further landing of French regulars on Anglesey to cut William's communications and to either trap him between the two halves of his invading force as he pushed up through Lancashire, or else compel him to fall back on London. The stage would then be set for James to unite both wings of his army and to drive on towards a final confrontation with his foes outside the gates of the capital. With speed of the essence and resistance seemingly at an end in Ireland, this strategy had much to recommend it, not least the hopeful reports that continued to flood in from Claverhouse's Highland army. However, the entire logistical success, and indeed the feasibility, of such a strategy relied on the commitment of the French and the willingness of de Seignelay and Louvois to devote two fleets and a substantial military force to a campaign in England, which had neither been foreseen nor budgeted for when James set sail from Brest. The King had assumed that his allies held exactly the same war aims as he did, and that they would selflessly pursue them to his ultimate advantage. Unfortunately, neither supposition was actually true. D'Avaux's instructions had made it plain that Ireland was to be a sideshow, not the cock-pit, of a European war, at best a milch cow for the French Treasury, and at least a running sore in the underbelly of the Williamite war effort. Expeditions to Scotland and England were not part of this stratagem, as the involvement of French forces was to be as limited and as costless in terms of money and lives as was possible. As a result, Château-Renault, having accomplished his mission, wasted little time in weighing anchor and setting sail for home, even choosing to ignore a small English squadron under Sir George Rooke as it passed them on the horizon, on its way to disrupt the flow of Jacobite communications between Scotland and Ireland. Equally damaging was the disinterest with which d'Avaux regarded the King's ambitious plans, and the refusal of de Seignelay to commit himself to the deployment of additional naval forces, in his response to the King's letters, assuring him in only the vaguest of terms that a landing in Scotland would depend entirely upon the success enjoyed by Claverhouse's troops over the coming summer. Thus the course of the war in Scotland – upon which James believed all of his hopes to be founded – would, for the time being at least, be forced to develop without his direct involvement and, more significantly, without the help of the French military backing which he had always believed to be decisive.

At the Revolution, the challenge to James's authority had been every bit as dramatic in Scotland as in England. As Melfort began his precipitous flight to France on 10 December 1688, troops opened fire on rioters at the end of the Royal Mile, and the mob broke down the doors of Holyrood House and abbey. Houses owned by Jesuits were sacked, their printing presses destroyed and fires lit in the nave of the abbey church. Though Edinburgh Castle continued to be held in the King's name, by the Duke of Gordon and a small garrison, the Scottish Privy Council – which quickly restructured itself, rejecting James's pro-Catholic policies through the co-option of new Protestant members and the arrest of the Lord Chancellor, the Earl of Perth – was singularly unable to maintain order, or to prevent fresh Covenanter risings from sweeping the south and the west. While the Earl of Breadalbane, one of the new powers in the land, rode hard for London, intending to pledge continuing loyalty to James and to attempt to excuse the arrest of his leading councillor in the land, Cameronian rebels marched unopposed across the Lowlands, ejecting Episcopalian clergymen from their manses almost at will, and raising bonfires from the 'popish' altars, railings and vestments that they had stripped from their churches. Initially, the demands of Breadalbane and the other councillors were limited and of a profoundly conservative nature, envisaging no major alteration to the constitution, with James continuing as sovereign but undertaking, upon the advice and guidance of William of Orange, to dispense permanently with the services – and to destroy the influence of – the Earl of Melfort and his brother the Earl of Perth. However, the pitch of events, culminating in James's escape to France, had moved so fast in England that the certainties upon which Breadalbane had been prepared to negotiate had all but been destroyed by the time his coach nudged its way through the London crowds on its final approach to Westminster. The slow but sure realisation that a change of central administration was underway in Whitehall prompted the exodus south of many nobles and Crown servants, eager to steal a march quite literally upon their rivals in securing their places within the new political order. As a result, the Privy Council was denuded of personnel, talent and any real authority, as popular politics were reasserted on the streets of Edinburgh, and as the confidence of the élites in their rule virtually evaporated amid constitutional crisis. The demands of privy councillors for the calling of a free Scottish Parliament, to mirror the actions and debates of its English counterpart and to similarly settle the succession, were ignored in December 1688, as William and his English supporters had no appetite for conceding parity with a rival elective body that might well seek to broker a different constitutional settlement to Westminster. Consequently, the Scottish Parliament was called for March 1689, after the English Convention had safely taken the lead in its deliberations and decisions. Surprisingly however, despite attempts by Presbyterian magnates such as the earls of Crawford and Cunningham to pack the Scottish Convention with their supporters, roughly half of those members returned could be classed as being among James's natural supporters and of having no urge – whatever might have passed in England – to remove the crown from their King.

The Parliament met in the shadow of the gun, with Gordon's Jacobites still controlling the artillery high up on the castle walls, and Claverhouse and his brother officers lodged about the town, waiting upon events. With the militia disbanded by order of council, the Scottish army drawn south in December in the forlorn attempt to shore up James's monarchy, and with many regular units – as we have already seen – prepared to openly rebel against their new conditions of service, Whig members of the Convention turned to the Cameronians to protect parliament from any attempted counter-revolution. Three thousand of these hardened guerrilla fighters, whose sect had been driven underground during the 1680s, and whose leadership – of such fiery prophets as Richard Cameron and Donald Cargill, and such youthful visionaries as James Renwick – had been extirpated at the hands of the government, now guarded the doors to the Great Hall of Parliament House, openly patrolled the streets of the Scottish capital, and faced down the cat-calls issued by the bolder souls among Claverhouse's troopers, as the Members of Parliament took their seats. Though its meeting had been called on William's authority rather than by James's, the volatile nature of the proceedings and the potential for the return of the King was emphasised from the outset, as the

Bishop of Edinburgh commanded all of those present to pray earnestly for the soul of James II and for his speedy restoration to his kingdoms. Though this gave heart to the King's partisans and raised the concern of the Whigs, who had grouped uneasily around the Duke of Hamilton, of far more serious intent was the move to check the resurgent power of the Campbells and to bar the young Earl of Argyll from taking his seat, on the grounds that his father had died a rebel and his title was still under attainder. Due to the influence of Hamilton, a compromise was reached, whereby the circumstances of Argyll's position were noted but not acted upon and the Earl was able to take his seat unhindered, aware that his family might once more hope to take a controlling share in the governance of Scotland.

Both factions, Whig and Tory, looked to the struggle over the election of president as being decisive for the subsequent development of the parliament. Hamilton, though he was still choosing to hedge his bets and had not yet openly declared for William, was the Whig candidate, while the elderly Marquess of Atholl was the choice of the Tories, in the hope that his moderation, unshakeable espousal of Protestantism, and willingness to deal openly with William of Orange might all combine to recommend him to waverers. Unfortunately, Atholl, who had already incurred the bitter and undying wrath of James II on account of precisely this willingness to compromise, was singularly ill-equipped to fulfil the role expected of him. Numerically his candidature seemed assured, but at the last minute his nerve failed him and, realising the dangers and responsibilities inherent in playing power broker with the fate of the nation, he suddenly took fright and attempted to withdraw from the contest, protesting himself unworthy of such an honour, and leading twenty of his supporters across the floor to vote for Hamilton's appointment to the position. Stunned by this unexpected development, and effectively left leaderless, the Tory vote crumbled. However, while it is an indication of the strength of their original position that they lost by only forty votes, the Tories did little thereafter to regain either their cohesion or the political initiative. With Hamilton installed as President, the Whigs successfully packed the parliament's election and military committees, fighting off Tory attempts to have the Cameronians dismissed and instead pushing through a declaration that firmly identified the garrison of Edinburgh Castle as the true enemies to the peace and which called on them to surrender forthwith. At this point, however, it was James's own intervention that was to prove decisive.

As he had lain aboard ship upon the Brest road, James had composed a letter to the Scottish Convention, with the help and advice of Lord Melfort, dismissing its basic legality yet still commanding its members to uphold his rights and 'to declare for us your Lawfull Sovereign'. The problem was that, while William III's address to the parliament, which was also read out to members on 16 March 1689, was conciliatory, promising to safeguard Protestantism but refraining from offering a potentially divisive blueprint for the future remodelling of the Scottish Church, James's communication appeared imperious and hectoring, raising the spectre of civil war and threatening the trial and execution of all those who did not return to 'their duty' to him by the end of the month. He made no concessions to his subjects regarding religion, and had Melfort – the architect and almost universally excoriated symbol of the former regime – sign the letter, adding fresh fuel to the critics' fire. Worse still, while he refused to acknowledge the authority of the parliament, he clearly expected it to function as a legislature until such a time as he could convene a new one. Moreover, he expected its members to put themselves upon a war footing, raising taxes and looking to their own defence against 'any foreign attempts' until such time as he could render them 'speedy and powerfull assistance' from Ireland and take the fight back into the enemy's camp.[12] Such a letter to his 'faithful and loyal Subjects; generous . . . and true hearted Scotchmen' might, indeed, have held the vigorous power to command had James still been sitting as King at Whitehall, and had the Scottish Privy Council still been functioning in his interests. However, the magnates were keen to avoid bloodshed and unwilling, as yet, to throw around such epithets as 'traitor' or 'rebel' when partisan allegiances were still uncertain and extremely fluid. The injection of violence into Scotland, as the result of largely external forces and the meltdown of James II's English government, was something which few, if any, of those present in the parliament were prepared to countenance, while even those such as Claverhouse, outside its walls, were still endeavouring to secure favourable terms from the nascent Williamite government, and were not yet fully committed to the course of armed struggle. As a result, James's letter shocked the members of the Scottish Convention by its brusqueness and by the brutality of its tone and decided many Tories upon a policy of sudden *rapprochement* with their Whig and Williamite foes, as the only means by which to prevent civil war and the future settling of scores by the winning side, whoever they might have been.

Thoroughly dispirited, many Scottish Tories began to drift home, leaving their seats in the Convention vacant and, on 14 April 1689, Hamilton and the Whigs experienced no great difficulty in passing a vote which pronounced that James had forfeited his crown and the government of the nation through his misrule and utter disregard for the liberties and freedoms of his subjects. On 11 May 1689, William and Mary were offered, and accepted, the Scottish throne, as joint monarchs and in accordance with the precedents already established in England. With the legislatures and the constitutional settlements of England and Scotland now seemingly back in step, regular Scottish troops under

Major-General Mackay had been landed at Leith and had restored order
to the capital, before fanning out towards Stirling in an attempt to secure
a vital arsenal and the gateway to the Highlands. In the meantime, a plan
to establish a Jacobite assembly at Stirling to rival the Convention had
collapsed, with one of its possible ringleaders, Charles Erskine, 5th Earl
of Mar being seized as he attempted to ride out of Edinburgh, by William
Cleland, the son of a Lanarkshire gamekeeper and a former Covenanter
rebel who now led one of the Cameronian detachments guarding the
approaches to the capital. However, Claverhouse, who had pressed for
the raising of the clans in rebellion to secure the safety of the alternative
Jacobite parliament, had waited only until James's letter had been
definitively rejected by the Convention before galloping north, at the
head of officers and fifty troopers from his old dragoon regiment, to wait
upon events and for a more auspicious moment at which to raise James's
standard in rebellion. Now without the chance of a Scottish Jacobite
parliament to act in concert with that summoned to Dublin and to
challenge the legitimacy of the Lords and Commons at Westminster,
James's cause would have to rely on a combination of the willingness of
the Highlanders to wage war on its behalf, the force of Claverhouse's
personality to maintain their cohesion as a fighting force, and the
possibility of re-supply from Ireland and France, in order to guarantee its
survival and eventual export.

At the beginning of April 1689, James had received word that the clans
were in a position to raise an army of more than 5,000 men in a short
space of time, if only support from France and Ireland was immediately
forthcoming. Though this figure would be proven to be wildly over-
optimistic, James was extremely impressed by the claim and attempted to
broker a compromise deal with d'Avaux, whereby three Irish regiments
would be immediately transported across St George's Channel, with the
firm commitment to despatch a large number of other units as soon as
the opportunity presented itself. Even though these troop movements
were subsequently blocked through French intransigence and by military
failure before Derry, it is doubtful if the landing of anything less than a
full-strength army would have produced any considerable alteration in
affairs, for initially at least, there appeared little appetite for the
projected rising in Scotland.[13] Claverhouse failed to secure Stirling Castle
and, while the western clans mustered in respectable numbers at
Dalcomera on the River Lochy, the solidly Episcopalian north-east, of
which much had been expected, failed to stir against the resurgent
Presbyterian threat. Moreover, an opportunity to engage Mackay's
regulars upon favourable terms as they fell back from Strathspey in
disorder was squandered and, amid unseasonably bad weather,
Claverhouse was struck down with dysentery. His Highlanders, who had
not received the anticipated supplies from Ireland, fell to looting. By the

time the Duke of Gordon finally surrendered Edinburgh Castle, on 13 June 1689, the rising was on the verge of petering out, with pay and powder, food and forage, all in cripplingly short supply. Many clansmen chose to return home with their prizes or to go raiding after the cattle of rival chieftains, rather than seek a decisive engagement with Mackay's redcoats, who had pursued them every step of the way and enjoyed some considerable success in containing the rising to its original recruiting grounds, between the Moray Firth and the Tay. Yet, even as Claverhouse prepared to disband his handful of remaining followers, the embers of the revolt were sparked once again by the seizure of Blair Castle by Stewart of Ballechin, which effectively cut the government supply lines across the Highlands, and prevented Mackay's forces from uniting with Argyll's clansmen as had originally been envisaged. Throughout June, Jacobite propaganda leaflets were found nailed to kirk doors, while a large consignment of coin, bound for the insurgents, was discovered by government forces only the day after Edinburgh Castle had fallen, stashed away in the bottom of a coffin. Furthermore, although Vice-Admiral Rooke fell upon the handful of transports that contained the arms and supplies finally sent over from Ireland by the French, most of the powder and the 400 men of Colonel Purcell's dragoon regiment, together with a number of Irish officers, had already been hurried inland and escaped capture off the Isle of Mull.[14]

Meanwhile a fully recuperated Claverhouse had raised a scratch force of Highlanders, including the Camerons, the Macleans, and the Macdonalds of Glengarry and Clanranald, and driven into the heart of Atholl, recruiting new adherents en route and heading, unwittingly, straight into the path of Mackay's pursuing forces. The two armies met at the pass of Killiecrankie on 27 July 1689, in an engagement which, though subsequently heavily mythologised in the Jacobite, Highland, and Scottish Nationalist pantheons, was a sharp and scrappy affair, a true soldier's battle that witnessed the triumph of group morale and personal bravery over military strategy, or even the tactics advocated by the rival commanders. For much of the day, the two sides had been content merely to watch and to wait, noting each other's deployments, as the government forces, flanked by streams and with the River Garry to their rear, stretched themselves out across the wide plateau in front of Urrard House, and the rebels, bunching around the strong central detachments of Clanranald, Glengarry and Lochiel, occupied the Orchil ridge running underneath the summit of Creag Eallaich. Mackay had some grounds for confidence, as he had taken the Jacobites by surprise, driving his army and its large baggage train through the narrows of the pass without incident, and had succeeded in reforming his columns into line without being hit by a thunderous Highland charge while they were still deploying or strung out on the march. However, his concern to protect his wings had led to the thinning of his ranks and to his regiments becoming isolated, one from the other, with large gaps of dead ground opening up in between them. This should not have presented too much of a problem for well-trained troops, with units able to afford each other fire support and to close up in the event of an advance or attack, but save for the three regiments drawn from the Scots Brigade, the majority of his soldiers were either newly levied or – like Hastings's Foot, the one English regiment present – recently purged of several of their officers and unused to experiencing irregular warfare.

For his part, deficient in firearms and with the sun still shining brightly in his men's eyes, Claverhouse preferred to attempt to draw the government forces on up the hill, using a handful of sharpshooters to pepper the enemy lines with shot in the hope of bringing down Mackay's conspicuously mounted figure, or of provoking a major attack upon the ridge-line. Though refusing to be drawn, the government officers were similarly concerned with forcing an engagement and feared that the Highland army, whom Purcell's men had reinforced, but which was still outnumbered by their own regiments, might wait until nightfall before slipping away from the field to either fall back on pre-prepared positions about Blair Castle, or disappear entirely back into the mountains. As a consequence a cannonade was ordered with a view to softening up their positions and possibly inciting a disorganised charge by some or all of the clans upon their guns. However, while salvoes from the three small leather cannons, laboriously carried up the pass on the backs of packhorses, inflicted little damage on the rebel lines and broke away from their poorly constructed mountings after only their third firing, a party of fire-lock men drawn from Mackay's own regiment were able to quickly dislodge a nest of Jacobite marksmen who had taken cover in nearby cottages, killing several of their number and sending the rest fleeing back up the slopes in utter disorder. It would appear that it was this action, coming just as dusk was falling, which finally forced Claverhouse's hand and led him to commit the clans to a wild and desperate charge down from the heights. Confronted by a furious, rolling wall of slashing and shouting men, the government troops fired a single devastating volley into their massed ranks, flattening hot lead into the wooden targes and breastbones of the approaching clansmen and engulfing the front ranks of Lochiel's Camerons in a wreath of smoke and fire. For a moment the Highland mass shuddered and wavered, as Leven's regiment poured steady volleys into the exposed flank of Clan Cameron and as Mackay put himself at the head of his cavalry and led them out through the centre of his position, in wide arcs that threatened to break through the heart of the clansmen and to turn the enemy's increasingly ragged lines on both the left and the right. Then disaster struck, as Claverhouse committed his own troop to meet the threat, and

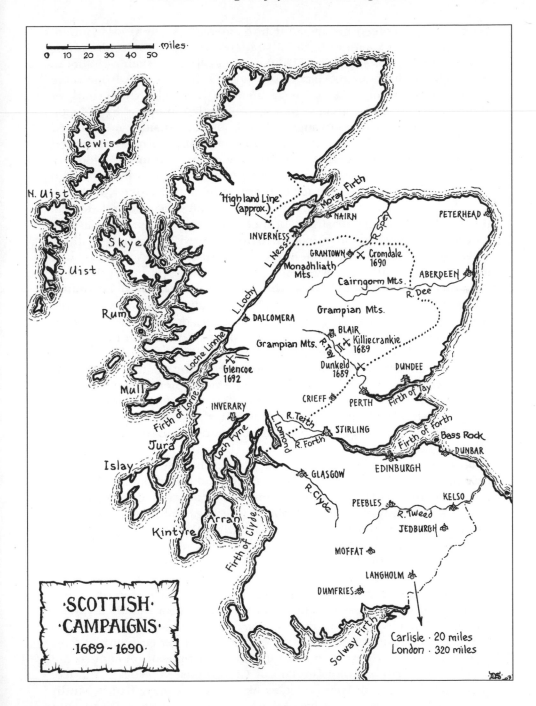

·miles·

0 10 20 30 40 50

Lewis

N. Uist

Skye

S. Uist

Rum

Mull

Jura

Islay

Kintyre

Arran

'Highland Line'
(approx.)

Moray Firth

NAIRN

PETERHEAD

INVERNESS

L. Ness

GRANTOWN

R. Spey

Cromdale
1690

ABERDEEN

Monadhliath
Mts.

Cairngorm Mts.

R. Dee

L. Lochy

DALCOMERA

Grampian Mts.

BLAIR

Killiecrankie
1689

Grampian Mts.

R. Tay

Loche Linnhe

Glencoe
1692

Dunkeld
1689

DUNDEE

Firth of Lorne

INVERARY

CRIEFF

PERTH

Firth of Tay

R. Teith

L. Lomond

STIRLING

Firth of Forth

Bass Rock

Loch Fyne

R. Forth

EDINBURGH

DUNBAR

GLASGOW

R. Clyde

PEEBLES

R. Tweed

KELSO

JEDBURGH

Firth of Clyde

MOFFAT

LANGHOLM

DUMFRIES

Solway Firth

Carlisle · 20 miles
London · 320 miles

·SCOTTISH·
·CAMPAIGNS·
·1689 ~ 1690·

as the inexperienced government horsemen took fright and bolted, leaving their Commander-in-Chief suddenly alone in the midst of his foes, while his cavalrymen trampled down or swept away their own foot in their indecent haste to get clear of the field. Only yards away from where Mackay was attempting to push his way through 'the croud of Highlanders' that now assailed him, and entirely unnoticed by the men of either side, a stray shot caught Claverhouse in his side and tumbled him from his saddle. As clansmen and Jacobite troopers streamed through the gaping hole that had suddenly opened up in the middle of the government position, Mackay's regiment of foot was overwhelmed before the soldiers had a chance to properly fix their bayonets, and fled. Elsewhere, discipline collapsed, with sergeants and officers unable to beat the increasingly desperate stream of frightened and broken redcoats who had fled from the front ranks back into line with the flats of their halberds and spontoons. While the centre first fractured and was then torn apart, the entire left wing dissolved under the splintering blows of claymores and Lochaber axes, with hunter and hunted becoming inextricably mixed as the battle dissolved into individual combats and the struggle to reach the baggage train and the banks of the River Garry first. One young soldier from Balfour's regiment later summoned up his impressions of the chaos and carnage that engulfed him, as the clansmen closed 'on us like madmen, without shoe or stocking . . . and were in the middle of us before we could fire three shots apiece, broke us, and obliged us to retreat. Some fled to the water, and some the other way', but he added, laconically: 'I fled to the baggage'.[15]

With his servant, and only remaining companion, shot down at his side, Mackay spurred his horse on towards the safety of a small knot of redcoats from Leven's regiment and, uniting them with the balance of Hastings's Foot who were still in reasonably good order, managed to ford the river and march to safety under the cover of darkness. The Highlanders, many of whom had fallen to looting the baggage train, were too exhausted and too disordered by the casualties that they had suffered, and by the temporary collapse of their chain of command, to mount an effective pursuit which might have proved decisive and thrown open the road to Edinburgh. As the Camerons fanned out across the battlefield in search of booty, one party began to strip the dead and wounded of their valuables, uncovering the body of a wounded cavalry officer who made to stir on their approach. As rough hands tore at his buff coat and at the straps that still held fast the bloodied remains of his cuirass, his groans were silenced forever by a single pistol shot to the head. Thus perished John Graham of Claverhouse, Viscount Dundee, killed not by a fabled silver bullet, as his foes would have had it, but by the greed and ignorance of his own friends. In the years which were to follow for the Jacobite cause in Scotland, marred by treachery, grim pragmatism and painful defeat, his name could only grow in stature, attracting an aura of romance and claims of greatness which were conspicuously absent during his short and, for the most part, brutal life. A competent soldier, who commanded in only two limited and irregular battles – one of which he had lost disastrously – Claverhouse had possessed the spirit and charisma necessary to weld the clans into an effective army, capable of toppling the Edinburgh government, and disciplined enough not to entirely alienate the civilian population of the south thereafter. Moreover, as a Lowland gentleman able to command authority with both James II's council in Dublin and with the clan chieftains in Highland Scotland, he was a rare and valuable figure in the movement to restore the exiled King through the exclusive use of military action. His famous victory, purchased at the cost of his own life and those of approximately 700 of his men, was in truth a pyrrhic affair, which had severely mauled his forces, rendering more than a third of them either dead or wounded, without completely destroying or even entirely routing those of his foes.[16] This said, the defeat of the government army came as a profound psychological shock to the administration in Edinburgh and prompted many among its servants – and even some among its leadership – to reconsider their choice of allegiance, while fresh recruits poured into the rebel camp, tempted by the hopes of further victories and the attendant accumulation of spoil, making good the losses suffered at Killiecrankie.

However, Colonel Alexander Cannon, Claverhouse's successor as Commander-in-Chief of the Highland army, squandered both the military initiative and the goodwill of the clan chiefs over the course of the next three weeks, and was forced into making a precipitate and strategically worthless assault on the small garrison of Dunkeld, in an attempt to maintain the momentum of the rebellion into the harvest season. With 5,000 men ranged across the low band of hills that surrounded the town, and in possession for the first time of a respectable train of artillery, Cannon threw his cavalry across the Tay early on the morning of 21 August 1689, cutting off the garrison's last line of retreat, before giving the order for heavily armed assault parties to go in as the spearheads of a general assault. The town itself appeared entirely forsaken, deserted not only by almost all its civilian population, who feared its speedy fall and a general massacre, but also by a party of government dragoons who had clattered through its lanes the day before, under orders to withdraw to the south, seemingly unconcerned that they were leaving the garrison to its fate. If the seriousness of their predicament was not lost on the red-coated infantrymen, who now took to stripping the lead from the cathedral roof and melting it down for musket balls to make good their desperate lack of ammunition, then neither was the fact that they were among the least liked or trusted units of the British Army. Raised only four months before, at a muster at the parish church at Douglas, the Earl of Angus's regiment was better known as the 'Cameronians', on account of the large numbers of former Covenanter rebels and members of Richard Cameron's sect who had chosen to enlist in its ranks. Fractious and disputative at the best of times, the regiment believed – with some good reason – that it had been led into a trap and that it was to be deliberately sacrificed in order to appease a resurgent Presbyterian establishment who, since Edinburgh and the parliament buildings had been secured, had little need for such intensely independent souls.[17] Consequently, led by their field preachers, the soldiers mutinied, demanding that they be permitted to fire the town and march away to safety before disaster could overtake them. The situation might have deteriorated further and all discipline broken down, had not their commanding officer, William Cleland, threatened to shoot his own horse in front of them, in order to prove his determination not to abandon his men, and to stand beside them in a fight to the bitter end. This restored a semblance of order and allowed the soldiers to return to their task of repairing the dilapidated series of ditches and low stone walls which ringed the perimeter of the town.

As the Jacobite guns opened up on the town, the Highlanders, with close cavalry support, drove in Cleland's pickets and rushed at the barricades, discharging a single volley before throwing down their muskets and drawing their broadswords. Recoiling before the onslaught – not having been issued with either bayonets or side-arms of their own – the Cameronians were compelled to give ground and fell back to prepared strongpoints about the cathedral close, kirkyard, and Dunkeld House. Though some were separated from their comrades and cut down in the streets as the barrier beside the market cross was overrun, others took up positions on the roof tops or in the attics of cottages, pouring down a withering fire on the attackers at point-blank range, hindering their attempts to fight their way into the centre of the town and emptying the saddles of horsemen who had charged too far forward, believing the day to be already won. Amid the confusing maze of streets and ramshackle yards, made worse by the smoke continuously disgorged from the barrels and priming pans of some eight hundred muskets, the Highland charge lost momentum and, as it broke itself against granite walls and casualties began to mount, Cleland and his officers launched a series of sorties, pushing the clansmen back step-by-step at the point of their pikes. With his men already inside the town, Cannon could no longer make use of his artillery from its existing vantage point, without the possibility of hitting his own side. However, as his guns fell silent, he made no attempt to reposition them or to move them up into Dunkeld itself, in order to provide covering fire for those clansmen who were now pinned down at the road junctions, flattening themselves against doorways or contours in the ground for protection against the disciplined volleys which had repeatedly swept through their ranks and littered the cathedral close with their dead. Every new rush was beaten back, with marksmen picking off officers and fugitives alike, while Cleland dashed from point to point, stopping any gaps in the defensive line and cheering on many a grim-faced redcoat, with a bloodied halberd in his hand and a psalm upon his lips.

Deprived of fresh orders, many clansmen fell back, dragging their wounded behind them and, unsure how best to proceed, contented themselves with milling about the streets for the rest of the morning, impeding the passage of reinforcements and fresh supplies of shot. However, others, of a more aggressive and inventive disposition, smashed their way with successive charges into the rows of cottages that overlooked both Dunkeld House and the cathedral, slaughtering defenders and occupants alike. They then began to return fire down on the Cameronian positions, focusing their particular attention upon Cleland's flying column and dropping many of the officers about him. After an hour's fighting, two shots from these snipers transfixed the young commander at almost the same moment, bringing him to his knees and lodging musket balls – each of which might have been fatal on their own – in his liver and in the side of his head. With morale at a premium and the majority of the regiment's officers now either dead or wounded, Captain Munro assumed command without comment or ceremony, and prepared to make a fresh sortie, while Cleland attempted to drag himself back inside Dunkeld House so that his men might not see him die. Though his life drained from him before he could reach the steps, Cleland was at least granted his final wish, as the news of his death did not spread through the ranks to create alarm, and the pace of Cameronian fire only redoubled – thundering the last and most fitting of salutes – over his crumpled body.

With communications in danger of being completely severed between the cathedral and the house, and with sharpshooters continuing to rake his lines, Munro led a series of fresh counter-attacks which succeeded in stabilising the situation and setting light to a number of houses in which the enemy musketeers had sheltered. Wattle, daub and thatch burned all too easily, as Dunkeld was consumed by flames.[18] Roof-beams split and small stores of powder exploded, drowning out the screams of those unable to get out of the buildings in time, while the Highlanders only added to the confusion by lighting their own fires in retaliation, in the hope of finally smoking out the remaining bands of Cameronians who still clung tenaciously to a handful of houses beside the cathedral. Several times more the clansmen stumbled out of the fiery haze which had descended on the town, to attempt a new storm, but each time their front ranks were shot down in the narrow alleyways, the hammer-blows of their

swords and axes made little impression on solid oak doors, and the force
of their charges faltered before they had even reached the kirkyard wall.
By eleven in the morning, after four hours of hard fighting, and with
powder running low on both sides, Cannon finally sent orders through to
his captains, authorising yet another frontal attack. This time, however,
the tired and choking Highlanders refused to go into the fray again, and
drew off with their cartloads of wounded, leaving more than 300 of their
dead behind them in the shattered and still burning town.

     The defeat at Dunkeld effectively spelled the end of the campaign, with
the shattering of the Highland army's reputation for invincibility and the
swift surrender of Blair Castle to Mackay's troops at the end of the month.
Henceforth the activities of the rebellious clans would be limited to a
destructive cycle of low intensity raiding and, by the time the chiefs
disbanded their followers for the harvest and set out on the trek back to
their homes, their hearts had largely gone out of the fight. Their
commitment 'to assist one another to the utmost of our power' in the
raising of a fresh rebellion in the coming year belied the fact that they
were unwilling to pledge, even on paper, more than token numbers of
troops to the future struggle. Of more significance was a stampede among
both the lairds and magnates to take advantage of the amnesty offered by
the government, if they would appear in the Scottish capital before
10 September 1689. Breadalbane, who had in turn over the past months
sought Melfort's downfall, been disappointed by the lack of favour shown
to him by William III, and turned Jacobite plotter, now acted once again
as a political barometer, seeking an accommodation (however temporary)
with the surprisingly durable administration in Edinburgh. There would
not now be a French landing in support of a Highland rising, or the
uniting of the Irish and Scottish armies under the command of King
James. Indeed, the ignominious rout of Cannon and Buchan's last field
army at Cromdale in May 1690 would merely serve as a footnote,
confirming in the minds of James's French advisors the wisdom that they
had shown all along in refusing to support his costly and impractical
schemes for the opening of a new front in his northern kingdom. Yet, if a
major element of James's grand strategy had fallen at Dunkeld before the
roar of Cameronian guns, his dreams of leading his armies back through
Scotland and of a triumphal descent upon London had already been seen
to founder and split asunder upon the walls of Derry.

II

In the spring of 1689, James had had good reason for believing that he
would soon be the master of all Ireland. Enniskillen, though defended by
a full regiment of Fermanagh men, ably led by Thomas Lloyd – whom

James would later scoff at as a 'little Cromwell' – and by Gustavus Hamilton, the town's militant governor, was not initially perceived as offering a great threat to Jacobite supply lines. Its castle, sitting squarely on Lough Erne, lacked the ravelins and demi-lunes necessary to render its walls impervious to modern artillery fire, while the small settlement that had grown up on the banks of the lake was not thought capable of either quartering troops, or of withstanding a siege for long. Robert Lundy, the new Governor of Derry, was equally dismissive of its value and urged its immediate evacuation so that its vital resources and manpower might be better concentrated in the defence of his northern city. Only the repeated and vociferous objections of the iron-willed garrison prevented a withdrawal similar to that which had gifted Sligo to the Jacobites several weeks before, and it came as a definite surprise to Lord Galmoy, in March 1689, that the surrender of the town and castle could not be immediately accomplished through the threatening, and subsequent committing, of war crimes in order to frighten its defenders into submission. Even Derry, with its impressive city walls and redoubts newly strengthened as the result of Lundy's foresight and industry, was not expected to hold out for long. A deep sense of pessimism pervaded the defence committee, who had no wish to die traitors' deaths, and feared the consequences of standing out so brazenly against a King who had once ruled over them, and possibly would do so again. Despite the derision his memory is accorded in Ulster tradition, Lundy was no coward, but a competent if rather unimaginative career soldier. As such, he was left in no doubt about the city's capacity to resist. After the barring of the gates against Antrim's troops, Derry was seen as a safe haven for Protestants fearing, and fleeing, possible massacre. Consequently, up to 30,000 refugees had sought sanctuary behind the city walls, throwing up tented encampments and placing a serious strain on already stretched food stocks. It was this consideration, and the belief that the city could not survive a formal siege, conducted by regular troops under the direction of French military engineers, which had led him to reject the services of two English regiments that had been newly landed at Lough Foyle as reinforcements, and to pen such a grim appraisal of the city's condition that the government in Whitehall refused to authorise a future re-supply, in the belief that the capitulation of Derry was both inevitable and imminent. Furthermore, Lundy had planned to evacuate the officers of the garrison along with many of the leading citizens, and urged that negotiations should be opened immediately with the Jacobite army in the hope of securing relatively favourable terms for surrender.

It was hardly surprising therefore, that James should turn his attention to the fortress city, or believe that he had merely to show his face before its walls to secure Derry. Tyrconnel, however, already feeling himself edged out of both the government of Ireland and James's affections by the presence of Melfort, advised against the venture, believing that he knew the temper of Derry's citizens – and that they would fight – and fearing that the King would lose a great deal of face in the eyes of his loyal Irish subjects, if he were to return from the city empty-handed. With his mind firmly set on expediting a landing in Scotland through the swift crushing of resistance in Ulster, James assumed responsibility for the direction of the forthcoming campaign, leaving Tyrconnel behind in Dublin, and leading the army north in person. However, it is at this point that the weaknesses and ambiguities which plagued James's exercise of command began to reveal themselves in stark clarity. As his columns pushed on towards Omagh and Strabane, James maintained only a dilatory pace at the rear, nudging his horse across potholes and over muddied tracks, leaving any tactical consideration as to how best to pursue the pockets of enemy troops who fell back before the Jacobite advance to the individual initiative of those of his general officers who accompanied the advance guards. Thus, while the King reached Newton Stewart on 15 April 1689, and on finding 'his own foot extreamly haras[s]ed with their long marches and bad we[a]ther' ordered a halt for the rest of the day, his generals, Richard Hamilton and Conrad von Rosen, simultaneously encountered strong resistance along the river lines of the Finn and Mourn respectively, and were drawn into fighting significant engagements in order to gain a crossing. With the bridges broken, and the King's son, the Duke of Berwick – newly promoted to the rank of Major-General – estimating as many as 10,000 'rebels' entrenched on the opposite banks, James could hear from his camp the sudden spluttering of musketry that greeted Hamilton's 600 horsemen as they broke from cover and attempted to swim the divide.[19] Yet still the King did not march to the sound of the guns. The indecision that often overcame him when responsibility rested solely on his shoulders, and when events outstripped or failed to conform to his preconceptions of them, appeared once more to paralyse his command. No fresh orders to engage were issued to the army under his hand that day. Fortunately, however, in this case numbers did not tell, as Hamilton's cavalry swept over the levee, gaining 'the opposite bank with the loss only of one officer and two private [soldiers] drowned', and scattering the enemy before them. Just 3 miles upriver, von Rosen's action had been attended by even more spectacular success, as the General had led his men in fording the river, routing a far larger force of insurgents after the briefest of struggles and capturing a small earth fort and some artillery pieces.

While the fugitives streamed headlong back to Derry, abandoning their arms and equipment, and blaming their commanders for their own flight, James reacted surprisingly to developments, preferring to dwell on the presence of one English frigate, the *Swallow*, and the troopships on Lough Foyle, rather than on the victories newly gained at such little cost. The movements of the two English regiments came to assume a decisive position in his mind, despite the fact that he had at his back an expeditionary force that was many times larger, and believing that Derry would not now surrender without a protracted siege, he left both his command and the 'honour' of capturing the city to von Rosen and turned back upon the road to Dublin, offering only the briefest and least satisfactory of explanations for his conduct, claiming that the preparations for the opening of the Irish Parliament necessitated his return to the capital. However, no sooner had he started for Dublin than post horses were sent galloping after him, in an attempt to make him change his mind. The Duke of Berwick, who had seen for himself the terror in the eyes of his foes, and the lack of resolve that they had shown in defence of their fortifications, concluded that they would show a similar reluctance to fight to preserve their friends, families and homes within the beleaguered city. James, escaping from the rain showers which had dogged his progress, had reached Charlemont in County Antrim, and lodged there overnight, before Berwick's despatch finally reached him on the morning of 17 April. The words of his son, discounting any reports of a major landing by English forces, stressing the ease with which the recent victories had been won, and begging the King to reconsider and to go through with his original plan to appear in person before Derry, certainly wrought a miraculous and near instantaneous lifting of James's mood. Calling for his horses, he turned about once again and, abandoning all trace of lethargy and gloom, threatened to outpace his escort as they raced back towards Derry. Though Berwick would subsequently attempt to downplay his influence on his father, the letter had served to galvanise the King because it touched upon his concerns and, more importantly, told him exactly what he wanted to hear.[20] Though James had never wanted for physical courage and had proved himself, in his youth, as a competent junior officer, he had never led an army into battle and was painfully aware that the only campaign in which he had enjoyed personal command had dissolved into turmoil and rout, amid dissention, betrayal and crippling inaction on Salisbury Plain. However, while James may have been aware of his own limitations as a general, and certainly feared and resented the demands that command had placed upon him, he had certainly not lost his taste for *gloire*. Hard fighting and serious military planning appear to have held little attraction for him in Ireland, but the promise of quick and easy victories, which would provide additional lustre to his reputation as a great and valiant soldier, and serve to spur him on his way to the conquest of Scotland, certainly delighted him and accounted for his sudden – and otherwise largely inexplicable – change of heart.

Riding hard, James finally sighted Derry on the morning of 18 April 1689. By frequently changing horses, he had managed to cover more than 60 miles of bad and winding roads back from Charlemont in little more than twenty-four hours, receiving en route a despatch from Lieutenant-General von Rosen, which informed him of the successful opening of negotiations with the garrison. As the King surveyed the city's defences, he felt sure that it would be a matter of hours before he could take possession of Derry and bring the rebellion against his authority to a sudden, and extremely satisfying, conclusion. Though the River Foyle coiled protectively around its northern and eastern sides, and a stretch of marshland would prove a stubborn obstacle to entrenchment outside the western walls, the promontory of Windmill Hill (rising sharply just 500 yds to the south of the city's Bishop's Gate) provided an ideal position for the sighting of batteries, which could then concentrate their fire to destructive and decisive effect, raking the walls and pouring shot down at will on Derry's streets. Fearing the destruction of the city, the corporation had already outlined 'a treaty for their submission' and sent Archdeacon James Hamilton and Captain Nevill to negotiate the final terms with their foes. For his part, von Rosen was prepared – in consultation with Richard Hamilton – to guarantee that both the citizens and the garrison would be protected from reprisals, and that they might continue to live peaceably in the city. However, the rebellion had to be seen to be broken, and as a result no military compliments were to be observed, no evacuation was to be permitted, with drums beating and colours unfurled, and the soldiers present were to surrender all of their horses and arms to the waiting Jacobite army. Furthermore, von Rosen had no intention of allowing negotiations to drag on, and gave the citizens until noon on 18 April, to either accept or decline his offer. The only stipulation that the defenders had made, fearing that a sudden, treacherous storm might overwhelm the garrison and deliver the city to their vengeful enemies, was that for the duration of the truce the Jacobite troops should not pass within sight of Derry's gates.[21]

James's arrival had appeared extremely auspicious to his followers, as he assumed authority for the negotiations and pleased both himself and his soldiers by staging a review of his foot regiments early that morning. However, a sharp disagreement broke out among his general staff as to how best to expedite the surrender and whether or not the terms of the truce should be strictly adhered to. Von Rosen was firmly of the opinion that a show of force, bringing the army slowly forward in order of battle, would be enough to break the spirit of the garrison and frighten them into surrender. However, Lieutenant-General Hamilton begged to differ, explaining to the King that if they were to show their true strength before the city, then they would not only run the risk of breaking the truce, but would also reveal their woeful lack of sufficient mortars and cannon with

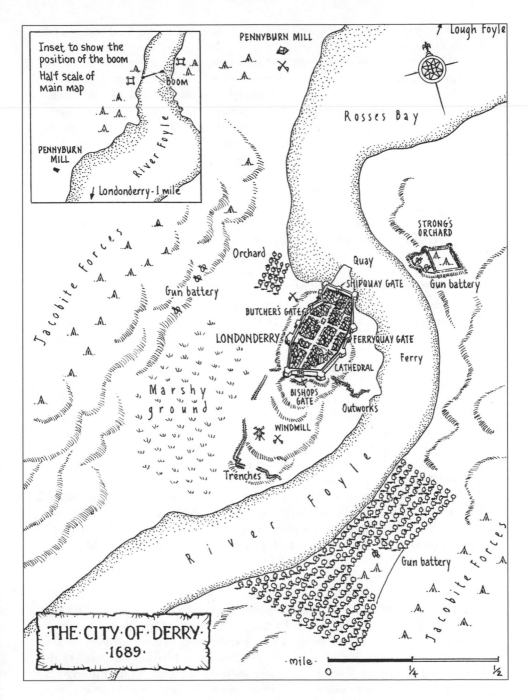

Inset to show the
position of the boom
Half scale of
main map

Boom

PENNYBURN
MILL

River Foyle

↓ Londonderry - 1 mile

↑ Lough Foyle

PENNYBURN MILL

Rosses Bay

STRONG'S
ORCHARD

Gun battery

Jacobite Forces

Orchard

Quay

SHIPQUAY GATE

Gun battery

BUTCHER'S GATE

LONDONDERRY

FERRYQUAY GATE

Ferry

Gun battery

CATHEDRAL

Marshy
ground

BISHOPS
GATE

Outworks

WINDMILL

River Foyle

Trenches

Gun battery

Jacobite Forces

THE·CITY·OF·DERRY·
·1689·

·mile·

0   ¼   ½

which to reduce the walls, and the poor state of both their siege and artillery trains. It was far better, he argued, to let the threat of the Jacobite army remain undeclared, so that uncertainty might breed fear in the minds of the citizens and soldiers, rather than to lay down an explicit challenge which might be rationally assessed and dealt with. Unfortunately, the subtleties of his argument failed to convince James who, buoyed up by his expectations of success and by the acclamations of his troops that morning, decided upon the unambiguous use of force to overawe the city. As the noon deadline drew close, the drums of the Jacobite army began to roll, soldiers began to form their columns, and the King galloped out of the camp at St Johnston at the head of the cavalry and dragoons. Later, James would attempt to blame von Rosen for the delay in delivering a summons to the stricken city, but there is little evidence to suggest that, as his horse regiments showed themselves on the skyline and his foot pushed up behind them on the ridges to the south of Derry, the King was in anything other than complete concordance with his General. With still no word from the garrison, James led his horsemen in procession towards the Bishop's Gate, while dragoons spread out in advance of their path, and a single trumpeter lighted out from the ranks and drove his horse on towards the city, bearing an order for the surrender.

However, the approach of the King's army had thrown Derry into confusion, with the war council divided, Lundy's authority challenged and the garrison – believing themselves about to be betrayed – preparing to take matters into their own hands. To the sentinels, and the anxious citizens who now thronged the walls, James's actions appeared to have clearly violated the spirit of the truce and threatened the start of a general assault. Alarms were sounded, powder and arms distributed, and cannon run out by a people who no longer either trusted, or respected, the assurances of their leadership regarding the intentions of the King. Above all, they had been implored to hold their fire against the approaching horsemen, but emboldened by the enemy's lack of artillery cover – there were only two mortars, two siege guns and three field pieces in their support – and fearful that the initiative would soon pass to their foes if they were permitted to reach the city gates, the decision was taken to clap burning linstocks to the cannons' touch-holes, igniting powder charges and sending an explosive wall of shot screaming into the very midst of James's bodyguard. In an instant the situation changed completely for the King's party, from a calm and orderly progress to a state of horror and confusion, amid the shrieks and flailing limbs of both horses and riders cut down by the cannon balls' sudden flight. Pulling up sharply, James was reminded (if he had ever truly forgotten) that artillery fire was no respecter of either titles or persons, as one of his staff officers was cut down by his side. Amid the smoke, the dragoons opened up on the walls in hesitant response, but they were heavily outgunned and as their casualties began to mount, they wheeled about, covering the retreat of the King and the main cavalry force back up the slopes. Stunned and soot-stained, James seemed hardly able to comprehend the nature of his new misfortune and clung stubbornly to the belief that, despite the fusillade, the city would be surrendered to him that day. Initially, he had some grounds for hope as Lundy had been horrified by the action and the corporation had sent out messengers to beg the King's pardon for the behaviour – and the murderous intent – of their men. A further communication was promised within the hour, the deadline for the surrender having now expired, and this served to renew James's hope. However, as the rain began again and the hours ticked by, the King began to appear as a forlorn figure on the hillside. Sitting motionless on his horse, the dark brim of his travelling hat pulled down over his brow, he spent the rest of the day watching and waiting in vain for word that would never come. As the afternoon drew on, James finally acknowledged von Rosen's repeated pleadings and gave permission for the army to stand down, and to find dry cover in and about St Johnston.

The garrison observed them as they went on their way, turning their backs on the walls of Derry and slipping back behind the hills, the way that they had come. If the cry of 'No Surrender!' had stuck uncertainly in many a throat after the debacle at Bandon, it now assumed a profound resonance and political power in the affairs of Ulster, serving in place of a manifesto as a declaration of uncompromising intent (and barely concealed fear) to unite and define the Irish Protestant cause. It was shouted after James's retreating troopers that day and turned against Governor Lundy, in the evening, as the city government was overthrown and the citizens broke into the council chamber, scattering their representatives before them. Over the following days, Lundy was formally replaced as governor by Major Henry Baker and, in a less formal though even more keenly felt sense, by the Revd George Walker, and was allowed, by accident or design, to escape from the city disguised as a common soldier.[22] With the power of Lundy and the council shattered beyond all repair, the defence of Derry fell to far more militant souls, who would brook no talk of capitulation and who were prepared to fight to the end if the need arose, be it through starvation or the point of a gun. James's staff officers had some glimmering of the changes sweeping the city, as they convened their own council of war 5 miles away at Monglevin Castle, on the evening of 18 April. Yet the King was prepared to offer further concessions in the hope that negotiations might be swiftly resumed the next day. Passes were issued for up to twenty of Derry's leading citizens to pass freely through the Jacobite lines, so that they might resolve matters, and Richard Hamilton extended the promise that if they would undertake the 'delivering the Keys of your City to his [i.e. James's] Royal hands [then] you shall be treated as Favourites, and Finishers of this difficult siege'. Loyalty would be richly rewarded, with the commissioned officers allowed to continue 'in the same Posts at least, if not advanced to a better', while all the Protestant landowners in Derry would have their estates confirmed and restored to them by act of parliament. The fact that that body had not yet been convened in Dublin, and would show nothing but hostility to any suggestion that the iniquitous land settlements of the 1660s should be perpetuated, does not seem to have occurred to either James or Hamilton, though it certainly did little to persuade those already left unconvinced of the value of the King's word following his abortive ride into their city. However, sweetened promises were backed by graphic threats towards the close of Hamilton's letter, for the council members were left in no doubt that 'if you continue obstinate, your Ruin seems inevitable, by withstanding an Army so well-disciplined and so powerful; which resolves, if you continue obstinate, to give no Quarter to Man, Woman or Child . . . [though] once our Cannon and Mortars have rent the Walls in pieces, and the Town is taken by Storm, then thousands of your Wives and Children shall fall upon their knees, and with repeated Sighs and Groans implore our pity'.[23] Certainly, such a combination of hopeful promises and dire ultimatums worked well on those members of Derry's élites to whom the letter had been addressed, but by the time of its arrival power had already effectively passed from their hands, and the twenty commissioners they had appointed to negotiate with the King were prevented from leaving the city by the threats and rough-handling delivered by the militant bands of soldier-citizens who now commanded in their place. Furthermore, though the promises of amnesty had been far from ineffective in drawing out from the city almost a third of the fugitives who had crowded the streets, the reduction in numbers had also served to partially alleviate the food shortages, while many of those among the élites who might have proven influential in negotiating a settlement had also left, effectively purging Derry of its moderate party and ceding authority to firebrands such as Baker and Walker.

James did what he could, making a gracious show of pardoning and offering protection to all those who sought him out at Monglevin Castle. With scores being bloodily settled in the countryside, his willingness to intervene often did mean the difference between life and death. One prisoner, who was subsequently amnestied, witnessed an 'unnatural peace of cruelty' on the outskirts of James's camp. Word had spread among the cavalry troopers that an attempt had been made to bewitch their horses and 'a poor old woman [of] at least seventy years' was run to ground, beaten and robbed, before being shot down at point-blank range.[24] In such a climate of endemic and often entirely random violence, James's desire not to show partisanship – in the hope that he might continue to rule in the name of both Protestants and Roman Catholics – dismayed many of his followers and led to charges that he 'had played the Englishman' too strongly. D'Avaux sneered at his leniency, while an anonymous Irish Jacobite held that: 'No experience will make him behave himself towards those traitors as he should do. He spoiled his business in Ireland by his over great indulgence towards them . . . [for] he was infatuated with this rotten principle – provoke not your Protestant subjects'.[25] Though it was only in the bitterness and disillusion of his latter years that James would seek to define the defenders of Derry and Enniskillen as 'the most obstinate and bitter ennemys he ever had', by the time his overtures were finally rejected on 19 April, and his weary trumpeter told that he would be fired on if he attempted to return again, the King had good cause to dwell upon the nature of 'that spirit of Rebellion . . . [that] was forced to canton itself in the North'.[26] Now reconciled to the idea that Derry could not be delivered without the opening of a formal and costly siege, the King wasted no time in outlining a rudimentary plan for the deployment of his artillery and the gathering in of corn, meal and cattle from the surrounding countryside, before announcing that he would be returning to Dublin to attend to the parliament, even though its opening was still almost three weeks away. Von Rosen left with him, probably due to the objections of James's Irish officers, who feared both his rough methods and his savage tongue, and the command of the siege operations fell almost by default to Maumont, who had been newly promoted Lieutenant-General in a bid to counteract the influence and ambitions of Richard Hamilton.

Had he had the time, the Frenchman might well have proved himself to be an inspired choice. He enjoyed good relations with his Irish subordinates and, while acknowledging the difficulties that he faced, in terms of supply and equipment, he was almost alone among his brother officers during the campaign in refraining from undue complaint and in applying himself energetically to the task at hand, making the best use of those advantages – of manpower and fighting spirit – which he did possess in abundance. Without the artillery to make a practical breach in the city walls, he turned his attention instead to the earth fort at Culmore, 5 miles downstream, that acted as a choke point upon any traffic wishing to travel further up the river. Massing all his available forces before the stronghold, Maumont accepted the surrender of Culmore from its isolated and thoroughly dispirited garrison without a shot being fired, before pushing Hamilton's soldiers down into the village of Pennyburn, on the outskirts of Derry. However, a counter-attack was immediately launched by the city's garrison, catching the Jacobites off-guard while their cavalry were away foraging, and leaving the General to put himself at the head of two thin troops of horse and dragoons, in an attempt to stem the citizens' advance. Caught by a burst of fire from the surrounding hedgerows, the horsemen were scythed down in the narrow lanes – the officers to the fore suffering particularly heavily – with Maumont receiving his death wound, allegedly at the hands of the enemy commander, Colonel Murray. His death deprived James of the one French commander who seemed to unquestioningly accept his own rationale for pursuing the war and the need for speed in reducing Derry, and ushered in a period of almost incessant raiding by the garrison. Four days later another engagement at Pennyburn saw the Jacobites suffer further heavy losses, with the Duke of Berwick taking a heavy blow to his spine and Major-General Pusignan receiving a grievous though potentially not life-threatening wound in the fierce hand-to-hand fighting. Yet while Berwick, with a touch of hubris, boasted in his old age that: 'this was the only hurt I ever had' in battle, Pusignan was carried to the rear, only to suffer dreadfully at the hands of amateur local surgeons and die piteously cursing the want of a French doctor to dress his wounds. James dryly observed that his generals were far too valuable to be wasted in such a manner, and urged them to exercise caution and to refrain in future from leading from the front. Such advice, however, sat ill with his desire for haste and limited Maumont's rival and successor, Richard Hamilton, to a policy of mere containment until such a time as sufficient artillery could be brought up to prove decisive.

Hamilton had not been slow to throw a cordon around the city, and in establishing his mortars – when they finally arrived – in an orchard on the eastern banks of the River Foyle, he was able to rain down shells upon Derry, both day and night, ploughing up the roads, as George Walker was to acknowledge, and breaking down the houses 'so that for our citizens it meant death met them at every corner and in their closets and bedchambers they could be no more secure'.[27] However, for all his bravery, Hamilton had little understanding of the art of siege warfare, and overlooked the importance of Culmore Fort entirely, neither refortifying nor sufficiently garrisoning its walls in order to block the river traffic and frustrate any attempts at re-supply. Had he done so, and achieved these aims, then the siege of Derry might well have had a very different outcome. As it was, the Jacobites struggled to regain the initiative, storming Windmill Hill on 5 May 1689, only to lose it again the very next morning. Further assaults against the position failed over the course of the next two months, and by the time the Earl of Clancarty's regiment had been driven off the bastion outside the city's western gate on 28 June, it had become glaringly obvious that the capture of Derry by storm was not only beyond the scope and resources of the Jacobites, but also outside the immediate interests and wider policy objectives of their French sponsors. From then on, the city's survival depended primarily upon its ability to feed its inhabitants and to ward off the ravages of starvation, which had become the principle weapon of the Jacobites as they attempted to tighten the blockade about its walls. However, such a strategy would take time to effect, and if both Derry and the Lowlands of Scotland were not to be quickly secured by James's armies, then the King would be forced to accept that the only realistic option – in the short term at least – was to consolidate his regime in Ireland, at the expense of his involvement in his other kingdoms. For this he required a parliament that was not only loyal but compliant, and above all generous with its finances.

III

Since the arrival of the King, Dublin's goldsmiths and jewellers had been kept busy with commissions to replace the lost royal regalia in time for the opening of the Irish Parliament. Slowly but surely, as they worked away throughout the spring months, the character of both the city and of Irish politics had perceptibly changed about them, with the establishment of a new royal court providing a powerful and stimulating focus for the native aristocracy, and a source of almost continual employment for dressmakers, tailors, travelling actors, musicians and footmen. As Christ Church was hastily re-consecrated for its (albeit brief) role as a Roman Catholic cathedral, and the remaining Protestant members of the corporation were purged, patrons such as Frances, Lady Tyrconnel and Lady Mary Butler came forward either to re-endow existing religious houses, or to provide the funds and political influence necessary for the foundation of new monasteries and convents. Trinity College, deserted by the overwhelming majority of its Fellows, was used as a prison for captured soldiers and for suspected insurgents, though damage to its fabric and to its superlative library was limited due to the industry of James's new Dean and Provost, who clearly believed that a fresh generation of Roman Catholic students and masters would soon take up their places there. Most dramatically, the influx of large numbers of troops, disproportionately quartered on Protestant homes, served to lend Dublin the aspect of an armed camp, and led to a marked escalation in food prices and in the cost of even the most basic of commodities. Though the Huguenot community lacked both the desire and the capacity to go on its travels once again, and busied itself filling orders for the hundreds of woven stockings required by the King's new soldiers, other Protestants baulked at their loss of political power – symbolised by the growing numbers of confident and well-fed monks and priests now in their midst – and feared what the imposition of martial law on the city would hold for them. While Macaulay would later charge d'Avaux with plotting to launch a St Bartholomew's Day-style massacre upon the Protestant population of Dublin, there would seem to be little truth to this story, although d'Avaux's repeated appeals to the King to show far greater stringency in the use of the treason acts, separating 'loyal' from 'disloyal' Protestants, might (had they been heeded) have proved every bit as bloody, as random, and as thoroughly divisive as the sanctioning of this type of military pogrom. However, even though the French soldiers regarded the 'heretics' with whom they were forced to lodge with nothing less than contempt, and cases of rape and violence were often inflicted during the free quartering of the troops, the imposition of martial law was used every bit as much in an attempt to maintain military discipline, as it was to break the resistance of Dublin's Protestant community. James appeared, throughout his time in Ireland, to be incapable of imposing order on his men. Duels, brawls and running battles, which frequently erupted as the result of the simmering national rivalries of the soldiers who fought beneath his colours, appear to have been endemic in his army. D'Avaux sniffed that two-thirds of the Irish regiments should have been mustered out of service, as they behaved like brigands and robbed those that they met upon the roads, yet he did nothing as two of the King's guardsmen were dragged by their hair outside his window and were soundly beaten by the soldiers of another regiment. Overstaffing, underemployment, and the late arrival of their wages resulted in an officer corps that saw individual acts of violence as a means of alleviating their boredom and of wining personal renown for their bravery, in the absence of the opportunities afforded by regular warfare. In spite of d'Avaux's condescension, the French were particularly prone to squabbles over pay and promotion, while James's own staff and immediate family offered some of the worst possible examples of lack of restraint. Tyrconnel beat senseless one junior officer whom he had found stealing fruit from the trees outside the house of the French Ambassador, while the King's 17-year-old son, Henry Fitzjames, Lord Grand Prior – who, whether through fear or simple enjoyment had taken to burying himself deeply in his cups – provoked a fight with Walter, Lord Dongan over his refusal to drink a health to the Earl of Melfort.

If many of Dublin's citizens, from both denominations, had cause to fear the swaggering recklessness of the soldiers, or resented having to pay increased taxes for the 'improvements', such as the draining of St Stephen's Green, that James had ordered to be made to their city, then the Roman Catholic population were willing to overlook such discomforts and invest their hopes in the coming parliament, which they felt would do much to confirm their growing sense of nationhood and to remedy many of their old grievances. There was, however, to be no contested election for its seats.[28] Candidates would be nominated from an approved list drawn up in advance by Tyrconnel and the King, while the borough corporations had already been thoroughly refashioned in order to return representatives drawn predominantly from among the Roman Catholic 'old English' and Gaelic communities. Consequently, though the election may well have reflected the ethnic and religious composition of Ireland more accurately than any of its predecessors, it certainly cannot be regarded as being more 'democratic'. Although several members later criticised the calling of the parliament as a diversion, while Derry and Enniskillen still held out, Tyrconnel despatched election writs to the sheriffs and mayors in all of those counties and boroughs that acknowledged the authority of Dublin, and some 230 members from a full quota of 300 names were duly returned. Where the influence of central government was weak, or strongly opposed, elections were not held and, as a result, there were no county representatives for Fermanagh, Donegal and Derry, while a number of boroughs, concentrated mainly in Ulster, similarly failed to make returns. Though a mere five Protestants took their seats in the parliament – more had been nominated but had thought it far wiser and safer to stay away – the nature of James's concept of the government of Ireland was underlined by his decision not to amend the laws barring Roman Catholic bishops from sitting in the House of Lords. Despite the fact that the King was engaged in a desperate struggle to rebuild his power and regain his thrones, it was continuity and, at best, gradual change that James was to emphasise to his Gaelic and 'old English' allies. Furthermore, any revolutionary – or conceivably even counter-revolutionary – overtones that the parliament might have assumed were to be played down and avoided at all costs. Thus one member, who had sought to draw strident parallels between the problems facing Masaniello's radical revolt of 1648 in Naples and those that now beset the King in Ireland, found himself quickly removed from the floor and impeached. Property and social order had to be seen to be sacrosanct under James's kingship.

At the opening of the parliament, James commended its members for their readiness to serve him, liberally praising their courage and zeal, which 'made me resolve to come to you, and vent[ure] my life with you in defence of your liberties and my own Right'. However, while his commitments to framing 'such Laws as may be for the good of the Nation' and encouraging 'the improvement of trade' were as vague as they were uncontroversial, he left no doubt about his unwillingness to please his natural constituencies of supporters in Ireland. In the knowledge that his words would be reported and commented upon in England, he declared that 'I have always been for libertie of Conscience, and against invadeing any man's Right or libertie . . . for . . . nothing shall ever perswade me to change my mind as to that; wheresoever I am Master I design God willing, to establish it by Law, and have no other test or distinction but that of Loyalty'. By attempting to re-forge the complex new set of alliances that he had hoped would unite Roman Catholic with Dissenter and Tory in the period from 1687–8, James was following his deep-seated convictions that only the granting of toleration could resolve the agonising confessional struggles that since the Reformation had destabilised the God-given system of monarchies across Europe. If only, he reasoned, a level playing field might be created, whereby all the faiths might compete equally for souls, then the intrinsic correctness of Catholicism would inevitably lead other converts back to Rome – in exactly the same manner that he had experienced as a young man – to be more 'sensibly' touched by the divine presence and 'to live up to the height of Christianity'.[29] Unfortunately, while this vision of universal toleration might hold great appeal for the smaller and more heavily persecuted of the Dissenting sects, such as the Quakers, it did nothing to recommend itself either to those Irish Catholics who wished to break once and for all the Protestant hegemony over their land, or to the half-famished defenders of Derry who had set their faces against any form of compromise with their foes. The King's dilemma in pushing for toleration, as d'Avaux acutely observed, was that while the Roman Catholics were 'certainly the only faithful subjects of his Britannic Majesty' it was extremely difficult 'to distinguish between the Protestants who are faithful and those who are not'. Moreover, though the Gaelic and 'old English' interests could unite in agreeing on the need for reparations for the lands that they had lost over the course of the last century, and clamoured for the seizure of Protestant estates, James stopped short of redistribution and was only prepared to offer relief 'for such as have been injured in the late Act of Settlement, as far . . . as may be consistant with . . . the publick good of my people'.[30] The reinstatement of Roman Catholic power in Ireland was thus to be of a political but not a financial nature and it was as a result that the Dublin, or 'Patriot', Parliament was soon to be at loggerheads with the King.

James's speech had certainly drawn applause and received both the fulsome thanks of Sir Richard Neagle, the newly elected Speaker of the House, and the immediate vote of a £20,000 grant to the King, to be made every month for the next thirteen months. However, no sooner had the cheering died in his ears, than James and his advisors began to recognise that these sums had been granted as a testimony of the members' approval, rather than as a genuine reflection of their willingness to levy new taxes and to actually pay him the subsidies that had been promised. Having only ever envisaged the parliament as a means to fund his war and feeling well pleased with his performance in the chamber, James was slow to recognise the need for finding competent business managers to harness support and build a powerful voting lobby in his interest. As a result he was surprised to discover that many in parliament had a far wider definition of their purpose than the simple voting of subsidies, and was thoroughly taken aback by the raft of legislation that was quickly tabled and which threatened not only to destroy the Act of Settlement but also to fundamentally renegotiate the future division of powers between the legislatures in Westminster and Dublin. 'It appears', wrote d'Avaux, 'that the King of England slept at a time when his affairs demanded the greatest action and forethought'.[31]

James had always been closely identified with the re-division of Irish lands after 1662, and had been a major beneficiary of the Act of Settlement. He had accumulated enormous private estates and had made sure that his closest friends, such as Tyrconnel – whose own lands now spread right across Dublin, Kildare and Leath – shared in his good fortune. Furthermore, there were many Irish Catholic noblemen, judges and merchants who had bought up the estates belonging to former Cromwellians, and who were horrified by the tumultuous cheers that greeted the bill to overturn the hated act and to have it burned by the common hangman. They now joined with the King and Tyrconnel in attempting to force a compromise through the House of Lords, on 13 May 1689, which would have permitted a measure of compensation and allowed roughly half the current landowners to keep their property. Yet the mood of the Lords was so bellicose that even this motion – known to have royal support – was heavily defeated, and the King's partisans, led by the bishops of the Church of Ireland, were forced to fight a long and laborious rear-guard action, which succeeded in delaying the passage of the bill for almost two more weeks, while individual peers registered their own detailed appeals in an attempt to preserve the integrity of their estates. Fearing that the increasingly strident claims of Roman Catholic priests for the return of their property and buildings might be taken up by the parliament, inevitably leading to the destruction of the political influence and the eventual pauperisation of the established Church, the Bishop of Meath became the leading and most articulate opponent of a bill 'that unsettles a former Foundation (upon which this Kingdom's Peace and Flourishing was superstructured) and designs to erect another in its stead; the success whereof is dubious and uncertain'. Consequently, he chose to attack it on the grounds that it represented a threat to the existing fabric of society, challenging inheritance and property rights, and ignoring the improvements that the new proprietors had made upon the lands. 'It is unjust', he declared, 'to turn Men out of their Possessions and Estates, without any fault or demerit', while it was 'not for his Majesties Honour to consent to the Ruining of so many Innocent, Loyal Persons . . . [and] to rescind those just Acts of his Royal Father and Brother'. Furthermore, he claimed that the legislation was not only impractical and ill-considered, but would prove an insurmountable obstacle to both the King's return to his English throne and to the building of a stable government in Ireland. It would destroy the ability of the State to tax, by overturning the wealth of the leading families of the nation, and would 'neither preserve him in the Kingdom that he enjoys, nor restore him to those he has unhappily lost . . . [for] the Protestants in England and Scotland [would not] joyn heartily in restoring him to his Crown, when they understand how their Brethren here are used'. The interest of the King, he argued, should be paramount, for it was not a time for personal greed 'for Men to seek for Vineyards and Olive-yards, when a Civil War is raging in the Nation, and we are under Apprehensions . . . of Invasions from abroad'. Yet all his arguments were in vain for, as he had feared, the parliament was minded 'to divide the Spoil before we get it, to dispose of the Skin before we catch the Beast'.[32] James, who had been deluged with petitions from anxious landowners, threatened to prorogue the parliament if he did not get his own way and have the legislation dropped. However, the Irish MPs calculated – accurately – that he needed their subsidies far more than they needed to continue their debates in the chamber, and effectively called his bluff, tying all future consideration of parliamentary grants to the passage of the bill. Thoroughly outmanoeuvred, James admitted defeat, instructing the bishops not to vote against the legislation, as that would imply faction within his parliament and he would not countenance such an 'Evil' as party, 'that Good might come on't'.[33]

Royal assent was finally given, on 22 June 1689, to the repeal of the Act of Settlement and Explanation, with James grumbling disconsolately that: 'he was fallen into the hands of a people who rammed many hard things down his throat'.[34] Under the terms of the new legislation the heirs to lands seized after the rebellion of 1641 were to receive a full pardon for the actions of their families and were to have all of their original lands returned to them. Those owners who had bought property during the reign of Charles II were to be compensated with land confiscated from the Williamites now in 'rebellion' in the north, and James was personally to be heavily recompensed for the loss of Crown lands through the expropriation of Lord Kingston's estates in Cork and Roscommon. Significantly, as R.G. Simms has shown, the iron works at Knappagh in County Mayo were exempted from the provisions of the act, being judged to be far too vital to the war effort to have their production disrupted in any way, while the King was to continue in possession of Phoenix Park and the royal lands at Chapelizod.[35] The Dublin Parliament had intended for the legislation to set in motion a massive redistribution of wealth in Ireland, but in fact no action was taken to do anything that might have turned the provisions of the act into hard reality. James temporised, pleading with some justification that the need to direct the war effort came first, and doing nothing to create the planned court of claims that was to have overseen the division and re-allocation of Irish lands. With no cases heard, the legislation remained on the statute book, while society was not immediately remoulded and it would be left to the outcome of the war to effectively decide the issue.

The Repeal of the Act of Settlement had handed Whig pamphleteers a golden opportunity to justify their vision of James as the brutal servant of the papacy, in thrall to a wild and murderous people, and intent upon destroying the lives and property of every law-abiding Protestant in his former kingdoms. Unfortunately, the terms of the Act of Attainder, pushed through parliament in the teeth of James's opposition, did nothing to mitigate this impression. More than 2,000 individuals were identified by name, including Archbishop Marsh of Dublin, together with five of his bishops, the Duke of Ormonde and over 400 gentlemen, held culpable alongside large numbers of yeomen farmers and tradesmen of high treason. It was not the prospect of seeing men hang that provoked such a mighty fury in James that his nose began to bleed again, but the attempt by parliament to limit his prerogative as to who the Crown could – or could not – pardon. The conditions for the surrender of the named individuals and the time set for them to comply were so disadvantageous that the list was obviously never intended to compel the obedience of his subjects, but to act as a rough guide to score settling once the Protestant risings were finally broken. Having observed the willingness of the King to give safe conducts and free pardons to the streams of pitiful refugees who had fled out of Derry, the parliament was unwilling to allow him to carry on permitting their foes to go unpunished forever.

However, James was successful in heading off what he saw as other potentially damaging legislative measures. To the horror of his Irish subjects, and to the incredulity of d'Avaux, he reaffirmed England's dominant position over Ireland's trade, including the right to impose prohibitive restrictions on its growth, and refused to divert the valuable wool trade to France, as had been expected in order to hamper William's gathering of English tax revenue and to pay back the French Treasury for its already heavy expenditure in his cause. D'Avaux noted that: 'he had a strange envy of France, and earnestly wished that they should get no credit for bringing him in here', but it is not hard to see in this stand how a proud and intensely nationalistic King of England sought to preserve his dignity and independence, through refusing to give ground to his foreign and equally self-interested patrons.[36] True to his word at the beginning of the parliamentary sessions, James was also able to abolish the Test Acts that had excluded Roman Catholics from both civil and military appointments, and, to the dismay of some of his English Tory followers and the French officers and specialists in his suite, proclaimed a liberty of conscience for all denominations. Furthermore, to the bewilderment of many who saw him as one who had suffered much for the Roman Catholic faith, he refused to permit the seizure of Protestant churches and continued to defend the institutional integrity of the Church of Ireland.

Even before the parliament met, James had been aware of the demands for increased Irish independence among his followers, and indeed there were many – not least of whom were Tyrconnel and Sarsfield – who rather hoped that the King would forget his other territories and settle for the establishment of an autonomous Ireland under the protection of France. Unfortunately for them, this was the one thing to which James never could, or would, agree. Central to his concept of his office was the inviolable nature of the union of his crowns, and he therefore set his face firmly against parliament's attempts to repeal the Poynings Act, which had guaranteed the English executive the right to make laws for Ireland, and made the Dublin body entirely dependent upon Westminster for both its existence and legislative programme. Here, in James's own terms, was what he felt to be his greatest success of the parliamentary session, as he first heavily modified the draft proposal and then stringently opposed the bill for repeal. However, it was the challenge to the royal prerogative arising from this move by Irish MPs that particularly stung the King, as he demanded the right to scrutinise any projected legislation in advance and to have the right to approve or deny its passage before it ever reached the stage of being debated on the floor of parliament. Having crawled its way through the House, the passage of the bill was finally killed off on 21 June 1689, when a statement from James was read out to the MPs asserting his right to use his prerogative, in such a manner, upon all future legislation. Unable to oppose this notion of the King's veto, and all too well aware that James would never knowingly pass any bill that was contrary to his interests, the move to repeal Poynings's law was quietly allowed to drop.

Yet this small triumph was won at the cost of forfeiting the enormous reserves of goodwill that James had enjoyed since his arrival in the country. The King had made it abundantly clear that in the event of his victory, Ireland was to remain as little more than an English colony, subordinate in almost every way, and with his religious reforms representing the only major gains for the Roman Catholic majority. However, if his popularity had been seriously damaged by his refusal to put native Irish and Roman Catholic interests to the fore during the sitting of the Dublin Parliament, then his management of his own cabinet was no more assured. Every night at seven o'clock, James met with his closest advisors, Tyrconnel, d'Avaux, and Melfort, in his council chamber in Dublin Castle, but it was hardly ever a harmonious gathering. D'Avaux and Tyrconnel hated Melfort with a passion that was fully reciprocated, desperately resenting the effect of his silken words upon the King and attempting to retard his plans for the projected landing in Scotland. Yet they could seldom make common cause against him, as Tyrconnel was withdrawn and thoroughly uncommunicative, still nursing his hurt pride now that he was no longer the sole master of Ireland. For his part, d'Avaux surveyed the old warrior with disdain, noting how much weight he had gained, the difficulty with which he mounted his horse and how his limbs were swollen with gout. Without any visible emotion, the Frenchman concluded that he was hardly worth courting; it would be a wasted effort, as the Irishman would soon be dead. It was in this climate that Melfort – who save for the King and his sons was almost entirely friendless – wrote to complain to Lord Waldegrave on 8 May 1689, that there were already 'clouds arising against me'.[37] Indeed, neither his contemporaries nor posterity had much that was good to say of this vain, arrogant, and habitual intriguer, whose uncompromising and singularly uncomplicated brand of ultra-royalism and proselytising Catholicism had already wrecked the King's administration in Scotland, and looked fully capable of similarly destabilising his government in Ireland. Yet his devotion to the monarchy and his profession of personal piety were the very things that bound James to him and gained him a trust which was not entirely misplaced. Though not particularly gifted in anything save the flattery of his master, and often negligent of business, Melfort was at least relatively honest as regards the management of his master's finances. At the particularly impecunious court in Dublin, where peculation was often regarded as a mere perk of office, he took charge of the secret service money and, as far as can be gathered, made sure that it was properly distributed, running a network of spies and agitators throughout Ireland, Scotland, and England.[38]

However, the accumulation of sufficient money to properly promote the Jacobite movement, and to pay and equip the new Irish army, lay outside the expertise of James and his cabinet. With tax returns falling well below that which had been envisaged by the Dublin Parliament, Tyrconnel had gone so far as to suggest that his troops should be paid in kind, although James and Melfort had moved fast to rule out such a desperate expedient. Meanwhile, at the height of the financial crisis, d'Avaux had devoted his energies and a considerable amount of spleen in trying to obtain the dismissal of the coiner of the Dublin mint, having discovered that the man was a Huguenot. Only the prompt intercession of a gang of workmen, who drove the Ambassador's appointee back out of the workshop with a flurry of blows, saved the French exile's job. Far more serious was the decision to recall and re-mint the entire Irish coinage. As a temporary solution to an appalling lack of resources, the measure had much to recommend it, especially in terms of resolving the desperate shortage of small denomination coin required for everyday transactions, the bare maintenance of a market economy, and the buying and selling of foodstuffs. James had not been slow in recognising the danger presented by the flight of capital out of Ireland. He issued a proclamation at the beginning of June 1689 in an attempt to encourage back 'several merchants and other inhabitants of Belfast [who] have quitted their homes either by the instigation of persons ill affected to us, or out of fear . . . [leading] to the depopulation of the said town and lessening of trade therein', but he did nothing to address the fundamental problem of Ireland's economic subjugation to England, or the sobering fact that three-quarters of the nation's wealth was concentrated in the hands of merchants and nobles who lived overseas. Indeed, his defence of Poynings's law and his refusal to renegotiate the terms of the wool trade had, if anything, made matters worse.[39]

With mints established at Dublin and Limerick, the emergency coinage – known to posterity as 'gunmoney' due to the melting down of old brass cannons to supplement the supply of base metals culled from everything from city bells to cooking pots – was minted in pewter, brass and copper, to the value of somewhere between £1.5–£2 million. Even then, it did not entirely resolve the shortage of ready cash, with Tyrconnel continuing to write mournfully to Mary of Modena that the supplies of the new coin were still failing to keep pace with demand. However, the provision of 'gunmoney' did at least ensure that the government would henceforth be able to pay its troops adequately and on time, while James's proclamation of 4 July 1689 made it a criminal offence to refuse to take the brass coins as tender. The problem with the new currency lay not only with the soaring international price of bullion, which equally affected France and Holland – and over which James could have no control – but in its failure to be accepted abroad, rendering it valueless among the mercantile community and leading to the stockpiling of gold and silver by society's financial élite. More damagingly, many Protestant traders off-loaded their supplies of the new currency to buy up relatively inexpensive staples such as wood, tallow and corn from the (usually) Roman Catholic producers, while deferring or simply hiding outlay on more expensive goods, which would have necessitated the change-over of their funds. Equally divisive was the decision to pay the French troops, whose numbers dramatically increased after autumn 1689, in gold and silver, while the Irish soldiers had to make do with the base metal substitutes.[40] Yet although the new coinage would pass into Anglo-Irish folklore as being synonymous with the sour and spoiled fruits of popish rule – which sought to forcibly impose 'brass money and wooden shoes [i.e. the sabots, or clogs, worn by the French soldiers]' upon the people – the recourse to currency reform was far from an extraordinary measure, being utilised by the supporters of Charles I during Britain's civil wars, and by William III as a means to pay for his European wars after 1695. As with land reform, the success of the re-coinage in Ireland depended ultimately on the stability and longevity of James's regime and stood every chance of gaining acceptance, especially among the servants of the Crown, if only the civil war could be brought to an end.

The enormous strain placed on the Irish economy by the need to raise and maintain a large army had been compounded by the failure to keep accurate muster lists, or even to establish an effective network of depots, magazines and arsenals. As a result supply lines frequently became stretched to breaking point, while the general staff were never entirely sure how many men they had under arms at any given time, often permitting relatively small detachments of the enemy to surprise and overwhelm their positions due to their shocking inability to concentrate their forces in good time at the point of greatest need. While James had been at Derry, Tyrconnel had conducted a tour of inspection throughout the army, noting the lack of standardisation of equipment, the poor quality of the firearms shipped over to them by the French, and the enormous variation in the strengths of the individual regiments. Captain John Stevens, an English Jacobite who served in the Lord Grand Prior's regiment, was clearly overwhelmed by the 'common computation [which] was incredible, for most men reck[o]ned the whole nation, every poore country fellow having armed himself with a skeine, as they call it, or dagger, or a ropery like a halfe pike, weapons only fit only to please themselves . . . under pretence of suppressing the rebellious Protestants'. As a consequence of such disorder, and in an attempt to professionalise the service – choosing quality over sheer quantity – James and Tyrconnel agreed on a remodelling of the army, with a reduction in the establishment from approximately 100,000 men to somewhere in the region of 35,000, comprising forty-five regiments of foot, eight of dragoons, seven of cavalry, and a Life Guard of Horse that included a troop of mounted grenadiers. Many of those dismissed joined the 'rapparees', the bands of guerrillas who were named after the ubiquitous cut down pike that they carried, and who looted Protestant homes and raided the Williamite supply columns with impunity. Some found a place within the ranks of the irregular army formed from among the Gaelic communities of Ulster and north Connacht by Tyrconnel's sworn enemy, Hugh 'Balldearg' O'Donnell, who stubbornly refused to acknowledge the authority of Dublin. However, despite the complaints levied against Tyrconnel by the large numbers of officers displaced through the army reforms, by the summer of 1689 James was in possession of a superlative cavalry arm, which had benefited enormously from the recruitment of large numbers of gentlemen's sons and from the recent improvements in horse-breeding in Ireland. The foot regiments, often with strong regional allegiances, were however still inexperienced, in part as a result of the shortage of black-powder, which limited their firing practices and meant that, as von Rosen observed, 'a single cannon-shot passing at the elevation of a clock-tower throws a whole battalion to the ground'. Melfort accurately summed up the situation when he wrote that 'there is no want of raw men to be found here, if we but had some old troops to show them how to do well'.[41]

In June 1689, James received an unwelcome reminder of his reliance on France, as Louis XIV wrote tersely to him about the need to put his army into a state of readiness and to deal immediately with Enniskillen and Derry, before an expeditionary force could be landed by the English fleet on the shores of Ireland. Suspecting that d'Avaux's increasingly despondent reports had brought about this unexpected censure, the King of England replied dryly that he had done everything in accordance with the wishes of the French Ambassador. Yet this was scarcely the truth, as he had steadfastly refused to heed d'Avaux's counsels to proceed against the Irish Protestants far more firmly, and to leave them nothing but scorched earth, buying up all the food, forage and supplies that he could in the north, before destroying what was left, so that his enemies might be denied its use.[42] His son, however, suffered from no such compunction, raiding the estates of known rebels in early July, and burning homes and property as a warning to other Protestant landowners. Having missed capturing one insurgent, the preacher Andrew Hamilton, he allegedly commented that: 'if they had got himself [i.e. Hamilton] they would have made him meat for their hawks'. He was forced to content his soldiers with firing the clergyman's manse – together with his properties in ten separate villages – before driving off 'above a thousand cows, two hundred horses and mares, and about two thousand sheep' taken from the neighbouring estates. To Berwick, and the young gentlemen who rode by his side during his sweep through Donegal, destroying enemy magazines and routing a large party of horse and foot outside Enniskillen, it seemed as if the war was as good as won.[43] All that remained to be conquered were the lakes and marshes of Fermanagh and Derry's defiant walls.

Though a relief expedition led by James's former protégé, Major-General Kirke, had set sail from Liverpool and had been anchored in Lough Foyle since the beginning of June, often pushing as far upriver as Culmore Fort, no serious attempt had been made to come to the assistance of the city or to break the siege. Undoubtedly, the wooden booms connected by iron chains and stretched across the river by de Pointis's engineers presented a formidable obstacle to the English vessels, especially when backed up by the fire from heavily entrenched Jacobite cannon, but Kirke's failure to commit himself to action rested upon more than just this. His personal bravery and ruthlessness had never been doubted, either in his skirmishes against the Moors before Tangier, or during his brutal suppression of Monmouth's revolt, but he seems to have been utterly ill-equipped for an independent command, where strategy and collected thought (as opposed to bullying violence) were needed to carry the day. Though he could see the beacon lit on the steeple of Derry cathedral, to acknowledge and speed on his advance, he neither sailed against the boom nor landed his regiments to bring succour to the garrison. Inside the city, the situation was now desperate. With ammunition and foodstuffs running low, chippings of brick were being used in among the shot, while all the dogs and domestic pets had already been eaten, and supplies of horsemeat, tallow and mice were running dangerously low. Amid the constant rainstorms and heavy bombardments, overcrowding, poor shelter and bad diet all combined to undermine immune systems and to raise sickness to near epidemic levels. After contracting a fever following a long night watch, Governor Baker died, worn out by the fatigue of over-work and the burden of his enormous responsibility. He was buried with full military honours in the vault of St Columb's cathedral. His successor, Colonel Mitchelburne, and his great rival in that position, Revd Walker, could only watch as Kirke's ships sat immobile near the mouth of the Lough, while von Rosen firmly assumed both the conduct of the siege and, for the time being, the military initiative.

Having witnessed his assaults repeatedly driven back and his attempts to mine the city walls defeated by marshy ground and waterlogged earth, von Rosen – who had always believed the conduct of the siege to be misplaced and wasteful – tired of James's continued policy of offering the garrison ever more favourable terms to surrender, and despising such 'weakness' prepared to teach Derry's citizens a hard lesson in the waging of war as it was practised on the Continent. Though, in theory, he was only present as an advisor to Hamilton and knew full well that the King had offered his protection to the Protestants in the surrounding community, von Rosen issued an ultimatum to the garrison, that if they did not surrender before 1 July 1689, he would round up every Protestant he could find – man, woman, and child – between Inishowen and Charlemont, and drive them before his army, as though they were a herd of cattle, to the walls of Derry. There they could be permitted entrance by the garrison, swelling the city's population by several hundred more hungry mouths, or allowed to starve to death between the siege lines. It is not known whether von Rosen was a student of Caesar and had read his Gallic Wars, but Derry was not Alesia and, in the twenty-four hours left to them before the deadline expired, Mitchelburne and Walker planned their own bleak act of reprisal. As the huddled country folk were forced through the lines, a gallows was hoisted up on the walls and word was sent from the garrison threatening that unless the prisoners were allowed to return to their homes, they would begin to hang their prisoners one by one and regardless of rank. Hamilton, whose authority had already been challenged, now chose to intervene and a ferocious argument broke out between the two in the Jacobite council. At last, the Irishman prevailed and von Rosen rescinded his order, allowing the civilians to steal off home, but not before several hundred of the city's old and infirm had slipped out of the gates and in among their ranks, and several young men had chosen to join the garrison in their place. It was a humiliating climb down by the besieging army and, worse than that, served as an indelible stain upon James's reputation for the conduct of war. Ever protective of his military fame, the King recognised this danger immediately and brought von Rosen to account, supporting Hamilton's conduct and thundering against the Lithuanian as a bloody and 'barbarous Muscovite', whom he would have had hanged for disobedience had he been his own subject.[44] Unsurprisingly, there could be no reconciliation between James and his most senior commander, and though they would continue to work together for almost eight more months, the General's credit was thoroughly broken and he soon let it be known that he wished to be allowed to return to service in France.

If cruelty had failed to deliver Derry, then James still clung desperately to his belief that fresh offers of talks might result in a surrender, and he went so far as to give Hamilton permission to grant whatever terms he liked in order to gain possession of the stronghold. On 8 July 1689, the King wrote to offer the Irishman advice, returning to stratagems that had already been tried – unsuccessfully – before condemning the failure of 'your French engineers, tho' very able in their trade, [who] may have been so used to have all things necessary provided for them and to want nothing that they are not so industrious, as other lesse knowing men might be, and that they do not push on their worke as they might do, having so much to say for themselves upon account of their being so ill provided'. Certainly, the correspondence of de Masse, the Engineer-in-Chief at Derry, was rarely graced with optimism as he lamented his own poor health, the frequent confusion in the Jacobite ranks, and the inability of the army to enforce even a rudimentary blockade of the city. However, it is remarkable that James – who had created such a powerful mystique about his own professionalism – should be so dismissive of the skills of the small body of specialists that remained beside him. Moreover, it is indicative of his subsequent conduct that he chose to fall back on precedents from his own service as a young man, half-recalling his experiences at the siege of Mousson, where charges shattered the walls 'which I have seen done to a stronger towne than Derry, and where we [similarly] wanted cannon to mine their defences'.[45] Such retreats into a glorified and romanticised past, in order to sustain a flagging military reputation, would become an increasing feature of his writings as the Irish campaign, and his subsequent attempts to retake his throne, gradually exposed his failings and severe limitations as a commander. For the moment, however, despite all his well-meaning advice, the situation in the Jacobite camp remained only marginally less critical than the plight of the city's garrison. The weather had been exceptionally cold and damp, and conditions had been made worse for the besiegers by the lack of tents and warm bedding. Many soldiers had been forced to construct huts from sods of turf, or had hollowed out holes in the ground in which to sleep, protected in part from the elements and in part from enemy fire, until the rising water table flooded them out and forced them to build new shelters. As sickness swept the camp, a Williamite prisoner wrote of 'the bloody flux, smallpox, fever and agues being among them, they die extremely fast in the Irish camp; the generality of their sustenance being nothing else but oatmeal and water, with some raw lean beef'. The 'ammunition bread' promised for the soldiers, and contracted out to a Mr Auffroy in June, had obviously not been delivered. Discipline, too, had begun to fray, and had not been helped by James's willingness to pardon deserters, allowing them back into the service, while the authority of their officers was not supported in any way.[46]

In the meantime, Kirke's inaction had not gone unnoticed. Marshal Friedrich von Schomberg, who had once served alongside James in the trenches before Etampes and Mousson, had been charged by King William with leading the expedition to regain Ireland, and was currently assembling his army of Dutch, British, Huguenot and German regiments about the ports of Chester and Liverpool. Now in his seventy-fourth year, the old veteran was regarded as something of a figurehead for all those career soldiers displaced by the Revocation of the Edict of Nantes and, realising both the importance of Derry and the need to take the war to the enemy, he gruffly dismissed all Kirke's excuses and wrote to him, urging that he should go immediately to the assistance of the city. Tentative contact had been established between the garrison and the relieving forces by the middle of July, and it would seem that Kirke was finally spurred into action by the news – which would soon transpire to be largely false – that the booms had already been broken by storms and that the Jacobites had shifted the last of their cannon back from the river line, in an attempt to bombard the city into submission.[47] Under the spreading cover of evening's gloom on 28 July 1689, the frigate *Dartmouth* shepherded two supply vessels, the *Phoenix* and the *Mountjoy*, together with a longboat packed with soldiers and sailors equipped with grapples and cutting gear to sever the booms if the need arose, up the River Foyle and into the path of the enemy guns. Despite the fact that Culmore Fort had not been significantly reinforced, a massive fusillade swept over the decks of the approaching vessels, felling the Derry-born master of the *Mountjoy* as he encouraged his men to ram the boom, and sending a jagged splinter into the thigh of the boatswain as the longboat crew hacked at the barrier's wooden beams. In launching the attack, Kirke and his commanders had been concerned that transport ships might have been sunk in the channel, effectively barring the passage of all shipping upriver to the city, but although this had been urged upon Hamilton by his commanders, he had stopped short of such a drastic if potentially decisive measure, fearing that once Derry was taken it would have destroyed its trade for no good purpose, depriving King James of the valuable tax revenues that he so earnestly desired. As a consequence, the attackers made good progress and soon discovered that the river defences had been built in far greater haste, and with far less skill, than they had ever dared to hope. It appears that one of the booms had already disintegrated under the action of the winds and the tide – though there remains an element of doubt as to whether it was ever completely finished in the first place – while the other succumbed quickly to the blows of the sailors and the sudden, jolting impact of the bows of the *Mountjoy* as she tore away the chain that linked it to either bank. Yet, as the *Phoenix* sailed through unscathed in her wake, the *Mountjoy* recoiled sharply as a result of the collision and, briefly snarled by the shattered links of chain, she thudded into the riverbank and settled in the mud. For a moment it looked as if the Jacobite cavalry, who had seen their chance and charged out from among the trenches, swirling about and firing into the stranded vessel, might succeed in boarding her, but a broadside from the guns of the *Dartmouth*, bearing up behind her, scattered them in an instant and sent them racing back the way that they had come, while the crew of the longboat quickly attached a line to the *Mountjoy*'s fractured bows and towed her away to safety. Covering the advance of the little supply vessels, the *Dartmouth* continued the artillery duel with the defenders of Culmore Fort, punctuating the night with sudden bursts of thunderous flame, until it was certain that the ships had reached the quayside at Derry. With the siege effectively broken, the citizens of Derry raced down to the dock to embrace their deliverers and to rush ashore the supplies of peas, meat, brandy and cheese, that were worth far more than riches to a people who had been down to their last two days' worth of rations. Hamilton and von Rosen could do little more than watch, while one Jacobite sought to contrast the 'shouts of joy the town gave hereat' with the grievous 'pangs of heart it gave to the loyal army'. Unsurprisingly, recriminations flew thick and fast, with allegations that the gunners in the fort had been drinking since the morning 'which caused them to shoot at random', that treachery had had a part to play, or that the cannon themselves were to blame, being 'so small and so few that they could not sink a ship in the passage'.[48]

For three more days King James's army continued to pepper the city walls with shot, but all chance of starving the garrison into submission had now gone, and Hamilton made preparations to lift the siege. However, even as the Jacobite army drew off towards Lifford and Strabane, burning their camp and leaving behind them in shallow graves almost 2,000 of their men – including de Masse, the cheerless officer of engineers, whose sufferings had been brought to an end by a cannon ball just days before – a fresh disaster was breaking over their comrades who been sent to subdue Enniskillen, which gifted the entire North of Ireland to the Williamites. Supplied with arms and ammunition through Ballyshannon, Gustavus Hamilton and Thomas Lloyd had made full use of their cavalry by launching near continuous raids on the outlying Jacobite encampments, and by constantly harrying the line of communications between Dublin and the siege lines at Derry. As a consequence, James had sought their destruction and had planned to lead an army against Enniskillen in person, until persuaded by d'Avaux (perhaps a little too easily) to entrust the operation to the hands of his former favourite Justin Macarty instead. Unfortunately, though Macarty was a serious and competent officer, he was handicapped in his movements through Fermanagh by James's prescriptive orders and by the bad service rendered by his subordinate, Anthony Hamilton, brother of the siege commander at Derry. Having failed to reconnoitre the enemy positions before him, Hamilton led his over-confident dragoons straight into an ambush on the morning of 31 July 1689, before fleeing from the field without making the slightest attempt to rally his broken and savaged men. Forced into giving battle at Newtown Butler that same afternoon, Macarty saw his remaining cavalry broken and his guns overrun by the furious charge of the Enniskillen men. Amid the confusion his horse was shot from under him, and only the timely recognition of his identity by a brother officer saved him from being clubbed to death, as he lay pinned down by his fallen mount. For James, coming so fast on the heels of the relief of Derry it was a terrible setback, securing the whole of Fermanagh for his foes and marking the destruction of an entire Jacobite army, with all its artillery and the baggage train captured, along with more than 500 prisoners. Forgetting his recent coldness towards Macarty – which had been provoked by the Irishman's willingness to side with Tyrconnel against Melfort – the King sent two of his surgeons and a physician to tend to his wounds, and a present of wine and money to restore his spirits. However, even though he enjoyed James's trust, he was probably lucky to be in captivity while, in the Jacobite camp, the grim hunt to apportion blame for the defeat and to identify scapegoats was begun. Anthony Hamilton and Captain Lavallin, a gentleman from Cork who had been accused of contributing to the flight by misinterpreting his orders to turn 'left about', were arrested and duly court-martialed before a panel led by General von Rosen. While Hamilton – who had not stopped running till he had reached Navan, almost 50 miles away from the fighting – had an influential brother and many friends at court, and was speedily acquitted, Lavallin, who had neither, was condemned. With James refusing to offer a pardon, the unfortunate officer went before a firing squad still protesting his innocence, and fell (we are told) much lamented by his comrades throughout the army.[49]

With the war in the north practically at an end and the Jacobites effectively robbed of the military initiative for the first time, an extremely favourable set of circumstances had been created for Schomberg's arrival in Ireland at the beginning of August. Having set sail from Hoylake, near Chester, von Schomberg made landfall at Bangor after only little more than a day at sea. No attempt had been made to obstruct his passage by the French navy and the winds had been so favourable that his craft had surged ahead, without waiting for the subsidiary convoys carrying horses, supplies and artillery which were supposed to rendezvous with him en route. Carrickfergus, 'smothered with dust and smoke occasioned by the bombs', fell quickly before the combined bombardment that he launched from both land and sea. Riding through the ranks of the 'country people' who had gathered in order to take their vengeance on the garrison, who had lived off the land for the past months, the Marshal had been forced to draw and brandish his pistol to prevent a general massacre, and to ensure that the terms of surrender he had granted were fully respected by his own side. Realising that the Enniskillen men and the defenders of Derry would soon swell the enemy's ranks, and that Belfast was already as good as lost to him, James wrote to his son-in-law, Lord Waldegrave, of 'the flame which Schomberg's landing in this kingdom hath kindled here' and prepared to take d'Avaux to task.[50] The King's French advisors had already concluded that Dublin could – and indeed should – no longer be held against von Schomberg's approach. The prompt burning of the city and the employment of a scorched earth policy would, they argued, allow James to slip west into Connacht with his army intact and to wear down his opponents through sheer attrition, over the course of years rather than months if needs be. Yet James, who felt that he had invested both time and effort, through the heated sessions of the Dublin Parliament, in legitimising his rule in Ireland, had no desire to destroy his own capital and to pauperise the entire kingdom just so he could live as a virtual outlaw. Nevertheless, this ruthless approach to war was to yield impressive results for Sarsfield, Tyrconnel and St Ruth after his departure, and would effectively ensure that a Jacobite army remained in the field for two more years.

Unfortunately, during the course of these discussions the King could no longer count on the support of his loyal servant, Melfort. Tyrconnel and his clients had sought to blame him for the failure to take Derry, while d'Avaux's unremittingly hostile reports of his laziness and crippling mismanagement of the war effort had completely destroyed his credit at the French court. Increasingly, James's own rule was becoming compromised by his association with Melfort's presence and malpractices, with his Irish officers beginning to grumble that he should never have come to Ireland, and at the end of August the King was reluctantly forced to agree to send his Secretary of State back to France, for a short time only, in order to give an account of the campaign and to lobby for fresh aid. Surprisingly, d'Avaux was almost sad to see him go, for he had heard whisperings of a plot among the army to have him assassinated and was somewhat disappointed that his least favourite courtier had not stayed long enough for the plan to take effect. However, he need not have worried, for no sooner had Melfort arrived in France than Mary of Modena was prevailed upon by Louis XIV to send him on an embassy to the court of Rome, removing him permanently from the realm of Irish politics and further strengthening the hand of those on James's Privy Council who would have turned that body into an unthinking instrument of French foreign policy. Disconsolate, James (not for the first time) openly voiced his doubts about the future of his government in Ireland, and his continuing presence in the country. While Melfort had still been at his side, he could still entertain hopes that, although the Scottish campaign was now out of the question, a winter landing in England backed by a string of local risings might be possible, permitting him an honourable way out of Ireland and the chance to sweep William away as quickly as he had come. Deprived of his friend's support, and of Melfort's unerring capacity to aid and sustain his master in all of his self-deceptions, James was forced to accept that his immediate future lay in Ireland and that – as Tyrconnel daily pressed upon him – he had little other choice than to fight, if he wanted to maintain himself in his capital.

Putting himself at the head of the army, James established his operational headquarters at Drogheda, determined to concentrate his forces along the Boyne Valley – which acted as a major natural barrier for any force attempting to surge southwards – and fully intending to project his own military power forward as far as the pass at Dundalk, in order to harass the enemy at every conceivable turn. The campaign started well for the Jacobites, as Berwick led raiding parties back through Armagh and County Down burning everything in their path, leaving Schomberg to enter Newry only to discover, to his horror, that everything of value in the town had been destroyed and that its buildings had been reduced to little more than smoking ruins and piles of rubble. His regiments, clearly shaken by the sight, were forced to camp that night on the north side of the town. Unfortunately a storm which rose that evening not only put out the fires in the town but also blew down most of the soldiers' tents, leaving them to shiver in the wind and the rain.[51] Pushing forward into an unknown and devastated territory, which had come to resemble a moonscape as the retreating Jacobite cavalry screen pitted the roads, pulled down the farms and destroyed the bridges in their wake, von Schomberg's advance was both slow and uncertain. A handful of Berwick's troopers appearing on the hillsides, or sounding 'a flourish' with their trumpets, was enough to hold up the progress of the entire army for hours at a time, as the old warhorse painstakingly reconnoitred the ground ahead of him and meticulously dressed his lines, in constant expectation of a sudden and devastating attack. With the weather worsening all the while, stores running low, and a commissariat that was clearly unequal to the task of re-supplying his army, von Schomberg called a halt at Dundalk in the hope that he could have fresh provisions run in to him by the fleet. However, while storms kept the ships which should have re-supplied them standing out to sea, the Marshal chose the worst possible site on which to pitch his camp, on marshy ground which was prone to flooding. It afforded small comfort to soldiers already drenched to the skin, and disease spread like wildfire among the ranks. If ever there had been a time to attack, with sickness, desertion and attempted mutinies all threatening to destroy the morale and cohesion of von Schomberg's army, then it surely must have been now, but as James led some 22,000 men through County Louth in the middle of September, he appeared to share in his opponent's curious reluctance to force a general and potentially decisive engagement.

Having advanced to within 3 miles of Dundalk, the King had ridden out to observe the trenches that the enemy were throwing up outside the town, before establishing his own encampment and interrogating a lieutenant and a handful of soldiers, who had been brought in by his skirmishers, as to von Schomberg's strength. Writing much later, Berwick thought that the Jacobites had an advantage of some 2,000 men over their foes but that this was effectively cancelled out by their being 'but very indifferently armed'. James, though heartened by the spirit of his troops who he found 'resolute, and convinced that nothing but Victory could secure them from loosing [sic] their liberty, their estates and Religion', seemed to be awed by the professionalism of the enemy forces and by the size of their artillery train. However, while he refused to sanction a direct assault on their fortified positions, for almost three weeks he tried to tempt von Schomberg's troops out from behind their defensive lines to give battle on the open valley floor. The Jacobites regularly foraged close to the enemy pickets, burning those supplies that they could not bring back to their own camp, and launched swift (if limited) raids on their lines, with the aim of snatching prisoners and gaining word of von Schomberg's intentions. False alarms had constantly troubled the peace of the Williamite camp both day and night, and a handful of deserters – who had conceivably been instructed to go over to their foes by their officers – brought with them, on the morning of 20 September, intelligence that the Jacobites planned to mount a major attack on their emplacements the next day. It was no surprise, therefore, when James's army mustered at first light and advanced, at beat of drum and in 'great numbers', to within musket shot of the trenches. The King's artillery opened up a desultory bombardment of the Williamite positions, as the forewarned soldiers quickly formed ranks, but the elevation of their guns was too high and their cannon balls sailed harmlessly over the heads of their enemies, falling well to their rear.

Skirmishers deployed well to the fore of the Jacobite regiments, but their uncoordinated fire made no impression on von Schomberg's foot who 'shew'd great forwardness and impatience' to begin the fight and whose volleys soon scattered the would-be marksmen, killing a handful of their number and sending the rest hurrying back behind the bulky security of James's pike-blocks. Drawing back out of range, the King's army continued to wait patiently for signs that their enemy would consent to give battle, but despite the excited pleas of his junior officers, von Schomberg remained impassive all morning and would not consent to stir himself or any of his soldiers into action. As first minutes, and then hours, passed by without event, James decided not to press matters any further, giving the order at approximately 1 pm for his men to ground their arms and to return to camp. A similar anti-climax followed two days later on 23 September, when the Jacobite army showed itself once more before von Schomberg's lines, again failing to provoke a battle, and drawing off under cover of a smoke-screen from haystacks fired in the neighbouring fields by the retiring troopers. Clinging to the belief that von Schomberg might still be induced to sally out into the open, James remained in his camp until 6 October, unable to rationalise his opponent's refusal to be drawn in to the fight, and increasingly tormented by fears that a rising was planned by the Protestants of Dublin and that a naval landing was about to be made to his rear, cutting off his path of retreat. One might have thought that such concerns would have induced James to launch a full-scale attack on Dundalk, clearing the road back to Ulster and destroying the immediate threat that he had to face, but he did nothing of the kind, being perfectly prepared to join von Schomberg in playing the waiting game and continuing to repeat the same tactics – of sudden advance, followed by swift retreat – which had already failed to produce the desired results. Only when his cavalry had finally exhausted all the forage in the area, did James belatedly decide to burn his camp and fall back upon Ardee, where he and his army continued to wait, holding the line of the Boyne Valley, in expectation of an attack that would now never come.

Even though his new base offered the army adequate protection against any projected assault, James had taken as little care over his choice of site as had his rival, and the driving rains soon washed out the fragile shelters in both encampments. Melfort's replacement, Sir Richard Neagle, had proved himself to be no more efficient in the maintenance of the supply lines than his much-reviled predecessor, while the King and his generals had not learned the hard lessons of Derry and had done nothing to set up proper depots for the re-equipment and re-provisioning of the thousands of increasingly ragged and hungry soldiers who felt the edge to the autumnal chill. As 'the bloody flux', or dysentery, swept the camp, the cavalry exhausted their remaining forage and had no idea where to search for fresh hay, oats and barley; promises of new tents came to nothing, and officers estimated that a half of their men marched barefoot, while a third braved the downpours with both feet and legs bare. There was widespread fear of famine as the harvest failed – mainly because nothing had been planted in the spring – and the countryside was torn apart by rival gangs of soldiers forced to pillage for their very survival. D'Avaux sadly noted that: 'The King of England does not like us to draw attention to the disorder of his affairs no matter how respectfully and humbly it is done', but the truth was that James was not there to see the ruin of many of his regiments over the winter months. He had returned to Dublin in early November, rightly concluding that the campaigning season was well and truly over and there was no more fighting to be done that year.[52]

It was of no consolation to the soldiers he left behind him at Ardee that, if anything, the Williamite army was in an even worse condition than their own, or that both before and after retiring to Lisburn for the winter, von Schomberg's forces were ravaged by a combination of the cold, lice, and pneumonia. Fever, allegedly spread by the survivors from the siege of Derry, also coursed through the cantonments, carrying off hundreds of malnourished soldiers whose immune systems had already been broken by months of hard (if thoroughly inconclusive) marches and counter-marches. By the spring, perhaps a third of von Schomberg's army – as many as 5,600 men – had sickened and died, a testament not only to the harsh weather, but also to the limitations of seventeenth-century military logistics and the failure of their elderly commander to realise that speed was of the essence in bringing Jacobite Ireland to its knees.[53]

Though James would later seek to claim that: 'the Campagne ended very much to the King's honour and advantage', delighting in the fall of Sligo in mid-October to Patrick Sarsfield's horse and a party of Sir Neil O'Neill's dragoons, the two sides had become – quite literally – bogged down in their defensive lines, having settled nothing and achieved no more than a heavy loss of life through the unchecked spread of disease.[54] Furthermore, while von Schomberg had been unable to deliver any sort of knockout blow to the Jacobites, his successful landing and the relief of both Derry and Enniskillen had ensured that Ireland was far less secure in its allegiance to James by the winter of 1689, than at the time of his first coming. His performance before the Irish Parliament, and his refusal to set aside English interests in favour of those of his new hosts, squandered his political capital and tarnished his reputation, while the spread of the war had been effectively contained within the thirty-two counties and all but snuffed out in Scotland. James was now very much on the back foot, in no position to invade England and increasingly willing to invest all his hopes in what he believed was France's limitless resources of men and munitions. He had already negotiated a troop exchange with Louis XIV, who had promised him 5–6,000 veteran reinforcements for the new year, in return for roughly the same number of Irish soldiers, though this had been a point of some controversy as the French had originally demanded a far better return for their outlay in manpower and resources. However, it was with these fresh regiments in mind that James heard reports of William III's preparations to carry the war to him in person, and contemplated fighting the final battle with his enemy (who was both nephew and son-in-law) upon Irish land. As the yule log burnt low in the grate before him, and the candles were extinguished one by one in the Great Hall of Dublin Castle, there is little to suggest that the thought of the struggle to come brought James II, twelve months gone from his palace at Whitehall, any sort of Christmas cheer.

CHAPTER FOUR

The Banks of the Boyne

I

Parliaments, as William III was coming to appreciate with ever-growing clarity, could be troublesome things. He had watched with dismay as the proceedings of the English Convention had devolved into bitter wranglings over his revenue and as the Whigs had tried to hold up the promised Act of Indemnity, in an attempt to purge local government for good of their Tory rivals, and to confer an inbuilt majority for their own partisans in any future parliament. More disturbing to the Dutchman, who had the blood of the House of Stuart flowing through his veins, was the decision of MPs to turn the Declaration of Rights into law, transforming sentiments which William had been led to believe were merely the restatements of customary privilege into far more radical attempts to transfer power from the Crown to Parliament. By December 1689, the dispensing power – so closely identified with James II's resurgent monarchy – had been declared illegal and removed from the arsenal of royal prerogatives. For a King who had hoped to pass on the throne with all its powers still intact to his eventual heir – at this point, likely to be his nephew, the little Duke of Gloucester, who had been born to Princess Anne in July and named in his honour – such moves came as a particularly heavy blow. They were interpreted by William as representing nothing more than a singular mark of ingratitude from a legislature that he alone had saved from ruin. Furthermore, while £2,000,000 had been earmarked by parliament in October 1689 for the prosecution of the war in Ireland, much of the money had already found its way into the seemingly bottomless pockets of the Chief Commissary, Henry Shales, whom some suspected of Jacobitism and all noted as showing utter indifference to the plight of the soldiers who sickened at Dundalk and Lisburn. Just as serious was the Whigs' intention to use the question of supply for the war in order to tie the King's hands, and to compel him to rubber-stamp their ambitious legislative programme, which included the remodelling of the boroughs. Even though the Corporation Bill eventually went down to defeat in the Lords in the new year, the threat to hold up the granting of loans for the war now compelled William to act in order to reassert his will, dissolving the Convention in February 1690 and calling for fresh elections, so that he might preserve both the power of the Crown and his chance of leading an army into Ireland during the forthcoming campaigning season.

With his envoys shuttling from one north German and Baltic court to the next in an attempt to hire troops, settle subsidies, and preserve the fragile patchwork of alliances that had maintained the League of Augsburg, William remained fearful that, in his absence, the States General of Holland might undertake to negotiate a separate peace with France. Louis XIV had taken the Dutch invasion and the overthrow of James II as the signal for the outbreak of hostilities with both England and Holland, though it was not until 5 May 1689, after the battle of Bantry Bay had actually been fought, that a formal declaration of war was delivered on behalf of the English, by William's diplomats. Yet William's luck held, with the allied generals slowly consolidating a series of gains along the disputed Rhine Valley, re-garrisoning the fortresses of Kaiserwerth, Cologne and Bonn, and inflicting a sharp rebuff to de Humieres at the battle of Walcourt in August 1689. Of far greater value was the 'Grand Alliance' concluded between the Dutch Republic and the Empire at The Hague, on 12 May 1689, and the successful courting of both Bavaria and Denmark over the summer months. By the following year, as William was preparing to sail for Ireland, alarm at Louis XIV's territorial ambitions had driven Spain into the arms of the allies and persuaded Pope Innocent XI to advance large sums of money to finance the expedition. Further delays, resulting from the visceral electioneering of February and March 1690, had led William to despair of the inefficiency and faction that beset English politics, declaring that: 'One loses patience in seeing the slowness of the people here in all they do, although I hurry from morning to night'. Nevertheless, the heavy defeat of the Whigs at the polls, and the return of large numbers of Tories to office – who, in their desire to secure place, privilege and the dominant position of the Established Church, had reconciled themselves to the revolutionary settlement – actually served to ease the pressure on the joint monarchy and permitted Queen Mary, clearly petrified at the prospect of taking executive power in her husband's absence, to be gifted the services of Danby, the one familiar counsellor in whom she could trust.[1] William, though often overcome with exasperation at his wife's obtuse nature, had now good cause to be thankful for her gifts and for her ability both to soothe the tempers of the quarrelsome magnates who sat on her council, and to salve English national pride, which had been sorely dented by the flight of the native king and the importation of a foreign one. Indeed, if the slight, silent, and – more worryingly – Calvinist, William had distinctly failed to impress his new subjects, carrying with him always the dignified reserve of a stranger, then Mary fitted almost perfectly the Tory ideal of a monarch, English to the core and devoted with every fibre of her being to the rituals and doctrine of the Anglican Church. Almost entirely without guile, she combined the deference and modesty expected of a dutiful wife with feminine tact and good grace, and acted as a valuable counterbalance to her sister Anne, who was both attempting to found a rival polity based about her own Household, and preparing – under the tutelage of Sarah Churchill – to play the national card without the faintest trace of shame or scruple. It was this consideration, and the knowledge that her dull and moon-faced husband, Prince George of Denmark, had managed to change his allegiances within the space of the last year, with scarcely a blink or any certain reflection, that decided William upon taking his brother-in-law with him to Ireland, where he would be out of the way of temptation and, as a staff officer with no real responsibilities, could do no significant harm.

William had hoped to sail first to Scotland, thoroughly securing and pacifying that nation, before landing his reinforcements in Ireland. However, the winds dropped away, leaving his fleet stranded off the Cheshire coast for several days at the beginning of June 1690, and effectively removing all remaining possibility of the voyage north, while adding appreciably to the King's mounting sense of frustration. William had been deeply disappointed by von Schomberg's failure to press the campaign in Ireland to a successful conclusion. He had always valued the Marshal's combination of far-sighted judgement and bluff bravery, but this unexpected reversal, coupled with what he believed to be the dereliction of duty among his general officers, only confirmed in him the desire to take the conduct of the war into his own hands. One of the most troublesome and intractable of problems was presented by the presence of James himself, for if he fell in battle his blood would surely be seen to cling to the hands of both his daughter and son-in-law, while if he was captured he might become as great a nuisance, and as forceful a rallying point, as he had been before his escapes from London and Rochester. Furthermore, it was the more personal and devastating vision of 'how terrible it must have been', if 'my husband and my father would fight in person against each other, and if either should have perished in the action' that tore at Queen Mary's thoughts, as she agreed to the cancellation of a joint coronation in Edinburgh and chose to overlook the graffiti chalked on the gates of Kensington Palace – under cover of dark by some Jacobite wit – promising that by midsummer the place would be open 'to let' again to a new tenant. However, a plan had already been drawn up that seemed, at face value, to offer a solution to these problems, by endeavouring to lure James on board a 3rd rate which had supposedly defected from the Williamites, before weighing anchor and racing out of Dublin Bay, effectively kidnapping the hapless monarch and eventually landing him safely in either Spain or Italy, as he 'should desire', and pressing upon him some £20,000 for his future subsistence.

Bishop Burnet believed that William 'thought it was a well formed design, and likely enough to succeed; but would not hearken to it', saying that he would have no hand in treachery and fearing that a scuffle might break out and shots be fired, once the subterfuge was discovered, which might have resulted in the former King bleeding his life away upon the decks of an English battleship.[2] If James could not be dislodged from Ireland, in good conscience, without the use of force, then William was prepared to make clear to the House of Lords in January 1690, that high taxation and the ills currently afflicting his lands could only be curbed quickly by the ending of hostilities, while he was the only commander who was both fully willing and capable of delivering the knock-out blow. Thus, he declared, to expedite 'the speedy recovery of Ireland . . . and to preserve the peace and honour of the nation, I am resolved to go in person' to Ireland. However, had William been a suspicious general he might have felt – as the fog closed in about his yacht as soon as it got out into the Irish Sea, obscuring it from the anxious sight of the look-outs aboard its escorts – that the new campaign appeared to be extremely ill-starred. For days the convoy struggled to edge its way forward against prevailing winds, and it was only after sheltering in Ramsey Bay, at the north-west tip of the Isle of Man, early on 14 June 1690, that the King's luck and the winds changed, with the gathering breeze suddenly filling sails and pushing the fleet on towards its destination. That same afternoon some 300 ships, troop transports, supply vessels and men-of-war, together with scores of rowboats and pleasure craft loaded with curious spectators, crowded into the harbour at Carrickfergus, as William III was slowly rowed ashore and the guns of the fleet answered the salute given by the cannon run out on the castle walls, intoning both a welcome obeisance and the thunderous intent of a second King who had arrived in Ireland to claim what he believed to be his by right.[3]

Knowing that a fresh (and much more significant) challenge was to be launched against his power in Ireland that year, it is all the more remarkable that James had made no effort, in the intervening months available to him, to break the deadlock and destroy von Schomberg's forces before they could be properly reinforced. He had spent the winter in Dublin, presiding over a little court which, with its attendant pages, gentlemen ushers, grooms, cooks and confectioners, attempted to replicate the functions and formulas of his old Household at Whitehall. College Green had become a fashionable area for courtiers to live, with the King's faithful valet, de Labadie, moving quickly to take possession of a mansion sequestrated from Viscount Charlemont. Scurrilous tongues at Versailles would credit James with keeping two of his Irish mistresses – allegedly but poor creatures, all skin and bone – close by, while later aristocratic visitors to Dublin would accord him only the far more mundane honour of introducing spaniels into the land, and with popularising the breed, after a little pack of the animals was seen to be constantly trailing in his wake. Far more telling was the absence of goods and livestock from the capital's markets, and the fact that the great estates and parklands had been swept long ago for horses with which to mount cavalry troopers and pull siege guns.[4] James had attempted to enforce a blockade on the enemy's ports and to disrupt von Schomberg's naval communications, but he had refused to license privateers to disrupt English trade, and he could only lead his soldiers down to the quayside and look on as a helpless spectator as Sir Cloudisley Shovell seized the Pelican – the only frigate belonging to the Jacobite navy – after a brief fight in Dublin Bay and carried her back out to sea as a prize for his daring.[5]

James had been troubled by the late arrival of the French fleet and resolutely clung to the belief that the landing of crack French regiments would not only restore the military balance in his favour, but also assist in the training of his own soldiers, providing the necessary reservoir of expertise that his army had hitherto struggled to make good. Though it seemed that the King had won his battle with Louvois to make a straight exchange, with numerical parity of forces on either side, he bitterly resented the attempt by the French military to strip his army of its best officers. Although James had never particularly cared for Sarsfield, whom he had considered stupid, he had grown to value his usefulness and bravery after his capture of Sligo, and refused to be parted from him. Conversely, the French had heard quite enough of the failings of the Hamilton brothers, from the pages of d'Avaux's increasingly Jeremiah-like despatches, to want nothing to do with them, rejecting their services after James had offered them. It is conceivable that the King might have been prepared to send his son Berwick into France, if he could have been guaranteed the command of the Irish Brigade, but his allies were not inclined to trust such an important post to a youth, who although recognised as a promising and courageous officer, still lacked wide-ranging experience of independent action. The natural choice to lead the Brigade had been Justin Macarty, who was competent, well-bred and respected by both parties, but whose gifts would not outshine or provoke the jealousy of too many French officers in the constant search for preferment, honours and titles. Unfortunately, his capture at Newtown Butler had effectively removed him from the frame, until he chose to break his parole in the most controversial of manners, and rejoined a clearly delighted King James in Dublin in December 1689. From then on, it was Macarty's hand that was to be instrumental in the shaping of the Brigade, bringing five heterogeneous foot regiments up to strength, and fighting hard to raise the issue of their pay and conditions with their new masters. The regimental names of Clare, Mountcashel and Dillon would win battle honours from Italy and the Alps to Catalonia, Flanders, and the Rhine over the next twenty-five years – their illustrious pedigrees finally being eclipsed only by the tide of Revolutionary warfare in France – but for the moment, as just over 5,000 unarmed men were herded aboard transports, the success of these first 'Wild Geese' to flee the shores of Ireland was far from certain, and their leaving was accompanied by 'a great deal of howling' and the wails of distraught families who feared, with good justification, that they would never see their loved ones again.[6]

The Irish Brigade left in early March 1690 on the same vessels that brought the long-anticipated French reinforcements to Cork, and were accompanied not only by Macarty, but also by von Rosen and d'Avaux, who could barely contain their relief at their return to the Continent. James, too, was happy to see them go. He had had nothing but contempt for von Rosen since his brutality at Derry, and subsequent defeatism when confronted by von Schomberg, and he had sought to hold d'Avaux personally responsible for the recall of Melfort, which had effectively soured their working relationship and rendered it increasingly untenable since the close of the previous summer.[7] With his original appointees to James's general staff now either dead, like Maumont and Pusignan, or thoroughly discredited, like von Rosen, Louvois was forced to give his grudging approval to the King's original choice for the commander of the French forces: the comte de Lauzun, who had been promoted to field rank and had arrived in the troop convoy with almost 7,000 men, including officers, artillery men and surgeons. Unfortunately, James's joy at seeing his friend was soon eclipsed by his dismay at the quality of the troops that he had been sent. He had expected veterans, but had been delivered instead the tired and dispirited soldiers of the regiment Tournaisis, who had been transferred directly from the front in Savoy, and a mixture of expatriate troops in French service, many of whom were Walloons or German Protestants who had originally been prisoners of war but who had enlisted as a means of securing their freedom from Louis XIV's jails and prison camps. Like James, Louvois had no intention of gifting away his best officers and men with no real hope of return and, by April 1690, he was informing his master that 'unless God works a miracle to the King of England, the Prince of Orange will accomplish the conquest of Ireland with far greater ease than he imagines'.[8]

Such fears appeared to be fully vindicated, as Berwick's regiments had been surprised in a dawn raid on their quarters at Cavan in February 1690. They had been scattered by the Enniskillen men, leaving both the town and their magazine to be fired, and their shaken general to limp back to Dublin with the survivors, and make as good an account of the affair as he could before his father's war council. Equally debilitating were von Schomberg's repeated attacks on Charlemont Fort, the last significant Jacobite stronghold in Ulster, after the town of Cavan had fallen. Though the settlement underneath its walls had been laid waste by the Williamites, the fort at Charlemont had held out all winter, becoming a safe haven for Roman Catholic refugees driven in from the surrounding countryside. However, with women and children accounting for one fifth of all those sheltering within its ramparts, food supplies soon ran critically low and famine threatened the garrison. A small relief force was despatched in May 1690, but it had been ambushed in the surrounding swamps and routed, while James appears to have done little to keep the route into Armagh open or to re-supply the garrison, once famine took hold. Without any word of hope from Dublin, Governor Tadhg O'Regan concluded that he had done all that honour required of him and negotiated favourable terms with von Schomberg. Though he was forced to leave behind a considerable artillery train, which would have been of great assistance to the Jacobite army, O'Regan and his men were allowed to keep their arms and rejoin James's army. They were received as though they had won a victory rather than suffered an entirely avoidable defeat. Impressed by O'Regan's tenacity and fighting spirit, the King bestowed a knighthood upon him, although it might have been of far more account had he mobilised his forces earlier and attempted to send well-protected supply convoys deep into the heart of the enemy's territory, before the fortress that had made the new knight's reputation had actually fallen in the first place. Once again, Melfort's failure to provide the army with adequate logistical support was blamed, but he had been gone for over six months by this time and neither James nor Neagle had done anything to remedy the situation. Moreover, if one anonymous Jacobite could praise von Schomberg for drawing out of winter quarters early in the new year and taking the war to his enemy before Charlemont 'like a vigilant general', then James was painstakingly slow in gathering his army about him again at Dundalk. Even then, he failed to concentrate his forces effectively, worrying unduly about controlling the castles and towns to his rear and bottling up valuable troops in garrisons, when their numbers and experience would have counted far more decisively in the field.[9] This said, he had taken a commanding position overlooking the Moyry pass, key to any advance upon Dublin, and had taken steps to fortify ground that was already naturally extremely formidable. It was argued that had the King pushed on just 4 miles further along the road to Newry, where the causeway narrowed and was hemmed in by bog, he could have threatened to completely sever William's communications and to have virtually guaranteed the necessity of fighting a battle upon his advantage. Even if his foes pushed themselves through the 'Gap of Ulster', by merely holding on to his entrenchments at Dundalk, James was dictating the terms of the campaign and would still compel William to fight every step of the way if he wished to break out of the north and begin the advance on Dublin.

The Jacobite army had the advantage of the terrain and of pre-prepared positions, but Lauzun advised against the King giving battle, fearing that an outflanking movement through Armagh might cut their supplies and plant a Williamite army to their rear, capable of beating their own in a rush back to the Irish capital. Certainly the Governor of Dublin, Colonel Luttrell, was fearful of a rising within the city limits, imposing a curfew on all Protestants between 10 pm and 5 am, and banning more than five of them from meeting together at any one time, threatening: 'Death, or such other Punishment, as a Court Martial shall think fit'.[10] However, with William breaking up the five thinnest battalions of von Schomberg's army, which had been weakened over the winter by disease and desertion, and asserting his considerable authority over his multi-national forces of Danes, Dutch, Finns, French Huguenots, Brandenburgers, Swiss, Irish Protestants and Englishmen – who would probably have been unmanageable in the hands of a lesser commander – it was obvious to all that he would seek to press a decisive engagement upon James at the first available opportunity. All that was in doubt was exactly when, and where, the battle would be fought. James had already committed himself to preserving Dublin at all costs, and had discounted the possibility of slipping away to the west, living off the land, and fighting a protracted rearguard action. In order to fulfil his stated objectives, he would be forced to fight either at Dundalk or on the river line of the Boyne, the only other defensible barrier between Belfast and the capital. Unfortunately, James appeared to be curiously reticent about fighting; during the previous autumn, at almost the same spot, he had rejected von Rosen's urgings to sanction an attack, and now his resolve broke down once again before Lauzun's largely unfounded fears, and he gave the order to abandon his heavily defended position and fall back towards Dublin.

No one was more surprised by this decision than the first party of Williamite dragoons who edged through the Moyry pass, expecting all the time to be hit by an ambush or to encounter the main body of the Jacobite army, drawn up for battle. As anxious minutes passed by, and they met with no more than token resistance from a handful of skirmishers, who quickly beat a retreat when it became apparent that they were outgunned, scouts were sent tearing back along the advancing Williamite columns bearing news that made their commanders scarcely believe their luck: the Jacobites had abandoned the 'Gap of Ulster' and the empty camp at Dundalk was theirs for the taking, for the price of only boot leather, sore feet, and a brisk march under a sweltering Irish sun. In the meantime, James was in good spirits, thoroughly enjoying the long hours spent in the saddle and the easy camaraderie of soldiers, and now reconciled to the impending reality of battle and confident of victory. He had hoped that his army would quickly strip the surrounding countryside of food and forage, holding up William's advance and drawing him further from the coast, forcing the English and Dutch dragoons to scour the land for fodder and the commissariat to send fresh pleas to the Westminster Parliament for an urgent re-supply. Unfortunately, William's conduct of war did not mirror that of von Schomberg; there were to be no grand manoeuvres or protracted set-piece sieges, aimed at the maximum preservation of military strength and the conquest of territory. Instead, there was merely to be the grim and determined pursuit of his quarry, as the allied army occupied the deserted depots first at Dundalk and then Ardee, following all the while – at one day's remove – the clouds of dust that indicated James's line of retreat, and reaching, on the morning of 30 June 1690, the wooded heights that overlooked the Boyne.

II

James had established his headquarters in the dilapidated church that crowned Donore Hill, with his army encamped on the surrounding slopes, and a large garrison anchoring his right flank on the nearby town of Drogheda. The key to his position was the loop in the river at Oldbridge, where a small village (which despite its name had no crossing other than a ford) set among cornfields, gardens and meadows, ran right down to the waters of the Boyne. Rough breastworks had been hurriedly thrown up along the river line and three thin batteries, comprising eighteen six-pounders, had been sighted in order to sweep the opposite banks and cover the two small islands that lay midstream. The nearest bridge, at Slane, 9 miles to the west, had already been pulled down, enabling the King to formulate a plan of battle that depended upon tearing apart the Williamite attack before the first assault troops could gain the safety of the southern shore and close with the raw Jacobite regiments. Yet the supposition that the Boyne represented an impenetrable barrier, which would disorder any advance and allow the enemy to be raked down as they floundered amid the fast-flowing currents, depended on a combination of the absence of fordable crossings, and the ability of James's army both to obstruct any reconnaissance of the shallows and to concentrate a devastating barrage upon those columns foolhardy enough to attempt to find a way across. The Jacobite army had used the Boyne Valley as the base for its operations during the previous summer, so one might have expected James and Tyrconnel to have thoroughly reconnoitred the area and to have been prepared to defend the river line in depth. However, it appears that neither of these relatively routine tasks had even been considered as the King and his French and Irish generals made their dispositions on 29 June 1690. The discovery that the Boyne was not an insurmountable obstacle, but that it was actually criss-crossed by multiple fords at Drybridge, Oldbridge, and Rosnaree, appears to have come as a great surprise to James, who had implicitly trusted that the Oldbridge promontory would serve as an impregnable natural bastion towards which any attack would have to be focused and upon which any storm would be surely be broken. This is particularly surprising as James had splashed across the ford without difficulty that morning at low tide, while his drummers had not even had to break their rhythm during their passage, or to lift their instruments out of the water. Despite the evidence to the contrary, the King was so confident of the strength of his dispositions that he had neither fortified the northern banks of the river and the surrounding hillsides, so that they could act as forward positions, nor left even a token force on the high ground in order to obstruct William's deployment. The narrow gorge running from Tullyallen to the ford at Oldbridge – known to posterity as 'King William's Glen' – could, if held by only a few troops of dragoons and several companies of foot, have obstructed the advance of the enemy for hours on end. However, James had refused to sanction all such measures and had withdrawn all his regiments back across the river, allowing the Williamites to deploy and to launch reconnaissance missions at their leisure. Furthermore, having decided to anchor his army upon Oldbridge, James had done precious little to fortify the place. Despite his plentiful manpower and the presence of French engineers, there were no rows of partially submerged stakes to slow the advance across the Boyne, no forests of *chevaux de frise* to disorder a charge on the opposite bank, and no fields sown with spiked caltrops to bring cavalry charges to a sudden and potentially murderous halt on the outskirts of the village. Similarly, those few rough earth walls and barricades that blocked off the entrance to Oldbridge inspired but little confidence in the soldiers who sheltered behind them, peering over the parapets into the darkness for a sight of the approach of their foes, or sheltering around spare camp fires to keep warm against the chill of the night.

James had set great store by the advice of his war council, but it remained divided between those senior officers, led by Lauzun and Tyrconnel, who were still advocating the sacrifice of Dublin and a retreat to the west, and an influential group of junior commanders whose views were given voice by Berwick and Sarsfield, and who urged the fighting of a battle upon their chosen ground. In halting on the Boyne, it might be thought that the King had signalled his intention to follow the recommendations of the latter grouping, but still he vacillated, alternating between thoughts of a fair fight for his crown and of a complete flight from the shores of Ireland. This lack of any clear battle plan permitted Hilaire Belloc, acting as one of James's foremost modern apologists, to evolve a complex and influential hypothesis that recast the

Boyne as a model fighting withdrawal, conceived from the first as a rearguard action by a King concerned to preserve the cohesion of his army when faced by overwhelming numbers of better equipped foes, and executed to near perfection, with James saving his army and inflicting far heavier casualties on his enemies than he suffered in the course of the action. James himself had first put forward this view in his official biography, claiming with hindsight that he knew in advance that the Boyne offered only 'an indifferent good' post and hinting that Oldbridge was 'not to be mentained' but would be held 'to hinder the Enemies . . . as long as possible'. However, even then he did not try to argue that he was only attempting to fight a retreat, making it abundantly clear that he had been 'determined . . . to hazard a battle'.[11] Moreover, had the King wished to simply draw off, he might have been expected to make better use of his head start over William's army, or to have slipped away under the cover of dark on the night of 30 June/1 July, leaving his campfires and slow-matches burning as a diversion. As it was, he remained rooted to his position, issuing no new orders as the first elements of the enemy's vanguard appeared on the hillsides above Tullyallen in the early morning of 30 June and began to probe at his defences.

While their artillery was being brought up from the rear, one party of dragoons galloped towards Slane to see whether the bridge there still held, and other scouts returned to report that the bridge into Drogheda was so heavily defended that it precluded an assault, and that the Jacobite cavalry troopers had turned their horses out to graze in the meadows east of Oldbridge, and had been spotted sunning themselves beside the river. The leading Dutch regiments issued forth from the glen in parade ground order and pushed on to the banks of the river, where they presented an all too tempting target for the Jacobite gunners, who soon sent them scurrying back to cover, though it seems that the powder, shot, and sheer effort they expended was not in the end proportionate to the casualties that they managed to inflict. As the afternoon wore on, a Williamite battery of four six-pounders and four howitzers was dragged into position on the north bank. It opened up a bombardment on Oldbridge, puncturing the sides of cottages and killing a Jacobite officer who was lying on his sick-bed in an upstairs room. The Jacobite guns returned fire, signalling the beginning of a fierce long-range artillery duel that would last until evening, while William lit out from the ranks – accompanied only by a small staff group – to inspect the enemy's positions for himself. Having noted the depth of the river and that many of the trenches ordered had only been half-dug or else left incomplete, he turned back and dismounted close to the neck of the glen, to eat lunch and to watch the movements in the enemy lines at his leisure. He had, however, been observed by Tyrconnel, Lauzun, and Berwick through the lenses of their telescopes, and they now put themselves at the head of a troop of cavalry and trotted warily across the ploughed fields east of the village, coming to a halt when they were directly opposite their counterparts, separated only by the winding stretch of river.

For almost half an hour, William and his friends sat beside the water's edge, quite unconcerned by the proximity of their foes, while the dragoons from their escort tied up their horses and went down to the river to drink. However, several Jacobite marksmen had crept in among the tall reeds that grew at the edges of the bank, and opened fire upon their approach. As the surprised dragoons dropped their canteens and hats and grabbed at their weapons, Tyrconnel and his staff wheeled away to the sides of the field, revealing two artillery pieces whose approach had been masked by the stationary cavalry. These now gave fire, sending two cannon balls screaming into the midst of William and his picnicking officers. The Prince of Denmark's horse was struck across the throat by the first cannon ball and pitched down lifeless in the dirt, while the second shot clipped the top of the northern bank, losing much of its force, but still ricocheting upwards, striking William across his right shoulder as he mounted up, tearing away a piece of his buff coat and both the skin and flesh underneath it, before continuing its flight and smashing the top off the pistol of an officer who rode beside him. As William swayed in the saddle and the Paymaster General, Thomas Coningsby, stuffed his handkerchief under his coat to staunch the flow of blood, the entire party was obscured by sulphurous smoke, and a great cheer rose from the Jacobite army as word that the enemy commander had fallen rippled through their ranks. There were anxious moments for the Williamites, with the dragoons scrambling back up the riverbank and attempting to provide a covering fire, as their King spurred his horse back towards the rear – protesting all the while that the wound was 'nothing' but requesting his cloak be pulled tight about him, so that his men might not see him hurt – while George of Denmark, wig in hand, floundered about in the dust and called for a fresh steed to be found for him.

News of William's supposed death flew fast to Dublin and, from there, on to Paris, where the windows were illuminated, the citizens celebrated, and mobs forced passers-by to drink a draught to commemorate the killing of France's greatest enemy, and to charge the health of James and his son. While images of the King and Queen of England were burned in the streets, a satirical print was quickly produced, showing William's lifeless body carried from the field by Halifax, while his soul descended into the spirals of Hell. As the bells of Notre Dame peeled out a thanksgiving, and tales of the losses inflicted on the Anglo-Dutch army grew wilder by the hour, only Louis XIV seems to have maintained a sense of proportion, making clear his disdain for those courtiers who showed their joy at the death of a fellow prince, and preferring to wait for firm confirmation of the scope of James's victory before sending his congratulations to the King.[12]

The tumultuous noise rising from his troops had drawn James from his tent and, believing that his nephew was dead and that the tremors running through the enemy lines might lead to the retreat of their army, he formed up his cavalry ready to make a charge, with the intent of turning the disturbance into a full-scale rout. However, the troopers perceived no further disorders among the Williamite regiments, who maintained their positions and then began to raise their own cheers and cries of 'God Save the King!', as the Jacobites strained forward in their saddles to discern the cause of the commotion, before finally abandoning their watch and trotting back disappointedly to their lines. In the meantime, King William had retired to his coach, losing 'near half a spoonful of blood' and having his wound dressed by his private surgeon. Battles had been lost over lesser mishaps and, as he dismissed the doctor who suggested he should be bled and allow himself time to recuperate fully, William may well have contemplated his earlier refusal to begin the fighting that day, on the grounds that Mondays had always been particularly unlucky for him and it would have invited certain disaster. Within the hour, however, he was back in the saddle, showing himself before men who had feared the worst and who now raised the wild and joyful shouts that so surprised the Jacobite cavalry on the opposite bank, as he rode repeatedly through the middle of his regiments with only von Schomberg for company, waving his hat in answer to their cheers, as proof that his arm had not been damaged beyond repair.

With William still very much alive, and the nerves of his soldiers restored, the fire of the rival batteries at last began to slacken, with two of the Jacobite cannon knocked out of action and James's gunnery officers starting to worry about conserving their ammunition for the fight on the morrow. In the evening, William's officers met among the ruins of Mellifont abbey to formulate their plan of attack, but they were anything but united. Von Schomberg, who had been out of favour due to his failure at Dundalk – and who had been virtually ignored by William since the King's arrival at Carrickfergus – advanced an ambitious strategy that relied on a feint being made against the Jacobite positions at Oldbridge, keeping them occupied and pinned down, while the main Williamite force marched upstream to Slane, fording the Boyne there, and swung back to hit the enemy in the flank, rolling up their line from east to west and preventing any chance of escape by cutting off their only line of retreat through a seizure of the pass at Duleek, in their rear. Far blunter measures were called for by Count Solms, who regarded the Marshal's plan as mere artifice, leaving far too much to chance and placing insufficient faith in the fighting qualities of their men. He argued for an all-out frontal assault, using their superior numbers – there were roughly 36,000 Williamites to 25,000 Jacobites – to forge across the river, charging down the enemy guns and driving them back from their entrenchments at push of pike and by club of musket. With the majority of English officers backing von Schomberg, and the Dutch siding with Solms, William attempted to broker a compromise, whereby the Marshal's son, Count Meinhard von Schomberg, would lead a diversionary force towards Slane, hoping to draw off some of the Jacobite troops in their wake, while the main force of the army would punch its way through to Oldbridge with the King at its head. Just to make sure that his commanders held to their orders next morning, and would not be able to pursue their own strategies by claiming that they recalled the evening's debates somewhat differently, William had the decisions of the war council minuted and sent out to them during the night, provoking the slow-burning fury of Marshal von Schomberg, who muttered 'that it was the first order of the kind that was ever sent to him', as he stomped back through the tent lines to his supper and uneasy sleep.[13]

Written orders might have been of even more use to the Jacobite commanders up on Donore Hill, as Lauzan repeated his belief that the presence of the fords at the heart of their line rendered their positions untenable, and that it would be best to withdraw while they still had time. However, James thoroughly disagreed, arguing that the attackers would be scythed down by their musketry and case shot long before they reached the shallows and appreciating, correctly, that his army had to stand and fight sometime, if Dublin really was to be saved. The French had observed that the Williamite army appeared to be extending its right flank further out along the valley, threatening to cross the river at Slane where the eight squadrons of Sir Neil O'Neill's dragoon regiment had been posted to keep watch. James, who had had to be very forcefully persuaded to despatch O'Neill's men in the first place, agreed to lengthen his position westwards but made it clear that such a manoeuvre would have to wait till the morning to be carried out. Unfortunately, beyond this measure of stretching a frontage that was already over-extended in places, and a reiteration of his commitment to holding the river line at Oldbridge, James appears to have issued no other commands, or to have made any contingency plans for either reinforcements or counter-attacks to ease the pressure on his front ranks, if his entrenchments were breached, or his flank turned, at any point. There is simply no evidence of any significant tactical or strategic considerations having been discussed in the King's tent that night and, while it may be that the defeated commanders had no wish to record their mistakes for posterity, it would seem more than likely that it was no oversight, but a failure by James – who had never before led an army into battle – to elucidate any kind of plan at all.

At first light on Tuesday 1 July 1690, William's army got underway, the soldiers pinning sprigs of greenery in their hats as a field-sign to distinguish themselves from their foes. Coat colours and even banners would be of little use for recognition once battle was joined, as both Williamite and Jacobite regiments claimed to represent the legitimate British Army and sought to appropriate its symbols: the red coat of the infantryman, the cross of St George emblazoned on the King's colours, and the cantons of the individual companies. Furthermore, the hues of individual uniforms – the blues of the Brandenburgers, Danes, and Dutch – could easily be confused with the same coloured cloth worn by some privately raised Jacobite units and Zurlauben's Germans, while the undyed woollen coats of those Irishmen who had not received their red uniforms in time could be mistaken for the white coats of the French regulars, or for the plain coats favoured by many of the Enniskillen men. Consequently, the Jacobites also decided to use a field-sign as the surest means of telling friend from foe and attached slips of paper to their brims. Meanwhile William – who had been forced to abandon both his breast and back plates on account of his wound – was perhaps the most conspicuous figure on the field, wearing all his decorations, including the Star and Garter, though he trotted forward on a brown horse, rather than the white one that would soon become firmly imprinted upon the myths and iconography of Protestant Ulster. Through the lifting darkness, Meinhard von Schomberg led almost 10,000 men out of the camp and began the diversionary march upstream towards Slane, while anxious reports of the enemy's movements roused the Jacobite commanders from their tents on the heights of Donore, and compelled their King to summon a fresh council of war. James appears to have been in a state of confusion as to the intentions of his foes, which was only compounded by both the heavy mist that lay on the Boyne and the contours of the valley, which ensured that William could mass his regiments in the hills before Tullyallen without being observed, and that James could only follow their march to the west for a short time, before losing all sight of them beyond the curve in the river. Fearing that his flank was about to be turned, James again alternated between making fresh plans for defence, ordering the main body of his army to move westwards to shadow the progress of the younger von Schomberg, and preparations for escape, hitching up his heavy artillery and rushing it to the rear together with his baggage train.

Having surveyed the broken piers of Slane bridge, Neil O'Neill had been quick to reason that the enemy would not waste their time and effort by attempting a storm there, but would first try the shallow ford at Rosnaree, which was not tidal and which was much closer on their line of march. Accordingly, he withdrew his regiment to guard that crossing, planting three artillery pieces on the southern bank of the Boyne as, at

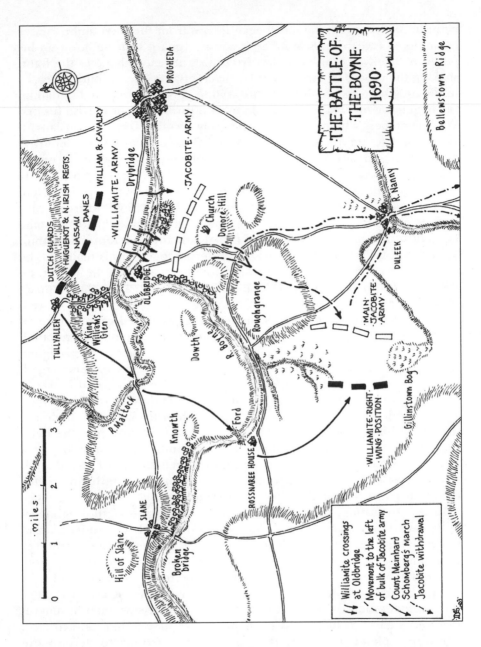

THE·BATTLE·OF·
THE·BOYNE·
1690·

Bellewstown Ridge

DROGHEDA

Drybridge

WILLIAM & CAVALRY

WILLIAMITE·ARMY·

NASSAU

DANES

HUGUENOT & N.IRISH REGTS.

DUTCH GUARDS

JACOBITE·ARMY·

Church

Donore·Hill

R. Nanny

DULEEK

TULLYALLEN

King Williams Glen

OLDBRIDGE

Roughgrange

MAIN·
JACOBITE·
ARMY·

Dowth

R. Mattock

Knowth

Ford

WILLIAMITE·RIGHT·
WING·POSITION

Gillinstown Bog

Hill of Slane

SLANE

Broken bridge

ROSSNAREE HOUSE

miles

3 2 1 0

Williamite crossings
at Oldbridge

Movement to the left
of bulk of Jacobite army

Count Meinhard
Schomberg's march

Jacobite withdrawal

eight in the morning, the mist began to rise from the surrounding water meadows to reveal von Schomberg's advance guard bearing down on his position. The first powder flashes from his guns gave flame to the fight, shaking the repose of the ancient Celtic chieftains who lay buried nearby in the long barrows which broke the skyline at Newgrange, and signalling the beginning of a battle that would mark a turning point in Irish history. Von Schomberg's men seem to have barely recoiled from the onslaught, returning fire almost immediately, while their own dragoons deployed across the opposite banks and a hundred horse grenadiers trotted, boot-to-boot, to the water's edge and in to the attack. Hopelessly outnumbered, and with several of his troopers already dropped, O'Neill decided that only a furious reply, catching the enemy midstream and completely routing them before their main body had a chance to come up, might enable him to hold his position for any length of time. Swinging himself into the saddle and gathering together his regiment, he quickly dressed his lines and prepared for the charge. In an instant, he led his men pitching into the shallows, breaking against the compact ranks of the heavy cavalrymen and turning aside from a flurry of well-aimed blows. The narrowness of the crossing point had caused many of the Irish dragoons to bunch up, crushing and tumbling into one another, and as the force of their charge was deflected amid scores of struggling troopers and riderless horses, the mounted grenadiers counter-charged, driving straight through the centre of their already disordered ranks. In vain, O'Neill attempted to rally his men, still brandishing his sabre when a downward thrust from one of his foes ran him through the thigh and transfixed him in his saddle.[14] His troopers carried him from the field, bleeding profusely, as Meinhard von Schomberg spurred his own horsemen across the ford onto the southern banks of the Boyne, scattering the Jacobite dragoons before them for 2 miles in either direction across the surrounding countryside.

In the meantime, the French brigade – consisting of the regiments Tournaisis, Forez, Famechon, La Marche, and Zurlauben – under Lauzun was marching steadily towards the sound of the guns in the west, while King James, who could gauge nothing of the nature of the fighting from his command post, continued to denude his position at Oldbridge of troops, bringing whole regiments and their accompanying artillery out of the line and sending them off on the road to Rosnaree without having yet received a clear picture of what enemy forces they would have to face. Tyrconnel pleaded to be left with adequate troops to defend the trenchworks around the village, but it was to no avail, and his forces were further reduced in number to about 5,500 men, comprising seven infantry and three cavalry regiments, together with just two troops of the household cavalry which had to be quite literally begged from the King. As the sun rose in the sky, burning its way through the early morning haze on what was to become the hottest day of the year so far, James's anxiety grew to the point that he chose to put himself at the head of his bodyguard to lead the remainder of his reserve and the cream of his army down from the hillside after Lauzun's men. However, the march – conducted in full view of the enemy and well within the range of their guns – was not only difficult but surprisingly protracted, as the regiments sweltered in the heat and were forced to scramble across broken and steep ground. The only consolation was that the younger von Schomberg's troops were having no easier a time; their advance was reduced to a crawl after they tried to strike back eastwards and ran straight into the middle of a bog. As a result, it was several hours before both sides managed to edge their way towards each other across treacherous and uncertain ground, finally coming to a halt separated by a series of marshy ditches, narrow ravines, and a steep-sided stream that fed into the mire from the Boyne itself. While Sarsfield tried to find a path through all these obstacles and James reinforced the French lines, the rival armies stood and watched one another, uncertain now how best to proceed. At the rear of the Jacobite force, artillery had begun to rumble ominously, but the King appeared to pay it no heed, convinced that he was facing the main body of the Williamite army and that the decisive battle was about to unfold before him. Thus, the two sides continued to stare each other down, separated at their closest point by no more than a musket's shot until, a little after two in the afternoon, a messenger kicked his horse over the rough ground to James's side, bringing with him the news of the disaster that had overtaken the Jacobite forces left behind at Oldbridge.

With almost four-fifths of the army away to the west, Tyrconnel had been left to face the full force of the Williamite attack. No sooner had the last of his men gulped down the shot of rum issued with their rations that day, than the enemy guns began their long, rolling bombardment, targeting in particular two substantial houses surrounded by high garden walls which sat squatly on either side of the way down to the ford. With the Williamite artillery positioned on the high ground overlooking both the river and the village, and the Jacobite guns transported away to the west or to the rear, Tyrconnel's men were soon pinned down behind their breastworks, or forced to quit their stations behind the garden walls, as fire raked the town. The loop of the river, which had been thought an advantage by James and his commanders when they made their dispositions, was now revealed as a serious liability, as cannon balls enfiladed the village from three sides. By ten in the morning, the roof of the church at Oldbridge had been stoved in, several of the garden walls were breached, and most of the cottages had either been demolished or left as smoking and burnt-out shells. The frontages of the two main strong points had been blown apart, strewing debris across the main road and sending the garrison cowering under cover from the unremitting hail of howitzer shells. With the defenders pinned down, and messengers racing in bearing news of the successful crossing of the Boyne at Rosnaree, William gave the order for the first wave of assault troops to attempt to ford the river in front of Oldbridge. The honour of spearheading the attack, to the disquiet and barely disguised jealousy of the English regiments present, fell to the three battalions of the Dutch Blue Guards under Count Solms, who led them forward to the strains of 'Lilliburlero' piped and beaten out on scores of fifes and drums. If the bagpipers and drummers who had accompanied the Jacobite regiments struck up their own rough refrains in response, then no one afterwards thought it worthy of recall, while 'the Dutch beat a march till they got to the river's side', where Solms reigned his horse back at the last moment, allowing his soldiers to push past him. The music finally ceased as they plunged into the Boyne 'some eight or ten abreast', submerged up to, and above, their waists in the water. Wisely, the Jacobite musketeers waited until their foes were halfway across the ford, the press of their bodies almost choking up the flow of the river, before they re-occupied their firing steps and loopholes, and issued an ear-splitting volley that rent the air and shrouded the Boyne in smoke, but which did little actual damage, the musket balls skipping harmlessly across the water or streaking high above the Dutchmen's grenadier caps. More effective was the fire from sharpshooters who, holed up in the church tower or in the upper stories of those houses still standing, were able to target the officers and brought down one unfortunate lieutenant as he directed his men across. Tyrconnel had already committed his remaining infantry reserves, with James's Royal Regiment filing into the village and forming up to charge the Dutch Guards as they struggled ashore. A fierce hand-to-hand fight quickly developed about the water's edge, with the Jacobite officers leading in an attempt to stem the enormous onrush of humanity that was now bursting over the Boyne's southern bank. Major Arthur managed to run an enemy officer through with the point of his spontoon, but as he called on his men to follow him into the fray, he was felled by a volley from the guardsmen that effectively served to clear the way ahead. As grenades were hurled through windows, and the half-finished trenches were carried at point of bayonet, the Jacobite foot began to crumble, yielding their positions and crying 'to their own for horse to sustain them'.[15]

Tyrconnel had massed his cavalry among the folds of the neighbouring hills, in an attempt to shelter them from the enemy guns, but as the Jacobite infantry were driven from the village and the Dutch Guards reformed in the surrounding fields, he sounded the charge and watched as Berwick and his brother swept forward at the head of a wall of horsemen which engulfed the blue-coated lines. He was not the only one who witnessed the scene with a mixture of hope and trepidation, for William – on the other bank – was looking on as his Household troops disappeared under the swirling mass of horsemen and was heard to exclaim to himself, in no more than a faint whisper, 'my poor Guards, my poor Guards'. However, the Dutchmen did not break but maintained their lines and, as the enemy horsemen thundered past them, delivered repeated volleys by platoon with near perfect discipline, destroying the cohesion of the charge and plucking many a young gentleman from his saddle. While Berwick tried to rally his horsemen for a fresh attack, William was heard to utter an audible sigh of relief as he ordered the Danish regiments and Colonel Cutts's Dutch regiment across the river to offer assistance to his beleaguered guardsmen. Two Huguenot regiments had already been despatched to carry out the task, but they had been caught by the Jacobite cavalry as they struggled ashore and, lacking pikes or bayonets, were thrown into disorder as the horsemen crashed through their ranks doing a dreadful execution and shooting down Colonel Caillimotte, who had made a brave stand. As the colonel was carried to the rear, mortally wounded but still urging defiance to his men, Marshal von Schomberg – who had been flying about the battlefield all morning, in spite of his years, encouraging his troops and directing the advance – ploughed through the water and threw himself into the path of the retreating regiments. Pointing at the cavalrymen and the Jacobite infantry busily reforming in their wake – wearing their paper field-signs in imitation of the Bourbon white cockade – he shouted to the fleeing Huguenots, evoking all their sufferings since the Revocation of the Edict of Nantes, 'Come, gentlemen, there are your persecutors!'.[16] His words struck exactly the right note: soldiers who had been on the verge of slipping away returned to the colours, stubbornly clinging to their tenuous position along the riverbank and stepping up their ragged fire against the cavalrymen who continued to wheel about them. The fury of the first Jacobite charges was now spent, and some horsemen, having pushed their advantage too far and followed Dutch fugitives back into the village, now found themselves cut off in the alleyways and quickly surrounded by the reinforcements who continued to wade ashore in ever greater numbers.

Coming to Berwick's support, Tyrconnel now gathered together his last cavalry reserves – his own regiment and that of Lord Galmoy – and led them downhill to the attack. Though the village seemed to have been secured for the Williamites, the Dutch Guards and the Huguenots had barely been able to stabilise their positions, while the Danish reinforcements had been all too slow in coming up. Harried by fire from dragoons on the southern bank, they had missed the line of the ford and were left floundering in the mud, with many of the soldiers struggling to keep their heads and their weapons above water, while their commander, the Duke of Wurtemberg-Neustadt, was spotted being carried ashore on his grenadiers' shoulders. No sooner had the Danes gained the safety of dry land than they were hit by the fresh cavalry reserves and their leading companies scattered, causing William to intervene personally in an attempt to alleviate the pressure on his faltering lines. Putting himself at the head of a body of Dutch and Enniskillen cavalry, he attempted to ford the Boyne downstream at Drybridge, but his horse's hooves stuck fast in the mud on the river bed and the frightened animal refused to move any further. As Jacobite horse and foot began to pepper his troops with fire, one of the Enniskillen men intervened to lift the struggling little King out of his saddle, and set him down, bemired and gasping for air, on the far bank. However, William was quick to recover from his asthma attack and, having remounted, dressed his lines in preparation for a charge up the slopes of Donore Hill, in the hope of breaking through the enemy's right flank. Only a few hundred yards to the west of him, Tyrconnel's horsemen were surging through the ranks of the allied army, shooting and slashing at the depleted lines of guardsmen, routing some of the Enniskillen men, and attempting to surround the Huguenots as they pushed on towards Oldbridge. Marshal von Schomberg had already spotted the danger and, shortly before William's crossing, had charged in to the midst of the developing mêlée so that his men might see him and once more take heart. However, he had long since outstripped his escort and staff officers and, unarmoured, proved a conspicuously easy target for the Jacobite troopers who now milled about him, mistaking him for King William on account of his blue sash, and hacking at his exposed face and head as he struggled to ward them off with his sabre. Though badly cut and bleeding he appeared for a moment to be holding his own, scribing an arc through his foes, until a shot fired blindly by one of his own cavalrymen, who was still crossing the river to his rear, struck him in the back of the neck and sent him spiralling to the ground. The Danish Ambassador saw him fall, and thought that his impact on the cobbled path to the village hastened his end, but in truth he was probably dead before he hit the ground. The young captain who dismounted to try to help him was in no doubt as to the matter, while the first physician on the spot declared that he had died immediately without ever uttering a word.[17]

The news of the Marshal's death had not had a chance to spread through the allied army by the time that William arrived on the southern bank, and consequently the King was able to steady his forces and drive his cavalrymen on up the hill, scattering the remaining Jacobite dragoons before him and gaining the crest, despite the best efforts of the enemy horse. With the heights above them taken, Tyrconnel, who had charged repeatedly that day, realised that the end was in sight. His remaining foot had begun to slip away, and his cavalry were exhausted after repeatedly hurling themselves on the phalanx of Dutch bayonets and the unbroken Huguenot lines. Though Williamite writers were later to sneer that their courage had derived merely from the spirits issued that morning, and that many troopers had ridden into the action fighting drunk, there was little that could be said against the gallantry of the Jacobite cavalrymen, who had continued to do far more than could have been expected of them long after all hope of a victory had been lost. The fields and meadows about Oldbridge were littered with their dead, including the Earl of Carlingford, who had charged as a gentleman volunteer, and Lord Dongan, scythed down by a cannon ball as his dragoons fell back, together with many of the junior officers. The two troops of Household cavalry left behind by James had been virtually annihilated with (it was claimed) no more than sixteen of the original 200 troopers escaping from the battle without some wound. Berwick's horse had been shot from underneath him during one of the last charges, and though he rolled clear of his flailing mount, he was ridden over by the enemy cavalry and spent anxious minutes behind their lines before he was recognised by one of his troopers, who helped him onto his horse and got him away to safety. As Cutts's regiment reinforced the bridgehead at Oldbridge and still more troops continued to pour across the Boyne, Tyrconnel, red-faced and blown from his exertions, rallied the shattered remnants of the once-proud Jacobite cavalry and gave the order to begin the retreat back to the pass at Duleek. On the heights, Richard Hamilton tried to hold the walls of the burial ground and the church – from which James's standard of St George still fluttered – and mounted a series of desperate counter-charges with the remaining troopers left to him. Amid the smoke and confusion, William almost suffered the same fate as von Schomberg, as an Enniskillen man presented his pistol to his head, before being coolly informed of his identity, while musket balls shattered one of his pistols and tore away the sole from his boot. Nothing, it would seem, could prise the day from William's grasp, or deny him the triumph that his industry deserved, as his horsemen weathered one last Jacobite assault and pitched a stunned and badly wounded Hamilton at his feet. It was said that it was only the King's hurried intervention which saved him from the wrath of the Ulster men who closed in about him, but William, mindful that this was the courtier whose duplicity had destroyed the chance of a negotiated settlement in the winter of 1688–9, eyed him coldly, reminding him of his compromised honour and his broken promises and parole as he was bundled unceremoniously towards the rear.

As Tyrconnel frantically attempted to stem the headlong flight of his infantry, who were now discarding both weapons and equipment in their haste to get away, James was receiving the news that his flank had been turned and his army had been broken at Oldbridge. The enormity of the

disaster overtaking his men to the east does not immediately seem to
have shaken him; he still believed that the main business of the day lay
before him in the breaking of Meinhard von Schomberg's division, and
ordered his Household cavalry to prepare for an immediate charge that
might secure him the victory he craved. However, Sarsfield – who had
spent the best part of an hour exploring the morass in front of their
position – strongly voiced his opinion that such a charge was not only
impractical but would bring disaster upon all who made it. Lauzun,
whose secret orders had been to preserve the French regiments at all
costs, decisively vetoed any such measure and urged a general retreat.
James appears not to have known what action to take, but while his staff
officers debated the point before him, the Williamite forces suddenly
began to draw off and appeared to strike out across country, heading for
the Dublin road in an attempt to bar their avenue of retreat. With the
choice of action so abruptly taken from him, James was forced to
acquiesce in the withdrawal and could only watch as one of his cannon
became bogged down in the marshes and had to be abandoned. The
French officers on the King's staff would later blame him for ordering
the retreat back through Duleek – sure to become a bottleneck due to
the fact that the fugitives from Tyrconnel's army were heading to the
same narrow pass – when the road from Slane still remained free of
traffic and open to them. As it was, James was adamant that the broken
nature of the terrain made this route extremely hazardous, and
maintained that the way through Duleek would allow him to preserve his
army intact. Very soon, however, the order of the retreat began to break
down, as 'scattered and wounded horsemen' fleeing from the battle at
Oldbridge got in among the column, spreading their tales of alarm
before galloping off at speed. Fearing that William might be about to
seize the pass and effectively bottle up the entire army – resulting in
either its total surrender or a bloody last ditch stand – Lauzun urged the
King to abandon his foot and artillery and make straight for Dublin,
riding hard with the Horse Guards and dragoons who comprised his
vanguard. Imperceptibly at first, Lauzun had begun to increase the pace
of the cavalry escort, soon outstripping the soldiers trailing behind and
leading to the opening up of yawning gaps in the column, as some of the
infantrymen tried to follow suit and broke ranks in an attempt to run on
ahead. Only the marquis de la Hoguette tried to remonstrate about the
fate of the foot soldiers, but he received short shrift from Lauzun, who
ordered him to worry about the preservation of the King and nothing
else. With these instructions, the nobleman was entrusted with James's
safety and, together with the King and Sarsfield's regiment of horse,
which was detached to act as their escort, galloped on ahead. They raced
through Duleek and made good their escape long before the bulk of the
fleeing army had the chance to choke up the road to Dublin.

The men of the Lord Grand Prior's regiment had not seen action that day but, as they approached the pass through a narrow lane 'enclosed with high banks', tired and footsore yet still maintaining their column ten-abreast, they were hit from behind by Tyrconnel's broken cavalrymen, who discharged their pistols at their comrades in their attempt to clear the road. They charged in among the now frightened and disordered soldiers, trampling over some and scattering far more in their reckless and pell-mell flight. John Stevens, who had already seen his colonel abandon the regiment that morning so that he might serve with more honour among the cavalry, could hardly contain his horror and shame as his soldiers: 'took to their heels no officers being able to stop them, even after they were broke and the horse passed . . . I wonderd what madness possessed our men to run so violently, nobody pursuing them'. With their sense of discipline gone, he begged the fleeing infantrymen 'to stand together, and repair to their colours, the danger being in dispersing; but all in vain, some throwing away their arms, others even their coats and shoes, to run the lighter'.[18] Seeing their columns disintegrating under the impact of successive waves of terrified fugitives into an uncontrollable mass of struggling and shouting bodies, the French regiments tried to re-impose some semblance of order. The officers beat the fleeing Irishmen out of the way with the flats of their swords and spontoons, while the soldiers shot both into the air and into the very heart of the mob in order to clear the lane in front of them. Faced with such utter confusion, few of King Louis's officers were now disposed to be charitable to their Irish allies, and one wrote shortly afterwards that: 'These savages here, who are unaccustomed to war, were taken completely by surprise, and terror soon took hold of them. The officers did no good and showed bad example. Such terror and such a rout were never heard of. It was impossible to rally them'.[19] However, the sudden use of force succeeded in its aim, as the road quickly emptied of the absconding soldiers and Colonel Zurlauben was able to form up his regiment across the road, in order of battle, to bar both the Williamite advance and the further onrush of the Irish fugitives. To his rear, the other French regiments began their retreat through the village and across the river Nanny, bearing away their artillery without further hindrance. Close by, the enormity of the defeat had finally struck Lieutenant Stevens, who 'thought the calamity hade not been so general, till, viewing the hills about us, I perceived them covered with soldiers of several regiments, or scattered like sheep flying before the wolf, but so quick, that they seemed to cover the sides and tops of the hills'.[20]

There was, however, to be no general pursuit. It was later alleged that William had chosen not to press his victory too hard, being content to possess the field and let his father-in-law escape, rather than risk a possible check to his advance by the unbroken French regiments as night fell, or the death of King James during the flight. Yet the truth would seem to have been far less calculating. The assault troops who had fought their way across the Boyne at Oldbridge were too exhausted to give chase, while the younger von Schomberg had attempted the pursuit, swinging his regiments back east in order to catch James at Duleek, only to discover that the ground before him was so difficult that it would be several hours before he could finally crawl towards his objective. As darkness fell, the Williamites camped in the fields surrounding Oldbridge and – having left their baggage train far to their rear – collected together vast bundles of pikes and muskets abandoned by the Jacobites, piling them up to form enormous bonfires around which they sheltered to fight off the encroaching chill of the night. Some 500 of their comrades had fallen in the battle, including Marshal von Schomberg, Colonel Caillimotte, and Revd Walker, the self-styled governor and bishop-designate of Derry. As William returned to his coach he was reported to have sniffed that the clergyman had had no place on the field of battle, but he received Meinhard von Schomberg with generosity and feeling, as he offered his sympathies on the death of his father and promised to take care of his family. However, the legacy of his mismanagement at Dundalk still clung to the Marshal's memory and he never received the state funeral which he had deserved. It was left to Dean Swift to raise a fitting monument to his memory more than forty years later, in the face of the utter indifference of his rapacious 'kith and kin'.[21] Jacobite losses were more severe, with approximately 1,000 of their dead left behind them on the battlefield and many more nursing serious wounds as they limped away on the road back to Dublin. Some, like Berwick, had no more than fresh bruises and a battered sense of pride to show for their defeat, but others – like Sir Neil O'Neill, who died of his wounds eight days later at Waterford – were not so lucky. Though James and his son would subsequently attempt to downplay the significance of the battle, reducing it to the status of an inconclusive skirmish, it scarcely appeared that way as allied soldiers rifled through their discarded baggage train that night, seizing hold of the King's silver dinner service, his pocket watches, and some of the unused military gifts that had been lavished upon him the year before by Louis XIV. If the majority of the artillery train, the French brigade and the battered nucleus of the Jacobite cavalry were salvaged from the disaster, this had nothing whatsoever to do with James – who had removed himself from the action at the first available opportunity – and everything to do with the forethought and professionalism of Colonel Zurlauben and the French regulars who had secured the line of retreat, and the bravery of Tyrconnel, who had spent the evening rallying his shattered regiments and organising their orderly withdrawal to the walls of Dublin. Moreover, the King's reputation as a bold and resourceful soldier had suffered a blow from which it would never fully recover. James had decided to fight at the Boyne, but in retreating behind the river line and failing to conduct anything more than the most rudimentary of reconnaissance, he had permitted William to take complete control of the situation and to choose the time, place and nature of each assault on the Jacobite positions. Every one of James's responses had been passive; apart from his abortive order to charge the younger von Schomberg's cavalry, he had never once sought to seize the initiative and had acted with a mounting sense of disquiet which quickly turned to panic as the day wore on. If his lack of concern for his soldiers and his willingness to desert them when his own life appeared to be in danger cast a cloud over his tactical abilities, then his failure to hold the pass at Moyry, and the ease with which William duped him into dividing his army and sending the greater part of it off on a pointless route march through marshes and bogs, did little to recommend his grasp of military strategy.

Leaving both the remnants of his army and de la Hoguette's party of French officers far behind him, James had sped on through the evening shadows, protected by the tight defensive ring of Sarsfield's escort, until he reached the safety of Dublin Castle, bringing with him, as John Evelyn was later to quip, 'a speedy flight and the sad tidings of his own defeat'. He found Colonel Luttrell and his garrison worried and jittery, and quickly summoned a meeting with those of his privy councillors who were still close at hand in the city. A later (and almost certainly apocryphal) story claimed that Lady Tyrconnel sought to pithily upbraid him for his abject cowardice after he had tried to blame the timidity of the Irish for his defeat, but accounts of the King trotting back into Dublin with his shoulders bowed that night, and refusing the meal cooked for him at the castle, would seem to possess far more validity. Similarly, James would subsequently claim that the large bundle of mail from his Queen, delivered to him on his arrival – informing him of Marshal Luxembourg's dramatic victory over Count von Waldeck and the allies at Fleurus ten days earlier – made him think of returning to France in order to exploit the military success in Flanders. Even assuming that James had received this news, quite what he hoped to achieve by abandoning his last remaining kingdom and returning to the Continent, when the French victory might well have released more troops for service in Ireland, is far from clear. It probably amounts to no more than an exercise in self-justification, or at best self-deception, by the King and his editors long after the event.[22] James went to extraordinary lengths to emphasise the unanimity of his Privy Council over the need for his immediate departure from Ireland, as he ran 'a great risque of being taken by the Enemie, who they believed would be there the next morning', and even claimed that Tyrconnel's private chaplain, Fr Taafe, 'a very honest and discreet Clergie man', had pressed upon him the need for flight. From these reports it would almost seem that the King had no will of his own and that he relied totally upon the advice offered to him by his councillors. Yet James knew far more about the military situation to his rear, and about the Williamite pursuit, than Secretary Neagle or the Duke of Powis, who had spent the day of battle safely ensconced within their drawing rooms in the heart of the capital, and who knew nothing of the true state of the army as it trailed back towards Dublin through the darkness.[23] It seems fair, therefore, to assume that having galloped from the Boyne in mortal terror of his life, James had already resolved to quit his kingdom and obtain a safe passage to France long before his councillors began to file into his chamber.

At midnight, Berwick's aide-de-camp brought the news that about 7,000 infantrymen had been rallied several miles outside the capital and were in desperate need of cavalry cover, in case the Williamites appeared and endeavoured to press home their advantage. James did what he could, despatching Luttrell's dragoons and three thin troops of heavy cavalry to their aid, but with daylight Berwick discovered that most of the foot had slipped away from their makeshift encampment and had headed back to their homes and families. John Stevens awoke to find himself left with just twenty men and the colour guard, all that remained of the Lord Grand Prior's regiment of 800 men, the rest of those who had not taken to their heels at Duleek having gone long before the morning light. In the meantime, the King had called together the magistrates, aldermen and city councillors to reassure them that, while Dublin would now have to be surrendered to his enemies, it would on no account be burnt by his retreating army. However, this excepted, the rest of his parting speech was so petulant in tone, and of such a bitter and hectoring content, that it can only have further dismayed, confused and humiliated his remaining followers. He informed the city fathers that: 'tho I have been often cautioned, that when it came to the touch, they [i.e. the Irish Roman Catholics] would never bear the brunt of a Battle, I could never credit [it] . . . till this day, when having a good Army, and all Preparations fit to engage a Foreign Invader, I found the fatal Truth of what I had been so often precautioned; and tho the Army did not desert me, as they did in England, yet when it came to a Tryal, they basely fled the Field, and left it a spoil to my Enemies, nor could they be prevailed upon to Rally, tho the loss in the whole defeat was but inconsiderable; so that henceforth I never more determine to head an Irish Army, and do now resolve to shift for my self, and so, Gentlemen, must you'.[24] If James had arrived in Dublin to almost universal goodwill among his Roman Catholic subjects, then the delivery of this speech certainly killed off the last of their residual affection for him. It was but little recompense for the bankrupted city coffers and the deaths of so many of Ireland's sons, of both sides, who lay buried in the shallow earth around Derry, Dundalk and Enniskillen, or whose bodies – already robbed and stripped by the country folk – were stiffening in the summer's heat along the banks of the Boyne.

Troopers from the King's Life Guard were still clattering into Dublin, some mounted double, others lacking sabres or pistols, as James was preparing to leave the castle at five in the morning on 2 July. Having requisitioned the last of the fresh horses from the stables as mounts for his bodyguard, he could – or perhaps would – not spare any others for de la Hoguette and his small staff of French officers, who had become separated from him after the flight from Duleek and, having failed to regain contact with Lauzun's main body, now arrived to ask if they could accompany the King on his ride to the coast. However, despite the need to make haste in order to be clear of Dublin before he could be brought to account, either by Williamite troops or by his own general officers (for he had made no attempt to contact either Tyrconnel or Lauzun since they had parted on the Boyne), as soon as he got out into the open countryside south of Dublin, James's pace slackened to a 'leasurely' trot, as his mood alternated between relief at the prospect of escape and fresh panic at the thought of being pursued. At each river crossing his cavalrymen were ordered to stay behind, for several hours at a time, to guard the fords and to make absolutely sure that the King was not being followed, before attempting to rejoin his party as best they could. Years later, a story told by a labourer named Coghlan would be taken down, claiming that James, easily distinguishable by his height and his fine horse, had stopped in the dust of the highway near Arklow to eat some cold meat and drink a jug of strong beer, but had been overcome by a sudden and violent nosebleed, which had doubled him up and spattered the post supporting the porch on which he had been sitting. The post, stained by the blood royal, was preserved for many years afterwards and apparently became something of a local curiosity, before a careless servant, heedless of its value, burnt it for firewood. Though such an account, told third-hand, has much of the folktale about it, and may be no more than a re-setting of the well-known account of the King's earlier seizures on Salisbury Plain in order to add dramatic incident to the story of his escape from Ireland, it is entirely possible that James, fearing once more for his life and feeling the burdens of command too onerous, suffered a similar attack which temporarily incapacitated him on the road south. Indeed, Francis Randall, a Quaker who was forced to provide the King with a change of horses at Enniscorthy, testified to the strain under which he appeared to be suffering, noting the fully cocked pistols stuffed into James's holsters, primed so that they could be drawn and fired in an instant, but far more likely to be triggered by a sudden jolt on the uneven road surface and to send a bullet spinning into either the horse's flanks or the rider's shins or foot. James, however, was not the only one that day whose nerves were fraying, for de la Hoguette, remembering Lauzun's

injunction to protect the King, had managed to find new horses in
Dublin and raced after him, bearing frightening tales of Williamite
troopers fanning out over the surrounding hills. James apparently
assured him that he had seen only groups of farmers and peasants, who
were quite inquisitive but nevertheless simply going about their business,
yet there is still the sense that the Frenchman's arrival served to inject a
greater sense of urgency into the King and his now dwindling band of
followers, for they began to pick up their pace and rode through the
night, arriving at Duncannon at dawn.

Once there, there was a discussion about how best to proceed, as James
rejected both an overland journey through Waterford to Kinsale, and a
voyage straight to France, preferring instead the more cautious method of
taking ship for the southern port, where he felt sure he would find French
warships ready and capable of conveying him safely to the harbour at
Brest. De la Hoguette was sent ahead to requisition a suitable vessel and
found the aptly named *Lauzun*, a French privateer lying just off the coast,
laden with supplies of corn for the army. With 'the wind being good and
the coast cleere' the King set sail from Duncannon that evening and was at
Kinsale by the following morning, where he found the harbour packed
with a convoy of merchant ships and their escort of three French frigates
under the command of the younger Duquesne. James spent the day
dictating letters to Lauzun and Tyrconnel, which offered them virtual carte
blanche to continue the war or to secure what terms they could from
William. Wishing to be done with Ireland, James sent them 50,000 gold
pistoles, which was approximately £40,000 and 'all the mony he had', but
nothing in the way of instructions or advice other than the vague promise
that he would use his time in France to lobby for more aid and logistical
support to be sent across to them. At midday on 4 July 1690, James,
accompanied by a handful of gentlemen and his son Henry Fitzjames (who
had wasted little time in fleeing from the battle), slipped out of port at
Kinsale and began his voyage back to France. He busied himself with
trying to justify his actions as best he could, pointing to the French navy's
victory off Beachey Head on 30 June – which saw an Anglo-Dutch fleet
ripped apart in the English Channel – and reviving his old project of
leading an invasion of the south coast in a sudden push towards his former
capital, while William was still tied down in Ireland.[25] Certainly the plan
had something to recommend it, as for the first time the French had
control of the sea-lanes and the Londoners, who had been thrown into a
state of abject panic by the destruction of Torrington's fleet, daily expected
the landing of French troops. However, James failed to appreciate the fact
that though it was now possible for such an expedition to be launched, the
French were bound to be wary of entrusting it to the hands of the
individual who had just squandered their resources in Ireland, by fleeing
precipitously from the action when there was still much to be decided.

James II in Ireland, *oil on canvas by John Riley, c. 1690. Although James had never actually commanded an army in battle, he continued to appropriate the imagery of a successful general and confidently looked forward to the campaign that lay ahead of him.*

The Fatal Embrace. *Louis XIV receives James II at St Germain, 1690, an anonymous engraving.*

Sir Neil O'Neill in Gaelic dress, oil on canvas by John M. Wright. Although painted some ten years before the Boyne, this magnificent portrait represents a powerful restatement of Irish nationhood, and shows the nobleman as a Gaelic chieftain, with his piper, hunting equipment and faithful wolfhound. The Japanese armour at his feet may serve as a comment upon the persecution of Catholics in that land or may simply reflect O'Neill's taste for the new and exotic.

Richard Talbot, Duke of Tyrconnel, oil on canvas, c. 1690, School of Rigaud, attributed to François de Troy. Though grown corpulent and prematurely aged, Tyrconnel maintained his soldierly bearing and was to prove his ability and valour, in James's cause, throughout the disastrous campaigns of 1690–1.

William III, portrait bust by Anna Maria Brannin. This eerily life-like wax image captures perfectly the King's aquiline features and the sense of keen intelligence and deep melancholia that were hallmarks of his character.

The Cruelties of James II in Ireland. *A Dutch propaganda print by Schoonebeek, c. 1690. By way of contrast, James was to show himself scrupulous in his conduct of the war.*

King James leads his household cavalry at the battle of the Boyne.

The Battle of the Boyne, oil on canvas by Jan Wyck, c. 1690. While King William and his staff gallop past their blazing guns, their infantry columns forge across the river line and take possession of Oldbridge.

LE ROY IACQUE DÉLOGE.

J'avois fait un ragoust pour tout L'Angleterre:
sans que ie me suis trop hasté.
J'aurois demon renom rempli toutte la terre;
Mais un ORANGE a tout gâté.

The displaced King, anonymous Dutch engraving, 1691. James is shown dressed as a Jesuit priest while, in the background, a devastated countryside is dominated by his fortress and still smoking fires.

Battle of La Hogue, *oil on canvas by van Dienst, 1692. The destruction of the French invasion fleet at La Hogue brought an end to James's hopes of a military solution to his troubles.*

John Drummond, Earl of Melfort, dressed as a Knight of the Thistle, oil on canvas by Sir Godfrey Kneller. Melfort's boundless self-confidence, as attested to in this portrait, could – and indeed was – equated with hubris and insufferable arrogance.

Blank commission for the Jacobite army, signed by James and Melfort, and distributed to their English supporters in 1692, in the expectation of a popular uprising and the beginnings of a new civil war.

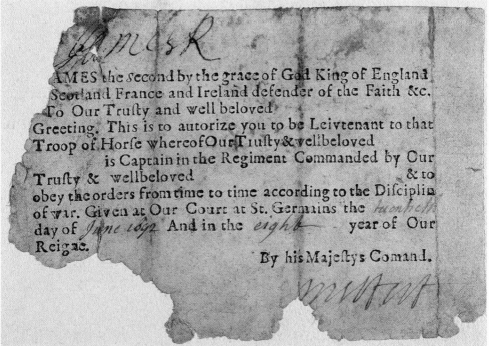

The clock tower and keep of St-Germain-en-Laye before restoration, engraving by A. Brunet-Debaines. Note the salamander badge of King François I on the turret. James did little to stamp his own personality on his last residence.

The Royal Penitent, *engraving by Antoine Trouvain, Paris, 1694, once owned by Samuel Pepys. Although such displays of piety served to inspire his existing followers, they did little to win new support for King James's cause.*

While James would choose to speak of the Irish campaign as being effectively over at the time of his leaving, with his army destroyed and nothing more to hope for from 'so shatter'd and dishearten'd a body of men, as now remain'd', his pessimism did not in any way reflect the truth of the situation. His flight from Dublin had provoked a crisis in the city, and the general exodus of the troops under Governor Luttrell had allowed several thousand Protestant prisoners to break out of Trinity College and begin exacting a random form of revenge, by ransacking the houses of courtiers prominent in James's administration. Without a government, Robert Fitzgerald assumed authority and hastily opened negotiations with the advancing Williamites, in an attempt both to preserve the city from being sacked by the approaching troops, and to prevent further reprisals by the Irish Protestant mobs. However, William's caution in securing his rear – by summoning and receiving the surrender of Drogheda before even considering a march on Dublin – and ruling out the possibility of an immediate pursuit had bought time for 'the shadows of [Jacobite] regiments' who had limped away from the Boyne. They regained something of their cohesion and rallied a number of their men back to the tattered colours that were unfurled outside Dublin's walls to signal that very purpose. Despite their defiance, the city was glad enough of William's protection from further violence and destruction and surrendered without a fight on 4 July, leading to a domino effect among other garrison towns such as Wexford, Duncannon and Waterford, which were either evacuated or rushed to seek terms. However, the elderly Governor of Athlone, Colonel Richard Grace – a veteran of the English Civil Wars and the Cromwellian conquest, who had charged alongside James at the battle of the Dunes – further fortified the town and prepared to offer resistance to Lieutenant-General Douglas's advancing troops. Though Tyrconnel was at this time urging the resumption of negotiations with William, in an attempt to salvage some guarantees for the native Irish from the wreckage of James's regime, Grace typified the views of the opposing Jacobite party, led by Sarsfield, Berwick, and the Bishop of Killaloe and Limerick, who were adamant that the war should be continued by any means necessary. Exhibiting as little concern for military conventions as had von Rosen, Grace shot over the heads of the party of Williamites who came to the walls of Athlone under a banner of truce, and yelled after them that he would refuse to either give quarter to, or accept terms from his enemies, even if it meant chewing through the leather of his boots after the last of his provisions were exhausted. With the chances of a negotiated settlement and of William peacefully gaining control of Ireland through the sudden implosion of the Jacobite movement receding, Douglas invested Athlone and engaged in a furious artillery duel with the garrison, which lasted until he had burned through the last of his powder a week later, when he was forced to lift the siege (abandoning his smashed gun carriages and the corpse of his chief gunnery officer) to rejoin the main body of the Williamite field army. With Athlone preserved, the river crossings along the middle of the Shannon were secured for the Jacobites, and the regiments which met at Limerick under Tyrconnel and Lauzun were saved from encirclement and able both to consolidate their positions and to make good their losses.

William had believed that the fire had gone out of his opponents after the Boyne, and that terse proclamations commanding his Irish subjects to obedience and threatening them with the treason acts if they did not obey would bring the kingdom to heel with no more bloodshed. However, for once he had seriously misjudged the mood of his opponents, and as resistance continued and the numbers of 'rebels' taking advantage of his amnesty remained negligible, he was finally forced to invest Limerick and to prepare for what he hoped would be a short siege. Unfortunately, the overconfidence that had stemmed from the victory at the Boyne would now seem to have been the undoing of the expedition to the west. Taking advantage of the appallingly lax security which had begun to characterise the Williamite encampments, Sarsfield led a daring cavalry raid in the early hours of the morning of 12 August 1690, which caught the Williamite siege train out in the open and succeeded in overrunning it before any sort of defence could be organised, blowing up the guns and ammunition and killing the draught horses, gunners, and a number of camp followers, before triumphantly withdrawing back to the city without incurring any significant losses. This defeat effectively served to force William's hand, denying him the possibility of reducing the walls of Limerick through a conventional siege and leading him to sanction a reckless general assault as soon as the first practical breach was opened on 27 August, in order to maintain the momentum, crush the last resistance and bring the campaign to a successful conclusion before the weather closed in around him. Consequently, he threw regiment after regiment against the city walls, but lacking adequate artillery to cover the advance, the assault parties quickly stalled, failing to exploit their initial successes and being repeatedly scythed down as they attempted to clear the breach, before finally retreating after several hours of hard fighting and leaving some 2,300 casualties behind amid the rubble, smoke and chaos that was Limerick. Despite such heavy losses, William stoically prepared for a second assault, but his luck deserted him at last, as the rains came, washing out his entrenchments and compelling him to break camp and lift the siege on 30 August. The successful defence of the city not only restored Irish martial pride and conferred upon the French Governor, the marquis de Boisseleau, a reputation for bravery and calm competence, but also served to bestow upon Sarsfield a mantle of heroism and the aura of legend, which he was never entirely to lose. The aspirations of the native Irish community – sustained by Roman Catholicism and a nascent, if still ill-defined, sense of nationalism – for a champion and a liberator, capable of breaking the Protestant ascendancy by force of arms, might have settled upon James II and, indeed, at the time of his coming to Dublin such heady ideas filled the air, but his refusal to extirpate his Protestant subjects, to challenge their economic power or, more importantly, to stand and fight when it was required of him, had entirely destroyed this possibility by the late summer of 1690. The lasting impact of the Jacobite wars now diverged sharply in Scotland and Ireland, with the clans of the Great Glen, who knew James only as a remote and idealised figure, uniting around the Stuart cause and projecting its imagery in order to combat the resurgent power of the Earl of Argyll, while Roman Catholic Ireland, which had directly experienced the King's rule, turned from him and looked instead to the Crown of France to obtain for them some lasting vestige of independence. Thus, James was exorcised from Irish mythology, his name suffixed with a scatological Gaelic curse, and his figure reduced to that of a craven foil to Sarsfield's valorous paladin, in both English and Irish popular plays and prose. While Lord Clare was busily confiding to Louvois that the King was more fitted to life in the cloister than to the exertions of commanding armies or to forging the policy of the state, Sarsfield established himself as the embodiment of the Irish Jacobite army, shouldering his way onto the military council in the face of Tyrconnel's grim disapproval, and establishing the principle that there would be no negotiated settlement but a fight to the finish for the very soul and future development of Ireland.

For weeks Lauzun, who had withdrawn back into Galway with his French regiments, had been looking for an honourable way of extricating himself from the war in Ireland and of securing his return home. Now that Limerick had been saved and the immediate danger to the survival of the Jacobite cause had been staved off, it was possible for him to arrange the necessary transports by 12 September 1690. Tyrconnel accompanied him, anxious to gain James's ear and to protect his flagging authority as Viceroy against the slanders and disdain of Sarsfield and his swordsmen, and from the marked indifference of Berwick, who recognised his honesty and 'good sense' but also his 'immoderate' vanity and innate cunning.[26] Despite the resurgent strength of the Irish Jacobite resistance and the possibility that the kingdom might still establish itself as an independent entity, James increasingly saw Ireland only as a useful sideshow, capable of ensnaring William and keeping him out of England and the Low Countries, while allowing him to build his party among the English nobility and lay the foundations for his return to Whitehall. After almost eighteen months spent governing Ireland, James seems to have gained little sympathy for, or understanding of, those diverse and mutually antagonistic communities over which he had tried to rule. His deeply Anglo-centric views were unchanged by his experience and, indeed, may have become more strongly held and more forcefully expressed as a result of what he believed to be the wilful ingratitude of his Irish subjects, both Catholic and Protestant.

In 1692, he outlined a set of instructions for the guidance of his son, the Prince of Wales, in statecraft, drawing upon what he felt to be the lessons from his time in Ireland and giving vent to his frustration at the demands made of him by the Dublin Parliament. The nation was to be utterly subordinated to English culture and polity, with the Roman Catholic Church there remodelled by English bishops and the practice of sending novices to be trained abroad in the colleges of Spain, Rome and the Low Countries discontinued. Given that these seminaries subsequently became instrumental in the promotion of ideological Jacobitism and the cult of the dispossessed Stuart King, it is somewhat ironic to read of James's fears of the 'evil' attendant on sending bright young priests out of their homeland, to be taught a doctrine of resistance to English power and a love and respect for the aims of French and Spanish foreign policy. Furthermore, while the garrisons were to be strengthened in the north and religious toleration secured 'for the good of Trade and improvement of that Kingdom', the Protestants were not to be trusted 'too far' as they were 'generally ill principlel'd, and Republicans'. Though Ireland might serve as a reservoir for recruits for the army, these men were to be used abroad and were not to be employed at home; only 'English, Scots, or Strangers' were to be posted there so as 'not [to] tempt the natives to Rebelle, they being of a very uncertain temper, and easily led by their Cheefs and Clergy, and beare with great impatience the English yoak'. In order to break this cycle of mistrust, James suggested that the common bonds of language and culture that bound the remaining Gaelic nobles to their peoples should be broken, for 'great care must be taken to civilise the antient familys, by having the Sons of the Cheef of them bred up in England, even at the charge of the Crown . . . in setting up Scholes, to teach the Children, [so that they] would by degrees weare out the Irish language . . . and would contribut much to lessen the animositys that are amongst them'. Indeed, the power of the monarchy should, in the King's view, come to permeate every area of Irish life 'to order it so as their cheefe dependance may be in the Crown . . . and [the people] be weaned from their natural hatred against the English, be more civilised, and learne to improve their Estat[e]s, by making plantations and improving their Land as the English and Scots have done wheresoever they have settled'. Under James, therefore, plantation was to have been an ongoing process and, remembering bitterly the struggle over the Repeal of the Act of Settlement, he despaired that 'one cannot beat it into their heads, that

Severall of the O's: and Macks, who were forfeited for Rebelling in King James the firsts time, and before, ought to be kept out of their Estat[e]s'. By this point, he even seemed to be in doubt as to the value of Tyrconnel's former services and advised his son that in future: 'No Native [was] to be Lord Lieut. nor no Englishman that has an Estate in that Kingdom, or great relations there', adding that the office was 'to be changed every three yeares' in order to prevent the establishment of any rival power base to that of the Crown.[27] James II had, therefore, left Ireland having learned little and forgotten nothing. Though he was glad to be free of that kingdom, he conceived of the struggle waged in his name as part of a larger civil war that would engulf all his former domains over the coming years, and which would surely restore him to his throne if only sufficiently monumental French resources were committed on his behalf. As he sighted Brest, however, he failed to appreciate that such support was entirely conditional upon his own behaviour and usefulness for the advancement of Louis XIV's power. Therefore it was perhaps a kindness that, as yet, James did not fully realise that it was not just the cream of his army that had perished on the Boyne, but also the reputation for bravery, diligence and military foresight that he had carefully and consistently laid claim to since he first saw action, tumbling in among the enemy horse on the outskirts of Etampes, almost forty years before.[28]

CHAPTER FIVE

The Temper of the Times

I

James's sudden and wholly unexpected arrival in Brest caused both consternation and confusion among many in the small army of his sympathisers scattered across Europe, not least the penniless Italian historian who would have received a commission to write a celebratory account of the King's victories in Ireland, and who now discovered overnight that the project had been cancelled and he was henceforth out of work and favour at the court of Rome. Indeed, many of those who watched James's coach hurtle through the Normandy countryside, bound for St-Germain-en-Laye, still believed that the battle of the Boyne had been a great victory for France and that, as William's body lay next to that of von Schomberg in unconsecrated ground, the restored King of England was racing to report his latest success – and to give his grateful thanks – to Louis XIV. Even those French officers and courtiers who were bold enough to press the King for details about the battle were left none the wiser as to what had actually occurred; monsieur de la Rongere was shocked by James's indifference to the fate of the French regiments that he had left behind and by his startling confession that he had 'no idea' what had become of them, while the intendant of Lower Normandy, who accompanied him for part of the way on his journey south, was surprised that he talked cheerfully of his future plans and of his exciting adventures in Ireland, but seemed utterly oblivious to the cataclysm which had overtaken the nation in his wake, and which had come to overshadow all of his affairs.[1]

Though James discovered his court in mourning for the death of his son-in-law Lord Waldegrave, a man of promise and utter loyalty, he seems to have done little to console his daughter Henrietta, who found herself a widow at only 23, and instead expressed his delight at the news that King Louis was to visit him the very next morning, believing that such a meeting could only signify the decision of the French to send an invasion fleet against England, with him at its head. Failing to realise that his credit had sunk so low, or that there were many in the War Ministry who agreed with Marshal Luxembourg's terse assessment that: 'Those who love the King of England should be glad to see him in safety, but those who love glory will deplore the figure he has made of himself', he made himself busy with preparations for his immediate departure for the coast, only to be shaken to the core of his being when Louis XIV received his plan for the landings coldly, declaring that he could do nothing until he had further intelligence from Ireland. Attempting to press matters, James urged that they should arrange another conference to discuss the invasion, as there was 'in reality no need of an account from Ireland to convince the world, that England was naked and disgarnished of troops, or that the French, being now superiour at Sea, had it in their power to transport the King thither', but Louis's demeanour suggested that their interview had come to an end and James's increasingly desperate messages to him at Versailles, delivered with ominous regularity over the following days, received but little in the way of response. He had never doubted for a moment that Louis XIV would continue to support him with men, money, ships and munitions, but the discovery of the mild illness that now prevented the French King from receiving him came as a terrible and unforeseen blow to his self-esteem and all his hopes for the swift reversal of his fortunes. Indeed, his official biographer reflected that: 'When the King . . . perceived the true motive of this delay, tis certain his patience never underwent So great a tryal in the whole cours[e] of his life, as he afterwards owned to a person entrusted with the secret: the defection of his Subjects, the loss of battles, and the desertion of his favorits, had never thrown him into dispair, but [the discovery that] the Prince who was his only friend and support, was a declareing a dis-resolution to hazard nothing upon his management for the future . . . sunk his hopes and expectations the Lower'.[2] Given that much has been made of the perilous state of James's mental health at the time of the unravelling of his administration in England in 1688–9, it is somewhat surprising that this passage from his memoirs has been almost entirely overlooked, especially as it seems to hold the key to the nature of his future relationship with Louis XIV, and accounts for the subsequent shift in his self-perception. Indeed, it is not going too far to suggest that James's ego was utterly shattered by King Louis's public rejection of his services and criticism of his abilities, and that this prompted a re-evaluation of his position in France, and a major seachange in his affairs and personal priorities. As reports reached James which suggested that the victory at Beachey Head was not being properly exploited – with only a small landing at Teignmouth undertaken, which accomplished little more than terrorising the civilian population – he saw his chance to 'breake the neck of the war' being squandered and Admiral Tourville's original objective, to ensure the safe landing of a French invasion force, going unfulfilled. Consequently, James waited impatiently until Louis XIV 'could hould out no longer' against seeing him and then chose to press his case further, citing promises offered when the first flush of victory at Fleurus had been foremost in the French King's mind and when it was still believed that James was the master of Dublin, and asking to be permitted to join the fleet as soon as possible, with or without an army. Such was James's confidence that he declared that: 'He was certain his own Sailors would never fight against one, under whom they so often had conquered' and urged that if only he was allowed to show himself before the English fleet, then they would be sure to mutiny and to lead a triumphant French fleet up the Thames, ending the war at a stroke. It might have been thought, given Louis's extreme reluctance to discuss the matter any further, that James would have let his project drop quietly, but he did nothing of the kind and continued to pressure his host to sanction the longed-for descent on the coasts of England. As a result a difficult scene ensued, with James once again reminding the French King of promises made and Louis XIV again coolly parrying his arguments, before bringing the discussion to a close with a reminder of his guest's true position, combining a clear warning with a gesture of his continuing regard, letting him know that this was 'the first favour he had refused to his friend, and it should be the last'.[3]

Such a humiliation was almost more than James's pride could bear and it is noticeable that, in subsequent weeks, the French courtiers and even Mary of Modena, upon whom much of the day-to-day running of the exiled court had devolved during her husband's absence, became far more dismissive of the King than they had ever dared to be before. During a pleasure trip to St Cloud, James had attempted to censure the frivolous chatter of the duc d'Orléans, dismissing his talk of riches, jewels and furniture with the assertion that: 'I had lots [of money], but I never bought gems or furniture with it. Nor did I build palaces. I spent it all on making great ships and cannons and guns'. Having heard this refrain many times before, his Queen cut him short with a grave reminder that 'a lot of good they did you. Why, they have all been used against you!', while the Duke's wife, leaning into their carriage, noted the ensuing silence and that: 'There the subject ended'.[4] If James could no longer seek to justify his record of kingship before even his own Queen, then he was indeed in a sorry condition. His reputation for safeguarding the English national interest through the pursuit of a strident foreign policy, backed up by his own military genius and might, now hung about him in tatters. Having been humbled before Louis XIV, he had the choice either of accepting his reduced place in the world and adjusting to his utter dependence upon his patron, or of attempting to continue to assert his independence, remaining for the moment with his French hosts but casting around for fresh allies, whether in Rome, the other princely states of Italy, or even in the courts of Spain and Austria, who might, in time, be prised from their alliance with William. Yet James unreservedly chose the former course, accepting Louis's stinging criticism and acknowledging his authority over him, while internalising the reasons behind his fall from power and increasingly coming to locate them – as we shall see in later chapters – within his sense of religious guilt. As it began to dawn on him that there would be no sudden return to his throne, he started to reconcile himself to the idea that his stay in France might be a long one and that his fate was particularly ill-starred, constantly reminding his followers, in his gloom and self-loathing, that: 'He was born to be the sport of fortune'.[5]

Certainly, reverse seemed to follow reverse in the weeks following the King's return. Dismal reports of the collapse of Cannon's Highland army after the defeat at Cromdale, and of the dissention that pitted Tyrconnel against Sarsfield and Luttrell in Ireland, compounded the impression of defeat and disillusion that had been created by the Boyne, leading the Duke of Modena to commiserate that these events had quite: 'destroyed the cheerfulness of our mind . . . by representing the reality as different, change joy into sorrow and plunge our mind into inexpressible trouble'. James attempted to sublimate his own despair by spending long hours in the saddle, pursuing the stags, boar and deer which populated the enormous forest of St Germain. More often than not, he was to be found giving chase and hurtling through the thickets down to the banks of the Seine in the company of the dauphin, a portly and rather unimaginative figure who was to become his firmest friend among the French royal family, and who shared his inexhaustible appetite for hunting, being credited with the single-minded destruction of every wolf in the countryside about Paris. Yet if James was attempting to fight off the depression that had clouded his thoughts since his humiliation in front of Louis XIV, this did not equate to a collapse in his mental faculties. In August 1690, he had spoken to the Bishop of Autun of his desire to visit the Paris Observatory, and towards the end of the month the clergyman arranged for him to be received by the members of the French Royal Academy of Sciences. By all accounts the visit was a great success and the King took a lively interest in the observations made of five of Saturn's moons during the previous evening, although unfortunately as he and the newly returned Melfort visited in the morning, James never got to look at the stars for himself through the powerful new telescope. Nevertheless, as he discussed the work of Galileo and proudly championed the theories of English astronomers and scientists such as Flamsteed, Halley, and Newton, for which he felt partly responsible through his deployment of patronage, his hosts recorded their impressions of his knowledgeable and animated conversation, which transcended the realms of conventional court flattery. In particular, James turned his attention to the uses of astronomy and telescopes in navigation, and soon had the assembled scholars unrolling large maps for him on the floor of the East Tower. He asked eagerly how French nautical charts and their accuracy of measurement related to those used in England, reflecting on his own calculations of topography and distance made on the voyage to Ireland

and making a present of them to the Academy. Wondering how Canada could be so much colder than France, yet on the same latitude, he discussed the search for the North-West Passage, and the voyages of English merchantmen through the Straits of Magellan, complimenting the work of the Jesuit mathematicians in Siam and delighting in the little model that he was shown of a prefabricated military bridge. His hosts were delighted when he noted two devices, made by Charles II's former Master-Mechanic Sir Samuel Morland, 'which served to identify the days of the week in a chosen year many centuries ago in the Julian Calendar and the other in the Gregorian. But he said that the second was inaccurate and would not work after the end of the century since no thought had been taken to select the day to be lost in the year 1700'. His guide, Giovanni Cassini, rushed to show him a perpetual table for the Gregorian Calendar that would work perfectly in the next century and, as the King showed his evident delight, he presented it to him. After a little more than two hours, James departed from the observatory with his gift, leaving the scientists 'filled with admiration for the wide knowledge of his Majesty' and praising both the consideration he had shown them and his 'great intelligence in all these matters'.[6]

Unfortunately, such praise and careless interludes in the King's routine were all too rare. During the same period, the first real sign of a change in James's approach to his affairs manifested itself in the reorganisation of his Household, so as to 'have made a stranger forget the King's condition and [to] have fancyd him and his at Whitehall'. Up until the summer of 1690 there had been a certain impermanence in the Household's structure and position, stemming in part from the fact that the King had established his own court in Dublin, and in part from the belief that the establishment at St Germain would be expected to quickly uproot itself, if the opportunity arose, and return to England post haste. However, with such plans now put on indefinite hold, James confirmed his servants and advisors in their posts, and created an inner cabinet consisting of his principle Secretary of State, Lord Melfort; Sir Richard Neagle, whose loyal services in Ireland had already commended him as the minister best fitted to take charge of the affairs of that nation; Fr Louis Innes, who held the portfolio for Scotland, and John Caryll, the St Omer-educated courtier and poet, who continued as Secretary to the Queen. Flying in the face of received wisdom, Melfort had managed to re-establish himself at James's side, with his reputation enhanced by the success of his mission to greet Alexander VIII, the new pro-French Pope. However, the strains that would mar the development of ideological Jacobitism were already clearly delineated between those who conceded the need for compromise with the beneficiaries of the Revolution Settlement, in order to preserve the Church of England and see the King restored without reprisals or a fresh civil war, and those who were determined to challenge the Anglican monopoly of power and to advance unambiguously pro-Catholic policies regardless of the cost, without any dilution of James's policies of 1687–8. Given the composition of his council, with Melfort well to the fore, it is unsurprising that during his early years of exile James consistently pursued the aims of the latter party, known as the Non-Compounders, rather than those of the former grouping, styled as the Compounders. This was perhaps not too surprising, as those who had followed him unquestioningly into exile were largely representative of people who had staked everything in his cause – army officers, former ministers, personal friends, priests and servants, and increasingly a body of Irish and Scottish refugees – and lost it all amid the wreckage of his regime. Given such circumstances, they were hardly likely to countenance the deals which the Compounders recommended with Tories such as Godolphin and Churchill, who had already betrayed them and grown rich by their treachery, yet who now sought to profit again by a change of government, while sitting safe at home and running few of the risks in forcing the pace of counter-revolution. Unfortunately, it was precisely this group who had made dramatic gains in the late election, overturning Whig majorities and driving the radical consciences of the Revolution, such as the younger John Hampden, to bewilderment and despair. They were now the power in the land, grumbling at William's alleged mismanagement of the economy, and capable of acting as the motor for future dramatic upheavals in the governing of the state.

On one level, things had gone awkwardly for William ever since his coronation in April 1689. The Archbishop of Canterbury had refused to officiate, claiming James was still King, and instead the Bishop of London had to be drafted in to perform the ceremony. The new Queen Mary dismissed it as being tiresome and 'all vanity', while her husband had his pocket picked on the way to Westminster abbey and his champion mocked by an old woman in the crowd. James, for his part, had attempted to warn his daughter off taking such an irrevocable step and tried to reassert himself as patriarch, writing to her that 'if she were crowned while he and the Prince of Wales were living, the curse of an outraged father would light upon her, as well as that of God who had commanded duty to parents'. With only thin ranks of peers attending the coronation in England, and the ceremony cancelled in Scotland, the dual monarchy suddenly appeared vulnerable as rebellion flared across two kingdoms, and almost the entire energy of the state was geared to the prosecution of both domestic and foreign war. It was scarcely a wonder that some hankered after the return of the former King, or that the government at times came close to fearing it was about to lose control of even its own supporters. At Newcastle-upon-Tyne, captains Hayford and Killigrew took matters into their own hands, addressing the crowds along the quayside – to the horror of the civic authorities – and leading them in the destruction of the enormous brass statue of King James that stood there, throwing ropes around the figure and plucking it from the saddle of its horse, informing onlookers who peered through the windows of Hedlam's coffee house that 'our laws, liberties and properties were taken away and all by that picture', as the people closed in about the battered image, showering it with handfuls of stones and repeated blows. One unfortunate bystander, a yeoman by the name of Robert Maddison, who said that he thought it a shame to see the statue destroyed and the remains hurled into the waters of the Tyne, was chased off down the quay by 'a soldier or officer in a blue coat, [who] made a pass at him with his sword'.[7] If central government was particularly anxious to contain outbreaks of lawlessness, and to fend off complaints from aggrieved private gentlemen when 'the common people . . . are sometimes apt to make escapes in what they think is service to a cause they are affected with', then it found positively threatening the drip-feed of accounts from local magistrates concerning resistance to the new establishment.

Such was the concern that the theatres were watched and Shakespeare's *King Lear* banned for fear of the audience drawing obvious parallels, while *Richard II* and its account of a king-killing was simply censored of any provocative comments. One anonymous Whig playwright might recast James as 'Cullydada', king of 'New Hungary', who murdered his way to the throne in an attempt to force Islam upon his people, only to be routed by 'Prince Lysander' and driven into exile 'at which the Skies clear up, the Sun shines, and all the enchanted Pagan Mosques, Priests, [and] Jesuits [that populated this strange nation] . . . Vanish[ed] in a Moment', but the Jacobites soon replied, portraying William as a soul tormented by the ghosts of all those he had wronged, driven by fears of assassination and taunted by his alleged homosexuality and foreign birth, while 'the English had been harrassed almost to utter Ruine . . . [and] nothing can restore Peace, Trade, and Safety to the Nation but the Restauration of K[ing] James, which in all reason will make him too welcome to a wearied People'.[8] Dryden was replaced as Poet Laureate, but a dying Aphra Behn turned her hand to producing a stream of polemical Jacobite verse that found a ready market in those of the fashionable new London coffee shops where James's name was still revered. Bromfield's coffee house was closed down in 1690 for being a hotbed of dissention, but its proprietor simply continued to sell his drinks to his existing customers from the comfort of his own home. Even the capital's Jacobite drinking dens – such as the Dog in Drury Lane, the Half-Moon in Cheapside, and the Blue Posts in Spring Garden – were rarely subjected to forced closures or raids, with the government preferring to rely on the services of informants and paid agents, who drew no comment as they noted down what was said and what toasts were made, as the would-be conspirators sank deeper into their cups. Only when prolonged drinking bouts led to civil disorder, as in 1695 when Sir John Fenwick and his companions sounded trumpets and forced passers-by to drink a health to King James in Drury Lane, did the authorities move to take action. However, the young gallants who were at the root of the trouble had already been thoroughly scattered by the ready fists of a gang of butchers – called out from the nearby Clare Market by loyal Williamites – long before any beadles actually appeared on the scene.

In the summer of 1689, Jacobite agents landed at Cockerham Sands in Lancashire, bringing with them declarations to raise the north in the name of the fallen Stuart King, and commissions empowering the local gentry to raise regiments of horse and foot in the expectation of civil conflict. However, even though a 'great Quantity of Arms and Warlike Equipage . . . Kettle Drums, Trumpets, Jack Boots and . . . Saddles' were bundled ashore under the cover of night, the Tory gentry were unprepared to rise in advance of James's return to England, while the local militias rounded up many of the most uncompromising adherents to the old regime with little by way of fuss or resistance, before marching them south and placing them under house arrest in Manchester until autumn, when the threat of immediate invasion from Ireland had largely receded. It was reported that, under the cover of a bowling match, some 150 well-armed gentlemen had met in Northumberland to discuss the timing of a rising, while clusters of 'disaffected persons' were spotted flitting through the forest around Knaresborough bearing arms. Jacobite officers, bearing commissions and letters from their King, were captured in Chester and on the coast of Flintshire, while Sir Adam Blair, Lord Melfort's brother-in-law, was seized in June 1689 in the act of distributing James's declaration, but was bailed in the spring of the following year. Large sureties secured freedom for the earls of Castlemaine, Salisbury, and Peterborough, who had been accused of trying to forcibly re-Catholicise the kingdom, while Lord and Lady Griffin (together with their unfortunate cook) were held after false bottoms, containing intelligence bound for the court of St Germain, were discovered in pewter bottles found in their possession. Far more serious was the silent war conducted by coin-clippers who, in the privacy of their own homes or workshops, attempted to debase the currency and bring William's government to financial ruin. They could expect to face the capital penalty with far greater regularity than the handful of disaffected rural squires who were brought before the bench for attempting to foment rebellion. The reasons are not hard to discern, as the latter usually retained something of their influence among the Justices of the Peace and county juries, which made their convictions fraught with difficulty, while those charged with sabotaging the economy came largely from the artisan class, and lacked any such powerful protectors.

Anglican political opinion had fractured over the fate of King James's person, if not his policies, with a substantial minority of the clergy and a significant number of the bishops – including White of Peterborough, Frampton of Gloucester, Lloyd of Norwich, Turner of Ely, and Ken of Bath and Wells – refusing to take the new oaths of loyalty to William and Mary. Many more clergymen were sympathetic to their stand but, looking with fear and concern at the destruction of the episcopacy in Scotland, they chose to follow Bishop Lloyd of St Asaph, who felt he had done all he could by the old King and retreated into sophistry, taking advantage of the ambiguity in the wording of the oath which distinguished between the *de facto* monarchs, William and Mary, and the *de jure* king, James. However, the hardened group of Anglicans who could not compromise their consciences, or break the vows that they had sworn before God to their former sovereign, developed into one of the most formidable obstacles to the consolidation of the new government in England. Bishop Cartwright of Chester had chosen to accompany James to Ireland, only to sicken and die at Dublin, but others such as Bishop Turner of Ely remained at home, throwing themselves into uncomfortable new roles as plotters trying to overthrow the existing temporal authority, and using their influence in attempts to re-forge shattered alliances, in order to bring home the exiled King upon binding conditions. Turner had already been spotted by government agents in Covent Garden, meeting with Feversham, Dartmouth, William Penn the younger, and John Ashton – a former servant to Mary of Modena who was now acting as the group's link to St Germain – in order to thrash out their terms. Potentially such an alliance, between the hierarchy of the Church of England, the former commanders of the army and navy, and representatives of both the Protestant and Roman Catholic Dissenting communities, was extremely formidable, with the power to both compel respect and wield physical force in the struggle to return James to his throne. By December 1690, the meetings of leading Protestant Jacobites had become a regular occurrence in Covent Garden, at premises owned by Ashton's father-in-law, while several conferences had been held with Members of both Houses of Parliament as to the best manner of restoring the former King with French help. As a prelude to a planned invasion in 1691, Turner and Lord Clarendon – who had by now established themselves as the prime movers in the plot – urged that James should persuade Louis XIV to re-establish toleration for the Huguenots, thus taking the sting out of the argument that the persecution of Protestants was the objective of the former King's policies. They also advised that upon landing James should keep his French troops in the background, so it might not appear as an invasion, and that he should declare his resolution to preserve the Church of England and to govern according to law and through parliament.[9] Moreover, it was decided that Richard Graham, Viscount

Preston, the former Secretary of State and devout Anglican who had clung on to his seals of office ever since the Revolution, should be despatched immediately to carry their proposals to James and to negotiate with him on their behalf.

At first sight, Preston seemed to be the ideal courier. He had served as a diplomat at Versailles and had close contacts with the court at St Germain, while his loyalty to the Jacobite cause was without reproach, as he had spent the spring of 1689 distributing French funds and preparing to launch a rising, which led to him spending several months in the Tower of London. However, while he had proved himself to be a thorn in the side of the authorities – and was jailed again after attempting to claim that his baronetcy, conferred by James after his fall from power, was legally valid – he lacked the skill and nerve of a natural conspirator. Pretending to represent a gang of smugglers, John Ashton hired a fishing smack, the *James and Elizabeth*, in order to carry himself, Preston and Major Edmund Elliott over to France, guaranteeing its owner (a Quaker from Wapping) a return of thousands of pounds for just the one lucky trip. Though a sixpence was broken and the deal duly sealed, Ashton's wild promises of riches had aroused the suspicions of the owner and his wife, and they rushed to tell Danby, the elderly and somewhat beleaguered Lord President of the Privy Council, all that they knew. Having already had the conspirators under surveillance for several weeks, as they crossed the piazza at Covent Garden on their way to their regular meetings at the Seven Stars, Danby was thoroughly unsurprised by this fresh evidence of intent but let the plot progress to its fruition in an attempt to catch the messengers with their incriminating evidence upon them. Preston and his companions had been excessively nervous when they boarded the fishing boat near the Tower, but as they sailed safely down the Thames on the stroke of New Year 1691, leaving in their wake both a government frigate lying off Woolwich and the blockhouse at Gravesend, the mood of the conspirators lightened visibly and, leaving his secret correspondence in the hold, Preston rushed to unpack a seasonal hamper, handing out roast beef, mince pies and wine to his friends. However, no sooner had they sat down to eat, than the look-out raised the alarm that a swift vessel, packed with armed men, had set out from Tilbury and was pursuing them. The letters had been tied together by a lead weight, so that they might be easily jettisoned over the side in just such an emergency, but Preston seems to have lost his head entirely and did nothing to retrieve them while the boat was being boarded by the search party. Ashton, who appears to have been made of far sterner stuff, edged his way below decks, snatching up the packet and hiding it under his coat as Preston and Elliott dived for cover behind sacks of ballast on the deck. Unfortunately, Ashton was seized fast before he had a chance to throw the letters overboard, and he could only watch as Elliott fumed impotently and Preston attempted, without success, to bribe their captors into letting them go free.[10]

Viewing the correspondence, Danby had every reason to be delighted with his haul, for the letters implicated not only their bearers but also almost all the leading Protestant Jacobite grandees – Clarendon, Turner, Penn, and Dartmouth – together with James's former mistress, Catherine Sedley, Countess of Dorchester in treasonable practices. To make matters even worse for King James's adherents, having been sentenced to death, Preston vacillated between resolution and fear before turning king's evidence on all his former friends and accomplices, in return for a pardon, the restitution of his estates and the irrevocable destruction of his reputation. Elliott and Sedley were thought to be of no account, but it was rumoured that the soldier's lucky escape owed much to his own complicity in the investigation, as well as to the omission of his name from the correspondence. Turner and Penn had fled in terror for their lives, though in truth the authorities had little interest in prosecuting either of them. William voiced his desire to see Penn remain at liberty while Turner, awkwardly numbered as one of the seven bishops who had defied James in the summer of 1688, was conveniently smuggled away to France by his friends. However, Dartmouth and Clarendon, who commanded respect and had wielded significant power in their own right, were quickly taken and committed to the Tower. Within weeks, Dartmouth – who had revealed the exact dispositions of the English fleet – had succumbed to a stroke as the result of the stress incurred by his imprisonment and the thought of his possible trial for treason, while Clarendon, despite the relatively lax conditions under which he was being held, began to complain of his own failing health. His brother, the Earl of Rochester, pleaded tearfully on his behalf and William, who had little appetite for a show trial which could only end in spilling the blood of his wife's uncle, eventually saw to it that he was removed to the country under house arrest, having convinced himself that Clarendon's credit was all but destroyed. Only Ashton emerged from the proceedings with his dignity still intact, though it did him precious little good and a great deal of harm. He steadfastly failed to give evidence against his companions and, lacking friends or family who could lobby effectively for him at court, he went to the scaffold unrepentant and owning his utter 'dependance on king James, and his fidelity to him'.[11] When it was believed that Preston would go to the scaffold, his sympathisers had scattered about the streets of London papers threatening that Mountjoy, still languishing in the Bastille, would be broken on the wheel as a reprisal, but no similar threats on Ashton's behalf were heard from King James or his ministers, and he died without appeals for clemency, while his children, if not perhaps his widow, appear to have ultimately received slight recompense for their sufferings at the court of St Germain.

The immediate effect of the discovery of the plot was to tar the non-juring clergy with accusations of disloyalty, enabling those Anglican clergy who had taken the necessary oaths, but whose sense of decency had prevented them from stepping in to fill offices and stipends vacated by those of their fellows who had been stripped of their livelihoods, to assume positions that had remained empty since the winter of 1689–90. Furthermore, with Turner's departure from the shores of England, the less confrontational brand of resistance championed by Sancroft, the Archbishop of Canterbury deprived of office, met little by way of a challenge from the more militant wing of the non-juring Church. Conversely, Melfort's hardline followers on James's council drew strength from the destruction of Lord Preston and the Hyde brothers, who had sought to place restrictions upon their King, and it would be some time before Lord Middleton could establish himself firmly in their place as the new leader of those Protestant Jacobites who remained domiciled in the British Isles. Yet, even if Preston's mission had managed to get through to France, it was debatable just how warm a reception would have greeted its proposals among Melfort's circle at St Germain, and more importantly among the courtiers and ministers of Versailles. James himself had realised that a hard series of discussions would have been necessary once Preston had arrived 'in order to accommodate these seeming contradictions' contained in the proposals to guarantee his return. While it would be wrong to conceive of him being ideologically wedded to Melfort's Non-Compounders – for he was more than capable of shifting his favour towards whichever wing of the Jacobite movement seemed the more likely to secure his return to power throughout the 1690s – the plotters appear to have wildly overestimated the extent of his influence over Louis XIV. They had good reason to be worried that religious intolerance would spread in the wake of the Sun King's armies; not content with the forcible conversion of his own subjects, Louis XIV had already compelled the young Duke of Savoy, with the threat of invasion and possible annexation, to destroy the Protestant enclaves within his own alpine borders. Moreover, if the opprobrium of successive popes and his fellow princes, the threat of bloody guerrilla wars in the Languedoc and Piedmont, the defections or forcible retirement of some of his best commanders, and the debilitating effect on the French economy of the emigration of some 200,000 citizens, including many in the silk-working and glass industries, had done little to dampen Louis's desire to extirpate Protestantism from his lands, then any appeals for toleration of the Huguenots from his English client-king might appear preordained to failure. Indeed, despite the continuing reiteration of his commitment to religious toleration in Britain, and his welcome reception of the Huguenots between 1685–8 on primarily economic grounds, James's defence of the rights of his exiled Protestant subjects was equivocal and muted, to say the least. After his arrival at St Germain, his intervention on behalf of the French Huguenots – tarred in his mind with 'Antemonarchical and resisting' principles – was practically non-existent. A unilateral declaration by James to safeguard the liberties of his Protestant subjects might have sufficed, and been forthcoming, but the main flaw in the plan, which James was not apparently prepared to acknowledge to his English partisans, was that everything hinged on him making a landing with French support, and by 1690–1 an army and a navy were the last things that were being offered to him by Louvois and the King of France. In encouraging his supporters to count on a level of military support that he could not hope to deliver, James had acted in an extremely disingenuous manner toward Anglicans such as Clarendon, Dartmouth and Turner. He may have thought they could provoke widespread civil resistance, a rebellion, or a naval mutiny in England, which could subsequently be exploited by France, or perhaps he still believed that, having secured some sort of deal with the English opposition, he might be able – against all the odds – to prevail upon Louis XIV to change his mind and commit the necessary forces to a campaign which, as yet, existed nowhere save in his own head.[12] Either way, James could be seen to be making policy based on optimistic hopes rather than on any solid guarantees of support, whether from the French or even from the English. It must be thought that, as Preston prepared to leave for France, the King had more than an inkling that his false promises might not ultimately be enough to reunite the ultra-Tories in his cause, or to speed him homewards.

Indeed, James's stock had fallen so low at the French court that he was even forbidden to follow Louis XIV to the siege of Mons in the spring of 1691. Enormous preparations had been undertaken over the winter months to ensure the success of the action, with vast quantities of food and forage stockpiled in a series of depots throughout Namur and Hainault, and an overwhelming force of artillery, engineers, and some 46,000 men carefully assembled along the border by Louvois, to ensure that the 6,000-strong garrison might be quickly and very publicly crushed. It was intended as a set-piece action, designed to showcase the power, majesty and military genius of Louis XIV, and the pre-eminence of the French in the art of war. Thus, the courtiers of Versailles clamoured to be allowed to witness the spectacle, the dauphin prepared to leave the table and the hunting field to follow his father into the camp, and even Monsieur – who had been consigned to a life of uselessness once his victory at Cassel and his appetite for war had threatened to outshine his brother and nephew – was allowed to witness the opening of trenches and the fearsome bombardment of the town. After his defeat at the Boyne, James had longed for the opportunity to rebuild his reputation as a soldier and saw, in the plans for the investment of Mons, the chance to taste the excitement of battle once more, without the onerous constraints of personal command, and with the prospect of victory practically assured in advance. Having sat through a performance of Molière's *Bourgeois Gentilhomme* at the Trianon – an experience he probably did not relish, due to his aversion to the theatre and to comedies in particular – James had managed to obtain another audience with King Louis. He pushed once more his scheme for an invasion of England, clutching at the hope that Marlborough's sudden disenchantment with William's governance and the opening of correspondence with St Germain – stemming from his failure to obtain the expected rewards from his new master – might signal the general disaffection of the English army, and the potential for Marlborough to initiate a major mutiny among the military at any given moment. As his friend the dauphin spoke of his preparations for the coming campaign in Flanders, James, 'thinking I was right to expect it for more than one reason', hoped that an appearance in the trenches before Mons might serve to re-establish him in the good graces of Louvois and the French military establishment, and to expedite a descent upon England. However, his hopes were quickly shattered in March 1691, as he revealed to his closest spiritual confidant, the abbé de La Trappe, when he admitted that: 'I am not asked on the trip to Mons with the King, when I was really looking forward to going'. He had argued with Louis but 'eventually was unable to gain my point'. To James this was 'a great mortification which has descended upon me which touches me where I am most sensitive' and faced once more with rejection at the hands of the French King, and the unsettling knowledge that his military career appeared to be on the wane, he found that despite burying himself in St Francis of Sales's meditations upon patience, he could not entirely rid himself of feelings of bitterness and loss, telling the abbé that 'I who hardly complain' could not help but express the sadness that he felt and look to the monk for reassurance.[13] Mons duly fell to the French army after less than a month's siege, but it was a victory that was to be owned by Louis XIV alone. It was his figure that was portrayed – with more than the usual operation of artistic licence – directing the assault from the forward positions, surrounded by death and destruction yet miraculously preserved from all harm. Whether through the desire to allow no one to share in his moment of triumph, or because it was felt that his brother monarch might be something of a liability in the siege lines, there was no place for James at his side. As the very epitome of tact and discretion, the abbé sympathised with his friend, saying that he 'was not surprised at the displeasure your Majesty felt at seeing the King depart for Mons, without your going with him', before attempting to put the best gloss possible on events, arguing 'that the opposition he [i.e. Louis XIV] made to your Majesty's being of that party was only the result of consideration for you, and of his care for the preservation of your person . . . What grief had it been for the King if he had seen with his own eyes that happen to your Majesty which may happen to persons who expose themselves, which everyone knows you would not have failed to do'.[14] This combination of reassurance over Louis's continuing love for his cousin and the careful flattery of James's courage failed, however, to explain why the King of England might have been at far more risk during the siege than the French monarch, his heir, or any of the great magnates who followed in Monsieur's train. It was clear that the possibility of returning to a professional military career in Flanders, revisiting the scenes of his youth, was entirely closed off to James, and increasingly he chose to focus his attention on the politics of England and on the narrow devotional, recreational, and domestic constraints of a world based around the respective centres of La Trappe, Versailles and St Germain, largely shuttering off from his vision the problems and opportunities presented by the rest of the European continent.

II

In part, the increasing Anglo-centricity of his efforts was a reaction to the final destruction of his cause in Ireland and the subjugation of resistance in Scotland amid the bloodied snows of Glencoe. Since James's premature departure from Kinsale, the administration that had continued to rule in his name had attempted to confront, as best they could, many of the logistical and financial problems that the King had left in his wake. Confidence in James's brass money had collapsed completely after the fall of Dublin; many small traders and farmers had reconciled themselves to the eventual re-establishment of English rule, and quantities of sterling had been injected back into the Irish economy by the resumption of trade with Britain, helped by the presence of large numbers of Williamite troops who paid for their goods in coin fresh from the Tower mint. Facing complete financial collapse, Tyrconnel chose to attempt to stimulate commerce by devaluing the discredited coinage, but while this pleased the remaining merchants of Munster and Connacht, the measure served to drive a further wedge between the Viceroy and his army, who saw their remaining bargaining power over already scarce markets virtually destroyed, rendering their infrequent and paltry wages of even less consequence in their struggle to ward off the pangs of hunger. The need to secure substantial French subsidies in order to pay his troops properly and stave off a mutiny – which he suspected Sarsfield may even have welcomed – provided a further crucial incentive for Tyrconnel to cross over to France in person as quickly as possible. Since the Boyne, he had left the management of the war to Berwick, who had continued to employ a ruthless policy of slashing and burning crops in an attempt to slow the Williamite advance and bring on the menace of famine with the coming winter, until his foes threatened him with similarly grim reprisals unless he immediately desisted from this widely deplored practice.

In the meantime, a fresh expedition had left Portsmouth bound for the south coast of Ireland, under the command of Marlborough, who had lobbied hard for the honour now that he did not have to risk facing his former patron in the field. Landing before Cork, the kingdom's second city, at the end of September 1690, he was reinforced by Wurtemberg and some 5,000 men drawn from the Dutch, Danish and Huguenot regiments already serving in Ireland. Marlborough speedily seized an outlying fort, dragging up naval artillery and pounding the city walls, virtually at will, from the surrounding heights. Realising the danger that Cork was now in, Berwick struggled to mount a relief expedition but, finding himself badly outnumbered, declined to risk a battle and drew off, leaving the city to its fate. On the afternoon of 27 September, storming parties waded across the two branches of the River Lee and pushed their way through the marshes that protected the city's breached west wall. Despite the heavy fire tearing through their disordered ranks, the sodden infantrymen reformed and carried the counter-scarp, throwing the defenders back into the town and preparing to launch a final assault, before the garrison beat a hurried parley and surrendered without the promise of terms. In contrast to the slaughter experienced at Limerick, it had been a remarkably successful operation, which had delivered a significant Jacobite stronghold and its garrison of 4,000 trained soldiers to the Williamites for a relatively slight cost. Leading from the front, the Duke of Grafton – who had lost his command of the Guards as the price of voting against William becoming King – had ventured ashore with a detachment of sailors, and had been raked down by an unexpected wave of musket fire at the height of the storm. He clung to life for eleven more days, lamenting only that he could not leave his 'country [by which he meant England, rather than Ireland] in a happier and more tranquil state'.[15]

Kinsale fell shortly afterwards, as Sarsfield's cavalrymen watched helplessly, and the Jacobite commanders rushed to attribute blame for the year's failures, to seek credit for their rare successes, and to finally settle the deeply divisive scores that had split their command. Even from his remove at St Germain, King James seemed singularly loath to resolve these disputes. By arriving in France well ahead of his detractors, Tyrconnel was able to put his own side of the argument before both James and the French court without the fear of contradiction. He recommended himself warmly to Louvois by blaming Lauzun alone for the disaster on the Boyne, and made a favourable impression on the French King, who – although he refused to send him fresh regiments – promised him a new staff of general officers, a full re-supply and a further consignment of silver and gold. James was glad to see him, and on their parting made him a Knight of the Garter – ironically in place of the newly deceased Lord Grafton – and accorded him the title of Lord Lieutenant of Ireland. It might have seemed that the tall Irishman had reached the very summit of his career, enjoying James's complete confidence and being entrusted both with overseeing the affairs of the nation and with the ongoing conduct of the war, but as his coach rumbled back towards Brest, a delegation with a very different agenda was already preparing to land in France. Berwick had already headed off one plan by Sarsfield and Colonel Luttrell to have Tyrconnel arrested, but sensing that further trouble was afoot, he had moved to assert his authority, summoning 'all the principal Lords, as well of the clergy as laity, and all the military officers, down to the Colonels' and having them pass unanimously a resolution that Luttrell, together with his elder brother Simon, the Bishop of Cork and Colonel Nicholas Purcell, should leave immediately for France 'in order to represent their real condition and necessities' to King James. Having rid himself of most of the opposition to his rule at a stroke, Berwick resolved that Purcell and Henry Luttrell, 'the two most dangerous incendiaries', should not return to trouble him again, and added Major-General Thomas Maxwell, a Scotsman, to their suite, bearing secret instructions to the King that the pair were to be arrested as soon as they set foot in the palace at St Germain.[16] However, James's nerve appears to have failed him when confronted by the mission and he decided not to implement his son's request, fearing that the Irish might seek reprisals against Berwick, Tyrconnel and their servants if he dared to raise a hand against their representatives. Worse still, he played for time, initially refusing to see them before changing his mind, hearing out their litany of complaints and weakly urging concord in an attempt to maintain the balance of power in Ireland between the rival groups, but serving in effect only to undermine Tyrconnel's all too recently ceded authority. Thus, he agreed that the new French commander – the marquis de St Ruhe, known to posterity as St Ruth – should supersede his Viceroy in military matters, while he honoured Sarsfield with the earldom of Lucan in an attempt to counteract the impression of favour created by Tyrconnel's recent advancement. Yet one wonders whether James really believed that he could reconcile the two parties so easily, as he decided to recall Berwick, 'not choosing to leave [him] in a country so full of troubles', while despatching the Luttrells back to Ireland without censure, and sending Neagle over with Tyrconnel to assume a position in the administration and to guard his interests in the absence of his son.[17] Deprived of his first taste of independent command, Berwick arrived back in France in February 1691, only to leave almost immediately – much to his father's jealousy – for the siege lines at Mons, as a gentleman volunteer.

One individual who was, however, heartily welcomed in Ireland was General St Ruth. He had commanded Justin Macarty and Lord Mountcashel's fledgling Irish Brigade during the hard fighting through the mountains of Savoy against the Protestants of the Vaudois, where warfare took on the harshest edge of confessional conflict and where quarter was seldom given by the Irishmen, who won ecstatic praise from their French comrades but suffered appalling losses as they were used repeatedly as assault troops, striking fear into, and gaining the hatred and utter opprobrium of, their foes. Yet the myth glibly propounded by King James, that his Irish subjects could not fight, had been destroyed forever, and St Ruth had won the love and respect of those he had led, which was soon communicated back to their fellow countrymen at home. Meanwhile, Sarsfield's tenacious defence of the Shannon throughout the autumn and winter months had further served to bolster his reputation and, while Berwick and Tyrconnel might choose to sniff that too much praise had turned his head and rendered him both uncontrollable and largely insufferable, there can be no doubt that he had become the living symbol of Irish resistance to English rule, and that his combination of great personal bravery and unyielding vigilance had ground down the repeated attempts of Douglas and Kirke to stove in the Jacobite positions along the river line and to establish permanent bridgeheads on the west bank of the Shannon.[18] Unfortunately, he lacked the skills of a politician and could not bring himself to make common cause with St Ruth, who had swiftly supplanted the Viceroy in the management of the army after his arrival in May 1691, and thereafter consolidated his authority by conscientiously trying to resolve the problems of supply and communications in a manner that was wholly foreign to the halting and uncertain measures previously undertaken by von Rosen and Lauzun.

With Tyrconnel withdrawn to Limerick and his influence effectively confined to the civil administration, St Ruth gathered together his forces and took up a strong position behind the fortress of Athlone, which had been threatened by a fresh enemy offensive. Since William had left Ireland in September 1690, command of his army had passed rapidly from Count Solms to Baron de Ginkel, who had been left to hold together the regiments, depleted and demoralised after their check at Limerick, over the course of yet another dank Irish winter. Clearing the way through the Jacobite outpost of Ballymore, Ginkel sighted his heavy siege guns before Athlone on 20 June 1691, and unleashed a ferocious bombardment on the castle and the two halves of the town that straddled either bank of the Shannon. Amid a firestorm, the Jacobites were quickly forced to abandon the town on the eastern, or Leinster, side of the river, but stubbornly clung to their fortifications on the opposite Connacht bank, as a fierce struggle developed for control of the shattered bridge that spanned the waters of the Shannon. Despite the best efforts of the

Williamite engineers, who edged their way forward under cover of darkness to repair the arches and throw new planking across the yawning gaps in the structure, as the prelude to a general assault, Irish cannon continued to rake their exposed positions and raiding parties undid much of their work, setting fire to the timbers of the bridge with a sudden hail of grenades and piles of burning faggots, hurled in among the planking as the Williamites fell back. To Major-General Mackay, newly come over from Scotland, Ginkel's obsession with seizing the bridge was a costly mistake when fords existed, both up- and down-stream of Athlone, that might be crossed easily and with only light casualties. Unfortunately, his superior officer refused to give the time of day to his well-considered advice and continued to throw men and materials across the arches, in the fruitless attempt to repair the damage daily wrought upon their work by the now well-honed aim of the Jacobite artillerymen and grenadiers.

However, if Mackay and Ginkel neither liked nor trusted one another, the Jacobite command was similarly torn by internal dissention, as St Ruth's deputy, Lieutenant-General d'Usson, was targeted as Tyrconnel's friend, and Major-General Maxwell had still not been forgiven for his attempt to have Luttrell and Purcell stripped of their commands. Tyrconnel made one last attempt to win back the army, appearing in the trenches only to find that Sarsfield was raising a petition against him. News that he had been negotiating with Louvois for a fresh exchange of 'Wild Geese' for French regiments and equipment had been leaked to the troops and embroidered, to the point that many soldiers believed that the Viceroy was scheming to sell them like so many head of cattle, to enrich himself and to curry favour with his foreign paymaster. Denied his wish to lead the King's Life Guard into action one last time, Tyrconnel left the Jacobite camp without ceremony and set his horse on the road back to Limerick, his spirits having 'sank prodigiously' in the words of Berwick, now that both his King and his army had turned from him, leaving his only refuge to be found in the company of his remaining friends, and in the temporary solace afforded by fine foods and the liberal passing of the brandy bottle.[19] If, after a lifetime's devotion to the frequently conjoined causes of the Old Irish nobility, the Roman Catholic faith and the House of Stuart, Tyrconnel had become a forlorn and divisive figure, St Ruth might conceivably still have been in need of his advice and experience over the coming days, as he misjudged the nature of the troops now under his command. Used to the complicated manoeuvres conducted by the highly drilled regiments he had led on the Continent, he attempted to accustom his Irish regiments to the effects of a cannonade by rotating the regiments serving in the trenches each day. In theory the idea was sound, providing valuable combat experience for the new levies that could be turned to good account in the heat of any forthcoming battle, but amid the smoke and confusion of the disintegrating fortress, which was being daily reduced to mountains of brick and rubble, the continued movement of regiments from post to post bred bewilderment among the rank and file, and proved to be a recipe for disaster.

With time at a premium, Ginkel began to lose hope that a successful crossing of the Shannon could be effected and seriously considered raising the siege. Only strong representation from Mackay and Wurtemberg prevented this and committed the General to hazarding a fording of the river underneath the still-smouldering bridge beams. Accordingly, under the cover of dusk on 30 June, Ginkel committed his grenadier companies to a storm of the town and had them wade, chest deep, across the Shannon. Their surprise appearance, when the newly exchanged regiments had just settled down for the night, threw the entire garrison into confusion. A sharp bayonet charge cleared the first line of entrenchments and sent the Jacobites scurrying back into the town with all hope of a rally gone, and every man thinking only of how best to preserve himself. While English regiments formed up and doubled across the bridge, with the gaps in its boards quickly filled, now that there was no one left to obstruct their crossing, Lieutenant-General d'Usson attempted to stem the flight of the regiments, but was caught up in the stampede and swept back towards the Jacobite camp before being finally trampled to the ground and knocked out by the weight of the panicking soldiery. Before the rout could become general and engulf his entire army, St Ruth pulled his troops back off the heights behind the town and sounded the retreat. Though it was subsequently alleged that the Scotsman, Maxwell, had been negligent in his duty, standing down his men and letting them go off to hunt larks just as the attack was about to go in, the charges against him owed everything to national prejudices, the need for a scapegoat, and the hatred that a large section of the Jacobite staff bore him. If blame was to be attributed, then it could not be denied that St Ruth should have shouldered much of it, having constantly re-ordered his lines and then failed to do anything to fill the walls with fresh regiments or to take a lead in rallying his frightened and stunned men once the extent of the Williamite attack had revealed itself. A year before, Athlone had been a byword for the military resurgence of Jacobitism, but now it became synonymous with allegations and counter-allegations of duplicity, cowardice and treachery. Amid such sorry circumstances, it might have been a mercy if the town's original Governor, Colonel Richard Grace, who had fallen in the fight, had died before the fall of the town. As it was, he was pulled mortally wounded from the rubble and watched as Ginkel's staff cantered through the ruined streets that night, bringing a halt to the killing and taking possession of all that remained of the fortress in the name of William III.[20]

Hearing of the town's fall, Tyrconnel advised – for he was no longer capable of ordering – that the army should pull back to Limerick and prepare to weather a fresh siege. If they could hold out against Ginkel's forces until the autumn – and there was no reason why they should not, as the city had been heavily refortified since William's regiments had been shattered against its walls – then resistance could be prolonged for a further year, with the Williamites then forced back into winter quarters and the promise of French reinforcements being sent over in the spring of 1692. Unfortunately, St Ruth's pride had been stung by the loss of Athlone and he resolved, against the warnings of Sarsfield and the majority of his general staff, to give battle to Ginkel at the first available opportunity, in the hope of winning a decisive victory that would bring the war to a close and set the seal upon his reputation. The two armies met close to the village of Aughrim, on 12 July 1691. The Jacobites had assumed a formidable position, their flanks pinned on their left by the bulk of Aughrim Castle, and on the right by swampy and broken ground terminating on the slopes below the parish church. They had had time to entrench themselves on the wide frontage of Kilcommodon Hill, while the front ranks of their infantry occupied 'a parcel of old garden ditches', with the morass stretched out before them protecting almost the entire length of their lines, save at a narrow causeway and a ford.[21] Ever cautious, Ginkel probed at their positions before sending his Danish, Dutch and Huguenot regiments of horse trotting boot-to-boot across the ford in order to open the attack on the Jacobite right, and his infantry under Mackay coursing through the marshes to strike at the enemy's centre, a little after five in the evening. Yet no sooner had the cavalry emerged from the water than they were hit by the solid wall of Sarsfield's horsemen, who hurled them back in disorder but failed to break through their ranks. The infantry fared no better. Having dragged themselves clear of the marshes they were met by a succession of murderous and well-disciplined volleys from Jacobite foot soldiers hidden behind the low walls and hedgerows, which significantly thinned their ranks as they prepared to form up for the charge. Even then, the Jacobites melted away, falling back to a second line of pre-prepared positions and leaving their exhausted foes to climb up the slopes straight into the path of their guns. As they reeled back in shock and horror they were hit by a wild charge, which gained momentum as it rolled down the hill and swept the redcoats off the slopes and back to the very edge of the marsh. While the battle hung in the balance, Ginkel continued to feed his foot regiments into the marsh, hoping to reinforce his stricken advance guard, but in fact only adding to the general confusion as Mackay appealed for order and a flushed Colonel Cutts pushed his wavering troops back into formation, steadying their nerves as he and the General appeared immune to the cannon balls that churned up the ground all about them. At the same moment, an elated St Ruth was galloping through the ranks of the King's Life Guard, believing that the battle was already won and that it would only need him to set his horse regiments in motion to smash through the struggling knots of infantrymen who were reforming about the English colours. Riding over the ridge and exposing his silhouette against the skyline, he was still calling excitedly about him when a cannon ball skimmed over the Jacobite lines and struck off his head. Anxious that their soldiers should not discover that their Commander-in-Chief had fallen, the officers about him threw a cloak over his corpse, but were at a loss as to what their next course of action should be. Relations had become so strained between St Ruth and his subordinates after his refusal to retire back to Limerick, that he apparently had not thought fit to familiarise any of his staff with his battle plans. Consequently, while the Jacobite command suffered a curious paralysis, with the order to commit the Household cavalry to the charge suddenly and seemingly inexplicably rescinded, troopers sat idle in their saddles as Mackay, mud-splattered and cursing loudly, resumed his forward march, with 'the ridges seem[ing] to be ablaze'. The marquis de Ruvigny, a Huguenot commander, led the English cavalry across the causeway and on towards Aughrim Castle. Before their charge, Luttrell's dragoons offered only a spluttering and desultory fire as de Ruvigny's troopers stove in the Jacobite foot guarding the castle and poured over the brow of the ridge, getting in behind the forward units and rolling up the enemy lines from left to right.

As the Jacobite regiments began to fragment before this onslaught, Sarsfield, who had been holding off repeated attacks on the right flank, broke off from the fighting and wheeled back towards Kilcommodon Hill, uniting with Lord Galmoy's horse in an attempt to prevent the general massacre of their foot and to fight a rearguard action which would enable the remnants of some regiments to limp off the field in relatively good order, to make their escape under the cover of the encroaching night. However there was no getting away from the enormity of the catastrophe that had overcome the Jacobite army, with the fugitives abandoning their colours and artillery: 'Stricken with terror . . . fleeing in all directions across the countryside into the mountains, woods, bogs and wilderness . . . the women, children and waggoners filled every road weeping and wailing'. Williamite writers subsequently claimed that some 7,000 Jacobites had fallen on the field, but while this may be something of an exaggeration, and James's own figure of 4,000 dead with probably the same number wounded might be nearer to the truth, it was clear to all the contemporary commentators that Aughrim had been the scene of unprecedented slaughter. One eyewitness serving with the Danish contingent recalled the sight of 'the many men and horses too badly wounded to get away, who when attempting to rise fell back unable to bear their own weight'. Ginkel's army had also suffered heavy losses, though his officers could not agree, even as the grave pits were dug, on an exact figure; it seems likely that no less than 3,000 of their comrades lay dead and wounded on the field. Significantly, however, the Jacobite officer corps had been hit disproportionately hard, with St Ruth and Lord Galway dead, the second-in-command de Tesse carried off the field with multiple wounds, and Major-General John Hamilton, the brother of Richard and Anthony, captured but already so badly injured that the help of the Williamite surgeons could not save him. St Ruth's hatred of the Protestants and preparedness to inject an overtly religious aspect into the war in a manner – to King James's credit – not previously sanctioned had encouraged many priests to serve in the ranks. Eighty of them had fallen that day, with Alexius Stafford, Dean of Wexford, 'an undaunted zealot and most pious churchman', scythed down by enemy fire as he led the Royal Regiment forward in their first charge of the day. While the Duke of Wurtemberg counted the fourteen standards and thirty-two flags taken, and cartloads of discarded muskets were wheeled back to Ginkel's makeshift camp by soldiers anxious to redeem them for the promised bounty, a bleak epitaph was being served upon the Jacobite movement in Ireland. Looters were in the act of stripping the body of St Ruth's secretary when they discovered the tattered text of the declaration he had read out to his troops that morning, promising that they would: 'bear no longer the reproaches of the heretics . . . be assured that King James will love and reward you, Louis the Great will protect you, all good Catholics will applaud you, I myself will command you . . . your posterity will bless you, God will make you all saints and his holy mother will lay you in her bosom'.[22] For the fugitives jamming the road to Limerick that night, it might have seemed that James II and Louis XIV were very far away and that their promises counted for little against the cold steel wielded by their pursuers.

Without substantial fortifications, Galway yielded quickly upon good terms, while the morale of both the Irish Jacobites and the independent Gaelic partisans collapsed. Hugh 'Balldearg' O'Donnell, who had been expected to go to Galway's aid, began to treat with the Williamites for pardons for himself and his men, while a packet of Henry Luttrell's correspondence was sliced open and read to reveal that he was preparing to strike a deal with his foes. Tyrconnel ordered his arrest and court-martial, but Ginkel's threats of reprisals saved him from the firing squad. The removal and discrediting of his foe was, however, to be almost the last act undertaken by the Viceroy. Despite the disaster at Aughrim, Tyrconnel continued to believe that Limerick could hold out for another year and that, through guerrilla actions, the war might still be continued long enough to drain away King William's resources, or until favourable terms might be prised out of his government for the Irish Catholics. Unfortunately, after coming home from a party thrown by his friend d'Usson, he suffered the first of a series of strokes that eventually deprived him of his power of speech and finally, after five days of wasting sickness, of his life, on 14 September 1691. A paper purporting without a shred of evidence to be 'Tyrconnel's Will' was soon circulated, which contradicted the entire tenor of the Viceroy's career in urging the army to abjure the French alliance and look to enlisting in the service of those Roman Catholic powers, such as Spain, Austria, Savoy, and Poland, currently engaged against the forces of Louis XIV.[23] However, the spirits of the Irish soldiery could not have sunk much lower as James's new administration – led by Neagle and two unpopular English civilians – failed to gain credibility, and Ginkel's artillery began to sound against Limerick's walls. The siege was prosecuted so hesitantly and the year was so far drawn on that it would have been a relatively easy matter for the garrison to have clung on until the end of the campaigning season, for despite the claims of some Jacobite officers there was no shortage of food, and Ginkel had neither the stomach nor the resources to sanction the storming of Limerick. Yet, surprisingly, it was Sarsfield who took the initiative in opening negotiations with the Williamites, preparing to surrender the city provided that permission for him to evacuate the army to France was granted, and basic – though as it would turn out, easily rescindable – guarantees for the civil liberty of Roman Catholics could be obtained. Early attempts to win concrete safeguards for religious liberty were refused outright by Ginkel, but surprisingly, and to the horror of both William and Bentinck, he was prepared to agree to the transportation of the Irish regiments to France, believing somewhat naively that the private soldiers would prefer to remain at home and might be prevailed on to enlist in his own army, rather than risk the uncertainties of exile. Sarsfield achieved what he wanted from the military clauses of the treaty, and let the civilian administrators know that they should conclude their negotiations quickly and as best they could, but without the exertion of his influence and the implicit threat of the force he could command, the provision made in the Treaty of Limerick for those left behind was poor indeed. Sarsfield's critics sneered that he had abandoned the city and ended the war only so that he might be able to bring over his regiments intact to France, creating what amounted to a private army with himself and his clients at its head. Though he may well have been dreaming of a marshal's baton, and Tyrconnel would surely have pursued an entirely different policy, he had brought off an extremely valuable diplomatic and military coup, establishing the right of more than 11,000 soldiers to retire to France together with their arms and equipment, their families and property. Undoubtedly, Sarsfield had decided that the best service he could perform for his nation was to ensure the survival of the army so that it might form the spearhead of King James's invasion force for England, thus guaranteeing the final victory for indigenous Irish political, economic and religious rights by other means. In the short term, as we shall see, his decision to bring the war in Ireland to an end at the beginning of October 1691 proved to give an enormous boost to James's prestige and usefulness in the eyes of the French court, as it effectively gifted him an army of highly motivated and experienced troops, ensuring him consideration once more in the councils of Louis XIV and the ability to retain an air of independence and to project his power across the battlefields of Europe.[24]

Unfortunately, the memory of the King's flight from Ireland – and his unwillingness to renegotiate fundamentally the basis for the nation's continuing relationship with England – left a lingering and unpalatable aftertaste to those who did not follow the 'Wild Geese' to St Germain. Though James would continue to appoint bishops to vacant Irish sees, and more importantly, the Vatican would carry on ratifying his choices, priests and people were more concerned with maintaining their faith and the cult of the saints, than with the promotion of any new forms of popular attachment to the House of Stuart, who had served them particularly ill in the recent past. Similarly, after 1692 Roman Catholic landowners were more involved in fighting legal cases in order to regain lost or to preserve threatened lands – which, before the adoption of the crippling Penal Laws in 1704, actually yielded positive results, ensuring that 14 per cent of Irish land remained in their hands – than in trying to foment armed rebellion in the name of the former King. Moreover, many of the natural leaders for any such rising were now either dead or in exile, or, like Henry Luttrell, had moved to accept a lasting accommodation with the governments in Whitehall and Dublin.[25] The military option still existed, and indeed would continue to do so for more than a century, but it was a continuation of armed struggle by proxy, fighting English power as the servants of France on foreign fields from Steinkirk and Landen to Blenheim and Fontenoy, denuding the land of would-be insurgents who conceivably might have kept a more vital and visible brand of Jacobite allegiance alive at home. It was, therefore, to Scotland that James's heirs looked for the outbreak of major rebellions to fuel their cause, but even there, by the mid-1690s, the potential for continuing warfare capable of depriving William and Mary of their crowns was remote indeed. It would only germinate once again when a new generation, recalling the manner in which rival and dominant clans had sought to break their resistance, found a common cause – and a means of attempting to preserve an already failing caste system – through their military and emotional adherence to the exiled Stuarts.

III

While the feudal clan ties between the Irish aristocracy and those that they ruled had largely been severed by the close of the seventeenth century, the same was not true of Scotland, where the clan muster might still bring hundreds of armed men onto the field through the belligerence of a single chief, and where raiding for livestock was an ingrained feature of Highland culture, of particular economic value (if not of necessity) in a land of scarce agrarian resources and frequent want. After Cromdale, where Livingston's troopers had put to flight an army of clansmen in a matter of minutes, James had ordered Cannon and Buchan, the generals responsible for the débâcle, to join him in France. The Edinburgh government had been only too willing to ensure that they, if not their men, were eventually equipped with the necessary passes to leave the kingdom. However, the plans and preferences of the former King had oscillated between a longing to keep the military struggle alive through the agency of the Highlanders, and the belief that a political accord might be struck with the Scottish Episcopalians, disaffected Presbyterians, and the members of 'the Club' – who also styled themselves more prosaically as the 'Killiecrankies' and haunted the fashionable Edinburgh coffee houses talking treason – bringing him both a more immediate and far more durable restitution of his fortunes. Unfortunately for him, the viewpoints of these groupings were mutually exclusive, and though Melfort repeatedly made plain to him the dangers inherent in seeking to play one set of his supporters against another, James had been perfectly prepared to sacrifice the interests of the pro-Stuart clans in 1690, in return for the support of the Earl of Argyll and his tenants. With the war in Ireland going badly wrong, the promise of the arrival of regular regiments to supplement the rebellious clans had already largely evaporated, while the chiefs began to appeal to St Germain for permission to accept the government's offer of indemnity. However, James temporised, still believing that the French might be persuaded to bring troops and supplies over to Scotland in the autumn and winter of 1691–2, and unwilling to stand down the clansmen when the war might still be rekindled in the Highlands, so that the period for the amnesty came and went with still no message from him returning to the chiefs. Just as damaging was the belligerence and pride of the clan leaders, who inflated their capability for threatening the power of the Edinburgh government in order to gain personal prestige, but only succeeded in provoking the further fear and rage of Lowland society and in allowing the Presbyterians in the resurgent Scots Parliament to destroy any chance they had of negotiating more favourable terms for the lasting pacification of the Highlands. It was a recipe for disaster, made all the worse by the government's inability to harness the funds necessary for a military solution to the clans' raiding, and by the Parliament's refusal to even countenance a political formula that might have ended the worst of the feuding and re-established a measure of peace in the north. The soldiers sent to garrison the new fortress rising slowly at Inverlochy –

soon to be named after King William – were woefully and fitfully paid, while their numbers were continually thinned through the effects of poor diet and rampant dysentery. Without the threat of a Jacobite field army to instil fear for the safety of their property, the merchants of Glasgow and Edinburgh shut tight their coffers, and the promised subsidies, needed to ensure that the government troops could enforce the rule of law beyond the Highland line, effectively dried up. Whitehall had been prepared increasingly to cede authority for Scotland to a single minister, Sir John Dalrymple of Stair, who was thus gifted an enormous degree of leeway in the settling of private scores. William III, who knew little of conditions in the north, sent repeated demands that hostilities should be speedily brought to an end so that the regiments, currently tied down in mundane garrison duties, might be redeployed for potentially decisive service on the Continent during the coming year. It is likely that he did not even read the bundle of documents presented for his signature by Dalrymple, including one containing the order that: 'If Mac Ian of Glen Co and that tribe can be separated from the rest, it will be a proper vindication of public justice to extirpate that set of thieves'.[26]

The collapse of formal military operations had cast those clans who remained in arms more firmly in the guise of traitors and criminals, while the continuing proclivity of the Highland rebels, in particular the Macdonalds of Glencoe, for extortion and plunder – which went largely unpunished – was a continuing reminder to the government, and to Dalrymple in particular, of the weakness of the executive's power. Despite James's reticence in making his commands known, a combination of hefty bribes and the desire to take advantage of the amnesty, in the hope of biding their time till more favourable circumstances for a general rising emerged, led the majority of the clans to come slowly in to take the oath of allegiance to William before the deadline of 1 January 1692. The harshness of the winter had also served to compel obedience, as James's instructions permitting the submission of the clans arrived in the final days of 1691, prompting a last-minute rush of Highlanders into Fort William to make their peace with the authorities, including Alasdair MacIain of Glencoe, who had simply followed the lead of his chief, Macdonald of Glengarry.[27] Unfortunately, Dalrymple was intent upon inflicting a lesson on the recalcitrant Highlanders and urged Livingston 'not [to] trouble the Government with prisoners' after the planned destruction of Appin, Lochaber and Glencoe.[28] Originally it had been intended that Invergarry Castle would also be taken, adding a solid military objective to the vengeful raids, but unfortunately the siege train did not arrive and Dalrymple's murderous gaze settled solely upon Glencoe.

Dalrymple suppressed letters that would have proved that MacIain, however belatedly, had taken the necessary oaths, and concurred with the

Scottish Privy Council in declaring that his submission was to be treated as invalid and that, henceforth, the old man and his tenants were to be placed outside the normal operation of the law. Raiding and the attendant reprisals that it provoked were nothing new to the Highlands, while the use of overwhelming force against the civil population, to act as an example to other communities who harboured insurgents, was an established, if less than edifying, military technique in the hardened theatre of European war. Moreover, MacIain and his men were no strangers to inflicting violence and robbery on rival districts, and had always accepted the dangers that they ran in living by the sword. Consequently, the concept of Glencoe as a punitive raid – even though, to date, Scotland had been spared the type of atrocities that had marred the Jacobite war in Ireland – would have shocked few in either the political nation or the wider Highland community. What marked out the government raid on Glencoe as an act of singular brutality was the manner in which it was conducted, with the military establishment at Fort William effectively looking the other way while Robert Campbell of Glenlyon accepted the hospitality of the laird of Glencoe and his tenants, announcing that he and his men had merely come on a tax collecting mission, before launching a premeditated and murderous assault on their hosts in the early hours of 13 February 1692. It left thirteen men – including MacIain, who was slain in his nightshirt at his own bedside – and more than thirty-two women and children shot, bayoneted, or left to die of exposure amid freezing temperatures and heavy snows. While the village burned and the war cries of clan Campbell subsided, the Governor of Fort William noted dryly that 'I have ruined Glencoe', as the buildings were destroyed, the livestock driven off, and the goods of the Macdonalds left 'a prey to the soldiers' of Argyll's regiment.[29] The random nature of the killings, which failed to kill or capture the overwhelming majority of MacIain's fighting men but butchered many of their families, ensured that the manner of retribution, though certainly sudden as intended, could not be kept secret for long. The massacre of innocents, combined with the duplicity involved in the breaking of all customary taboos regarding the welcoming of strangers, managed briefly to transform Lowland society's response to the Highlander from terror and loathing to sympathy for a foe grievously wronged. Subsequent inquiries in 1693 and 1695 were forced to consider – but largely fought shy of apportioning – blame for the murders, and cast a long shadow over the record of the civil and military administration of William's northern kingdom, and those of his servants who had shown little compunction in misleading their sovereign in their haste to extract a private and bloody price for their past sufferings and humiliations.

Though the glens may well have been pacified far earlier and more effectively had Dalrymple listened to the advice of Major-General Mackay, and authorised a vigorous conventional military campaign over the previous summer, the thought of fresh massacres certainly helped to concentrate the minds of other clan chiefs and to significantly lessen their appetite for further resistance to the Williamite government. Over the following months the last sparks of rebellion were allowed to go out, but although many of Claverhouse's former officers chose to go into exile, offering their swords to their King at St Germain, the clan system remained subdued but intact, prohibiting – even if the desire or the means had existed to effect it – the mass exodus of Highland soldiers to France in order to serve alongside their Irish counterparts. One hundred and fifty Scottish officers, veterans of Killiecrankie, Dunkeld and Cromdale, did manage to seek out their sovereign at his new residence, but without their men behind them there was little hope of finding them suitable employment, and to avoid becoming yet another drain upon the King's already overstretched resources, they took service as private soldiers in a specially raised Scottish company in the French army. Receiving orders that the new regiments were to leave for the war in Spain, James summoned them to his palace, on the eve of their departure, for one final review. As drums rolled, the King appeared before them theatrically wrapped in the folds of a long black cloak, to bestow on them the parting blessing 'of a King and a father', commiserating with their misfortunes and loss of status – for 'I cannot express to you how terrible it is for me to see so many brave and worthy gentlemen, reduced to the rank of simple soldiers' – before walking through their ranks, speaking a few brief words of encouragement to each man in turn, promising that he would not forget them and pledging that: 'If it pleases God for me to be re-established on the throne, I will compensate you for your sufferings and repay you for your devotion to me'.[30] As they marched out of the gates of St Germain and down the tree-lined avenue that would set them back on the road to Paris, and eventually to the frontier fortresses, James withdrew into his private chamber for the rest of the day, shedding hot tears at the thought of their sacrifice, and in the recognition of his own reduced circumstances which had made him powerless to help them in their time of greatest need. Three years later a touching sequel to these events would be played out, as a handful of survivors from this group returned to St Germain from the battlefields of Catalonia and, seeing the little Prince of Wales taking his exercise in the castle grounds with his governor and attendants, thrust their arms through the palace railings, calling out to the child and wishing him well. Though Jacobite propagandists would later seek to stress the gravity and maturity with which the 7-year-old addressed the bedraggled party of his father's soldiers – thanking them for their services in unrealistically high-flown terms – the Prince certainly followed, with little prompting, the lessons on the necessity of charity repeatedly taught to him by his parents, throwing to the men the purse containing his pocket money – 12 pistoles, or slightly less than £10 sterling – and commanding them to drink a health to King James, as the grown men pressed forward to kiss his small hand.[31] Such examples of devotion, emphasising the selflessness of both the exiled Stuarts and those who sought to serve them, were to become the staples of Jacobite hagiography, stirring the emotions and inspiring the love and fidelity of those who had given up much to follow their cause. However, such deeply sentimental motifs, bordering at times upon the maudlin, played less well outside the exile community. They exuded a particular form of tragedy and hopelessness which only struck a truly popular chord in England and Scotland with the Romantic revival of the nineteenth century, when the Cardinal Duke of York slumbered safely in a tomb paid for by a Hanoverian king, the Jacobite cause was safely dead, and all that was expected of its new and largely bourgeois 'adherents' was a sense of melodrama, rather than a commitment to a life of covert and treasonable action which threatened poverty and the tug of the hangman's noose at every turn.

Yet if James had been unable to provide for those pauperised remnants of his officer corps that had come over to him from Scotland in the latter half of 1692, there had been every hope at the beginning of the year that his own political fortunes were on the rise once again. The marquis de Louvois had always been one of the exiled King's sternest critics, his intuition backed by the damning empirical evidence of d'Avaux's reports and by the shattered wreck of the Franco-Irish venture in Ireland. His sheer appetite for disciplined hard work had made him indispensable to Louis XIV's Ministry of War, despite the disapproval of madame de Maintenon, and his word had counted for much in destroying the credit of James II's fresh schemes for the invasion of England, almost as soon as they were presented to his master for discussion. However, his continual labours, coupled with his irregular yet gluttonous diet, led to the sudden and dramatic collapse of his health in July 1691. Appropriately enough for one who had devoted his life and all his professional energies to the service of the French Crown, he was gripped by stomach pains as he worked at his desk alongside his King, and despite the despatch of the royal surgeon to his bedside, he was dead of a seizure within a matter of hours. Coming so soon after the premature death of his rival de Seignelay, the Minister of the Marine, Louvois's unexpected demise created a void at the heart of France's military affairs which could not easily be filled by any one individual. Ordinarily it might have been expected that his son, the marquis de Barbezieux, would succeed him in his office, but even though he had gained valuable experience serving at his father's side, the young man as yet lacked the years and the necessary gravitas to assume such a major responsibility in the state. Next, Louvois's former assistant, the marquis de Chamlay, was offered the chance to buy the position but declined on the grounds of conscience, feeling that he could not act to dispossess the son of his old friend of that which was rightfully his. Consequently, a compromise was arrived at whereby Barbezieux would hold the honour of the office, while Chamlay would act as the principle military advisor to both the Minister and the King. However, the result of this division of responsibility was that Louis XIV became more closely involved with the day-to-day direction of the war, as even relatively routine matters of military policy and logistics were forwarded to him by Barbezieux and Chamlay for his final decision. Unlike Louvois, the King of France felt an emotional debt to his exiled cousin that went far beyond any clinical assessment of his advantage as a pawn in the diplomatic struggle for dominance in Europe, or as an instrument for the destruction of English power. He held it a sacred duty to undertake, as far as it was possible, the restoration of the legitimate King of England, and as 1691 came to a close he was greatly encouraged in this endeavour by the conjoining of his personal sentiments with growing evidence from his ministries (and the spy network they employed) that the opportunity clearly existed to fulfil his obligations to James II and, at the same time, to deliver the knock-out blow to one of the most formidable powers in the coalition ranged against him. If in the summer James had begun to appear something of a forlorn figure at the festivities of the French court, then by the winter of 1691 he was once again at the centre of its policies, closeted for long hours with the King, and gratified almost beyond his dreams that plans for the invasion of England were again being considered. 'I have lost a good Minister', Louis confided gruffly to his cousin, 'but neither your affairs nor mine shall go the worse for it', and so – for a time, at least – it seemed.[32]

The quality of intelligence flowing into St Germain had given good reason to believe that a major cleavage in the royal family between Queen Mary and her sister Anne might serve as a catalyst for further dissent. The parliamentary sessions that year had been bitter and niggardly, with the subsidies for the prosecution of the war and for William's own supply being fiercely contested. Criticisms levelled against the awarding of English honours, offices, and commands to the King's Dutch favourites and commanders – such as Bentinck, Ginkel, and Solms – increased enormously in terms of their frequency and venomous strength. Meanwhile, Marlborough was smarting after being denied the position of Quartermaster-General following his successes in Ireland, and refused to accompany William to the Continent in order to oversee the coming year's campaign. Regular meetings in the Cockpit at Whitehall united Shrewsbury, Russell and Godolphin in the interest of Princess Anne and moved them, along with Marlborough, to maintain a regular correspondence with St Germain through their friends and kinsmen.

Despite his betrayal of James on Salisbury Plain, Marlborough now contemplated turning his coat once more and delivering the control of the army back to his former master. He hoped to obtain a pardon from the former King, partly in recognition of his following within the English military establishment, and partly as a result of his hold over Princess Anne – through his domineering wife, Sarah – and his close personal contacts with the exiled Jacobite court through his sister-in-law, Frances, Lady Tyrconnel and his nephew, the Duke of Berwick. At the beginning of December 1691, Anne had taken the dramatic step of writing to her father begging forgiveness for deserting him in 1688, for 'if wishes could recall what is past, I had long since redeem'd my fault', and pledging that she was 'very desirous of some safe opertunity to make you a sincere and humble offer of my duty and submission to you, and to beg you will be assured that I am both truly concern'd for the misfortune of your condition, and sencible as I ought to be, of my own unhappiness as to what you may think I haue contributed to it'.[33] As several of the major players who had turned their backs on James three years before struggled to build bridges to make amends with their fallen King, William III now appeared to be the monarch deserted by his followers, surrounded only by an isolated clique of foreign advisors. History seemed to be on the verge of repeating itself, with society's élites preparing to jettison another unpopular monarch with the assistance of an outside power. It seemed a highly auspicious moment to contemplate military action on behalf of King James, as Melfort wrote to Louis XIV in January 1692: 'That, at first, the prince of Orange was beloved. But that now he is much hated and despised; and that they publickly speak ill of him every where', while the troops were ill paid, the militia unreliable and the High Churchmen ready to come to terms and to act on James's behalf.[34] At the same time, Queen Mary's demand that her sister should dismiss Lady Marlborough from her service led to a final and very public breach in their relations, with the heavily pregnant Anne refusing to abandon her friend, even though she was threatened with having half of her parliamentary grant revoked. The following day, Marlborough was deprived of his courtly offices and military commands, on charges of corruption and extortion, while Princess Anne, forced out of her lodgings in the Cockpit, left for the country soon afterwards with Sarah Churchill defiantly at her side, and Godolphin loudly protesting against the wrong that had been done to his friends.

None of this intelligence was missed by King Louis's ministers, who received extremely sanguine reports from their agents, such as the abbé Renaudot, that: 'The number of . . . [James's] servants increases from day to day, and in some places they are three to one. It has been necessary to send a Regiment of thirteen Companies to Norwich, for fear of a rising. Several towns and counties have elected members well

affected to the King to vacant seats. Everything tends to the same design
. . . but the different opinions as to the methods for obtaining this end
are the greatest obstacles, and it is to be feared it will be impossible to
unite them unless the King arrives in person, with a good body of troops'.
This latter caveat appeared to be less of an obstacle now that Sarsfield's
Irish soldiers were arriving in large numbers on the coasts of Brittany,
and the French navy, chafing after a year of relative inactivity in which
they had failed to press their advantage over the English fleet, looked
expectantly to the optimistic plans of their new minister, Pontchartrain,
to seize the initiative, destroying their foes piecemeal, catching the
English and Dutch fleets before they had time to join together and
mounting a successful invasion of England in the window of opportunity
provided. As Louis XIV signed the orders authorising the expedition,
even James's personal life seemed to contribute to the prevailing climate
of hope and expectation, with his wife announcing her pregnancy to the
court. The birth of a second surviving child to James and Mary of
Modena would, it was felt, lay to rest the allegations of the King's
infertility and the slanders – which had already begun to abate – that the
Prince of Wales had been no more than a suppositious infant.[35] While
William and Mary remained childless, and Anne had only one surviving
and frequently poorly son, James might conceivably be the father of two
healthy young sons within a matter of months, adding to the impression
(shared by many Tories) that the future lay securely with his own exiled
bloodline, rather than with the withering stems of his first family, cursed
by God for their impious betrayal of their remaining parent.

Sarsfield had sailed out of Cork harbour with the last of the 'Wild
Geese' on 22 December 1691, having been taken aback by the
determination of his men to embark for France alongside their wives and
children. Although he had only ever envisaged the officer corps taking
advantage of the clause in the Treaty of Limerick that permitted the
'families' of soldiers to accompany them into exile, he quickly came to
realise that he would have to acquiesce in allowing the hundreds of
dependants who thronged his camp to go aboard the transports, if he did
not want to see mass desertions or experience the mutiny of his troops.
Due to this increase in numbers, and the tendency of Ginkel and the
administration in Dublin to place fresh bureaucratic obstructions in his
way, he arrived in France later than planned. James had clearly been
troubled by Sarsfield's failure to appear before him at a rendezvous of
senior officers in Rennes at the beginning of January 1692 – fearing with
some reason that he might be seeking to establish his own authority over
that of the King with the new army – and ordered him to report to him
immediately on his arrival, so that colonels might be appointed to the
embryonic regiments on his advice, 'provided you arrive in any
reasonable time'.[36] James had already sent his envoys Colonel Lee and

John Kearney to Brittany in order to survey the quality of the troops and to find them food and lodgings, but their tasks were far from easy. Units had been broken up and despatched from Ireland at different times and on different transports, while the Breton villagers on whom they were quartered were anything but welcoming, given that they had barely enough resources to see themselves and their own families through the harsh winter months. It was reported that after weeks spent in transit camps, and several days cramped in the holds of the transports, more than 1,500 soldiers had fallen ill, while many came ashore clad only in rags and were reduced to begging in the countryside until supplies were made available to them from the French depots. James had argued forcefully that his army, although paid for and armed by the French, should be largely autonomous, with its regiments being permanently brigaded together, and himself arbitrating on all matters of discipline and having the final say in the appointment of both senior and junior officers. Unfortunately, while Louis XIV was prepared to countenance James the privilege of awarding his own commissions, he would reserve for himself the final say in their dispositions, dividing the regiments between different theatres of war as he saw fit, and ensuring that they swore an oath of loyalty to France rather than to Ireland and the British Isles. Furthermore, James had hoped that by keeping the numbers in each company relatively small and having sixteen rather than fourteen companies allocated to each regiment, he might be able to find fitting employment for the large numbers of displaced officers who had sought to resume their profession at his side. However, once again, Louis refused to allow the Irish Brigade preferential treatment and, in a measure which would also minimise the cost to the French treasury, ruled that contrary to previous agreements the 'Wild Geese' would receive parity of wages with the French conscripts, which was substantially less than they had been receiving (in theory, if not always in practice) according to James's English establishment. Sadly, the King was forced to acknowledge that the pay of his men 'will fall short of what they were to have in Ireland', while attempting to sweeten the pill by promising 'that all field and other officers and all private soldiers . . . when it shall please God to restore him to his kingdoms, shall receive so much in money or lands as shall complete their full pay'. However, some of the more intractable problems deriving from their change of political masters, and the corresponding alterations in their terms of service, had fortunately already been solved by the experience of Mountcashel's Brigade on their arrival in France, almost two years previously. Though nothing could prevail upon the French authorities to issue the Irish soldiers with bayonets, and until the late 1690s they were forced to stream into the attack wielding their muskets like clubs, the decision to issue the Regiment Clare with the cast-off grey uniforms and white cockades from various units of Louis XIV's army provoked a mutiny, which was only resolved when it was promised to equip the soldiers with the scarlet coats befitting men of the regular British line. Thus, it was comparatively easy for James to oversee the standardisation of dress in his new regiments along previously established models, and to preserve the fiction that his redcoats actually represented the legitimate British army, albeit an army that was, for the time being, very much in waiting.[37]

James had not been slow in leaving St Germain for the coast in December 1691, setting up his headquarters at Nantes, overseeing the disembarking of his soldiers and establishing training camps for them inland. Though recognising the difficulties Sir Richard Neagle was facing in 'regulating our troops . . . [with] so many deserving men being to be provided for, and so few places to be disposed of', he busied himself with signing batches of commissions for his new army and confirming those who had been prominent in the Irish war – such as Berwick, Sarsfield, Galmoy, Simon Luttrell and Lord Grand Prior – with colonelcies. In expectation that a series of large risings would greet his landing, with, it was claimed, 'great numbers of armes . . . privately bought by Catholicks and other Loyal persons, men listed and Regiments formed; so that in some of the Northern Countys particularly Lancashire they were so zealous, that eight Regiments of horse and dragoons completely formed', James also sent over a commission to the Earl of Montgomery, the son of his Chamberlain, Lord Powis, authorising him to raise his own cavalry regiment, together with a large bundle of counter-signed but otherwise blank commissions which allowed him to appoint his junior officers as he saw fit. At the same time, as the French expeditionary fleet and transports began to assemble in the north off the coasts of Normandy, and in the south at Toulon, James appointed Thomas Stratford to act as his consul at Brest and to take charge of receiving the tenth share of all prize money from newly licensed Jacobite privateers – appropriately named the *Prince of Wales*, *Berwick*, *Sarsfield*, *Benediction* and *Providence* – which operated out of that port and St Malo. Through the late winter months and on into the spring, the Irish regiments were trained and drilled under the watchful eyes of officers drawn from the Gardes Françaises, while the Duke of Berwick put the reformed Horse Guards through their paces and made sure that Sarsfield and his circle did not use the absence of the King to ease their own nominees into prestigious appointments to command the cavalry troops. Nine infantry regiments, each of two battalions, three companies of Scottish foot, two regiments of horse, two troops of Horse Guards, and two regiments of dismounted dragoons – who presumably would have been found mounts once they were landed in England – were thus established, and at the beginning of April they began the march to Normandy and the invasion ports, to await their transports across the Channel. The landing was to have taken place before the campaigning season had opened in Flanders, so that the Dutch would have to wait for their forage to ripen before sending their reinforcements back across to England. The initial plan, conceived in utmost secrecy in January 1692, had envisaged the fleet navigating a course through the Irish Sea to the Clyde, before landing the troops and munitions in the sheltered anchorage at Glasgow, and beginning a march down through the Lowlands and into Cumberland and Lancashire, where James and his commanders felt assured they would meet with plentiful recruits and the chance of major strongholds declaring for their cause. In such a light, it is easy both to understand the King's reticence in the winter of 1691–2 to let his Highland forces disband themselves, and to absolve him for much of the blame in allowing the chiefs to accept the Williamite amnesty ('to do what may be most for their own . . . safety') so late in the day and with such fatal consequences for the inhabitants of Glencoe.[38]

The King had counted on a force of between 25–30,000 men, including 3,000 horse and dragoons, in order to successfully prosecute the campaign, and argued that: 'if I come with . . . smaller, I shall run a great risque of not being joined by the English, who, in that case, will wait for the issue before they will hazard themselves. Whereas, on the contrary, if they see me at the head of such a good army, they will not hesitate to join me immediately upon my landing'.[39] Unsurprisingly, however, the French, with a mind to both their rapidly emptying financial reserves and the need to wage a war in Flanders that year, declined to authorise such an overwhelming use of force and granted instead a contingent of approximately 7–8,000 Frenchmen, alongside the Irish Brigade, who were brought under the unified command of Marshal de Bellefonds. With the defeat at the Boyne – which saw the quality of his generalship sharply questioned – still uppermost in his mind, it is significant that James was now concerned to obtain the greatest possible advantage over his foes, and to try to convince his hosts of the need to make him the master of such a powerful army that his victory would be assured and his military reputation restored before a shot was even fired. The projected landing in Scotland was quickly abandoned, with a much smaller descent – undertaken by the newly returned Major-General Buchan and his three companies of Scots, conveyed in a handful of transports and convoyed by two frigates – envisioned upon the east coast, with a landing in Aberdeenshire or the Mearns, and with approaches made to Lord Keith and Alexander Nairn of Sandford, to raise troops and seize Slains Castle until they were relieved by the invading forces.[40]

James had wanted Ambleteuse to be the site of the embarkation, on the grounds of the potent symbolism that it inspired – so that he might be seen to have landed as a fugitive and to have returned a conqueror from exactly the same spot – and favoured a quick crossing of the Channel and a landing in Kent, preferably at Dover. From there he would have led a lightening march on Rochester, to seize the fleet stores, equipment, and those ships that lay at anchor on the Medway. Believing, as did Louis XIV, 'that the Army would be directed by Marlborough, the Fleet by Russel, and a great part of the Church by the Princess Anne', James thought that if he got that far inland London would surrender before his army, and the rest of the country, taking its lead, would quickly submit. Initially the threat of invasion had not been taken particularly seriously, but as word of the preparations taking place on the coast of France reached England – the roads choked with supply columns, and the ports crammed with ships – something approaching panic set in. John Evelyn recorded rumours that a rising was felt to be imminent and that, at the beginning of May, 'the reports of an invasion being now so hot, alarmed the city, court and people exceedingly', while the abbé Rizzini thought that: 'if a landing is effected, the least good to be hoped from it . . . will be the lighting up of a Civil War in that kingdom, whence the most useful consequences will arise for France, in diverting Orange's forces, combined with a vigorous attack upon his confederates, who finding themselves abandoned by him, will be forced to sue for peace, which could not fail to be advantageous to the English King'. Livestock was driven inland to avoid it being seized to provision an invading army, the militia was called out, and regiments of the line were concentrated outside Portsmouth. Meanwhile, Lady Ailesbury paid a visit to Princess Anne – recovering from the death of her latest child shortly after his birth – to warn her that a Jacobite invasion force would be landing in England within twenty-four hours and that 5,000 troops had been detailed to escort her back to her father, if she so desired.[41] Marlborough, along with many other Jacobite suspects, had been confined to the Tower of London, while the home of the Bishop of Rochester was turned over by government agents searching for incriminating evidence. Regiments were hastily prevented from taking ship for Flanders, as King William had his private yacht made ready at The Hague so that he could race back to assume command of the defence of England if a landing did, indeed, take place. Yet, while many of the nobility and even some among her Privy Council began to reconsider their allegiances, Queen Mary's courage held firm. Despite being cursed by a debilitating cold that had laid her low over Easter and had caused her to miss church attendance for the first time in more than a decade, she took steps to discredit her father's manifesto, smuggled into the country in large numbers as a prelude and a rallying call to the counter-revolution.

Melfort's was the guiding hand behind the drafting of the King's declaration and, unfortunately, he stamped the document with a vindictive and unyielding tenor that was wholly counter-productive and completely out of step with the temper of the times. If James was to provoke a mutiny in the fleet and drive his coach largely unopposed from

Rochester to his palace at Whitehall, then it was the backbone of Tory England that he needed to win over to his cause, with assurances about the future survival of the Anglican Church and the promise of pardons for all those among the ruling élite who had forsaken him in 1688–9. The document did manage to highlight several areas where William's government was genuinely unpopular, pledging to send home the Dutch and German regiments 'as soon as we shall be fully settled in the quiet and peaceable possession of our Kingdoms' and underlining the damage that had been done to the nation's economy through the waging of a major European war, with 'more money . . . drained out of the purses of our subjects in the compass of that time, than during the whole reigns of many of our predecessors put together . . . transported in specie into foreign parts, and for ever lost to the Nation'. However, despite prohibiting the 'collecting or paying any of the illegal taxes lately impos'd upon the Nation' and promising to 'protect and maintain the Church of England, as it is now by Law Established', the declaration was over-long, convoluted, and extremely bitter in its reiteration of the wrongs done to James at the time of the Revolution, the threats made to his life while he was at Rochester, and the ingratitude of those of his family, friends and subjects who had connived in his downfall. While the King's enduring commitment to 'Liberty of Conscience' might have eased the fears of the Dissenting community, in the eyes of the Tories it seemed to counteract the earlier pledge to protect the Anglican faith, and when combined with the generally threatening tone of the document towards any who did not 'return to their duty, and repair to our standard', might appear to have destroyed any credit the King's promises might have won with the Dissenters. James and Melfort would seem to have learned nothing from the experience of the successful Restoration of 1660, where conciliation, tact, and an air of ambiguity had achieved far more than a force of arms ever could. By way of contrast, the declaration of 1692 appeared to accept that the crown was to be won back primarily through military action, with the King's subjects being exhorted to seize 'any of our forts', or to bring 'over to us any ships of war, or troops in the usurper's army, or any new rais'd and arm'd by themselves' in order to atone for past misconduct. Far more damaging, however, was the impression given by the long list of names exempted from a general pardon, that the return of the King was to be accompanied by a bloody settling of scores, which would send not only leading figures of the Revolution – such as the earls of Sunderland, Bath, and Danby – to their deaths at Tower Hill or Tyburn gallows on charges of treason, but would also seek to extend the capital penalty to a host of lesser figures – such as the jury that had sentenced John Ashton to the scaffold, and Edwards, Napleton, and Hunt, the fishermen 'who offered personal indignities to us at F[a]versham' – who were of no account in the affairs of the nation, but had nonetheless attracted the vengeful ire of an unforgiving sovereign. It seemed to many that terror and conquest, with the help of a foreign army, were to be the hallmark of James's rule once he was successfully restored, and though William was compared to the Emperor Nero in the body of the text, it was clear that in seeking 'the re-establishment of the greatness of the English monarchy' it was his uncle who appeared to envisage the more absolute style of kingship. While a commitment to a parliament was implicit in the declaration, the earlier commitment to that body being 'free' to decide on the fate of the constitution was now withdrawn, and the 'illegality' of the legislatures that had sat since 1689 was clearly held to have invalidated all the legislation passed since that date. Faced by such a bleak and uncompromising document, some English Jacobites tried to comfort themselves that the declaration was actually a government forgery and issued their own more temperate manifesto that pretended to have come straight from the presses of Paris and St Germain.[42] James's declaration was, consequently, a propaganda gift to his opponents and Queen Mary made sure that it was widely reprinted under the government stamp and circulated together with a comprehensive reply and exegesis, which sought to demonstrate the ruin and bloodshed that James and his Franco-Irish army would wreak upon his subject peoples, if he was ever allowed to return.

However, while the disastrous nature of the declaration and the corrosive impact that it had on the King's potential followers among the crucial High Tory constituency was later to be recognised and debated at some length even by his official biographer, James appeared to be unaware of the destructive character of the document he was promoting, and continued to authorise the despatch of fresh copies to Scotland and England throughout the spring and early summer. The princely courts of Europe were becoming receptive to his envoys once more, and Sir John Lytcott set out for Rome at the end of April, to lobby for funds from the Pope and to attempt to prise Innocent XII further from his alliance with the Emperor. Thus it was with a sense of optimism that James presided at a brief ceremony in the chapel of St Germain shortly before his departure for the army, creating his 4-year-old son a Knight of the Garter, together with Lords Powis and Melfort.[43] In his absence, the plans for the invasion had changed once again, for with the army concentrated in the Cotentin peninsula of Normandy, it had been decided that the cavalry should go aboard their transports at Le Havre and that the foot should embark from La Hogue, for a general rendezvous with their escorts off the Isle of Ushant. Consequently, James hurried to Caen on 14/24 April 1692 together with Marshal de Bellefonds and the Duke of Berwick, to oversee the naval preparations. Unfortunately, at this point his luck failed him, with contrary winds bottling up his ships for the best part of four weeks and a number of his transports being damaged by a storm that suddenly blew up at Le Havre. James had always realised that everything depended upon the speed and secrecy with which the two halves of his escort met – having assembled at Brest under Admiral Tourville and at Toulon under Admiral d'Estrees – but the Mediterranean fleet had failed in its first attempt to slip through the Pillars of Hercules and had been severely battered by the elements, losing two ships off the Spanish enclave of Ceuta in North Africa. As a result, all chance of preventing the English and Dutch fleets from uniting, and of bottling up the Portsmouth squadron while embarkation was taking place, was lost as d'Estrees's ships struggled to make progress against contrary winds in the Bay of Biscay and Tourville's uncompromising instructions from Louis XIV to seek out and destroy the English fleet assumed an importance and dimension, as regards the expedition, that had never been envisaged originally. Tourville had been stung by de Seignelay's bitter criticisms of his conduct at the battle of Beachey Head two years before, and now determined that his reputation as the King's loyal servant should not be tarnished any further through a refusal to follow his orders to the letter. Louis XIV had confidently predicted to his courtiers that a great naval battle would decide the fate of the invasion, but his enjoinder (passed through Pontchartrain) 'to engage [the enemy], whatever their strength' and the hastily scribbled postscript in his own hand, confiding that this 'is my will and I wish it to be exactly followed', certainly did not anticipate the uniting of the allied fleets and the failure of d'Estrees to reinforce Tourville's now heavily outnumbered men-of-war.[44]

It therefore came as something of a surprise when James and the Duke of Berwick were stirred from their lodgings at La Hogue on 19/29 May 1692, by the sound of the distant rumble of guns out at sea. All day they waited on the cliff tops for a sight of their fleet, but it was not until the following morning that they saw a line of ships flying the French fleur-de-lys standards edging their way towards the shore. They let out a cheer of welcome, believing 'that our victorious fleet was come to transport us to England'. Unfortunately their joy was short-lived, as it soon became clear that these vessels were just one component of Tourville's fleet that had scattered before the allied fleet. Realising the danger that lay in the Admiral following his orders precisely, Pontchartrain had already written to Tourville rescinding them, but the despatch had not reached him by the time that he had sighted Russell's fleet off the Normandy coast at Cape Barfleur and given the instructions to engage his foes. It may be that he had hoped that the English Admiral, who had given repeated assurances to the court of St Germain of his goodwill, might have chosen that moment to signal his change of allegiance and to lead his ships over to their side. However, while it is likely that the contents of King James's declaration had sent a chill through Russell's heart and thoroughly shaken his resolve to betray his joint sovereigns, he was also a man of heady ambition, and it was probably the realisation that his combined fleet of 88 ships and galleys exactly outnumbered the French by a ratio of 2:1 which proved decisive, causing him to emphasise his devotion to William and Mary before battle was joined by making his crews swear the oath of allegiance afresh upon their quarterdecks.[45] Tourville's fleet had the weather gauge and closed rapidly with the allied ships, till the lead vessels were separated by no more than the distance of a musket shot. Aboard one of the French vessels, the King's son Henry Fitzjames watched the mute approach of his foes, until a Dutch battleship unilaterally broke the tension, firing a ragged broadside in the direction of the French line. It did little damage, but was answered by a general fusillade that buried both sides under a thick pall of smoke and flame, as guns belched shot across the decks and into the hulls and rigging of their foes. Despite his lesser numbers, Tourville initially held the advantage as he managed to concentrate his fire more effectively on the point at which the converging lines of ships eventually collided with one another but, as the morning slipped away and afternoon came on, Sir Cloudisley Shovell managed to nudge his ship through the French line, threatening to cut off the entire enemy rearguard (or Blue Squadron) as other English vessels followed suit and attempted to envelop their foes on all sides. Realising the danger immediately, Tourville – aboard a flagship whose decks had been ploughed into jagged shards, and whose cables had been cut in an attempt to avoid collision with one of the fireships that had been loosed on the French fleet – took advantage of a rapidly descending sea-fog to signal to his captains to break off the engagement, and to fight their way clear as best they could. The allied vessels continued the pursuit until nightfall, but by first light the sound of Tourville's signal gun was enough to reunite the majority of his fleet and to allow it to flee in relatively good order towards the fortified coastline of Cape La Hogue. Three detached ships, including the Admiral's former flagship the *Soleil Royal*, ran in to the harbour at Cherbourg, but were caught by English fireships and longboats in the shallows and, lacking artillery support from the shore, were burned to the waterline. The country folk watched as flames licked the stern of the *Soleil Royal* and the proud frieze, depicting a triumphant Louis XIV trampling enemy princes underneath his horses' hooves, slowly cracked in the heat, before catching flame and disintegrating, showering the waves with droplets of burning paint, gold leaf, and swirling clouds of charcoal and dust.[46]

Despite this setback, the French navy could still comfort itself that, although heavily outnumbered, it had fought the English and Dutch fleets to a standstill and had managed to extricate itself, with the only losses occurring directly as the result of the executive's failure to properly

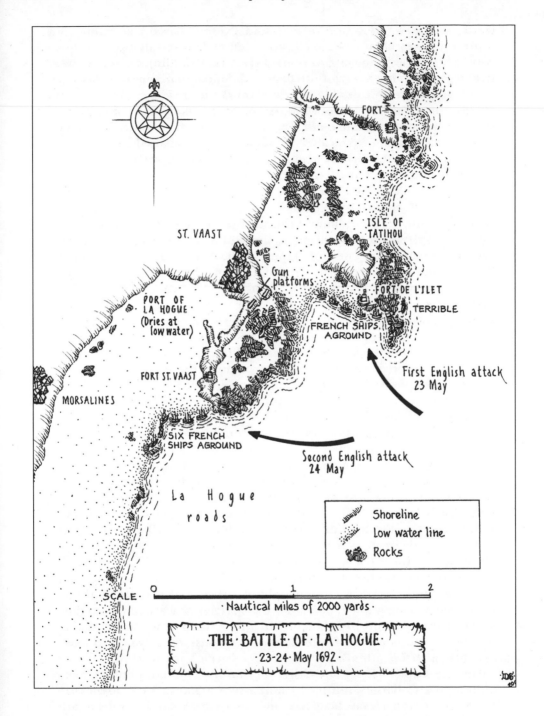

FORT

ISLE OF
TATIHOU

ST. VAAST

Gun
platforms

FORT DE L'ILET

PORT OF
LA HOGUE
(Dries at
low water)

TERRIBLE

FRENCH SHIPS
AGROUND

First English attack
23 May

FORT ST. VAAST

MORSALINES

SIX FRENCH
SHIPS AGROUND

Second English attack
24 May

La   Hogue
roads

	Shoreline
	Low water line
	Rocks

SCALE

0   1   2

· Nautical miles of 2000 yards ·

THE · BATTLE · OF · LA · HOGUE
· 23-24 · May 1692 ·

fortify the ports along the Norman and Breton coasts. Unfortunately, while those vessels that were either faster or had simply suffered less damage were able to outrun their pursuers, rounding the cape and stealing away to the safety of the heavily defended harbour at St Malo, a dozen ships under Tourville – now aboard the *Ambitieux* – could not weather the headland without the risk of being taken. They stood in to shore in the safe anchorage of La Hogue, taking refuge under its coastal batteries. There, three days after the disaster, James chaired a meeting of the war council at which he and Tourville reached agreement that the battleships should not be beached, but should be saved and defended at all costs, by building new gun emplacements along the shore and calling up reserves of powder from depots across Normandy. Unfortunately, at some point the French Admiral reconsidered his judgement and decided to run the vessels aground, stripping them of their cannons and stores, a decision which James does not appear to have argued with, or even to have questioned, though it flew in the face of all that had already been agreed. Furthermore, once he had seen the ships brought in to shelter underneath the guns of the twin forts of St Vaast and de l'Ilet, resting on the sands at low tide, James urged that use be made of the numerous troops that were camped around his standard – still expectantly awaiting their embarkation – on the surrounding cliffs. In this manner, the crews might be reinforced, doubling or even tripling the numbers of armed men on board, and greatly enhancing the firepower that might be hurled against any would-be attackers. Yet Tourville, according to James, declined even this offer, feeling that it was 'a dishonour to commit the care and defence of his Ships to any but the Seamen themselves'. However, even if the Admiral had felt obliged to stand on his pride – and we only have the word of the King that he behaved in this manner – it might be felt that James could have sought to use his influence further. As it was, he apparently merely withdrew his suggestion and meekly retraced his footsteps back to his own headquarters, some distance away.

The intent of the English squadron, anchored just off the coast, was not hard to discern, as since before dawn on 23 May/3 June 1692 a succession of small boats had rowed in towards the sands, packed with heavily armed sailors and officers who busied themselves taking soundings and measuring the draught at the entrance to the harbour. James had reputedly gone onboard the *Saint-Philippe* that evening to dine with the captain and his officers, but the sudden bombardment that began to issue from the English ships after dusk caused him to leave abruptly with his attendants and take a barge back to shore. In the meantime, Captain Peregrine Osborne, Danby's son, led a little armada of longboats, barges, pinnaces and several fireships towards the six French men-of-war beached on the eastern sands underneath the guns of Fort de l'Ilet. The *Terrible*, its hull already shattered during the battle at sea, made for the easiest target, and the crew of a fireship was able to quickly swarm aboard the stricken vessel and set its timbers aflame. However, a sudden cannonade from the fort managed to hole Osborne's barge, grazing his leg and leaving him and his crewmen to flounder in the rising waters until another boat could come up to haul them to safety one by one from their sinking craft. Initial disciplined volleys, fired through the raised gun-ports, stalled the assault for several minutes until the gunfire slackened, as the guns of the larger support vessels began to play on the hulls of the French ships and as a fresh swell propelled several longboats up the beach, their crews spilling out onto the sands and overrunning the gun emplacements within a matter of minutes. Numerous sloops intended to assist in the troop embarkation littered the harbour and, amid the darkness and mounting confusion, Tourville and his officers attempted to rally their fleeing sailors, and to launch them in these craft to engage their foes. Elsewhere, the skeleton crews left behind on the battleships were gradually abandoning their posts, while an English longboat ran ashore and for a moment looked as if it was about to be swamped by the onrush of French and Jacobite soldiers who charged down to the shore from their cantonments. However, an over-confident cavalryman was plucked from his horse by a boathook as the English pushed their vessel back into the shallows, and their assailants fell back, stunned by the trooper's sudden and unexpected end. The five remaining French warships had now been gained by the English storming parties and fires lit upon their decks. As James and his eldest son peered out into the night, a magazine aboard one of the men-of-war exploded, briefly illuminating the scene as their foes collected their wounded from the beach and retired back to their boats as the tide began turn, sending them back out to sea to the accompaniment of a salvo from the landward decks of one of the three-deckers, whose guns had inexplicably been left onboard and which now exploded, sending shot screaming into the fort on the cliffs above. Seeing the danger at hand, James was told by his staff to abandon his position beside the shore guns, and he was hurriedly being bundled out of the entrenchments by French soldiers when the full weight of this broadside smashed into the works where he had been standing only a few moments before, leaving the shaken King to thank the peculiar operation of providence that had once more acted to save him from his enemies.[47]

Daylight brought little respite, as the English crews were reinforced and sent out again to destroy the six remaining enemy ships that lay helpless on the western sands. In the intervening hours nothing had been done to bolster the defenders' flagging morale, and the French officers were hard pressed to persuade their soldiers to remain at their posts to serve the guns at Fort St Vaast, as the small flotilla of English boats bore down upon them. From the breastworks that ran underneath the walls of the fort, James watched as his artillerymen fired blindly, and at extreme range, expending much of their powder long before the boats presented themselves as viable targets. Even as the attackers pulled alongside the stranded hulks and began to swarm over the sides of the ships, the French crews attempted to make their escape, dropping over the opposite side into the bottoms of the cluster of boats that waited to carry them safely back to shore. Looking on as the English sailors stormed simultaneously across the decks of the *Galliard, St Louis, Bourbon, Tonnant, Fier* and *Fort*, scattering their enemies before them as though they were of no more account than handfuls of winnowed chaff, James found himself transported by a sudden patriotic joy that recalled his time as Lord High Admiral, and the ownership that he felt for the Royal Navy and all its achievements. Clapping wildly, the King excitedly exclaimed – in the midst of Marshal Bellefonds and his French staff officers – that 'none but my brave English could do so brave an action!'. As flames swept over the outlines of the beached warships and Vice-Admiral Rooke and Captain Osborne committed their fireships in order to burn the transports and shallops bunched up tightly together in the harbour, few outbursts of emotion could be said to have been so spectacularly misplaced, or so badly mistimed.[48] The response of Bellefonds and his men was unfortunately not recorded, but as the English boats bore away – with the sailors brandishing captured French colours and all the booty they could carry off the burning enemy ships – it was clear to them all that the chances for the successful invasion of England had, quite literally, gone up in smoke.

Surprisingly, almost the only person who continued to hope that a landing might still go ahead was James. Despite the wreckage of his fleet littering the rocks and sands of the bay, and every new tide washing up either fresh debris or the bodies of those French sailors who had been too tardy or too brave to make their escape in time, he refused to recognise his true predicament or to break camp, remaining for several more weeks on the coast of Normandy in the hope that Pontchartrain might still be able to conjure up a fresh fleet for him, and that the invasion could somehow be rescheduled for the late summer. Yet James, who had often led the English battle fleet out on campaign, must have known that for the time being French naval power had been broken in the Channel. He could not go on deceiving himself forever. His prime interest now was to keep his army together, and to this end he began to provide out of his own pocket for many of the Irish officers – and even two priests – who could not be found places within the French establishment. However, this could do no more than buy a little more time, some two months at the most, for his regiments to subsist in Normandy and to maintain the pretence that they represented an entirely separate force within the French army, which might remain under his direct and largely independent command. Such thoughts were to be sadly and finally dispelled in early June, when King Louis sent orders, from the siege lines at Namur, for the invasion army to break camp and disperse to the various theatres of the war – Flanders, Catalonia, and Savoy – where reinforcements were needed. His instructions brooked no argument and came as a shattering blow to James, whose dreams of reinvigorating his own military career and of maintaining direct control over the fate of his regiments were effectively destroyed by the flick of the Sun King's pen. Just as damaging was the impact that the news of the destruction of the invasion fleet had on domestic English political opinion. As the expedition was recast by Williamite propagandists as an exercise in aggression by a foreign power, preordained to fail through God's unerring providence towards his chosen Protestant people, it became a far easier matter to portray James as a 'hatchet-faced Jesuit', a religious bigot and the willing tool of the nation's enemies, who would take pleasure in visiting death and destruction upon his own subjects, were he ever to be restored. The vitriol that hallmarked the King's declaration of 1692 had certainly contributed to this impression, but it was the abject failure of James's military forces, and his French backers, that turned fear into derision and further eroded his reputation for personal bravery and competent generalship. It was his daughter Mary who was lauded as the hero of the hour, a second 'Gloriana' who had delivered England from a second Roman Catholic armada, just as surely as Queen Elizabeth had destroyed the first. Russell, the would-be traitor, was transformed into the champion of the Williamite nation, while Princess Anne hurriedly broke off all contact with her father and St Germain. Marlborough received his Whig relatives at the Tower and appealed to Danby, stressing his loyalty and begging for an early release. At Rome, Sir John Lytcott had been able to secure fresh subsidies for the exiled court and warm words of encouragement while plans for the invasion had been ongoing, but he noted the King's 'disappointment at La Hogue had cooled the zeal of his friends at Rome, and even of his Holiness himself', and that: 'Many here pretend . . . great inward zeal in their prayers for [James II]. But, if they do pray, they do it so as not to be seen of men, either in their closets, or, perhaps, the primitive grottoes and catacombs'. For the time being at least, the arms landed in the north of England were simply stockpiled, the orders for Major-General Buchan to set sail for Scotland were hastily rescinded, and the bundles of blank commissions, for regiments that were never now to be raised, were either consigned to the fire, or – as in the case of those entrusted to Colonel Parker at Standish Hall – simply bricked up behind the walls of a manor house, waiting for better times and for King James 'to come again'.[49]

The burning of his fleet and the dispersal of his army appears to have affected James's self-confidence far more seriously than the experience of his defeat on the Boyne. Indeed, to say that he was devastated by this turn of events might be something of an understatement, for he took the entire ownership of the catastrophe that had overcome the fleet at La Hogue upon himself. Yet while Hoffman, the Imperial Ambassador in London, was in no doubt that: 'The destruction of that Fleet is due to the Jacobites here, who gave King James, and consequently the King of France, false ideas of the English Fleet, assuring him it would never be ready to put to sea', James can be seen to have had nothing whatsoever to do with the decision of the French Admiral to fight at Barfleur, and can only be held responsible for failing to exercise his authority to the full at La Hogue, in not holding his staff accountable for their original decisions and for neglecting to push through his plan to reinforce the ships' crews with men drawn from his own ample forces. Yet, while Tourville was received graciously by Louis XIV and effectively absolved of his share of the blame for the disaster, James came to the conclusion that his own endeavours had been cursed by God and that it was his presence alongside the Franco-Irish battalions on the cliff tops that had precipitated the disaster. The 'hand of God', he declared, 'was most visibly apparent' at La Hogue, 'since without this the plan could not have failed, the King [Louis XIV] having organised it all so well'. The weather, he told the Bishop of Autun, had been the signal of the Almighty's displeasure, 'and nothing was anything more clearly shown . . . for, had not the winds been contrary to us and continually favourable to our enemies, the descent would have been made'. Indeed, so complete was his belief in the withdrawal of divine favour that he made a scene at the convent of Chaillot, snapping at the Abbess who had sought to commiserate with him that their prayers had not been answered, saying: 'It seems to me that you imagine that what you asked of God would have been better than what He did'. With his sleep pattern broken, he complained over the following months that he was often awake and troubled through the early hours of the morning and had no idea how best to combat his restlessness, asking the abbé de La Trappe if it was fitting, in his distraction, 'to rise to pray and praise God'. His profound disquiet manifested itself in his failure to report the news of his defeat directly to Louis – sending Melfort instead – and in the abject terms in which he addressed himself, as an unworthy supplicant, to his brother monarch in the accompanying correspondence, lamenting that: 'My evil star has influenced the arms of Your Majesty, ever victorious but when fighting for me. I entreat you therefore to interest yourself no more for a prince so unfortunate, but permit me to withdraw, with my family, to some corner of the world, where I may cease to be an interruption to Your Majesty's wonted course of prosperity and glory'.[50] The virtual destruction of James's self-confidence, which had begun upon Salisbury Plain, now culminated in the collapse of his military ambitions at

La Hogue, and marked a steady but nonetheless dramatic shift in his personal ambitions, away from the hopes of securing a temporal crown once again, to thoughts of salvation and the gaining of a spiritual one which could not be taken from him by the hands of men. This did not, however, spell the end of his determination to protect his own prerogatives as the rightful King of England, or those of his young son and heir, in whom all his worldly aspirations now came to be vested.

This growing 'cult' of family, centred on the royal exiles, was what finally prompted James to leave Normandy and head back to St Germain to be present at his wife's lying-in. The new child had been eagerly expected, with the King and his wife sending out invitations to the entire English court – including everyone from Queen Mary and Princess Anne, through to the members of the House of Lords and their wives, and the wife of the Lord Mayor of London – to come to their palace to witness the birth, under the protection and safe passage of the King of France. In the event, however, with the threat of invasion first waxing and then dramatically waning, only three individuals attempted to take advantage of the offer. Dr Hugh Chamberlain, a leading Protestant obstetrician – who had pronounced the Prince of Wales's birth to have been without taint – and Henry, Earl of Peterborough were simply refused passports by the English government, but the request of Theophilus, Earl of Huntingdon was treated with far greater suspicion and, while his house was ransacked for incriminating evidence, he was arrested and sent to the Tower. For Mary of Modena, the pregnancy had been a long and difficult one. The courtiers at Versailles feared that the hours she devoted to her prayers, continually on her knees, might further damage her health, and she herself sniped sourly at her husband's lack of attention, for: 'The King has not chosen to return from La Hogue, though he has nothing to keep him there, and my condition speaks for itself to make him come to me. In the meantime, he would not resolve upon anything'. To make matters worse, Catherine of Braganza, en route from London to Lisbon, paid her a visit during her long progress through France, and though she appears to have been delighted by the attentions of the little Prince of Wales, who came out to meet her at Pontoise, the atmosphere between the two queens, who had never got on despite their shared faith, was somewhat strained and their meeting was brief. With the baby already a fortnight overdue, Mary of Modena miserably declared that she trembled in dread of the birth 'and long for it to be over for everyone's sake'. This delay permitted James – who had managed to convince himself that the child would certainly be another son – to return to her side, just four days before she went into labour. Yet even though his intuition failed him, and his wife was delivered of a baby girl, the King's joy in holding a healthy child quickly outweighed his disappointment at her gender, and he declared in his clumsy, if not ham-fisted, manner that God had given them a 'consolation' in the time of their utmost distress. The name stuck, and though the infant would be baptised as Louise Marie Stuart, she would often be referred to as 'La Consolatrice' in the years to come.[51] It was an entirely fitting epithet, as during his last exile James's two young children represented his only real triumphs. The birth of his daughter seemed to give the lie to the claims that the Prince of Wales had been substituted at birth for the true, but stillborn, infant, and appeared as a fitting recompense for the two girls from his first marriage whom he felt had betrayed him.

Consequently, despite the tribulations of fresh defeat and the need to accommodate himself to the life of a permanent exile, it was with unfeigned delight and a rare sense of hope for the future of his line, that James entered the high-vaulted chapel at St Germain to celebrate his daughter's christening. The news from Flanders had been nothing but positive, with the fortress of Namur falling before the heavy French siege guns, and the army of William III failing to make an impression on Marshal Luxembourg's positions at Steinkirk. Amid the fearsome slaughter, the luckless Lord Mountjoy – only recently released from the Bastille in an exchange of prisoners – had received his death wound, while Major-General Mackay's appeals for help had gone unheeded by a stoical Count Solms, leaving the intrepid Scotsman to fall still shouting encouragement and breathing defiance as his brigade was overwhelmed on all sides. Such victories had added further lustre to the King of France's laurels and Louis had made it plain that, far from allowing his cousin to slip into obscurity, he would continue to honour him as he had in the past and would stand as sponsor, together with the duchesse d'Orléans, to his new child. Thus it was that – scarcely noticing the oppressive August heat that so troubled the ladies of the court – James took his place beside the French King, as the Archbishop of Paris scribed the sign of the cross on the brow of the struggling infant, and the statues of his ancestors the Capetian kings looked down from the walls upon a ceremony that even the exacting madame was forced to admit was a model of quiet dignity.[52] Yet if the life of Princess Louise Marie pointed the way ahead for a King anxious to preserve and stress his precious legacy, then just as important for James was the example of St Louis, whose stone figure loomed large in the chapel, emphasising that supreme virtue and salvation could only be achieved through suffering and resignation. It was a lesson that would not be lost on the former King as he struggled to chart his uncertain path in the years that still lay ahead.

CHAPTER SIX

The Shadow Court

The château of St-Germain-en-Laye was situated just 12 miles from Paris, on a commanding plateau above the river Seine. Since the twelfth century there had been a royal castle on the heights, but by the time of James's arrival all that remained of the medieval fortress was the much-modified shell of Charles V's keep and a deep moat that surrounded the residence on all sides. François I had initiated a comprehensive rebuilding of the site in 1539, sweeping away the mediaeval outbuildings and raising a renaissance palace about a central courtyard and the chapel of St Louis. It had not been substantially altered since, despite the addition of five rather disfiguring corner wings in 1680. Thus, the palace still bore the unmistakable imprint of its former owner, with François's personal badge of a fire-breathing salamander stamped on the enormous brick chimney that both dominated and heated the ballroom, and on the moulded balustrades and the clock-tower that overlooked the approaches and the quadrangle. Louis XIV had been born in the New Castle, and had occupied St Germain as his principal residence between 1660 and 1682. However, after the removal of the court to Versailles, the old palace had gone into rapid decline and had to be hurriedly renovated prior to Mary of Modena's arrival in December 1688. Long boarded-up windows had to be thrown open and set with new glass panes, while door locks had to be oiled or replaced, and scuffed and splintered parquet flooring was reset and waxed.

Yet, the major problem facing the royal exiles in their new home was, as Thierry Boucher and Edward Corp have pointed out in their studies of the court, an acute lack of space. This required the King to make greater use of his Bedchamber for the reception of visiting ambassadors and dignitaries, and ensured that the key personnel of the Jacobite court lived and worked in close proximity to one another. In this manner, the Duke of Berwick occupied a suite of rooms directly underneath those of his father, while the Duke of Powis was lodged below the Prince of Wales's apartments – which before 1682 had been occupied by the dauphin – and Lord Melfort's chambers adjoined those of Berwick, allowing him easy access to both the King and the Queen, whose quarters were above his own. Even though the royal family did not own any of the furniture at St Germain, and simply used that left behind or specially loaned to them out of store by Louis XIV, their

surroundings were certainly in keeping with their station, affording
King James a suite of rooms hung with a series of heavy tapestries
depicting the life of Joseph, and decorated throughout in crimson, with
his bed, armchairs and drapes matching in 'red . . . velvet, lined with
gold mohair'.[1] A vaulted balcony ran around the outside of the King's
apartments; this was once taken advantage of by the child of the Prince
of Wales's future governor – Francis Plowden – who, shut out of doors
by her mother as a punishment for a misdemeanour, had shinned over
the dividing balustrades and edged her way along the gallery until she
reached the glass doors that led into James's private suite. The frantic
search for the infant came to an end when Mrs Plowden was ushered
into the King's presence to find her errant daughter playing blissfully
on James's knee. However, while the royal couple might have chosen to
fill their rooms with exotic and highly ornate examples of Japanese
Imari ware and Chinese embroidery, it was this sense of barely
contained chaos – resulting from the cramped lodging of English, Irish,
Scottish, French, and Italian courtiers and servants cheek-by-jowl – that
appears to have prevailed at St Germain. On their first arrival at court,
Lord Ailesbury's bearers had to step gingerly over piles of timber stored
on the King's privy stairs, while in 1693 the French authorities were
presented with the bill for dredging and repairing the moat, after the
townsfolk complained of the smell occasioned by the mounds of refuse
dumped there by the castle's inhabitants, and the country folk looked
askance at James's laundry maids hanging their washing up to dry from
the boughs of their orchards. One solution might have been to have
moved the overspill from the royal household to the nearby New Castle,
but unfortunately the grand façade of the building could scarcely
conceal the dilapidated and dangerous state of its walls and rooms,
which had remained unoccupied since the departure of Louis XIV.
Without the resources to repair its crumbling fabric, James was unable
to provide lodgings for the poorer members of his entourage, who
crowded into the surrounding town, almost doubling its population and
reviving its declining fortunes, but also to some degree rendering it
ungovernable.

    While James provided subsidies for those courtiers prepared to forsake
life at the Old Castle and to rent rooms in the municipality, the Duchess
of Tyrconnel was among those lucky enough to possess sufficient
resources to buy an imposing residence in the centre of the town. The
majority were less fortunate, as rents rose in line with the explosion in
demand for accommodation, and the existing provisions for health care
and basic public amenities struggled to keep pace with the needs of this
new and rapidly expanding immigrant community. Though the general
hospital was enlarged in 1690, and the road linking St Germain to Poissy
was properly paved later in the same year, such developments were far

outweighed by the opening of new chapels to cater to the exiles' spiritual, rather than physiological, needs. The religious orders began to return to the town, well aware that the pressing requirements of dispensing charity to the growing numbers of the poor were more than offset by the chances of securing fresh patronage. While entrepreneurs, local craftsmen, and manufacturers provided the exiles with both the luxuries and the staples they desired for life at court, there was a sharp divide between the 'haves' and the 'have-nots' who rubbed shoulders at St Germain. They were pitched in bitter competition for the employment opportunities, offices, and titles that would enable them to adopt the latest fashions in clothes and furniture, and to acquire the trappings of gentility – through the employment of cooks, private tutors, and fencing and dancing masters – that would distinguish them in a society of displaced aristocrats. Thus, while there were undoubtedly fortunes to be made by those with an inclination to hard graft, such as Richard Cavanagh who rented a 'shop shaped like a hut' next to the guardroom at St Germain; financial speculators like the Irish bankers who set up business in Paris; or the French investors who set up a new brewery outside the walls of James's castle, to satiate the émigrés' thirst and to profit from the unexpected scarcity of the local grape, those without the taste for work and whose pretensions to gentility had worn perilously thin, or those who had been attracted to St Germain primarily as a means of making an easy living, were quickly disillusioned and often sought recourse to crime or to violent disorder. Moreover, the increasingly strict moral code that Louis XIV had attempted to impose upon his subjects, which found its mirror image in James II's equally strict admonitions to his followers, presented further difficulties for both the heterogeneous collection of exiles gathered about his court and for the local authorities who attempted to restrain and condition their conduct. Even the influx of numerous Irish priests after 1691 provided the French police with a fresh headache, as Fr Thomas Sheehy was arrested after spending the night with a prostitute, before saying the Mass at Versailles, and Alexander Campbell, a Franciscan, was seized after attempting to blackmail his order, claiming that he would reveal the names of all their operatives in England unless they immediately promoted him to the post of provincial superior. The wife of one of James's servants fell pregnant by the superintendent of the duc de Bourgogne's household and left her husband and fled towards Paris. However, she was apprehended and sent to a convent so that her reappearance at St Germain might not further embarrass King James and her cuckolded spouse. Demobilised and impoverished Irish soldiers haunted the neighbouring woods, robbing unwary travellers on the highroad and cutting purses in the town. Lord Galmoy's valet was murdered after one such robbery went wrong, and his assailants, Thomas Murnahan and Thomas Welsh, took to their heels in an unsuccessful

attempt to avoid detection, while in just one day Francis O'Neil and
four other 'Wild Geese' were broken on the wheel for crimes of robbery
and violence. James was not blind to the endemic poverty of many of his
followers, whose children died in disproportionate numbers compared to
those of the French townsfolk, and who received a decent burial only
thanks to the charity of the exiled nobility and religious benefactors. As a
result, it was not uncommon to hear of the King calling certain of his
unemployed soldiers to him in his cabinet, in order to press small folded
pieces of paper to the value of '5, 10, 15, or 20 pistoles [between £4–£16],
more or less, according to the merit, the quality, and the exigency of
each'.[2]

James quickly evolved a daily routine that gave his life in exile the all-
important structure that he craved, allotting set times for his rising ('at
seven or half past' each day), his morning prayers, constitutional walks,
attendance to business and private reading, before entertaining guests
and finally retiring to sleep, resolving 'never to spend more than eight
hours [a night] in bed'. Hunting still took up much of his time and
served as an appropriate outlet for his violent energies, and he was
indeed fortunate to have the sprawling forest of St Germain on his
doorstep to provide him with an almost limitless number of quarries to
chase and trap, including deer, foxes, wolves and even bears, as well as
large numbers of heron and wild duck to shoot along the banks of the
Seine. Luckily, James had quickly forged a solid friendship – based on a
shared interest and the mutual respect of seasoned sportsmen – with
King Louis's Master of the Hunt, the duc de La Rochefoucauld, who
ensured that he was soon equipped with a proficient retinue of huntsmen
and beaters, fine stables, and replacements for all the hounds, hawks, and
falcons that he had been forced to leave behind in England. When
William III's Ambassador subsequently had the temerity to ask
La Rochefoucauld for the loan of a pack of hunting dogs, he was curtly
informed that he could not comply, for as the Master of the Hunt he was
exclusively at the command of James, the rightful King of England, and
that he could not find it within himself to oblige the servants of a
usurper. However, even though some six million trees had been planted
over the last two decades in order to provide the game with cover in
James's newly acquired Great Park, it is doubtful if in the course of a
pursuit he ever paused for long to admire the romantically overgrown
ruins of the castle of La Muette, which had been left to decay as a
picturesque folly by his predecessor. It is more likely that the hunting
lodge at Le Val, buried in the heart of the woods, was of more use to the
King and his companions during sudden downpours, and that the shrine
at Mount Valerian, on the road back to Paris – known as the 'little
Calvary' – was far more to his personal taste. Similarly, though the
sweeping terraces and formal gardens, designed by André Le Nôtre in

1672, provided the most marvellous panoramic views of the Seine Valley, James merely noted wistfully that the scene reminded him of the countryside that stretched from Richmond Hill to Windsor, and begrudged the extra expense for the upkeep of the many formal fountains and cascades which adorned his grounds.[3]

Aside from the Households of the King and Queen, an independent establishment was also set up in 1695 for the young Prince of Wales, when his education was removed from the hands of his mother and his nurses, and firmly entrusted to his governor and his tutors. His early years had been spent in the care of Lady Strickland and Lady Powis, reliable pillars of the exiled aristocracy, whose husbands enjoyed exalted positions in the royal service, whose commitment to Roman Catholicism could not be questioned, and whose own families mirrored the fecundity and stability aspired to by James and Mary of Modena. It was this profound sense of family as being the building block upon which orderly societies were built, with 'a good Christian . . . Subject' equated with 'a good parent, a good Sonne, a good Wife, [and] a Good Husband', that informed James's concept of politics and his own crucial role as patriarch at the apex of the social pyramid, guiding, admonishing, and praising his peoples as needs be. The rebellion of his daughters from his first marriage had not only overturned the 'natural order' of civil society but had also threatened to destroy James's dual image as the universal father and sovereign of the British people, rendering him – in an analogy that was not lost on many of his propagandists and partisans – as an unnaturally forsaken and Lear-like king. However, his children by Mary of Modena offered him a second chance to raise a dynasty which might be completely faithful to his person, his political legacy, and to the Church of Rome whose credo he espoused with every fibre of his being. Unsurprisingly, the development of the child who might, it was fervently hoped by all at the court of St Germain, one day sit on the throne of England, and on whom the future of the Jacobite cause ultimately depended, was of the utmost importance and debate among the King's followers. Many of the Compounders still at work in England entertained hopes that the Prince might eventually convert to Protestantism, or at least seek to disguise and dissemble the nature of his Catholic faith in order to pave his way back to the crown, but such thoughts were anathema to James, who hoped that his son would become 'a zealous Catholick of the Church of Rome' and advised him that he should 'let no human consideration of any kind prevaile with you to depart from her'. He entrusted the boy's development to the Drummond clan, the most unyielding and strident of all the Non-Compounders lodged at St Germain. Such an intent was discernible early on, when the dowager Countess of Errol, kin to lords Melfort and Perth, was appointed for a short-lived period as his son's governess, and confirmed when, in the summer of 1696, he created Perth as the child's governor and charged him with overseeing not only his curriculum, but also his personal development.[4]

It was James's gravest fear that his son, exposed to the disappointments and enforced idleness that attended every exile, might grow into a dissolute youth, the image of those swaggering, drinking, and wenching cavaliers whose company he himself had once enjoyed in Paris and Brussels during the 1650s. Increasingly, James sought to locate the reasons for his own ill fortune in the withdrawal of God's favour, occasioned by his 'predominant sin' of womanising to which he had 'so very foolishly and indescretly exposed [him]self' from the time of his early manhood onwards. 'Nothing', he declared, 'has been more fatal . . . to great men, then the letting themselves go to the forbidden love of Women, [as] of all the Vices it is most bewitching and harder to be master'd if it be not crushed in the very bud'.[5] Were his son to follow in his errors, then disaster, he believed, would surely attend him in exactly the same manner, for 'none ought to be more on their gard then you . . . for the greater men are, the more that they are exposed' to sin, and he urged that the boy should 'remember always that Kings, Princes and all the great ones of the world, must one day give an account of all their actions before the great tribunal, where every one will be judged according to his doings', adding the stern warning that he should: 'Consider you come into the world to serve God Almighty, and not only to please yourself, and that by him Kings reign, and that without his particular protection nothing you undertake can prosper'. Unfortunately, James was all too well aware of the march of time, which had already robbed the boy of the services of two of his governesses, and worried that if he were to die before his son's majority, then the ministers and tutors about the Prince might soon be changed and his wishes quickly forgotten, ignored, or – more dangerously – overridden. Consequently, the King, whose own education had been interrupted by civil war and flight into exile, was determined to outline a guide to personal conduct and the art of politics, that was to be adhered to as a blueprint for the Prince in the event of his premature death and, while he still lived, to cast the sternest and most prescriptive of eyes over the boy's intellectual studies and physical pursuits. The two resulting documents produced definitively in 1692 and 1696, known respectively as instructions 'For my son the Prince of Wales' and as the 'Rules for the family [i.e. Household] of our dearest son', delineated an upbringing that was both highly authoritarian and prohibitively restrictive.[6] Though James Francis Edward had initially been regarded as a spirited child, who had landed a blow on the nose of the dauphin when he bent down to kiss him, and who threatened to hold his breath whenever he did not get his own way with his mother and her servants, he quickly developed into a sullen and withdrawn boy, who was once scolded by the Earl of Perth demanding of him why he had 'to learn by study the affability which your sister has by nature?'.[7]

Such a profound alteration in the child's character owed much to the deadening prescriptions of the 'Rules' laid down by his father, which ensured that little of the outside world could reach the Prince without the prior approval of his governor. No-one could give the child food or sweets, flowers or toys, without the express permission of Perth, while: 'No children must be permitted to come into . . . his lodgings, upon the account of playing with him, but when they are sent for . . . and not above two or three at a time'. Moreover: 'None are to be permitted to whisper in . . . his ear or talk with him in privat . . . No books, written papers, or any thing of that nature must be ever given to the Prince without shewing them first to the Governor or preceptor . . . and no songs must be taught . . . but such as the Governor shall first approve'. A timetable was given to him, outlining the hours to be spent at his prayers, his books, and at play, but although he was permitted to learn to dance it was his spiritual well-being that was held to be paramount, with the memorising of his catechism and his instruction in 'Christian doctrine', together with stern injunctions against any of his servants uttering anything in his presence 'that is rude and not decent for him to hear', well to the fore. While his father's abhorrence of plays ensured that the French nobility would later remark, with a mixture of surprise and amusement, on the boy's failure to comprehend what was meant by the 'theatre' (a fine stage mouldered away unused at St Germain), it is not hard to see that his upbringing stifled whatever creativity he may have had, and equipped him to turn evidence against his tutor in the winter of 1703–4, when Mary of Modena had the unfortunate John Betham called to account on the grounds of his doctrinal 'errors'.

The Prince's education had pitted the Jesuit Order against the English secular clergy and, in particular, its Jansenist adherents, in producing guides for his instruction and in forwarding their own candidates to serve as his tutors. Yet, if the Jesuits were broadly in favour of accepting that England was unlikely to witness either mass popular re-conversions or the legal re-establishment of the Roman Church in the near future, then the Jansenists appeared to be far more militantly ambitious, as they were not content to confine themselves to missionary work, but looked instead to the re-creation of a national Church with an overt hierarchy in the British Isles. Such an approach had fitted well with James II's attempts to promote Roman Catholicism in his domains from 1685–8, and won the Jansenists many formidable supporters at the exiled Jacobite court, including the Earl of Perth. Furthermore, the stress laid by the movement on internal moral reform, austerity, and a withdrawal from the world, when combined with a pervading sense of pessimism about human nature, an element of pre-destination, and a sense of heady mysticism both conformed to, and shaped, many of King James's personal religious ideals, right down to a common disapproval of actors and a desire to ban all theatre performances. As a result, James had been prepared to countenance the propagation of Jansenism – a sect that had been explicitly condemned by Pope Urban VIII in 1653–4, and had found its most formidable opponent in Louis XIV – at his court, and saw fit to appoint John Betham, a priest and educational propagandist of profoundly Jansenist sympathies, as one of the tutors to his son. However, the narrow, politically uncompromising and self-abnegating curriculum taught by Betham, with its insistence on sharpening the memory, utilising travellers' tales from India and China only to demonstrate the folly of men who 'follow their own imaginings and the dark side of their souls', and the need 'to take care not to instil such a curiosity in [children] which could be dangerous' in the study of natural history and anatomy, did little to counteract the limitations already imposed on James Francis Edward's intellectual development. It served to ensure that he would never emerge as an inquiring and imaginative prince of the nascent European Enlightenment, of the stamp of Eugene of Savoy, Philippe II of Orléans, or even of Peter the Great of Russia.

However, if James's male heir was subject to an almost stifling array of commandments and regulations, then the education of his daughter Louise Marie passed largely without comment and received but scant attention from her father. Though she learned a little of history and Latin, she was only otherwise equipped with those social skills that would allow her to shine at court, and to express a conventional but surprisingly moderate and unremarkable personal piety, given the intense devotional climate at St Germain. Emerging into adulthood as a vivacious and charming young woman, who displayed all of her father's recklessness during the hunt and enough of her mother's fragile beauty to captivate the hearts of French courtiers in the salon, she was considered as a prospective bride for the warlike and Protestant King Charles XII of Sweden, whose sabres, it was hoped, would add force to the legitimist arguments of the fallen Stuarts, at a time when French support was already threatening to turn cold. Tragically, the same preoccupation with her brother's interests to the neglect of her own, which had allowed her character to emerge from childhood virtually unscarred by the misfortunes of her House, was also to result in her early death. A visit to the convent at Chaillot in the spring of 1712, to comfort a nun who was seriously ill, resulted in first her brother, and then Louise Marie, contracting smallpox. Yet, while Mary of Modena and her physicians fussed about the stricken young man, the rashes spread across the Princess's body unchecked, without much in the way of either notice or comment, and by the time the severity of her condition was fully realised she had been so terribly weakened by the effects of her illness and by chronic diarrhoea that the attentions of the doctors – which took the form of bleedings and the administering of large quantities of pain-relieving opiates – merely speeded her decline, and she passed away on the morning of 8/18 April 1712, just a few months short of her twentieth birthday.[8] King James's consolation was no more.

The impression of a court held in thrall to a combination of unyielding gloom and constant disappointment has coloured the approach of successive generations of historians from Macaulay to Miller towards the Jacobite exiles at St Germain. However, this vision of a perennially impecunious, priest-ridden and thoroughly bigoted Household, governed by an elderly and failing King, owed much in both its inception and propagation to a short yet devastating critique of the émigré community written by John Macky, a Williamite agent and propagandist. It was published anonymously in 1696, at a time when criticism of the conduct of the war was growing apace in England and a new French invasion once more threatened. The primary targets for Macky's withering pen were those disparate Protestant Jacobite communities, ranging from Anglican to Dissenter, which still hoped that James's return to power would be accompanied by either firm guarantees for the preservation of the national Church, or an unprecedented extension of religious freedom through a comprehensive toleration enshrined in law. To Macky, who sensed that these two sets of aspirations were to an extent mutually exclusive, all such promises were illusory, designed to divide loyal Protestant subjects from their King and to endeavour 'to lull them a-sleep, under the specious pretence of liberty of conscience till all his [i.e. King James's] engines were ready to give the fatal blow'. In an attempt to make the political movement synonymous with Roman Catholicism, he confided his hopes that 'ages to come will hardly believe, that in England there should be found one single Protestant Jacobite', and added that 'the reformed nations abroad are at a loss what to make of that unaccountable species of men'. St Germain, in his eyes, was a benighted place where priests might be found 'buzzing' about the deathbeds of James's Protestant followers, ready to ignore the last wishes of men such as Major-General Cannon, who refused to abandon their faith but who, nevertheless, had communion wafers rammed down their throats at the last moment so that it might later be given out that they had died as good Catholics. Denied Christian burial, succour, and advancement, the King's Protestant followers were slighted and pauperised, being forced to choose between sacrificing their religion, and dying as pariahs in empty attic rooms or in the depths of the Bastille. James was held personally culpable for the climate of incessant proselytising and sudden persecution, for he was not even prepared to 'keep on the old mask' of the apostle of toleration, spinning out the 'imaginary hopes' of those misguided English Jacobites, and 'since he went to France, he has taken all pains imaginable to let the world know his inveterate aversion to all those of the reformed religion'.[9]

However, many of Macky's case studies were ill founded. The widow of John Ashton, though failing to find employment with Mary of Modena, had not been unduly persecuted or left to die in poverty on account of her faith, while Bishop Gordon's conversion to Rome was the result of Bossuet's stern and compelling logic, rather than the threat of force. Political and personal, as opposed to religious, disagreements led to Colonel Fielding, Captain Maclean, and Sir Andrew Forrester returning home of their own volition to make their separate peace with the Williamite government. Similarly, the notion that James was driven by an unshakeable and austere desire to forcibly extirpate Protestantism from among his subjects was a cruel caricature of a King who, throughout his last exile, continued to uphold his rights – bestowed by God through his coronation vows – as the 'defender' and head of the Church of England. He stood by his commitment to maintain religious toleration in Britain, in the belief that it was not only a matter of simple justice, but a social and economic necessity which formed the proud basis of the achievements of his kingship. James was thus a man of deep contradictions, who might shock his hosts by suddenly unsheathing his sword as the host was elevated in his chapel of St Louis, and standing mute and bolt-upright in order to emphasise his position as the Supreme Governor of the Anglican Church, but whose greatest delight was in seeing a fresh convert received into the Roman Catholic Church – for 'I do aver as a great truth and of my owne knowledge, that I never knew a true convert, that did not visibly mend his way of living' – and who would often break off from his daily routine to force little devotional tracts into the palms or the pockets of his Protestant courtiers. There was little doubt that the King was a great proselytiser for his adopted faith, a fact not lost on those clergymen who were to preach his epitaphs, and evidenced by his continual rejoinders to the Earl of Middleton to forsake his faith and embrace Catholicism. However, this did nothing to stem the flow or dim the ardour of those Quakers – known as 'tremblers' to the French courtiers – who continued to cross the Channel to present their compliments and to offer their services. Thus, Guli, the wife of William Penn, became a regular visitor to St Germain, bearing and spiriting away intelligence reports, while the young Dr William Bromfield risked his life by despatching 300 cavalry horses to France, and suffered imprisonment for acting as a Jacobite courier, before finally seeking refuge at the exiled court.[10] Moreover, the number of Protestants actually employed in James's household at St Germain was proportionally greater than that of his former court at Whitehall, and would increase as the 1690s wore on. Unfortunately, the problem lay not in the fact that James gave employment to Protestants while in exile – for even Macky had had to struggle to shed a dim light on the Earl of Middleton's advancement – but in English domestic opinion. In a land where a mere 5 per cent of the population was Roman Catholic, it was hard to see the overwhelming preponderance of Catholics in the King's service at St Germain (some 84 per cent in 1693, falling to 81 per cent in 1696) as the product of anything other than an inordinate display of personal and religiously motivated favour, and a desire to thoroughly marginalize James's Protestant subjects and remove them from the levers of power. In part, the preponderance of Roman Catholic over Protestant servants could easily be explained by the exigencies of life in France, where the available pool of labour for manual jobs in the kitchens and stables was exclusively Catholic, and by the fact that several ladies of the Queen's Household, such as Pellegrina Turini, had followed her from Modena to England at the time of her marriage, and had remained with her ever since. The displacement of so many Irish soldiers and their families by the war of 1689–91, and the 'Flight of the Wild Geese', further added to the inbuilt Catholic majority, while James's attempts to re-enfranchise the Roman Catholic nobilities of England, Wales and Scotland had tied many families, such as the Stricklands, the Carylls, the Douglases and the Drummonds, far more firmly to the King's fate, making exile a slightly more palpable and rational consideration for them, than for their Protestant friends and neighbours. Furthermore, the co-option of foreign noblemen and priests into the royal Household – most notably James's friend the comte de Lauzun and the Italian Fr Don Giacomo Ronchi – also served to contribute to the feeling that despite the King's determination to recreate precisely the courtly ceremonial of Whitehall, the culture of St Germain was far from Anglo-centric. It owed much, in terms of the arts and music, to Mediterranean Europe, while its English personnel were far outnumbered by the combination of the King and Queen's Scottish, Irish, French and Italian servants.

If James had seen toleration as a simple ruse by which to divide and confound his Protestant subjects, paving the way for forcible re-conversions, then he might not have been expected to have enshrined religious liberty at the heart of Jacobite policy and to have so forcefully recommended its promotion to his young son. 'Be not persuaded by any', the King instructed his heir, 'to depart from [religious toleration]; [for] our blessed Saviour whipt people out of the Temple, but I never heard he commanded any should be forced into it'. The inherent perfection and correctness of Roman Catholic doctrine, as perceived by King James, rendered the logic of its arguments insurmountable by any who approached the faith with an open mind. Thus, there was no need to have his peoples 'frighted', forced or cajoled into a change of faith, when 'gentlenesse, instruction, and good example' would naturally lead men and women to it by 'a particular grace and favour' shown by the

Almighty. 'I make no doubt', he added, that 'if once Liberty of Conscience be well fixed, many conversions will ensue, which is a truth too many of the Protestants are persuaded of, Church of England men as well as others, and so will require more care and dexterity to obtain it'. Yet, it was precisely this sense of tact that James had always conspicuously lacked when dealing with the heartlands of Protestant England, curiously reinforced by his earlier injunction to his son that toleration might only be secured if he was 'never without a considerable body of Catholick troops without which you cannot be safe'. The experience of the Exclusion Crisis and of his reign had clearly done nothing to warn the former King of the potent – and from his own point of view, wholly destructive – emotions that the dual terrors of resurgent Roman Catholicism and a large standing army had always aroused in the minds of his Protestant subjects. One cannot doubt the sincerity of James's commitment to religious toleration (for why else would he have abandoned his Tory backers, natural supporters of the restored Stuart monarchy, in order to pay uncertain court to the fragmented Dissenting communities, who had been deprived of political and professional office since 1662?) but his judgement as to the implementation of this policy may be questioned in two major areas, which reflect on his inflated expectations for its success as he himself chose to define it, and on the manner in which it was to be practically achieved after 1689. James had experienced at first hand the evangelical delight with which the arrival of the Vicar Apostolic had been greeted by the English, and how, in the north country in particular, young and old alike had thronged to him for the performance of blessings and baptisms. Unfortunately, there was a marked difference between a sudden thaw in official persecution, allowing many so-called 'church papists' who had previously compromised and dissembled their beliefs to publicly espouse Catholicism once more, and the gaining of entirely new converts, Anglicans and Dissenters from outside court circles, to the Roman faith. Aside from James's simple equation of Dissenters with trade, his rationale for toleration depended entirely upon the premise that there would be an inexorable slide towards the re-conversion of the British Isles, based on the example of his own moral conduct and that of other leading converts (including his late brother, Charles II), and on the persuasive power of Roman Catholic teaching. While this might have been possible in England in 1536, 1553, 1558, and even conceivably in 1603, the complete collapse of Protestantism across the land was far more difficult to envisage in the late seventeenth century and had been made far more improbable as the result of the anti-Catholic backlash of 1688–9. Moreover, while the Jesuit tactic of concentrating on the conversion of social élites, in the hope that they would either force or convince those whose lives they controlled to follow in their wake, had proved spectacularly successful in Poland, Bohemia, and the fragmented German states – where the people's faith mirrored that of their Prince – it was far less assured in England, where the collapse of Presbyterianism among the aristocracy and gentry after 1660 had resulted not in a wholesale return to Rome, but in a rejuvenated Anglican Church. As a consequence, the best that James might rationally expect from his policy of toleration was the amelioration of the plight of the indigenous Roman Catholic communities in Great Britain and Ireland, and the gradual replenishment of their numerical strength through a steady trickle of new converts. This meant that his plans for the re-forging of the religious composition of his kingdoms would take place over decades, rather than months or even years, and seems to explain in part his concern that his son and heir should undertake to continue and complete his commitment to toleration.

Yet, the problem remained that James's entire religious policy presupposed that his subjects would react to his initiatives in exactly the way that he expected them to. He made no real allowance for potential resistance to his moves towards toleration, such as that mounted in 1688 by the Church of England. Moreover, his entire concept of his own Divine Right monarchy ensured that his rule was to be proprietary, if coloured by a sense of paternalism. Thus, every individual liberty was the result only of the monarch's graceful concession, or of the precedents established by his (or her) predecessors. There was no right that was the inalienable property of the subject, but rather a series of privileges that might be given – or rescinded – by the sovereign, as God's representative to the nation, upon consideration of their merits. James, therefore, was emphatically not a liberal of the type beloved by Victorian novelists and writers such as Harrison Ainsworth and Fr John Lingard, or a libertarian conservative of the stamp enthusiastically applauded by today's dominant brand of revisionist historians.[11] Given that James's temperament afforded him little understanding of any viewpoint contrary to his own, and that he would brook no opposition, however constructive in intent, then it was all too easy for him to mistake principled criticism for treachery, and to conflate political and confessional opposition with the sin of rebellion, which he believed was being constantly urged on his unwitting subjects by those 'disaffected, turbulent, and unquiet spirits' who were ever at work spreading the distemper of republicanism throughout the world. Indeed, it was primarily as the best means of securing social control that James had originally been drawn to Roman Catholicism. The abbé de La Trappe had not been slow to summarise his guiding sentiments, arguing that: 'if there is no divine authority who judges opinions, and the doubts which can arise, at all times, and which particular things it is right to know: all religion would be an arbitrary affair, everyone would have his own views and follow his own imaginings, and fantasies, for the rules of his own belief, this would be the greatest of all confusion'. Authority and rigid certainty were the qualities that James desired from his faith, and his concept of God was primarily the military one of a grand captain – 'the Lord of Hosts, the God of Battles' – who might command His servants as He willed, without either argument or question, and to whom total obedience was required at all times. If the Roman Church 'should be recognised as the one true church' in the King's mind precisely because it resolved confusion and brooked no debate, then at some point it might be expected that James's hopes for toleration and the reality that this would entail – a continuing increase in the number of non-conformist sects – might well come to a clash.[12]

The King had shown little compunction about directing Judge Jeffreys to enact the most severe of sentences on Monmouth's rebels in 1685, and three years later he had not baulked even for a moment at confining his Anglican opponents, in the form of the seven bishops, to the Tower for daring to oppose him. Consequently, there were many in the political nation who feared that James's return, despite his well-meaning promises of toleration, would only serve to spark a fresh confessional conflict. They were quick to deduce from the text of his declaration of 1692 that his experience of exile had enabled him to recall every slight that had been offered to him, but to learn nothing of the reasons that had initially prompted them. Far more disturbing in terms of the future of toleration were the conditions under which the King was likely to be restored. By 1692 it had become clear that the internal opposition was far too weak, and bitterly divided over the question of aims and objectives, to bring down William III without foreign military aid, and that this vital ingredient could only be provided by the armies of the King of France. Consequently, it was the Revocation of the Edict of Nantes – which had sought to root out the Huguenots from every level of the state apparatus, forcibly baptising the children of Protestant parents, sending objectors to the galleys, and resulting in the annihilation of whole communities in the Languedoc and Bordeaux – which limited James's room for manoeuvre once he arrived in France, and coloured the attitudes of many Britons towards the question of his independence in civil and religious matters, were he to be ushered back into Whitehall by an escort of Gardes Françaises.

While Louis XIV had turned a blind eye to James's pretensions as the supreme governor of the Church of England, he was not prepared – as middle age stiffened his sinews, and the influence of madame de Maintenon effectively narrowed the parameters of his mind – to permit the court of St Germain to openly play host to Protestant services. It has been argued that James chose not to argue this point of principle at the time of his arrival in France, in the belief that it would not develop into a live issue as he expected to be quickly on his way again and to be restored to his thrones within a matter of months. Even if this had been the case (and the King's reluctance to antagonise his only friend and supporter is certainly understandable) then it would appear from what we have already seen that the initiative in sending James into Ireland was taken by the French, and that from the time of his first embrace with Louis, the exiled King was willing to defer to the judgement of his brother monarch in almost every matter of policy. His psychological abasement before Louis XIV, coupled with his almost complete political dependence, had virtually ensured that the question of the religious rights of the Protestants quartered at St Germain would not even be raised in the privy cabinet of the Sun King, or discussed by the idle courtiers in their salons at Paris and Versailles, save in terms of denunciation. James's high-minded commitment to toleration for his subjects in Britain and Ireland would not, it seems, be extended to them during their exile in France, a fact that was largely acknowledged by his acceptance of 'the Lawes of the Country [which] would not permit the same priviledges as publick prayers' and his concession that he could only attempt to mollify 'what he could not obtain a total relaxation of'. Unsurprisingly, many wondered if religious prescriptions would be levied on the returning King by his French masters, and that when the moment came James's character would be found lacking in the requisite fibre to prevent persecution. As John Macky and similar Williamite propagandists knew full well, it was a dismal and uncertain fate that awaited any Protestant who settled at St Germain. Subject to the open scorn of French courtiers and Irish soldiers, and to the angry suspicion of the inhabitants and tradesmen of the surrounding town, they were marginalised from the mainstream of polite society and denied the privilege of openly practising their religion, or of receiving any sort of formal burial. Forbidden from following a trade or a profession, there was no way for a Protestant from the lower or middling classes to make a living at St Germain, save through direct patronage or domestic service, with the result that those non-Catholics who did find refuge at King James's court were predominantly men and women of independent, and frequently very wealthy, means. In these respects at least, Macky's pamphlet did accurately reflect the truth that the King's Household was far from conducive to the maintenance of individual Protestant belief. Lord Middleton and Sir Edward Herbert were forced to hold covert services in their private apartments, constantly in danger of discovery and the sudden accusation of the *lettre de cachet*, while death really did lead to secret burials in the night, where the form of Anglican or Dissenting liturgy was hurriedly said over the corpse as it was consigned to an unmarked grave in the corner of a dark field, or on the waste ground beside the highway.[13]

Roman Catholicism undoubtedly set the tenor of the increasingly stern moral code that was enforced at the court, with a 'great many

Chaplains . . . [lodged] below staires' and six to eight more priests housed above. Fr Petrie's influence over the King had been decisively broken due to his display of abject cowardice when faced by William III's advance in December 1688; James had been quick to turn from him, and attempted to lay the blame for his loss of power squarely at his door as early as January 1689. Having been appointed as the rector of the English College at St Omer, Petrie had returned incognito to St Germain for slightly more than a fortnight at the close of 1693, but even though the Compounders feared that his presence had been both divisive and wholly destructive, he was something of a spent force and was unable to force his way back into James's councils. Indeed, the King's experience of relying on this overly ambitious and proud Jesuit may conceivably have prejudiced him against favouring other confessors from that order during his latter years. However, it is probable that the unyielding asceticism of the Capuchins was more in keeping with the spiritual rigour desired by the older James, than were the reassuring words, comparatively light penances, and cultured discourses favoured by the more worldly Jesuits. Unfortunately, even then the King had trouble containing the faction that grew from the rivalry between his chaplain and confessor. Although both were Capuchins, Fr Mansuet, the King's former confessor, had convinced himself that his rival, Fr Dominic White, had gained James's ear and connived at his removal from his post. To make matters worse, it was alleged that White had sought to obstruct the efforts of the Irish branch of their order from recovering the convents at Charleville and Sedan that rightfully belonged to them. As a result, the King was forced to issue a certificate to White at the beginning of 1693, expressing his utmost faith in the probity of his servant, and affirming that his dismissive comments about a cluster of missionary priests who had gathered at La Hogue in preparation for the abortive invasion carried his full approval. White nevertheless chose to leave the King's service, 'to retire to a convent, much to his edification', but James had salvaged much of his reputation and demonstrated that sense of protective tenacity that coloured his relationships with all those of his servants who had pleased him, however controversial and damaging their wider reputations might happen to be. In part, this explains the intense personal loyalty that the King was capable of invoking in individuals as different as John Ashton (who would choose to mount the scaffold defiant and tight-lipped to the last), Captain Middleton and his handful of soldiers, whose obstinate stand on the windswept Bass Rock still afforded the Jacobites a British garrison in the winter of 1693–4, and Lawrence Dupuy, a courtier who had served James since the early 1660s, sacrificing everything to follow him into exile, and who was eventually appointed to the Prince of Wales's fledgling Household as a 'Gentleman Waiter' in 1695.[14]

However, the King's attempts to extend his own inflexible sense of personal morality into the life of his court, and to make it general, produced results that were as unfortunate as they were unexpected. James had been disturbed by reports that his son Henry – who was later to be branded as 'the stupidest man on earth' by the duc de Saint-Simon – had taken to the bottle again and had fallen among low company in the suburbs of Paris, keeping two humbly born mistresses, the daughters of the King's tailor and of a poulterer at St Germain respectively, and making promises to marry the former. At roughly the same time, Berwick had begun to pay court to Sarsfield's 19-year-old widow Honora, rejecting the pleas of his father, who would have preferred a far more advantageous match for his son with a French or Italian princess. Berwick married Honora at Montmartre in 1695, undertaking to raise her small son, who had been named after the Prince of Wales, as if he was his own. It was left to James to reluctantly mount his coach, the Sunday before the wedding, and journey to Versailles in order to offer a shame-faced explanation of the young man's conduct to a particularly taciturn Louis XIV. A similar disagreement was to erupt five years later when, after his wife's premature death from consumption, Berwick went behind his father's back to ask – without success as it turned out – for the hand of the daughter of the comte d'Armagnac. Yet, these rejections of parental authority seem to have troubled the King far less than Berwick's failure to heed his spiritual advice, or the scandalous conduct of his newly widowed daughter Henrietta. For while Berwick's affairs of the heart eventually resulted in two contended but entirely respectable marriages – to Honora, Countess of Lucan and to Anne, daughter of Henry Bulkeley, the master of the King's Household at St Germain – and even Henry Fitzjames was finally prevailed upon to marry the daughter of the marquis de Lussau, there were some transgressions among his children that James was far less willing to either comprehend or to forgive. In 1696, a casual conversation with Berwick – who, James recognised, 'seeme[d] to . . . endeavor to live as becomes a good Christian' – both shocked and shamed the King, who could not comprehend that his son, having 'looke[d] death so offten and so boldly in the face' in skirmishes in Ireland and Flanders, at the siege of Budapest, and at the battles of the Boyne and Landen, could express his reservations about expecting death and being 'desirous to Dy'. Considering himself still a soldier, James began a paper to his son, which, though it was seemingly neither finished nor delivered, sought to upbraid the young General, marvelling at his 'want of consideration . . . and want of having read anything on that subject' that might have led him to order his affairs, and to reject the world and everything in it as mere show. 'What paines, [and] what dangers', the King exclaimed, 'dos not those of our trade undergo, to gain a little reputation in the world, and to capacitat[e] them selv[e]s to command armys all w[hi]ch we cannot be sure of enjoying one moment', adding that was 'it not the last degree of folly and madnesse, not to take the same pains, the same care, to arrive at such an estat[e] of perfection', in actively welcoming death, 'w[hi]ch percevering in, we are sure of Eternal happynesse'.[15]

Yet if James fretted that death stalked his son across the battlefields of Europe and might snatch him unawares – a fate which did eventually overtake him at the siege of Philipsburg, though not before he had gained his baton as a Marshal of France and become an old man – then he had little cause to fear for either his son's continuing sense of filial piety or his devotion to the Church of Rome, which led him in later years to encourage two of his own boys to take holy orders, and to make large financial bequests to numerous monasteries and abbeys across France and Spain. While Berwick might have been brought to heel by his father's hurt and angry missive, no such peremptory commands were able to bring his sister, Henrietta, Lady Waldegrave back to obedience. Since the death of her young husband, she had found the atmosphere of St Germain increasingly stifling and had railed against both the King's failure to secure her a fresh marriage and his suggestions that she might prefer to retire to the cloister. Having taken refuge in the arms of a series of young gallants, she finally fell pregnant to Lord Galmoy, but scandalised her father and his court by failing to divulge the name of her lover or to accept her incarceration in a convent, and the taking of holy orders. Within two months she had escaped, marrying Galmoy in March 1695, and fleeing into Flanders. Enraged and clearly embarrassed, James and his wife refused to ever see her again and, as Galmoy's passions for her cooled and he abandoned her in order to resume his career with the French army on the Moselle, she was forced to appeal to William III to alleviate her poverty and to allow her a safe haven in England. By November of that year she was back in London with her children, staying at the home shared by her mother, Arabella Churchill, and her new Whig stepfather, Colonel Charles Godfrey.[16]

While James's personal pursuit of piety might have driven a wedge between himself and his natural children it was, at least, an extremely useful attribute in obtaining relief for those of his followers that he could not hope to support, and whose loyalty had rendered them otherwise destitute and friendless in a foreign land. The King, and in particular the Queen, were to make good use of their contacts with the College of Cardinals and with the French bishops, in order to channel funds for 'the poor Irish families who had fled to this kingdom' and to activate the networks of patronage controlled by the Church. Thus, money was found to keep Fr Walter Innes at Rome under the protection of Cardinal de Janson, and Fr Jeremy O'Reagan and his curate Mr MacCarty, lately come from Ireland, asked to be provided with a benefice by the Archbishop of

Bordeaux. Meanwhile a veritable flood of requests was submitted to the bishops of Chalons, Tours, Le Mans and Treguier, and to the abbesses of Dunkirk, Remiremont, Caen and of St Georges de Rennes, beseeching that places might be found in their convents for the daughters of the Copleys, Butlers, Dillons, Dowdalls, Berminghams, Magners, Macdonnels and Millefonts, all Jacobite families of 'gentle birth' who could not hope to provide the necessary 'portions' to secure their entry into leading religious institutions. In the cramped and relatively expensive, rack-rented tenements of St Germain there were many heads of large and extended families – such as Mr Halpenny, 'an Irishman, who has numerous family . . . and is a worthy object of . . . compassion' – who sought to lessen the numbers of mouths to feed around the table, and to attest to their continued faith in God, by sending their daughters to take the veil. As a consequence, Mary of Modena was able to secure a place for Halpenny's daughter at Xaintes and thanked the Abbess of Cambrai for 'her kindly reception of Miss Michel de Latte, whose father and mother have long served the King and herself' but had to appeal that she might be 'admitted to the habit on the recommendation . . . by Father Joseph Aprice, her chaplain' on confirmation of her 'promise . . . that, when God shall restore them to their kingdoms, she will provide for her portion by paying them a yearly pension of 25 l., till she gives them 400 l. for the extinction of the same'. Moreover, as casualties mounted among the exiles serving with the French armies in Catalonia, Flanders, Savoy, and along the Rhine, the Queen was forced to make additional appeals for the religious houses to offer support for the widows and orphans of those Jacobite officers who had 'died in the service'. In the summer of 1698, Fr Cloche, the General of the Dominican Order, was petitioned by Jeanne MacCarthy – 'three of whose brothers have been killed in the king's service since the revolution' – so that she might have leave to join the house of the Irish Dominican nuns near Lisbon.[17]

Ill-equipped to meet the educational needs of the growing number of children left dependent on the exiled court, James and Mary of Modena turned to the Church to provide places so that a new generation of exiles might be able to learn their letters. In this manner, places were found for worthy young students at the English Colleges at St Omer and Rome, with preference being given to George Collingwood and Christopher Piggot, two of the Queen's 'Chapel boys' at Whitehall, who had fled to France and been educated in Latin there at a cost to her privy purse. Others were not so lucky and, having seen his pay constantly cut back, Ensign Cook of the King's Life Guard wrote despondently to the Bishop of Metz, fearing that he could no longer fund the education of his young sister at a nearby convent. However, while this emphasis on a religious education maintained and indeed strengthened the organic connection between St Germain and the Church in France, Spain and Rome, it also

meant that some of the brightest and best sons and daughters of the
leading Jacobite families became dedicated servants of the Curia and the
mendicant orders, rather than directly serving the exiled Stuart court
and devoting their talents entirely towards the restoration of James II and
his son. Moreover, the practice of sending their younger children away to
become priests and nuns eventually led to the failure of the bloodline of
several noble Jacobite houses, while the restricted curriculum and
orderly, disciplined way of life did not sit easily with all those youngsters
who were schooled by the divines. Thus, Mary of Modena was forced to
apologise to the Abbess of Dunkirk for the unruly behaviour of one of
her pages – Roger, the adolescent son of Lady Strickland – who had been
put into her charge, conceding that: 'I desired you to take upon you a
charge so difficult and improper to your state of life' for 'I know how
impossible it is for a Religious person in inclosure to guide the actions of
a young man abroad'. Promising that she would forward payment
forthwith for the disruption and damages caused during the boy's stay,
the Queen added that the quartering of a youth in the convent 'is not
likely to happen again', and attempted to strike a positive note in her
correspondence by confiding that she was 'fully persuaded that without
the care you had of him, he might have fallen into greater
inconveniencies'.[18]

James's rather anomalous position as both the *de jure* head of the
Anglican Church and as a proselytising Roman Catholic, increasingly
concerned with his personal salvation and that of all those about him,
unsurprisingly produced a series of rather awkward expedients at
St Germain. The King continued to make appointments to vacant sees
in the Church of England – which William had begun to fill with
greater decision since the discovery of the non-jurors' connivance in
Lord Preston's plot – though he had made sure first to ask the advice of
the Catholic bishops of France about the legality and morality of this
move before embarking on it. Although the crisis in the Anglican Church
had lessened slightly with the death of Archbishop Sancroft in 1693, and
with the unedifying spectacle of Thomas Sprat, Bishop of Rochester,
dissembling his allegiance to James from the witness box and pleading
that his 'weak memory' did not permit him to recall the details of his
overtures to St Germain, James was still approving the appointments of
the deprived Bishop of Norwich in the mid- to late 1690s, and saw to it
that Denis Granville, the Anglican Dean of Durham, served him as his
personal chaplain, in his capacity as 'defender of the faith', alongside his
regular phalanx of Capuchin confessors.[19] However, for as long as
Granville's presence was barely tolerated by the French authorities, and
his ability to preach and polemicise thus severely limited at St Germain,
there was as little hope of the non-jurors significantly informing the
King's policies in France as there was of them breaking out of their

insular and increasingly marginalized ghetto mentality in England.
Unfortunately, James's interest within the Roman Catholic hierarchy was
no less bitterly contested, with the cardinals and bishops who owed their
allegiances to either the Empire or Spain opposing his appointments on
the grounds that they were simply the agents of French foreign policy.
Successive popes, while expressing their personal admiration for the
former King's qualities and sorrow at his plight, feared both the effects of
his counter-productive zeal on the Roman Catholic community in
England, and the risk to the Papal States in being seen to decisively
favour a client of Louis XIV, or even for that matter of Leopold I. James
was certainly fortunate in having the loyal support of both the young and
inordinately ambitious Cardinal de Bouillon – who headed the College of
Cardinals, and should have been a decisive voice in choosing a new
pontiff – and of Gabriel de Roquette, the Bishop of Autun (and Bossuet's
nephew), in furthering his personal and political cause, although neither
enjoyed the full confidence of Louis XIV. His other allies, Cardinal de
Noailles and Cardinal d'Estrees, devoted themselves primarily to
undermining the Jesuit stranglehold on the French court. Far more
serious was the frequently strained relationship between James and Philip
Howard, the Cardinal of Norfolk, the foremost English clergyman at the
court of Rome. Tactful and diligent, Howard had spent his entire career
in the conjoined service of the Church and the English Catholics, only to
have his office as Protector of England stripped from him at the court of
Rome on James's initiative in 1688 and awarded, instead, to Mary of
Modena's Italian uncle, Cardinal Rinaldo d'Este. If this were not bad
enough, James then lost further credit with both the English Catholic
community and the Curia by wildly apportioning a share of the blame for
his fall from power to Howard – for failing to harness the power of the
papacy firmly against William III – and then by watching helplessly as his
nominee, the Cardinal d'Este, promptly sought to set aside his vows and
marry, following the death of his nephew Francesco II and his
inheritance of the duchy in his own right. It was almost a grace that
Howard, who had died in the summer of 1694, did not have to witness
the confusion caused in the administration of the English Church by
Rinaldo's decision, or the unseemly family squabble that was soon to
break out between uncle and niece over the unpaid balance of Mary of
Modena's marriage portion, a sum which many hungry exiles realised
might now be used for their maintenance at the court of St Germain. As
it was, James had attempted to ensure that the renewal of the powers of
the four Roman Catholic bishops charged with overseeing the pastoral
life of England might be achieved by Howard 'with as little noise as
possible', so as not to excite adverse comment or raise the confessional
temperature in his former kingdom, while hoping that the Cardinal
might continue to forward his interests in Rome. However, for the most

part, the King preferred to use Ellis, the titular and far more pliable Bishop of Adrianople, as the conduit of intelligence from the Papal States to his own Household.[20]

Yet while secret correspondence continued to crawl perilously across the Channel until the defeat at La Hogue, from courtiers such as Marlborough and Godolphin – who hoped to salvage their careers in the event of King James's return – the Jacobite secretaries of state, under-resourced and continually overstretched, were constantly in danger of losing the covert war to undermine William III's government. Melfort had managed the King's intelligence-gathering service during the first years of the Jacobite exile with relative efficiency and considerable diligence, commanding those clergymen and gentlemen of whose loyalty he was sure to enter into covert activity as a matter of duty, and easing the consciences of those whose devotion to the cause wavered by the generous distribution of bribes and subsidies. Yet Melfort's sense of proud independence and his willingness to fight tenaciously to preserve his master's influence made him a large number of enemies at the French court, which had previously been well-disposed towards him and had served to counterbalance the disapproval with which many of his fellow exiles had always regarded his activities. While Louis XIV's ministers enjoyed his cultured conversation and were prepared to forgive him his occasional displays of overbearing arrogance, they became concerned and felt that they could not afford to overlook his activities when these began to cut across their own ministerial briefs. In particular, the abbé Renaudot, who had been placed in charge of controlling the spy network in England by de Seignelay, bitterly resented any attempt to subordinate his own activities to those of Melfort, or to establish dual control over intelligence-gathering between Versailles and St Germain. Thus, while the exiles thought primarily in terms of advancing the day of King James's restoration and harnessed their activities to that end, assuming that French support would be a constant in all their schemes, the foreign policy objectives of the French Crown were to break the series of European alliances arrayed against it, and to knock England out of the war at all costs. As a result, there were many hard choices to be made among King James's former subjects as the 1690s wore on, as to whether their allegiance lay with the 'rightful' sovereign or with the nation itself. With trade disrupted by French privateers, and English and Scottish soldiers daily spilling their blood in Flanders, it was difficult for many patriotic men and women in the constituent kingdoms of the British Isles to applaud foreign victories which threatened them with higher taxes, bankruptcy, and the deaths of husbands and sons, in order that their exiled monarch might be restored at an unspecified future date. Moreover, for a monarch who identified himself with an unambiguous form of English nationalism which sought to extend the frontiers of empire and to supersede the cultural traditions of the regions, James was apparently unable, or entirely unwilling, to recognise that his position as the ally of his country's foes was in any way anomalous. Though he might choose to maintain that the English state was indivisible from his own person and office, the reality of wartime – when his servants were engaged in espionage that was primarily intended to furnish military assistance to a foreign power – was one that might not easily be reconciled to the principles of a patriot. The failure of James and his supporters to fashion a distinctive image for English and Irish (as opposed to Scottish) Jacobitism, which could harness cultural aspirations and pre-existing national mythologies to its cause, only served to increase the distance between the King and those whom he had once ruled, and to render his cause a fringe movement which acted merely as an umbrella for a variety of discontents and localised concerns. With Melfort dealing directly with agents across the British Isles, the exiled court could maintain organic links with its followers at home, while, conversely, operatives in the field could continue to believe that they were engaged in the struggle to return their King to power, rather than simply furthering the territorial ambitions of Louis XIV's France. However, Melfort's position was systematically undermined by the Compounders and by those among his former allies at St Germain who either looked with jealousy on his friendship with the King, or had lost all faith in his judgement after the declaration of 1692 had rebounded so disastrously on them all. Thus, Renaudot's scathing appraisal of his rival's competence, and his conclusion that 'the court of Saint-Germain has proved so often wrong about the faithfulness of some or the dishonesty of others that we take no risk by not trusting it blindly', gained a wide currency among James's followers, hastening Melfort's fall and the subordination for the time being of the King's ability to gather intelligence outside channels recognised and supervised by the French authorities.

If Melfort had enjoyed some success in coordinating plans to destabilise King William's government in England and Scotland, he and – more damagingly – his successors were far less adept at controlling the leaks that emanated from their own supporters. The unwelcome truth was that the court of St Germain crawled with spies in the way a hedgehog is alive with a multiplicity of ticks and fleas, draining away the lifeblood of its unwitting host. Failure to find advancement at King James's court led the unscrupulous, or the simply disillusioned, to settle both their personal and financial accounts by selling information to their erstwhile foes. In this way, the aforementioned Fr Campbell sought to bolster his flagging career, while John Simpson cheerfully sold secrets to either side, and William Fuller – who had served as a page to Mary of Modena, and had frequently shuttled correspondence in and out of

England – finally lost his nerve and, upon capture, agreed to act as an informant, fabricating ever wilder tales of conspiracies and incipient invasions in order to justify his retention on the government payroll. Yet it was the inability of the members of James's extended Household to refrain from idle boasts and loud conversation in very public places that led to Bentinck – who had gathered the reins of the intelligence services to himself – to harvest the choicest and often the most accurate streams of information. The Jacobites' employment of simple codes and pseudonyms to protect their agents could hardly withstand the attentions of the mathematician John Wallis, who was retained by the Williamite government to break their ciphers. Melfort was denoted by the number '16', Middleton by '10', James by '300' and his Queen by '302'. Unfortunately, the code names adopted by the Jacobites, with their paternalistic sovereign known as the 'good farmer', the Prince of Wales as 'the bold Briton', and Princess Anne and her husband the Prince of Denmark waspishly styled as 'Charles and Mrs. Chirchill', would hardly stand up to critical scrutiny for more than a few minutes. Worse still, a lack of care bordering on sheer incompetence bedevilled the Jacobite intelligence services at every level. The luckless Fergus Graham scribbled an address to Lord Middleton at 'the Court of England', and was surprised to discover that the postmaster of Liège, knowing no better, had simply redirected his reports to Whitehall, while Melfort's list of active Jacobite agents, destined for the scrutiny of his brother at St Germain, was caught up in a parcel of English mail and was subsequently published by William III, as evidence of the continuing malignancy of the movement. When the Jacobites were not busy scoring such spectacular own goals, the English embassy in Paris served as a centre for counter-espionage throughout Bentinck's tenure in 1698, and his secretary, Matthew Prior, regularly haunted the city's pastry and coffee shops 'becoming acquainted with half the starving English and Irish about Paris'. He duly filed his reports, contrasting the hardships suffered by the émigré community with the cancerous distemper that he felt to be at the heart of their cause. Even more successful was John Macky, who slipped in and out of St Germain and its environs almost at will, and who authoritatively confirmed that the French naval operations of 1692 had aimed at landing an invasion force on the coasts of England as opposed to Scotland, which had originally been thought to be the target by the Admiralty.[21]

Though James had agreed to the banishment of Fergus Graham 'on some disgust the Queen had taken' to his habitual drunkenness, and he was held to be 'a great enemie to drinking, gameing and indeed all such pleasures as were obstructive to business, and which commonly render men wholy incapable of it', he was far less successful in containing the passions and petty jealousies of his followers. One of the failings of the

Jacobite court, which Prior had been quick to identify, was its propensity for violence in order to settle even the most minor of quarrels. It was hardly surprising that in such a heavily militarised community – where numbers were swelled each winter by officers and volunteers returning from the front, every gentleman wore a sword, and where poverty added a harder edge to questions of honour and precedence – that fights would flare with sudden intensity, but James had always been curiously ill-equipped to preserve order among his followers. The closest companions of his youth, men such as Jermyn and Tyrconnel, had been inveterate duellists who scorned the attempts of the civil authorities to limit their private score-settlings. Yet while advancing years had swept apart their fates – with Tyrconnel dying in harness as the loyal servant of the House of Stuart, and Jermyn slinking off from St Germain in 1692 to engineer his return to a comfortable and undistinguished retirement in England – James retained to the last both an unwillingness to clamp down on 'killing affrays' and a certain inclination towards accepting duels as a necessary part of the soldier's life. As a result, such fights punctuated the monotony of life at court and the marquis de Dangeau noted in February 1691 that: 'A few days ago, a dreadful duel took place at St. Germain; two Englishmen, the brothers of the earl of Salisbury, quarrelled, fought and wounded each other dangerously'. Though they quickly set aside the reasons behind their dispute and asked each other's pardon, they 'sent for a priest, and abjured the protestant religion'. The Frenchman added a doleful postscript, that 'the elder, nineteen years of age, is since dead of his wounds, and the younger is extremely ill; [and] he only waits his recovery to enter the society of La Trappe'.[22]

In a society with a fluctuating and mobile aristocratic population, many of whose members arrived and left in conditions of secrecy, issues of identity and pedigree also loomed large. The King continued to maintain a College of Arms, and charged his Herald, James Therry, to settle all such cases and to adjudge who could, and who could not, bear arms. Certificates proving that the Carys, Ogilvies, and Hanmers were indeed noble families were quickly forthcoming, but matters were further complicated by the tendency of some itinerant exiles – who shared no ties of blood but did possess the same surname – to claim an aristocratic lineage in the hope of thereby securing a share of scarce patronage and preferment. There was a similar tendency among some French families to claim English patents of nobility, taking advantage of the general confusion to advance spurious claims of kinship, or to assert their ownership of titles that had long fallen vacant through tenuous claims to descent from junior or long-separated branches of once-great families. In this manner, Louis and Pierre Becquet, and Julian Campain, laid claim to English titles and estates, and while the pedigrees of displaced Irish gentlemen such as Matthew Crone were relatively easy to

check, James wrote tersely to his Herald about the need to examine
carefully 'the pretensions of John Jacquenot Jackson, Sieur des Auches,
a captain of the French army, to bear the arms of the family of Jackson
of Hickleton in Yorkshire, Baronet, of which he pretends to be a
cadet'.[23] Such disputes arose primarily not through petty criminality and
the desire to defraud a court that had found itself in greatly reduced
circumstances, but stemmed instead from the realisation that in the
event of King James's restoration it was more than likely, given the
unforgiving tenor of the declaration of 1692, that estates would be
sequestered from leading Williamites and re-allocated to their original,
or more deserving, owners. Moreover, the realisation that the returning
King would be in need of a great many loyal appointees to reinvigorate
the organs of state and to help govern the regions, after a successful
counter-revolution had all but swept away the current personnel, led
many exiles to retain their hope in better days to come, and to engage
in internecine battles over apparently academic titles and empty
privileges with far greater vigour than would otherwise have been the
case. This explained, in part, the eagerness with which the émigré
community watched James's appointments to the Jacobite peerage and
court, with intense interest and considerable expectation. As English,
Irish, and Scottish titles fell vacant – or were held to have been forfeited
through disloyalty – the King appointed his core followers to reflect the
composition of the peerage in his lost domains. However, for the most
part, he was sparing and realistic in his appointments and carefully
avoided the dangerous temptation of creating a new and entirely titular
nobility in the hope of binding his aristocratic servants more closely to
him. Thus, the majority of his appointments occurred during the first
years of his exile, when he attempted to fashion a fresh government
about him at St Germain – raising William Herbert, the former Earl of
Powis, to a dukedom and conferring the rank of baron on Melfort and
Preston – and when the war in Ireland necessitated rewarding Tyrconnel
with a dukedom, Sarsfield and Galmoy with earldoms, and Macarty with
the honour of Viscount Mountcashel. On the death of the thoroughly
dissipated Christopher Monck, 2nd Duke of Albemarle in 1696 and the
extirpation of his line, William III had appointed his handsome young
favourite Arnold Joost van Keppel to the honour of 1st Earl of
Albemarle, forcing James to retaliate by creating his son Henry
Fitzjames as duke in his stead. Political reality was also reflected in the
desire of the exiled King to further reward Melfort for his friendship
and loyalty with a dukedom, just at the point (in 1694) when his
political support was haemorrhaging away at both St Germain and
Versailles, and when the ascent of John Caryll in his place virtually
demanded the latter's advance to the dignity of Baron Caryll of Durford
five years later.[24]

The claims to the legitimacy of the Jacobite 'government' in waiting were likewise kept alive by the manufacture of new seals of office and a fresh coinage, intended to rival and to eventually supersede those recast in England after 1688. James recalled that the regalia of the Lord Mayor of Dublin was still in the possession of Sir Terence Dermot, the former incumbent, and demanded that it be returned immediately to Sir William Ellis, one of the few remaining Irish Protestant Jacobites, as 'we have not yet determined in whose custody the . . . chain and medal ought to remain during our absence from our kingdoms'. The master engraver John Roettiers and his two sons, James and Norbert, had fled to France at the Revolution and continued to serve their patron 'as engravers general for the king of England', producing in January 1689 a new Great Seal to replace the die that he had recklessly cast away in the Thames during his initial flight from Whitehall. Without the possession of the correct die James clearly believed that any orders issued under his hand – or under that of his rival – would be invalid and 'knowing the necessity of having a Great Seal of England with us' carried the new die with him into Ireland, 'wherewith we ordered several patents and grants to be sealed in our royal presence'. Unfortunately, however, the King quickly discovered that 'that Great Seal, as being made in haste, was imperfect in the graving, and the impression made thereby not so beautiful as the impressions of our Great Seal of England used to be' and, while still in Dublin in May 1691, he ordered John Roettiers to start work on a more fitting replacement. As soon as the craftsman had finished his work, James ordered that the old seal should 'be broken in our presence, which was accordingly done' so that there could be no chance that forgeries could be made from it and so that the work of his government might proceed without a halt or inconvenience. By the close of 1695, James had also envisaged the production of an entirely new coinage and had authorised Roettiers and his sons to engrave 'punchions and dies for coining five pound pieces, forty shilling pieces, guineas and half-guineas of gold with the royal arms on one side, and the picture of the King on the other', together with stamps of like design, 'for coining crowns, half-crowns, shillings and sixpences'. However, while it is unclear if examples of the fresh Jacobite currency were ever produced in large numbers, it is probable that their propaganda value exceeded their practical use, and that the dies were only intended to be shipped to Britain and Ireland in the event of a successful invasion. Far more effective were the series of commemorative medallions that the Roettiers family, and later Dassier, produced in order to glorify the King and his young son. These could be slipped easily into a pocket or hung round the neck, so that the memory of the fallen Stuarts might not fade so easily in their lost kingdoms, and so that the images of James and his son might serve as a constant reminder of the continuing need for service and personal sacrifice on the part of their erstwhile subjects. Consequently, at the same time as William Weston's print shop at St Germain poured forth a stream of pamphlets, broadsides and books from its presses, often purposely produced small enough to hold in the palm of a hand or conceal easily about the person, the little foundry that served the court turned out medals to be smuggled into the British Isles – often by the Roettiers themselves – which served as similar political manifestos, albeit in gold, silver, copper and bronze.[25]

Certainly the exiled court was not an arid place, intellectually barren and bereft of any sense of aesthetic beauty, for its inhabitants, drawn predominantly from among the élites of Stuart society, were highly literate and desired to emulate their near neighbours at Versailles. Melfort adapted easily to life in the opulent suite of apartments that had previously been home to madame de Montespan, and filled its walls with large canvases collected from the studios of a rising generation of Italian artists. Under James's patronage, Innocenzo Felde, the master of music, ensured that new Italian scores also predominated in the repertoire of the small ensemble of professional musicians who gave recitals at the court and, when required, provided the accompaniment to religious services held in the castle's large chapel. Moreover, while John Caryll and Richard, Lord Maitland proved themselves adept as translators of reflective, religious and classical works, an altogether lighter and more worldly note was struck by Anthony Hamilton after his return from Ireland, as he set down a series of scandalous recollections of the intrigues and passions that had characterised Charles II's Household at Whitehall. Yet it was noticeable that as Hamilton attempted to recapture the gallantry and hedonism of his long-vanished, carefree youth, he chose to draw an unflattering contrast between the court of the Restoration and the jaded and oppressively introspective atmosphere that he felt prevailed at St Germain. In sneering at the scores of priests who seemed to haunt the corridors and backstairs of the castle, and in characterising the court as 'the very worst place in the world', where widows in their weeds begged shamelessly for charity, he may have been doing no more than looking back to a vanished age of plenty before the hard reality of exile, and recalling a period of sexual and personal licence that had withered away before King James's increasingly forbidding gaze. However, it is significant that this account of life at St Germain – with its bores and bankrupts – from the pen of a committed Jacobite largely echoed the tone conjured by that of Macky the Williamite agent.[26]

Despite his unexpectedly protracted residence at the Old Castle, James did remarkably little to renovate the fabric of his palace, or to raise monuments to himself and his young family in terms of bricks and mortar, or to commission great works of representative art. The former may be explained by the scarcity of funds, an already crippling wages bill, and an understandable reluctance to tamper with a property that was only on loan to him, but the lack of a tangible imprint of his stay upon the architecture of the building was not lost on later visitors – who hoped to imbibe something of the faded grandeur and tragedy attached to his latter years – and resulted in King François's salamanders continuing to leer down on his throne, rather than the lion and the unicorn, as might have been expected, being installed on the brickwork and panelling of the walls above his audience chamber. Having taken great pains during both his youth and kingship to promote himself as a warrior of exceptional professionalism and prowess, it is both notable and surprising that James largely abandoned the use of his strident personal imagery after his return to France in the summer of 1690. While on campaign in Ireland he had still been happy to have John Riley portray him as a victorious commander, his tightly down-turned lips offering the only clue to his recent setbacks and the belated discovery of the harshness of war (see Plate 1). As cavalry troopers wheel about him on a darkened canvas, shot through with the streaks from his blood-red plume and gaudy sash, the King is caught in motion turning to view those unknown eyes which have the temerity to regard his armoured and still-trim figure, his gaze as impassive as ever and only a faint crease on his brow betraying his advancing years. Relaxed and thoroughly in his element amid the sudden din and dislocation of battle, James appears as the master of the situation, his right hand clad in the kidskin and tassels of a fine leather glove, gripping his baton of command and signalling the direction of the advance, while he rests momentarily on his plumed cuirassier helm. His open left hand, fringed only by a finely cascading seam of lace that is at odds with his blackened cavalry armour, reaches instinctively for the rapier that hangs loosely at his side, in expectation of action.

Yet defeat at the Boyne had laid bare the King's failings as a general and revealed the all too slender grounds on which his reputation as a formidable soldier had been built, rendering his recourse to military symbolism and authority untenable literally overnight, as the brutalising reality of a shattered Irish army and real men rather than painted forms lying injured and dying in the lanes about Duleek, deserted by their commander, impinged on the carefully crafted artifice of James's martial genius, making it the redundant object of bitter scorn. Unable to effect an immediate return to active service as the result of King Louis's refusal to include him in his entourage at the siege of Mons, James was faced by the wreckage of his personal imagery and declined to sit for further martial portraits. When his Household servants, such as Sir Thomas Strickland, wished for new canvases of the King clad in armour, clutching his baton of command, and swathed in the folds of a military cloak, they were forced to turn instead to existing images, painted by artists like

Sir Godfrey Kneller before the Revolution, and to have them copied by artists attached to the court of France. If it no longer seemed appropriate, in the short term at least, to depict James as a warrior, then the King was increasingly painted, drawn and engraved in the mid-1690s as a companion figure to his wife and children, fulfilling the roles of either royal patriarch or holy penitent.[27] Even then, the stimulus for these new developments came primarily not from James himself, or even from any of his closest adherents, but from the King of France and the court of Versailles.

It was Louis XIV who willed the commission of an enormous canvas depicting the exiled royal family, and sent his brother Monsieur to accompany James and Mary of Modena to the door of Pierre Mignard, the foremost French portrait painter, in order to persuade him to engage in the endeavour. Unfortunately, Mignard was old, perennially overworked and seriously ill, and complained mournfully after several sittings at St Germain that he could not continue with his work on account of the damp, fearing that 'the air was too cold for a man whose chest was infected'. Initial sketches, with bold strokes of red chalk offsetting the delicate black outlines of the figures, showed the King standing supported by a walking stick, while his little daughter clung to her mother's shoulder. The Prince of Wales was shown as a precociously self-confident young boy, clad in a miniature breastplate as an indication of his desire to emulate his father in the waging of war and pointing towards the royal regalia, in order to underscore the themes of the continuity and legitimacy of the exiled House. However, it seems that the dimensions of the King's chambers at St Germain where the canvas was to be displayed necessitated an alteration to the composition, while James's personal preferences ensured a subtle reworking of the figures, with formalism triumphing over the relative naturalism of the artist's original treatment of the group. Thus, the chubby and babyish face of the Princess Louise Marie was slimmed to conform to adult proportions, and she was shown gesturing towards the King with a calm composure which was mirrored even in the gaze of a faithful spaniel that regarded its master with a mixture of awe and loving intent. The elderly servant who had originally carried the train of the young Prince's cloak was now replaced by a crouching black page, while James was shown seated in his Garter robes, bolt upright in his armchair as he gathered towards himself the folds of his cloak and the hilt of the court sword that had replaced his cane (see Plate 17). The result undoubtedly differed from King Louis's original conception of a grand yet relatively informal canvas that would form a fitting companion piece to the portrait of the dauphin's young family, completed by the same artist just six years earlier. Under James's direction, it was the majesty of the monarchy, transcending all human frailties, embodying the values of family and dependent on the virtues of the patriarch at its core, that was most firmly emphasised. It offered a vision of a new and, he believed, 'rightful' Stuart dynasty that, given time and the Grace of God, would push aside the dishonoured and spoiled fruit of his first marriage that he was now forced to reject through their connivance in the usurpation of his throne. Consequently, the 'cult' of the exiled House of Stuart, centred about an idealised family unit of the wise old father, the beautiful but demure and devoted mother, and two well-behaved and serious children who promised much for the future, came to replace the image of James, the original 'Jacobus', as the defining element in the cause that bore his name. Though the King would always represent the fount of authority for Jacobitism, it was a gradually encroaching sense of his own mortality, added to the fear that his children might be permanently stripped of their birthrights and confined to eking out meagre livings at courts on the outer fringes of Europe, that led him on to revitalise the artistic reflection of an unyielding and single-minded political objective which, in the next hundred years, would commit itself entirely to the regaining of everything that had been lost in a few short weeks in the winter of 1688–9.

The last sitting for the picture had to be completed in November 1694 at the studio attached to the painter's home, as Mignard's work was quite literally killing him and his strength was no longer sufficient to permit him to continue his tiresome journeys to Versailles, let alone to the inhospitable palace further downriver on the Seine. However, it was some time before the finished portrait was installed at St Germain; James appears to have been in no great hurry to take possession of the work, and the canvas remained half-forgotten at Mignard's Parisian home following the death of the artist and the settling of his estate. Louis XIV took possession of the original sketches for the study, along with numerous pictures by Mignard of his own family and the French court, while the painting was finally removed to St Germain after James cleared his debts with the artist's daughter three years later, in a manner that was both equitable and to her evident satisfaction. Serving as the model for numerous copies and lesser, derivative versions of the same scene, Mignard's last great work appeared to mark a sea change in the King's use of personal imagery. It redefined James in the eyes of his English supporters and would-be adherents not as a man of war, whose every energy was geared to the promotion of fresh conflict, but as a man of advancing years who, despite the slights offered to him by an ungrateful people, still intended to rule for all as the father of the nation.

Yet this far more inclusive and pacific image of the King, widely disseminated from the mid-1690s onwards and based around the conventions and taste of the French court, could still strike entirely the wrong chord with James's former subjects if uncritically applied. Thus, the delicate pair of engravings executed in Paris by Trouvain in 1694, showing the King and Queen at their prayers, might well have charmed the émigré community and French courtiers with their depiction of the fidelity to God continually expressed by the royal couple, but might also have reinforced the dominant impression already created by the King's Protestant foes and the beneficiaries of the Revolution of 1688–9, that James's commitment to his peoples and to his kingship would always come a poor second to his overriding loyalty to the Church of Rome and to the prevailing political agendas espoused by the current pontiff. Indeed, while copies of the print were smuggled into Britain in large numbers and even found their way into Samuel Pepys's secluded library, the vision of James in the costume of the French court – complete with high-heeled shoes of the type popularised by Louis XIV, which given James's naturally imposing height would have made him a truly towering figure – did little to visually distinguish him as the 'Roy d'Angleterre' of whom the accompanying text made proud boast. Moreover, his portrayal as a humble supplicant attending to his private religious devotions, with his hands opening up his breviary at the correct page for that day's order of service, his arms crossed on the stall supporting the precious book and his face frozen in an expression of blank deference to the operation of the divine will, firmly located him within the culture of European Catholicism, despite his claims to be the head of the Church of England. It reinforced the sense among his erstwhile Protestant subjects that he was personally and spiritually dependent on hostile foreign powers for both his sustenance and for his basic political orientation (see Plate 14). Worse still, the link between James and his faith had already been established at the time of the Revolution by hostile English and Dutch artists, who had attempted to emphasise the King's role as an unthinking pawn of the Roman Church, constantly surrounded by hordes of squabbling, craven priests, and prepared at a moment's notice to sell his peoples' lives and liberties in order to propagate his faith and to introduce the harsh and unforgiving stamp of the Counter-Reformation to the British Isles. Thus, earlier engravings of the armoured King were re-cut so that a mock papal tiara might be shown suspended above his head, and in 1691 a print appeared in Holland that actually sought to show James clad as a Jesuit priest, the curls of his long wig spilling out from underneath his cap and tumbling out onto the shoulders of his dark uniform cape. The only inhabitant of a wasted landscape, illuminated solely by the palls of smoke and flame belched forth by the brazier suspended from his fortress's walls, James was recast as an apostle of religious terror and hatred, intent upon imitating the practices of Louis XIV's dragonnades and making forced re-conversions through a recourse to the noose and the gun (see Plate 9).[28] As a result, for those British viewers of Trouvain's serenely elegant print who were among the middle ground of Anglican and Tory opinion that James needed to cultivate if he was ever to secure his own and his son's restoration, what was intended to evoke thoughts of the King's personal piety might have simply reinforced the notion that his faith, as the single defining element of his kingship, carried with it an implicit commitment to a violent re-ordering of the state religion.

Furthermore, while Mignard had worked on a preparatory sketch showing the King in armour which was then abandoned, on account of either royal displeasure or the artist's death, by the close of the seventeenth century James – whose confidence in his military gifts had been reawakened by working on the early passages of his memoirs, at Cardinal de Bouillon's instigation – chose to return to his former martial imagery and had himself depicted by François de Troy as a warrior standing beside his crown. Clad in a somewhat stylised suit of armour, the manner of his portrayal had changed little over the course of almost forty years. Only the opulence of his wig, the lengthening of his jowls, and the fact that his sash and breastplate now barely disguised his spreading waistline bore testament to the ravages that time and disappointment had wrought on an individual who had come to despise his physical form and to seek a release from the cares of the world.[29] Yet it would be entirely wrong, and the result of no more than hindsight, to probe too deeply behind the apparent deadness of the King's heavily lidded eyes, or to project a sense of profound loss and utter hopelessness upon a man who, despite his retreat into asceticism, still felt the need to project the myth of his military genius and to impress his claims to political and religious vision upon both posterity and his son and heir, in whom he had invested so much (see Plate 18). Indeed, if James's failure to concentrate on refashioning his personal image – or to consistently promote any sort of visual image at all after 1690 – ceded the initiative to his foes, who distorted his intentions as readily as they had changed his garb from a kingly mantle to Jesuit robes, then through the production of a constant stream of images of the titular Prince of Wales and his sister Princess Louise Marie, James was at least able to chart their growth from babies to young adults, for his own benefit as a loving father and for the benefit of his supporters. The images emphasised beyond a shadow of doubt the strong family resemblance that both children, but most importantly his son, bore to their parents.[30]

If James succeeded in dispelling much of the ignominy and slander that had surrounded the birth of his heir, then it was this promotion of his own family, coupled with his passionately espoused faith, that directed his patronage of the arts, rather than any over-riding desire to collect or commission major works for their intrinsic beauty, or to sponsor any remarkable new developments in the field. The halls of St Germain were decorated with busts of the King in stone and terracotta, while carvings of

James's friend and confidant the abbé de La Trappe sat alongside his collections of holy relics and gems in the cabinets of his private rooms. It is notable that the King, with his profound aversion to novels and works of fiction and his habitual exhortations to his friends and supporters to read 'good books', did not maintain a library of any size; those volumes that he did own were overwhelmingly standard books of religious devotion, breviaries and conduct books, which served to order his day and to provide him with both the necessary thoughts for reflection when he retired to read after his lunch, and the words he needed 'to say the prayrs out of the manual for the evening'.[31] It was therefore unsurprising that paintings with religious themes should be produced by the series of artists employed at St Germain. However, it is significant that Poussin's enormous rendering of the 'Last Supper', hung in St Louis's chapel, was a legacy of the French King's tenure, and that it was Mary of Modena rather than James – who had never taken a particular interest in commissioning art of any kind – who took the lead in ordering new devotional canvases that were to be painted by Gennari and de Largillière and gifted to Louis XIV, Catherine of Braganza (by then resident in Portugal) and the sisters of the convent of La Chaillot. In addition, it was she who commissioned Gennari to produce a charming study of the Virgin and Child, which possibly hung in her private chapel alongside a large canvas by de Largillière (also ordered in 1692) depicting at prayer the St Margaret who had introduced Roman religious practice to Scotland in the eleventh century. However, the majority of commissions received by the artists in residence at St Germain came from private rather than royal patrons, and consisted of portraits of the exiled Stuarts which acted as keepsakes and badges of allegiance, as well as members of their own families. As a consequence images of the royal family, both separate and linked within a single design, proliferated in Jacobite households, while the luminaries of the court – such as the Waldegraves and the Stricklands, the dukes of Berwick and Albemarle, and Captain Macdonald – all sat for formal portraits before continental masters.[32]

Through the re-establishment of his court in exile, James II consciously sought to evoke the atmosphere of his former palace at Whitehall and to distance himself from William III's utter rejection of his administrative reforms. Despite the constraints imposed by his relatively reduced financial means, and the need to abandon his residence at St Germain at once if a recall to his kingdoms was forthcoming, James was able to create a dignified setting for his government in waiting, which had the power to impress the impartial visitor and which also reflected his own interests and preoccupations, in terms of his love of the hunt and his quest to secure the salvation of his soul. Moreover, while there was little that was innovatory about his limited artistic and literary patronage, it would be wrong to characterise St Germain as a doleful, threadbare, and thoroughly bigoted outpost of Counter-Reformation thought. For those of means who could still rely on an independent income drawn from their estates in the British Isles, or who could find employment through the patronage of King James and his Queen, life at St Germain could be both agreeable and rewarding, with access to the glittering society and entertainments of Versailles on hand if desired. However, for those without a fortune to trickle away on lodgings and ultimately fruitless plans for the restoration, or for those whose Protestantism jarred too roughly on the sensibilities of an increasingly intolerant French state, the émigré court could be just as harsh and as sorry a place as Anthony Hamilton had claimed. If the scramble for patronage formed the mainstay of politics in every royal household, then this process became far more savage and bitter in exile, where appointments were all too rare and a sense of defeat and omnipresent danger was far too common. After the mid-1690s, the hopes of both the King and his courtiers focused on the titular Prince of Wales, while the feeling grew that the return to power of the fallen House would be accomplished through steady work over a long period of years, rather than as the result of a sudden and spectacular collapse of the Williamite government that could be achieved in a matter of weeks. James, therefore, took on the aspect of the patriarch, effectively combining the sense of his legitimate inheritance from both his father and brother and the consistency and sacrifice that he had shown in upholding his office, with the more novel sentiment of renewal through his transference of insight and wisdom to his young son.

Yet, if James was in no doubt that his heir would one day be crowned as King James III in Westminster abbey, he also increasingly let it be known that he did not expect to live to see his family and Household returned back to England in triumph. This prospect of a deferred victory, though accepted by many at his court, came as scant comfort to those who struggled to make their living in both the château and the town of St Germain, and as the 1690s wore on there were increasing requests from the King's adherents, such as Sir Miles Cronly, that they might be naturalised as French citizens. Furthermore, while the first generation of émigrés, like Sir Thomas and Lady Winifred Strickland, might be prepared to settle into a quiet retirement in rural France, devoting themselves to charitable and religious concerns, a far starker choice faced the rising generation of Jacobite nobility. They might choose to continue to inhabit King James's shadow court, eking out a half-life that mirrored the practices of Whitehall from 1685–8 in the hope that their longed-for return to prominence might one day come to pass, proffering their swords and talents to France in the meantime, or they might consider abandoning the cause in which they had been raised, and negotiating their return home through a compromise with the Williamite authorities that would allow them to resume both the management of their estates and their part in the government of their localities. Such blunt choices were faced by the Strickland's own sons, and while their heir Walter, who had been Groom of the Bedchamber to James II, obtained permission to leave St Germain in 1699 to secure the family estates in Cumberland, his younger brother Roger – who had once caused such trouble for the nuns of Dunkirk – took service with the Prince de Conti, before obtaining a commission in the French army and dying before his twenty-fifth birthday during an outbreak of smallpox at Toulon.[33] Yet as political disappointment and military disaster threatened to eclipse the court, James's will to impose direction on his movement even after his death, and to refashion the historical record to suit the image of his kingship – as soldier, patriarch and humble penitent – found its expression not in the stones, the artwork, or the elaborate rituals of the palace of St Germain, but in the pages of the King's own writings, which would come to exert both a lasting influence and a dramatic fascination upon generations of propagandists, authors, and historians, of which their tired and care-worn author could only have dreamt.

CHAPTER SEVEN

Eclipse at Ryswick

I

In June 1694, the Earl of Perth and his wife broke their journey to Antwerp, leaving the comfort of their coach so that they might explore the battlefield of Landen. Almost a year before, King William's army had defended the streams and river tributaries that criss-crossed the terrain and anchored their flanks, dug in behind hastily improvised fortifications that linked together a chain of four villages, but which eventually had proved inadequate to repel the enormous weight of the French regiments, which had punctured their lines and swept over their trenches. The allied commander, Count Solms, had been carried from the field early in the day, faint from loss of blood, and mortally wounded by a cannon ball that had severed his right leg below the knee. King William – as even his enemies had been forced to concede – had led by example, stiffening his men's increasingly desperate resistance and placing himself at the head of his cavalry regiments, his diminutive figure often lost amid the crush of his foes, his wig and sash both shot through, as he launched repeated charges against solid walls of enemy troopers who far outnumbered his own. On two occasions, French regiments had occupied the crucial stronghold of Neerwinden on their left flank, only to be driven back from the burning village with heavy losses. However, at the third attempt, Marshal Luxembourg committed his crack troops, the Swiss Guards and the Gardes Françaises, to spearhead an attack that drove the allied defenders back in utter disorder from their emplacements and abandoned gun positions. By nightfall, Luxembourg surveyed more than sixty captured standards and, later still over his breakfast at Tirlemont, thought to toast the 'good King James' and to hope that the fruit of his victory would be realised through the consolation of that King and his swift re-establishment, God willing, upon his throne.[1] Landen should have been the greatest triumph in a year that had seen substantial victories for French arms in every theatre of the war against the allies. The fortresses of Rosas in Catalonia, Charleroi, Huy in Flanders, and Heidelberg on the Rhine, had all fallen before their siege guns, while Marshal Catinat broke the Savoyards at the battle of Marsaglia in October 1693, throwing open the road to Turin and forcing Duke Victor Amadeus to begin to reconsider his choice of alliances. Worse still, from the perspective of the English government, Admiral Tourville fell

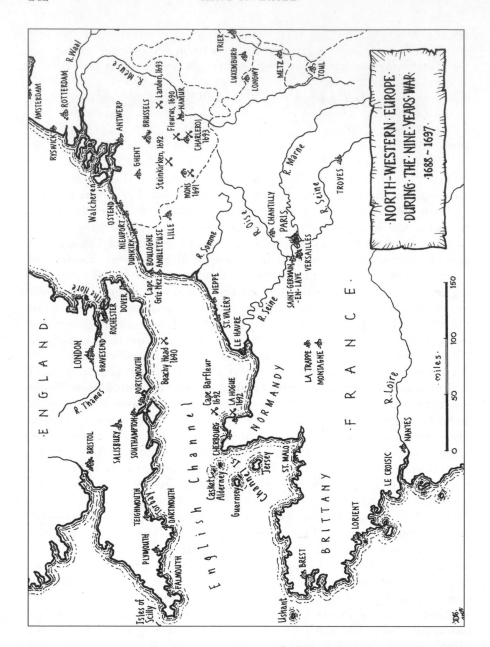

NORTH·WESTERN·EUROPE
·DURING·THE·NINE·YEARS·WAR·
·1688 ~ 1697·

upon the Smyrna convoy off the bay of Lagos, destroying the supply vessels and capturing a large amount of bullion, though the majority of the Dutch and English escorts fought their way clear in a running battle along the coast of Portugal.

Yet, as Perth walked 'over the field where the battle was fought last year', he derived no sense of satisfaction from seeing the 'heads and bones of limbs, skellets [i.e. skeletons] of horses, old hatts, shoes, holsters [and] saddles' that were strewn across the still-cratered landscape. Instead, he noted – with remarkable prescience – that poppies had sprung up amid the remains of the shattered trenchworks of Flanders, 'and where it is lying untilled a scarlet sheet is not of a deeper dye nor seems more smooth than all the ground is with these flowers, as if last year's blood had taken root and appeared this year in flowers'. The truth of the matter was that Luxembourg had failed to pursue his broken foes, allowing William to escape back across the River Geete with his baggage train, and regroup his regiments about Louvain. His ferocious defence at Landen had effectively torn the guts out of the French army, blunting the force of its strike against the frontier fortresses and saving Brussels and Liège from investment for at least another year. Losses on both sides, as Perth came to appreciate during his tour of the stricken field, had been appalling, but the impact of such high casualties among their officer corps had caused particular dismay to the French commanders, causing them to pause for some six weeks in the prosecution of their offensive, while the court of St Germain felt keenly the loss of those of their gentlemen volunteers and King James's Foot Guards who had been mown down by point-blank artillery fire in the struggle for the breastworks. Colonel Barrett, a member of the 1689 Dublin Parliament and a veteran of the siege of Cork, had fallen at the head of the Guards, while Sarsfield had been shot through the chest as he directed the attack on Neerwinden, and Berwick had been separated from his men during the struggle for the village. Discarding his white cockade, Berwick took advantage of his red officer's coat and tried to thread his way back through the enemy regiments to his own lines. He might well have succeeded in his task had he not been recognised by his own uncle, Brigadier George Churchill, who arrested him and his aide-de-camp at once and delivered them, impassive and curt, to the side of King William. Despite the thunder of battle that raged all about them, the King extended the gentlemanly courtesies of war towards his captives and, 'after looking steadfastly at [Berwick] for an instant', he ordered him to be conveyed safely off the field under heavy guard.[2]

In similar fashion, the victory at Marsaglia had been purchased with a disproportionate cost to Irish life. The initial charge of the 'Wild Geese' carried all before it but could not be adequately controlled, as the soldiers clubbed and battered their way into the enemy redoubts, momentarily threatening to overtake the Duke of Savoy as he spurred his horse from the battlefield, and utterly oblivious to the burning shot that tore through their ranks and shredded their colours even at the moment of victory. Two Scottish officers, Major-General Thomas Maxwell and Brigadier John Wauchop, had died leading King James's dismounted dragoons, while Brigadier James de Lacy and Colonel Daniel O'Brien (newly created 4th Viscount Clare) had suffered mortal wounds as they led the Irish Brigade within range of the enemy guns. Moreover, even as the Earl of Perth clambered back into his coach and continued his leisurely journey back through the Low Countries, Justin Macarty – half-crippled from the wounds he had suffered at Newtown Butler and in subsequent campaigns along the Rhine – had taken leave from the French army to take the curative waters of the Pyrenees. Unfortunately the treatment proved of no avail and, as Perth returned to his comfortable lodgings in Antwerp, the Lieutenant-General's constitution finally failed him and he breathed his last in a rented room at the spa town of Barèges. Fate was to treat others among James's followers even less kindly, as several of his privateers were taken at sea and their crews tried and hung as common criminals in the autumn of 1693, though they pleaded before the Council of State that their commissions had been lawfully obtained from the court at St Germain and that they should be treated in the same manner as other prisoners of war. Although the deaths of Sarsfield, Macarty, and their brother officers would be duly lamented in the pages of Parisian newspapers – and James would spend anxious days wondering if his son would be conveyed to the Tower of London, before word finally reached him of Berwick's exchange for the Duke of Ormonde – the fortunes of those private soldiers wounded or maimed at Landen and Marsaglia passed without a murmur. Many, if not most, were forced to seek charity from religious foundations, while their families braved as best they could the shortages and famines that afflicted France as the harvests failed in 1693–4. With the wage bill for his retainers spiralling at St Germain and the French War Ministry already footing the bill for his regiments, James was largely unable and – judging by the lack of formal bequests made to his invalided soldiers among his Household accounts – somewhat unwilling to acknowledge the need for the systematic relief of his destitute followers.[3]

To make matters worse, as Louis XIV's victories were revealed to be increasingly hollow and the French King began to cast about for a means of extricating himself from a conflict that had the power to ruin his carefully crafted state, James's own attempts to capitalise on the cycle of allied defeats and to foment domestic unrest across the British Isles suddenly started to appear forlorn and tarred by a streak of cynical, or possibly desperate, opportunism that had previously been largely absent from his considerations of policy. Following the defeat at La Hogue and the devastating failure of the Declaration of 1692 to speak to James's former subjects in a moderate, constructive and appealing language which they could readily understand, the political initiative within the Jacobite movement began to slip away from Melfort and the hardliners, and to vest itself for the first time since the Revolution in the disparate groups of Compounders who clustered about the rival earls of Middleton and Ailesbury. In the New Year of 1693, both noblemen had slipped independently out of England and made their way to St Germain, hoping to gain the confidence and favour of the King. The timing of their arrival could hardly have been more propitious; Melfort was locked in a bitter struggle with the abbé Renaudot over control of the intelligence services, and had been widely censured for the political failures of the previous year. Furthermore, James was all too well aware of the growing desire for peace at the court of Versailles and, fearful at the thought that the French Crown's support might suddenly be withdrawn from him, he was now far more willing to acknowledge the advice of King Louis's ministers on pursuing policies that embodied tact and compromise. With resistance in Scotland and Ireland effectively crushed, it had become painfully clear to James that English Jacobitism, in its current incarnation, was far too limited in terms of both its popular appeal and its ability to turn covert activism into full-scale insurrection, to ever successfully challenge the Williamite state. Furthermore, if there was now little chance of his followers initiating a new English Civil War, the cumulative effects of the defeats at the Boyne, Aughrim, and La Hogue – coupled with the over-extension of French military power across Spain, Flanders, Italy and the Rhineland – had served to rule out the decisive use of foreign arms in his restoration to the throne. If the military option, and all thought of the reconquest of his errant peoples, was denied to James for the foreseeable future, then he was henceforth compelled to reconsider his whole strategy for regaining power. He would have to invest far greater time, thought and patience in forging a viable negotiated settlement which would satisfy the concerns of enough of the leading magnates to provoke a haemorrhaging of support for King William's government, in order to send the usurper and his treacherous wife away with exactly the same speed and sense of clinical efficiency with which they had arrived.

James's confidence had been buoyed by the failure of Marlborough and, more surprisingly given his willingness to preside over the destruction of Jacobite hopes at Barfleur and La Hogue, Admiral Russell, to completely sever their contacts with St Germain. As a result, the King's belief that the army and navy might be induced to declare for him, or at least to maintain a state of wary neutrality once William's administration had begun to falter, remained largely undaunted. Moreover, the willingness of the Earl of Middleton, who had been imprisoned in the

Tower alongside Marlborough and Huntingdon during the invasion scare of the previous summer, to rush to St Germain at almost the first available opportunity following his belated release from custody, not only served to furnish the fallen King with up-to-date knowledge of the mood of the English opposition, but also suggested that all that was needed to capitalise on the disaffection of the High Tory nobility was a suitably attractive and accommodating blueprint for the re-establishment of his personal government. However, while the subsequent arrival of the Earl of Ailesbury at James's court undoubtedly served to confirm this impression, that nobleman's cause had already been largely compromised by Middleton, whose arrival far sooner and in conditions of much greater secrecy had enabled him to gain the King's ear without fear of contradiction or opposition from other Compounders. Another trait, which he rather surprisingly shared with Melfort, had also served to endear Middleton to James and to signal the beginnings of his ascendancy in the service of the exiled King. Put simply, he avoided – as Ailesbury most certainly did not – disagreeing with James's judgement or challenging his notions about the foundations on which his support in his former kingdoms was built. Thus, Ailesbury, who sought to circulate a new manifesto from King James throughout the fleet, and who had come to St Germain with promises of assistance from admirals Killigrew and Deval, found himself subjected to a most uncomfortable, and to his mind unproductive, interview with his sovereign. Things began badly as James pressed the nobleman to reveal what he thought of the Declaration of 1692; the King was 'a little stunned' when Ailesbury tactfully refused to answer the question directly and, with noticeably less delicacy, added that 'there was little occasion of giving my opinion, since the declaration was printed some time since in London, and the printer [Mr Darby of Bartholomew Close] was or would be soon hanged'. Regardless of the King's evident displeasure, Ailesbury pressed on, asking James if he was prepared, as many English Jacobites believed he was, to 'go over with a competent force' to back his words with the threat of force. Terse and agitated, the King replied in his 'short dry way . . . "Over? Over? You know the contrary"', waving aside the nobleman's protests that he had 'never read . . . of a declaration set forth and published until that King or Prince was ready to support it either by a legitimate right or a usurping one'. Noting that Middleton was at James's side, Ailesbury ventured one last gambit in an attempt to compromise his rival and to salvage some practical advantage from the publication of a new declaration, which suddenly seemed to have neither a solid political purpose nor a particular constituency within the realm to which it would directly speak. Promising to carry Middleton's fresh declaration 'on board the Fleet, that so the Admirals may accept and declare for you', he made this action conditional upon 'the composer of it' accompanying him on his mission so 'that he can assure the Admirals, viva voce, that he saw your Majesty sign it'. For a moment the King, who had grown 'greatly silent', considered the proposition that Ailesbury had no intention of actually performing in person, before Lord Middleton – who was ready to throw himself at his master's feet to beg him not to allow him to go – 'recovering a little' of his composure, diffused the danger and tension inherent in the situation and made light of the suggestion, suggesting that it was but a 'jeer' and bringing the interview to a peremptory conclusion. A similarly unproductive, if far more congenial, meeting followed between Ailesbury and Louis XIV at Versailles. However, with the King of France unwilling, and probably also wholly unable, to commit further resources to an invasion of England, the Earl started his long journey home empty handed, complaining of the poor lodgings he had been afforded by the exiled court and caustically regretting that although he would never see Middleton again, 'I wish I never had before'.[4]

James was left with a declaration penned in accordance with Middleton's demands, which was ready to be printed by the spring of 1693 but which did not accompany a fresh wave of Jacobite activity, either political or military, and which he had no means of adequately distributing to any but his already committed followers. This had certainly not been Middleton's intent when he had begun work on the document that was to supersede all of the King's earlier manifestos, and in particular the disastrous Declaration of 1692. Though he had been unable to press upon the King the need to raise his son and heir as a Protestant, in order to allay Anglican fears, he had otherwise been extremely successful in exorcising Melfort's influence from the paper and in redefining Jacobitism for a predominantly English and Lowland Scottish audience. Consequently, it referred to the reform of the constitution, the securing of a general European peace, and commitments to protect 'the Church of England, as it is now established by law' together with its hold on the 'Universities, Colleges and Schools', combined with undertakings to limit the prerogative and to bow to the will of Parliament, and to 'give our Royal assent to all such bills as are necessary to secure the frequent calling and holding of Parliaments, the free elections and returns of Members, and provide for impartial trials'. Indeed, it almost appeared that James, through the medium of Melfort's Declaration, was providing a thorough critique of his own practice of government in 1687–8, and was acknowledging both the durability and the popularity of the Revolution Settlement, promising to 'ratify and confirm all such Laws made under the present usurpation as shall be tender'd to us by that Parliament' and apparently attempting nothing in terms of the ordering of the state save for the removal of the present executive. However, if Middleton had successfully identified the unpopularity of the additional taxes levied on King William's British and

Irish subjects in order to pay for his potentially ruinous foreign wars, and promised 'to exchange' Chimney Money 'for any other assessment that shall be thought more easy', then there was still little to recommend the new Declaration to James's supporters in Ireland, or among both the Protestant and Roman Catholic Dissenting communities that stretched across his former lands. Even though he refused to abandon his personal commitment to religious toleration, James now sought to downplay its significance in his legislative programme, merely promising to 'recommend to . . . Parliament such an impartial libertie of conscience as they shall think necessary for the happiness of the Nations'. Yet, this measure was immediately and completely contradicted by the next clause in the document, in which James pledged himself to retaining the Test Acts, which barred non-conformists from the professions and the offices of state. The concerns of his hard-line supporters, and especially those of the 'Wild Geese', over such mutually exclusive commitments were further exasperated by his willingness to invalidate much, if not all, of the legislation that had been passed under his hand by the Dublin Parliament of 1689. Were he to be restored, Ireland would remain economically dependent upon England, while the confiscations of native Irish property that had been enshrined in the Act of Settlement of 1662 would be respected and confirmed.

Thus, despite its failure to speak to James's existing supporters, and Irish Catholics in particular, the new statement of policy in the Declaration appeared to embody the lessons learnt from the criticisms directed at its predecessor, and was framed in such a way as to persuade those Anglicans who had always represented the natural constituency of the Stuart monarchy to re-engage with his cause. Unfortunately, while its terms would almost certainly have been enough to heal the breach within the Tory Party in the autumn of 1688, and to have saved James's crown for him, the political landscape had changed almost beyond recognition in the intervening years. In appearing to acknowledge his past mistakes, and in overturning policies announced less than a year before, the exiled King might seem to have recognised the grievances of those Tories, such as Danby and Marlborough, who had directly connived at his fall from power. Similarly, the Declaration of 1693 might have capitalised on the unpopularity of the war, and the resurgence of Tory sentiment, had it been issued as part of a coordinated plan of action aimed at restoring James to his throne. Without the unfavourable legacy created by his earlier manifestos, it might have reaped substantial political rewards and succeeded in extending the umbrella of Jacobitism to include those large and potentially decisive Anglican and Tory constituencies that had been alienated from the King since he turned to the Dissenters in the spring of 1687. James's promise: 'That on our part we are ready and willing wholly to lay aside all thoughts of animosity or resentment for what is past, desiring nothing more than it should be buried in perpetual oblivion', and his offer of 'our free pardon and indemnity to all our loving Subjects . . . who shall not by Sea or Land oppose us', might well have served to finally allay the fears of many of those who had come to reconsider the wisdom of their past desertion of him, had it not come so soon after the earlier declaration which had personified the spirit of vengeance.[5] As it was, the value of James's word had been seriously compromised, and the sudden reversal of his intention to inflict the full vigour of the treason laws on all those who had incurred his wrath only served to cast him in a vindictive and somewhat cowardly light, as a petty tyrant who might swagger and threaten when backed in 1692 by the force of French arms, but who, when this was withdrawn a year later, would choose to seek forgiveness from his erstwhile subjects, aiming to ingratiate himself back into their affections through the use of honeyed words.

James was clearly uneasy about the wisdom of issuing the new Declaration, and began to seek a means of distancing himself from his responsibility for a document that bore both his seal and signature. Worrying that he might be criticised for his promises to protect the Church of England, and that his actions could even endanger the salvation of his soul, the King put the draft sections of the Declaration before a panel of four English Roman Catholic divines who were an integral part of his court, including his own confessor, the Jesuit Fr Sanders, and his son's tutor, Fr Betham. Though the handful of Anglican clergymen domiciled at St Germain, and the non-juring parsons and bishops in England, might have felt it incongruous that the future of their Church was to be decided by those of a different faith, it appears James saw no such conflict of interests in his decision, adhering to the belief that in every question of doctrine the Roman Catholic clergy held an unquestionable and unrivalled authority. The panel duly returned their judgement that while: 'The King could not promis[e] to protect and defend a Religion he believed erroneous', he might continue to oversee the operation of existing laws with regard to the Anglican Church, and to make appointments to sees and benefices as he thought fit. Unfortunately, in removing the basis for James's claims to be the 'Defender' of the Church of England, the priests had left their King dissatisfied, and he looked for further reassurance from the French clergy. However, their lack of understanding of the intricacies of the legal basis for the Established Church, and its curious historical evolution, rendered their findings of little value to the anxious sovereign. It was only when Bishop Bossuet pronounced that the final text of the Declaration was indeed justified, comparing it to what Henri IV 'had promised to the Huguenots in the Edict of Nantes' almost a century before, that James finally received some peace of mind, though he grumbled that Cardinal Janson had not deigned to reply to his queries from Rome. If he had absolved some of his feelings of disquiet regarding his relationship with the Church of England, then the King could not so readily remove from his mind his misgivings about the other clauses in the Declaration. Rather, he sought to place the blame for promoting such an ill-considered and divisive document with those treacherous English lords who had promised to support Middleton's scheme but who abandoned all trace of their resolution once that Lord's 'back was turn'd', and with Lord Melfort who had delivered the Declaration to Versailles and had championed it there out of a sense of loyalty, even though his every instinct and prejudice had revolted against its central provisions. Melfort – who had attempted to argue that the Declaration was a mere expedient, for it would be 'far easier to argue the business of the Catholics at Whitehall than at Saint-Germain' – was thus scapegoated as the King's leading Roman Catholic minister, who should have raised sufficient objections to the finished text but did not, in his eagerness to curry favour with the English and Scottish Protestants who had always hated him.[6] In a letter to the abbé de Rancé in December 1693, James went even further, alleging that: 'there was too much precipitation in printing it, that it might have been better worded . . . but he was so press'd . . . by those who sent the proposals, and the Ministers of the French Court who thought the occasion so favourable, as not to be neglected; that he had not time to correct it as it ought to have been', while insisting that by offering to preserve the Test Acts, 'there was no injury done to Catholicks, but keeping them out of imployments, whereas it would certainly be a great advantage to them to have a Catholick King upon the Throne'.[7] In this, James was either being extremely disingenuous or had become, somewhat late in the day, a hardened disciple of Machiavelli, hiding his retreat from principle behind a smoke-screen of words. Whichever case was true – and it certainly seems that the former was far more likely – it is clear that the King had embarked on a major exercise in self-justification that even sought to make Louis XIV an accessory to the failure of his latest political offensive, by blaming his host for placing undue pressure on him to do anything that might disrupt William III's war effort and prevent that King from collecting the necessary revenues to support his armies from his British and Irish subjects. Once again, James chose to portray himself as a victim of tragic circumstances over which he had no control, alleging that had he 'refused those proposals how hard soever they apear'd' from the French court, then the clamour of the 'whole Kingdom, weary of the war as well as the Ministers . . . almost ruin'd by the great taxes, together with the scarcety of wine and corn . . . would have been so great his Most Christian Majesty [i.e. Louis XIV] could not have been able to have resisted it, and probably the King [i.e. James II] would have been sent out of the Kingdom as an opiniatre [opinionated] bigot, who prefer'd some points of his prerogative . . . [to] the peace and quiet of all Christendom'. On these grounds, James sought – after the event – to dissociate himself from the text of his Declaration of 1693, claiming that he had been failed by Melfort, who had dispatched the manifesto, rather than by Middleton who had drafted it, and that Louis XIV had mistakenly forced his hand in a rare and tragic lack of judgement. The King of France had, he alleged, been misled by his courtiers and his desire for peace into 'grasping at . . . shaddows for support'. On consideration, he might have concluded that such a scathing comment might equally have applied to his own desperate attempts to rally support in the winter and spring of 1692–3.[8]

Without the recourse to a fresh plan for invasion, which many English Jacobites believed would deliver French regiments to their shores by May at the latest, James's Declaration was condemned to become no more than a point for conversation and heated debate, alienating the King's Roman Catholic supporters and bringing him, in the words of his official biographer, nothing but 'blame from his friends, contempt from his enemies, and repentance in himself'. The non-juring bishops of Norwich, Bath and Wells, Peterborough, and Ely had been startled and dismayed by the appearance of the document, and joined together with the Earl of Clarendon and the Marquess of Worcester in advising James to refrain from acting in the spirit of the Declaration, or from undertaking any fresh policy initiatives without prior consultation with them. At the Imperial court, Prince Charles Henri de Vaudemont did much to publicise the Declaration, using it to demonstrate to Leopold I that the cause of King James could no longer be presented as a Roman Catholic crusade, while – after transferring himself to Rome – he similarly used James's own words against him with the Pope, arguing that if even James no longer saw the Test Acts as an obstacle to be removed, then the Catholic community in England was hardly facing any threat or disadvantage. The intrusion of realpolitik into the King's self-image as a martyr for the Roman Catholic faith had proved disquieting, and had thrown into stark contrast not only the limitations of his support – for no recognisable upsurge in new Jacobite activity was initiated by the publication of the manifesto, let alone the spontaneous uprising that had been promised by Middleton with such confidence – but also the realisation that: 'the fewer friends he had left, the harder it was [for James] to content them, those jarrings, and animosities of parties, made it exceeding difficult to propose or embrace any thing, which did not meet with contradiction and opposition from one side or other'.[9]

James was certainly increasingly constrained by the collapse of the independent military operations conducted by his followers in the British Isles. In July 1691, a handful of Claverhouse's former soldiers, with the aid of two of their jailors, seized the prison on the Bass Rock in the name of the fallen King and, having availed themselves of the well-stocked arsenal and a number of small sailing boats, began to harass the shipping in the Firth of Forth. Secure in their windswept island fortress, they quickly attracted recruits to their little garrison from the Jacobites on the mainland, and made good their lack of provisions through seizing merchantmen and establishing irregular supply runs by a swarm of French privateers. However, while their defiance permitted James to maintain a symbolic territorial presence in his former kingdoms, and to invest the barren outcrop with a military significance which it lacked in reality, the activities of its garrison amounted to no more than nuisance value for the authorities in Edinburgh. Though they had captured a sergeant and a small band of soldiers who had been sent across the Forth to request their surrender, and had succeeded in luring a Danish ship to within range of their guns, before stripping it of its cargo 'of provisions and what els[e] they wanted as due to their little independent state', their decision to intercept a bride and her maids en route for a wedding party in March 1693 led to dissention over the 'want of pretty women' by those who had not succeeded in forcibly securing a companion, and the defection of roughly half the garrison back to the mainland, in search of a more comfortable and sexually rewarding lifestyle. A year later, as supplies were running critically low and starvation threatened, James wrote to Captain Michael Middleton, the Governor of the Rock, informing him of his decision to send across his brother, Major Robert Middleton, in order to advise him and to 'conjointly manage all things to the best for our service by keeping the garrison in union and discipline and encouraging all our subjects under your command to stand firm to their duty, letting them know they may assure themselves of a due reward of their services and sufferings whenever we shall be in a condition to do it'. While the Major was duly despatched, together with Fr Nicholas who was 'to perform the duty of a priest to the garrison', James was only able to respond to the soldiers' increasingly shrill pleas for food with a vague commitment to 'send you from time to time what supplies can be conveniently transported to you from this place', and with the suggestion that they should 'purchase [in effect this would be translated to 'take'] provisions for yourselves by making incursions on our rebel subjects, whenever you can without endangering the loss or ruin of the garrison'. Unfortunately, Major Middleton was immediately seized after landing in Scotland and was swiftly condemned to death for high treason. His only hope, as the authorities informed his brother, was if he were to be exchanged in return for the fortress on the Bass Rock. Though tired, ill and half-starved, Captain Middleton still thought of his duty and wrote to James for permission to surrender the island, before opening up negotiations. With the naval blockade of the garrison holding firm and no other means of saving the life of a valued officer, the King acknowledged the futility and the increasingly ruinous cost of keeping the Bass supplied by sea, and sadly gave his consent to the surrender of his last outpost in the British Isles. The promise of free pardons and £200 in expenses to allow the soldiers to settle wherever they wished undoubtedly spurred the garrison on their way. However, although the Major was duly released from custody, the Middleton brothers were to prove curiously ill-starred. By the time they reached St Germain, Captain Middleton's health was already broken after successive harsh winters spent on the exposed Rock. Nevertheless, the brief celebrity that his stubborn defence of the stronghold had brought him at court might still have proven to be some recompense, had not he and his brother quarrelled violently with a group of the French King's guards in December 1694. The brief affray, sparked by national animosities, resulted in swords being drawn and both brothers falling, after a running battle, to a barrage of blows and savage kicks. Their deaths threatened to pitch the rival groups of officers lodged at St Germain and Versailles against one another, as the French soldiers absconded without waiting for the results of the promised enquiry, and as Louis XIV felt impelled to visit the court of his fellow monarch to remonstrate with James and to demand that he should in future preserve better order among his followers, in order to curtail the climate of habitual violence that he felt coloured the behaviour of his Household.[10]

In the meantime, increasingly desperate memoranda had been prepared for the consumption of both James and the French War Ministry over the winter of 1693–4, alleging that England was seething with discontent, and that up to 4,000 horse and dragoons were ready to rally to the King at his landing, while the garrisons of Exeter, Bristol, Hull, Tilbury, and Languard were all on the verge of declaring for him, and virtually the entire administration was willing to desert their posts en masse in order to aid him. However, the rather sorry admission buried within the text that: 'It is true, there are not convincing proofs of all this', was unlikely to incline such hard-headed administrators as Chamlay and Barbezieux, let alone Phelypeaux and Louis XIV, to commit already scarce resources to such an ill-considered action. Thus, while Sir John Fenwick might continue to urge that James could 'never come too soon' and that his success would be assured if he landed with not 'less than 30,000 men [and] a good train of artillery', such armies, which would have to be gifted to him by the French King, were simply not his to request or to command. His overtures to Admiral Russell and lords Godolphin and Marlborough were resumed, but reaped ever diminishing returns as their empty promises of loyalty and affection never actually transferred into the realm of domestic political action. Although it is possible that Marlborough sought to betray General Tollemache's raid on the port of Brest in the summer of 1694, which resulted both in the assault troops charging into the mouths of Vauban's waiting cannon and the death of the Earl's nearest rival, his contacts with the Jacobite court were certainly severed to all practical purposes soon afterwards, while Admiral Russell cheerfully patrolled the Mediterranean that year, scooping up French prizes despite his undertakings to the contrary. Similarly, Godolphin, secure in the favour of Princess Anne, was content to sit tight, giving what encouragement he could to his former master in case he might at some point return, but extremely unwilling to break cover or to significantly further King James's cause until his landing had become an imminent reality.[11] Though the network of leading Jacobite activists, including Colonel James Graham, Sir William Penn and Sir Theophilus Ogelthorpe, remained largely intact as a conduit for intelligence and smuggling – and had benefited from the collapse of the trial of eight Lancashire gentlemen for treason, which made local authorities far more reluctant to bring political prosecutions – the covert links between the courts of St Germain and Whitehall became increasingly strained, to the point at which aristocratic, rather than gentry, connivance at a restoration became a fringe pursuit for figures like Ailesbury, Clarendon and Marlborough, who had been denied the great offices of state to which they so ardently aspired.

However, if James's claims to sovereignty in his former domains were faltering, the death of his brother-in-law, Duke Francesco II of Modena, opened up the possibility of his succession to the Italian principality in the autumn of 1694. James had hardly known how to break the news to his wife, and had only undertaken the task that was 'much against his will' with the help of Fr Sanders, his confessor. They had disturbed the Queen while she was at her prayers in the palace of Fontainebleau, though tellingly she inferred from the doleful expressions on their faces, and those of the surrounding courtiers, that their discomfort was caused by 'some reverse in the army or at sea', rather than by a bereavement, and refrained from enquiring any further upon the matter. When James finally summoned up the strength to explain the circumstances of her young brother's death, which had followed after months of ill health, 'she had the strength to overcome the first movement of anguish, and, being on her knees, offered her great sorrow as a holocaust of resignation to Almighty God'. Yet, as the abbé Rizzini explained, once 'in bed, she gave way to her tears but did not refuse to receive the consolation which the Most Christian King [i.e. Louis XIV] came to offer her'. Yet, the King of France's sympathy was not entirely disinterested, for the unexpected vacancy of the ducal coronet conjured up the possibility of establishing a client who would be entirely dependent on the force of French arms in a pocket state that straddled the borders of the duchy of Milan, the papal territories, and the republics of Venice, Florence, and Genoa. Threatening the flank of Savoy, the duchy held the potential to tip the balance of power across the entire Italian peninsula in favour of France. It was this knowledge that had prompted Louis XIV to offer his support for Mary of Modena, in the event that she pressed her own claims to sovereignty. The bloodline of her own House had withered dramatically, leaving Mary and her uncle, Cardinal Rinaldo d'Este, as the only two possible candidates for the ducal throne. While Rinaldo benefited from being the male heir and from his close contacts inside the Modenese court, he was only the younger brother of a previous duke, and a prince of the Church who might not marry or be expected to beget heirs. As a consequence, his succession could only result in the eventual extinction of the male line and the passing of the title, in time, to either his niece and her husband, or to one of their children. Mary, on the other hand, was both the daughter and the sister of dukes – the last direct descendant of Alfonso IV – who had already provided the duchy with would-be successors and whose claim, in the absence of Salic law in Italy, was far stronger than that of many of the rulers whose lands lay to the south of the River Po. Consequently, as soon as her initial grief had subsided, Mary began to consider the best means of securing her inheritance and determined to lay joint claim to the duchy, with her husband as the senior partner. With Louis XIV prepared to back their succession with both men and munitions, and several of James's Irish regiments already engaged elsewhere in northern Italy, the project might have stood a reasonable chance of success, had it not been for the sustained opposition of Pope Innocent XII and Cardinal Rinaldo, and for the surprising reluctance of the former King of England himself to be drawn into any such engagement. On the death of his nephew, Cardinal Rinaldo had wasted little time in proclaiming himself Duke of Modena, and in suppressing the details of Francesco II's will. Backed by the Pope, who dreaded the further incursion of French influence into Italy, he renounced his vows and opened negotiations with the House of Brunswick-Lunebourg for a bride. Even then, James might still have staked his own counter-claim to sovereignty and, though the matter would necessarily have entailed hard fighting over several campaigns, he might have hoped to be eventually rewarded with both the dukedom and a treasury that could have been put to profitable use in stirring up domestic opposition and in financing fresh descents on the British Isles. Queen Mary offered 'pressing instances to oblige her husband to go to Modena to take possession of that duchy', but James refused. He was unwilling to engage in protracted hostilities in which he had no heart, and believed – reasonably enough – that the assumption of a foreign title would weaken his claim to the thrones of Britain and Ireland, and might destroy the commitment of his supporters there and at the court of Versailles to continue working for his restoration to his lost domains. However, his willingness to defend his own concept of his divinely ordered rights was, on this occasion, balanced by his refusal to fight for his wife's inheritance. He thus passed over the only opportunity he was afforded of leading a French army into combat that year.

Hurrying towards Rome in order to attempt to wring further subsidies from the papacy, the Earl of Perth unsurprisingly received short shrift from Duke Rinaldo, who was busily consolidating his position by offering support to the allied war effort and preparing to recognise William III as the legitimate King of England. However, Perth for his part was distracted by other matters and was more willing to overlook the bitter slights that he had suffered at the hands of the new Duke, now that his brother had fallen victim to his enemies at the exiled court and had finally been deprived of his offices in the royal household. Since Middleton's arrival at St Germain and his appointment as joint Secretary of State alongside his rival, Melfort's position at the heart of the Jacobite government had become increasingly untenable. Shared religious conviction counted for little as John Caryll and the Duke of Berwick joined with Middleton to mount a concerted putsch on King James's beleaguered first minister. As the severe frosts that had dappled the clock tower and roofs of St Germain abated and the spring of 1694 turned to summer, rumours which had probably emanated from the office of the abbé Renaudot circulated through the émigré court, suggesting that Melfort had been prepared to leak correspondence implicating prominent Compounders in plots to destabilise the English government, in order to strengthen his own party in that land. Even though his monopoly of the King's favour and his steely reluctance to acknowledge criticism, or to offer concessions in the hope of securing new allies, had already destroyed his reputation among British and Irish Jacobites, and severely eroded his remaining support at St Germain, it was the collapse of confidence in his abilities at the French court – where previously he had been regarded as a valuable and trusted figure – that finally compelled James to recognise the opprobrium in which Melfort was held by the overwhelming majority of his followers, and to reluctantly move to dismiss his favourite. In May 1694, he was relieved of his seals of office and left the court, settling finally at Rouen. As Perth explained, though he carried with him 'all the expressions of goodness for him imaginable' from the King, Melfort had 'had so many enemies that it was not possible [for him] to hold out any longer'.[12] However, his removal and the accompanying triumph of the Compounders at St Germain did not, as might have been expected, signify a seachange in Jacobite policy and tactics, for Middleton had secured office at a time when the fortunes of King James looked to be at their lowest ebb, with French aid severely curtailed and few independent initiatives – aside from the now routine overtures to the fleet and army commanders, and wishful incitements to armed risings – being issued at the behest of the exiled court.

A measure of just how desperate things had become for King James was registered by the ill-contained delight with which news of the death of his daughter, Queen Mary, was greeted by his supporters, and the manner in which their revived hopes found expression in the belief that the entire Williamite administration would surely implode under public criticism and the sheer weight of the tragedy. However, at the start of the winter of 1694–5 it had been King William's health that had given concern. He had returned exhausted from campaigning in Flanders, his fragile constitution worn thin through the rigours of constant marches conducted in the face of tempests and extreme cold, and by the worries attendant upon battlefield command. Wracked by chills, talking quinine for his ailments, and placed on a sorry diet of apples and milk by his doctors, he saw the Triennial Bill through its last stages in Parliament and oversaw the appointment of a new Archbishop of Canterbury after the death of John Tillotson. Meanwhile the smallpox virus, which had haunted him since childhood and carried off both his parents, made its reappearance on the streets of London. In the midst of the epidemic, Queen Mary – who, unlike her husband, had never been stricken by the disease as an infant – felt unwell after waking on the morning of 21 December 1694, and noticed the spread of the tell-tale rosy blotches that had appeared overnight upon her arms. That evening she burned the majority of her private correspondence and prepared calmly for death. William, however, was distraught, telling Bishop Burnet through his streaming tears that he was now 'the most miserablest creature upon earth' and writing to the Prince de Vaudemont that if he should lose his wife, he 'should have to retire from this world'. Refusing to leave her side, he had his military camp bed dragged into her room and kept a constant vigil in the hope that she might rally enough to fight off the disease. His prayers, and those of the assembled Anglican divines, appeared to have been answered as, on Christmas Day, the fatal spots disappeared and she regained something of her strength, disappointing the fun of at least one Jacobite lady who had planned a ball that evening in order to celebrate her death. Sadly, however, her respite was of short duration as her rash returned, confounding the hopeful diagnosis of her physicians who had ventured that she was only suffering from measles, and effectively condemning her to death. Feeling no pain save that inflicted on her by the clumsy attentions of those who attempted to save her, Mary was able to take communion from Thomas Tenison, the new Archbishop of Canterbury, and to lucidly record her steadfast devotion to the Church of England, thanking 'God [that] I have from my youth learned a true doctrine that repentance is not to be put off to a death-bed'. Falling in and out of consciousness as Tenison softly intoned the psalms by her side, she spurned the last of the medicines that were proffered to her and died peacefully in the early hours of 28 December, 'after two or three small strugglings of Nature without such agonies as are usual'.[13] It appeared that the inconsolable William would soon follow his wife to the grave, as he retreated deep into his apartments in Kensington Palace, unable to sleep and 'not capable of minding business or of seeing company'. Fearing that he might have to preside over a double funeral, Archbishop Tenison remained close at hand, while the Earl of Danby hurried through the snows to plead with the King on behalf of his Council, to look after his health for his own sake and for that of the nation. As anxious servants threw open the shutters to air rooms that had grown stagnant during the final days of the Queen's illness, and the King was carried out into the gardens in an attempt to reinvigorate his wasted lungs, orders were despatched for 6,000 yards of black cloth to be hung in mourning throughout the royal palaces, and Sir Christopher Wren was given charge of directing elaborate preparations for Mary's lying in state and burial. At Bristol, Jacobites sounded a peel of bells in celebration at her demise. In the Lords, her own uncle, Rochester, pressed the argument that the joint reign had come to an end and that, as such, parliament should be prorogued pending fresh elections and a re-ordering of the succession.

To the exiles at St Germain, however, word of the Queen's death came as a ray of hope, dispelling the worst effects of a winter that had been so severe that 'wine as well as water' had frozen in their glasses, and leading many to believe that there had never been such a propitious time for either a rising or a new political offensive to brush aside their beleaguered and thoroughly dispirited foes, and usher in a counter-revolution. James had noted with disapproval the appearance of French courtiers in dark hues and black ribbons and 'insisted very strongly' that neither his own Household, nor that of Louis XIV, should go into mourning at her death, as had been widely expected. The duchesse d'Orléans thought that he 'showed no signs of sorrow . . . which surprised me very much, because I cannot understand how one can forget one's children, however wickedly they have behaved towards one'. There was certainly little sign of forgiveness, or the rekindling of former affection for which the duchess had hoped, in James's correspondence with the abbé de La Trappe. It would appear that de Rancé rather than the fallen King had first broached the subject, but while James conceded that her death had come as 'a great surprise, [for] she was only thirty-three and appeared to be in constant good health', the circumstances of her passing and the fate of her soul – which he believed was condemned to eternal damnation – were the themes which exercised his concern and strong disapproval. His daughter had had, he declared, 'the ill fortune to die in a religion which offers no hope for the good of her soul', while to make matters worse: 'I have it on good authority that she swore at her death that she did not believe she could be charged with any great sin'.

Such 'false reasoning', James believed, was 'unhappy for the transgressor and worse for those [i.e. the clergy of the Church of England] who let her transgress so strongly'. Though her resignation to death was eerily prescient of that to which he would urge the Duke of Berwick to aspire, the King still judged hers as a worthless end, for he believed her to have renounced her duty to him and to have fallen 'for the false promises of the world' as though there was 'no God, no eternity or [no] hell'. As a consequence, Mary's passionate espousal of Anglicanism and her failure to recognise on her deathbed that the wrongs she had done to him had served to remove her from his family circle – for he pointedly distinguished between 'the Princess of Orange', and James and Marie, 'my children' – and to deny her any hope of salvation.[14] Personal and religious slights combined, hardening the King's heart and ruling out any possibility of reconciliation between him and the memory of a daughter who, both now and in the hereafter, had simply ceased to exist. Such an attitude, seemingly deprived of all human feeling, might have sat well with the austerities of La Trappe, but did little to recommend James's character to the worldly and vivacious Elizabeth of Orléans, who held that at Versailles: 'All those who knew the Queen sing her praises'. Neither did it make the actions of the King any more comprehensible to his former subjects, who in the main responded to the death of their sovereign with spontaneous outpourings of grief which matched those of her husband in terms of their genuineness, if not perhaps in their life-threatening intensity.

Hundreds filed through the gates of Whitehall Palace each day to pay their last respects to the Queen, whose embalmed body lay under a heavy canopy, surrounded by the regalia of state, and by a mass of burning candles whose light scarcely served to dispel the oppressive sense of gloom that settled on her subjects as they passed her bier. The Duke of Shrewsbury wrote to Admiral Russell that: 'there was never any one more really and universally lamented', while Bishop Burnet thought that she was deeply mourned and deserving of popular grief, 'the best to be so, of any in our age or in our history'. Moreover, instead of depriving King William of the last vestiges of his legitimacy, as the Jacobites had confidently predicted, the death of Queen Mary had actually served to bring him far closer to his British subjects, for, as the Emperor's representative in London noted: 'this sad occurrence has effaced the bad impression they had of the King, for they thought he only loved the Queen because she had helped him to the succession, but now people are quite undeceived about that'. As William slowly began to regain something of his strength, escaping the smoke of London for the hunting fields of Richmond in Surrey, the calls of the Earl of Rochester for the prorogation of Parliament fell on stony ground, and the members of the Lords and Commons prepared to march in procession behind

Queen Mary's cortège, to the sound of Henry Purcell's sombre yet ethereal requiem. Loyalism and not treason appeared to be the order of the day, as not a sword was drawn in James's service and those disaffected tongues that continued to wag and heap scorn on his daughter's corpse were either smothered by the voices of the multitude, or else were held to have been silenced by divine intervention, as in the case of the Southwark artisan whose curses were immediately followed by a seizure and a sudden end.[15] Without French military backing, the exiled King could do no more than watch as his other estranged daughter, Princess Anne, severed her communications with his court and moved to heal the breach that had opened up between herself and William III. She refused to meet again with her uncle the Earl of Clarendon until he had pledged himself to the King's service, and even promised to dismiss Sarah Churchill, her truculent and nakedly ambitious shadow, from her Household. Even James's apologists were subsequently forced to concede that: 'his Majesty made no particular effort' to spark a new cycle of activity aimed at toppling William from his throne, and held only the hope that 'the government might shake and unhinge of it self'. Such behaviour might be thought to signal an attitude of passivity and utter despondency, but it may have reflected more accurately a realisation on the part of the King of the limited power and appeal of Jacobitism, and a tendency to recall – and an attempt to apply uncritically – the lessons of the Restoration of 1660. In that year, James felt, the will of God had revealed itself and become manifest in the miraculous implosion of the British Republic and, increasingly, he began to invest in his misfortunes a sense of the operation of providence, the withdrawal of divine favour, and the passionate quest to secure its return.

II

Allowing the day-to-day administration of his court to fall to his wife, and entrusting matters of policy to Middleton, James was now afforded the time and leisure for introspection that he had previously lacked, which 'made him turn St Germains into a sort of Solitude' and prompted the later editor of his papers to mark in their margin in 1695 that the 'King applys himself wholly to Devotion'. Concerned that time was pressing hard on him, James believed that it was particularly beholden upon him, 'more than the others', to reconsider his past life 'since I started so late to apply myself to everything good to achieve my salvation I am very aware that this very reason should make me more careful and assiduous to do this, and work at it without relaxation [as] it is the only necessity'. He stated that he 'abhor[red] and detest[ed] my self for having so offten offended so grasious and mersifull a God, and having lived so many years in almost a perpetual course of sin, not only in the days of my youth when I was carried away w[i]th the heat of it, and ill example, but even after when I was come to yeares of more discresion', and he determined to practice 'a complete submission and resignation to the will of God'. He wrote more frequently and fully to the abbé de Rancé, fretting that a letter he had sent from Fontainebleau 'was lost on the road', and setting aside the summer months for his annual retreat to the monastery of La Trappe. Yet if James welcomed ever greater personal austerities, and railed against the 'errors I had been bred up in' and 'those dangerous cources I embarked my self in . . . and so very foolishly and indiscretly exposed my self to sine', he was certainly not prepared to reject all his early exploits prior to his conversion in the late 1660s. Indeed, while he attempted to locate the root cause of his political adversities in his sexual promiscuity, the 'predominant sin' of his youth which had brought down upon him the wrath of God, he clearly distinguished between his private and public career, and continued to regard his early military service as marking the high point of his life.[16] His tales of the battles and sieges of the Fronde, retold incessantly with – it must be said – diminishing returns at the courts of Versailles and St Germain, had, however, reached the ears of Emmanuel-Theodose de La Tour d'Auvergne, and prompted the erudite and ambitious Cardinal to tentatively approach James in 1695 with a view to recapturing something of the past glories of his own princely House.

As the son of the duc de Bouillon and the nephew of Marshal Turenne – whose conversions had surprised and devastated French Protestantism, depriving the Huguenots of their champions among the Princes of the Blood and confirming the resurgent power of Roman Catholicism in the years before the Revocation of the Edict of Nantes – the young Emmanuel-Theodose had enjoyed a meteoric rise through the ranks of the Church that had earned him the epithet of the 'Red Child'. A canon at fourteen and a doctor of theology at the Sorbonne by the age of twenty-three, his uncle's patronage had secured for him both a cardinal's hat and a post as chaplain to Louis XIV two years later, while as the Duke d'Albret he was numbered in his own right among the first flight of the French aristocracy. Unfortunately, Turenne's death at the battle of Salzbach in 1675, and the bitter animosity that Louvois showed towards his House, combined with the grave reservations held by the King regarding his fierce independence of spirit and religious vision, acted to place a check on the Cardinal's further promotion. Though he continued to accrue benefices and had become Bishop of Albano in 1689 as the result of papal favour, he lost his royal chaplaincy, experienced a period of exile and had his hopes of securing the Prince-Bishopric of Liège disappointed as the result of Louis XIV's personal intervention. Meanwhile the Bourbons, a dynasty whose pedigree was junior to his own, gradually eroded the patrimony of his House, having already stripped away Bouillon control of the city state of Sedan and ridden roughshod over the family's claims to dominance in the Auvergne. As a consequence, the Cardinal sought to capitalise on his uncle's growing reputation as a national hero, divested of his status as a foreign prince and one-time rebel, and transformed by the time of his death into a model of the disinterested professional soldier, a servant of the state who had served faithfully as his King's sword-arm, 'the terror of the Empire and Spain, the adoration of his soldiers, and the admiration of all Europe'. According to this concept of his endeavours, Turenne's conversion appeared as the crowning triumph to an already illustrious career, removing the last barrier to his military advancement in the service of the French Crown, winning the praise of Bishop Mascaron for his 'great heart, his uprightness, and the ingenuousness of spirit in which he was moulded', and conferring upon him the promise of eternal salvation. Such a powerful legacy might be effectively deployed by his heirs – and by his favourite nephew in particular – as a means of bolstering the independence and fortunes of their House, and of establishing a 'cult' of family that could free the Bouillons from the unwelcome attentions of the King of France and the jealousies attendant upon life at his court. This is not to say that the Cardinal did not act out of a powerful sense of affection for his late uncle, and a desire to protect and enhance his already glittering reputation. Indeed, Emmanuel-Theodose had been so overcome at the news of Turenne's unexpected death in action – overheard by mistake when the official despatch had missed him on the highway – that he had fainted and had to be revived, with some difficulty, by his friends. As a result, James's talk of 'several particulars, and a few considerable actions in the life of the late Monsieur de Turenne . . . which were unknown to me, not being reported in the memoirs I have of him, written in his own hand', both thrilled and delighted the Cardinal, who begged the King 'to set down in writing, at the hours that would be least inconvenient to him, the particulars and actions of which I had no knowledge'. To his surprise, James was flattered and only too pleased to comply, taking the Cardinal to one side and telling him 'that he would do [him] this favour with joy, as soon as it should be possible', and even confiding to him that 'as he had already written pretty exactly year by year in English the memoirs of his own life, he would extract and put into French all that concerned the campaigns in which he had served in the French Army commanded by Monsieur de Turenne and those in which he had next served in the Spanish Army, in the Netherlands, until . . . the Peace of the Pyrenees'.[17]

Amid the chaos of the Revolution and the crumbling of his regime, James had made sure that his roughly sketched memoirs, of which he was inordinately proud, were spirited out of the country on board the Tuscan

Ambassador's yacht. These papers provided him with the basic source material for his narrative and, over the autumn and winter of 1695, he dictated his military reminiscences to Mr Dempster, one of his secretaries, weaving together a tight and compelling narrative from his existing notes, and imbuing his work with such a sense of immediacy and excitement that each successive generation of historians which has chosen to revisit his career since that time has been captivated by its pace and gift for graphic exposition, often setting aside critical judgement in their eagerness to embrace the author's viewpoint and particular martial code. This is hardly surprising, as it would be the task of the meanest and most jaded of imaginations to seek to deny the vigour of the King's prose. For, in undertaking to produce a series of reminiscences of the campaigns conducted by 'the greatest captain of his age', which he had experienced first hand as a young man, James had freed himself from the need for self-justification and was able to retell, in the best manner he could, the evolution of strategy around the council tables of the vicomte de Turenne and the prince de Condé, and to recall the unleashing of brutalising and at times almost random waves of violence across the battlefields and siege lines that came to pockmark the countryside of northern France and Flanders. Though no general, James had learned his trade as a soldier at the sharp end, amid the dust, rubble and withering shot of skirmishes in the suburbs of Paris, and had thereafter proved himself as a valuable staff officer, acting upon the orders of others in a manner that was consistently dutiful and distinguished by great personal bravery. From 1652 to 1659, his had been a world of sudden forced marches, of swift judgements as to the quality of horseflesh and men, and of the camaraderie and the new sense of belonging which had been forged amid the extremes of exhaustion in camp and the adrenalin-soaked uncertainties of the battlefield. Thus, he might recall his service as a volunteer alongside Count Schomberg in the storming parties at Etampes, or in the trenches of Mousson, without comment or the censure born of hindsight. In the main, he was capable of refraining from refashioning his earlier sentiments, save where he felt it necessary to decry 'the ridiculous stories' and criminal curiosity 'put out by' fortune tellers, and where he felt he had to emphasise his hatred of rebellious subjects, seeing in the slaughter of Frondeurs 'a fitting judgment of God'. Untroubled by the need to take far-reaching decisions, and revelling in the exhilarations of the fight, James had found in Turenne a role model worthy of his particular respect and affection. Indeed, the passage of more than forty years since their first meeting had done nothing to dim these sentiments and, in making the Cardinal de Bouillon a present of his military memoirs, James emphasised that through 'all his life' the memory of his former mentor had been 'very dear and very precious to him, because he regarded him as the greatest and most perfect man he had ever known and the best friend he had ever had'.

In seeking to recapture something of the exploits and glories of another, and to lay claim only to the tutelage and occasional praise of his 'hero', James was able to report on events in a manner that is strikingly forthright and accessible to a modern readership. With the unmistakable whiff of gunpowder evoked on almost every page, he speaks directly to his audience of 'the dust which the balls, which were falling like hail, raised under the feet of the attackers', of the 'great rattle of musketry' which invariably preceded an assault, and of the keen frosts, flash floods, and clay-churned roads that hindered an advance, bogged down supply wagons, and rendered 'roads impracticable'. Far from being paragons, his soldiers starve and grumble about their desire to return home, fighting over miserable and tattered cabbage leaves, looting the civilian population almost at will and drinking themselves into oblivion after seizing wine and brandy from a little boat beached at Nieuport.[18] James permits himself to be glimpsed only at key junctures, riding to war on a borrowed horse, buckling on his armour immediately before a surprise attack, and plunging repeatedly through the ranks of his foes at the battle of the Dunes, losing himself in the swirling mass of troopers that vainly slashed and hacked at his passing. Few other collections of military memoirs from the seventeenth century would transcend so successfully the existing conventions of the genre – which aimed at recreating the classical styles of a Quintus Curtius, an Agricola, or an Arrian – to impart something of the author and of the conditions under which the officer corps had served. As a result, his work complemented that left unfinished by Turenne at his death, for where the Marshal was judicious in his appraisals of his rivals and conscious of the need to convey the broad sweep of military and political planning which had underpinned all of his victories, James's focus was far more narrow, descriptive, and withering in its treatment of those commanders, such as the duc de Lorraine or Don Juan of Austria, whom he neither liked, nor respected.

Considering that James had set about dictating his memoirs at the virtual nadir of his career, it comes as no surprise to discover that he chose to revisit his past endeavours with a marked fondness and a desire to recapture for posterity the impressions generated by his long-vanished youth. Far more remarkable, however, given James's decision to reject the trappings of the world and to mortify his flesh through fasts and savage scourgings, all at the very time that he was narrating his tales of battle, was his ability both to acknowledge and to re-create on the page the blistering impact of war and hardship upon his senses. Sappers work to undermine the walls of Mousson wreathed in 'smoke and dust', powder wagons explode with a fury that lights the horizon and an intensity which scorches the surrounding horses, while kettle drums beat and trumpets sound to call the charge, as storming parties break themselves upon the ditches of Arras.[19] Over the course of 290 manuscript pages James honed his personal image as an able and energetic young warrior, and firmly attached his own fame to that of the Marshal whom he had sought to honour, effectively conjoining the fortunes and the dynastic reputations of the exiled Stuarts and the House of Bouillon. At the end of January 1696 (New Style), the King invited Emmanuel-Theodose to St Germain and, after the necessary formalities were completed, beckoned his guest through into his private cabinet. There, with an air of theatre and mystery, he produced the bundle of papers on which he had been working from his bureau, and presented it to the clearly delighted and extremely grateful Cardinal, receiving his fulsome thanks and extracting only the promise that they would not be published, or consulted by any but their new owner, until after the death of the King. If James had, as we have already seen, precious little use for new visual depictions of his military skill after his defeat on the Boyne – and increasingly expressed himself as a man of sorrows, utterly divorced from temporal concerns, rather than as the soldier he had once been – this did not preclude him from seeking to justify his past conduct of operations and to promote his claims to martial genius. The unwelcome hours of inactivity, forced on him by the disappointments and exigencies of exile, were now turned to good use as the King worked his way through the writings of Jean Croiset, St Theresa of Avila, St Francis of Sales, the life of 'brother Palemon' and uplifting stories concerning 'the marvels and bounties' attendant upon the salvation of 'great sinners'.[20] He also began to set down, albeit intermittently, his thoughts on religious matters and continued to add to his personal memoirs, concentrating disproportionately on his role as a commander at the battles of Lowestoft, Sole Bay, and the Boyne, and stressing his claims to have been instrumental in the development and projection of English naval power. However, with the exception of the manuscript that he had handed to the Cardinal de Bouillon, he never actually managed to finish any of these extensive prose works, and for the most part the thread of narrative broke off after a few pages, once he had communicated the point at hand, or when his train of thought had been interrupted. In spite of these drawbacks, his writings, which focus primarily on the areas of his public life – his faith, his military record, and the betrayal of his kingship by those who seemed to owe him everything – which he felt most comfortable exploring, began to be fed piecemeal to the publishers of St Germain and Paris within a few short weeks of his death. They became the mainstays not only of Jacobite and romantic hagiography, but also of substantial works of scholarship and biographies of the King's life, right through the eighteenth and nineteenth centuries and, to an extent, on into the twentieth. If James emerges from the pages of many of these works as an example of youthful heroism and constant enterprise and endeavour, whose sorry record in office and failure to provide leadership at both Salisbury Plain and the Boyne seems to sit uneasily with such rich early promise, then the answer to the conundrum would appear to lie in the nature of the source materials, and in the King's ability, late on in life, to effectively edit the tales of his exploits and to fashion the self-image of the successful general and admiral that he had always aspired to be. At the heart of all his writings, and in his early military memoirs in particular, there is a genuine sense of promise unfulfilled and of the savage workings of providence, which repeatedly stripped from James that which he held most dear at the very moment when his success had seemed to be assured. In this manner, he had been removed from Turenne's side and forced to fight in the ranks of his foes in the campaigns of 1657–8; had been forbidden from exploiting his advantages and had seen his command of the fleet settled on others after his pyrrhic victories of 1665 and 1672; and had been humbled by the loss of his offices after the passage of the Test Acts; before losing his crown to his daughter and nephew, and his reputation as a commander and a politician in Ireland. Yet, rather than seeking to blame his own failings as soldier and statesman for the checks to his career, and for his final devastating fall from office, James could only make sense of his sufferings if he attributed them all to the forfeiture of the grace of a 'jealous God', Himself a commander of armies, who 'seeks to keep us attentive and uncertain'. If the papers that Cardinal Bouillon clutched tight to himself as his coach bumped and jolted its way back towards Paris along uneven roads bore testament to the King's remembrance of better and less complicated days, then they also provided a powerful testimony to James's true vocation and genius, as a fearless regimental commander and as a dedicated staff officer who might be expected to follow orders without question, to efficiently reconnoitre the most savagely defended of enemy positions, and to press home an attack regardless of cost or consequence.

III

If French intransigence had condemned James to a period of frustrating political inactivity, sidelining him from the war councils at Versailles and putting on hold any serious attempt to secure his restoration, then by the winter of 1695–6 the increasing insolvency of Louis XIV's government and the unexpected fall of the fortress of Namur to the allied army had necessitated yet a further reversal of French policy, which served to bring the King back to prominence and conferred on him a key role in bringing the European conflict to a swift and successful conclusion. As early advantages failed to be exploited, and the Sun King's armies resigned themselves to further attrition and to fruitless campaigns of march and counter-march from Catalonia to the Rhine, the need to open up a significant new front, capable of knocking Britain out of the war at a single stroke and of bringing the allies to the conference table before the French Treasury could be finally bankrupted or William III had the chance to capitalise on his gains along the Meuse, led to the revival of plans for the invasion of England. Reports of domestic disquiet resulting from the re-minting and devaluation of the coinage, and of the disloyalty of the great magnates – Sunderland in particular – combined with the belief that a new Whig-dominated parliament would both obstruct King William's management of the war and drive many Tories straight out of office into the waiting arms of the Jacobites, to further swell their ranks and heal the breach in Anglican opinion. These views were amplified by James's supporters and widely propagated at Versailles and St Germain. It was certainly the case that William had denuded the country of regular troops in order to strengthen his army in Flanders for the coming campaign, and that an English fleet that might otherwise have guarded the Channel was still lying, inactive, at Cadiz. However, while Middleton and the abbé Renaudot drew comfort from the reduction in the number of French regulars requested to be sent over to England in order to support a successful rising, and concluded that this reflected the resurgent strength and potential military power of Jacobitism across the land, the fact remained that the commitment of Louis XIV and his ministers to mounting such an invasion was now wholly conditional on the ability of King James's supporters to initiate and then sustain a popular rebellion in England, until such time as their own troops could be safely landed and deliver the *coup de grâce* through a successful march on London. Already committed to waging protracted struggles across several fronts on the Continent, and with the possibility of Carlos II's imminent death prompting a fresh explosion of violence in Spain, King Louis had neither desire, nor use, for a client king who could not sustain his own regime, once re-established, without a massive injection of French aid, and who might not be expected to achieve even that in the first place without an enormous effusion of blood and the squandering of the state's remaining treasure.

Although James continued to set great store by the prospect of a large revolt in the north, and the Duke of Berwick certainly believed that the King's 'friends . . . had found means to raise two thousand horse, well appointed, and even regimented, ready to take the field on the first notice', there was confusion and disagreement from the outset as to who would take the lead in initiating hostilities. The French, while assembling a fleet, forwarding James some 100,000 louis d'or, and setting aside 12,000 seasoned regulars under the marquis de Harcourt to expedite the landings, remained unshakeable in their resolve to venture nothing until 'the King's friends would rise first and possess themselves of some considerable town or at least embody themselves in some good post'. Unfortunately, as Berwick dutifully reported, those 'persons of the highest distinction . . . engaged in the business . . . all were unanimously agreed not to throw off the mark, before a body of troops was actually landed in the island'. With 'neither the one nor the other choosing to recede, the good intentions on both sides would produce no effect', and an impasse was reached that was only broken when James decided to send his son back into England in February 1696 on an intelligence-gathering mission, in order to ascertain the true levels of support for the projected rising and to coordinate the activities of the individual plotters. Yet, while Berwick had no difficulty in stealing unnoticed across the Channel and in making contact with 'some of the principal noblemen' at their London addresses, he could not surmount their fears that they and their men would be cut to pieces by line regiments long before any help could come to their aid, and he failed to convince them of 'the necessity of not letting slip so fine an opportunity' for the seizure of power. Finally forced to concede the logic of their arguments and to recognise that 'they continued firm in their resolution not to rise', Berwick chose not to tarry any longer in the capital. He started back for the coast of France, suffering no more than a single moment of alarm when, on waking suddenly in the gloom, he mistook a group of heavily armed men – hired to protect him by the master of his waiting vessel – for a government search party, and started up to grasp at his sword and to gain the light of a lamp, before realising his error.[21] However, it is significant that before leaving he had established contact with a group of plotters who aimed at seizing, or killing, King William.

Having been progressively denied the means of waging conventional warfare against their foes since the early 1690s, a significant minority of Jacobite activists – located primarily among James's former officers, and strengthened by the arrival of former guardsmen despatched from St Germain to orchestrate a rising – began to consider far more desperate measures in order to destabilise the Williamite administration. Talk of assassination and kidnapping, though often no more than the product of wishful thinking and of the ale cup, became commonplace among these disaffected elements as the scope for civil war of the type envisaged in England by Louis XIV and Barbezieux declined. Sir John Fenwick, styled rather grandly as a Major-General in expectation of his leading the newly raised cavalry in the field in 1696, had in the past chosen to frequent Hyde Park with his companions; there they had refused to doff their hats to Mary II as she drove past, mumbling threats and making obscene gestures until the gates were at last closed to them, and a watch was placed on the route regularly taken by the Queen's party. At the same time, his accomplice George Porter – the nephew of James's

Vice-Chamberlain at St Germain, who had attempted to orchestrate Jacobite activity in the capital in the early 1690s and had gladly accepted a commission from the exiled King – quickly established himself as a spokesman for the conspirators. He envisaged an all-out attack on Kensington Palace and the murder of William III while he slept, only to be overruled by his companions on account of the sheer impracticality of the scheme. Unlike the brash but soldierly Fenwick, and the scholarly Charnock – who had lost his academic sinecures at the Revolution and had limped back to England after the failure of the Irish campaign 'a poor grumbling Jacobite and younger brother' – Porter seems to have had a love of violence for its own sake, having been convicted of manslaughter in 1684 for an unprovoked attack on a fellow theatre-goer. He cajoled his colleagues towards this savage expedient, while Brigadier Sir George Berkeley, a veteran of the war in Scotland and La Hogue who had been sent over by James in the New Year of 1696 to provide military expertise for the rising, set about formulating the plan to waylay William's coach as it prepared to cross the Thames at Brentford on the King's return from hunting at Richmond. The conspirators would take advantage of the cover provided by the hedgerows that bounded Turnham Green to launch the attack and scythe down the King and his handful of attendants in the confines of a narrow lane. Though earlier plans had been made and there had already been an attempt on King William's life by a French soldier, the sieur de Grandval, who had tried to surprise him at his headquarters in May 1692, the attention to detail and deadly seriousness which characterised Berkeley's plot, when allied to the desperate need of the Jacobites to provoke French military intervention, lent it a far greater significance than the previous schemes and thoroughly recommended it to Berwick as a means of accomplishing a change of regime. Berkeley was well known and respected by the young Duke, having served in his own troop of horse, and though Berwick later recalled that he 'did not look upon the affair to be as certain' as Berkeley and the other conspirators thought it was, he met with the Brigadier three days after his arrival in London and 'thought myself bound in honour not to dissuade him from it'.[22]

With the 'men chosen, and even the day fixed for the execution of this project' at the end of February, Berwick hurried back to Calais, but due to the casting of a wheel on the road to St Germain he was unfortunately too late to reach his father before the latter had committed himself to leading the invasion forces. For weeks James had hesitated, for even though a select band of his Household officers had been detailed to lead the revolt and had left his palace, individually or in pairs, after a last interview with the King, he already knew full well that there was little hope of an English rising taking place as the prelude to the invasion. James had already categorically assured King Louis, on the basis of a hurried interview with one of his intelligence agents – a Mr Noseworthy, who operated under the alias of Powell – that just such a rebellion was imminent. It was on this information, delivered in the New Year, that the French King had committed himself to giving the go-ahead for the project, but when James thought to examine Noseworthy's written report, which had been compiled shortly after his arrival at St Germain, he was horrified to discover that no such undertaking to embark on a civil war independent of French involvement had ever been made by his friends among the English nobility, and that such forces as existed to mobilise in his support were small and widely scattered. However, rather than risk losing face before a fellow monarch, James – by his own subsequent admission – chose to hide this crucial piece of intelligence from Louis XIV and his ministers, in the blind hope that 'the misunderstanding betwixt the Prince of Orange and Parliament might encreas, and afford perhaps an occasion, that might encourage the French to send the King over first'. He blithely continued to issue orders for an invasion that he knew should never be allowed to take place by either his military backers in France, or by his would-be partisans at large in England. Impressed by the formidable fleet assembling in conditions of utmost secrecy along the Normandy coast, and by the willingness of the Anglo-Dutch authorities to believe that a French attack was imminent on the coast of Zeeland, rather than on the south-east of England, James appears to have been in little doubt, as he prepared to set off for Calais to rendezvous with his army, that victory could be obtained and his throne restored to him, if only he could force the French into landing him and exposing their own troops to the dangers of the fight. Such confidence was not, it seems, shared by his Queen, who stopped rouging her cheeks during his absence and consequently appeared both ill and prematurely aged to the more observant and sharp-tongued of her friends at Versailles.[23] By the time Berwick was able to intercept his father's coach on its way north to the coast, both men were fully committed to courses of action over which they had little or no control, and which they knew to be at best risky expedients and, at worst, preordained to a ruinous failure of such magnitude that it might spell the final destruction of both their cause and their individual reputations. Berwick's doleful report on the English Jacobites' reluctance to rise can only have served to confirm James's misgivings, but it is not known whether he confided to his father the details of Berkeley's conspiracy to assassinate King William. The duchesse d'Orléans certainly thought, a few months after the event, that Berwick – 'who is a little inclined to be brutal' – had taken an active part in promoting the plot 'in the name of the two Kings', despite the fact that neither James nor Louis XIV had instigated it or given it even their tacit approval, and she attributed the brief cloud that he fell under at the court of France in the spring of 1696 to his willingness to mire himself in the blood of his own royal family. It is certain, however, that James took great pains to entirely dissociate himself from the would-be assassins, publicising his decision to dismiss from his service a certain Mr Vane, who had come to him with a similar plan for the murder of William III, and ordering his arrest, for 'we cannot prove whether he has been instigated to this by our enemies, or by an indiscreet zeal'. Yet, while there can be little doubt that James was entirely free of guilt in initiating attacks on his nephew's life, there is reason to suspect that he was not so adverse to the use of political assassination to further his needs, provided that he was not directly implicated in the act and stood at least at one remove. As a young man he had been prepared to sanction the murder of Oliver Cromwell, and he had shown little compunction in training his guns on William at the Boyne. Moreover, in February 1700, it was reported that James had gone out onto the terraces at St Germain to observe the discharge of a prototype of an airgun, 'without fire or noise', and that on his wondrous exclamation as to: 'What execution or mischief may not this engine do?', he was told by his son Henry, the titular Duke of Albemarle that: 'It may do the Prince of Orange's business [i.e. assassinate him]'. Though the information came from a government informer, and may have been coloured to reflect popular prejudices – with the King's Jesuit confessor, Fr Sanders, providing the impetus to the plot – the evidence had already been delivered to the English Ambassador in Paris, via another source, by the spring of the following year.[24] At the very least, this further corroboration of the story suggests that James's overriding passion for weaponry and new technologies that could be made to service the art of war had not deserted him with the passing years, and that he was prepared to consider the arguments for the sudden and violent removal of his nemesis.

Significantly, the wording of James's commission to Brigadier Berkeley in December 1695 had been couched in particularly vague terms, whether through accident, necessity or design, permitting a wide variety of interpretations to be read into it. Thus while Berkeley and all those who joined him were empowered 'to rise in armes and make war upon the Prince of Orange', they were also permitted 'to do from time to time such other acts of hostilitie against the P[rin]ce of Orange and his adherents, as may conduce most to our service, we judging this the properest, justest, and most effectual means of procureing our restoration and their deliverance'. This would appear to sanction the murder of King William if it was thought to be necessary in James's service and, at the same time, permit Berkeley to subsequently argue that he acted in good faith, scrupulously observing the letter of his instructions but without the express knowledge, or approval, of his master. Such ambiguities were certainly not lost on those of King James's officers, some eighteen in number, who were despatched to England fully expecting to be engaged in drilling new recruits and leading their fledgling regiments into action, only to discover that they were now being asked to conspire against the life of an enemy prince, and that they were expected to make the leap from professional soldier to hired assassin. For some, such as Brigadier Ambrose Rookwood, it was almost too much to countenance, and he admitted that if he had not already been under orders from a superior and had known what was expected of him in advance, he would have sought to 'have begged his majesty's pardon for not coming' across the Channel. Other Jacobite gentlemen in London, such as Robert Ferguson and Sir John Friend, were no less troubled by their consciences, and were henceforth quietly excluded from the meetings of the conspirators chaired by Berkeley and Porter. Friend, with a sense of grave authority and dreadful foreboding, thought that such measures reflected the utter desperation and intellectual bankruptcy of the movement to which he had been committed, and predicted that whether or not the plot was successful, 'it would ruin King James's affairs, and all his friends'.[25] However, for Berwick the necessity of engaging French troops in a war for his homeland and his father's crown obviated every other consideration, and it is difficult to believe that during his brief conference with James on the highway outside Clermont, he thought to entirely hide from him the existence of the conspiracy, when according to his own account he was prepared to divulge all the details to Louis XIV at Marly, less than twenty-four hours later. James had been concerned that his son should report directly to the King of France, thereby delivering the unwelcome news of the refusal of the English Jacobites to rise unaided – news that he himself had chosen not to communicate – and to make sure that the responsibility for launching the invasion, or standing down the waiting troops, rested solely on the shoulders of King Louis. The knowledge that resistance to the expansion of France's borders hinged largely on the fragile figure of the Stadholder of Holland and King of England, and that in the event of his death the succession to the crowns of Britain and Ireland would be thrown open once more, to be decided in a contest between James II and his young children on one side, and Princess Anne and her ailing progeny on the other, was not lost upon Louis XIV. Indeed, if Berwick is to be believed, then his willingness to keep the invasion fleet together depended entirely upon the news coming out of England and the possibility that King William would fall victim to the knife or the gun.[26]

In the meantime, James had established his headquarters at Calais and appointed the marquis de Harcourt as the Captain-General of his forces, and Richard Hamilton as his Lieutenant-General for the coming campaign. Yet, even as he paraded his regiments and worried that he would have to celebrate the papal jubilee at sea, and as his son confidently predicted the offices that he would gain, and the reparations that would be made to the King of France upon their victory, Berkeley's conspiracy was already beginning to unravel from within. For the plan to be successful, both William and his guards had to be overwhelmed by the sheer number of their assailants. Unfortunately, this meant widening the circle of their acquaintances and permitting George Porter – who was, at the best of times, never the most circumspect of plotters or the most acute judge of men – to continue to recruit new members to the conspiracy in the days that led up to its execution. On paper, at least, one of those whom he had latterly approached, Captain Thomas Prendergast, appeared to possess every quality that was required. Porter had counted him as a friend, a Roman Catholic and a fellow officer, familiar with handling weapons and useful in a fight, who had long been active in the Jacobite cause. Unfortunately, if Rookwood, coming straight from St Germain, had been able to surmount his qualms about committing regicide, Prendergast, only newly come to London from Hampshire at Porter's specific request, could not. Furthermore, unlike Rookwood he did not conceive of himself as a serving soldier and, perhaps more importantly, did not feel that he had King James's tacit blessing for his actions. As a result, on the evening of 14/24 February 1696, after attending a meeting of the conspirators, Prendergast marched straight through the gates of Kensington Palace and demanded that he should be granted an immediate interview with Hans Willem Bentinck, William III's boyhood friend and confidant, on a matter touching the King's well-being. Once he had presented himself to the surprised and sleepy Dutchman, who had been on the verge of turning in to bed, his approach was no less direct. Declaring himself to be a Roman Catholic and a Jacobite plotter, he expressed his absolute horror at the thought of king-killing, which he believed struck not only at the basis of his religion but also at the base of civil society. His evident candour convinced Bentinck to take his allegations of a conspiracy seriously and guaranteed that, when King William heard his story related in a similar manner, he was taken with the informant's honesty and was prepared to guarantee that he would emerge from the affair with his honour intact and his liberty assured, and that he would not be called upon to turn evidence against his former colleagues. There was now no question of William making his customary hunting trip to Richmond on Sunday, and security would be tightened about his person but, the King added, although the immediate danger of assassination had been removed, while the conspirators were still at large there was every chance that they might formulate a new plan to kill him. If Prendergast really wanted to demonstrate his abhorrence of the crime of regicide, and to remove the threat from the King once and for all, then what was required of him was a definitive list of names. Having already gone so far on the road to betrayal, it was now hard for him to hold back or to still his tongue, in the face of such inexorable logic and such a subtly disarming technique of interrogation. By the time the night was out, Prendergast had duly compiled a file detailing all the known addresses, whereabouts, and personal particulars of the would-be assassins.

Within forty-eight hours the trained bands had been called out to secure the capital, Admiral Russell was hurrying to the south coast to put the fleet on an invasion warning, and messengers were embarking for Flanders bearing orders authorising the recall of two line regiments. Receiving word that the plot had been discovered, Berkeley rode hard for Romney Marsh and, together with Captain Holmes, one of his brother officers, took a smuggler's boat back to France. The rest of the conspirators were not so lucky. Robert Charnock awoke to find a King's Messenger and a party of dragoons standing at the foot of his bed, while – for appearances' sake – Prendergast was taken together with Porter, and Rookwood, though brought in by accident, had his identity betrayed by a former friend. Deciding that a traitor's death was not for him, Captain Porter broke and turned King's Evidence against all those that he had engaged in the plot, appearing as the lead prosecution witness at their trials in return for his life. As the government net widened, the counterfeiters of government coin joined the owners of safe-houses in the cells of Newgate gaol. Sir John Fenwick who, at best, had operated on the fringes of the conspiracy and had effectively talked himself onto an arrest warrant was hauled in for questioning, and thereafter threatened to implicate a large swathe of the Tory aristocracy, including Marlborough, Russell, Godolphin, and Shrewsbury, for corresponding with St Germain. In Parliament, the Whigs, already resurgent after their success at the polls, seized the opportunity to discredit the most recalcitrant of their foes and backed an Instrument of Association, which pledged the signatories to defend their King and country against all enemies, whether foreign or domestic. Jacobitism thus became associated with treachery not just to the person of William III – now purposely styled in the document as the 'rightful and lawful' sovereign, rather than just as the *de facto* monarch – but to the Protestant faith and the country at large. Consequently, those Tories who had salved their consciences and hedged their bets by seeking to distinguish between the *de facto* and the *de jure* king were now faced with a stark choice in putting their names to, or withholding their signatures from, the Association. In the event, more than eighty members chose to abstain and opened themselves up to charges of betraying the nation in its hour of need. Local documents of Association were drawn up, often spontaneously, in the regions and municipalities – and even in the American colonies – with tens of thousands of signatures collected; the wearing of red ribbons became fashionable as a sign of loyalty to the state and as a visible testimony of having signed the pledge. In order to symbolise his concordance with his people and his desire to make common cause with them in the defence of the realm, William appended his own signature to the Association when it was presented to him at Kensington Palace by the Speaker of the Commons and a delegation of MPs. Amid such a hostile climate, all support for Jacobitism, whether political, military, philosophical or merely emotional, could be equated with treasonable criminality and the desire to murder, and might be easily identified on the grounds of failure to sign a letter of Association. Unsurprisingly, many of those among the Tory county élites and the aristocracy who had kept their lines of communication open with the exile community, through real affection or simple prudence, now stampeded in a panicked attempt to dissociate themselves from any taint of Jacobitism. The flow of intelligence to St Germain virtually dried up overnight, leaving James complaining that it was now almost impossible for him to coordinate any action with his followers in England. In an attempt to restore his lines of communication, he authorised Middleton to shower gold on the merchants of Calais, in order to ensure that his pacquets would still be carried across the Channel, and entrusted 500 livres per annum to Mr Nowell – an agent whose allegiance had already been called into question – so that he might 'make the best interest you can among the sailors [of the port]; and procure [the King], by that means, the best intelligence you are able'. Unfortunately these initiatives, smacking as they did of desperation, failed to re-forge the shattered links between King James and the British aristocracy. Such was the terror of being implicated in the plot that Shrewsbury begged to be relieved of his offices, confessed all that he knew, and retreated into the fastness of his country estates, a broken man. Ailesbury, having considered fleeing to St Germain, similarly divulged the nature of his contacts, though in the event it was not enough to save him from a further spell of imprisonment. George Churchill, with a somewhat colder appraisal of events, hoped that a means might speedily be found to 'thrust a billet down [Fenwick's] throat', for: 'Dead men tell no tales'.[27] Marlborough was indeed fortunate in having his impeccably Whiggish brother-in-law, Colonel Godfrey – who had married Arabella Churchill, King James's former mistress and the mother of the Duke of Berwick – to attest to his loyalty on the floor of the House of Commons, and he lost no time in following the advice of his brother, George, in directing all his influence to securing the conviction of Fenwick for treason, before the latter could inflict still more damage on his reputation for patriotism.

Charnock went to his execution with grim dignity in March 1696, taking care to buy a new coat and to powder his wig, though he knew full well that they would soon be splattered by the mud as he was dragged through the streets on his way to Tyburn. Sir John Friend, who had advanced money to the plotters, was briefly reprieved only to go to the scaffold a month later amid the cold and frost, having refused to implicate anyone else in his crimes. Rookwood had attempted to claim that he had been merely fulfilling his orders as a soldier of King James, but was convicted of treason in any case and met his death with a similar martial resolve and detachment. Fenwick, however, struggled almost till the end in order to save himself. His attempts to flee to St Germain, and to bribe Porter not to testify against him, had resulted in failure, and had led to both his capture amid the Kent marshes and to the double agent pocketing a large sum of money, gifted by Fenwick's anxious family, before informing the authorities of the details of the attempted perjury. However, while Fenwick had certainly been committed to participating in a military rising, the arrival of Berkeley in the capital appears to have marginalised his influence within the Jacobite underground, and there was no compelling evidence that he had ever committed himself to participating in the attempt on the life of the King. Unable to secure a certain conviction in a crown court, the authorities employed the use of a Bill of Attainder for the last time in English legal history, to try him before the Bar of Parliament. Faced not only by the animosity of the Whigs, but also by the deadly fear of a significant number of Tory peers who had no wish to be dragged down by his further glib confessions, which gave too much information for the well-being of his friends and too little to secure his pardon from his foes, Fenwick's position was hopeless. He was duly convicted of high treason in November 1696, and fell to the headsman's axe on Tower Hill early in the following year.[28]

The collapse of the plot and the eventual execution of nine Jacobite activists inflicted enormous, and extremely sudden, damage on King James's cause. It directly linked him, rightly or wrongly, in the popular imagination with an attempt to murder a fellow Christian prince, and destroyed much of the infrastructure – along with many of the actual personnel – of the Jacobite underground, which had been absolutely vital if any rising in the name of the King was ever to actually take place. Moreover, the climate of fear and suspicion engendered by the government through the use of informers, the suspension of Habeas Corpus and the use of the treason statutes had done much to weaken the group solidarity of those among the gentry, local élites and aristocracy who might have been prepared to rally to James. They were encouraged to consider their own personal survival, and the salvaging of their family estates, before venturing assistance to a remote, and increasingly friendless, dynasty. In similar fashion, the claims of the Jacobites to moral probity and the defence of legality appeared to have been severely compromised by their apparent willingness to visit arbitrary judgement and murder upon any who might dare to oppose them. From the safety of Paris, in the summer of 1697, George Berkeley might choose to compose any number of memorials, testifying to his sole responsibility for formulating the plot and exonerating his royal master from any responsibility therein, but what really mattered to many of James's former subjects, if not the overwhelming majority, was the impression that the King had been prepared to utilise any methods, however brutal, to regain his thrones, and to visit civil war and foreign invasion on them to that end. Indeed such sentiments were not merely the projections of Whig propaganda, as James subsequently did nothing to distance himself from Berkeley or to remove him from his service, while Berwick openly flaunted his closeness to the Brigadier and the other surviving conspirators before the English Ambassador at Paris, scarcely a year later. By that time the King's policies, and those of his followers, had failed to bring down William III, and James – the son of the martyred King Charles I – was now widely held to have been prepared to sanction regicide in order to regain his power.

For the French administration, the exposure of the plot had served to remove the final rationale for launching their invasion fleet against the coasts of England. There would now be no rising in support of King James and as a result there could be no justification for sacrificing the small expeditionary force, which was still camped in Normandy, on what would be at best an adventurous raid and at worst a massacre, as every town turned out its militia and every cottage and hedgerow hid an English musket. The only person who failed to acknowledge the reasons behind the disbanding of the expeditionary force, and the transfer of the individual regiments to the front in Flanders, was James. He blamed everyone for his predicament: from the English Jacobites for their divisions and failure to rise, to the French for not taking the invasion seriously enough and for only ever considering it as a feint. Finally, he even criticised the conduct of the European war by Louis XIV and his marshals, declaring that had he been in command, the French armies, rather than being frittered away along the Rhine, would have driven deep into the Low Countries that year, bringing the conflict to a successful close and handing control of the continent to the King of France, while permitting James to return to his own lands and titles without placing a further strain on the finances of his hosts and allies. The limitations of such bluster were probably not lost on Marshal Choiseul as he entrenched his siege guns before Philipsburg, or on Vauban as he set off to take up his post on the frontier, and it was certainly not welcomed by the Parisians, whose taxes had gone to fund the ambitious schemes and the privileged lifestyle of the former king. In March 1696 they crowded the Pont Neuf to protest about his imminent return to the capital and to sing derogatory and scatological songs about his person. As criticism of his conduct, and open amusement at his continual running to the coast in order to oversee invasions that never actually happened, became commonplace at Versailles, three gentlemen who had been overheard to say that King James would be forced to return to St Germain 'with his breeches on his head' were arrested and conveyed to the Bastille on the orders of a furious Louis XIV, whose own lustre was in danger of being tarnished by the tragi-comic failures and posturings of his luckless client. The humiliation of returning empty-handed to his court was more than James could bear, and he set about delaying the moment when he would have to admit to himself that the invasion had been cancelled and begin the long and dispiriting journey back from Normandy. On April Fools Day 1696, the duchesse d'Orléans commented that the 'French cannot lose the habit of mocking at people', and noted that a series of satirical placards had gone up across the capital proclaiming: 'One hundred crowns reward for anyone who can find an honourable excuse to bring the King of England back to Saint-Germains'. She went on to note mischievously that: 'The idea of this struck me as so comical that I could not help laughing at it, although I feel a lively compassion for the poor king'.[29] In the meantime, James had followed his transports down to Boulogne and determined to wait with his remaining troops until practically the last company had started out for Flanders, and the last tent in the camp had been taken down, in the hope that Louis XIV might still have a change of mind and call out his fleet after all. In further prolonging his absence, he had succeeded only in deluding himself and in amplifying the amusement, and sly looks, with which the French courtiers – and even some of his own Household – greeted his low-key and decidedly sheepish return. As ever, he attempted to put on a brave face and to attribute his failures to the workings of divine providence. On 2/12 May 1696, he wrote to the abbé de La Trappe announcing his return to St Germain in the following terms: 'Here I am, having returned from Boulogne several days ago. God did not wish to restore me again. May his will be done always, it is our part to submit without complaint or regret. The project was well, I had the same duty to the King, my brother [i.e. Louis XIV], for having carried things out having to his cost done all that he was expected to do, but God who is master of the winds as he is of the rest of creation, did not wish them to be favourable either in the Channel or in the Mediterranean'.[30] Making no mention of the failure of the English Jacobites to rise, upon which the project had been conditional, and more pardonably refusing to acknowledge the destructive impact of the abortive plan for King William's assassination, James thus attempted to view the collapse of the invasion purely in terms of the adverse operation of winds and tides, which had hindered the progress of Château-Renault's warships up from the Mediterranean in order to act as escorts for the convoy. As James knew only too well, this was at best only a half-truth and it did nothing to hide the fact that in choosing not to authorise the landing of his regiments in England that year, Louis XIV had abandoned all hope of achieving a crushing military

St Margaret of Scotland, oil on canvas by Nicolas de Largillière, 1692. This devotional work once formed the centrepiece of James's art collection.

Mary of Modena, oil on canvas, attributed to Alexis-Simon Belle after François de Troy.

The Cult of Family: James II, Mary of Modena and their Children, *oil on canvas by Pierre Mignard, 1693–4.*

James II in 1698, oil on canvas by François de Troy.

James Fitzjames, Duke of Berwick, anonymous English engraving, eighteenth century. The most able and charismatic of the later Stuarts, Berwick would become a naturalised Frenchman, and one of the most successful generals of his age. His death in battle, in 1734, would be mourned not only by the Jacobites and the King of France, but also by the foremost philosophers of the Enlightenment.

JAME S.
Duke of Berwick.

The Abbé de Rancé, engraving after Rigaud, 1696. Though his sense of austerity forbade him from sitting for a formal portrait, de Rancé was tricked into meeting Rigaud by the duc de Saint-Simon. The artist then quickly sketched his image from memory, and within two days had produced his masterpiece of the monk in his cell.

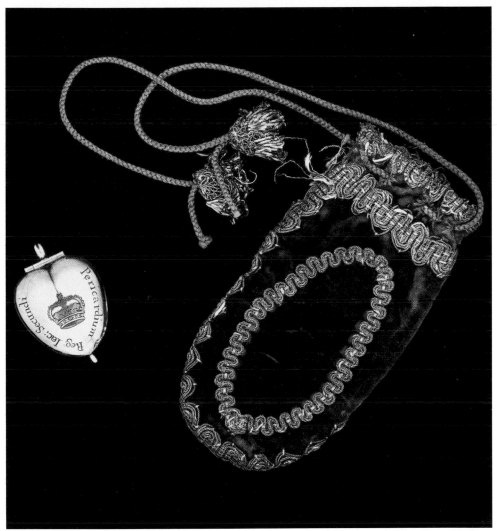

Silver reliquary containing a piece of James II's heart. As calls for James's beatification grew louder, his followers sought out his relics and attributed to them – in their grief and abject defeat – the most miraculous of healing powers.

Opposite, above: *Jacobite buttons, containing strands of James II's hair. These were given to Henry Fallowfield, a Lancashire Jacobite, by the Old Pretender in 1715.*

Opposite, below: *A reliquary containing a piece of the King's Sash, dipped in his blood by his guards immediately after his death. The symbol of the Sacred Heart is here appropriated in the service of James's own sanctity.*

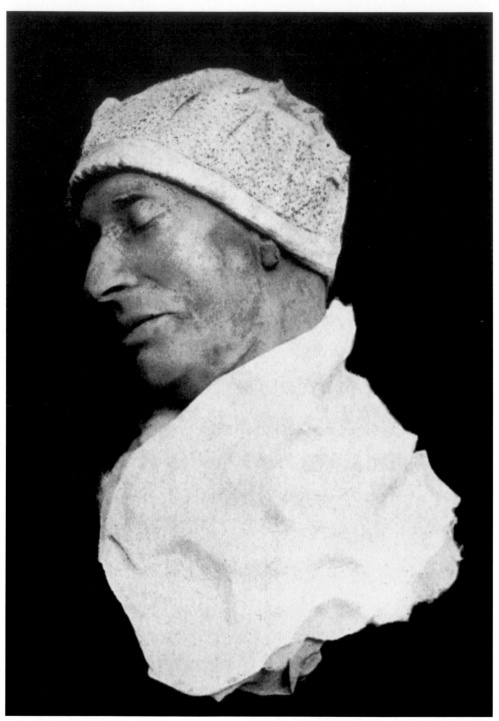

King James II's Death Mask, wax, 1701. Sadly this fascinating artifact became just one more chance victim of the barbarity of fascism when enemy artillery destroyed the museum at Dunkirk in May 1940.

The Death of James II at the Palace of St Germain, *oil on canvas by Robert Westall, 1833. Surrounded by the Archbishop of Paris, his sons and King Louis XIV, James takes his leave of the world. Though still shown as a religious visionary, James – without his long beard – has more of the aspect of a nineteenth-century gentleman than a seventeenth-century ascetic, who had renounced all hope, vanity and honour in the service of God.*

In a more secular age, the dispersal of the King's body, and the veneration that surrounded it, assumed a decidedly grisly and darkly comical air, as shown in this 1956 cartoon by Don Pottinger.

The King's tomb at the Church of the English Benedictines, Paris, engraving by F. Guerard, c. 1701. With his crown shrouded, and his coffin left above ground – in the hope that it would be returned to England one day – this shrine to James II became a place of pilgrimage for his followers and the centre of the cult of his 'sanctity' throughout the early years of the eighteenth century.

blow that would end the war, and by the same token had emphatically rung down the curtain on the last realistic opportunity for his client to regain his crown through the use of French arms. The war would now be destined to drag on until it could be resolved through a negotiated settlement at a peace conference. Any such conclusion of hostilities would entail significant compromise and could not fail to be detrimental to the interests of the exiled King, whose political survival lay almost entirely within the personal discretion of Louis XIV, and who had nothing left to bargain with at the council table, save for a few tattered privateers sheltering at St Malo, and the regiments of 'Wild Geese' which were still engaged in the scattered fighting along France's borders. James acknowledged as much when he noted as 1696 wore on that: 'there was never a more dismal prospect of affairs in Christendome then now, to see it involved in so almost an universal war', but he continued to blame the truculence of his former subjects for refusing to return to their allegiance to him, and for persisting in hostilities, as: 'the Generallity [of the people] so insensible of the heavy hand of God that is and has been upon them, for now these seven years, by war, pestilence and famine . . . are now become more stif necked and incorrigible then the Jews, for they, when any of these visible marks of Gods heavy displeasur fell upon them cryd to the Lord, in their trouble and he delivered them out of their distresse'.[31] However, even at this low ebb, with peace talks only a matter of months away, James was still afforded two wholly unexpected opportunities to reverse the decline in his fortunes; the first through the agency of Louis XIV and foreign nobility, and the second through an extraordinary offer that was to be made by William III. All that was needed was the vision and the strength of character to grasp at them.

IV

In June 1696, the last of a series of heart attacks claimed the life of Jan III Sobieski, and threw open the succession to the elective crown of Poland to a large field of prospective candidates. The failure of an attempted coup, launched by the King's eldest son with indecent haste and scant preparation while the old warrior's body was scarcely growing cold, had further destabilised a rudderless and tottering state and ensured that power would reside during the interregnum with Michal Radziejowski, the Cardinal-Primate of Poland, and with a small but similarly Francophile coterie of nobles who initially gathered themselves about the widowed Queen and her younger son, Alexander. While a self-interested aristocracy prepared to sell their votes in the senate to the highest bidder, and the rival factions of the Sobieski dynasty persisted in destroying the last remnants of their authority in the land, Louis XIV lost no time in preparing the way for the nomination of a French candidate to the throne by entrusting large subsidies to the Cardinal, to be used at his discretion as bribes in return for electoral support. With the war going badly for France, the last thing that Louis XIV now needed was the succession of a candidate favoured by the Emperor, such as Lewis of Baden, or the Duke of Lorraine, which would bring Poland into the Grand Alliance and mobilise the nation's economic and military power against him. However, with Radziejowski coordinating French interests in Warsaw and several of the provincial diets returning votes in favour of nominating the former King of England to the vacant throne, the French Ambassador – the abbé de Polignac – informed his master that a real possibility existed of establishing James II as their client ruler in Poland. Though he was completely without any pre-existing form of influence among the nation's political élite, of the type normally conveyed by close familial ties or by the operation of independent patronage, such failings may have actually served to recommend James to both the Polish nobility – who regarded him as being malleable to their own domestic agendas – and to Louis XIV, as a figure who would be entirely dependent upon external support and favour in order to remain in power for any length of time. Furthermore, as a passionately committed Roman Catholic, who believed that he had lost his former kingdoms on account of his personal piety, and as a prince who had always stressed his accomplishments as a soldier, the Poles could claim to have found a worthy successor to the late Jan Sobieski, while the French – who were under no illusions about the prospects for the peaceful seizure of the throne – might hope to have found a candidate who would be prepared to fight to secure his claim. As a result, the scheme to settle the Polish crown on James had much to recommend it, at least at face value, to all parties. It would permit Louis XIV to faithfully discharge his duties to a brother monarch, by securing him a new crown in place of that which had been lost, while removing James from France as the testimony to his good faith in the run-up to negotiations with Great Britain and Holland. Moreover, it would ease the conclusion of a peace treaty without the need for a prolonged and wholly divisive discussion about the nature of the Stuart succession, while at the same time guaranteeing Louis a new and unshakeably loyal ally in the East and permitting the Polish aristocracy an agreeable figurehead, capable of re-establishing order in their rapidly fragmenting state.

Faced with the likely destruction of his remaining international influence as the pre-condition to any lasting European peace, James might have been thought to be well-disposed to a plan which, if successful, would have restored him to his former dignity and authority – albeit in an entirely new geographical and political setting – and which would have raised the prospect of him continuing to press his claim to kingship in Britain and Ireland, with the backing of an independent treasury and military establishment. Yet it was James himself who proved to be the stumbling block to the entire project, as monsieur Pompone, the King of France's envoy, quickly discovered when he arrived at St Germain in September 1696 to sound out James's commitment to regaining a measure of temporal power. It became readily apparent over the course of their interview that James could not conceive of laying claim to a crown that was not his by hereditary right. Thus, while he had a God-given right to rule in England, Scotland, and Ireland – those lands that had been administered by his grandfather, father, and elder brother in their turn – and would fight tooth and nail to preserve his own prerogative, he had no valid claims to kingship in foreign lands, save by the right of imperial conquest. In this manner, he might seek to lay claim to new territories, whether in Africa or the Americas, in order to increase the wealth of a fledgling British Empire, but he might not dispossess a legitimate sovereign in pursuit of purely private gain. This after all had represented his entire critique of William III, who had usurped a throne that was patently not his, and if James was now to thrust himself forward to seize an office to which he was not entitled, then this would not only weaken his attempts to regain his 'rightful' thrones but would also entirely compromise the moral and religious basis upon which his kingship had been built. For James, therefore, the acceptance of the crown of Poland also entailed 'a formal abdication' of the crowns of Great Britain and Ireland, and though the French diplomats 'said to me that they really expected me to take it on', he felt that despite this pressure, the advice of his friends at Versailles, and even the opinion of at least one of his own closest advisors, he could not in all conscience give his consent, 'being fully persuaded that I would lose completely the interests of religion and of my family in taking on another role'. James was, however, greatly touched by the regard in which the Polish nation appeared to hold him and which, as the editor of his memoirs noted, 'gave the world a just Idea of his merit, and how well he deserved to wear that which had been so unjustly torn from his head'. Aside from such considerations of keenly felt principle and sheer pride, it would appear that James also had sound practical reasons for declining so tempting an offer, and for risking both the censure of the Poles and the displeasure of his French backers. Constantly preoccupied by a sense of his own pressing mortality and the decay of all living things, he knew that it was unlikely that he would live to see his son achieve his majority. In such an eventuality – and in the light of the abject failure of such an adept and successful statesman as Jan Sobieski to secure the hereditary succession – then even if he had been able to establish himself as the King of Poland it would have been virtually impossible for him to bequeath that office to James Francis Edward, and to thereby fulfil his duty in perpetuating his royal line. To abandon what he conceived to be his son's solid and legitimate claim in order to pursue a purely adventurist policy in the East, which might not even result in his guaranteed election, seemed but a poor and remarkably short-sighted expedient to the former King of England. James was well aware that Poland, though in theory a crowned republic, was in reality governed by a rapacious and notoriously corrupt oligarchy, whose actions were increasingly leading to their country becoming no more than the plaything of the great powers.

Certainly, the fate of King Louis's alternative candidate for the throne, François Louis, prince de Conti, appeared to confirm the accuracy of his assessment, as the young Bourbon could do nothing to stop either Cardinal Radziejowski lavishing French funds upon himself, his family and his immediate circle – instead of judiciously using the money to buy the necessary votes in the assembly, as had always been expected – or to prevent the other foreign ambassadors, and even Sobieski's eldest son Jakub, from shifting their allegiance to Augustus of Saxony, who now appeared as a compromise candidate capable of checking the influence of France. With the prince de Conti showing a marked reluctance to hurry to Poland to press his claim, despite his previous bravery on the battlefield, the rival factions of nobles could not be made to agree on the result of the election and eventually opted to announce the succession of their own candidates, with Radziejowski proclaiming Louis François as King in Warsaw, while his deputy declared Augustus to be the King at Wola. By the time that Conti finally landed near the port of Danzig at the close of September 1697 (New Style), Augustus had already had the summer months in which to consolidate his position in Poland, rushing Saxon troops into Warsaw and Breslau, and orchestrating his own coronation at the cathedral in Cracow. It took only the appearance of the combined Saxon and Polish cavalry arm, before winter finally set in, to scatter Conti's advance guard and to send the French Prince back on his way home across the Baltic Sea, with no more than a customary form of regret from him or his erstwhile backers. James might – and indeed did – derive an element of satisfaction from seeing that his caution had been justified, and made what scant political and religious capital he could out of his refusal of the throne, declaring that: 'I have made my choice, [for] I much prefer to live as I am, although at present there is little sign that I will ever be reinstated . . . I hope that one day God will re-establish me or my son in all our rights, well aware that when it pleases him, he can do it, when one expects it least, and if he does not wish to do it, then all the kings in the world could not though they joined together for this result, they could not accomplish it'.[32] Yet the line between a prudent resignation to misfortune and an almost crippling passivity, which could lead to the squandering of good opportunities, was all too fine and subjective a matter, and even the abbé de La Trappe chose his words carefully in acknowledging James's willingness to contravene the wishes of Louis XIV, venturing that: 'God must have granted you very particular graces to be so absolutely at His disposal, that you place your happiness and peace in depending upon Him'. Alongside the general revulsion felt at Versailles for the greed exhibited by the Polish aristocracy, there was also a feeling that had matters been expedited more firmly on the ground (whether by James II or the prince de Conti) then the result might have been very different, allied to a sure knowledge that the former King of England's refusal to play the part required of him had thrown him back once more upon the largesse of their own sovereign.

If the fate of the eventual succession to the crowns of Great Britain and Ireland had precluded James from seizing the throne of Poland, then it impacted no less on the long-term considerations of William III. Following the death of Queen Mary, he had been urged to remarry by his friends, but having already set aside his mistress, Elizabeth Villiers, and declined the hand of Elizabeth Charlotte, the only daughter of the duc and duchesse d'Orléans, ostensibly on religious grounds, it appeared that his grief precluded any thought of matrimony, whether based upon passion or the dynastic considerations of begetting an heir. William had made himself personally responsible for the children of Princess Anne and Prince George of Denmark, but only one frail and sickly little boy, William Henry of Gloucester, had survived for more than a matter of weeks. Although he was raised – without mention of either his exiled grandfather or his uncle, the titular Prince of Wales – to aspire to be the epitome of the militantly Protestant, warrior prince that the majority of the English people so earnestly desired, few were convinced by the façade of unity which the ruling House espoused in both print and verse as a counterblast to the successful Jacobite propaganda celebrating the fecundity of James II and Mary of Modena. While William might affectionately preside over the manoeuvres conducted by the boy and his companions amid the pasteboard fortifications and miniature cannon provided for him in the palace gardens, and turn an indulgent blind eye to the activities of his diminutive grenadiers when they took to holding up passers-by on the road from Kensington to London, demanding money and presents, he could disguise neither the antipathy he felt for the child's clumsily ambitious mother, nor his concern at the fits that wracked Gloucester's slender body and the build up of fluid on his brain that had disfigured his skull, and which would latterly render the wearing of his wig intolerable. As a result, William feared for the child's survival and began to look for another means by which the breach with his father-in-law might be healed and the Protestant succession permanently secured. Having never publicly subscribed to the fiction that James Francis Edward had been smuggled into Mary of Modena's bed through the stratagems of the Jesuits, he was now able to open up a tentative dialogue with the court at St Germain, in the hope that the desire to protect the birthright of his son would outweigh the exiled King's devotion to the Church of Rome, and to a French alliance which had brought him nothing, to date, save for disappointment and defeat.

Thus, in August 1696, William's agents at the courts of France and the Stuart exiles began to spread the idea that he might be willing to acknowledge the titular Prince of Wales as his heir, and to adopt him as his own son. Though the offer would have removed a major barrier to the conclusion of a peace, offered a form of recompense to King James and his supporters – fulfilling their major long-term objective of guaranteeing the eventual sovereignty of James Francis Edward – and would have ended almost a decade of political instability in Ireland and the British Isles, it would also have entailed the exiled King renouncing all his rights to sovereignty, condemning him to eking out his last years in France as an entirely spent force, without the chance of ever returning home in triumph. Moreover, it also entailed on the boy's behalf the renunciation of his Roman Catholic faith and a commitment to his upbringing as a Protestant, under the firm direction of William III and the Anglican bishops. Unsurprisingly, this was anathema to both James II, who had recently reasserted the link between his son's kingship and his practice of Roman Catholicism before departing to join the invasion fleet at Calais, and to Mary of Modena, who had poured scorn on the proposal in front of the abbé Rizzini, remarking that of the 'two usurpers' created by such a deal, 'she could more willingly suffer the present one [i.e. William III], than her own son'. Yet the child represented James's strongest remaining asset, the only trump card he had left to play, and his ability to quieten the rumours that had dogged the Prince's birth and to prove his legitimacy could be counted as the most tangible successes of the old King's years in exile. A more pragmatic statesman, and a less tender father, might have been prepared to sacrifice custody of the 8-year-old boy in order to secure him a throne as an adult, and to have judiciously waited in the wings until time or a turn of good fortune had laid aside King William and either permitted the return of the exiled King, or allowed his son to practise, in the open or in the privacy of his apartments, his devotions according to the Roman rite. However, James, though perfectly capable of dissembling in other matters, was entirely opposed to any ambiguity regarding the nature of his own faith, or that of his heirs. To permit his son to abandon Catholicism in the cause of political expediency would, in his mind, rank among the greatest of sins, for it would not only destroy the purpose of his life's work – the personal practice and public propagation of that faith in the British Isles – but would also mean sacrificing the child's spiritual salvation and condemning him to eternal damnation in the hereafter, in pursuit of a worthless and short-term temporal advancement. As both father and King, James felt himself unable to sanction such a disastrously radical action, which would destroy at a stroke the very fabric of his patriarchy, in his family and Household as well as among his faithful subjects, and would remove the last vestiges of his moral and political authority across his three former kingdoms. If he had fought to defend his prerogative, and had dreaded losing custody of his son more than he feared losing his own life in the winter of 1688–9, then the thought of abandoning his God-given rights as King and surrendering the custody of his son to his bitterest enemies was no less palatable to him, as he contemplated William III's offer in the safety of his study at St Germain. Though his bluff and pragmatic natural son the Duke of Berwick might scoff that it was 'a great imprudence to refuse such an offer', and his wildly ambitious brother-in-law Duke Rinaldo of Modena – who could barely conceive of principle overriding that which was politic – declared that he was a fool for not jumping at King William's generous offer, James was adamant that he would neither abandon his rights as sovereign and father, nor bargain with his son's immortal soul. Consequently, news of his refusal slowly filtered back to England through diplomatic channels and the intelligence community, while the abbé Rizzini was left to lament that: 'Peace is drawing near, and if it is to bring a day of serenity everywhere else, it will be for their Majesties a night of bitter mortification'.[33] Just how fatal the coming negotiations were to be for the fortunes of King James and his little court was to become all too apparent as the winter of 1696–7 shuddered to its close, and the agents of the belligerent powers prepared to traverse a war-ravaged continent in order to discuss terms at the secluded mansion of Ryswick, that lay amid the woodlands on the road between The Hague and the potteries of Delft.

V

The thought of a general peace had filled James with a sudden and pressing dread that he simply could not ignore. Resented by the Parisians and by sections of the populace of St Germain, who demonstrated in front of his palace for bread and, on occasion, even stoned his guards in the belief that he was the root cause of the war and an avoidable drain on their taxes, he attempted to mount a defence of his cause through a flood of memorials and letters issued by the Earl of Middleton and the abbé Renaudot, and the belated despatch of monsieur Dem as his private envoy to the talks. James, however, was under few illusions that these initiatives would prove successful without the backing of French diplomacy. Confiding gloomily to the abbé de La Trappe that: 'according to appearance, I am to once more suffer a reverse' he let it be known that he was preparing for those 'consequences which in the language of the world will not be very advantageous to me', but begged his friend not to

divulge the nature of his fears for 'no one has said any more to me of the
course of the negotiations which are under way, [and] that it was why it is
necessary for me to keep the secret'. James's exclusion from the French
King's counsels, and the barring of his representatives, including the
luckless monsieur Dem, from both the preliminary discussions and the
formal peace talks, probably accounted for the uncertainty and at times
complete incomprehension with which he regarded King Louis's decision
to enter into negotiations with his foes. The Duke of Savoy's decision to
break decisively with his allies and to conclude a separate peace with
France in the summer of 1696, which committed him to providing troops
for Louis XIV's war effort and enabled Marshal Catinat's army to be
released for service in Flanders in the following year, had convinced
James that the Grand Alliance was about to crumble and that victory was
at hand. His surprise and pain were clearly evident when he noted that,
at the point 'when his Most Christian Majesty seem'd to have got a
perfect superiority over his enemies by so many victories, and now a
separate peace with Savoy, he should however grasp so greedily at
a general one, as to abandon for the sake of it, the cause of a Prince, his
near relation, his friend and Ally, whose protection as it gave lustre to his
actions, so the glory of his restoration seem'd to be what was only wanting
to compleat his Character'.

His entire faith in his protector appeared to be on the verge of being
shattered as, in a state of bewilderment, James considered that all of the
'reasons and resolutions' given by the King of France for his support 'had
vanished of a sudden' and that 'whether it proceeded from secret Court
intrigues, or aims at popularity in some persons of greatest credit about
him . . . [it] is still a Mistery'. Yet in the event, such was James's physical
and psychological dependence on his host that it took little more than a
testimony of King Louis's continuing 'friendship and consideration' to
prompt James to abandon his critique and to proudly boast to his circle
that his protector 'comes to see me often'. Rather than heralding the
triumph of French arms, the Treaty of Turin now appeared to him,
upon reflection and advice, to signify the beginning of a retreat from a
war that France could no longer hope to win. The 'state to which his
[i.e. Louis XIV's] affairs have been reduced', James now considered, 'will
force him to take steps for the good and ease of his kingdom, which he
will hate doing, and will cause him as much grief as it will cause me'.[34]
However, while James was willing to accept King Louis's sympathy for his
plight, he was certainly not prepared to defer to the objectives of French
foreign policy or to accept that the agreement of the peace was a forgone
conclusion, over which he could exert no independent influence.
Consequently, with the 'storme comeing so fast upon him', he
despatched his own envoy to Emperor Leopold I in December 1696, well
in advance of the start of the negotiations, in an attempt to set the

agenda for the talks and to prompt a split within the ranks of the allies. In essence his case contained nothing that was new, and desperately reprised many of the same tired and unsuccessful arguments that he had first offered to the Emperor in the spring of 1689. James began by advancing evidence to show 'how unjustly he had been oppressed by this Confederacy', before stating 'how shocking and mysterious it apear'd to the Christian world, that his Imperial Majesty and other Princes of the house of Austria, so famed for their piety and religious zeal, should contribute to the dethroneing of a Catholick Prince, and substitute in his place a professed enemie of the Church'. In order to remedy these wrongs and to guarantee his position as a true Roman Catholic sovereign, the Emperor was urged to work tirelessly for the restoration of James II and the destruction of William III, in emulation of the King of France. If this was not acceptable – and though James did not acknowledge it, it certainly flew in the face of the reality of the balance of power in Europe, and the heavy losses suffered by the Empire on both her western and eastern borders over almost a decade of constant warfare – then Leopold might resolve to conclude a separate peace with King Louis, which 'promised better terms than could be expected by a general one'. Well aware that he had nothing to gain by entering into an agreement to derail the peace talks with an exiled monarch who could offer nothing to the Empire, and who could hardly claim to speak for his patron the King of France, Leopold refused to grant a private audience to James's envoy and instructed his confessor Fr Millingatti to deliver a reply that was at once as hypocritical as it was dismissive and brutally frank. While the Emperor had 'always looked upon [William III's] invasion as unjust and impious, and heartely prayd for King James's restoration', he also maintained 'that he enter'd into that league against France for Self preservation, against an unjust aggressor' and that 'in acknowlidging the Prince of Orange for King, he follow'd the consent of the whole Nation and the example of other Princes, who had done the like to Queen Elizabeth and Cromwel'. Though James's hopes of unilaterally breaking the Grand Alliance had been unrealistic to say the least, this fresh rebuttal at the hands of a Roman Catholic prince, from whom he had always expected assistance based upon their shared confession, came as nothing short of a fresh insult. The blatant insincerity of the Emperor's concern for the well-being of the fallen King evoked in him rage at such 'mysterious casuistry', which 'looked like Charles the 5th's making publick prayers for the Pope's delivery, whilst he himself kept him prisoner in the Castle of St Angelo'.[35]

Over the Christmas of 1696, James had comforted himself by watching the French regiments drill and by concluding that so far 'the winter [had] passed in preparations for war more than peace'. However, by New Year his spirits had again been laid low by the news from Vienna and by 'a very heavy cold accompanied by a fever which lasted two or three days until the thaw', rendering him 'very poorly' and unable to answer the bundles of correspondence that grew daily upon his desk until the beginning of March (New Style). In order to safeguard his interests at Ryswick, the King pushed once more to be allowed to send the Earl of Middleton as his minister to the peace conference, while circulating further declarations to the Roman Catholic princes, listing the grievances he had suffered at the hands of William III and revisiting his idealised successes as Duke of York. However, neither the heart-rending tales of his sacrifices for the faith, nor the familiar accounts of his past military glories, were capable of eliciting much in the way of a favourable response from his brother monarchs, and Louis XIV held fast in his resolve to forbid James from sending to the imminent talks a representative who might exercise a veto and destroy any chance of a negotiated settlement. Dismayed by the attitude of his host and protector, as much as by the utter failure of his appeals to harden the attitudes of the Catholic states and to instil a sense of unity among them, James now set his hopes on the collapse of the negotiations at Ryswick and was gratified to learn of the gulf of expectation that separated not just the foreign policy objectives of Louis XIV from those of William III, but also those of Great Britain and Holland from the rest of their allies. While the Swedish diplomat, Count Lilienroth, attempted to mediate between the different sides and factions, acting as an honest broker, the Emperor tried to stall proceedings in the expectation that his armies would win fresh gains in the East which might be bargained away later in return for Strasbourg. Meanwhile the Duke of Lorraine, who had been permitted to make representation to the conference, argued long and hard that his hereditary lands should be restored to him. Worse still for King William – whose financial crisis barely allowed him to maintain his armies in the field, and who was forced to fight a defensive campaign in the midst of the negotiations, while the French drove on towards Brussels – the Spanish plenipotentiary insisted on acting upon his own initiative and presenting every obstacle in the way of progress, and the Electors of Brandenburg and Hanover consistently pursued their vendettas against one another, obstructing the flow of troops and vital supplies for the support of their common cause.[36]

Everything, as the Imperial Ambassador forcefully pointed out to Bentinck – who was now acting as William's chief negotiator – hung upon the fates of the two displaced princes, James II and Duke Charles V of Lorraine. Neither side wished to abandon a trusted ally, but without adequate representation, and with Louis XIV forced to recognise the reality of the Revolution Settlement as a pre-condition to the making of any peace, James was in much the weaker position by the summer of 1697. Moreover, while it was a relatively uncomplicated matter to settle

Duke Charles back into his sliver of a frontier state, thus displacing
French troops but not a distinctive rival claimant, the Channel and
William III provided an altogether different, and far less surmountable,
problem for James II and his adherents. It might have served the King
better had he recognised the extent of his dependency on France and
maintained a dignified silence for the duration of the talks, putting his
faith entirely in Louis XIV's goodwill and working quietly behind the
scenes with Marshal Boufflers to ameliorate the worst of the treaty's
provisions. However, subtlety was never James's particular forte, and he
attempted once again to circumvent the diplomatic process and to appeal
over the heads of the rival delegations to all the 'Princes' and 'Potentates'
of the world to reject the legality of the negotiations and to guarantee
him the participation of his servants at Ryswick, in order 'to assert our
undoubted right by a Sollemn Protestation against whatever maybe done
to our prejudice'. Unable 'to let our silence be interpreted as a tacit
acquiescence' in the terms of any potential settlement, he urged his
fellow monarchs to 'weigh how dangerous the pre[c]ident they make may
prove to themselves', adding that 'since ours is the common cause of all
Sovereigns, we call for their assistance in the recovery of our Kingdoms',
and calling on them to 'reflect how glorious such a resolution would be,
and how sutable to the true interest of those who are born to govern'. It
was for them, James thought, to judge 'whether the former Treatys
(which we offer to renew with them) will not prove more lasting; and
whether the peace now treated of, will not be better secured by our
guarantee, than if they accept of the like offers from a Prince, who has
neither title nor succession'. Thus, no peace could ever be had at the
hands of William III, 'the Usurper of our Kingdoms . . . being null by the
default of a Lawfull authority', and no agreement made at Ryswick could
ever hope to bind James and his heirs 'to the subvertion of the
fundamentall Laws of our Kingdom, [and] particularly those relateing to
the Succession to our Crowns'. As James carefully reminded his chosen
audience 'no extremity shall oblige us to renounce or compromise' and
the only settlement that would ever fully satisfy him would entail the
resumption of a universal war until such a time as King William's power
could be decisively broken and his own crowns returned to him.[37] Talking
as if from a position of strength, rather than the one of extreme weakness
in which he found himself, James's declaration of his rights offered little
to princes and peoples alike, who were already weakened almost beyond
their endurance by a war of attrition that neither side now appeared
capable of winning. Though, as we shall see, James's pleas might reach
the coasts of Africa, where they evoked the sympathy of the Emperor of
Morocco, their reception in Europe was far more muted, and the King
now appeared to be markedly out of step with the pressing concerns and
harsh political realities of death and dearth which motivated his fellow

monarchs, finally causing them to consider breaking off hostilities and
driving them, however unwillingly, to the peace table to treat with one
another.

If the King's best hope had been to sow discord among the allied
powers so that the talks might stall in the face of a barrage of conflicting
demands, and to focus the negotiations on his own plight, then his
stratagem in firing off yet another hastily constructed epistle that
hectored rather than reasoned – appearing to reduce the entire conflict
to no more than a question of James's kingly rights – was never likely to
provoke a major re-ordering of European alliances in his favour. In truth,
it was now no more than a gambler's final throw, pitched in a desperate
attempt to escape at long last from the constraints of French diplomacy
at a time when both Louis XIV and William III were struggling to satisfy
the client princes who had attached themselves to their rival camps
(whether for expediency or the need for sheer survival) and who now
wished for a share in the meagre spoils of the war to justify their
sacrifices. To make matters worse, Vauban's swift and almost textbook
capture of the fortress of Ath in Flanders, with little cost in terms of the
lives or even the sweat of his soldiers, had served to harden the position
of the French negotiators over the summer months, while even the
discovery by William's agents that the Spanish delegate had been wilfully
misrepresenting the position of his government did not save Barcelona
from falling or serve to break the deadlock. James's declaration had been
timed to coincide precisely with these developments, but he had failed to
capitalise effectively on the moment and his refusal to acknowledge the
legality of the negotiations at Ryswick had further isolated him from the
diplomatic mainstream and condemned him to fulfil no more significant
a role than that of a virulent and somewhat petulant critic. Having cast
himself as the faithful ally of the French Crown, his belated attempts at
unilateral action convinced no one of his independence and damaged his
reputation for gratitude and plain dealing towards his hosts. Thus, it was
as a mere spectator, stripped of his vestigial influence and denied his
claims to moral authority, that James spent the anxious weeks as summer
turned into autumn, shuttling between St Germain and Fontainebleau in
an attempt to glean information on both the progress of the talks and his
eventual fate. For a time it almost seemed that the deliberations of the
plenipotentiaries at Ryswick were of a secondary consequence when
compared to the manoeuvres of the French and allied armies, as they
wheeled across the plains of Flanders in dogged pursuit of a solid
strategic advantage through the conquest of cities and the destruction of
their enemies' supply lines and forage. Yet if the fall of Ath had raised
French hopes that the campaign might be concluded with the surrender
of Brussels, King William's skilful defence of the canals and his spirited
night march had acted to save the city, focusing attention once more on

the talks and the need for the diplomatic impasse at Ryswick to be broken before winter could set in to confine the armies to camp and raise the prospect of another year of depredation and want. However, the personal trust and friendship that existed between Bentinck and his former captive Marshal Boufflers allowed informal negotiations to take place, in full view of the rival hosts, as soon as the guns fell silent before Brussels. A series of truces were declared that permitted the enemy commanders to meet in the surrounding fields and orchards and to communicate directly, without fear of misrepresentation or dissembling, the core demands and reservations of their royal masters. Having initially showed deep scepticism about the value of these discussions, William – whose relationship with Bentinck had been on the wane – started to realise, as one obstacle to the peace after another was brushed aside, the true value and significance of these informal talks. Bentinck had already reaffirmed William's commitment to concluding a peace with France in the name of the British Isles and Holland, and that he would venture to commit both Spain and the Empire to the process. However, if these powers insisted on further prolonging the talks to his detriment, with their unrealistic demands on French domains and colonies, William now let it be known that he was perfectly prepared to abandon his allies and sign a separate peace with King Louis that would immediately pull the Anglo-Dutch brigades out of the war, easing the drain on his treasury, and ultimately compelling the Emperor and the representatives of the King of Spain to treat more favourably with their foes.

From the outset, the territorial concessions offered by Louis XIV had appeared to William to be both sensible and extremely equitable. He was prepared to restore Lorraine to its ousted Duke, and to return Luxembourg to Spain, the principality of Orange to William III, and the fortress city of Strasbourg to the Emperor. Moreover, though in his official communications Louis still insisted on styling King William as merely 'the Prince of Orange', as a condition of the peace he would henceforth recognise his enemy's rights as the legitimate King of England. Unfortunately, this commitment did not go so far as to renounce the French Crown's intervention in the internal affairs of Great Britain and Ireland in order to re-establish the fallen King James; nor did it provide a specific undertaking to remove French military and financial assistance from him. Without such pledges, and the physical expulsion of James and his followers from France, the draft treaty appeared to offer no firmer guarantees for the security of the British and Irish peoples than a form of words which acknowledged the existence of William III, for the time being at least. The person of King James, and his eventual fate, therefore assumed a central importance in the discussions between Bentinck and Marshal Boufflers, with progress being made only when Louis XIV accepted that William could not reasonably be expected to accept the return of the exiled Jacobites en masse, and with William for his part undertaking not to make Orange a safe haven for the Huguenots. James had made it known that he would not leave France quickly or quietly, and yet it was this which his foes most earnestly desired and which now placed Louis XIV in a most difficult and embarrassing position, as his troublesome guest presented the only intractable obstacle left in the way of signing the peace. In this light, the former King's stubborn refusal to pursue his admittedly tenuous territorial claims in Modena and Poland might have appeared all the more inconvenient and galling to those who counted themselves among the peace party at Versailles. William had made it plain that James should be specifically named in the treaty as his mortal enemy; that the French should curtail all aid, whether direct or indirect, to both him and his cause; and that he should be presently sent out of France, to take refuge at Rome or in one of the cities of the other Italian princely states, where he would find it far more difficult to charter vessels for a prospective landing on the English coast. However, Louis's honour as a King who had given his word and bound himself to offering selfless assistance to a fellow monarch, and the genuine friendship and sympathy he felt for his sad and beleaguered cousin, led him to reject all these demands and to refuse to explicitly abandon his support for King James's person, if not perhaps – as Boufflers was keen to intimate to Bentinck – his cause. Accordingly, William and his emissary proposed a compromise, whereby intent to observe the underlying spirit of the treaty, rather than binding commitments to honour its prescriptive clauses, would be recognised as the crucially defining issue. As a result, while King Louis would not permit James to be named in the final document, he could be persuaded to undertake to refuse direct or indirect assistance to 'the enemies of Mr. le Prince of Orange, without any exception', just as William had wished. This, if properly observed, would destroy the Jacobite threat from France and, as Bentinck clearly hoped, might oblige James to remove himself from beyond her borders. As he confided to Lord Shrewsbury, Bentinck had continually stressed 'the necessity that king James should retire from France . . . even from the first interview', and while that stipulation could not now be written into the treaty out of 'consideration' to Louis XIV, 'they should cause king James to depart, as soon as a peace should be concluded, without the appearance that the king of France was obliged to adopt this measure'. If this was not expedited by the French government, and the necessary pressure brought to bear on a defiant James, then Bentinck warned that 'it must be concluded that he [i.e. Louis XIV] cared not for the duration of peace; since the king, my master, could never suffer king James to be so near England, as this would foment cabals, which the king of France promised, by this article, not to countenance'.[38]

With Boufflers hinting that James might be persuaded to quit St Germain and seek refuge in the papal state of Avignon, William urged his servants to bring the talks to a speedy conclusion, telling Bentinck of his 'great inquietude seeing in what a crisis all the affairs of Europe are' and taking a far more strident line with his ally, the Imperial Ambassador Anthonie Heinsius, who – after a further attempt at delaying negotiations – was curtly informed that: 'We could no longer continue the war, [and] that peace must be accepted on the conditions offered, within the term proscribed'.[39] Both sides had determined that the talks should end, even if no settlement had been reached, on 21/31 August 1697, but as the deadline approached William wrote gloomily to Bentinck that 'certainly the French will play us some dishonest trick about which I am not a little anxious' and his fears were realised when Louis XIV suddenly revised his demands, refusing to hand back Strasbourg to the Empire as had been previously agreed, and claiming French sovereignty over its formidable walls and the up-to-date fortifications that had straddled his borders. However, William was in no mood to re-ignite the war in order to salve Austria's belligerent pride and chose to overlook Louis's fresh provocation, accepting it at face value as brinkmanship, while single-mindedly pursuing his own objective of securing the treaty. Accordingly, though both servant and master chafed at the brusqueness and duplicity of the French plenipotentiaries, and fretted at the 'immoderate desire' shown for a settlement purchased at almost any cost by the English parliament, and more seriously by the Estates General in Amsterdam, William and Bentinck extended the life of the talks at Ryswick and duly acquiesced to the new French demands. Thus, on 10/20 September 1697 the peace was finally signed at Ryswick by the representatives of France, Holland, Great Britain and Spain, while the Empire – unable to hold out for the concessions it had desired – was forced to acknowledge the loss of Strasbourg and to sign a separate treaty a little more than a month later, which finally brought the Nine Years' War shuddering to its awkward and untidy close. Colonial prizes were returned to those of the European powers that had held them at the outbreak of hostilities, with the French repossessing both Pondicherry, their enclave in the Indian sub-continent to the south of Madras, and Port Royal, the capital of Acadia in modern-day Canada. However, elsewhere their gains were far more muted, with Charles of Lorraine restored to his duchy at the price of acknowledging the right of the French armies to free passage through his lands, and the return of Breisach to the German princes and the Knights of St John, signifying France's recognition that in future the extension of its eastern borders would be primarily limited and defined by the meandering course of the River Rhine. The re-establishment of Dutch garrisons in the barrier fortresses of Flanders came as a humiliating blow to Marshal Vauban, who was in no doubt that an impending victory had been needlessly thrown away and that the interest of France had been greatly damaged by the conclusion of the treaty.[40] Yet, while Louis XIV might claim to have saved his state from financial collapse, secured all those territories to which he had laid claim in 1688 – with the notable exception of Lorraine – and gained Strasbourg by what amounted to no more than a last minute ruse, the prince who appeared to be facing irreversible ruin as a result of the provisions and prescriptions laid down by the Treaty of Ryswick was none other than James himself.

It had been customary for James to visit Louis XIV at Fontainebleau every autumn, for anything up to two weeks at a single stretch, but his timing in arriving at the palace on the same day that the signing of the peace was officially announced was singularly unfortunate, and could not have been designed to have been more awkward or embarrassing for all the parties concerned. Though he let it be known that he and his wife 'had prepared for this moment for a long time' and claimed that the ratification of the treaty 'did not surprise me at all', the force of the blow was scarcely lessened for James by the care shown by Louis XIV in arranging a private audience for him, or by his host's careful explanation of the reasons behind his decision to concede so many points at Ryswick that appeared to be to his utter detriment. For, while James was prepared to accept 'that the king was very pained to tell me [of the conditions upon which the peace was based] as I was to hear him', and was grateful that it had been forbidden for 'the musicians to sing any songs of rejoicing until after the English court had left Fontainebleau', nothing could disguise the discomfort experienced by the former sovereign amid the firework parties and public celebrations that lit up the Paris skyline and even brought the French residents of St Germain out onto the streets. As his official biographer grudgingly admitted: 'it was hard to gild over such a pill', and James, taciturn yet dignified, withdrew to the confines of his study, more confident than ever of the correctness of his decision to place his trust not in the shifting affairs of temporal princes but in the 'King of Kings', who had taught him the value of the inner spiritual life and the virtue of complete resignation to his misfortunes, without which, he declared in early October 1697, 'I would never be as placid as I am now'. Unfortunately, religious certainty did not render James, even in the midst of his troubles, an easier or less severe master to serve. Indeed, his identification of his own past failings only appeared to have made him far quicker to judge the conduct of others, and far less tolerant of all those who seemed intent upon emulating his mistakes by refusing to sufficiently acknowledge the calling of God. As a consequence, while he 'was very obliged at so many of my friends who sympathised with me over the state of my affairs', he chose to spurn the goodwill of others as 'there was amongst them [a number] for whom I had more sorrow, those who had learned so little, as they should, [of] the duties of Christianity' and who had had the temerity to urge him to more active courses, rejecting the acceptance of his fate and with it 'the life which our Lord designed for us'.[41]

It was perhaps just as well that James chose to emphasise spiritual power at the expense of the temporal, for after September 1697 his recourse to the latter was in perilously short supply. While he might attempt to brush off his well-wishers at both Fontainebleau and St Germain, and seek to minimise the extent of the disaster that had befallen his cause at Ryswick by comparing it to the far greater danger that he believed would have befallen him had he not accepted 'all the crosses which it has pleased the good God to place on me, with both patience and joy', there was no disguising the fact that the French court's recognition of William III as King of Great Britain and Ireland had further weakened his already faltering authority. It also appeared to remove Louis XIV's commitment to recognise and back his son's claim to the throne. If the negotiations at Ryswick had effectively destroyed James's remaining hopes for his own restoration – a fact that he had grimly acknowledged to Louis XIV when, on a visit to the stables, he had noted that from now on they would see many fine English horses led out to pasture in France – then his resolve not to broker any compromise with his foes, or to sacrifice any element of his prerogative, even though it now operated only on an intellectual level, entailed grave consequences for both the survival of peace in Europe and for the lasting constitutional settlement of the succession in his former domains. Contemporaneous with the talks, there had been a renewed attempt by William III to persuade James (through the apparently willing agency of Louis XIV) to allow his son to return to England, in order that he might be formally invested as the Prince of Wales and acknowledged as the heir to the crown. This time it would seem that the conditions for the boy's education and possible adoption were left deliberately vague, and no mention was made of the necessity for his conversion to Protestantism, in order to tempt James into a dialogue. Significantly, the editor who, at the behest of his son, later provided a commentary to his memoirs, voiced his opinion – which would necessarily have been sanctioned by the 'Old Pretender' – that 'had the King taken leasure perhaps of reconcileing that apparent incongruity [of the Prince benefiting from William III's 'usurpation'], and for the sake of his Son and posterity, have overlooked the injustice done to himself'. However, such thoughts came more easily to the followers of James Francis Edward as they contemplated the prospect of a third decade spent in exile, than to his father the King, who 'could not support the thoughts . . . of making his own Child a complice to his unjust dethronement'.[42] On the rejection of this overture, James was free to continue to raise his son in the manner that he desired, and to further develop his own militant vision of a rival Stuart dynasty locked in perpetual struggle with the ruling branch of the family, defined by its unflinching commitment to the maintenance of the royal prerogative, the lineal descent of the crown based upon divine right, and an attachment to Roman Catholicism that could not be compromised by thoughts of temporal gain or political expediency. However, there was a price for James to pay in letting it be known that he could never be reconciled to the Williamite government, in that henceforth his removal from France became the primary objective of English foreign policy. Though the peace had spelled the end of his active political career, destroying all prospect of his restoration through the force of French arms and eclipsing his influence at the council tables of Europe, James was keen to demonstrate his intention to fight a protracted rearguard action in order to maintain the profile and cohesion of his cause, and to pass on to his son a legacy of unbroken struggle and conscious self-sacrifice that he believed would, if faithfully pursued, evoke widespread sympathy and result in the eventual return of the young Prince to his domains, as the rightful King of Great Britain and Ireland.

Unfortunately, in the wake of the Treaty of Ryswick, the continued survival of the royal Household at St Germain was still very much in doubt. A scheme was advanced whereby English subsidies, advanced in the form of the backdated payment of a jointure of £50,000 per annum to Mary of Modena, would serve to lessen the financial blow occasioned by the removal of French support, should she be forced to remove herself and her family to Modena, Rome or Avignon. The acceptance of such payments, which had been laid down for her by the English Parliament of 1685, would provide an element of stability for the Jacobite court and maintain James's dignity in the years to come. However, it would also commit the exiles to financial dependency on the British Crown and entail the acceptance of Mary's widowhood, acknowledging that her husband had been deposed and was, consequently, dead before the eyes of the law. It is all the more surprising, therefore, given the fierce opposition shown by James and his Queen to any assault on their rights, and their utter refusal to acknowledge the legality of the proceedings of the Convention Parliament, that the couple were prepared not only to welcome the payments but also to lobby for them to be made with strict regularity from King William's Treasury. Indeed, Mary of Modena was startled by such apparent generosity and wrote anxiously to her contacts in Vienna in an attempt to discover if the Emperor had had a hand in securing her such exceptionally favourable terms, while Middleton lost little time in informing the French government at the beginning of October 1697 that as: 'the Queen of England shall be paid what is due to her, we are persuaded, that his Majesty will be sorry that she should be deprived of it'. Rather than being alive to the irony of his situation – as the willing pensioner, albeit by proxy, of the one man whom since the autumn of 1688 he had set out to destroy – James was concerned with receiving tangible proofs of King William's good faith, 'for it will not be difficult for him to invent quirks for eluding his promise'. He requested that the abbé Renaudot should make it plain to the plenipotentiaries at Ryswick that the monies 'be paid at quarterly terms . . . [and] it is desired that the first quarterly payment should be made for Christmas next'. Moreover, provision was to be made 'in case they fail to pay punctually every quarter as it become due, it is desired [that] application should be made to the prince of Orange for redress, by the ambassador of his most Christian Majesty [i.e. Louis XIV]'. The inconvenient fact that payment of these sums was to be made at King William's 'pleasure' was for the time being overlooked, as was Middleton's warning that in accepting the money the royal couple were giving 'a handle to the English to use shifts' against the exiles.[43] For a Queen who had been reduced to selling her diamond buttons to provide charity for her friends and supporters, and whose correspondence with the former Mother Superior of La Chaillot betrayed her anxiety that although it appeared that 'nothing is changed with regard to our remaining at St Germains . . . I say, seems to be, for in truth, after all we have seen, how can we be sure of anything in this world?', the prospect of a steady stream of funds with which to provide for, and comfortably regulate, a Household swamped by dependants and overburdened by private debt appeared to be tempting indeed.

The convenient fiction that the transfer of funds represented no more than part of her legal dues from her unpaid dowry, rather than the payment of an endowment upon the official demise of her husband, made the receipt of the money palatable in the eyes of the exiles. However, their readiness to accept King William's coin did not translate into a similar willingness to fully reconcile themselves to their reduced place within the world, or to the provisions of the peace treaty. Even though James's sustained denunciations of the talks over the course of the last year had not served to ameliorate his condition in any tangible way, and had struggled to find a receptive audience, he felt compelled to issue a further 'protestation' in November 1697 against the signing of the peace, which testified to his paternal regard for his people, whom he looked upon 'as our children, even with a hearty and sincere desire of retaining the disobedient', and declared 'the sufferings of the dutiful among the most sensible of our afflictions'. However, the King's terse commitment to ensuring that 'all outlawries against [the Jacobite gentry] might be reversed; and they restored to the full and quiet possession of their estates' and his 'sensible compassion of the pressures [that his subjects] lie under' with regard to the taking of 'unlawful' oaths against his person were swamped by a lengthy and rather clumsy exposition of what he believed to be the false rationale that had prompted the ending of the war, and by his concern to show that the 'misfortune that happened to the French fleet at La Hogue' had fatally undermined morale at the court of Versailles and wrongly convinced the ministers there of the 'insuperable' difficulty of launching a successful invasion of England. Such warlike language was hardly in keeping with the spirit of the times, but James went even further, dispelling any doubt as to his true attitude towards the signing of the treaty by declaring that: 'We cannot suppose that any of our good subjects can harbour such disrespectful thoughts of us as to imagine that we were consenting to this peace. If any have such, we pity them, as the ravings of distempered people; and, without doubt, will be set right by reading our protestation'. Despite James's hopes, it is unlikely that these injunctions served to harden the attitudes of significant numbers of his erstwhile subjects towards the peace process. They revealed nothing save the absence of the King's ability to back up his polemical bluster with either well-reasoned argument or the force of arms; hope alone would therefore have to sustain the Jacobite movement. There could now be no promises of an imminent return for, while James gave voice to his 'sensible compassion', he could only seek to call upon their services at some future and as yet undisclosed time, 'when we have occasion for it'.[44] Such nuances were not lost on those former Jacobites and members of the political classes who had simply hedged their bets up until this point, and who rushed to pay court to King William on his triumphal return to London in December 1697, pledging their support and the loans necessary to underwrite the shortfall in the government's reserves that had been created by the war.

By way of painful contrast, James was forced to spend the winter contemplating the destruction of his independent forces, as by the terms of the Treaty of Ryswick the French Crown was to withdraw its support from his military establishment. The handful of his privateers that had survived the onslaughts of tempests and the fire of British frigates were either mothballed, or transferred into the service of France, depriving the King of a valuable stream of revenue from prizes, but throwing back on his charity far fewer displaced sailors – who generally had not been recruited from among his own subjects – than was threatened by the sudden withdrawal of employment from thousands of his predominantly Irish soldiers. There was no question of James finding sufficient resources to alleviate their poverty, once their regiments were disbanded, or to even begin to attempt to find fresh posts for both officers and men either at his own court or in foreign military service. Even Louis XIV's offer in the spring of 1698 to streamline the Irish Brigade, by amalgamating units that had traditionally been under-strength and far too heavily officered, and to incorporate several regiments within the French Royal Army, barely contained the problem. It was also far from being motivated purely by the sense of altruism and affection for the exiles that he attempted to communicate to James during their private meetings. The 'Wild Geese' had repeatedly proven themselves to be fearless and hardened soldiers, capable of turning the course of a battle by a well-timed charge or of storming the most heavily defended bastion through their total disregard of cost. As a consequence, the King of France was loathe to relinquish their services and sought, through their absorption into his regular military establishment, to not only evade the prescriptions laid down at Ryswick by claiming them as his troops rather than James's, but also to dispense with the cumbersome and costly existing system of command, which gave their colonels – and by extension their master at St Germain – a high degree of political and operational independence. James, whose methods of accountancy had been kept necessarily opaque in order to disguise the true weakness of many muster roles, to gain the maximum amount of subsidies from his hosts, and to maintain the largest possible number of officers in employment as befitted their station, had no choice but to reluctantly consent. His army was broken up, with Berwick gloomily reporting that a 'Great number of the Irish troops were disbanded', with just one regiment of cavalry and six of infantry, amounting in total to some 6,000 men, being retained by the French Crown. The independent companies were merged with the dismounted dragoons, and all that remained of the Athlone regiment after sickness and successive ruinous campaigns had taken their toll, in order to create a new regiment specifically for the Duke of Berwick. They were supplemented by 500 veterans, now serving 'as cadets with their former pay', who had been drawn from the Life Guards, which had been split apart and its companies dispersed throughout the brigade in order to strengthen the weaker or fledgling units.[45] Unfortunately, this was still not enough to satisfy large swathes of King James's former army, and by May 1698 a number of officers had presented their sovereign with a petition: 'to inform him of the state they are in, and to entreat assistance from him . . . [having] remained silent until now, in expectation of what it might be his Majesty's pleasure to order respecting them; but that the extreme necessity, to which they have been reduced, has constrained them to break that silence, in order to lay before his Majesty the pitiable condition of their affairs. That they had fought, during 10 years, in defence of their religion, and of their legitimate Sovereign, with all the zeal, and all the fidelity, that could be required of them, and with a devotion, unparalleled, except among those of their unhappy nation'. Yet, with wives and children to support, 'by the Peace they not only found themselves deprived of the properties to which they had legitimate claims, but were likewise prohibited returning to their country under pain of death'. Worse still, the officers feared that now 'they could not look for an asylum among the other Christian Princes, to whom they could assign no other reason for their unhappiness, but that of having

served his Majesty, and their own Sovereign, against them. That those
Princes would have no regard for them under existing circumstances,
since, during the war, they had refused to enter their service . . . [and]
neither could they any longer remain in the service of their Master, since
he had not been mentioned in the Peace, and he was not in a condition
to help them'. James duly forwarded their petition to Louis XIV, who
agreed to create a special unit within the French establishment entirely
comprised of commissioned officers, which could be used as 'shock
troops' or, later, as military specialists accompanying Philip V to Spain.
However, not all were so lucky, and while some old soldiers lamented the
replacement of their 'national' colours by French patterns, others took
service with the Roman Catholic powers, spreading the range of the
Jacobite diaspora still further to encompass Portugal, Spain, the Italian
states, Poland, and the Empire. Deprived of their profession, some of
these 'fierce and hungry partisans who had followed the standard of
James' banded together in gangs of housebreakers and footpads, striking
fear into those among their fellow countrymen, such as Dr Doran, who
wished to 'venture abroad by night' from St Germain without the threat
of 'pillage and murder'.[46] The thought that death on the wheel, or a life
eked out in the galleys, was poor recompense for veterans of the Boyne,
Aughrim, and Limerick appears to have been utterly alien to the good
doctor and to the householders of St Germain and the suburbs of Paris,
as they took to shuttering their doors after dark, and joined with King
James's courtiers in urging the local magistrates to sentence such bloody
and habitual malefactors according to the full rigours of the law.

However, the true cost of demobilisation could be measured not only
in terms of personal misery, hardship and want, but also in the removal of
a further prop to James's authority and the seemingly irrevocable loss of
his ability to inflict substantial military damage upon his foes. While he
still held control over regiments which were in theory at least directly
accountable to their King, and which represented a royal army in exile, a
useful source of patronage, and the instrument by which he might one
day hope to reconquer his lost dominions, he could still seek to project
himself as a formidable force in European politics. Once stripped of the
opportunity to wage war, the fundamental attribute of monarchs, James
would henceforth have a far more difficult task in claiming parity with his
fellow princes. St Germain would no longer be seen primarily as the
headquarters of a government in waiting, a microcosm of the state
apparatus which he once again hoped to control, complete with its own
army and diplomatic corps, but as the King's private Household, capable
of pursuing little in terms of either policy or statecraft which had not
already been sanctioned, or even initiated, by the rulers of France. James
faced a political landscape that had been changed entirely to his
detriment by the conclusion of the peace. Louis XIV was now prepared to

recognise William III as the King of England, *de facto* if still not *de jure*, and his own claim to sovereignty, together with that of his son, had been severely eroded as a consequence. If James's kingship had been denied and discredited, his right of residence in France threatened, and his defence of his rights could not now be pursued through a recourse to military action, then it would be beholden upon him to redefine the grounds on which his sovereignty was based, and to emphasise the moral and increasingly devotional nature of the contract between God, King, and people, which he believed had been compromised by his past failings and broken asunder by the wanton aggression of William III. It could only be restored for the benefit of posterity – along with social harmony and a true and just peace – by the return of James, or in due course his son, to their lost thrones. The war for the crown would now not be conducted on the battlefield, or even primarily in the council chamber, but in the solitude of the cloister or the chapel, where a King's prayers and the personal example of fortitude, acceptance and willingness to suffer, offered by one of the great laid low, might heal the breach between God and man and reconnect with the Divine will, allowing James to once more become the agent and beneficiary of a providence which, for the past decade, had turned so decisively against him and all his endeavours. James would dedicate his last years to this task, painstakingly laying the foundations of an atonement which he believed would secure his own salvation in the afterlife, and the happiness and good fortune of his young son here upon earth.

CHAPTER EIGHT

The Royal Penitent

I

It was raining steadily when James first ventured into the woods that surrounded the monastery of La Trappe, on the morning of St Cecilia's Day, 22 November 1690. Anxious to seek a conference with a hermit who had once, like himself, been a soldier in the service of Louis XIV, he had made an early start, navigating a path through the marshes and stagnant pools that pockmarked the valley floor, before leaving the trackway entirely and forging his way through the thorns and thickets to the spot at the heart of the forest where the old campaigner had made his home. Tired and a little flushed, James asked him when he heard Mass. 'At half-past three in the morning', came the reply, an answer which did not entirely satisfy all the King's companions and which prompted Lord Dumbarton to enquire how he managed such a feat in the midst of winter, when it was raining or snowing and the path ahead, which was difficult enough to follow in the daylight, could no longer be seen. With scarcely a hesitation, the hermit informed him that this would never happen as, having made many difficult route marches when a soldier, he could not now allow himself to fail in fulfilling a similar duty in order to try to pay back that which he felt he owed to God. While James nodded his vigorous approval, observing that it was all too common that 'so much should be done for an earthly king and so little for the king of heaven', Dumbarton persisted with his line of questioning, asking him if he ever tired and became bored with his isolation. Having renounced his profession, his fame, and all of his goods, the hermit told him that the passage of time amid the fastness and solitude of the woods meant nothing to him at all, as he thought only of eternity and of the quest for salvation. Much taken with his words, James embraced the penitent and bade him pray for his family, confiding to him that: 'Your condition is more fortunate than that of the great . . . [for] You will die the death of the just'. He regarded him with a look of unfeigned affection and regard, in which his courtiers detected almost an air of envy, as he took his leave and disappeared back through the trees.[1]

James was not by any means the first individual to have gone on retreat to Notre Dame de La Trappe. Indeed, ever since the early 1660s, when the abbé de Rancé had forcefully re-established the severest form of the rule of St Benedict in the crumbling Norman monastery, the site had become a magnet for between 6,000 and 7,000 visitors every year. Pilgrims, tradesmen, reformed brigands – such as the famous Dom Muce Faure – and those who were merely curious had all flocked to its gates, in order to witness the brothers' practice of harsh asceticism and to seek their salvation through this 'single oracle of the Desert'. At the palace of Versailles, Monsieur had fascinated the assembled noblemen by withdrawing from his coat pocket – normally filled with the sweets and savoury delicacies on which he habitually snacked – a hard and blackened lump of the bread on which the monks subsisted, and which he thought to pass from hand to hand amid cries of admiration and wonderment from the ranks of privileged and overly pampered courtiers.[2] Situated some 84 miles from Paris, amid poor and frequently waterlogged soil, the monastery had been substantially rebuilt by de Rancé, who sold off the silver plate and fine furniture, and attempted not only to return to the founding principles of the Cistercian Order, but to improve and indeed to surpass them in terms of the austerities practised under his direction. The monks were stopped from preaching and from hearing confessions, and swore to maintain a strict vow of silence, achieving the virtues of charity, humility, and inner peace through contemplation, stillness, and prayer. Private study was discontinued in favour of hard manual labour, while food was rationed to a bare minimum and fast days were regularly and scrupulously observed. Meat, fish, and eggs were all banned, together with butter and condiments, 'whose only effect is to excite sensuality', while vegetables such as green peas, artichokes and celery were also prohibited, on the grounds that even a vegetarian might 'be a gourmet'. The picturesque dovecot that stood in the courtyard until 1674 was demolished in order to underline the prohibition against eating flesh, though – as James was to note with approval – the watermill continued to be worked by the brothers to ensure their self-sufficiency and thus avoid a further source of contact with the outside world. Monks slept in their hoods and were encouraged never to raise their eyes, going 'to and from work, one behind another, seeing nought save the steps of those who walked before them'. Fear of incurring the disapproval of the abbé was at a premium and it was reported that some of the brothers had 'dared not even separate the leaves of their book, stuck together by the binding, without asking permission'. However, it was the positive courting of ill-health by siting the monastery amid low-lying swamps, the practice of 'patience' during sickness, and the provision of meagre – and during the early 1670s, near starvation – rations, combined with a refusal to seek the attention of doctors or to take medicines of any sort, that served to define de Rancé's radical monastic reforms. The development of a palpable sense of morbidity and a preoccupation with decay that clung to the monks of La Trappe stemmed directly from the shockingly high mortality rates to which they were subjected, and which was calculated to focus their thoughts solely on 'the things of eternity, which the wasting away of our health keeps unceasingly before our eyes, as well as the number of our brethren whom God has . . . called to Himself by a happy death; wishing to prepare ourselves to appear before the tribunal of Jesus Christ'.[3] These themes of the welcome death and the extirpation of all pride, ambition and desire as the pre-conditions to salvation would increasingly come to shape James's own religious writings, but there is no reason to suppose that he had been anything but receptive to these sentiments before Marshal Bellefonds suggested that he should accompany him on his visit to the monastery, as a means of coming to terms with his loss of power and his crushing defeat in Ireland.

James carried with him into exile an unshakeable commitment to Roman Catholicism, which lay at the very core of his being and which gradually began to assume the role of the connecting thread that linked together all his past endeavours and sufferings, making them not only intelligible and far more bearable for him, but also investing them with a guiding purpose and continuity which they may have wholly lacked at the time of their occurrence. Thus, every reverse inflicted on the former King was interpreted as reflecting the workings of a divine providence, ordered so as to offer a challenge to James's faith at particular junctures in his life. This could be met and then successfully surmounted only if he was able to accept the judgement of God and to work correctly in order to fulfil His will upon earth. Thus, the sorrow occasioned by his being driven 'early out of my native count[r]y', and by the convulsions of the Civil War and Revolution, had a positive and indeed happy effect, in that necessity brought him to live for 'most of the twelve years I was abroad in Catholike Kingdomes, by w[hi]ch means, I came to know what their religion was' and in time led to his conversion. As a result, he saw history as conforming to an orderly pattern – though it was discernible to God more readily than to the intellect of Man – and his own personal exploits as characterised by a sense of marked progress that brought him ever closer to a realisation of the love and power of his Lord, and to his ultimate goal of eternal salvation. Accordingly, his conversion to Roman Catholicism in the winter months of 1668–9 served as the defining moment of his life, and as a break with all those 'errors' in which he had been schooled, whether by his Anglican tutors in Oxford who had sought to obscure religious truth from him, or by his hardened companions in the military camps of France and Flanders, who had taught him the arts of war and love in roughly equal measure. His preservation from harm in battle, 'the wonderfull Changes' that had so unexpectedly laid low the Republic in 1660 and restored the monarchy to England, and his personal triumph in returning to prominence and in inheriting the crown after his reputation had been all but destroyed at the height of the

Exclusion Crisis, all combined to furnish him with the belief that those adversities to which he was subjected would, ultimately, always result in a successful resolution and his return to temporal power.[4] It was the failure of his political and military initiatives in the period from 1688 onwards to conform to what he believed to be this established pattern that caused James to experience the haemorrhaging of so much of his self-confidence during his final years of exile, and prompted him to undertake a major re-examination of his priorities and devotional practices, as the deadening hand of old age and disappointment settled firmly upon him.

Initially, however, the freedom occasioned by his further removal in 1688–9 from the virulently Protestant mainstream culture espoused by the English, to an atmosphere characterised by a resurgent, militant and supremely self-confident form of Roman Catholicism – albeit of the Gallican type – at the court of Louis XIV, appeared to be nothing short of a liberating experience, and one which permitted James to redefine the religious legacy of the 'legitimate' Stuart dynasty in line with his own thoughts and actions on the subject. The continuity of the entire period from 1660 to his fall from power was stressed, at the expense of the widely held view that his break with the Tories and the escalating advancement of Roman Catholics in office in 1687–8 marked a decisive rejection of the past. Moreover, James was so convinced by the reasoned logic behind his own conversion – which forcefully rejected the schism between the Papacy and the national Church, originating under Henry VIII, as unlawful and entirely unwarranted on doctrinal grounds – that he could not conceive for an instant of any of his subjects not being similarly convinced by exactly the same line of argument. If such enormous – and, if his own word is accepted, almost immediate – changes to his own way of thinking had taken place, which emphasised the overwhelming dependency of all temporal authority on strong spiritual foundations for the maintenance of peace, plenty and restraint, then he considered that all that was needed to begin the restoration of his fortunes was to win the propaganda battle, by placing the explanations for his conduct, and the importance that he attached to the Roman Catholic faith, before his ignorant and errant peoples. To this end, in 1690 and again in 1700, he ordered the re-publication of an account of Charles II's conversion to Catholicism from the 'short but sollid' papers he had discovered after his brother's death, 'one in the strong box, the other in the Closet, both writ in his own hand', and which he had ordered carried into exile with him. Appended to these documents, which sought to undermine the authority of the Anglican Church and to establish the reputation of Charles II as a devoted and thoughtful Catholic, who had made a 'good' end and died professing his faith, was a short paper written by Anne Hyde, James's first wife, which outlined the reasons on which her own rejection of Protestantism had been based. The core of her argument – that the

breach between the Churches of England and Rome had proceeded only
from human ambition, and that Transubstantiation, Papal Infallibility,
and the saying of Masses for the dead were 'all things necessary to
Salvation' – had been readily accepted by James in 1669, informing not
only his decision to convert but also shaping the foundations of his
thought on the matter and his subsequent reasoning over both the
superiority of Roman Catholicism to all other creeds and its ability to
heal the social conflicts which had torn at the fabric of the monarchy
since the late 1630s. So powerful had been the evidence amassed by his
late wife that James felt compelled even in the early 1690s to paraphrase
her conclusions in his own instructions to 'new converts'. He also sought
to link her writings to those of his brother in an attempt to demonstrate
that the restored House of Stuart had always represented a Roman
Catholic dynasty, that was passionately committed to re-converting its
subjects and saving them from the 'heresy' – and by implication the
disloyalty and fractiousness – espoused by the new Protestant sects.
Unfortunately for James, his religious insights and youthful readings of a
handful of key texts – primarily those of the Anglican divines Heylin and
Hooker – appeared to give the lie to the need for the Protestant
Reformation of the Church, but lacked both the intellectual rigour and
the widespread currency to spark a major re-assessment of the national
Churches in the British Isles and a return to the Roman Catholic fold.
More serious still, few of the King's former Protestant subjects were now
prepared to believe a word that he said or, indeed, to acknowledge that
the accounts of Charles II's conversion – frequently retold and
substantially embellished at his brother's behest – were anything more
than crude and hastily constructed forgeries, designed purely to
further James's own proselytising agenda and to expose the nation to the
worst depredations of the Counter-Reformation. At a distance of more
than three hundred years, with the loss of the original documents that
were allegedly in Charles II's hand, it is almost impossible to judge their
authenticity, or to conclude anything more than that the King
was received into the Roman Catholic faith on his deathbed by
Fr Huddlestone, and that James was in attendance. Whether James was
capable of justifying a forgery on the grounds that the ends would
eventually outweigh the means – a sentiment that was certainly at odds
with his profession and understanding of Catholicism – or, more
probably, was capable of deluding himself that the papers, whatever their
origin, represented a true reflection of his brother's religious feelings, is
ultimately a matter of personal judgement.[5]

However, in October 1685, a year before the original publication of the
documents in pamphlet form, John Evelyn recorded that James had
taken Samuel Pepys into his closet 'where, opening a cabinet, he showed
him two papers, containing about a quarter of a sheet, on both sides

written, in the late King's own hand, several arguments opposite to the doctrine of the Church of England, charging her with heresy, novelty, and the fanaticism of other Protestants'. Yet, while Evelyn thought it impossible to dispute that the writings were anything other than genuine, as they were 'blotted and interlined' by Charles II himself, he found it hard to believe that these jottings represented the King's own thoughts, as they were 'so well penned as to the discourse . . . [that they] did by no means seem to me to have been put together' by him, but represented instead a series of rough notes taken down from the direction given to him 'by some priest . . . from time to time, and here recollected'.[6] According to this account, James seems to have seized on the existence of these loose leaves to try to make his own vision of the Stuart dynasty general, and to project upon the late King his own concerns and high level of commitment to the Roman Catholic faith. It was James's misfortune to consistently underestimate the strength of Protestant sympathies in the British Isles and to wilfully misread the testimonies of a small number of converts to Catholicism, drawn overwhelmingly from among the social élites, as denoting a general desire for reconciliation with Rome. As a result, while his account of his brother's last moments – graphically retold in September 1692 for the nuns of La Chaillot – might bring him approval from the religious communities on the Continent, and certainly held the power to move individual Roman Catholics in Great Britain and Ireland, its equation of Protestantism with rank 'heresy' and treason appeared to do little more than confirm the worst fears of his followers among the Anglican Tories and the Dissenters, who had hoped that his religious policies would not be used simply as a cloak for the militant, and possibly forcible, re-conversion of his peoples. Indeed, as happened with his Declaration of 1692, the Williamite authorities were keen to permit the widest possible circulation of The Writings of the Late King . . . and Anne Hyde (which had already been subjected to both angry scorn and pure indifference during James II's reign) once the war in Ireland had been won and he was safely ensconced again in his chosen place of exile. Consequently, by 1693 the further reprinting of the documents had been sanctioned by the government, with the effect that his own arguments were turned against him. The old controversy over James's supposed willingness to defame his brother and to forge his letters was forcefully resuscitated, and used to further discredit the motivations of his adherents among the Roman Catholic community.[7]

This commitment to an explicitly Roman Catholic vision of the Stuart dynasty, which bound the theory of a divinely anointed kingship passed on from father to son to an unbreakable commitment to the Church of Rome, was – despite all James's attempts to rewrite history and establish a tradition of Catholic sovereignty – an entirely new development which came into far clearer definition after the loss of his crowns. It had been perfectly natural for James, on his arrival in France, to reflect on his experiences of past exile and to compare the difficulties he and his family had faced between 1648 and 1660 with the fresh problems that began to assail him after his flight from England at the close of 1688. It required little imagination to perceive that in some respects his fortunes had turned full circle, or to appreciate that the tired and disappointed statesman who had so suddenly and unexpectedly found himself deprived of office in late middle age might wish to revisit the sites of his youth, and to invest them with a significance and a sense of romance, born of hindsight and a longing for a seemingly less complicated and more heroic age. Consequently, shortly after reaching France in January 1689, he had contrived to visit the Convent of the Grand Carmelites, so that he might call on mère Agnes Arnauld, the elderly nun who had first raised doubts in his mind as to the validity of Protestantism while he was serving as a soldier in the Spanish Netherlands. Their conversation was, unsurprisingly, characterised by a strong sense of nostalgia but it also served to highlight James's spiritual journey from an errant youth, marred by sexual excess and tainted by the pursuit of worldly ambition, to a maturity that was hallmarked by a sincere and deeply held devotion to the Roman Catholic faith, which flew in the face of temporal considerations and the need for gradualism and tact when seeking to re-order the balance of confessional power in England, and which purposely invited, if not practically ensured, the King's ruin and scorn at the hands of his former subjects. Though the Archbishop of Rheims, Charles Maurice Le Tellier, chose to paraphrase Henri IV's famous statement of religious realpolitik and mock James, as he shuffled down the steps of the cathedral of Notre Dame de Paris, as the 'good man' who had 'renounced three kingdoms for a Mass', his comments were informed by his position as a prince of the Church and the scion of a noble House that had set itself in opposition to James's friends the de Bouillons, and did not seem to reflect the attitude of the middle and lower ranking clergy, who found in the King's behaviour much that was entirely commendable.[8] Out of step with an age that was increasingly turning cynicism into a virtuous art, James's account of his sufferings, and his preparedness to sacrifice everything and everyone about him on a point of religious principle, struck a chord with the ascetics within the French Church and with the mendicant Orders in particular. What appeared to be folly bordering on insensibility to the courtiers at Versailles – and even, on occasion, to those at St Germain – could be seen as the finest attributes of a just and God-fearing King by elements of the clergy and his followers, who discerned in his willingness to do what he regarded as right, regardless of the consequences, a determination to seek out eternal rather than transitory values and objectives, and to return the Stuart monarchy to an earlier and far more theocratic model of kingship. Having been subjected to so much bitter personal criticism for his open profession of his religion, James was very receptive to all such praise and rapidly began to accentuate the extent, in both public ritual and private pronouncement, to which his kingship was divinely ordained and practised according to the will of God. That such a rigid and explicit definition of his claims to authority would potentially serve to alienate a great many of his former subjects who were not Roman Catholics, and who had little appetite to be branded as effectively 'second class' citizens in their own lands, or that such a vision had a narrow constituency of supporters, located primarily among the Jacobite exiles and those Catholic gentry families – such as the Shireburnes, the Tydesleys, and the Widdringtons – still domiciled in the British Isles, seemingly did not deter him from refashioning his image of monarchy along religious lines, and gradually abandoning his self-perception as a warrior in favour of that as a patriarch to his peoples and a living 'saint'.

It was in keeping with James's view of his kingship as a sacred trust, not to mention his enormous relief after escaping his enemies and surviving a hazardous Channel crossing, that his first public act upon landing in France had been to hear Mass, in order to give thanks for his seemingly miraculous deliverance. Yet, until he came to regard his exile as being of a long or even a permanent duration, after his return from Ireland in 1690, he had shown no particular favour to any one theologian or religious Order. He visited the churches of Paris in order to celebrate 'the great solemnities' of the Christian calendar, and journeyed out into the surrounding suburbs and countryside to seek 'out those Parishes and Convents where the Christian duties were perform'd with greatest regularitie and devotion, and as he drew hony from every flower himself, so he left a sweet odor behind him, to the edification even of those who had spent their lives in a perpetual study of spiritualitie; they were ashtonished to find a Prince born to command, bred in the nois[e] of wars, and the distractions of a Court, should have higher notions of submission and resignation than they had been acquainted with'. To this end, he maintained Jesuit priests as his confessors, retained Jansenist sympathisers within his Household (despite the growing disapproval of Louis XIV), showed his continued favour to the English Benedictines, who had proved to be of great support in both spiritual and financial matters during his first exile from 1648 to 1660, and would have gone in disguise to the Chapel of the Hearts at Val de Grace along with the comte de Lauzun, had they not been recognised and forced by the great crowd that gathered to see them to turn their coach about. At the parish church at St Germain the anniversary of Charles II's birth was celebrated each year, while prayers were said with great solemnity for the re-conversion of England and, after 1690, requiem Masses were held to speed the soul of young Henry, Lord Waldegrave through the fires of Purgatory.[9]

Yet, despite all these overtures – and the care with which Mary of
Modena redecorated her private chapel to reflect her devotion to the cult
of the Sacred Heart – it was the Convent of the Visitation at La Chaillot
that became the initial focus for the religious self-expression of the exiled
Stuarts and their followers. The fabric of the building had originally
served as the country house of Catherine de Medici, before the suburbs
of Paris began to creep up to its walls and Marshal de Bassompierre
transformed it into a large private palace, cramming its corridors and
apartments with works of art brought home from his campaigns, and with
every conceivable luxury that he required to assist him in his latter years,
as he worked on the compiling of his voluminous memoirs. Subsequently,
the French Crown had gifted La Chaillot to James's mother, the dowager
Queen Henrietta Maria, in order that her own exile should be all the
more bearable and not without its worldly comforts. She, however, had
markedly different ideas and had presented the palace, together with its
vineyards, its farm, and its vast expanse of formal gardens to the Salesian
nuns of the Visitation, thus establishing a tangible link between the site
and the Stuart dynasty in terms of both tangible memory and physical
commemoration, while ensuring the lasting gratitude of the Order
towards the family of its unexpected benefactor. James's sister learned
her letters at the school run there by the nuns, and when, in due course,
Henrietta Maria died, her heart was encased in a precious reliquary and
placed beside the high altar as an object of veneration. Mary of Modena,
who had expressed her ardent desire to join the Salesian Order as a
young girl, had not been able to settle to her devotions at the abbey of
Poissy, which was much closer to the château of St Germain, and
discovered in La Chaillot not only a reassuringly familiar practice of piety
but also a firm friend and spiritual confidant in the Mother Superior,
Angelique Priolo, who shared with her a common Italian heritage.
During her visits, which began in Lent 1689 shortly before James's
departure for Ireland, Mary took over the suite of apartments formerly
occupied by Henrietta Maria, which had been newly refurbished for her
benefit by Louis XIV. She delighted in the company of the nuns, who
frequently hailed from the most illustrious of French noble families, such
as the La Fayettes, the Montmorencys, and the Ventadours, and often
timed her stays to coincide with the reception of novices into the
Order. Declaring that although God had declined her own wish to
become a nun, He had now given her 'the opportunity of serving the
whole establishment', she dutifully paid the sisters an annual rent of
some 3,000 francs for the use of her guest rooms – until the poverty of
the Jacobite court caused her to fall behind after 1709 – and made the
first of many gifts of plate, paintings, vestments, and religious sculptures,
which she could ill afford, but which served to further enrich the Order's
treasury and to transform the walls of the convent into a virtual

apotheosis of the exiled House of Stuart. Commemorative medallions, portraits in oils and marble busts of James, his wife and their children all competed for space alongside depictions of Henrietta Maria, Charles II and Catherine of Braganza, while specially commissioned allegorical works – mostly to be completed upon Mary's instruction after her husband's death – concentrated on the relationship of the royal couple with their children. In one canvas, the titular Prince of Wales was shown as the infant Moses, a foundling preserved among the bulrushes of France rather than of ancient Egypt; in another painting he became a new Emperor Constantine, handed a cross by his mother in the guise of St Helena, which bore the stern command that 'in this sign' he should 'conquer'. James was portrayed twice alongside his daughter, the Princess Louise Marie. On the first occasion, begun during their lifetime by Mignard and subsequently completed after the deaths of both the artist and the King by Gobert, James was depicted at his prayers as his daughter turned over a page in her book of psalms, to emphasise a stern passage that commanded her not to: 'Forget thine own people and thy father's house'. The second composition, painted in order to commemorate and mourn the princess's premature death in 1712, showed James beckoning to his daughter to join him in heaven, while the clouds parted above them in expectation of the joyous occasion and in promise of their life eternal.[10]

Yet, even though La Chaillot was destined to become the centre of a burgeoning cult that celebrated the holiness and devotion of the former King and Queen of England, James – in marked contrast to his closest confidants Melfort, Caryll, and later Middleton – went rarely to the convent, and exerted no direct influence on its development, preferring instead to allow Mary of Modena a free rein to become the nuns' undisputed patron and to use their buildings and high-domed church as the setting for her own personal displays of piety. Such a decision reflected in part the separation of religious patronage along the lines of gender, with the Queen's visits to the nuns of La Chaillot finding a subsequent mirror, as James himself recognised, in the King's own pilgrimages to the monks of La Trappe. However, it seems that the nature of Mary's discovery of the convent, immediately before James's departure to wage war, and the emotional intensity of the prayers for her husband's safety that she delivered there during his absence on campaign in Ireland, served to effectively preclude the King's easy or rapid involvement with the affairs of the Order on his eventual return. Though the nuns remarked that he had 'Honoured [the House] with his frequent Visits during the Life of the Late Queen, His Mother', his subsequent encounters with the Sisters of the Visitation appear to have been characterised by a sense of awkwardness, and may even have been uncomfortable for all the parties concerned. Following the destruction of his invasion fleet at La Hogue, James had returned to the convent in the company of his wife, but did little to recommend himself to the Mother Superior, purposely ignoring her heartfelt commiserations on his most recent defeat and tersely snapping his responses to all her subsequent questions. The sisters subsequently recalled that: 'At his first coming into France, he honour'd us often with his visits, coming to hear the good preachers that preach'd before the Queen, and other times at his return from hunting to carry back her Majesty; but fearing those frequent visits might be troublesome, by drawing too much company. He did us the honour to tell us, that to avoid this inconvenience, he was resolv'd to deprive himself of one of his sweetest consolations, which was that of coming often here'. As a result, La Chaillot was to remain Mary of Modena's private retreat and religious preserve, with her husband having no interest or reason to interfere with her sphere of influence among the genteel and cultured community of sisters, who displayed their unfeigned affection towards her with a shower of gifts of fruit, flowers and confectionary that came to verge on the embarrassing, and brought about her lasting delight with the simple request that one of their novices might take her name upon her admittance to their Order.[11]

The truth of the matter was that James had simply not had the time or the leisure to immerse himself fully in the religious life of France in the few short weeks that had separated his arrival at Ambleteuse from his departure with the fleet from Brest, still less to throw his weight behind any particular institution or individual within the Church. It was only on his return to France following the disaster at the Boyne, that he had the opportunity to think again in any depth on the religious direction of his life, the apparent withdrawal of God's favour towards him, and the steps that would be necessary in order to assist in the salvation of his soul. With the hunting field unable to divert James's energies indefinitely, his need to satiate his sexual desires apparently on the wane, and his mistresses left far behind him in Dublin, the invitation given to him by Marshal Bellefonds to accompany him on a retreat to the monastery of La Trappe seemed particularly welcome and possibly even auspicious. Every bit as brave, as quarrelsome, and as austere as the former King, Bellefonds was a man of enormous personal integrity and considerable learning, who was able to combine support for the Jesuits with an enduring friendship and admiration for many leading Jansenists. Despite Bellefonds' dislike for Marshal Turenne – and his outright refusal to serve under his command in 1672 – James was prepared to admire the respect and intellectual vigour with which he conducted his lengthy theological correspondence with Bishop Bossuet, and recognised in him the forthright military virtues and impressive service record to which he had always aspired.[12] For eighteen years, Bellefonds had been making pilgrimages to La Trappe and knew full well that in the hardened,

vigorous form of Armand de Rancé – who admitted to knowing no
greater joys than the chase of the hunt, fencing practice, and the touch
of a woman throughout a sinful youth – James might find a spiritual
guide, as he had, who could address the themes of temptation and the
fundamental need for repentance in a manner which an aging soldier
could readily understand.

Thus, James came to the monastery in the belief that he had already
suffered much in the cause of God but that, inexplicably, divine
providence had been withdrawn from him after so many years of success.
His initial reception, which saw the abbé prostrating himself before his
advance at the gates of La Trappe set the tone for the rest of the visit,
with de Rancé refusing the King's offer to rise to his feet and declaring
'with so profound a humility' that 'God visits us in your person', for it was
a tremendous 'happiness for us to see in this desert this great prince on
whose behalf we have so long continually offered prayers' and that 'we do
nothing more frequently or more ardently than ask God that He will
accord to your sacred person all the strength and all the protection
necessary to it . . . and that He will finally give you the immortal crown
that He has prepared for all those who have had the happiness, like your
Majesty, to follow Jesus Christ, and to prefer Him before all things'.
Reassured by these kind words, and by the regard in which he already
found himself to be held, James followed the monks into the church to
pray, before being engaged by the abbé in a long and private discussion
about the nature of salvation, in the shadows of the main hall. After
Complines, James brusquely waved aside the concerns of his courtiers,
who feared for his health amid the draughts and damp of the nave, and
made a deep and lasting impression on the brothers as the result of both
his resolve to stay in the church, alone if need be, in order to complete
his required number of meditations for the day, and through his
surprising eagerness to set aside all social distinctions and to willingly
share in their privations, tackling without murmur or complaint their
meagre 'fayre' of roots and vegetables for supper. Though the monks'
savage pursuit of poverty and self-denial struck an immediate chord with
the King, it was their observance of a near total silence that appeared to
be the most novel and unsettling, yet entirely commendable and
profoundly moving, aspect of the spiritual life of La Trappe. Anxious to
make the best use of the remainder of his stay, James saw nothing
incongruous in his behaviour as he repeatedly drew the abbé to one side,
his questions, observations, and marks of respect tripping over his tongue
as, watched by the silent monks, he initiated conversation and eagerly
sought to discover the source of their steely resolve and unshakeable self-
control. He observed their methods of work out in the fields and 'the
product of [their] gard[en]ing', and spoke approvingly of their ability to
bear the extremities of heat and cold in the spirit of 'Christian

patience'.[13] Noting that the brothers had evolved a complex system of sign language to make plain their needs, he registered his approval that the only noise that they made was to 'sing the office in the Church, [which] keeps their thoughts as continually fixed upon God, as their tongues are permitted to utter nothing but his praises'. He felt that his own predicament was directly explained and a resolution of his sufferings provided for when, the next morning, the choir of monks intoned the verses of Psalm 118 during the communion, declaring that despite being surrounded on every side with foes 'like bees; they blazed like a fire of thorns' it was 'better to take refuge in the Lord than to put confidence in mortals [and] . . . better to take refuge in the Lord than to put confidence in princes'. Thus might James, like the people of Israel before him, 'look in triumph on those who hate me' and recognise not only that: 'The Lord is my strength and my might; he has become my salvation' but also that though 'The Lord has punished me severely . . . he did not give me over to death'.[14] Writing only four days later, de Rancé thought that the text 'could not have been more appropriate and explicit if it had been done deliberately', for it reminded the King that 'the proud may be confounded with the injustice with which they have treated me', and that his 'consolation will be to submit to' the commands of God. As the service progressed, the abbé noted that James had approached 'the holy table with a quiet unusual piety', praying 'during the office and throughout High Mass without a moment's interruption', and having 'left the carpet on which he was, [he] placed himself on the bottom step of the altar and rejected the cushion offered to him'.[15]

If the words of Fr Simeon and mère Agnes had once stirred his youthful imagination with the promise of an everlasting Paradise and the threat of the undying fires of Hell, then James now found their echo in the verses of the psalm, bursting out miraculously as he took communion, and in the uncompromising tones of the elderly abbé, whose calls to an unquestioning, anti-intellectual, and almost martial obedience to the most authoritarian of Gods conformed to his vision of a world torn between polar opposites – right against wrong, white against black, and the saved against the damned – that sat distinct from the weighty qualifications and incomprehensible failures to speak or act completely in his defence that had so marred his relations with successive pontiffs, the Emperor, Cardinal Howard, and even the mainstream of the Roman Catholic community in England.[16] Defeat, dishonour and rejection at the hands of his peoples could, indeed needed, to be experienced and borne, in order to make amends to God, whose love, unlike that of James's subjects, was to endure forever. In advancing this aspect of Christian doctrine, de Rancé had intuitively succeeded in striking just the right note with the fallen King, who had found respect and certainty grievously lacking in the world of late, and who craved

doctrinal clarity, a vision of social and spiritual order, and the promise
that his labours would be rewarded, if not with a temporal crown, then
ultimately with the far greater accolade of a heavenly one, which could
not be denied him, tarnished, or stolen away by the hand of man. This
fresh concept of the responsibilities that lay upon a King without a
crown, who might act as the conscience of his errant nations and secure
an everlasting victory, not through politics or triumph on the battlefield,
but through his relationship with God and success in the inner struggle
for his soul, was La Trappe's gift to James. It provided him with the
central insight that prompted the comprehensive shift in the emphasis of
his kingship in the last years of his life, onto ever more theocratic lines, as
the image of him as warrior and statesman was allowed to fade and be
replaced by that of the priest-king, who strove to act as the intermediary
between God and Man, and to take the weight of sin from his former
subjects and redistribute it upon his own, increasingly bowed, shoulders.

  However, this would be a gradual process; it found its first expression
when James, as he prepared to leave the monastery after his visit to the
hermit in the woods, excitedly proclaimed his belief before the monks
that: 'One must come here to learn how God ought to be prayed to and
served', and announced his intention to 'try to imitate you as far as it is
possible in my position'. Indeed, so taken was he with 'the order, the
modesty, [and] the silence of these holy solitaries', that he declared his
intention to have framed copies made of the rules governing La Trappe,
so that they might be hung up in the corridors and chambers of
St Germain, urging that speech should never be raised above a respectful
murmur and that access to the formal gardens should be restricted in the
mornings for the better edification of his courtiers and their ladies. 'God
willing', James told the abbé on their parting, 'this will not be my last
journey here' and de Rancé, for his part, lost no time following up his
visit with a letter to Marshal Bellefonds in which he revealed that he had
been 'dying to tell you my impressions of this prince who is so worthy of
the respect and compassion of all men of good will'. Though born out of
curiosity, the King's visit appears to have made a vivid and lasting
impression on all the parties concerned, with the abbé's promise that:
'After the King whom God has engraved in our innermost hearts . . .
[James] will occupy the first place in our hearts' appearing to reveal
more than just the extremities to which conventional forms of flattery
might be taken in the service of the great and the good. For while de
Rancé appears to have been alive to the advantages of having his
monastic reforms endorsed by a King – albeit one in exile – who might
argue his cause at Versailles and thereby increase the likelihood of the
survival and spread of his legacy after his death, it does not appear to
have been in his nature to explicitly seek out powerful new patrons, and
it seems perfectly reasonable to accept that his conclusion 'that if [James]

found some consolation amongst us, as he indicated, he has left us an edifying memory which we shall never lose' resulted from entirely genuine sentiments. Moreover, he went to great lengths to record his impressions of the King, confiding to the Marshal that: 'I saw in him a depth of piety and religion that surprised me, a detachment from all worldly things and a resignation to God's will which can only be the effect of his grace and the impression made by his Holy Spirit. He is fully aware of the degree and extent of his disgrace, when he looks at it with human eyes, but this realisation only causes him to offer to God a continual sacrifice and thus attract the protection he needs in so total and complete a misfortune'. From de Rancé's perspective: 'One cannot fail to see that what consoles him is that he is convinced that what he is losing he had only for a few moments, that he was bound sooner or later to be deprived of it, but what he awaits is eternal . . . [for] I was struck by the restraint and moderation with which he spoke of his enemies; he does not utter a word in that respect which is not in accordance with the strictest rules. Nature has no part in what he says about them, all its reactions halted. This is assuredly something that is not within the power of man, and there is no room for doubt that in such moments God is entirely master of his heart. The vigour of his faith and the ardour of his zeal for the interests of the Church and the service of Christ are without equal, and he deems himself happy in his misfortune to have been judged worthy to suffer for the glory of his name. He knows and feels that persecution is the mark of those who belong to Christ'.[17]

For the abbé, therefore, as for the King himself, James's response to his circumstances was entirely rational and offered not only a coherent explanation of his failure to hold on to power in his three kingdoms, but also contained the seeds of his triumph over his foes, to be enacted in the hereafter. In a far more secular age where, for Western Europeans, questions of faith, salvation and the possibility of eternal damnation do not, for the most part, inform every aspect of their lives and where death is a thing to be hidden away and avoided, rather than to be celebrated and embraced as marking the passage of the soul from a corruptible to an incorruptible realm, James's actions may appear extreme or incomprehensible, the manifestation of a deeper sickness that stemmed directly from a form of mental or sexual illness. Such an approach, which seeks to dismiss all that is discordant and unsettling from the King's latter years, and to equate his severe practice of religious devotion with a blind frenzy born of madness, is a dominant feature within modern historiography. However, while it provides a convenient and superficially satisfying explanation for both James's fall from power and his subsequent failure to regain his thrones, the tendency to perceive in all the King's actions the progress of a virulent degenerative disease, that increasingly rendered him pathetic and insensible, has served to strip the

significance from the period of his last exile from 1689 to1701. It imposes
on all James's initiatives an interpretative model which owes much to
hindsight, and which dismisses them out of hand as being by turns
comically ridiculous, hopelessly optimistic, or preordained to
unmitigated and embarrassing disaster. For Victorian commentators from
a liberal or Whiggish background, the depth and fervour of James's
Catholicism appeared as evidence of his violent extremism and the
decline of his moral fibre. If the equation of Roman Catholicism with
treason, senseless brutality, and the desire to erode national liberties is
today wholly, and rightly, rejected by scholars, then the tendency of the
modern academic community to exorcise the impact of religion from
James's public career and to seek to trivialise the nature of his beliefs is
no less imprudent or unjustifiable. In rejecting all that is uncomfortable,
arcane, or simply difficult from the past, and in forcing all James's
endeavours to conform to a narrow paradigm that equates his practice of
religion with a deeper sense of malaise, reducing his whole career to the
study of his supposed medical ailments, a sizeable number of
contemporary commentators have unconsciously sought to neglect or to
trivialise the King's concept of his faith, every bit as damagingly as their
illustrious Victorian forbears, and arguably with less justification.[18]

James's public adherence to Roman Catholicism, which flew in the face
of the prejudices and principles of the overwhelming majority of his
fellow countrymen, had required considerable moral courage and –
having cost him in turn his military commands, the custody of his elder
daughters, and his right to the crown – can be seen to have offered him
no tangible personal benefit save for the promise of the salvation of his
soul. If we are prepared to recognise that, from the time of his
conversion onwards, James was motivated to a large extent by the desire
to safeguard the promise of eternal life that he believed had been given
to him by God, then his actions and his willingness to place his religious
principles before political advantage, often pursued with a flagrant
disregard of the cost, become all the more explicable and even
commendable. The opprobrium of human beings, however strong, was
nothing to be feared by the King when compared to the displeasure of a
harsh and jealous God. It is my contention, therefore, that the increasing
tempo of James's religious devotions during his latter years was motivated
by entirely rational considerations, which grew not only from a pressing
sense of his own mortality and a need to rationalise his failings, but also
from the new set of constraints placed on him during his final exile.
Moreover, though he sought out de Rancé and eagerly adopted him as
his spiritual mentor, there is nothing, as we shall now see, in James's
relationship with the abbé that spoke either of gullibility, or of the entire
abandonment of his political acumen in order to promote his favoured
Order. The lessons that he imbibed through his contact with La Trappe

were not simply or uncritically observed by the King, but were incorporated into his own pre-existing view of the path to salvation, and rapidly put to use in the radical fashioning of a unique concept of, and justification for, James's own sovereignty and personal authority. This saw his abandonment of the world as the necessary pre-condition to his claims to profound religious insight and his transformation into the embodiment of a living saint, a priest-king whose every pronouncement carried with it the moral force of divine will and mandate. In this light, even though James might be forced to witness the defeat of his army and invasion fleet, and be compelled to acquiesce in the cessation of military hostilities against William III after the Treaty of Ryswick, he might still persist in the waging of spiritual warfare against his foe on another, ethereal plane, where he firmly believed his fortunes would be far more secure and could not fail to be rewarded with an ultimate triumph which depended on nothing save his own constancy, inner resources and doctrinal strength.

II

Within a fortnight of his return to his palace at St Germain, James had written to de Rancé thanking him for his kind reception and declaring that: 'I was so happy with all I saw at La Trappe and so edified to see with what devotion the Good God is served that I could not help acknowledging it to you myself and to start an exchange of letters with you, which I hope will be useful to me in the saving of my soul . . . as . . . I am cross with myself that I did not stay longer to benefit more and to talk with you more deeply about what I have done'. To his evident delight, his wish was readily granted and over the course of the following decade a remarkable correspondence developed between the King and the monk, punctuated by James's annual visits to the abbey and only brought to an end by the death of de Rancé in October 1700. James certainly invested these missives with an enormous significance, declaring that: 'it took that visit [to the monastery] to give me knowledge of myself and make me despise all that seems great in the world', adding that it was 'a pleasure to find in all your letters very useful instructions for our salvation', and asking that the abbé 'let me have your news from time to time'. As a testament to their growing friendship – possibly the only lasting and entirely satisfying attachment that James made outside his family circle during his last exile – their correspondence soon dispensed with stilted and highly formal manners of address and began to directly reflect the concerns and hopes of both men. Their discussion of major spiritual themes and practices thus came to be interspersed with the exchange of political advice and personal news, which included James's concern for de Rancé's health, as recurring fevers sapped his strength, a serious fall endangered his life, and a paralysis crippled his right hand, threatening the curtailment of their correspondence in March 1695. The majority of letters from the King ended with a request for the brothers to intercede for him and his family in the course of their daily prayers, but here the formulaic element, over-emphasised by some later historians in their consideration of his powers of self-expression, all but ceases.[19] Though he wrote hurriedly and seldom developed an idea very far, changing tack and emphasis without warning, such an approach is all the more revealing, and demonstrates the urgency and seriousness with which James struggled to come to terms with his own practise of sin, and to chart a sure path for his personal salvation.

Before de Rancé, an exemplary individual 'who is so enlightened and so pious, and who knows the world and its pitfalls', the King felt impelled to present himself as the most humble and errant disciple of Christ, whose pursuit of 'spiritual advancement' appeared to be destined to fitful progress, achieved through considerable sacrifice and by painfully slow degrees, while he still clung to his pride and vanity. Therefore, James required the abbé to prepare his 'advance on the good road' and pledged that: 'from now on I will strive earnestly for my salvation and work hard to gain it'. Given that the King had converted to Roman Catholicism more than twenty years before, and had made his profession and promotion of the faith one of the defining ingredients of his rule in England, it may seem strange that he was prepared to admit in December 1691 that he still felt he had failed to show sufficient ardour and application in his service of God; as late as June 1696, he was still expressing 'a need for those examples of piety and mortification which are to be seen at La Trappe, to affirm those good resolutions that I have taken to lead a more Christian life than I did in the past'.[20] The cumulative effect of his loss of power, exile, and repeated military defeats had, however, wrought a devastating change in James's confidence and self-perception, and had convinced him that all his misfortunes had stemmed from his wilful alienation of God. This had rendered him utterly fallen in the eyes of the Lord, and incapable of freeing himself from the shackles of sin. Finding himself in such a desperate predicament, James acknowledged that he 'must rely entirely on the grace of God . . . [for] we aught to apprehend that the devine goodnesse will withdraw his grace from us, if we presume to much of our owne strength, and thinke we can do any thing that is good of our selvs'. Moreover, he had come to despair of his own character and condition, declaring that: 'I abhor and detest my self for having so offten offended so grasious and mersifull a God, and haing lived so many yeares in almost a perpetual course of sin, not only when I was carried away w[i]th the heat of it . . . but even after when I was come to yeares of more discretion'. Having identified 'my predominant sin' – and the cause of his ruin – as his ferocious sexual impulses, which had driven him into a series of largely unsatisfactory extra-marital affairs, James now strove to sublimate his passions, recognising 'those dangerous cources I embarked my self in' and acknowledging that he had 'so very foolishly and indiscretly exposed my self to sine, w[hi]ch had already gott the better of me, and to w[hi]ch I had but to[o] much inclination'. Admitting that he had 'lived so long in a constant cours of sin and scandal', James voiced his resolve to master 'the world, the flesh and the Divele', while coming to the realisation that he was powerless to improve his situation without acknowledging both his absolute dependence upon a spiritual guide such as de Rancé, and his utter resignation to the will of God. Consequently, he informed the abbé at the beginning of winter 1691 that: 'I have begun to take communion more often than I used to do' and begged him, in the following summer, to: 'give me your instruction in regard to those distractions which do not assail me so often when I take Mass, and especially when I say my prayers to give me remedies against a too good opinion of myself'.[21]

The practice of devotions according to a rigid timetable could be used to impose an element of order and routine on an existence that was increasingly stripped of diplomatic and military duties, even before the Peace of 1697 administered the *coup de grâce* to the King's hopes for his restoration. The prospect of even longer hours of leisure and idleness was particularly unwelcome to someone as active, and as profoundly unimaginative, as James, who appreciated that it offered greater scope for lapses into sin. He recognised that in the strict observance of his faith, hearing 'Masse not only on days of Obli[gation]: but on all other days if not hindred by some unforseen accident', receiving 'the Blessed Sacrament . . . once a weeke or offtener by advice of on[e]s Conf[essor]', in the repeated saying of the rosary, and in the observance of regular fasts, he might seek to divert his thoughts from dwelling on more sensuous pleasures.[22] After 1694, he pledged to spend one day a month on a spiritual retreat, assisted on 'Sondays, Holydays and Thursdays in the afternone' at the services of Complines and Benediction at the parish church of St Germain, and made sure that he took part in prayers 'every third we[d]n[e]sday of the month, for restablishing Cat[holic] Reli[gion] in the three Kingdoms, and to fast that day'. By 1698, he was noting his intention 'to repeat the seven Penetential Psalmes one a day' and had extended his pursuit of a 'perfect' abstinence even into those areas 'w[hi]ch are not ill in themselvs, for mortification, even hunting, and other manlyke exercises, should be used with moderation'.[23] In order to atone for his past sins, and to suppress his seemingly unconquerable sexual urges, he began to scourge his flesh and to wear 'at certain times an Iron Chain with little sharp points which pierced his skin; and had not the discretion of his Confessor mitigated his zeal in this particular, he had certainly carryd it to excess, for the horrour he had of his past disorders made him think he could never do enough to make a reparation for them'. Yet it was not only the Jesuit, Fr Sanders, who was disturbed by the growing influence of the community of La Trappe on the character of the King, for the French authorities – who were advancing money and arms to further his cause – became increasingly concerned over the sense of fatalism and hopelessness that his contact with the Cistercian brothers had supposedly bred in him. It was left to the hapless Monsieur, having been taken to one side by Louis XIV and informed of his duty, to write to the abbé de Rancé early in 1691, in order to persuade him to lessen his contact with the exiled King, or at least to use his best endeavours to persuade James of the necessity for him to adopt a far more aggressive, and markedly less defeatist, attitude towards the ongoing preparations for his own restoration. Unabashed, de Rancé correctly observed that he had not sought out James's company and favour, but that as the King had come of his own volition to him in order to seek a closer relationship with God, the saints 'Antony and Arsenius would have spoken from the depths of their desert' for so righteous a cause. Unfortunately, the letter from Marshal Bellefonds praising James's retreat from the world had already been published and circulated in the streets, salons and coffee shops of Paris, prompting the soldier to mount a lengthy defence of his vision of the King who had borne his persecution 'with so much faith, constancy, and piety' and of the monks of La Trappe, who were best placed to 'publish God's greatness abroad'.[24] Yet, the spirited counter-attacks mounted by Bellefonds and the abbé did little to quiet the growing chorus of disapproval from the French populace, who resented their tax money going to support a foreign King who appeared to have exhibited no great desire to help himself. Meanwhile, to the dismay of Louis XIV and the embarrassment of his brother, the following months only served to bring James deeper into the orbit of de Rancé and his followers. Indeed, the influence of the abbé did nothing to mitigate James's harsh and unforgiving personality; he rebuked the King for writing charitably of his Protestant former subjects that some 'live morally enough', and sought to drive home his own message that 'the devil is an imitator of Christ . . . with his [own] martyrs and confessors' and that James should not, in future, be misled by their dangerous shams. Furthermore, on 2/12 November 1691, the abbé sent James a letter of Association, signed by his secretary and thirty-two of his monks, together with a timetable of their days at La Trappe – which he hoped would help him to regulate his life at St Germain – and a reassuring message that confided to the King that: 'God's hand steers the vessel, and despite all the reefs, all the storms on the way will not fail to make the voyage successful'. Indeed, James's joyful reception of the accolade and his promise 'to persevere in despising the world to the degree that all

Christians should' was hardly calculated to appease the withering criticism directed against him at the court of Versailles, or to silence the fears of some of his own partisans that he might even seek to swap his stately clothes, already stripped of anything that smacked of the 'extravagant', for the simple cowled habit of a Trappist monk.[25]

Such criticism was not unfamiliar to James; through both his letters to the abbé and his private theological writings, he wrestled with the problem of attaining his salvation without withdrawing completely from secular society. In his very first letter to de Rancé he had announced his opinion that: 'I will not stop believing that it is within the ability of those outside the cloisters to do this [i.e. to turn their backs on the world], if they are willing to work as hard, in this important matter, as is necessary, because there is nothing to prevent a king as any other [man] may, having the humility, the Christian charity, and the complete resignation to God's will, without sin either in their nature or in their actions, as it is for the good fathers of La Trappe'. He chose to return to these themes seven years later when, in 1697, he concluded that while 'I am over joyd when I heare of any that leave the world and retire thether [i.e. to La Trappe], and have found great reason to praise the devine goodnesse for having put it into my hart to see that place, since I have visibly found great advantage by it, yett I cannot be' so partial to it, as to thinke one may not worke out ones salvation in . . . the world, without retiring thether or to some strict order, seing that persons of all qualitys, of all callings, have been great Saints, and may be so still'.[26] Yet, if the King's decision not to forsake his office, his family, and his loyal partisans produced audible sighs of relief , not only from Perth and Middleton, as might have been expected, but also from such a devoted Roman Catholic and loyal servant as John Caryll, who wrote scathingly of his master's 'ramble of devotion' at La Trappe in July 1695, this did not signal a lessening of either his ascetic rigour or a retreat from his support for de Rancé, even as storm clouds began to gather over the monastery that he had done so much to shape.[27]

The need for validation arose again and again in James's letters to the abbé, as he anxiously questioned passages that had been badly copied from de Rancé's *Conduite Chretienne* which described the salvation of a grievous sinner. He appeared to experience a further crisis of confidence after the signing of the Peace of Ryswick, declaring that despite all his mentor's teachings he could not 'get near to leading my life as it should be' and expressing his embarrassment 'not to have followed your instructions better'. De Rancé had repeatedly urged that he abandon himself entirely to God, but James continued to fret 'that with the saints one learns sanctity, and that among sinners one runs a great risk of becoming like them', promising that he would endeavour 'not to fear what will be and not to wonder what will be, which might offend God's intent' and reaffirming his need to 'go to my father the Abbe as often as possible, since all the time I have the happiness to be in your presence and hear you speak, I can renew my enthusiasm which I first gained in this holy house'.[28] However, if the labour of answering James's persistent queries had initially threatened to overwhelm de Rancé, and had led him, at the height of the King's spiritual retreats in 1695, to excuse his failure to write more out of his wish to allow his royal patron to enjoy his 'peace despite all', the time was fast approaching when their roles were to be reversed and the abbé was to seek desperately for evidence of James's continuing affection and willingness to actively defend his vision of monastic reform.

The rheumatism that attacked de Rancé's joints in the winter of 1694–5 and curtailed the flow of his correspondence, to James's evident disappointment, had also served to precipitate a succession crisis at the monastery of La Trappe. The abbé, exhausted by his labours, duly announced his decision to retire from office in May 1695, less than a year short of his seventieth birthday, but chose to appeal directly to Louis XIV to allow him the rare privilege of nominating his own replacement, seemingly to ensure the survival of his controversial reforms. Permission was duly given by the King and, with papal approval also readily forthcoming, de Rancé handed in his resignation and welcomed his successor Dom Zozime Foisil to the monastery at the close of the year, believing that the work had been accomplished to his satisfaction. Unfortunately, the rejoicings of his supporters that the granting of royal approval and the smooth transition of power from one generation to another would show 'how wrong people were to imagine that La Trappe would go to the grave with de Rancé' quickly proved premature; Dom Zozime sickened in the harsh climate within weeks of his arrival, and was dead by early spring. Another appeal was made to Louis XIV to empower the former abbé to nominate a further successor and James, who had been hurrying to join his invasion force at Calais, wrote anxiously that he had heard: 'that the new abbot was dead, and that the King had of his bounty permitted the rest of you to name another and that you have chosen Dom Armand, who was a Carmelite before he came to you', giving voice to his concern that: 'I beg you to let me know what is going on and let me know the state of your sanctity'.[29] Even though the Crown, in accordance with de Rancé's recommendation, had quickly approved the appointment of Dom Armand-François Gervaise, and James's subsequent visit to the monastery – for once in the company of his wife – had been a triumphant success, it became clear that a retreat from public office was more easily envisaged than accomplished by the former abbé. Unwilling to retire entirely to the confines of his simple cell, de Rancé continued to publish tracts attacking his foes among the Cistercians, Jesuits, and Carthusians, rounding upon those such as

Fénelon, the Archbishop of Cambrai, who had written of the necessity of hope in the individual quest for salvation. More serious still, though Dom Gervaise was now officially the new abbé de La Trappe, de Rancé remained as the public face of the institution, reluctant to yield anything of his authority to his successor and, due to his infirmities, increasingly reliant on his secretary, the layman Charles Maisne, for the propagation of his commands, injunctions, and spiritual advice. Assailed by criticism from without, as Fénelon mounted his own vigorous counter-attack on de Rancé's gloomy practice of theology, and by dissension from within, as the rival partisans of Dom Gervaise and monsieur Maisne jockeyed for position, the survival of La Trappe suddenly seemed to be imperilled. The crisis deepened still further when, having sought to assert himself, Gervaise ordered de Rancé's secretary out of his presence and only stopped short of ordering the expulsion of his foe from the precincts of the monastery, incurring the wrath and lasting displeasure of his former patron. With the duc de Saint-Simon, the comte du Charmel, and the abbess of the Clairets all actively engaged in besmirching his name at the court of Versailles as a drunkard, thief, poisoner, and sodomite, Gervaise forwarded his resignation to the Archbishop of Paris and James was, unwillingly, drawn into the maelstrom of accusation and counter-charge.[30]

The former King of England had been surprised to encounter monsieur Maisne, 'an honest man', at Versailles shortly before setting out for his annual retreat to La Trappe in the summer of 1698, but he did not appear either to grasp that this meeting had been contrived, or to realise the depth of animosity that existed between Maisne and the new abbé. As a result, it was a relatively easy matter for de Rancé to obscure the true nature of the conflict and to prevail upon him – ironically claiming the blessing of Gervaise for his actions – not to raise the matter with Louis XIV, or to seek redress for the slanders circulating about the monastery. As the son of a Parisian doctor, Gervaise had few influential friends at court and this, combined with his decision to take over the abbey at Estrees as an extension of La Trappe, even though it had already been designated for use as a mission house, served to further compromise his position. Yet, it was with regard to resolving the latter scandal that de Rancé now called on the services of King James. Fearing that his allies had overreached themselves in calling for Gervaise's removal, he had come to appreciate that the volume and ferocity of the pamphlets issued criticising life at La Trappe might not only result in the dismissal of an unpopular abbé but also in the destruction of the community that he had founded. Consequently, he deferred accepting the resignation of the abbé for the time being, and was reassured by James's undertaking to smooth over the dispute about Estrees and 'to try gently to exculpate the new Abbot for his enthusiasm for the increase of their [i.e. La Trappe's] reform in other places, which has been pushed into action at too brisk a pace'. Unaware that the campaign to remove the abbé had been formulated in the first place by de Rancé and his secretary, James wrote that he was 'mortified to have learned of the matter of the clerics who made a great noise about his failings', and subsequently sought to dismiss the 'muffled complaints which have been current for so long' about the Order as originating with the Devil, who would not suffer the pious to go on retreat, or the survival of 'communities as a shelter for the blasts of the wind, of these sorts of tempests, which arrive so unexpectedly when you least thought of them'. Yet while the scandal over the settling of Estrees ultimately subsided when Louis XIV made it clear that the house would be put to use as had been originally intended, and de Rancé was at last able to accept Gervaise's resignation, there was now no hiding from James the disquiet felt by several of the brethren at the conduct of the founding abbé. By the time the humiliated and disgraced figure of Dom Gervaise finally left La Trappe at the start of 1699 – destined to limp from monastery to monastery until his death more than half a century later – de Rancé had been forced to admit to the exiled King that dissension existed even within the walls of his abbey, but that this extended only to two or three of the brothers, and had not succeeded in contaminating the whole of the community. Henceforth, however, he appears to have found that he could not take James's friendship for granted. He markedly altered the tone of his letters for the rest of 1699, requesting that the King should visit La Trappe once again, begging for a proof of his continued affection and favour, and finally upbraiding him for his failure to respond to his letters promptly enough.[31]

Fortunately for de Rancé, James's coolness towards him was short-lived, and during the last months of his life he was able to fully regain the King's trust, as the latter returned to La Trappe and resumed his correspondence as before. James seems to have concluded that neither the abbé nor monsieur Maisne, for whom he expressed a particular friendship, were to blame for the troubles that beset their monastery, and chose to commiserate with de Rancé in September 1700 over 'the state you are in through the bad condition of your sanctuary'. Indeed, his only note of censure for Maisne's behaviour stemmed not from the unscrupulous campaign to discredit the reputation of Dom Gervaise, but from a report he had had that on recovering from a 'dangerous sickness', the secretary had expressed anger at his indisposition rather than, as the King had hoped and expected, a marked sadness at being able to escape from the clutches of a welcome death.[32] Yet even though his experience of the austerities practised by the Trappists, and de Rancé's savage rejection of individual ambition and all that was of the flesh, were undiminished in the eyes of the King, and formed the core of his personal theology, they did not act to the exclusion of other religious currents, particularly Jansenism, in his quest for salvation. They did nothing to mitigate the boldest and most idiosyncratic of his initiatives, fuelled by the intense devotional climate of his last exile, to gain not just entrance to the gates of heaven but the mantle of sainthood itself.

III

In the spring of 1698, Sir Nicholas Shireburne noted with growing concern the ill-health of his 5-year-old daughter and the blotchy skin inflammations that rimmed her eyes, and which made her screw up her face against exposure to bright sunlight. There was little in the make-up of this proud and hard-nosed northern magnate – who, as a Roman Catholic and a confirmed Jacobite, had managed against all the odds not only to protect his lands from sequestration, but also to increase an already substantial family fortune by prudent investments and a willingness to sponsor new manufactures – to suggest that he was either exceptionally gullible, or a fool. Yet, this student of Seneca and connoisseur of the arts, who filled his homes with pottery, furniture and ivories from the Orient, and who had completed a 'Grand Tour' of Europe in his youth, found it a perfectly natural response, when confronted by his child's worrying ailments, to send her to St Germain to be touched by James II for the 'King's Evil', or scrofula, in the belief that she would be miraculously cured. During his short reign, James had touched well in excess of 6,000 individuals for the affliction, distributing silver healing pieces as gifts to the sufferers bearing the inscription 'Soli Deo Gloria / To the Glory of God Alone' and the image of St Michael slaying a dragon, and gradually stripping the ceremony of its associations with Anglicanism. In removing such accretions, James believed that he was returning the ritual to its mediaeval origins and was re-establishing the semi-magical symbiosis that had linked God to the legitimate sovereign of England, from the time of Edward the Confessor onwards, through the agency of the coronation ceremony. Through the invocation of the Virgin and the Saints, the use of Latin prayers, and the signing of the Cross, James had hoped to make Roman Catholicism synonymous with the practice of English kingship, and to accentuate the dignity, mystery, and moral obligation of the office. Through his healing of the poor by the laying-on of hands – an occupation that still commanded a mass popular appeal and acceptance during the late seventeenth century – James had been able, as had his father and brother before him, to emphasise his sacred trust as King, and to distinguish himself from other men. In staking his claim to the throne in both 1680 and 1685, the Duke of Monmouth had cited his ability to heal as one of the marks of his true kingship, and though William III had stubbornly refused to take part in the ceremony – ordering that the infirm who besieged his gates should be sent away with some money and an enjoinder to find better health and more common sense – James clung to the practice throughout his exile, as a means of distinguishing his divine mandate to rule from his nephew's usurpation of a thoroughly debased worldly power. As a result, he was adamant that the form of service should not be tampered with after his arrival in France, and having exhausted the supply of touch pieces available to him by 1695, he ordered a new minting of the coins from Joseph and Norbert Roettiers, to be modelled exactly on the remaining example that had luckily been retained due to the forethought of a member of his Household. Whether this re-minting reflected the pressures of a heavy ongoing demand for these tokens by the sick, testifying to a continuity of practice from the earliest days of exile, or represented a conscious decision to reinvigorate a ritual that had been allowed to lapse, cannot now be discerned.[33]

What is certain is that the use of the touch to confer legitimacy on a claim to sovereignty was not a novel tactic, as Edward III had revived the ritual more than three hundred years earlier specifically in order to press his title to the French crown. Unfortunately, the assumption that the healing gift belonged solely to the English monarch, and the willingness of those successive sovereigns – until Queen Anne formally renounced her claim in 1712 – to maintain the pretence that they were still also the lawful ruler of France, now created a serious problem for James. Strictly speaking, his decision to continue healing not just his own adherents, but also the sick drawn to St Germain from the surrounding countryside, implicitly entailed a challenge to both the spiritual and temporal authority of Louis XIV, who similarly administered the rite to large numbers of his subjects at Easter, Pentecost, and Christmas Day. This might have provoked a clash of interests, as French courtiers noted the anomaly of two sovereigns united in their political aims but laying claim to exactly the same hereditary powers, had not Louis preferred to overlook his guest's actions – and his impolitic boasts that his healings were the more efficacious – and to offer no check or hindrance to the crowds which flocked to visit James in search of a miraculous cure. Though James's Whig detractors sought to discount the quasi-divine properties of his kingship 'in so free and inquisitive Age', through an empirical study of the efficacy of the royal touch – and eventually sought to stress the impact of the placebo, concluding that it could not be 'otherwise supposed than that when a poor and miserable Creature, prepossess'd with the most eager Thoughts of Relief, shall see the Royal Majesty condescend to apply his Hands for the Cure of the Sores and Swellings he is diseas'd with, but that it must . . . produce an agreeable Alteration in the whole Constitution' – there appears to have been scant criticism of James's healing powers from those who sought him out.

Moreover, though many returned time and again in order to be touched at the royal chapel at St Germain, this does not seem to have lessened their belief that they would ultimately be cured, and only served to confirm their scorn for the limitations of medical science, rationed strictly according to an ability to pay and often administered inexpertly by those who practised for the benefit of the populace. Sir Nicholas Shireburne certainly appeared to be delighted in the change wrought on his little girl, when she returned to England in December 1698. Yet his willingness to pay for what was, in essence, a costly pilgrimage to visit the 'rightful' King at St Germain served every bit as much as a gesture of defiance to the English authorities – in the demanding of passes for the child and her retinue to leave the country, and in the unambiguous rejection of William III's moral right to rule – as it was a rush to secure medical treatment for a much-loved child. Significantly, on the return of his daughter in 'Good health' for which he 'prais[ed] God', Sir Nicholas chose to send a gold watch valued at more than £26 to Sir William Waldegrave, the King's chief physician, 'for his Extraordinary Kindnes and Care' of her. If Mary Shireburne had made a full recovery – and there is no suggestion that she was afflicted by poor eyesight in adult life – then her father understood full well that the act of affirming his allegiance, and the securing of the royal blessing, might also be complemented by the best medical attention that money could buy.[34]

For James, therefore, the survival of his kingship, even through the difficulties of exile, could be greatly aided through the use of ritual, and by the demonstration of his continued ability to utilise supernatural powers for the purpose of healing the sick, in a manner that William III allegedly could, and certainly would, not. At the core of James's concept of kingship was the belief that he had already been divinely ordained to govern, set apart from the great mass of humanity, and invested with sacred attributes drawn directly from God. However dismal his present fortunes appeared to be, and however exacting his forms of abasement before the monks of La Trappe might be, James continued to cling to the sense of his personal election and of his purpose in bringing about the fulfilment of God's will upon earth, by leading, exhorting or cajoling his recalcitrant and 'stiff necked' peoples back to obedience, as the need arose. Moreover, during his last exile, he also explicitly sought to take for his models those two medieval Kings among his ancestors – Edward the Confessor and Louis IX – whose supposed practice of touching for the 'King's Evil' was allied to an active rejection of the world and the achievement of posthumous sainthood. Recognising in the course of his own life something of their defeats, sacrifices, and willingness to place both the service of the Lord and an exacting pursuit of personal piety before the dictates of statecraft, James consciously strove to assume their mantles and made little secret of his claims to the possession of a particularly deep and compelling religious insight. As the author of prayers, advice for new converts to Catholicism, numerous spiritual meditations and rules for Christian conduct, all of which were ultimately intended for publication, the King sought to propagate his own markedly distinct theological views and to advance the image of his personal qualities as a living saint.

The French court appears to have been well aware of James's religious agenda but, initially at least, was unsure quite what to make of it. Madame, in particular, was quick to poke fun at the King's zeal, in the aftermath of his defeat at the Boyne, repeating a comment attributed to Charles II that James would lose his crown through his profession of Catholicism, and his soul as the result of his infidelities with countless wanton and 'unsightly' women. Unimpressed by his conversation, his paucity of wit, and his incompetence as a soldier, madame sniffed with a barely disguised sense of irony that: 'the worthy king will not even make a good saint'. However, though she continued to scorn James's attempts to restrain his sexual ardour and to 'play the saint' in public, she was far more impressed by his wife's quiet demeanour and profound, yet understated, attachment to the faith. Indeed, Mary of Modena's repeated sponsorship of young girls seeking to take the veil, and her long and affectionate connection with the nuns of La Chaillot, served to foster a cult of veneration for her own person among both the exiles and the Recusant community in England, which although less forcefully expressed, ran parallel to and at times even threatened to eclipse that of her husband. Unable to formally educate their children in their traditional faith as they would have wished, English Roman Catholic gentry and merchant families sought to import toys from the Continent that would aid in their religious instruction and enable them – in the absence of the opportunity to observe the real examples – to distinguish the costume of the different monastic Orders. As a result, dolls or little 'mannequins' were frequently sent from France, and St Germain in particular, throughout the late seventeenth and early eighteenth centuries, as presents to mark a daughter's first communion or birthday, or else as a reminder of an absent child or sibling who had crossed the Channel in order to enter a religious house. It seems that Mary of Modena not only promoted the fashion for giving these expensive toys, in order to foster a continuing religious and political attachment among the young generation, but also served as the model for one of the most popular and seemingly best-loved of the dolls, combining the virtues of feminine beauty and a taste for fashion with the roles of the ideal Catholic wife and mother.[35] Thus, the stalls in Covent Garden came to be stocked with these seemingly innocuous representations of Roman Catholic loyalty, and of the exiled Stuart Queen and her children, while examples found their way into the nurseries and display cabinets of

Lancashire families such as the Townleys, Swarbricks, and Heskeths, aiding in the perpetuation of an organic emotional link between the heartlands of English Catholicism and the wider communities created by the Jacobite diaspora. However, these gender-specific dolls, perhaps unsurprisingly, failed to represent the severe and martial figure of King James, whose pursuit of piety was compromised by sexual desire and whose ascent to spirituality was far more ambiguous and fitful.

Forcefully transplanted late in life into a largely unfamiliar climate of competing religious devotions at the court of France, James found himself dependent on Louis XIV not only for financial and political support, but also ultimately for the sanction of his vision of kingship and for his self-styled appropriation of sainthood. As we have already seen, Louis had chosen to overlook his cousin's defence of those titular rights that appeared to directly contravene his own, and it was precisely this willingness to be seen to actively approve of James's championing of a wholly individualistic brand of piety that eventually silenced those critics who attributed Louis's surprising display of generosity to his fondness for the former King's pretty wife, and who sought to equate James's heartfelt expression of religious zeal with a particularly bullish display of stupidity. Furthermore, the French King's validation of James's holiness and sufferings on account of his religion served to greatly enhance his claims to sanctity, and to permit his further religious explorations. Though incapable of advancing a systematic form of theological argument, James was more than capable of expressing his concerns about the nature of salvation with a forceful sense of urgency and economy that lent all his pronouncements on religion a stark clarity and an unmistakable air of moral certainty and authority. Used to the habit of command, the old King envisaged God as a supreme sovereign, combining the virtues of the successful general with a harsh sense of paternalism, which constantly demanded complete obedience and inflicted the severest of judgements for any perceived transgression. A single slip in thought, word or deed might be enough to damn a soul for eternity, as James reminded his audience that 'we are always in the presence of God . . . [who] do[e]s not only see all we do, but knows our very thoughts', and charted the manner in which the Lord 'punished those that offended him'. All of human history was thus reduced to a series of peaks and deep troughs, as the grace of God was first offered up to virtue, and then withdrawn as the result of the base transgressions of man. The world could be obliterated in a moment, 'reduced . . . againe to eight persons, whom [the Lord] saved in the Arke' and, just as in the past, a modern people might be sentenced for their misdeeds 'to wander up and down in the desert, till that whole generation of murmerors, from twenty yeares upwards were dead and destroy[ed]'. For James this pattern of destruction and horror had been repeated within his own lifetime, and the example of the Jews –

who after the death of Solomon, 'did not only rebel against their King but against God him self, letting themselves be carried away by reason of State, to their ancient sin of Idolatry, for w[hi]ch the ten tribe[s] were severly punished . . . with their King, Princes and people . . . led into captivity, their cheef towne and Temple burnt and destroyd, and the whole country layd wast[e]' – bore striking similarity to the predicament that he and his disobedient subjects now found themselves in.[36] Consequently, like Nebuchadnezzar before him, William III might be 'raised up' by the Almighty 'to be an instrument of his wroth against them, for having forgot the Lord God', and the remnants of the British and Irish nations could expect to be 'dispersed and transplanted in to forrain parts', forced to 'live like vagabonds over the face of the Earth', until such time as proper restitution and atonement could be made by both the rightful King and his peoples and the covenant that bound them to God re-established once more. At that juncture, James believed, God would be seen once more to have 'performed his part, and driven out the Heathen before them, and settled them in a land flowing with milke and honny'.[37] The manner that this atonement would take was what exercised James most in the course of his devotional writings, yet he never doubted for a moment that the fortunes of his House, and of all those who had struggled in his cause, would eventually be restored through the direct intervention of God in the lives, and more importantly in the hearts, of men. A key element in this process was to be the re-conversion of England to Catholicism, which he was proud to proclaim as his life's work to de Rancé, but which Middleton and even Caryll were desperate to avoid mention of in the preparation of propaganda materials for their beleaguered followers across the British Isles. In common with many long-term exiles, James came to be increasingly removed from, and insulated against, the prevalent political and religious concerns of his homeland. Committed to a dialogue primarily with those who already professed an element of sympathy for his cause, his religious writings reflected the ever-widening gulf between the illusion of a triumphant return – based on a process of spiritual and social healing between the exiled King and his peoples – and the reality of a disparate and oft-defeated movement that was being forced by its elderly leader into an ever more narrow conceptual definition of its character and tactics, which was certain to alienate far more centres of support than it could ever hope to attract.

If this boded ill for the claims of James's partisans that he wished for no more than the establishment of a comprehensive form of religious toleration in his former kingdoms, then it did at least empower him to act as a forceful spokesman for the civil rights of his co-religionists. In particular, the imposition of stringent penal laws on the Irish Catholics – enacted by a vengeful and entirely Protestant-dominated parliament in

Dublin, operating against the wishes of William III – swept away, or simply ignored, the fragile safeguards offered by the Treaty of Limerick and prompted a further wave of emigration that cut James to the quick. To his confidants, he portrayed a truly apocalyptic vision of a land devastated through the malice of the 'Prince of Orange' and the marquis de Ruvigny, who had used the Peace of 1696 as a smoke-screen to launch a massive assault on the civil rights of the Roman Catholic population. Threatened with charges of high treason, every bishop, vicar general, and regular priest was ordered to leave Ireland before May 1698, but while public prayers were said for them at Rome, the Pope stopped short of linking James with their cause, much to the chagrin of Mary of Modena and the other exiles at St Germain. Though they continued to regard James as 'the chief of those persecuted', all that he could do in the summer of 1698 was to lament that: 'In the way they are going, in a few years . . . if God takes no hand in the affair, there will be few Catholics in that land, and . . . the Protestants will make more progress every day'. Facing the sudden influx of some 'four hundred monks who have arrived in France, [together with] a bishop', he returned to this theme, adding that the 'persecution of Catholics in Ireland continues at full blast' and commending God, in his personal prayers, to: 'Have mercy on the distressed part of thy persecuted Church that is in the three Kingdoms' and to 'preserve them from the terrible Laws that have been made against them'. James was in no doubt that the legislation passed in Ireland in 1695 and 1697 was only a prelude to wider attacks on the faith in his other former domains, which 'would be easy to do, since the laws are already in place sufficient for them to be put into execution'.[38] Yet, while James maintained good relations with the Irish bishops, and continued to have his nominations accepted for their vacant sees, all he could now do in their support, and in that of their stricken congregations, was to appeal to the papacy for increased financial subsidies for their physical well-being and to recommend that they accept his own credo, to have the: 'resignation to performe, and cherfully submitte to . . . Devine will in all things, pacience to beare with Courage, losse of life, estate, and all things they possesse or are most deare to them, rather than fall from, or any way decemble thy faith, or do any thing unworthy of the true Roman Catholike, and Apostolike faith'.[39]

If James's loyal subjects were to be exhorted to make ever greater sacrifices, then it was incumbent upon the King, as the conscience of his nations, to shoulder his own share of the burden, or as he himself repeatedly put it, to carry 'his cross'. The crown had become his Gethsemane, and his sufferings, mirroring those of Christ, might contribute on Judgement Day to the salvation of the entire world. As Bernard and Monique Cottret have pointed out, James's coronation had taken place at Westminster Abbey on the feast day of the Discovery of the

Holy Cross, 23 April 1685 (Old Style), and it is not beyond the bounds of possibility that this theme of the Passion, and of Christ's progress through the stations of the cross, came to assume an entirely new importance during his final exile, as the metaphor for his kingship and as the means by which he might achieve salvation at last. Certainly, James reflected upon precisely this theme to the abbé de La Trappe, and the nuns of La Chaillot seem to have believed: 'that God had predestined him to be made conformable to the image of Jesus Christ crucified, whose Kingdom was not of this world'. Having determined to follow in his saviour's footsteps every inch of the way along the Via Dolorosa, with its attendant beatings, fastings, and self-mutilations, James expressed his belief that it was only through suffering that 'we can hope to attaine a happy Eternity' and added that 'tis no marke of Gods displeasur to send us afflictions and crosses, for he chastiseth those he loves . . . either to hinder our offending him, or punishing us for our past faults'. Furthermore, the King wondered at the fact: 'That he had often made reflection upon that which men do to preserve their health, and a temporal life which lasts but a very little time; and on the other hand, the little they do to gain eternity: men easily take up a resolution to let an arm or a leg be cut off, and to suffer other violent operations, but few have resolution enough to suffer pains for their eternal salvation'. James, however, numbered himself in this select latter grouping, and in Jansenism found an intellectual movement within the Roman Catholic Church that confirmed his belief in his own election. Though he had formally converted to Roman Catholicism under the guidance of a Jesuit priest, and had once found reassurance in the teachings of that Order – which emphasised the decisive importance of an individual's intention to commit a premeditated sin, thus making the committing of mortal sin a very difficult proposition indeed – it was the influence of Jansenism, imbibed from mère Agnes and the French court as a young soldier, that was so forcefully to reassert itself during his old age, leading him to visit Port Royal in September 1693, and to spend five days on retreat at St Gregory's College two years later. Frequent confessions and absolutions had proven to be wholly ineffective in stemming the mounting pace of King James's misfortunes, and Jansenism – which stressed the utter domination of human beings by original sin, and the powerlessness of the individual soul in its relationship with God – appeared to account, in a far more satisfactory manner, for James's enslavement to sexual desire and his repeated punishment at the hands of the Almighty. Furthermore, the Jansenist rejection of free will, and the belief that the individual was preordained to experience either salvation or damnation from the very first, appeared to reflect Calvinist tenets – albeit in an assuredly Roman Catholic milieu which took its inspiration from Augustinian approaches to guilt and sin – that was capable of striking a chord with a convert from Protestantism such as James, and may even have served to evoke distant memories of his half-learned lessons of Anglican creed and confession in wartime Oxford.[40]

Consequently, while hostile propagandists might continue to associate James exclusively with the partisanship of the Jesuit Order, it was the example of La Trappe and the teachings of the followers of Cornelius Jansen that informed the particular bleak and uncomforting approach to the world that was expounded by the former King throughout his final exile, in his chosen guise as a man of sorrows. Though he was certain that his sins had brought about the destruction of his worldly fame, and that his devotional practices were still not as rigorous or as pleasing as they might be to God, there would appear to be no room for doubt in James's mind that he was, indeed, among the saved. The nuns of La Chaillot noted that God had: 'power'd into his soul great sweetness and interior consolations, giving him a tast[e] in this world of the hundred fold he has promis'd in the Gospel, to those who have left all for him' and that 'his heart was fill'd with so firm an hope and confidence . . . that he doubted not of the pardon of his sins; [and] he said he felt a profound peace, because he was fully perswaded, that God was content with his good will'. However, such absolute certainty could manifest itself in ways that were disturbing to those of his followers who were either Protestants, or else wished for the restitution of their fortunes in this world as opposed to the next. In this manner, while his affirmation of deeply-held religious belief, with 'a sincere sorrow' for having offended God and a pledge 'that if it were to be done again, I had rather suffer all sorts of pains and torments rather than offend Him', might serve to advance his claims to sanctity, and draw favourable comparisons with Edward the Confessor – whose jewels he wore, and whose crucifix he venerated – his accompanying declaration that: 'I am not only content to have abandoned all for him, but I would sacrifice all the Kingdoms of the world, if I had them for his sake', might have struck a note of unease in all those who had hoped that he would use his years of exile to profit from the lessons of his political – as opposed to spiritual – mistakes.[41]

All that had befallen him since his exile had, according to this extremely Theo-centric view of the world, been part of a preordained divine plan, which could not be changed in any way, or otherwise argued with. For an authoritarian personality such as James's, obsessed with the need for order, strict rules and blind obedience, such a certainty – which largely absolved him of any responsibility for his mistakes and personal inadequacies as a statesman or a general – had much to recommend it, as it could serve to restore his sense of self-worth and make his experience of defeat far more intelligible and altogether less burdensome. Accordingly, James came to write that God had 'called me from the pit of Heresy' and 'oppend my eis to have known and embrased thy true religion'. It was only through the mercy of the Lord that he had escaped the bullets and sabre cuts of battle, and had been preserved when all those around him were scythed down by chain-shot on the quarterdeck of the *Royal Charles*. Similarly, when the frigate *Gloucester* had gone down, he had been saved (unlike the majority of his crew) from 'the dangers of the Sea' and 'the noise of its waves', and it was this sense of his invulnerability in situations of great danger, when 'lesser men' died in their scores all about him, that confirmed James in his belief in his own election. He was convinced that he had been chosen to live in order to fulfil a divinely ordered purpose, and that his loss of power in the Revolution of 1688–9 had been orchestrated by the Almighty for no other reason than to guarantee the salvation of his own soul, through his awakening from the state of lethargic sexual sin in which he had wallowed. Had this not happened, James thought, 'I should have been for ever lost' and this formula, which almost removed the need for self-criticism of the vital areas of his kingship and his role in the genesis of the political Jacobite movement, allowed him to turn his record of unmitigated disaster since 1688 into something approaching a personal triumph. What appeared to be humiliating defeat now became no more than a test, devised by God in order to temper the steel of his soul and lead him further along the path of righteousness. In these circumstances it was entirely fitting that he should now give thanks to the Lord for depriving him of his three kingdoms and acknowledge that 'out of thy goodnesse [thou] wert pleased to banish me into a forrain Country, where I learnt to know what was the dutys, of Christianity, and endeavoured to performe them', becoming progressively closer to God through both his contact with the brothers of La Trappe, who inspired him 'with such a portion of thy grace, as to endeavor to live as became a good Catholicke', and his own pursuit of religious devotion, which cleansed his soul of sin and increasingly invested every one of his actions with an aura of sanctity. However, the quest for 'that perfection as became me', the 'grace to performe it', and the final victory over his earthly foes, could only be purchased, as the King came to realise, through the conquering of death itself.[42]

Most disturbing of all, not only to modern sensibilities but also to those of Mary of Modena – who disliked the Jansenist movement in all its forms, and had been horrified to discover the iron chain that her husband used for his mortifications hanging up 'in a Closet he had forgot to shut' behind him – was the King's tendency to look forward to the hour of his death and to make ready to rush forward to embrace it. Unsurprisingly, as we have already seen, the expression of such a desire had led him into serious conflict with his ambitious young son, the Duke of Berwick, but James was to remain utterly convinced that in the act of dying, and more importantly, in dying well, as a good Christian, lay the

key to his decisive triumph, which represented the beginning rather than
the end of his existence. Secular society was for James a place of
unmitigated corruption and, as he wrote at the end of July 1700, 'I am
sensible that the longer I live in this world, I hazard ever[y] day more and
more my Eternity, being consious to my self, that as long [as] I am in this
world, I am never in safty , and can never be so, till I be freed from this
curruptable body and united to thee'. When, he asked, 'will that happy
day come, that I may enjoy, the beatifull vision, and be joyned to the
Blessed Saints, who praise thee with out seasing', and concluded that:
'the soner tho callest me to thee is the better'. A refusal to acknowledge
and even to long for death stemmed, in James's eyes, from a profound
lack of faith on the part of the individual concerned. 'Tis want of love of
God', he declared, 'and in some degree a doubting of Gods infinit mercy'
that produced such an attitude, and 'want of faith to think that the life of
a man was necessary' in any manner. If God was trusted and the salvation
of the soul not doubted, as was certainly the case with James himself, then
death was an event to be welcomed, as a release from the snares and
concerns of the world. As far as we can tell, he initially put forward such
views in November 1696, a year after experiencing the first significant
bout of ill-health that he had suffered since his attack of smallpox in
1667. It is entirely conceivable that the brooding sense of mortality
expressed in his writings stemmed from the shock occasioned by this
blow to his previously extremely robust constitution.[43] In response to the
criticism levied on him by his wife and natural son, James returned to his
theme and defended his 'desire to dy', reprising his former arguments
and making it plain that 'where we are sure of nothing but that we must
dy', no time could be lost in settling one's affairs and in seeking to atone
for sin, as it was impossible to know either the time or manner of death,
as we 'cannot know how we shall be prepared till the moment our soule
and body must part'. With 'tears in her eyes' Mary of Modena had
beseeched her husband to have some consideration of her and her
children, and what would become of them when he was gone, only to be
told by the King that: 'God will take care of you and my Children, for
what am I but a poor weak man, uncapable of doing any thing without
him, whereas he has no need of me to execute his designs', adding that
his apparent harshness was calculated in order to prepare the Queen in
advance for his death. 'According to all appearance and the cours[e] of
nature', he declared, 'I shall dy first, and a stroke which is foreseen
makes a slighter impression . . . if by desireing to dy, one can look death
in the face with an undisturbed countenance, and seem to be delighted
with that, which according to the cours[e] of nature carrys the greatest
terrours with it in the world'.[44]

Life should be lived, therefore, as if every moment were to be the last
and in a manner of devotion and seemliness that meant that it mattered

not when one should finally happen to be called to God. The Sisters of the Visitation recorded that the King 'never lost any opportunity of speaking . . . of the necessity of preparing our selves for death' and that he confided: 'That if a sinner newly converted were surprised by death, without having done the penance he purposed to do, he would for all that find mercy; because God would make an account of his good intentions', adding that 'I am a very great sinner, and notwithstanding, I desire death with all my heart'. It has often been thought that such attitudes were a unique expression of James's personal theology, or that his morbidity grew out of a diseased or faltering mind. However, as we have seen, an active desire for death formed one of the central tenets of monasticism as practised at La Trappe, where the brothers constantly strove to remind one another of their mortality, and of the corruption of all flesh. In advancing his own views on the subject, James was doing no more than reflecting a pre-existing trend within the Catholicism of the Counter-Reformation, which he had discovered through repeated readings of the *Little Book of the Holy Desires of Death* by Fr Lallemont, 'one of the Religious of St Geneveve', and the meditations on the difference between Time and Eternity, by Fr Nieremberg, a Spanish Jesuit.[45] Rather than adding to James's sense of distraction, these texts served to calm the fraying nerves of the King and, in the case of the latter book, could be eagerly recommended to his courtiers on the grounds that: 'since I have read it, I have slept quietly in the midst of my misfortunes'.[46]

Confident of his own salvation, and of his theocratic mission to his former peoples, James felt no fear at the creeping approach of death. Operating from within the mainstream of Roman Catholic devotional practice, he had sought to make sense of his predicament as best he could, and to combine his increasingly arcane, quasi-divine concept of kingship – steeped in precedent from Saxon and Plantagenet England and Capetian France – with a vision of personal and national redemption which was grounded in the example of the covenants established between God and the Israelites in the Old Testament. This was achieved in the present at the price of the sorrow, repentance, and suffering undergone by James himself, as the priest-king who was to recreate the passion of Christ, and in dying achieve personal immortality among the saints, while setting in train a series of events that would eventually return his son and heir to the thrones of Great Britain and Ireland, thought to have been so irrevocably lost. Clearly, then, the manner of his passing was of signal importance to the elderly King, and he sought to leave nothing to chance in the strict choreographing of his end. He told de Rancé, as his closest spiritual advisor, that he was always thinking about death, in order to be 'always ready' for it, but that he still had cause to fear that if the coming of the end was not welcomed and prepared for in exactly the correct manner, then the longed-for victory purchased by dint of all of his sufferings might still not be realised at the last, and that the atonement of the King and his peoples before God would not be heeded. As a consequence, James was struck by all manner of uncertainties about the manner of his passage into the afterlife, and wrote to the abbé in considerable anguish, expressing his concern at 'this idea which came into my head [and] about which I have never spoken to anyone . . . That is to know if a man such as me who has offended God by so many mortal sins . . . should . . . try to get God to shorten the time I must stay in purgatory'. To James's mind, it seemed that it might be far better 'to be content to suffer for the time which is ordained, and to give the money which is ordained, and which ordinarily one gives for prayer for one's soul, to the poor'. Moreover, the King wondered: 'if it is not better to give what is accustomed to give for works of piety or charity in your will during one's life, than to have it paid to one's heirs' as an unnecessary burden. He clearly intended that his 'penances and mortification' should continue, 'greater . . . then can be inflicted on me in this world', long after his death. Unfortunately, de Rancé's reply to his concerns does not appear to have survived, and it seems reasonable to suggest that James was, at any rate, not entirely satisfied by his advice on this matter – if indeed any was forthcoming – as he saw fit to reiterate his concerns in a small paper on his religious 'Queerys' that he compiled for his own private use.[47]

The vision of the King's supreme self-sacrifice, and of his conscious disregard for his own well-being in order that he might redeem his subjects and regain the throne for his young son, was certainly one that struck a chord with his adherents. If today, in an age that seeks to hide away from the inevitability of death, we find something morbidly unnatural in James's preoccupation with the process of physical decay and the final corruption of the flesh, then it was not always so. Indeed, through his adoption of the image of a royal penitent, prepared to abandon his costly apparel, his worldly wealth and all the personal comforts that privilege had afforded to him, James evoked a series of powerful emotional and intellectual responses among his Roman Catholic followers. These linked him directly to a line of beatified Medieval kings, who had striven to serve the poor, miraculously cured the sick, and attempted to bring their frequently mutinous and unwilling peoples to a closer understanding of God and their pressing need for a thorough-going redemption, of the kind that could only be secured through their own intercession and willingness to endure the extremes of pain and want, culminating, if needs be, in a brutal martyrdom. For many at the exiled court of St Germain, the spectacle of a King without a crown, who tore at his own skin in an attempt to expiate his sins and those of his wayward subjects, and who chose to deplete his meagre treasury both to support his destitute followers and to offer ungrudging charity to the starving French who came begging at his door, fitted perfectly with such a model of regal sanctity. All that remained was for the King to fulfil his allotted role upon his deathbed, calmly accepting his fate while providing guidance to his family and loyal adherents, commending them to persevere in the service of his cause – now in equal measure that of his son – and giving graphic personal testimony of his own uplifting Christian faith. Having accepted the austerities of La Trappe as his ideal, set aside increasing time for the practice of his religious devotions and retreats, and laboured unceasingly to secure the promise of salvation, James approached death well prepared to enact a striking piece of political theatre which would define the religious and political parameters of Jacobitism at least until 1750, and which would succeed beyond all his expectations in both revitalising his heir's claim to the thrones of Great Britain and Ireland, and in precipitating a major seachange in French policy, that would help to fatally undermine the provisions of the Treaty of Ryswick and to plunge the western European powers back into a further cycle of dynastic claim and counter-claim which could only be resolved through protracted warfare. Despite his belief to the contrary, James's display of sanctity was destined to bring about not peace, but a return to the rule of the sword.

CHAPTER NINE

The Death of a King

I

At the end of February 1698 two messengers bearing secret despatches for James II left the court of Moulay Ismail, Emperor of Morocco. Fearing that they might be intercepted, either by English frigates or by the pirate vessels that still prowled the coasts of North Africa, they divided on the road and took ship separately for France. Their prudence, together with a certain amount of good fortune, ensured that, unexpectedly, both communications from the Emperor to the fallen King – the first written in Arabic, the second in Spanish, yet each presenting essentially the same argument in case one of the couriers was overtaken or fell by the wayside – reached their stated destination of St-Germain-en-Laye. Perhaps unsurprisingly, James's Household lacked a secretary of languages capable of translating or even deciphering the unfamiliar calligraphy of the longer Arabic text, and the letter was duly passed to Louis XIV's own interpreter, Petis de la Croix, for scrutiny. It was not until June, however, that de la Croix was able to return his verdict on the Emperor's surprising overture, and forward copies of his translation to both his own master and James. It appears that, following the negotiations at Ryswick, James had managed to get word of his predicament to Moulay Ismail, either through a direct appeal or by a more circuitous route. The Emperor, unlike those Roman Catholic sovereigns such as Leopold I, Carlos II, and Maximilian II of Bavaria, of whom he had expected so much, had not only sympathised with his plight but had also determined to provide him with substantial military assistance for the reconquest of his lands. As Duke of York, James had prevailed on his brother to allow the captured corsair Admiral Abdallah ben Aaicha to return home without payment of the customary ransom, and this demonstration of princely goodwill and generosity towards a brave and implacable enemy appears both to have made a lasting impression on the Moroccan government, and to have provided the basis for a firm friendship between James and his erstwhile prisoner. The English evacuation of Tangier in August 1683 permitted a rapid rapprochement between the rival powers, and when James succeeded to the throne less than two years later, it seemed natural for ben Aaicha to travel back to Whitehall, this time in the guise of an ambassador anxious to congratulate the new King on his ascent to power and to promise him the Emperor's continuing friendship and favour.

With James's image as a chivalrous and scrupulously fair warrior seemingly crystallised in the collective consciousness of Morocco's courtiers, corsairs and diplomats, and with ben Aaicha – who had returned to Africa after the conclusion of his mission – continuing to champion the King's virtues before Moulay Ismail, the news of the Revolution of 1688–9 fell like a thunderbolt on the Emperor and his Household at Meknes. There was to be more than an echo of the resulting outrage in his letters to the King, as the Emperor bitterly mocked William III's nationality, implying the venality and cowardice of the Dutch, and sought to assure James that: 'your people and your subjects will never find such a good King as you, nor will you find such a good people'. Money, troops and supplies were to present no obstacle to James's restoration as Moulay Ismail strove to point out that he was a powerful warlord, possessed of a Western artillery train, and currently engaged in driving the last colonial armies out from the northern tip of Africa. 'Certainly', he declared – clearly relishing the memory of pounding British and Irish soldiers behind the walls of Tangier – 'we wished that [Charles II] had remained alive to see the work which God wrought at our hands at the conquest of Arache over the Spaniards, [and] to see the siege of Cueta which we are making today, he would see the extraordinary expense to which the Spaniards are put and the uncountable numbers of piastres which they have to spend for their provisions'.[1] If he could, the Emperor 'would write to the English [to urge them to reconsider their attitude towards their former King] and . . . would find troops with which you could make a descent on England, retake your possessions and remount your throne'. A fleet of galleys, 'a powerful enough force at sea', had already been put in a state of readiness to receive James's commands, and was to be put at his disposal in order to spearhead a possible invasion. First, however, the exiled King would have to accept a series of radical pre-conditions attached to Moroccan support. Moulay Ismail had obviously thought long and hard about the chances of achieving the successful restoration of his would-be ally, and had concluded that military victory alone would not be enough to secure James his crown. He therefore expressed his hope that he would now give serious consideration to the best means of regaining the affection of his former subjects, and identified two areas – James's Catholicism and his alliance with France – that would have to be re-negotiated as the first steps to that end.

Having outlined, with an impressive if highly partisan degree of theological clarity, his rationale for determining Islam to be a superior creed to Christianity, the Emperor declared that 'if you wish to stay in your infidel belief' then there was not a shred of advantage to be gained 'in being separated from your country, cut off from your people and your subjects' simply as the result of a continuing emotional – and to his mind, highly irrational – attachment to Roman Catholicism. Though 'in general all of your [Protestant] sects are a tissue of errors and misleading notions', there was no hope of reconciling the English to the Church of Rome and the only practical course that Moulay Ismail could recommend to him, was for James to return as soon as possible to 'your real sect . . . that of Henric [i.e. of Henry VIII and Anglicanism]', and to 'abandon that which earlier caused the rift with your people, since your subjects believe that it is a matter of conscience to disown you because of the religion, because of which you are at odds. Beg their pardon, overcome them with honesty so that they will let you return'. If this was not a bitter enough pill for James to have to swallow, the Emperor continued regardless, urging him to 'leave French territory, [and to] take yourself to Lisbon, in Portuguese territory'. Once there, he reasoned that James would have done enough to distance himself, both physically and politically, from Louis XIV's aggressive pursuit of foreign policy, to open up the possibility of fresh negotiations with the English Parliament. These could be conducted with Catherine of Braganza, the Regent of Portugal and a woman 'with voice and authority', acting as an honest broker between the two conflicting parties. A Portuguese exile, while still being conducive to the King's Roman Catholic followers, would ensure that there 'would be less distance and difficulty between you and your people', making it 'easier to confer with them about arrangements' for a speedy return, and facilitating, if needs be, a show of force by the Moroccan fleet, poised just beyond the Pillars of Hercules.[2]

However, despite his undoubted admiration for James's fighting qualities, Moulay Ismail injected an element of criticism and warning into his correspondence with the King, expressing his alarm at a rumour stemming from the provisions laid down in the Treaty of Ryswick 'that you intend to go to Rome' and urging that he 'take good care to take this resolution, since, if you go for a time, you will get used to the place and will not want to leave, nor will you be able to return to your own Kingdom'. It was a testament to the sincerity and depth of James's religious devotion that the image of him as humble pilgrim, ready to take the road to the Basilica of St Paul, and to eke out his last years as a pensioner of the Pope, could be disseminated and its veracity entirely accepted, as far afield as the coasts of Africa; but what was far more disturbing to Moulay Ismail – and appeared to be almost wholly incomprehensible to him – was the King's failure, when all had been lost, to die sword in hand, fighting for his crown. 'Why', he stormed, 'do you stay with the French, abandoning your people and your father's Kingdom, and that of your brother, for another, and suffer a Dutchman to be honoured with your crown while you yet live? By God almighty! I could not suffer that your home and your Kingdom should be in the power and under the rule of a Dutchman – nor anyone else'.

Unfortunately, such a combination of strident advice and none-too-veiled criticism of his kingly conduct was not calculated to influence a naturally stubborn and closed-minded ruler such as James, who was already separated from his prospective backer by the formidable barriers constructed by culture and religious faith. Having staked everything over the course of his last exile on the success of Louis XIV's military campaigns, and having increasingly sought to equate his kingship with the establishment and maintenance of a Roman Catholic dynasty in the British Isles, he was extremely unlikely now to abandon his allies, together with his core set of beliefs and commitments, for the distant promise of Portuguese assistance and the dubious services of a clutch of Moorish galleys. Whatever his faults, James was neither opportunistic nor unprincipled when it came to his practice of religion, and to his sense of loyalty to those who had treated him well. Furthermore, even if he had contemplated for a second Moulay Ismail's offer, then any possibility of James seeking to distance himself from Louis XIV, and to draw about him a different set of allies in a new place of exile, had vanished in the instant that the Arabic letter was handed over to de la Croix for translation.[3] Indeed, it must have been with a wry sense of discovery that first the secretary, and then his master, read the Emperor of Morocco's recommendation that James should gradually disengage from his contacts with Louis XIV, 'in such a way that the French have no inkling of what you are up to, because if they know of your plan and intention, they will not let you go and stop you for two reasons: the first is that they do not want you to abandon their religion to return to your people's faith, the other is that you will become their enemy and lose them the war'.

There is no evidence that James ever received a full transcript of the translated letter, but even so he must have been well aware of Moulay Ismail's ulterior motive in attempting to wean him away from France at precisely the moment when English influence in North Africa had been neutralised; Spanish power was on the verge of eclipse, and d'Estrees's fleet was all that appeared to stand in the way of a return to Moorish domination of the Mediterranean trade routes. However, while James appears to have allowed the matter of Moroccan assistance to quietly drop, he was a prudent enough politician to maintain cordial relations with the Emperor, and a sure enough friend to welcome ben Aaicha to the state rooms of St Germain when the latter was posted to France as Ambassador in 1699. There was little doubt in the minds of the French ministers that, as the former commander of the swarms of privateers that operated out of Sallee to afflict a continual attrition on Western shipping, and as 'the only Moroccan man who was knowledgeable about European affairs', ben Aaicha was primarily engaged in an intelligence-gathering mission for Moulay Ismail, pinpointing possible weaknesses in the state in case of a future war and compiling detailed reports on the strength of

King Louis's armed forces. Yet James appears only to have recognised in his frequent visits to his palace, and his ceaselessly probing questions, a desire to revisit the past: an opportunity to discuss old battles and to relive the highly charged moment when he had granted his prisoner his freedom. Whatever else ben Aaicha may have feigned, there appears to have been no element of artifice in his expressions of affection for James and in the sorrow he felt at taking his leave of his friend on his recall to his homeland. Begging the old King to accept a lavish parting gift, he threw himself upon his knees in the audience chamber of St Germain and sobbed his farewells, while James – who more than guessed that this would be their last meeting – cradled his head in his hands and wept like a desolate child.[4]

Far from wishing to leave France for Avignon, Rome, or even conceivably for Lisbon, James was desperate to be allowed to remain with his court at St Germain, and fought a protracted rearguard action in order to win the sympathies, and more importantly the support, of Louis XIV, his nobility, and his ministers for his continued residence in the kingdom, in flagrant violation of both the spirit and the letter of the peace treaty signed in 1697. During that winter, James had still been visible as a valued ornament and honoured guest at the ceremonies held in Versailles to mark the marriage of King Louis's grandson, Louis, duc de Bourgogne to Marie-Adelaide of Savoy. The match, between a 15-year-old boy who might one day be expected to become King of France, and the 12-year-old daughter of the Duke of Savoy, could be thought to have been conceived as a reward for Victor Amadeus II's timely change of allegiance at the close of the Nine Years' War, and James and his Queen took great pleasure in handing the young groom and his little bride their nightgowns, and watched the celebratory fireworks which, despite squalling showers, lit up the Place de Suisses magnificently. Louis XIV had already surprised his courtiers by vouching his opinion, when the ink was still scarcely dry on the Treaty of Ryswick, that James and Mary 'were unfortunate persons, to whom he had given asylum; that he truly considered them as his friends, and that he would not send them away from him', and his resolve to maintain their status at the French court was emphasised further by their prominent participation in the wedding festivities and by his particular concern to postpone a ball, held later in December, until their horses had picked their way along the frosted highway from St Germain to Versailles, and James (despite his dislike of dancing) had taken his place beside him in the ballroom.[5] Unfortunately, if the form and dignity of James's power had so far managed to survive the signing of a general peace, its substance certainly had not. The King's hopeful reiteration of his desire to provide the Scots College in Paris with '100 l. sterling yearly, sent within six months from the day of our restoration' appeared increasingly forlorn, while the delight of the

Jacobites in the reduction of the English armed forces, and the removal of the Dutch Guards, forced on William III by his Parliament as part of the peace dividend, barely disguised that fact that James was having to implement even more stringent economies on his own Household, dismissing servants and winding down the last remnants of his military establishment. Writing references for his loyal officers, the King commended Colonels Johnson and Livingston to their new employer, the Doge of Venice, for their 'good conduct and long service', adding that they had suffered imprisonment in his cause, but that he no longer had the resources to help them.[6]

Yet the hammer-blows continued to fall on him, as the Westminster Parliament – when not seeking to clip King William's wings – sought to bring in new legislation against correspondence with James and his exiled adherents, and issued a proclamation, on the passing of this legislation in January 1698, 'that no person may pretend ignorance of the Act' if their letters to St Germain were intercepted by the government. Altogether more worrying to the exiles was King William's decision to follow up the peace treaty by sending an embassy into France. Though long and ruinous hostilities had been brought to an end, to the general satisfaction of almost every European prince save for James, the central problem that threatened the establishment of a durable peace – the almost certain extinction, at any moment, of the Habsburg dynasty of Spain – had not been adequately addressed during the course of the negotiations at Ryswick. With Louis XIV showing no particular inclination to honour the promises made at the time of his marriage to Maria Teresa, that he would not use the match to claim the Spanish crown for himself or his descendants, and the Emperor Leopold I determined to see his little grandson, Joseph Ferdinand of Bavaria, firmly seated on the throne, William III needed no reminding that the impasse between French and Austrian interests would have to be broken quickly if a descent into a major new confrontation was to be avoided. To this end, he emphasised the need for Bentinck, his Ambassador to the court of France, to use his mission to remove those obstacles that stood in the way of the peace, and 'to find means of preventing a war, which might result if the King of Spain died childless'. In order to reassure British public opinion, and to convince William that the provisions of the Treaty of Ryswick were still being adhered to, the Ambassador was further instructed by his royal master to: 'do his utmost to induce the Most Christian Majesty [Louis XIV] to make King James and his family quit his dominions, or at least to send them as far from his Court and the seacoast as possible. And the same also above all things as regards the conspirators against my life'.[7]

Though Bentinck fretted that Paris might not be to his liking – with all the houses and lodgings judged to be 'very mediocre' and all the plate 'melted down last year' – and contrary winds held up his crossing of the Channel, equerries and servants had preceded him to ensure that he would be able to receive the French diplomats in style, 'with rich furniture and . . . hangings for a room' to reflect his status as the representative of a King. Even the unexpectedly cold weather, which left the ship carrying three of his state coaches and all his baggage icebound on the Seine, did little to hold up his mission for long, or to detract from the impression of splendour that he created as he conducted a stately progress through the Normandy countryside, accorded full military honours by the garrisons of every town at which he chose to halt. As he set his carriage for the gates of Paris, he was joined on the road by his son, Henry, Lord Woodstock and his tutor, the Huguenot soldier and historian Rapin de Thoyras. While his secretary, Matthew Prior, slipped unnoticed into the city streets, anxious to gather intelligence and to establish contact in inns, coffee houses, and attic rooms with disaffected Jacobites keen to come to terms with the English government and to secure a passage home, Bentinck received courtesy calls from Marshal de Boufflers and the comte de Grammont, and dined in a pavilion newly built onto his residence at the Hotel d'Auvergne in order to accommodate his teeming entourage. An initial interview was quickly scheduled with Louis XIV, but as the short winter's day drew to its close and the Ambassador took his leave of Versailles, he had cause to reflect that, despite the 'many very obliging things' that had been said to him, little of substance had either been gained or broached in the course of these necessarily formal initial exchanges. Bentinck had presented his credentials, and been assured by the King of France 'that all the harm that could be done had been done during the war', and that 'it was necessary to forget the past, and think only of doing good to one another in the future', but any further discussion, and a public audience, would have to wait until Louis returned from his pleasure trip to Marly. Introductions were made to the dauphin, the duc de Chartres, and to the duc and duchesse de Bourgogne, the young couple who had so captivated the court, but the duc d'Orléans thought that he saw through all such overtures and scolded his wife for indulging in these pleasantries, as the English 'Lord only pays you so much attention in order to try and worm things out of you'. It appears that James had expected his friends at Versailles – and Monsieur and Madame in particular – to close ranks around him, and to refuse to acknowledge the presence of the Ambassador and his embassy, shunning their company and ignoring their questions and requests. Yet, while the duc d'Orléans – whom Prior dismissed with ill-disguised malice as being no more than a 'little marionette' – attempted to bully his wife into a state of silence, telling her that any contact with Bentinck 'will be very displeasing to the King and Queen of England at St Germains', the duchesse bit back that though she felt pity for the exiles, she could not 'refuse admittance to an ambassador from a King who is recognised as such, who the King [i.e. Louis XIV] and yourself receive with such distinction'. Moreover, while everything 'deserves that I should treat him well and pay him civilities in my turn', madame thought that: 'In truth . . . the King and Queen at St Germains are in the wrong if they find anything to complain of in it'.[8]

For the time being, James determined to continue with his daily routine as though nothing of significance had occurred, barring all mention of the embassy at his court, and choosing to so thoroughly and firmly exorcise the event from his memory that the editor of his papers could only seek to attribute the despatch of Bentinck to the malice of his foes, for the continued presence of the exiled King in France had provided 'so near a sight' and a continual reminder 'of what obraided them continually with their injustice and infidelitie, and hover'd over their heads like a cloud that still threaten'd a storm'. Unfortunately for James, Prior and Bentinck appear to have experienced scant difficulty in making the acquaintance of his discontented followers. They duly reported to King William on the high prices of rooms in Paris and St Germain, and that James's decision to forbid the Jacobites to return home en masse had unsettled the English and Irish exiles and 'sets them against King James . . . because they are badly off and find it difficult to live here'. Worse still, it did not take the Ambassador long to press upon his hosts the necessity of removing James from their territories, as 'essential to the preservation of peace', and he raised again, before Marshal Boufflers, the notion that the exiled King might be prevailed upon to withdraw to Rome. Considering this point, Boufflers ventured that though it would be wholly unacceptable to sever all connections with James, the King of France might agree to his leaving for the papal city of Avignon, as it would remove him and his troublesome partisans from French jurisdiction, while permitting him to maintain his contacts with, and dependence upon, King Louis's officials, and to be within a few minutes ride of the borders of the French states should his situation happen to change once again. Seizing on this apparent concession, Bentinck quickly agreed to drop all suggestion of a Roman exile if James was to be sent to Avignon, adding that: 'as regards method, I would gladly fall in with the King's [i.e. Louis XIV's] wishes'.[9] It was left to Marshal Villeroy to inject a note of caution into the proceedings, lest his comrade-in-arms committed the government to measures which the King would be unwilling to fulfil, reminding the Ambassador that Louis was, above all, moved by a sense of compassion to his brother monarch. It was this rather more cautious attitude towards the lengths to which the King of France might be prepared to go to safeguard the peace which was to be proved correct, even more swiftly than Bentinck and his taciturn secretary might have feared. Louis XIV had determined to leave the

English in no doubt as to his intentions when he informed Bentinck, at their audience on 7/17 February 1698, that: 'he could not think why I asked him to make King James withdraw: he was his near relation; he was touched by his misfortune; he had helped him so long, [and] he could not in honour make him withdraw'. In an attempt to salvage something from this impasse, and to avoid an early and irrevocable breakdown in diplomacy, Boufflers interjected that the Ambassador 'ought to be satisfied if he [i.e. Louis XIV] gave his word that he would not aid him [i.e. James II], and would sincerely keep the peace'. Unabashed, Bentinck continued: 'that there was no need for compassion in the matter of [James's] withdrawal, since [William III] had undertaken to give to him or to the Queen, his wife, about 50,000 l. a year, to live elsewhere; that if he refused to withdraw on these conditions, it could only be in the hope of using this money in fomenting disturbances or something worse [in Ireland and the British Isles] . . . [and] that without this withdrawal the peace could not last'. Louis then asked: 'to what place it was wished that he should withdraw' and, after Bentinck had ventured Rome or Modena, he played his part (already briefed by the Marshal) and suggested that Avignon might be more acceptable, to which the Ambassador readily consented. Though worried that 'the Most Christian King spoke to me in a much colder tone on this, than on the first occasion', Bentinck was still confident after his interview that James would be obliged to quit St Germain and take the road south for Avignon, if William was able to exert the correct pressure upon both the exiles and their French backers. Accordingly, he wrote to his master that: 'without absolutely proclaiming that you will not pay King James unless he withdraws', and without making it clear that he would not 'allow any English adherents of King James to live in England contrary to the Act of Parliament [for their banishment]', his task in securing the removal of James would be hopeless. However, 'if your Majesty were to base your general refusal [to act according to French wishes in these two specific areas] on the refusal of King James to withdraw, I think this would make them very annoyed with him, and perhaps compel him to withdraw of his own accord, giving the money as the reason'.[10]

At this point, Bentinck was still far more concerned about the presence at the French court of those Jacobite officers who had been implicated in the recent attempt to assassinate King William, than he was about the possible failure to remove James from France, which had now been allowed to become the primary objective of his mission. He complained almost daily of the murderous glances and threatening behaviour of the Duke of Berwick and 'all the officers who are his creatures', such as Berkeley, Berkenhead, Harrison and Parker, 'whereupon . . . my blood ran cold', and made representation that they should immediately be forbidden from coming to Versailles and, ultimately, be banished far beyond the borders of France. In particular, Bentinck railed against 'the way in which English rebels were allowed to come to Court every day, publicly even when I was there, [which] was everywhere the subject of comment, especially among the English and Dutch here'. Yet, even on this issue, Louis XIV temporised and expressed his surprise and disbelief at the charges levelled against the plotters. Bentinck 'named to him the principal people in the proclamation [wanted for the attempt on William III's life, but] he answered that the D[uke] of Berwick could only have been in England for the landing, that S[i]r George Barclay was cashiered with the company, and that he did not know where he was, that of Harrison, he had never heard speak, although I told him that he had been made prior of an English convent here, and as to Berkenhead, his Majesty said that he had never been employed except to carry letters'. After a short silence, Louis intimated that he would not be drawn further on the matter, and Bentinck withdrew from his audience chamber, uncertain how best to proceed and with nothing to show for all his protests. Yet even though his moods alternated between wild optimism and deep despair at the sincerity of the French in securing the peace, he appears to have delighted in the opportunity for independent action and the chance to crown his success at Ryswick with an even greater diplomatic coup. Neither liked nor trusted by the English nobility – who resented his foreign accent, his stiff formality, and his status as a parvenu – he basked in the attention of the crowds who ran alongside his coach when he entered Paris, and delighted in the appreciative company of the French courtiers, who competed to gain a place at his table, and who were almost universally charmed by his polished manners, cultured taste, and animated conversation. Furthermore, Bentinck had not been blind to the rise of Joost van Keppel, from a stoical if spectacularly unsuccessful huntsman to Duke of Albemarle, exclusively through royal favour. Far younger, more handsome than his rival, and with a reputation that was uncompromised by a close political association with the Whigs, Keppel was now poised to supplant Bentinck in King William's affections, and it may well be that in the French embassy, his adversary saw a last chance to even the score and to reassert his position in both his master's heart and his councils. Unfortunately, while Bentinck relished the rare privilege of being permitted to light Louis XIV's way to bed, and the prospect of the balls and fêtes that were to be held in his honour, William was formulating a stern critique of his conduct, identifying his failings in pushing the matter of James's residence and the fate of his officers too early, and far too hard, while allowing the matter of the Spanish succession – which should have dominated the talks – to slip almost unnoticed from the agenda. At precisely the same time, Matthew Prior had drawn his own conclusions about the trustworthiness of the French, and declared that: 'These people are all the same, civil in appearance and hating us to hell at the bottom of their heart: they assure us one day of the continuance of their friendship, and tell King James the next they will never forsake him or let him go farther off than St. Germains'.[11]

As days and then weeks passed by, such sentiments began to colour even Bentinck's previously sanguine judgements, and though he expressed his relief that 'the English in attendance on King James will not be allowed in future to come where I am', he added that, for the moment at least, 'perhaps that is all that I can expect'. However, this did not prevent the Duke of Berwick expressing 'himself everywhere with extreme resentment' at being charged with plotting to kill William III, and an element of frustration and uncertainty as to how best now to proceed entered Bentinck's correspondence with his master, as he noted on 9/19 March that: 'As to the affair of King James the flattering courtiers palliate it; but with regard to the assassins everyone shrugs his shoulders, for everyone talks of it, though I don't say a word, good or bad, to anyone about it'. He still had reason to believe that James might be forced to quit his refuge in France and, as late as 7/17 May, he was continuing to file reports from his agents at St Germain suggesting that the chief topic of conversation at the exiled court was 'whether it would not be better to withdraw to Avignon', rather than seek to hang onto their apartments until the last minute, risking a far more uncertain and potentially humiliating fate, should Louis XIV ultimately be forced to withdraw his favour from them. However, while Bentinck conceded that 'I do not know yet the reason for this discussion nor the result', King James was adamant that he would brook no compromise with his enemies over his place of exile, and that he would not retreat quietly into the background for the duration of the English embassy, despite the advice of his friends at Versailles and even though his presence at the court of King Louis might jeopardise the future peace of Europe. Yet James knew all too well that the maintenance of his profile as a sovereign who had been wronged by his people and by a usurper's malice, combined with a fresh outbreak of hostilities pitting the strength of France against Great Britain and the United Provinces, might offer the only possible respite to his flagging cause and provide the means by which his son could, eventually, be returned to his throne. As a consequence, James did everything in his power to show his contempt for the Ambassador's authority and to reassert his own claims to political legitimacy: he and not Bentinck was to be seen as being the representative of the British and Irish peoples, and to be treated as such. Even though it had been reported back in February that Louis XIV had 'sent word to lord Middleton, who is at the head of King James's council, that he begged he would . . . avoid meeting the English ambassador', the exiled King appears to have gone out of his way to force a confrontation. He rode out regularly with the dauphin in order to deny Bentinck the opportunity of joining in the hunt at Meudon, and was beside Louis XIV when the first black kite of the season was taken at Vesine, and the head falconer richly rewarded.[12] Furthermore, he contrived to be at a review of the troops of the Maison du Roi at the Plain des Arches, in the knowledge that the Ambassador had been invited and that he very much wished to attend. Attempting to diffuse a potentially embarrassing and volatile situation, King Louis sent Marshal Villeroy to see Bentinck, who had been reluctantly forced to decline his invitation, to explain to him that he 'would have very much liked [him] to see his guards'. The Marshal, however, could not prevail on him to change his mind, and was informed by the Ambassador 'that I should not absent myself from the review for love of King James, but out of respect for his Majesty, I would not come; for fear of doing anything which might give him pain, particularly when King James would be with him'. In order to satisfy the curiosity of his teenage son, and to ensure that the English mission might be represented at the parade, Bentinck permitted Lord Woodstock to go in the company of his tutor, with strict instructions 'not to approach King James or the Queen, or the English in their suite, if he knew any of them'. However, amid the noise and dust created by the wheeling squadrons of Life Guards, and the clatter of arms grounded in precise unison by the massed companies of the King's Musketeers, James Francis Edward left the side of his father, and the assembled French princes, slipping off the stand and attempting to engage Woodstock in conversation. Taken aback, the young nobleman pretended not to notice the attentions of the anxious little Prince as he tried to catch his eye, and issued only a brief nod in recognition of the bows of the exiles towards him. Undismayed by his son's failure to spark a conversation, King James made his own way through the crowds, seeking out Lord Cavendish – despite his evident discomfort – and doing everything he could to engage his attention. Unfortunately, Cavendish and his companions chose to follow the example of Lord Woodstock and cut their former King dead, doffing their hats and issuing stiff little bows from a distance, but saying not a word to him. As the dauphin and Monsieur looked on, James hurried expectantly towards his stony-faced quarry, before stopping just short of them and, after an awkward and protracted silence, turning back upon his heel and moving away to rejoin the King of France on the platform, with his shoulders registering only a slightly more pronounced stoop.[13]

Though Bentinck might have shied away from direct contact with the exiled royals, Matthew Prior experienced no such inhibitions and found a subsequent encounter with them in the chapel of St Cloud, during the christening of the daughter of the duc de Chartres, both incongruous and more than a little amusing. 'There was', he declared, 'nothing so odd as to see the Duke of Berwick and Lord Middleton in the gallery on one side, and I and Lord Reay on the other side, each looking on the other with an air of civility mixed with contempt', while 'the gentlemen belonging to the Duc d' Orléans and Chartres were embarrassed enough to call him [i.e. James] one moment "le Roy d' Angleterre" to them, and speak to me the next of "le Roy Jacques"'. As for the exiled King himself, he informed Lord Halifax, in terms reflecting something of his partisanship, that: 'You never saw such a strange figure as the old bully [i.e. James II] is, lean, worn, and rivelled', while his Queen, who was still recovering from a sharp illness that had prevented her from hunting in the spring, 'looks very melancholy, but otherwise well enough, [though] their equipages are all very ragged and contemptible'. After almost a decade spent away from England, the people and places familiar to King James and his followers at St Germain had altered or disappeared entirely from both the political and physical landscape. At the beginning of the year, a fire had broken out close to Bentinck's apartments on the waterside at Whitehall Palace, and spread unchecked over the course of the early hours of the morning to engulf the ramshackle medieval structures, so that by the following evening everything except for the Banqueting House had either been burned to the ground or reduced to a blackened shell. Though William III sniffed that 'the loss is less to me than it would be to another person, for I cannot live there', the work commissioned from Christopher Wren by James II to renovate the Queen's suite of rooms and to extend the Chapel Royal had vanished amid the flames, disintegrating into no more than the piles of blackened brick, charcoal and ash that were so eagerly investigated by crowds of curious Londoners in the following weeks. The external symbols of James's regime had long since been removed, with Grinling Gibbons's marble sculptures stripped away from the walls of the Roman Catholic chapel in Whitehall and re-carved – with the dove representing the Holy Spirit completely struck off – before being removed to the relative obscurity of an Anglican parish church in Somerset. If the statue of the fallen King dressed as Caesar escaped vandalism – at least until the late 1990s, when some unknown hand finally twisted the baton of command out of James's bronze grasp – then it was certainly subject to neglect, and moved to successively less prestigious sites about the capital. Of far more pressing concern to James was the unremitting pursuit of his activists by the authorities, with the Earl of Clancarty – who had continued to serve as one of the King's Life Guards at St Germain – being seized in London when he attempted to visit his young wife, in the hope of consummating their marriage and in the belief that the influence of her father the Earl of Sunderland would be enough to gain him a brief exemption from arrest. Though the comte de Tallard reassured Louis XIV, from the French embassy in London, that: 'King James still has many friends in this country; [and] it is certain that if the enterprise of La Hogue had succeeded, the greater part of England would have declared for him', he also vouched that 'those persons who are opposed to his [James's] will, are not opposed to his government', and the fact still remained that the schemes for invasion in 1690, 1692, 1693 and 1696 had all failed, and that few now believed that the former King had any chance of regaining his throne. That redoubtable old Cavalier Lord Craven had closed his eyes for the last time in April 1697, and even though the marquis de Dangeau expressed his wonder that 'he was nearly one hundred years of age' – he was actually in his ninety-first year – and his appreciation that: 'He was very well known in France', it could not have gone without notice that, since his capitulation at Whitehall, the old man had done nothing to further King James's cause, devoting himself instead to his gardens, and signally refusing to squander his vast fortune in supporting the exiles at St Germain, in the same manner that he had once provided enormous and unredeemable sums as subsidy to both Charles II and the Winter Queen. Memories of the Civil Wars were becoming dimmed, while the generation of ultra-royalists who formed the core Jacobite constituency, and who had come to maturity at the time of the Restoration, were now middle-aged. For these potential rebels, it was not James who now mattered so much as the eventual descent of the crown, either to his grandson the Duke of Gloucester, or to his son, the titular Prince of Wales. Thus, Marlborough, deprived of high military command under William III, bided his time and gladly accepted office as the head of Gloucester's independent Household in the summer of 1698, relishing his position as mentor to a boy who might one day become King of England; while those English noblemen who had refused to take Bentinck's advice and had ridden in the chase at Vesine were similarly 'very eager to have a sight' of the exiled child who could conceivably rule over them in the years to come. The abbé Rizzini noted with pleasure that they were 'delighted' with James Francis Edward, 'for he is always pleasant to look upon, but on horseback he is seen to wonderful advantage for the grace, lightness and gallant daring which at his tender age give him a special dignity and charm'.[14]

Yet James, refusing to acknowledge the decline in his own political capital and determined that his son should not compromise his religion in search of a crown, fully appreciated that the application of French military power would be essential in some form if the boy was to be restored as a Roman Catholic prince. The loss of their palace at St Germain and their expulsion from French domains would, therefore, be more than a further humiliation to James and his heir, marking as it inevitably would a diminution of King Louis's active support and raising major new doubts over both the legitimacy of their claims to sovereignty and to their fitness even to rule. There were undoubtedly those at St Germain who were alive to the delicacy of the French position, and thought that the removal of the Jacobite court to Rome or Avignon might even be something of a blessing in disguise, freeing James from the obligation to follow slavishly the dictates of Louis XIV's overbearing foreign policy and affording him the option of opening up entirely new – and more importantly, independent – lines of communication, not only with English politicians, but also with those Roman Catholic rulers, such as the Emperor, Pope Innocent XII, and the King of Spain, who were all too wary of French motives. However, James was in no doubt that in leaving France he would be fatally weakening his cause and be seen to be retiring altogether from the political arena. Consequently, in his endeavours to prevent Bentinck from gaining access to the French King, and in his increasingly ham-fisted attempts to provoke a confrontation with the English mission, he believed that he was fighting a last-ditch struggle to prolong his political life, with no room for the niceties that normally attended such high-ranking diplomacy. The combination of his gift for publicising his own plight and sufferings, and the pressing need for King William to preserve the European peace and to find a solution to the Spanish succession crisis that might satisfy both France and the Empire, now served to act in James's favour. Though Louis XIV might have been prepared to sacrifice his cousin in the name of political expediency, his morganatic wife madame de Maintenon, as the power behind his throne, certainly would not. Having herself converted from Protestantism as a young girl, she recognised in James something of a kindred spirit, and was deeply moved by the extremes of devotion practised by him and his wife. She therefore took upon herself the role of protectress to the exiled court and, as Louis's commitment to the Jacobites began to wane, she attempted to restore his resolve and to harden his heart against that 'heretic' nation that had sought to deprive its lawful Roman Catholic sovereign of his crown. At the same time, frustrated by Bentinck's distinct lack of progress in the negotiations, William had written to his Ambassador urging him to abandon his emphasis on removing James and the group of officers who had coalesced about Berwick, and to concentrate instead on re-focusing the talks on the eventual fate of the Spanish Empire. The aged marquis de Pompone and the marquis de Torcy had already approached Bentinck on precisely this matter, and with Tallard communicating directly with King William at Kensington in a series of negotiations held in tandem with those in Paris, the two sides started to edge slowly towards a solution to this most intractable of problems. By May 1698 it had become clear that Louis could, and indeed would, not act against Berwick and the alleged Jacobite plotters, as any such move would be seen as an admission that he had been prepared to harbour a gang of murderers and would-be regicides. Furthermore, his argument that by allowing James to remain at St Germain he could keep a better watch on his activities and prevent his partisans from undertaking any measures that might prove hazardous to the peace effectively disarmed Bentinck, and brought an end to any serious discussion of the removal of the Jacobite court to Rome or Avignon. However, Louis was prepared to give ground on the more important matter of Spain, and indicated that he would consider waiving the rights of the dauphin to that crown in favour of the young dukes of Anjou and Berry, thus removing the fear that the thrones of France and Spain would be united under one individual. Moreover, he signalled that he might approve of the secession of the Spanish Netherlands to the Elector of Bavaria, in order to guarantee the security of the United Provinces, and would, upon William's advice, undertake to protect British and Dutch trade routes. These concessions, and the commitment from Louis to sanction the dismemberment of the Spanish Empire, were enough to establish a viable basis for further negotiation and to result, in September 1698, in a Partition Treaty that for the time being at least seemed to satisfy France, Great Britain, and Holland, if not perhaps the Holy Roman Empire or the Castilian aristocracy. Its guiding principle appeared to be the striking of a balance of power through the division of Spain's European possessions among the rival parties, while the state itself, together with its colonial possessions in the Americas, the Indies, and Africa would be gifted to the least formidable candidate, who could not be expected to disturb the new status quo. Consequently, Louis XIV and William III agreed to recognise the Emperor's infant grandson, Joseph Ferdinand, the Electoral Prince of Bavaria as the heir to the Spanish throne, while the dauphin was to be compensated for his loss with the Italian states of Sicily, Naples, and Finale, which on his eventual succession would be united with the French crown. As a further sop to the Emperor Leopold, his younger son, the Archduke Charles would receive the Duchy of Milan.[15] Unfortunately for Bentinck, however, he could claim little credit for the final form of the treaty, and he left France in June 1698 having gathered valuable intelligence from the French and Jacobite courts – largely thanks to the industry of Matthew Prior – but having failed to replicate his earlier successes or to have further capitalised on his friendship with Marshal Boufflers. Though he maintained a leisurely pace on his journey to the frontier, visiting fortresses and paying a call on the son of the Great Condé at his home in Chantilly, the salutes fired in his honour now rang somewhat hollow: King James would remain at St Germain for the foreseeable future, and his own political career could not now be rescued from a sad and inexorable decline. While William still lived, he would be saved from the indignity of impeachment, but no sooner had the last breath left the King's shattered frame than his enemies in the English Parliament would close about him, ironically using his part in negotiating the Treaty of Partition as the pretext for precipitating his fall.[16]

II

James had written to de Rancé, back in March, boasting of the continuing friendship of the King of France, and of his resolution to give 'short order' to the proposal 'that I should be forced to leave the Kingdom'. These sentiments received their definitive confirmation in December, when Tallard informed King William that Louis XIV's 'honour was engaged to leave the King of England, who had retired to St. Germains, free to remain there so long as he pleased; that [his] determination on that point was unalterable; but if ever the King felt a desire to go elsewhere, [Louis] would make no opposition'. Seeing through this statement for the bare-faced hypocrisy that it was, William was said to have exclaimed at once of James, that: 'the desire will never come to him, unless it is instilled into him!'. The only means now available to compel this most troublesome exile to abandon St Germain was through the withdrawal, just as Bentinck had suggested, of the annual subsidies that had been promised to Mary of Modena from the English exchequer. Matthew Prior, for one, was at a loss as to the official government position, asking Halifax: 'Do we intend to give her £50,000 per annum or not? If we do not, I should now be furnished with some chicaning answers when we are pressed on that point, for it was fairly promised'. Payment for the next two years had already been authorised by Parliament, but William had no particular inclination to grant such large amounts of 'money which he suspects will be used against him'. In order both to deny support to his foes and to circumvent the swingeing cutbacks in his expenditure demanded by an increasingly hostile legislature, he preferred to halt the transfer of the funds and instead to divert the £100,000, in conditions of utmost secrecy, to bankroll his private projects, achieving at last a measure of financial independence for the Crown.[17]

Yet while the Jacobites protested at the non-payment of the jointure, and continued to lobby hard for the delivery of the money to St Germain, James's financial position was helped in August 1698 by Louis XIV's granting of 500 pistoles to him for a subscription held to alleviate the plight of 'the poor Irish' under his protection, and by the promise of 200 more from the duc and duchesse de Bourgogne and the duc d'Orléans, whose friendship had amazingly endured despite James's increasingly shrill enjoinders for him to renounce and do penance for his homosexual practices.[18] Preparations were already underway for a massive display of force to be staged on the plain of Compiègne, allegedly in order to introduce the duc de Bourgogne to the army and to instruct him in the art of war, but in actual fact the manoeuvres were designed for the purpose of instilling a fresh sense of awe and fear in the foreign observers at the sight of French arms, and to demonstrate the continuing scope of King Louis's military power 'which, so his enemies

believed, had been exhausted in a long and widespread war'. James duly
set out from his palace and journeyed north-east along the banks of the
River Oise to the sprawling encampment built to accommodate some
60,000 soldiers, where he took up residence in one of the wooden guest
houses, 'furnished like comfortable Paris mansions, . . . [and] newly
constructed in perfect taste'. As the troops fanned out across the
countryside, recreating skirmishes, performing a textbook investment of
the old château, and preparing to mount a carefully choreographed
storm of its walls to order on Saturday 3/13 September, James was moved
to declare that it was 'a sight that was more worth seing, then anything of
that kind of our age', and noted that there had never been 'in our days,
an army . . . composed of such choise men . . . so well clad and so well
mounted'. However, though he examined the batteries and trenchworks
that had been especially constructed in order to reflect the latest
developments in the technology of siege warfare, and doubtless
acknowledged the acclamations of his former Irish soldiers, as he spurred
his horse past the windmill at the foot of the slopes, or climbed the
crumbling ramparts so that he might gain a better view of their mock
engagements, something was missing for him amid the familiar smells of
burning powder, the roar of the guns, the wearied curses of soldiers
yielding up their defensive positions, and the thunderous collision of
rival cavalry divisions emptying saddles and spilling dazed or shrieking
troopers onto the hard turf. Though he applauded politely, taking his
cue from the King of France, as successive regiments broke upon the
fortifications, sweeping the defenders before them at point of bayonet,
the exhilaration of warfare and delight in its glory that had gripped
James fast ever since he saw his father's regiments deploy on Edgehill as a
boy, now appeared to desert him entirely. It was no longer James but the
duc de Bourgogne who was cheered onto the field, resplendent in a
glittering cuirass and in the first flush of his manhood. Knowing that he
would never command again and was now no more than an elderly
observer, he soon tired of the feastings organised by Marshal Boufflers, of
the 'eager courtesy [offered] by his vast staff of servants', and of the
empty toasts drunk to a victory in which he no longer believed. What was
left of the professional soldier in James now feared the ruinous expenses
incurred by gentlemen in the course of these play-acted encounters and
lamented 'what pains nay what mony have not the officers spent, to
distinguish them selvs their Reg[iment]s and privat troups and companys,
to gaine their King's favor'. Yet it was as a man of God and of particular
religious insight that he chose to frame his critique of these enormous
manoeuvres, worrying about the worldliness of the soldiers and fearing
for their salvation. 'I cannot hinder myself from making this melancony
reflection', he wrote, 'how few amongst this great and formidable army
thinks of their duty to the King of Kings . . . who by their almost constant

way of lo[o]se living can with justice hardly be called or looked on as Christians, by any reasonable or thinking men, [and] can any one say anything so favorable of them, as to say they are so many mad men; for must not one be actualy so, that belivs any thing of Christianity and that there is an Eternity of hapynesse or misery, and what stronger tys of duty we have to God Almight[y] then to any other'. Thus, the Lord of Hosts was now far more important to James than any human commander-in-chief, and the rough camaraderie of the camp no longer exerted any attraction for him, when compared to the tranquillity and certainty afforded him by the cloister.[19] It was with a glad heart that the old King clambered back into his coach after four days spent in the field, and contemplated the letter that he would formulate for the benefit of the abbé de La Trappe on his return to St Germain, outlining his experiences, testifying to 'the enthusiasm of the officers' and 'the smartness and fitness of [King Louis's] troops', but wishing all the more that the soldiers, who were now busily dismantling their tents or marching back to their garrisons, would turn their thoughts to their mortality, and to the transcendent word of God.

At St Germain, the progress of the King's young children was still, understandably, watched and commented on with the greatest interest. Louise Marie had cried her eyes out for hours on end at the marriage of the duc de Bourgogne, having dreamed that the courteous older boy would one day marry her, and that, when fully grown, they would rule alongside one another as the King and Queen of France. In such circumstances, it was fortunate that her disillusionment was quickly forgotten among the renewed rough and tumble of the nursery, as her boisterous and energetic nature reasserted itself and led – to her mother's grave consternation – to her gaining a blackened and bumped nose as the result of a particularly hectic game of chase, which no amount of powder could adequately disguise. Long after the event, the exiles were prepared to credit her with the power of prophecy and took comfort from her dream, said to have occurred after her father's departure for Calais in 1696, that he had set out on the road in a red coat but returned to her in one that was blue, thus signifying that God had decreed that James would never regain his throne and that the shelter of his château walls would now have to encompass all that remained, and all that was best, of 'his' England. Of more obvious and immediate advantage to the Princess was the ready approval granted to her by the ladies of the French royal family and the court at Versailles. Even that most waspish of social commentators, the duchesse d'Orléans, could only think to criticise her imperfect grasp of the French language, the product of her inattention to her books and of her father's lack of concern in securing for her anything but the services of the driest and most stiflingly formal of tutors. Otherwise, the duchesse thought that she was blossoming into an attractive girl, who would come to have a pretty figure and who already possessed both a spark of charisma and a pair of dark and lively eyes that put her mother's Mediterranean beauty quite to shame. In a similar fashion, her brother James Francis Edward was also winning the praise of courtiers, though in his case it was for the gravity and maturity with which he conducted himself at state occasions, such as at his first communion at Notre Dame de Paris, or for the skill he displayed in guiding his horse and training his gun in the hunting field. There was little doubt that the old King doted on the boy, training him in deportment, riding and fighting, but also spoiling him dreadfully with the sweets and confections that caused him to have the first two of his adult teeth pulled due to their advanced decay, leaving his mouth entirely bare of milk teeth, before his eleventh birthday. Moreover, those with a critical cast of mind might have chosen to read behind the laudatory accounts of the child's tenacity in running to ground a wild boar in the woods near St Germain, and lodging a musket ball in its spine that drove the maddened animal to even greater ferocity, to consider that the child had halted once his quarry had plunged into the moat of the Convent of Poissy, and waited patiently until his adult groom Charles Booth joined him, and could be ordered to carry him on his shoulders safely through the icy waters to the other side.[20] Yet if, on occasion, the boy was petulant and lacked any great faculty for perception or a recognisable sense of humour, such shortcomings were not calculated to disturb or even register with his father, whose latter years he brightened; his future represented the King's final opportunity to triumph.

Rarely troubled by pressing business and, for all his injunctions to the contrary, preferring to leave the day-to-day management of his cause to his wife and his Privy Councillors, James hunted less – though with a ferocity that was quite undiminished – and allowed his religious observances to expand into those hours and days that would otherwise increasingly have remained empty of all purposeful endeavour. Moreover, the significance of the Castilian aristocracy's refusal to acquiesce in the destruction of the Spanish Empire, and the pressure that they brought to bear on the ailing Carlos II to sign a will in November 1698 in which he left his territories in their entirety to the Electoral Prince – threatening once more to fracture the delicate accord established between Europe's warring dynasties – barely appears to have registered with James and his followers at St Germain. Similarly, even the unexpected death from smallpox, at the beginning of 1699, of the little boy who had been named as the heir to Spain, and upon whose survival had depended the entire success of the Partition Treaty, necessitated no direct response from the exiled King. He would put his court into mourning for the passing of Carlos II in November 1700, and was still capable of causing consternation among the French nobility by choosing to wear violet alongside Louis XIV instead of the deepest black, because he continued to uphold the anachronistic claim of the English Crown to that of France, but he was not at Versailles to see the duc d'Anjou acclaimed as 'Philippe V' of Spain in accordance with the incendiary terms of Carlos II's final will, and he did not accompany the court and the Princes of the Blood to Sceaux to take.his leave of the French candidate for the now vacant, and soon to be sharply disputed, Spanish throne.[21] When he finally did get to embrace the newly proclaimed King, it is notable that his words of congratulation were prefigured by a mawkish consideration of his own plight, and that while he expressed relief that King William's demands that the Irish Brigade be disbanded and the individual regiments be farmed out by Louis XIV to the Italian princes had never been acted upon, there was never any suggestion that he would be required to advise the military mission sent to accompany Philip V across the River Bidasoa. At the same time, it was made abundantly clear to him that even if hostilities were to break out, there would be no opportunity for him to turn back the clock and to wrest control of those units away from the French general staff in order to reconstitute his own independent command.

Though James would never again lead troops in the field and, on account of his gout, was even having trouble sitting on a horse for any length of time, such concessions to hard political reality, past military defeat, and encroaching old age, do not appear to have unduly troubled the King. He had already recorded his memories of his youthful campaigns for posterity, and it might be thought that he was content enough to relive them, amid his piles of papers and notes, in the seclusion and comfort of his study, where he could not be contradicted and where his tales, rich in the tragedy of a promise unfulfilled, might come to delight the ears of a younger generation as yet unschooled in war, to whom the sights and sounds of battle were unfamiliar, and the names of Turenne, Condé, and Don Juan-José of Austria were as distant and alien as those of any heroes drawn from the Classical pantheon. Of even greater consolation was his faith, and the consideration shown to him by Louis XIV in granting to him, in the winter of 1699, the abbey of the Benedictines at Montmartre, a gesture which in itself cost the King of France little, but which meant the world to his exiled cousin, in terms of the recognition of his own piety and the possibility it afforded him to increase his religious patronage. This latter prospect was immediately recognised by the abbé de La Trappe, who wrote to James not only approving of his choice of Abbess and expressing his hope that his own brand of primitive piety may be seen to flourish there, but also recommending 'an honest man, who is capable, intelligent and rich . . . [who] may be engaged to give his services to the Abbess of Montmartre in all that concerns the temporal affairs of her house', adding as an afterthought: 'He does it disinterestedly, desiring neither salary nor prerequisites'. A more transparent request, and one which by this point was arguably far more welcome to the King, came from Captain Robert Sumerville, a Scottish gentleman and 'a good Catholic . . . [who] has always served with distinction and loyalty', asking to be granted a furlough so that he might journey to Rome in order 'to visit the tombs of the Apostles' and to take part in the papal jubilee. James, in his role as patriarch and spiritual advisor to his extended family of supporters, gladly granted his permission and forwarded the necessary paperwork for John Caryll, his Secretary of State, to complete.[22]

His court remained under surveillance by Williamite agents, but by the late 1690s there was less of note for the spies and intelligence gatherers to report on. Charles Montagu, the Earl of Manchester, had arrived in Paris in the autumn of 1699 as the new English Ambassador, but like Bentinck before him he decided that it would be prudent to defer the presentation of his credentials until James and his Queen had left the side of King Louis at Fontainebleau. He noted that a fresh sense of optimism had gripped the exiles, with the courtiers 'still pleasing themselves with hopes the nation will recall them at last' and James trusting that the failure of the Darien colony in Central America – which threatened not only to bankrupt the private Scottish Company but also the entire Scottish people and state – might provoke a seismic shift in the political allegiance of the nation, with the disaffected aristocracy and a ruined mercantile class uniting in their support for a popular Jacobite insurgency. In order to hasten the end of the colony – which was already stricken by disease, poor crop yields, and levels of investment that could never hope to keep pace with such ambitious plans for settlement and the rapid expansion of maritime trade – James aimed to harness Spanish support and deliver a *coup de grâce* by landing prominent Scottish Jacobites in order to prompt the colonists to reconsider their allegiance, or to face the possibility of an immediate military assault. Though it appears that James dusted off his maps of the area and debated with his Privy Council the best means to make an overture to the 'most considerable men' on the isthmus, Spanish reluctance to allow the encroachment of French power in their sphere of influence, coupled with their unilateral military success in slowly choking the life out of the colony, ensured that the scheme came to nothing. While the memory of the brutal example made of the Macdonalds of Glencoe appears to have deterred a Highland rising, for the time being at least, and Lowland discontent at the erosion of Scottish political and financial independence manifested itself in no more than an increasingly bitter sense of Anglophobia, James felt (with some good reason) that his northern kingdom was becoming a fertile recruiting ground for his cause, and that it might one day provide a back door route for the invasion of England.

Though the Duke of Melfort, who had been allowed to return to Paris in 1697, continued to act as a conduit for individuals and snippets of information to be forwarded to St Germain, and still maintained – as Lord Manchester was all too well aware – a regular correspondence with elements of the nobility, James knew that the aristocracy would only be prepared to act if the morale of the regular troops quartered in Scotland was substantially weakened, or better still if both the soldiers and their officers were collectively won round to his cause. To this end, his adherents began to smuggle buttons into the country, which looked innocuous enough in transit, but which contained a scroll bearing the initials of the rallying call: 'God bless King James and prosper his interest' which might be revealed by the sharp turn of a miniature screw and which were issued as an identifying badge to all those who engaged in his service. The prospect of soldiers – unnoticed – replacing their regulation buttons with these covert symbols, and spreading their influence throughout the regiments stationed in the north until called upon to defect en masse as the precursor to a general rising, certainly captured the imagination of the King, who saw in the promotion of this tactic the welcome chance to inflict the same type of complete military collapse upon his foes that had paralysed his army in 1688. Trial batches of the buttons were made up, and examples of a variant design – by which the gentry might wear strands of the King's hair on their cuffs, set secretly into the bezel of their studs, even as they were supposedly toasting the health of William III, or later Queen Anne – were being distributed among Lancastrian Jacobites in the early 1700s. However, due to the pressing need for security it is impossible now to gauge exactly how widespread this practice was among the army, or even if it permeated the ranks at all.[23]

Despite his claims to the contrary, and those of government propagandists who wished to show him as an impecunious and entirely spent force, the Earl of Manchester believed that James still maintained a financial reserve of some £200,000 and thought him to be 'in a very good humour' after his visit to Fontainebleau. Despite his advancing years, he still appeared to observers to be a remarkably strong and robust figure, refusing to miss a day in the hunting field at the beginning of 1699 despite running a high temperature, and priding himself that while he now habitually wore a pair of spectacles to correct his long sight, in order that he might still read and write, his vision had not substantially deteriorated since the mid-1680s. However, even though the King was not afflicted by serious illness, a recurrence of head colds and accompanying fevers appear to have gradually weakened his constitution and his appetite for sustained hard work as the century drew to its close. In May 1699, he wrote to de Rancé of the indisposition that had 'laid low' the majority of his court and 'obliged me to put back all my arrangements. . .

[and] to defer my visit [to La Trappe], which makes me cross as I was greatly looking forward to the pleasure and satisfaction of seeing you again'. He already took tea and had thyme stuffed into his mattress, on the advice of King Louis's physician Dr Fagon, in order that he might better regulate his pulse and manage to sleep straight through the night, but a further chill meant that he could only take part in a couple of short chases after the deer at Fontainebleau, and was forced to spend one day inactive, taking the air (but only from the comfort of his coach) beside the ornamental canal. In this, perhaps, he was fortunate, for he missed the disgrace of his son, Henry Fitzjames, who managed to tumble from his saddle even before the climax of the pursuit. Malicious gossips claimed that he had, once again, been thoroughly intoxicated, while the slightly more charitable put it down to a combination of his characteristic stupidity and awkwardness.

There were still moments of levity and delight to be experienced by the royal couple, as when Mary of Modena wrote of her pleasure in 'the constant changing of the flowers' and the newly laid out fountains at Marly; or when James could still summon the energy to run his quarry to ground and throw himself, tired but glowing, from his mount in order to administer the kill that would bring the hunt to its end. James gladly hosted the Assembly of the Clergy at St Germain, from June to September 1700, listened to the denunciations of Fénelon and took comfort from Bishop Bossuet's stirring sermon on the conversion of St Matthew, demonstrating that the most wonderful changes could come about if God so willed it, and that such a change might yet come to pass in England. However, while Mary could still turn heads and led the new fashion for small head-dresses, at Louis XIV's behest, she had become, by her early forties, paler and far more drawn, troubled by bouts of ill-health and the lump that had begun to grow in her breast. The court at St Germain was now seldom free from the black hangings that signalled a period of official mourning for the death of another European prince, and which did little to alleviate either the King's oppressive preoccupation with mortality, or the sense of gloom that permeated a Household that was forced to ponder both its own reduced circumstances and the possibility that it might not even survive the inevitable transition – and probable further diminution – of power from James to his son.[24] The King had communicated something of his foreboding to de Rancé, that: 'It seems to me that so many deaths that happen, arrive one after the other among the great of this world, as the Queen of Portugal, a young princess, virtuous and very charitable, to the King of Denmark who was only fifty three years old, [and] the Duchess of Modena, mother of the Duke of that name who is reigning at the moment. Both great and small should think themselves that no one is sure of life at any moment, and this should be a truth known and proclaimed throughout the world'.

Thus, one by one, the actors who had shared the stage with King James bowed and made their exits. De Rancé died in October 1700, seemingly broken by the storms that had raged about his successors, leaving Mary of Modena to re-read his letters and to console herself that from Heaven he would not forget to mention her and her husband in his prayers. The death of Pope Innocent XII, who had preceded him by only a few days, had thrown into doubt the payment of a large subsidy for the 'poor' of St Germain, and necessitated the sale of more of the Queen's jewels. Whatever the truth of Manchester's intelligence report about the King's financial reserves, and despite the fact that Duke Rinaldo had only recently paid the balance of Mary of Modena's dowry, James was certainly greatly relieved by the election of Cardinal Albani as Clement XI to the See, and quickly despatched: 'Our Right Trusty and . . . Intirely beloved naturall son' the Duke of Berwick over the Alps on a mission 'to represent the pressing necessitys of Our Subjects at or about St. Germains, who have lost their Estates, and are banished out of their Country for their Religion and their Loyalty, and whose number is great, that Wee, tho Wee spare all Wee can out of Our own subsistence allow'd Us by the King of France, are far from being able to releeve'.[25] Though James was prudent enough to instruct his son: 'In your first audience . . . not to ask any thing of him', Berwick was to leave the pontiff in absolutely no doubt 'that to avoid dayly importuning him for money, which the crying necessitys of those poor people would oblige Us to, it were to be wished that he would be pleased to appoint a certain sum quarterly, or yearly, to be pay'd for that use, of which an exact account from time to time may be shewn to his Nuntio that resides in the Court of France'.

The sense of urgency and purpose that spurred Berwick and his escort on towards Rome had been further sharpened by a wholly unexpected and tragic circumstance in the summer of the previous year, that had focused English attention firmly back on his cause, and on the person of his half-brother, the titular Prince of Wales. Amid the excitement of his eleventh birthday, Princess Anne's son, William, Duke of Gloucester had become hot and over-tired, and was hastily diagnosed as having smallpox and bled. Dr Radcliffe, a non-juring royal physician who had, ironically, once attended to James II's nosebleeds on Salisbury Plain, arrived late on the scene and finding that the withered and trembling child was actually suffering from scarlet fever, was provoked to a state of incandescent rage by the sheer incompetence of his colleagues, screaming at them that 'you have destroyed him and you may finish him, for I will not prescribe'. Afraid that he might be accused by his jealous rivals of being a Jacobite and a murderer if the little boy died, he effectively washed his hands of the entire sorry affair, and left Windsor Castle immediately. Unsurprisingly, within the week the child was dead, and his devastated parents were left to mourn the last of their nineteen children and along with him their hopes of perpetuating the Protestant Stuart dynasty. As the abbé Rizzini swiftly and perceptively grasped: 'The consternation is great in London, because the difficulties are foreseen as to finding a substitute with any right to the succession, to the exclusion of the legitimate king, and his incontestable heir, the Prince of Wales. By the death of the Duke, the Prince is freed from the most formidable rival he had, and were it not for the point of religion, he would perhaps be proclaimed at once, on condition of leaving the usurper [i.e. William III] in possession for his lifetime; meanwhile no calumnies are being uttered against his birth'. Though some of the more headstrong, if not entirely heartless, Jacobites began their celebrations immediately on receipt of the news, the death of the boy – who was, after all, James's grandson and realistically could not have offered him any offence, for the pair had never met – presented the exiled King with the problem of how to best proceed in a manner that was seemly, but still yielded a positive advantage to his son and did credit to his cause. Consequently, he put his Household at St Germain into strict mourning and saw that this mark of honour was extended to the French court at Versailles, while strongly rebuking James Francis Edward for his thoughtless decision to go out hunting on the same day that the Duke of Gloucester's death was officially announced. However, it was one thing to ensure that the correct pattern of ritual and etiquette was observed, and quite another for the old King to set aside his feelings of hurt and to recognise the pain and loss of another. He could not bring himself to refer to his daughter as anything other than the 'Princess of Denmark' and, on reflection, came to consider that his grandson's tragic end was actually something of a blessing in disguise. The appointment of 'such a governor' as Marlborough to look after the Duke could, he thought, have only resulted in the eventual corruption of the boy and while 'according to appearances he had taken part in the crimes of the rest of the country' against his grandfather, it was indeed 'lucky for this child to die so young . . . for . . . one can hope for him that the good lord will take pity on his soul'.[26]

Within days the King had placed an order with the Roettiers family for some 7,000 medals bearing the portrait of the titular Prince of Wales, which could be quickly smuggled across the Channel and distributed among his followers. At the same time, the Earl of Manchester was troubled by the perceptible increase in the daily flow of visitors to St Germain, and by the presence at the French court of a growing number of English noblemen keen to offer expressions of friendship to the exiles, and to establish a foothold in both political camps, now that it seemed more than likely that both William III and Princess Anne would die childless, and that the titular Prince of Wales would inherit the crown by default. In order to regain something of the diplomatic advantage, Manchester decided at the beginning of October 1700 (N.S.) to go in

person to Fontainebleau – while James and his Queen were still in
residence – to inform Louis XIV of the details of the Duke's death. As
more than two months had gone by since the child had breathed his last,
the Ambassador's mission had little to do with the imparting of
information and the need to perform diplomatic courtesies, and
everything to do with the need to dent the pride of the Jacobites that had
'grown to so great a heighth as is not to be imagined', and to demonstrate
to those aristocrats and place-seekers whose allegiance was already
wavering that the Williamite state was not prepared to capitulate in the
face of a fresh dynastic crisis and the mere image – now becoming all too
familiar through popular prints and medallions – of a plump-cheeked boy.
To this end, Manchester made sure to draw up his coach directly
underneath the former King's apartment, to the evident consternation of
its occupant, and sought out all those privileged souls who had tried to beg
further favours from him, and to trim their sails in accordance with the
changing political climate. His presence certainly had its desired effect, for
James's nerve appears to have deserted him and he made no attempt to
confront the Ambassador, while those English nobles who had expressly
come over to France in order to pay suit to his son shrank back at
Manchester's approach, their hopes of future honours outweighed for the
present by the fear that their duplicity would be reported and accordingly
punished when they returned home. The Ambassador noted with a grim
sense of satisfaction that: 'I saw several faces I knew in England, but I hope
never to see them there again', even as his master King William cast about
him for a means of resolving the potentially disastrous succession crisis.
Save for James Francis Edward and his sister, the direct Stuart line had all
but exhausted itself, while the closest collateral branches were all Roman
Catholic and included such wholly unacceptable figures as the duchesses
of Savoy and Bourgogne, the dauphin, and the dowager Empress of
Austria. By strict reckoning, only the fifty-eighth candidate in line for the
throne, the 74-year-old Electress Sophia of Hanover – the youngest
daughter of James's aunt, Elizabeth – was a Protestant and therefore
deemed suitable in the eyes of both William and his Parliament for
consideration for the crown.[27] Such a fundamental alteration to the
succession, even allowing for the provisions made to bar Catholics in the
Declaration of Rights, would essentially deal the deathblow to the Tory
belief in a divinely ordained, hereditary monarchy, driving the theory's
remaining adherents more firmly towards Jacobitism, but presenting the
remainder of the political nation with a far clearer choice to make
between a returning Roman Catholic dynasty; a Protestant potentate
cherry-picked from the House of Hanover; or the abandonment of
monarchy altogether in favour of some form of republican governance.
Unprepared to countenance either the first or the last option, William's
attempts to make one last overture to James to permit his son to return to

England to be raised as a Protestant were once again rejected, while his half-hearted pursuit of the Princess Dowager of Nassau as a new bride was similarly doomed to failure. As a result, he arranged to meet the Electress Sophia at Loo in October 1700, and promised her that, in return for the support of Hanover in any future action against the French, her claim to the thrones of Great Britain and Ireland, together with that of her son George, would be recognised in lineal succession after the death of Princess Anne, and that in the meantime a generous financial annuity would be granted to her by the English Parliament. Such were the concerns of both MPs and Lords, unwilling to yield the hard-won authority which they had clawed away from the Crown as the result of the Revolution of 1688–9, and fearful of what might result from a vacant throne, that they were prepared to steamroller the bill for a new Act of Settlement through both Houses, and to present the legislation for assent by King William in June 1701. Though the document amounted to a visceral critique of William III's personal rule, in seeking to preclude the appointment of foreign favourites to English offices, to entirely restrict the movements of the sovereign abroad without gaining advance permission from Parliament, and to ensure that all future monarchs would take communion only in the Church of England, thus barring a Calvinist of William's stamp just as surely as a Catholic of James Francis Edward's, it did not infringe on the powers of the current monarch and his Privy Council, while affording them the wherewithal to counteract any future constitutional threat from Jacobitism.[28]

Having repeatedly emphasised that his son's religion was non-negotiable, and that both the Bill of Rights and the new Act of Settlement would have to be repealed as the prelude to any restoration, James realised that he ran the risk of making his cause synonymous with political Catholicism, and of alienating his dwindling if disparate band of supporters among the Protestant Dissenters. Not only did he believe himself to have been grievously wronged by his subjects, but he had also come to view himself, with an element of justification, as a man whose intentions had been consistently misunderstood through a combination of malice and ignorance. Toleration, he declared somewhat forlornly, had always been his maxim. Yet to all around him, if not perhaps to the King himself, it now seemed that he was far further away from securing the restoration of his rights, and those of his son, than he had been at any point since he had stepped ashore at Ambleteuse more than a decade earlier. Madame noted that while the French court continued to 'live on good terms with these royalties . . . we do everything that King William wants us to'. More disturbingly, the dauphin, who had always been James's most consistent defender, was overheard referring for the first time (in January 1701) to William not as 'the Prince of Orange', as had previously always been the case, but as the 'King of England'. Moreover, even as the Electress Sophia prepared to set out for Loo, in order to conclude the deal that would keep his son from the throne and condemn him ultimately to life as a shifting, stateless exile beholden to the charity of others, James was busily expressing 'the whole time' his love for her, tears welling in his eyes and the words tripping inelegantly over his tongue and rendering his halting French all the more difficult to comprehend. As he raised his hands to heaven and stuttered his praise for his cousin Sophia, she, like so many others before, had already determined to forsake him.[29]

III

On Good Friday, 4 March 1701 (N.S.), James was hearing Mass, as was his practice, in the Chapel Royal at St Germain. Outside the walls of the château, the woodsmen and carters were still clearing away the damage inflicted by the recent high winds that had torn through the forest and uprooted hundreds of trees. Yet, if the King had paid any attention to the sound of the workmen's axes and gruff curses that morning, his mind was now entirely focused on the liturgy of the service and the words of the choir as they sang the first two verses from the last chapter of the Book of Lamentations:

> Remember, O Lord, what has
>   befallen us;
> look, and see our disgrace!
> Our inheritance has been turned over
>   to strangers,
> our homes to aliens.[30]

As they approached the crescendo, the King noticed a thin trickle of blood seeping from his nostrils, and fumbled distractedly in his pockets for a lace handkerchief to stop the flow. The officiating priest and several of the courtiers present turned in time to see James sway – the kerchief pressed to his nose slowly turning crimson, having failed entirely to staunch the bleeding that had now become a flood – and stagger forward from his kneeling position, and then fall, losing consciousness as the stone floor came up to meet him and the words of the psalm washed over him:

> The joy of our hearts has ceased;
> our dancing has turned
>   to mourning.
> The crown has fallen from our head;
> Woe to us, for we have sinned![31]

The coif worn by Mary of Modena had prevented her from seeing her husband collapse, but this made the shock of seeing James hauled still unconscious onto a chair all the worse, and for several minutes she gave him up for dead. However, having been given smelling salts and carried back to his bed, James appeared to rally. The bleeding stopped and within a few hours he 'seem'd perfectly well again', was sitting up and was entirely lucid. He returned to work, to his devotions, and to his riding, but exactly one week later, as he was dressing first thing in the morning, he collapsed with a stroke that paralysed his right side and left him bedridden. News of his predicament was immediately carried to Versailles, but Dr Fagon was otherwise occupied, and Louis XIV was forced to despatch the diminutive Dr Boudin, the dauphin's physician, poste haste to St Germain in his stead. He arrived to find the King in such a poor state that, on receipt of his report, Louis had cause to fear for his life and ordered the duc de Gesvres to ride out early 'the next morning, and to bring him tidings [of James's condition] at his levee'.[32] It appears that James's own doctors were not considered sufficiently expert to treat their master, and even Sir William Waldegrave retired into the background as first Boudin and later Fagon applied burning irons to blister the skin of his useless hand, and administered frequent salt water emetics in order to flush out his weakened system. After several days he began to regain some mobility in his fingers, wrote a few words with his good left hand, and was well enough to receive a visit from King Louis and the Princes of the Blood. It was noted that he 'walked pret[t]y well' and managed, with the aid of a stick, to edge his way along the long terrace which led out from his palace in a curve that mirrored the gentle arc cut by the course of the Seine far below. By the end of March, Dr Fagon thought that his patient had recovered sufficiently to withstand the rigours of a long coach journey, and prescribed a course of curative waters for him at the springs of Bourbon, more than 100 miles to the south. Louis quickly, and magnificently, offered the invalid expenses of 100,000 francs per month for the duration of his journey, and sent twenty-six of his best carriage horses to St Germain to speed him and his retinue – led by the marquis d'Urfe – on their way.

As soon as he had heard of his father's illness, the Duke of Berwick had abandoned his mission in Rome and hurried back to be at his side. In truth, his attempts to stitch together a series of alliances with the Italian princes and to obtain the desired subsidies from the Pope had met with little in the way of success. He had commiserated with Victor Amadeus of Savoy over the possibility of his sister being barred from the English succession, but wondered whether the Duke's failure to make the proper diplomatic protests through his ministers would be taken in London 'as an assent, and that it was neither consistent with his honour nor his interest'. His host agreed to make representation to the Parliament at

Westminster, but in the event an extremely temperate letter handed in by an ambassador and a notary at the height of the debates carried little weight one way or the other, and barely registered amid such heated domestic political argument, and against the background of attempts by the Tory members to impeach the leaders of the Whig 'Junto' of Somers, Orford, and Halifax. Moving from Turin to the court of Modena, Berwick's talk of a military alliance between the Italian princes with King James (and by extension with Louis XIV) to prevent the 'inevitable havock' of another war proved no more persuasive to Duke Rinaldo than it had to Victor Amadeus, and he set off from Rome with no more than the vaguest of promises that the Modenese would endeavour to 'act as the Pope desired'. Affairs went from bad to worse as Berwick, suddenly stung by the contrast drawn between his official position as the trusted emissary of a King and his illegitimate birth, decided to stand upon ceremony at the audience organised for him with Clement XI. Remembering his father's stories of his old mentor, and his reception into the Church of Rome, he demanded the same honours that had been accorded to 'the late M. Turenne' and 'expected that a stool should be given me at the Pope's audience . . . as was claimed by the grandees of Spain, to whom at the least I did not think myself inferior'. A fortnight of awkward and at times stormy negotiations passed, as the young Duke stalked impatiently about his apartments and the Curia attempted to broker a deal that might satisfy the dignity of this least humble and persuasive of petitioners. Finally a form of compromise was reached, by which 'having made my customary reverences, and kissed the Pope's slipper, he should embrace me, and rising from his chair, should walk with me in his gallery, and into his apartments'. After such an inauspicious start to the talks, it was little wonder that the negotiations soon stalled, and that Berwick's offer of his own sword and the services of several Irish regiments – apparently made unilaterally without authorisation from either James or Louis, as a means of maintaining a cohesive Jacobite force on the continent and providing himself with employment – was politely, but firmly, refused. The Duke, with some of the condescension of the natural soldier, thought Pope Clement was 'timid and naturally irresolute . . . convinced of the necessity of having troops, in order not to be exposed to the insults of either party . . . but cautious of offending the Emperor, to whom the Italians pay much deference'. The Pope was, he thought, minded only to raise 'a few bad regiments, which cost him a great deal of money, without being of any use' for 'priests were scarce capable of managing military affairs'.[33]

Amid the discussions of military aid and alliance, it seems that the primary objective of the embassy, the gaining of a regular supply of money for the subsistence of James's impoverished followers, was allowed to fade into the background, and that the matter was left almost entirely to be pursued by default through the offices of Cardinal Janson. At the Pope's request, Berwick was kept busy reviewing his troops and examining his general officers. Though flattered by being charged with such a responsible task, the Duke had nothing but scorn for Count Massimo, the Governor of the fortress of St Angelo, who had only seen service in Flanders as a subaltern, more than forty years before, and Count Paolucci, who he thought owed his command solely to the influence of his brother, a cardinal, and had never been 'any thing more than a Captain of horse, for a year or two in the Duchy of Milan, in time of peace'. Annoyed that he should be denied a command, while these elderly and (for all that he could tell) hopelessly incompetent aristocrats enjoyed the status and the opportunity for action that high office in the army of the Papal States afforded, Berwick did not seem to notice, or even to particularly care, that he had failed in the purpose of his mission, and that his energies and attention were being diverted so that the decision on the granting of subsidies might be indefinitely postponed. However, while he was a far more assured soldier than a diplomat, there was no doubt that the Duke adored his father and that the news of the King's seizure devastated him. Abandoning his embassy, he hurried back north 'with all speed' in time to join James's convoy on the road to Bourbon. King Louis had decreed that: 'the honours due to his dignity of king, be paid to him in all the towns he passes through', and as a result James's leisurely journey through the Loire Valley, stopping each night to rest at a convent or a bishop's palace, took on the aspect of a royal progress and pilgrimage. Illness and the cold thinned the elderly and fatigued from the King's entourage, with Lady d'Almond losing her voice entirely and being left behind on the road to recuperate, while James and his wife took comfort from the fate of William Berkenhead, their erstwhile secret agent, who had been confined to the infirmary of the monastery at Montargis, and had chosen to abjure his Protestant faith and to embrace Catholicism on his deathbed. Before continuing on to Nevers, the King had had to rest for several days at the convent of La Charité, due to a reoccurrence of the gout that had periodically afflicted his foot for the last two years, but he saw fit to dismiss a minor nosebleed as being of no account and was well enough to resume his journey and to submit to the punishing schedule of purgings and cold baths scheduled for him immediately on his arrival at Bourbon. His crippled arm was massaged and doused and, within a matter of days, the Queen was writing optimistically to John Caryll that her husband: 'grows better every day then other, his goute is quitt gone, he eats well, sleeps well, and his hand and knee are much stronger, then they were', adding that 'if the waters do but never so little good, he must go back quitt well'. Gifts of Burgundy wine and crystallised fruit arrived for James from the Bishop of Autun, and he amused himself in the evenings playing tric-trac with the Bishop of Dole. A new routine was quickly established to the King's satisfaction, whereby he heard Mass regularly in the parish church, or if it was cold, in a private chapel that had been expressly created for his use in the antechamber adjoining the royal apartments. When it was sunny he ventured out onto the terrace of the adjoining Capuchin monastery and here, it might be thought, he experienced a liberating form of religious vision, and a concern to abandon the trappings of the world, that he had not known since his first contact with the brothers of La Trappe. Amid the gardens of Bourbon, he prepared to disengage himself entirely from secular society and to shed the external trappings of his power, in order to complete his transformation from warrior and king to penitent and man of God, who would soon advance to embrace death gladly. He no longer cropped the wiry grey curls that sprouted underneath his wig, and increasingly chose to leave off his hairpiece altogether, affecting the simplest of costumes and going about bareheaded and unshaven in imitation of the monks, save for when his presence at ceremonial occasions and formal receptions demanded otherwise.

Yet before he could be at peace, he needed to settle his affairs and to guarantee that his memoirs – which would ensure that the past could be viewed from his own perspective, his claims to military genius might not be overlooked, and that his records as a naval administrator and champion of religious toleration could at last be understood – would be properly preserved and their contents widely disseminated in the future. Prior to leaving St Germain he had, in one of his last official acts, written to Louis Innes, the Queen's Almoner and Principal of the Scots College in Paris, desiring that his personal writings might be transferred into the safe keeping of the archives and 'remain there as a lasting mark of our trust in you and our affection for our said College'.[34] However, the fate of his papers continued to trouble him and, from Bourbon, he urged his wife to write to John Caryll again as a matter of some urgency, in order to discover if his request had been accepted and 'to putt [his Secretary] in mind of his memoirs'. Fortunately, Innes had, in the meantime, already written to assure James that the manuscripts were in the process of being transferred to the Scots College and that Caryll had been 'hard at worke about them', editing the King's disparate recollections into one coherent and authoritative biographical narrative. Even then, the King – with little else to occupy him save for his treatments – still fretted constantly about the fate of his precious papers and had Mary of Modena send to Caryll 'begging of you to go on till you perfect the worke', while he checked the translations for errors of style and content, and even put himself through great pain by scratching a note to the Cardinal de Bouillon, so that he might learn if the accounts of his early campaigns were still closely guarded and treasured in his possession. Finding it difficult to close the fingers of his right hand around a pen, and unable to write unaided for any length of time, James unsurprisingly chose to rely on his wife to maintain a correspondence with lords Perth and Middleton at St Germain, and to preserve contact with the French court through the weekly letters that she exchanged with her great friend and confidante, madame de Maintenon. Before starting back for Paris in May 1701, the Queen wrote that: 'all the Doctors hear assure us, that he will find yett mor benefit by these waters a month hence, then he does at present', but Berwick remained thoroughly unconvinced by their sanguine prognoses and saw only the spectacle of his father stripped of all dignity and left to shiver in a simple wooden tub, while a train of servants worked to refill their buckets with fresh supplies of freezing water. More seriously, Berwick, alone of all the King's retinue and physicians, was disturbed by the fresh haemorrhage which resulted in 'a spitting of blood' from James's mouth, which he believed had been occasioned by exposure to 'these waters', that 'instead of doing him service' were only acting to hasten his end.[35] Though the bleeding brought his treatment to a halt, and speeded his return home, James chose to downplay the incident and to pass it off as being of no consequence.

Arriving at Moulins on 14/24 May, he could barely descend from his coach without assistance and, exhausted by the rigours of his journey, he dozed for much of the rest of the day. In an attempt to supplement medical science with the working of a miracle, the royal couple heard Mass at every stage along their route. Mary of Modena maintained a lonely vigil, praying before the relics of the founder of the Order of the Visitation for her husband's return to health, while James, who was unable to take part in the religious procession on Corpus Christi, was observed propping himself up on a balcony overlooking the cathedral of Notre Dame at Moulins, in order to witness its progress through the winding city streets. Such exertions, however, seem only to have added to the King's fatigue and, to the Queen's evident sorrow, a planned visit to La Chaillot had to be abandoned in deference to her husband's weakened state. Death now seemed to be at his shoulder at every turn, for the ill news reached him from the French court that his friend the duc d'Orléans had succumbed to a stroke. Just hours before, King Louis had paid a courtesy call on James and Mary to welcome them home to St Germain, but on his return to Marly he had quarrelled violently with his brother, blaming him for the unfaithfulness shown by his son the duc de Chartres towards his young wife Françoise-Marie, the King's own natural daughter. Threatened with a reduction in his pensions and 'beside himself with rage', Monsieur returned home to Saint-Cloud, reliving the argument and declaring his intent that this time he would not be seen to back down, even as his hand began to shake, his crystal glass slipped from his hand, and he fell back into the arms of his son in a state of apoplexy. He was dead by the next afternoon, the quarrel with his brother barely forgiven, due to Louis's belated appearance at his bedside, and James was left to make a journey to Marly to express his condolences to the King that was every bit as emotionally uncomfortable as it was physically tiring. At a loss for words, and with Louis still in a state of shock, James 'remained but a moment with him', before starting back for St Germain through a balmy summer's evening that now seemed to be so desperately at odds with the sorrow that had descended so unexpectedly upon the royal exiles and their hosts.[36]

Though he no longer had his old companion to hunt with, and to compare and swap stories of exploits at the battles of the Dunes and Cassel, James still managed to mount a horse and ride out again through the woods on 6/16 August in search of game, acknowledging the cheers of the crowds of Parisians who had gathered at the château gates in the hopes of gaining a glimpse of the King, in the knowledge that they (as well as he) fully expected that it might be their last. Yet, 'all on a sudden he grew weak' again and, on Friday 2 September 1701 (N.S.), he collapsed once again during a Mass held in the Chapel Royal, rallying slightly the next day, but suffering a further seizure on the following Sunday afternoon, which left him 'for some time without life or motion, till his mouth being forced open, he vomited a great quantety of bloud'. This time, there could be no doubt that the end was near, and James – who had long prepared for this moment – determined to meet his death with a calm equanimity that might prove an inspiration to his followers, and a telling indictment of the behaviour of his foes. He had had the presence of mind to make a general confession before falling into his fit, but on regaining consciousness and 'fancying he could not last long' he despatched his confessor Fr Sanders to bring him the sacrament, and sent for his son and heir. Clearly terrified, the 13-year-old was brought into his father's presence, but seeing him 'with a pale and dying countenance, the bed all cover'd with blood', burst into floods of tears. His hysteria quickly communicated itself to the courtiers about him and it was several minutes before order could be restored to the chamber, the wishes of the King communicated, and the boy properly comforted and brought to his bedside.[37] Opening his arms to embrace his son, James told him, 'with a force and vehemence that better su[i]ted with his zeal than the weak condition he was in', that he was: 'now leaving this world, which has been to me a sea of storms and tempests; it being God Almighty's will to wean me from it by many great Afflictions' and that his heir should serve the Lord 'with all your power and strength, and never put the Crown of England in competition with your Eternal Salvation', adding that one could never 'lose too much for God'. If his political restoration was to come a poor second to his spiritual well-being, then James reminded his son that there was 'no Slavery like Sin, nor no

Liberty like his Service' and that only 'holy Providence' had the power to 'set you upon the Throne of your Ancestors'. The only sure course was to 'obey the Queen your Mother, and stick always close to the King of France', but if he were to gain the crown, then James Francis Edward should 'take pity of your misled Subjects' and remember that: 'Kings are not made for themselves, but for the good of the People. Set before their eyes, in your own actions, a pattern of all manner of virtues. Consider them as your Children, [and] aim at nothing but their good in correcting them', for: 'You are the Child of Vows and Prayers'. Having commended the child to honour his mother and be a kind brother to his sister, so that he might 'reap the blessing of concord and unity' among his family just as surely as among his subject peoples, James refused to allow his son to be taken from him until he had held him a little longer and given him his blessing.[38] No sooner had the boy retired than his sister Louise Marie was ushered into the royal presence, so that James might take his leave from her. She should, he commanded, 'serve your Creator in the Days of your Youth, and consider Virtue as the greatest Ornament of your Sex', being continually mindful to: 'Follow close the steps of that great Pattern of it your Mother; who has been no less than my self over-clouded with Calumnies; but Time, the Mother of Truth, I hope, will at last, make her Virtue Shine as bright as the Sun'. While there was little that was original in these gender-specific homilies, and it was uncertain just how much of their content was actually absorbed by his weeping and thoroughly traumatised children, overwhelmed as they were by his piteous physical state, James's determination to master nature and to turn that which was truly ghastly and terrifying into something serene and instructive, leaving nothing to chance in the settling of his worldly affairs, deeply impressed all those present, and was swiftly communicated to the French court in the most favourable of terms. Though James had not been fated to die at the hands of his enemies – and indeed had done everything in his power to ensure that this was the case – he was keen to emphasise that his death was still a form of martyrdom, performed in the service of his faith. 'My Integrity and Innocency', he told the members of his Household – and his sobbing and prostrate Queen, who was now 'sh[ru]nk down on the ground by the bed side' – 'has been Oppressed with Infinite Lyes and Calumnies. I never entertain'd a Thought which was not levell'd at the Good of my Subjects. O Sweet Jesus, of thy Infinite Mercy forgive the Authors and Forgers of them! I Offer up all my Sufferings in Union with Thine. Sweet Jesus, Sanctify them to me for the Eternal Salvation of my poor Soul!'. Remembering the teachings of de Rancé, he praised that 'Holy Providence, who by permitting me to be deprived of an Earthly, hast given me better means to gain an Eternal Crown', adding that: 'I thank Thee, sweet Jesus, for giving me the Spirit of Resignation among so many Calamities'.[39]

Having exhorted his Protestant followers, and Lord Middleton in particular, to convert to Roman Catholicism in order to better fulfil his behests and follow his example of a virtuous life, James began to slip in and out of consciousness, but he remained lucid and it was not until 4 September (N.S.) that Fr Sanders was finally ushered into his presence, together with the local curate Fr Bennet, in order to administer the host and to perform the act of supreme unction. The King eagerly affirmed his belief 'with my whole heart' in 'the real and substantial presence of our Saviour's body in the Sacrament', and told the Papal Nuncio Philip Gualterio, who hovered close by, to send Clement XI 'my profound Respects' and to let him know: 'That I die a Child of the Church'.[40] He then proceeded to offer a pardon to all of his enemies, naming William of Orange, Princess Anne of Denmark and Emperor Leopold specifically, and adding: 'that he reckon'd them his best benefactors', for through the injuries they had inflicted upon him they had unwittingly brought him far closer to an understanding of God. Yet despite his preparations for a seamless transition between the mortal world and eternity, the end did not come as quickly as had been expected. With Waldegrave and Fagon continuing to administer treatments, bleeding and scalding him afresh and placing cupping-glasses to draw the lesions from his skin, Mary of Modena was given cruel and false hopes that he might yet make a full recovery, while a constant procession of French courtiers arrived at St Germain to pay their last respects and to gain a glimpse of the dying King, whose passing seemed increasingly to exude an aura of sanctity. Stripped of his finery, 'this Holy Combatant' appeared to have 'entered the Lists' with death and impressed the crowds of onlookers who filed through his darkened and claustrophobic chamber, to the sound of prayers repeated for the 'Recommendation of the Soul', with the calmness of his demeanour and his stoical acceptance of pain. On 8 September (N.S.), Madame had 'found King James in a pitiful state' and noted that while: 'His voice . . . is still as strong as usual and he knows people . . . he looks very ill and has a beard [grown long] like a Capuchin'. With his transformation from statesman to ascetic so graphically underscored by the change in his appearance and costume, all that remained was for the King to perform one last official act: approving the text of his will, presented to him by candlelight later that same afternoon by Fr Sanders and his legal counsel Robert Power. Though unable to sign the paper, he still had the presence of mind to dictate alterations, ordering that the gaps left blank for his daughter's maintenance be filled in with the correct sums, and waving the completed document above his head to show that he was 'well satisfied' with the final text. It was vital that every act should be properly witnessed so that, after the event, not one of his detractors could allege that there had been anything suspicious or underhand about the manner of his passing. As a result of this need for transparency, the doors to his room were no longer guarded, so that the courtiers might come and go almost as they pleased, and the curtains to his bed were permanently thrown open so that he might be seen and 'all the circumstances of [his death] should be made public'. He held on only in the hope that he might more properly emulate Jesus by expiring on a Friday, and now that he had observed the appropriate rites and given his advice to his family, he preserved all his strength to that end, speaking little save to pray, and napping frequently. Though his young children were now kept away from his presence, in order to spare them further anguish and in fear that their cries might shatter his repose, the protracted nature of the King's illness ensured that those closest to him were all in attendance. The Bishop of Autun had hurried to his side, promising him that the prayers of the community of La Chaillot would be devoted to his honour, while the Prince de Conti – who had been sent from Marly to look after the Queen – remained in constant attendance, 'infinitely surprized and moved' by James's declarations of piety and by the quiet resolve with which he reiterated his desire to die. Berwick and Middleton remained close by, while madame de Maintenon comforted his distraught wife, and Lord Melfort arrived from his house in Paris in time to embrace his old friend and to be forgiven for his past misdemeanours. The duc de Bourgogne was greeted with a nod, but the King would not allow his wife, the little duchesse, to come too close to him, lest the smell of his corruption should overwhelm and disgust her.[41] Yet, it was the three visits made by Louis XIV to St Germain – which, for the sake of narrative quality, were later condensed to just one in the pages of the Paris Gazette – that were to be of the greatest significance.

The very public theatre of James's death, his magnanimity towards his foes, and his selfless fulfilment of the highest moral and religious duties of a King, had clearly inspired Louis and reinforced his belief that those chosen to rule by God were distinct from other men and imbued with supernatural powers. Yet, though he too could not refrain from tears as he pressed his hand into James's frail and clammy grasp, and 'expressed his Concern for the loss of so good a Friend and Brother', it was his interview with Mary of Modena on 5 September that proved decisive. Though Louis ventured that he already 'looked upon her husband as a saint', this was not enough for the Queen, who pleaded with him to recognise her son's claim to the throne, as 'King James III' of Great Britain and Ireland, so that he might not be dishonoured and condemned to 'return to the state of a private individual'. For the moment, Louis would not be drawn, claiming that he 'had a great inclination towards the Prince of Wales', but 'that the matter required some reflection . . . [and] he could not recognise him without assembling his Council'. This was done the very next day, with the dauphin, seconded by the duc de Bourgogne, arguing the young Prince's cause, and the Chancellor, the comte de Pontchartrain, leading the ministers in their opposition to any attempt to subvert the spirit of the Treaty of Ryswick. Though war clouds were already gathering, with the establishment of the French claimant Philip V on the throne of Spain, and the British, Austrians and Dutch poised at any moment to sign a Second Treaty of Grand Alliance at The Hague that would commit them to supporting the Emperor's claims to the Spanish inheritance, through force if necessary, Pontchartrain argued that any further provocation on the part of France could only be counter-productive. By recognising James Francis Edward as King, they would not only be breaking the commitment made at Ryswick to recognise the legitimate sovereignty of William III, but would also be stating their intention to overturn the new English Act of Succession and to directly challenge the right of the House of Hanover to the throne. Everyone present recognised that such an action would carry with it enormous consequences, threatening to hasten Europe's slide back into war, and to enrage English public opinion, in particular, to such an extent that parliamentary subsidies for re-equipping William's armies would be immediately forthcoming. Somewhat disingenuously, the dauphin re-floated the old Tory distinction between a *de facto* and a *de jure* king, which he had probably first heard from James himself, and argued that it was perfectly possible for them to abide by their treaty commitments while recognising William in the former capacity, and James Francis Edward in the latter. With the emotive example of the dying King fresh in his mind, and with madame de Maintenon and the Princes of the Blood united in their wish to see his son proclaimed as 'James III', Louis – for once – allowed his heart to rule his head, overruling his ministers and deciding to start back for St Germain, in order to reaffirm the principles of a divinely ordained and hereditary monarchy before the exiles, and to bring an element of hope to the old King, as the reward for his faith and constancy.[42]

Thus far, Louis had only intruded into the solemn spectacle of James's leave-taking as an observer, responding in a fitting manner to the plight of his ailing cousin and paying tribute to his qualities, but scarcely seeking to shape events, or to provide the focus for them. However, in returning to the palace of St Germain on the afternoon of 13 September, he intended to place himself firmly back at the centre of the political stage and to demonstrate that his own actions were similarly motivated by God, and that he was every bit as capable as his illustrious guest of performing a grand and sweeping gesture that would fly in the face of prudence and expediency, in order to fulfil his obligation to 'a Prince of [his] own blood, who sought, and so justly merited [his] protection'. As he had done before, he had his horses' hooves muffled on their approach to the château and left his coach at the gates, hurrying across the drawbridge on foot, so that James's repose might not be disturbed by the harsh clatter of carriage and escort across the cobbles of the courtyard. On his entry to the royal apartments, he first sought out Mary of Modena and informed her of his decision – and that of his Council – to recognise her son, on the death of his father, as the rightful King of England. Next, the titular Prince of Wales was summoned to his mother's room, to be told of this impending elevation and to receive Louis XIV's promise: 'That if it pleased God to call for the King his Father, he would be a Father to him'. Writing several days later, the abbé Rizzini recalled that: 'the young prince instantly embraced the King's knees, declaring that he would remember all his life that he owed the title to his Majesty . . . Then he threw his arms around the Queen's neck in a transport of sorrow at the thought of his father's approaching death, and of compassion with his mother's grief, so that the Most Christian King had to take him away almost by force'.[43] All that remained now was for Louis to acquaint James with these welcome developments and, determined to reveal his intentions in a manner that would redound to his credit and extract the greatest degree of political capital from the situation, he attempted to hurry to his side. However, the crush of bodies straining to get a glimpse of their master in the small chamber, and blocking up both the adjoining rooms and corridor, ensured that Louis had to make his entrance via the external balcony, through the windowed doors. Such an unexpected arrival provoked gasps of surprise from those assembled, but he immediately moved to signal the recall of all those courtiers who withdrew on his approach, out of deference and the belief that he intended to speak privately to the dying man. With James in a severely weakened condition, Louis now addressed his words as much to his followers gathered in the room, as to the King himself, announcing: 'that I am come . . . to acquaint you, that whenever it shall please God to call Your Majesty out of this world, I will take your family into my protection, and will treat your son the Prince of Wales in the same manner I have treated you, and acknowledge him as he then will be King of England'. On hearing this, the oppressive hush that had surrounded the palace for the past ten days was suddenly broken, and the pent-up anxieties of courtiers and servants released. In defiance of all protocol – and forgetting that their own sovereign still lived – James's captains began to acclaim both his successor and Louis, by repeatedly shouting: 'God save the King!', while the noblemen present, 'as well French as English', pressed forward to give their thanks. Caught between joy and despair, some 'threw themselves at his Most Christian Majesty's feet', while others raised their hands to heaven, or through their 'countenances (much more expressive on such occasions than words and speeches) declared their gratitude for so generous an action . . . [by] his Most Christian

Majesty'.[44] As the cheering redoubled, Louis withdrew from the chamber, acknowledging the thanks of Berwick and Middleton, and affecting to wipe a tear from his eyelids, while James, almost forgotten amid the noise and excitement, shifted uneasily upon his pillows and managed to give a stiff nod to signify his approval.

After the event, the scene was rewritten to emphasise James's overwhelming gratitude towards, and dependency upon, Louis, with eloquent responses of the kind that he was no longer capable of making inserted into his mouth. While it is conceivable that the King of France took his final leave of James with a tender embrace, wishing 'Adieu, [to] my dear Brother, the best of Christians, and the most abused of Monarchs', it is probable that, for the most part, the royal hagiographers chose to project forwards into their last and far more dramatic meeting the thanks given by the exiled King to his host in their earlier interviews. It took James a fortnight to die, and the long drawn-out process of sudden seizures, administration of last rites, unexpected rallies and brief hopes of recovery that were soon dashed, necessitated the repeat of certain of the rituals and royal commands, and the King's leave-taking of his wife and family more than once. Though the careful choreographing of his end had almost been upstaged at the last by the personal intervention of Louis XIV, James could take comfort from the fact that he had succeeded in establishing the 'piety and sanctity' of his Christian death, of the type that, since his encounter with the community of La Trappe, he had always hankered for.[45] Moreover, by the manner of his death he had achieved that which he had been singularly unable to do over the course of the last four years of his life: to extract from the French an unambiguous commitment to recognise and to restore his heir, and to force their hand in rejecting the treaty commitments they had made at Ryswick, to respect British sovereignty and to acknowledge the political legitimacy of William III. The exiled court was no longer threatened with sudden removal beyond the borders of France, and in the advent of a major European war, the Jacobite movement, fashioned in the image of its creator, could be expected to move back from the margins to occupy a useful and important place in the formulation of Louis XIV's foreign and military policies. Most importantly of all, through James's efforts, his son had been transformed from an object of mockery and potential shame into a Prince of enormous dynastic importance, whose legitimacy was no longer widely doubted and whose claim to the English throne was on the point of being formally recognised by France. Through the sheer chance of the failure of bloodlines and the ravages of a spectacularly high child mortality rate, James Francis Edward and his sister had also become the possible hopes for the continuation of the direct Stuart line on beyond the life of Princess Anne.

If one were to judge James II's last years on his own terms, then one might well be persuaded that he had been a great success. He had forged the new political movement that was Jacobitism out of the wreckage of the old pre-1688 Tory party, and had imbued it with a strong sense of identity and a guiding set of principles on the nature of government and the divine right of monarchy that drew their inspiration directly from James's own writings and the memory of his sufferings. Furthermore, through his advice 'For My Son' of 1692, and his deathbed exhortations, he had bestowed on his heirs a clear concept of their obligations and the foundations on which their government should rest. In marked contrast to that of 1660, any future Stuart restoration would be far from ambiguous. It would be characterised by a commitment to overturn the Anglican Church's monopoly of ecclesiastical power, a fundamental re-drawing of powers between King and parliament – entailing almost the complete overturning of the Revolution Settlement – and a willingness to rely, in the short term at least, on the power of a French alliance to effect such dramatic constitutional change. The Stuart monarchy was to become synonymous with the practice and promotion of Roman Catholicism, with – as we have seen – adherence to the faith to be placed before all other considerations, even if that entailed a further loss of power and the permanent distancing of the exiles from those peoples whom they claimed to represent. Furthermore, the strict rules for the conduct of his heir, which emphasised the importance of unshakeable piety and a strong martial bearing, virtually ensured that all James II's successors would be forced to model themselves to a greater or lesser extent on his paradigm, or risk destroying their claims to both moral and political authority. Such narrowly defined parameters may have been of great comfort to James, and led him to believe that his legacy had been safeguarded, as was indeed the case. However, his willingness to accept that a future European war, growing out of the Spanish succession but spreading to include the question of the English, would offer the only sure means by which his son might be restored, necessitated an acceptance of French military involvement in the British Isles and a return to civil war and bloodshed that the overwhelming majority of the political élites in his three former kingdoms were simply not prepared to countenance. More seriously, the manner of his flight from Ireland, the collapse of organised resistance there and the resulting imposition of a militant Protestant ascendancy, had ensured that there was little scope for a resurgence of Irish Jacobitism. France and not the exiled Stuart dynasty was now the repository for national hopes, while the Roman Catholic majority, impoverished after a century of confiscations and struggling to remain true to its faith in the face of draconian penal laws, was understandably more concerned with eking out a living and trusting to

God, than with remembering in their prayers the King who had once abandoned them to their fate. With English Jacobitism confined to a few scattered geographical areas, and only the north registering particularly strongly, opposition to the Revolution Settlement was to be found most securely rooted in the Highlands of Scotland. In part, this owed something to James's ability as his brother's Viceroy, his record as King, and the folk-memory of Claverhouse's brief campaign, which had brought the clans of the Great Glen an all too rare victory; but even then the resilience and potency of Scottish Jacobitism was far more the product of the systematic erosion of economic and political independence, the denial of nationhood, and the death-throes of a clan system that could no longer support a Highland population driven to ever greater extremes in the raiding and feuding that inevitably accompanied the struggle for increasingly scarce natural resources. At best, the distance of James and the Pretenders who followed him lent a certain enchantment to their cause, but every fresh attempt at rebellion that they sponsored resulted in further disillusionment and in the hastening of the end of a culture, as the chiefs knew only too well when they watched James Francis Edward bolt prematurely from Scotland in 1716, and went down on their knees to beg his son, Charles Edward Stuart, to go home immediately and leave them in peace, on his landing in the late summer of 1745.[46] It was the misfortune of James II, and his immediate heir who followed so uncritically – and with such diminishing returns – in his footsteps, that the individualistic chivalric virtues which he had espoused no longer had a secure role in a changing Europe that was increasingly dominated by long-range artillery and a nascent sense of competing nationalisms. As a young man, James might have fought against troops of the English Protectorate in the service of Spain, but he could at least claim that he did so as part of an independent English Royalist army in exile, and that he was waging war in support of the monarchy against a form of republicanism. No such excuses could be afforded to his son in the eyes of his English critics when, as the client of a foreign power, he charged with the French Maison du Roi at the battle of Malplaquet, riding down those he claimed as his own subjects and stemming the tide of the Redcoats' advance.[47] In bidding his heir to emulate his endeavours at every turn, and in making the appeal of Jacobitism synonymous in the popular mind with support for both an overtly proselytising Roman Catholic monarchy and a military alliance with absolutist France, it may not be overstating the case to suggest that, despite all his best intentions, James had hopelessly misread the guiding political and religious preoccupations of the majority of his former subjects, unwittingly bequeathing to his heirs and to Jacobitism a legacy which – despite short-term advantages – was nothing less than a poisoned chalice.

Without the gift of foresight, but convinced that he had established the means by which his cause might prosper, and secure in the belief that he was about to be vindicated through his meeting with God, James prepared once more for his end. The problem remained, however, that it was one thing to master one's fears and seek to control the circumstances surrounding one's death, balancing ritual with sage words of advice, but it was quite another to seek to die 'to order' after delivering a last speech or waiting until an appointed hour. Yet this was precisely what James had attempted to do. His problem was that two Fridays had now passed since his initial seizure, and his leave-taking from his family, which had been intended as the climactic event of his illness, now appeared to have been somewhat premature and to have been overshadowed by the dramatic personal intervention of Louis XIV. Having determined to ensure that his pronouncements would not be forgotten, and that his passing would not go without mention, he despatched Middleton to the palace at Marly to thank the King of France for his kindness towards his son, and called James Francis Edward back to his side. His courtiers feared that a fresh meeting might send the boy into hysterics and raise: 'such a commotion in him as was thought to do him harme', but the old King could not be deterred from taking his son in his arms for one last time, reiterating his previous commands, and conferring his approval on everything that Louis had said. 'Thus', his official biographer noted, 'did this holy Prince talk of his aproaching death not only with indifference, but satisfaction, when he found his Son and Family would not be sufferers by it, and so composed himself' in order to await 'that happy hour' with ever 'greater cheerfulness'. On the next day, however, his condition took a sudden turn for the worse, with his emaciated form convulsed by violent tremors that caused his hands, which had habitually been folded in an attitude of prayer, to continuously shake and tremble. As the hours passed, his breathing became fainter and far more irregular and, as he rarely opened his eyes so that he might be better able to conserve his strength, the crowds of onlookers who waited expectantly in the shadows just beyond the corners of his bed increasingly had difficulty in telling whether he was still conscious or not.

Yet, though he had been disappointed by so much in life, James II was to be granted his wish in death. Through a supreme effort of mind over fragile matter he survived a difficult night, and saw the sun rise on the third Friday of his illness. Whether through pure coincidence, a steely design or, as the Bishop of Autun would later have it, the will of God, James breathed his last at approximately three o'clock in the afternoon on Friday 16 September 1701 (N.S.), 'the day of the week and hour' it was later recalled 'wherein our Saviour dy'd, and on which [the King had] always practiced a particular devotion' to obtain the most beatific and Christian of deaths.[48] No sooner had the death rattle subsided and his shrunken frame stilled than the candles were extinguished one by one throughout his chamber, and the sound of prayers for the dead, solemnly intoned by the priests, gave way to the cries of the heralds proclaiming that one reign had come to an end, and that another had already begun. Even as these were taken up and echoed around the walls of the castle courtyard by the royal guards, a courier was already racing to bring Louis XIV the long-expected news, and Lord Middleton, having broken his staff of office, surrendered his seals of state to the Queen and awaited her pleasure as Regent for her son. Close by, the new King – forced suddenly into an unfamiliar, adult role – smudged the tears away from his cheeks, prepared to receive the officer of the Maison du Roi left behind on purpose by Louis XIV to communicate his respects, and stepped uncertainly into the pale and already failing light of the shortening autumn day.

IV

It had been James's desire, if he died in exile and could not be buried, as he would have wished, close to the shrine of St Edward the Confessor in Westminster abbey, to be interred with as little ceremony as possible in the parish church closest to the spot where he had departed life. There was to be no monument raised to his glory, and only the briefest and most factual of inscriptions should inform those who passed by his simple stone that: 'Here Lys King James'. However, the very public manner of his death, and the intense interest that it had aroused, appeared to demand a far grander commemoration of his piety and self-sacrifice, and Louis XIV quickly overruled James's dying wishes and the respectful protests of the curate of St-Germain-en-Laye, in order to authorise the raising of multiple memorials to the late King in far more prominent locations, and the dispersal of his remains as befitted a saint. His body lay in state for twenty-four hours 'in the room where he dyd, the Clergie and Religious singing the office of the dead by him all night, and all the morning masses were sayd at two alters erected on both sides [of] the room'.[49] An autopsy was conducted and the body dissected and embalmed on the afternoon of 17 September, so that relics of the dead King might be forwarded to those churches and convents with which he had, supposedly, been most intimately connected. His heart was to be sent to the Convent of the Visitation of La Chaillot, to reside in a reliquary beside that of his mother in the chapel, while his entrails were divided between the parish church of St Germain and the English College at St Omer, and 'the Braines and Fleshy part of the head' were despatched to the Scots College at Paris, where the Duke of Perth subsequently erected at his own expense 'a fair monument' to the King, consisting of a black marble sarcophagus, mourning cherubim, a trophy of arms, and a bas-relief portrait of James as a classical general. It is notable that the chapel of the monastery of La Trappe, which might have been thought to have been James's natural resting place, was pointedly excluded from this list, though whether out of a desire to confine the King's relics to those religious houses that had particularly strong ties with the exiled English and Scottish clergy, or a conscious decision by both Louis XIV and Mary of Modena to distance the Stuart dynasty from a community increasingly mired in controversy, is not entirely known. In the meantime, the body itself was to be transferred to the Church of the English Benedictines at Paris, but before this could happen and the embalming could take place, an unseemly scrum occurred as servants, courtiers and the King's own guards scrambled to cut souvenirs from the dead man's clothes, bedding, and Garter sash, and fought to dip their prizes into James's blood as it was being drained.[50]

With order restored, and the crowd slinking back into the evening gloom bearing their handfuls of bloodied cloth as though they were already treasured and holy relics, Berwick and Middleton, as chief mourners, prepared to lead the funerary cortège through the night to the gates of Paris. According to custom, his closest family kept away, and out of consideration for the Queen's grief and utter distraction, the procession contrived to start late from the palace and to reach La Chaillot – where she had taken refuge shortly after her husband's death – at midnight, when she might not be expected to be awake and could thus be spared from either seeing or hearing the coffin pass by. Despite the late hour, and the secrecy of their route, the cortège 'was accompanyed with the tears and lamentations not only of his own Subjects but of the people where it passed', who dropped to their knees on its approach, crossing themselves and uttering prayers for the dead King's intercession on their behalf. Even in the streets of Paris, the curious and the devout stumbled from their beds and filled the streets, impeding the passage of the carriages and the progress of Berwick and his out-riders. Reaching the steps of the church of the English Benedictines by torchlight, Dr Ingleton – Mary of Modena's almoner and one of the tutors to 'James III' – handed over the body on behalf of the royal Household to the Prior, Anthony Turberville, who addressed the courtiers, the priests, and the crowds, thanking them for the safe delivery 'of the joyful relics of a most Holy Confessor, perhaps even a Reverend Martyr'. The late King was thus already identified as a possible candidate for beatification, and his life once more explicitly linked with that of Edward 'the Confessor'. The body was not, however, to be interred, but remained above ground in a triple sarcophagus consisting of two wooden coffins and one of lead, in the hope that it might yet, upon a future restoration, be removed to Westminster. Before the lids were nailed down, the monks made a plaster imprint of his newly scrubbed and clean-shaven face – which barely bore the imprint of the stroke that had twisted the right corner of his mouth downwards – so that a series of wax death masks could be cast to keep the sanitised image of the King's serenity, triumphant at last over his earthly corruption, fresh in the minds of both his subjects and those pilgrims who would venture into this and other funerary chapels that were now being raised to immortalise his fame.[51] For forty days, the Benedictine brothers kept a constant vigil beside the sarcophagus, now veiled by a silver pall, but at the end of this official period of mourning, a new set of black draperies embroidered with the arms of England replaced it, together with a silver lamp, a gift from Louis XIV, that blazed constantly before the tomb.[52]

As one of his first public acts, the titular James III wrote to Pope Clement XI and his cardinals, to acquaint them with the circumstances of his father's passing, and to assure them that: 'His last charges to us on his death-bed will, we hope, never be forgotten by us, namely, that we should always prefer the eternal salvation of our soul and the profession of the Roman Catholic faith to all transitory things and to all temporal advantages whatsoever'. A far more hardnosed appreciation of 'the purport of the lecture King James gave his son' was provided by the duchesse d'Orléans who, when writing to the Electress of Hanover, viewed the injunction 'to die rather than change his religion' as a 'sentiment I expect your son [the likely beneficiary of a Protestant succession] will be in hearty accord'. Be that as it may, thanks were also duly delivered to the General of the Jesuits, Tirso Gonzalez, for commanding every member of his Order to pray for the departed soul of James II. Mary of Modena quickly calculated that 'the liberal and prompt application you have made' already equated to some '5,000 masses for [his] repose', forgetting entirely – or perhaps choosing to ignore – her husband's injunction that no prayers should be raised in his honour, and that the money saved thereby should be distributed among the poor. The three convents of the Visitation at Lyons, and the Dean and Chapter of St Martin's Cathedral at Tours, all offered up a series of requiem Masses, while even after the initial waves of public sympathy and interest had begun to subside, the notion that James's sufferings had endowed him with a unique religious insight, and that he might be compared to the sainted royals of the Middle Ages or the warrior kings of the Old Testament, continued to gain ground.[53] At the Irish chapel of St Anne 'the royal' at Bordeaux, on 15/25 November 1701, Dom Pierre de Sainte Catherine delivered a funerary oration for James, comparing him to David, attesting to the fact that St Louis had frequently interceded on his behalf, and styling him as 'a great King, a perfect Christian' and a 'martyr of the truth and religion'. All sense of the humility and self-loathing with which James had come to regard himself was now abandoned, as

Dom Pierre apologised profusely for drawing comparisons between him and Job, for Job had not been a king. However, he declared, the image of Job as the patient man of sufferings, tested yet faithful, spoke to the condition of a powerful prince, laid low through treachery and his unwillingness to compromise his truth. While William III was reviled variously as another Absolom who raised rebellion against his father, or as Julian 'the Apostate' who had sought to re-introduce paganism into the Roman Empire, James was the defender of Christendom, who had attempted to hold together his state despite 'every kind of fury' being hurled 'against this unfortunate isle, Socinians, Anabaptists, Independents, [and] Shakers . . . all the fanatics were combined there . . . To conspire together against the one, the unique religion of Jesus Christ'. After the King's return from Ireland, he thought that his life had been 'a blank' to everything save for God, whom James had consistently adored and begged not to 'spare me in my weakness' but to 'soak your darts in the blood of your servant'.[54]

It was, therefore, no longer imperative for James to have suffered a physical martyrdom at the hands of his foes, for the executioner's block or a stray shot delivered at the height of the battle could be considered lesser ordeals than a living martyrdom, suffered over many years through the ingratitude and scorn of the daughters and subject peoples who had forsaken him. This interpretative pattern spread, as the papal court held a requiem for the King in January 1702, and the church of San Lorenzo in Lucina was swathed in black and hung with shields bearing allegorical scenes illustrating passages from his life, as the Jesuit Charles de Aquino preached before an empty catafalque to an audience which included Mary of Modena, her son, and representatives of the Benedictine Order, on the subject of James's courage, religiosity, and virtue. Not only had the King had the power to heal the body politic but, it was suggested, he might also have had the ability to draw the malice out of individual souls and to heal the sick. The Bishop of Autun was to go even further in attempting 'to expose to your eyes a truly Christian hero', and shortly after the first anniversary of James's death, on 19 September 1702 (N.S.), with the Archbishop of Paris officiating at a requiem service at the Convent of La Chaillot, he spoke of those Christ-like virtues of faith, gentleness and constancy that he saw reborn in James, and of the King's sufferings for the honour of God exactly mirroring those of their Saviour. His sacrifice was made 'to the sacrifice of Jesus Christ', for having been able 'no longer to retain in his heart the captive truth' of Roman Catholicism, he had ventured everything against 'the genius of the nation [i.e. England], naturally proud and independent', in his 'burning sincere zeal for the conversion of his blind subjects'. Though this had resulted in revolution and the loss of his throne, James had still respected the judgement of God and held firm to his course, rejecting 'Love, in separating us from that which we hold dear, [and] hatred uniting in us against that which we find most odious'. While this might have been an effort for others, the Bishop thought this 'did not cost anything to the holy King. He forgave without sorrow in his life, [and] he forgave with pleasure at his death'. He was, therefore, to be ranked among 'the Joshuas, the Constantines, the Theodosius's and so many other sovereigns in whom the love of their religion prevailed over their human interests', but he also exuded 'the ardour of the early Christians . . . the zeal of the priests of the primitive church' in the same manner as Pope Leo or Gregory the Great. 'Wise and fortunate, great and modest', James could be compared, once again, to King David consoled by the tranquillity of his death and blessing, even at the last 'the God of Israel, who had saved his crown and put his son to the test'. Yet, the bishop wished to take these religious parallels even further, into far more controversial territory, and to equate James's end directly with the passion of Christ. The King had, he claimed, in death achieved 'the sacrifice of the lamb without struggle' and purified 'fully the heart already pure, so holy, so penitent, [and] so detatched', being led willingly to the sacrifice and place of slaughter at 'the very same hour as you [i.e. Jesus] breathed your last on the cross' and having conferred upon him 'this last sign of conformity in perfection, in the sainted King, your death as your life'. However, while: 'It is God who motivated the efforts for the canonisation of the King of England, [as] he had [already] purified him in the fire of tribulation as we purify Gold in the furnace', it was the duty of all active Christians – and by extension both Louis XIV and Clement XI – to work to ensure that 'the King will have at his end a Eulogy worthy of him' and a 'pastoral benediction'.[55]

Royal favour was indeed forthcoming, with madame de Maintenon, the duchesse de Bourgogne and the princesse de Condé all visiting the King's tomb, at the church of the English Benedictines in the Rue de Saint-Jacques, over the course of 1702. However, it was Mary of Modena who had initially advanced the cause of her husband's sanctity, informing the Abbess of La Chaillot in the hours immediately after his death that: 'we now have a great saint in Heaven', and single-mindedly orchestrating a campaign to achieve his beatification, together with the Bishop of Autun, the Duke of Mazarin and, to a lesser extent, the Archbishop of Paris and the Cardinal de Bouillon. First of all, the Queen needed to remove from the King's devotional legacy any doctrinal traits of which she did not wholly approve. Consequently, James's attachment to La Trappe was downplayed, ongoing contact with the monastery was discontinued, and the reverence of the Sacred Heart – which was a motif of her own piety, having never figured strongly in the King's – was emphasised. It was, therefore, this combination of élite stimulus, heavyweight patronage, and a somewhat partial view of the King's theological practices (which expurgated his

association with the Jansenists altogether), that enabled the cult of
'St James' to flourish in its devotional centres at Paris, St Germain and
St Omer, and to spread rapidly to the south and east of France through
the influence of the convents of the Visitation. Whether or not there was
a parallel development of a truly popular and spontaneous tradition
concerning the King's piety and miracle working is far more difficult to
discern. The English Benedictines and the Daughters of the Visitation
who sought to gather evidence in order to prove the veracity of the cures
attributed to James's intercession were far more concerned with obtaining
depositions from the wealthy, the influential, and the articulate, whose
testaments could not be so readily discounted, rather than from the poor,
the outcast, and the illiterate, whose claims might be dismissed as mere
superstition or found to be overlaid with elements drawn from pre-
existing folk tales. Therefore, while the peasants who worked the fields
about St Germain may have continued to venerate the person of King
James, and to pray for his intercession to cure their ailments, the
surviving records tend to suggest that the stories concerning his sanctity
were disseminated from the top down, and that his devotion was most
actively practised by the Jacobite community in exile, members of the
French court and the Parisian bourgeoisie who had had direct contact
with the King towards the end of his life, and the monks and nuns from
those religious communities that he – and just as significantly, Mary of
Modena – had chosen to patronise throughout the course of their
last exile.[56]

The first recorded cure attributed to the King's miraculous powers
supposedly occurred ten days after his death when, in the course of
saying a Mass at the convent of La Chaillot for the repose of James's soul,
the Bishop of Autun was cured of a fistula in his eye which had occluded
his vision for many years. Further cures were soon reported, as the
'intercession of the King of England' was said to have healed the palsies
in both legs of Gilbert Marais, a surgeon from the Auvergne; prevented
Passart de la Rotte, the King's counsellor in the supreme court at Metz,
from retaining urine; cured Catherine Dupré of deafness, and the wife of
the Duke of Saxe-Gotha's dancing master of rheumatism, while she was at
Paris. In the case of Philip Pitel, a Benedictine monk from the diocese of
Tours, who had been seized with a cough and a swollen throat in
December 1701, God was beseeched 'to cure me, and to grant me health,
through the merits and intercession of King James'. If his prayers were
granted, he swore on his sick-bed 'to have a mass said, as a thanksgiving,
in the Benedictine church, where his corpse lays, and to touch the mort-
cloth, which covers it, with my tongue', whereupon he fell into a profuse
sweat, which quickly passed and left him completely recovered. By June
1702, enough cases had been reported for Cardinal Noailles, the
Archbishop of Paris, to authorise a commission 'to examine the truth of

the miracles of the King . . . to serve his canonisation', and nineteen examples of the healings of French men and women of everything from paralysis and swellings to cancer and convulsions were quickly gathered in.[57] Unfortunately for James's prospects of sainthood, by the early eighteenth century the process towards beatification was both extremely rigorous and very slow. Since 1634, when Urban VIII had reserved the right to canonise to the pontiff alone, the power to create saints had largely been removed from the influence and interest of temporal sovereigns and national Churches. As the papacy fought to retain its independence, it had little interest in creating hostages to fortune by bestowing the seal of divine favour on the representatives of particular dynasties, and raising up princes whose heirs might one day turn against it, or use their new-found spiritual authority to force their own candidate onto the throne of St Peter. As the system became bureaucratised, and unofficial cults were suppressed or quietly allowed to lapse, a fifty-year rule was introduced, whereby evidence might be gathered and the durability of the candidate's reputation assessed. With only fifty-five individuals canonised between 1588 and 1767, and no saints created at all between 1629 and 1658, the chances for James's cult to take hold were slight in the extreme. Although Sister Dumanoir, an Ursuline nun at Bourg-Saint-Andeol, could still write to the Sorbonne in May 1703 (N.S.) alleging that 'a little piece of linen soaked in the blood of the most blessed king James' had cured her sickness, and the Benedictine Brother Hugh Weldon continued to compile his papers for a biography of the late King in order to testify to his holiness, the initial excitement that had accompanied the first reports of healings was quickly allowed to dissipate.[58] Mary of Modena lacked the financial resources to maintain the momentum for lobbying effectively at Rome and, madame de Maintenon excepted, the court of France was at best lukewarm about the prospect of saying masses to 'St James of England'; at worst, those who had known him as a promiscuous youth or as a garrulous old man were downright sceptical. However, while the duchesse d'Orléans scoffed in November 1701 (N.S.) that though: 'I am sure that King James is in Heaven now. The Parisians go farther and imagine that he can work miracles, but my faith does not go as far as that', Louis XIV would soon have good reason to be wary of inflating the reputations of princely dynasties which might threaten to eclipse his own.[59]

Ever since James had first served as an aide-de-camp to Marshal Turenne there had been a link between the houses of Stuart and Bouillon, and this was only strengthened over time as James attempted to bask in the reflected glory of his idol, and to show his appreciation for his favour by promoting junior members of his family in the royal service on his return to England. Unfortunately, the dignity of a royal pedigree and his position as a prince of the Church had not made the Cardinal de

Bouillon an easy or comfortable subject of Louis XIV's centralising state. Given the task of obtaining from Innocent XII a condemnation of the Quietist movement – with which de Bouillon was known to have sympathised – and a thorough refutation of Fénelon's *Explication des Maximes des Saints*, the Cardinal refused, and consistently championed both movement and book, until finally compelled to return to France to make his peace after Louis XIV had deprived him of his office as Grand Almoner and ordered the confiscation of all his property. After such a public humiliation, it was not to be expected that this great churchman, who Berwick considered 'the proudest man in the world . . . who plumed himself still more on his birth than on his dignity', would be reconciled to the Crown for long, and during the War of the Spanish Succession a cache of his correspondence with the Duke of Marlborough was discovered by the King's spies, and he was forced to flee into exile. In July 1710, a warrant was delivered to the monks of St Denis: 'commanding them to remove the arms of the family of Bouillon which were on the altar, in the [stained glass] windows, and on the roof of the chapel where M. de Turenne is interred. In this letter there is a high eulogy of the late M. de Turenne, but the King disapproves of the monks having permitted the arms of the family of Bouillon to be placed in the chapel; even those of the Cardinal de Bouillon, with the hat [signifying his office], were in the windows, and the King sends de Coste to efface the towers [which comprised the arms of the Bouillon family] which were painted with the fleur-de-lys'. The signal was clear enough; henceforth the abbey was to be devoted to one dynasty, that of the Bourbon kings of France and their ancestors, and there was little room to spare in which rival symbolisms and forms of devotion might be permitted to flourish. The monastery at Cluny, where he had served as Abbot and where the Cardinal had intended to be buried and to memorialise the rest of his family, was forbidden to inter any of them in the future, while a book containing the genealogy of his House was banned. Its author, monsieur Baluse, was prohibited from coming within 40 leagues of Paris and removed from his professorial chair. Amid the chaos of his dramatic fall from power, the Cardinal believed that the set of military memoirs presented to him by James almost fifteen years before had either been lost, or seized by the government. As a result, the conscious propagandising of the friendship and mutual dependence of James and Marshal Turenne suddenly fell under suspicion, while the 'precious gift' of the manuscript, 'which I believed I should never see again', was not returned to the Cardinal until shortly before his death in 1715, when 'an act of Divine Providence' restored it to his possession.[60]

In a similar fashion, the glut of laudatory accounts of the King's life, rushed off the presses and smuggled into England to satisfy a reawakened interest in his deeds in the months after his death, failed to be immediately capitalised on by more substantial and more effectively polemical works. The edited collection of Fr Sanders' notes on his life, stressing his attachment to Roman Catholicism and the sanctity of his last hours, might have fitted well with the devotional climate on the Continent, but succeeded only in reinforcing a simple equation of Jacobitism with popery among James's many opponents, and in simply recapitulating the already well-known list of his virtues for his friends. While the bulk of the King's own memoirs remained under lock and key at the Scots College, for reasons of State and the security of informants named, substantial portions of the earlier passages were presented for publication, and quickly began to establish a familiar image of the young James as an active soldier, naval administrator, and colonist.[61] Unfortunately, while curiosity about the manner of the King's death and a residual sense of loyalism had created a market for pamphlets and broadsides retelling the events of his last hours, those popular devotional works in both poetry and prose that were intended to champion James's sanctity were singularly bereft of the ability to either persuade or entertain. Though Weldon was not even able to secure a publisher for his lengthy panegyrics, elsewhere the King was once again presented as a Job, or as a new King David 'most sad and unkind in his Stars', who 'had his Cross on Earth, as well his Crown / Mislead by Friends, imposed upon by Foes'. One anonymous Jacobite lady attempted to write an epic poem, in the manner of Dante's *Inferno* or Milton's *Paradise Lost*, from the perspective of the 'Long-declining, Saint-like Monarch', who stood: 'Upon the Borders of Eternity' watching in anguish as that: 'Ungovern'd Ship' of the English state 'which now no course can keep / Is Dash'd upon the Rocks, or swallow'd in the Deep'. James was shown to have received his reward in paradise: 'thrice happy was thy Fate / To change a Worldly for a Heavenly State' as the result of his endeavours to destroy the 'pregnant Hydra' of rebellion and to maintain his faith. While William III would be condemned to eternal damnation as the result of having expelled 'God's Anointed from their Thrones', victory had already been assured for James's party, with his son living and reigning after him, on account of his decision to allow the boy to be raised as a good Catholic, and to be nurtured by his widow and Louis XIV.[62] Such sanguine pronouncements were, however, completely out of kilter with the fears and preoccupations of the great majority of James's former subjects, as the state tottered on the brink of a new European war that had been hastened in part by Louis XIV's decision to recognise James Francis Edward as the rightful King of England.

Though he had also been recognised by the kingdom of Spain, the duchies of Savoy and Modena, and by the Papal See as the *de jure* King, the reception accorded to the news of the 'succession' of 'James III' in London was anything but hopeful. Two of his supporters had dressed themselves as royal heralds and had ridden through the streets proclaiming his sovereignty, but they were soon cornered by the crowds that had come to jeer at them, and were pulled from their horses, rolled in the dirt, and had their tabards stripped from their backs. Copies of a new manifesto, dated 3 March 1702 (N.S.), were quickly smuggled into the country and widely distributed, arguing for the boy's claim and promising, alongside toleration for Catholics and Protestant Dissenters, certain safeguards for Anglicanism. However, the generous spirit of its conditions were seen to be undermined by the behaviour of Lord Middleton, which aptly demonstrated the gulf that now separated the court culture of St Germain and the dictates of the cult of King James II from the religious and cultural sensibilities of the greater part of the English nation. Since the death of his master, Middleton – who had never enjoyed the complete trust of the Queen – had been an increasingly beleaguered figure, and had sought to hang on to his offices by a sudden and, to the mind of many, entirely unconvincing display of piety. Claiming that James's dying instructions had set him thinking more deeply about the state of his soul, he explained that, while stricken down with a fever several weeks after the King's death, he had awoken suddenly to find his ghost looming over his bed, imploring him to remember his words and not to delay in his conversion to Catholicism. While conforming to the already established formulas for recounting the King's miraculous appearances, and succeeding in its primary object of returning its author triumphantly to office, the story failed to convince many of those at St Germain and provided further evidence, in the eyes of his movement's detractors, of the intolerance of the exiled court, where no Protestant – even one so illustrious as Middleton – could survive for long without being either expelled, or compelled to submit to a forced conversion.[63] Worse was at hand, as the Westminster Parliament had already rushed to pass a Bill for the attainder of 'the pretended Prince of Wales, and Mary, his pretended mother', and London led a series of English cities in raising fresh addresses of loyalty to William III, evoking memories of the responses to the assassination plot of 1696. It became treason, in February 1702, to correspond with James Francis Edward, or to send him any funds, and the boy could be executed without trial if he ever set foot in the lands that he claimed to own. At the same time, Mary of Modena had spurned an overture from Lord Belhaven, who had offered to raise Scotland for her and her son if she would seek to limit the number of Catholic priests admitted to the country after the Restoration. However, even though James Francis Edward was expressly not being asked to abjure his religion, any suggestion of a compromise over matters of faith, or any attempt to move away from the model of kingship that had been established in such rigid terms by his father, was henceforth to be dismissed out of hand.[64]

Unfortunately, if James II's legacy appeared to be singularly ill-equipped for transmission to a British setting, where so much of its religious and political imagery appeared wholly alien, or else to be couched in extremely arcane terms, then it was no more suited to survival in the increasingly rigid pattern of European devotion. Faced by papal indifference and the failure of the cult to spread far beyond its original geographic centres, Cardinal Gualterio wrote to the Queen's secretary in January 1718 that 'it is impossible to make any use for the present [of] those [documents] relating to the miracles, because these are the last in order of discussion [with the Pope] . . . and must be preceded by many other processes [for beatification] which are exceedingly lengthy, and in which many years are usually employed, between the first introduction of the cause and their examination. That which can be done at present is to keep an account of all that concerns such miracles, and to follow the usual course . . . which requires the utmost attention and diligence'. The problem was that by this point the supply of miracles, real or imagined, had all but dried up, and the original healing of the Bishop of Autun had long been the subject of ridicule, as it was alleged at Versailles that a few days after the 'curing' the fistula had reappeared in the clergyman's eye and he had been forced to rush back to his diocese to escape the embarrassment.[65] Few priests or petitioners now embarked on pilgrimages to visit the 'holy' relics of the King, and even the remnants of his court had been scattered in 1713 at the close of the War of the Spanish Succession, under the terms of the Treaty of Utrecht. The conflict that James II had longed for, and invested so many of his latter hopes in, had done no more than to occasion further bloodshed and want, and to send his son away to the remote exile which he himself had dreaded, first to Avignon and later to Rome. The candles that had once burned brightly in the grille before his tomb at the English Benedictines had been allowed to flicker out; tourists rather than pilgrims now made their way to his shrine, and in 1728 the chapel had been robbed, with an unknown hand stealing the silver lamp that had been Louis XIV's gift. The Duke of Berwick, who had evidently not visited the place for several years, was horrified by the news and determined to replace everything that had been either lost or damaged. The war had carried him into Spain and Portugal, and at Almansa he had decisively broken an Allied army and placed the Spanish crown back upon Philip V's head. However, he had done it as a subject of the King of France, and not as the counsellor of the exiled King of England. Lighting after the military career that he had always desired, he had become a naturalised Frenchman at the close of 1703, in order to increase his chances of a command. For those like John Caryll, who cared to remember and dwelt long upon the events of the past, it might have seemed a strange reversal of circumstances, for barely two years before, Henry Fitzjames's young bride had had to take English nationality as a pre-condition to King James's blessing of the match. Yet, Berwick appears to have abandoned hopes for the restoration of his half-brother early on, and the two had rowed bitterly over the conduct of the Jacobite risings of 1715, with the Duke rejecting the offer of the rank of Captain-General for Scotland. The rift had been imperfectly healed and it was probably for this reason that the old soldier decided to make his donations to the Church of the English Benedictines anonymously. Following the death of his friend Philippe of Orléans, the Regent of France, he had lost all his army commands and 'retired from affairs, and in the state of idleness to which he was reduced' spent his hours shuttling between the court, his lodgings in Paris, and his country retreat, maintaining a small circle of friends, going for long walks, and reading.[66] It was in these circumstances that he visited the funerary chapel again, after his servants had delivered a new set of plate to the Abbot, and seen to it that the canopies that shrouded his father's coffin were repaired and properly dusted off. If any of the Parisians or the small community of Jacobite exiles who worshiped there had cause to notice the presence of the simply dressed stranger at the back of the church, they did not think to note or to comment on it, though it is likely that the Duke lit a candle to his father's memory before heading back out into daylight and clambering down the steps to the waiting carriage, with only the slightest of difficulties that betrayed his advancing years. As the church door swung to behind him, all that now remained inside was silence and shadow.

Genealogical Tables

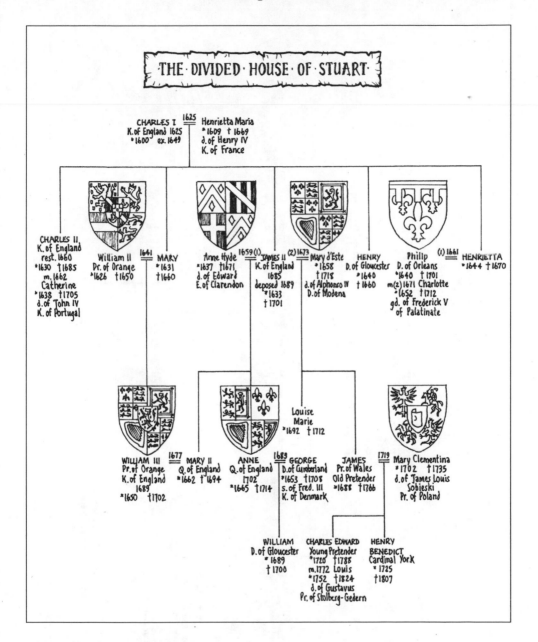

THE·DIVIDED·HOUSE·OF·STUART

CHARLES I —1625— Henrietta Maria
K. of England 1625 *1609 †1669
*1600 ex. 1649 d. of Henry IV
K. of France

CHARLES II
K. of England
rest. 1660   William II —1641— MARY
*1630 †1685   Pr. of Orange   *1631
m. 1662   *1626 †1650   †1660
Catherine
*1638 †1705
d. of John IV
K. of Portugal

Anne Hyde —1659(1)— JAMES II —(2) 1673— Mary d'Este   HENRY   Philip —(1) 1661— HENRIETTA
*1637 †1671   K. of England   *1658   D. of Gloucester   D. of Orleans   *1644 †1670
d. of Edward 1685   †1718   *1640   *1640 †1701
E. of Clarendon deposed 1689   d. of Alphonso IV †1660   m(2) 1671 Charlotte
              *1633   D. of Modena   *1652 †1712
              †1701   gd. of Frederick V
                                                              of Palatinate

Louise
Marie
*1692 †1712

WILLIAM III —1677— MARY II   ANNE —1683— GEORGE   JAMES   —1719— Mary Clementina
Pr. of Orange   Q. of England Q. of England D. of Cumberland Pr. of Wales   *1702 †1735
K. of England   *1662 †1694   1702   *1653 †1708   Old Pretender   d. of James Louis
1689   *1665 †1714   s. of Fred. III *1688 †1766   Sobieski
*1650 †1702   K. of Denmark   Pr. of Poland

WILLIAM   CHARLES EDWARD   HENRY
D. of Gloucester Young Pretender   BENEDICT
*1689   *1720 †1788   Cardinal York
†1700   m.1772 Louis   *1725
              *1752 †1824   †1807
              d. of Gustavus
              Pr. of Stolberg-Gedern

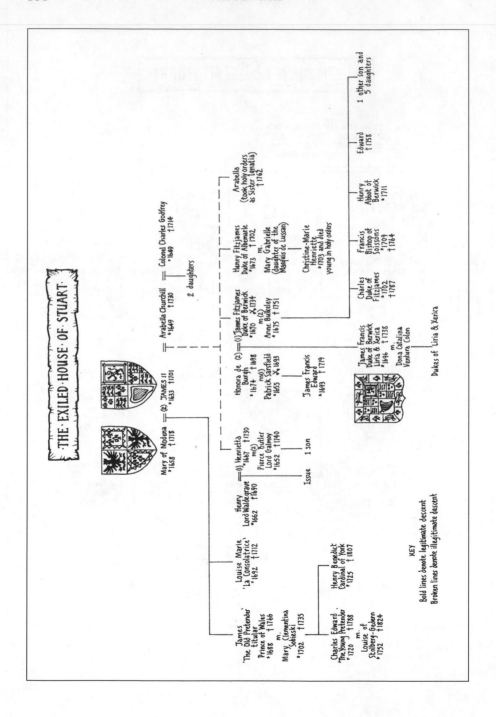

THE·EXILED·HOUSE·OF·STUART·

KEY

Bold lines denote legitimate descent
Broken lines denote illegitimate descent

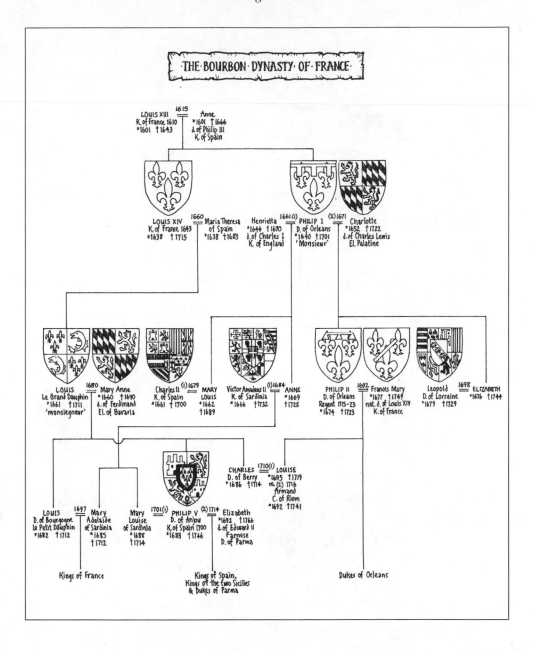

THE·BOURBON·DYNASTY·OF·FRANCE

LOUIS XIII — 1615 — Anne
K. of France 1610 — *1601 †1666
*1601 †1643 — d. of Philip III
K. of Spain

LOUIS XIV — 1660 — Maria Theresa
K. of France 1643 — of Spain
*1638 †1715 — *1638 †1683

Henrietta — 1661(1) — PHILIP I — (2)1671 — Charlotte
*1644 †1670 — D. of Orleans — *1652 †1722
d. of Charles I — *1640 †1701 — d. of Charles Lewis
K. of England — 'Monsieur' — El. Palatine

LOUIS — 1680 — Mary Anne
Le Grand Dauphin — *1660 †1690
*1661 †1711 — d. of Ferdinand
'monsiegneur' — El. of Bavaria

Charles II — (1)1679 — MARY
K. of Spain — LOUIS
*1661 †1700 — *1662
— †1689

Victor Amadeus II — (1)1684 — ANNE
K. of Sardinia — *1669
*1666 †1732 — †1728

PHILIP II — 1692 — Frances Mary
D. of Orleans — *1677 †1749
Regent 1715-23 — nat. d. of Louis XIV
*1674 †1723 — K. of France

Leopold — 1698 — ELIZABETH
D. of Lorraine — *1676 †1744
*1679 †1729

CHARLES — 1710(1) — LOUISE
D. of Berry — *1695 †1719
*1686 †1714 — m. (2) 1716
— Armand
— C. of Riom
— *1692 †1741

LOUIS — 1697 — Mary
D. of Bourgogne — Adelaide
Le Petit Dauphin — of Sardinia
*1682 †1712 — *1685
— †1712

Mary
Louise
of Sardinia
*1688
†1714

1701(1) — PHILIP V — (2)1714 — Elizabeth
D. of Anjou — *1692 †1766
K. of Spain 1700 — d. of Edward II
*1683 †1746 — Farnese
— D. of Parma

Kings of France

Kings of Spain,
Kings of the two Sicilies
& Dukes of Parma

Dukes of Orleans

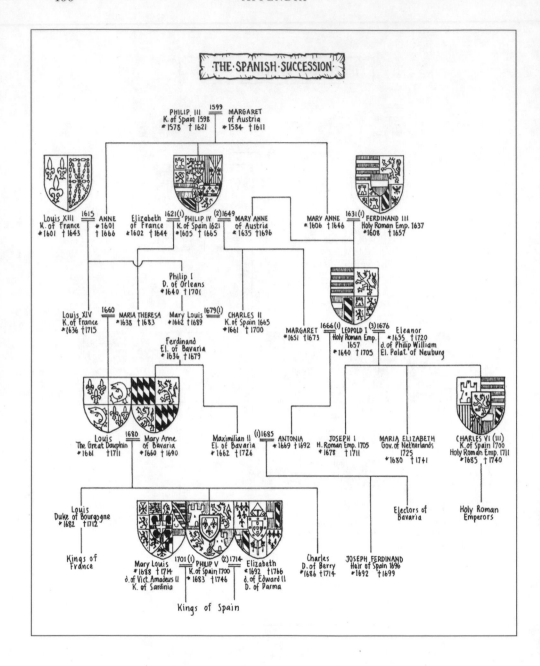

THE·SPANISH·SUCCESSION

PHILIP. III
K. of Spain 1598
✶1578 † 1621
— 1599 —
MARGARET
of Austria
✶1584 † 1611

Louis XIII
K. of France
✶1601 † 1643
— 1615 —
ANNE
✶1601
† 1666

Elizabeth
of France
✶1602 † 1644
— 1621 (1) — PHILIP IV
K. of Spain 1621
✶1605 † 1665
(2) 1649 —
MARY ANNE
of Austria
✶1635 † 1696

MARY ANNE
✶1606 † 1646

— 1631 (1) — FERDINAND III
Holy Roman Emp. 1637
✶1608 † 1657

Philip I
D. of Orleans
✶1640 † 1701

Louis XIV
K. of France
✶1636 † 1715
— 1660 —
MARIA THERESA
✶1638 † 1683

Mary Louis
✶1662 † 1689
— 1679 (1) —
CHARLES II
K. of Spain 1665
✶1661 † 1700

MARGARET
✶1651 † 1673
— 1666 (1) —
LEOPOLD I
Holy Roman Emp.
1657
✶1640 † 1705
(3) 1676 —
Eleanor
✶1655 † 1720
d. of Philip William
El. Palat. of Neuburg

Ferdinand
El. of Bavaria
✶1636 † 1679

Louis
The Great Dauphin
✶1661 † 1711
— 1680 —
Mary Anne
of Bavaria
✶1660 † 1690

Maximilian II
El. of Bavaria
✶1662 † 1726
— (1) 1685 —
ANTONIA
✶1669 † 1692

JOSEPH I
H. Roman Emp. 1705
✶1678 † 1711

MARIA ELIZABETH
Gov. of Netherlands
1725
✶1680 † 1741

CHARLES VI (III)
K. of Spain 1700
Holy Roman Emp. 1711
✶1685 † 1740

Louis
Duke of Bourgogne
✶1682 † 1712

Kings of
France

Mary Louis
✶1688 † 1714
d. of Vict. Amadeus II
K. of Sardinia
— 1701 (1) —
PHILIP V
K. of Spain 1700
✶1683 † 1746
(2) 1714 —
Elizabeth
✶1692 † 1766
d. of Edward II
D. of Parma

Kings of Spain

Charles
D. of Berry
✶1686 † 1714

JOSEPH FERDINAND
Heir of Spain 1696
✶1692 † 1699

Electors of
Bavaria

Holy Roman
Emperors

Notes

CHAPTER ONE: REVOLUTION

1. C. de Cavelli (ed.), *Les Derniers Stuarts à Saint-Germain-en-Laye* (Paris, London, & Edinburgh, 1871), Vol. II, p. 440; Anon., *The Life of William III, Late King of England and Prince of Orange* (London, 1703), p. 160; *Ailesbury*, Vol. I, p. 216; J. Dalrymple, *Memoirs of Great Britain and Ireland* (Edinburgh, 1771), Vol. I, Part I, p. 182; M. Haile, *Queen Mary of Modena* (London & New York, 1905), p. 224; & P. Rapin de Thoyras, *The History of England*, trans. N. Tindal, 2nd edn (London, 1733), Vol. II, p. 782; BL. Add. MS. 10118 f.196; BL. Add. MS. 36296 f.10; E. Bohun (pub. anon.), *The History of the Desertion* (London, 1689), pp. 101 & 103; *Evelyn's Diary*, Vol. II, p. 286; *Life*, Vol. II, pp. 264–5; & RA / M3 ff.693–4.

2. *Burnet*, Vol. III, Book IV, p. 797; *Evelyn's Diary*, Vol. II, pp. 285–7 & Vol. III, p. 299; A. Browning (ed.), *Memoirs of Sir John Reresby*, 2nd edn, preface by M.K. Geiter & W.A. Speck (London, 1991), p. 537; Dalrymple, *Memoirs*, Vol. I, p. 184; *Dangeau*, Vol. I, pp. 138–9; K.M. Chacksfield, *Glorious Revolution, 1688* (Wincanton, Somerset, 1988), pp. 112–15; *Hyde Correspondence*, Vol. II, p. 228; Cavelli (ed.), *Les Derniers Stuarts*, Vol. II, pp. 361, 363, 367, 373, 433–4; A. Evans, 'Yorkshire and the Revolution of 1688', *Yorkshire Archaeological Journal*, Vol. XXIX (1929), pp. 264–78; S. Wilton Rix (ed.), *The Diary and Autobiography of Edmund Bohun* (Beccles, 1853), p. 81; BL. Add. MS. 828 ff.11–12; BL. Add. MS. 36296 f.7; BL. Add. MS. 36707 ff.42, 49 & 51; & BL. Harleian MS. 6852 ff.402–3.

3. It is just possible that this prized relic was later returned to him, and that it was the cross discovered in the tomb of St Edward the Confessor just before James's coronation in April 1685. During his imprisonment at Faversham, the King seems to have been as concerned with its financial worth as he was with its spiritual and historical associations. See: BL. Harleian MS. 6852 f.403; Haile, *Queen Mary of Modena*, p. 520, & M. Hopkirk, *The Queen over the Water* (London, 1953), p. 162.

4. Anon., *An Address to the Lyon in the Tower* (London, 1689), p. 1; Bohun, *History of the Desertion*, p. 98; BL. Add. MS. 36707 f.52; Cavelli (ed.), *Les Derniers Stuarts*, Vol. II, pp. 417, 421 & 425; *Burnet*, Vol. III, Book IV, p. 797; P.J. Helm, *Jeffreys* (London, 1966), p. 177; R. Beddard (ed.), *A Kingdom Without a King. The Journal of the Provisional Government in the Revolution of 1688* (Oxford, 1988), pp. 175–6; Browning (ed.), *Memoirs of Sir John Reresby*, pp. 537–8; & H.W. Woolrych, *Memoirs of the Life of Judge Jeffreys* (London, 1827), pp. 305–6 & 362–3.

5. Historical Manuscripts Commission, *Twelfth Report, Appendix, Part VII. The Manuscripts of S.H. le Fleming Esq. of Rydal Hall* (London, 1890), p. 229; Bohun, *History of the Desertion*, p. 99; Cavelli (ed.), *Les Derniers Stuarts*, Vol. II, pp. 430 & 435–7; A. Hewitson (ed.), *Diary of Thomas Bellingham, an Officer under William III* (Preston, 1908), p. 37; R. Beddard (ed.), *A Kingdom Without a King*, p. 177; J. Childs, *The Army, James II and the Glorious Revolution* (Manchester, 1980), pp. 195–7; G.H. Jones, 'The Irish Fright of 1688: Real Violence and

Imagined Massacre', *Bulletin of the Institute of Historical Research*, Vol. LV (1983), pp. 148–53; P. Melvin, 'Irish Troop Movements and James II's Army in 1688', *The Irish Sword*, Vol. X (1982), p. 100; N. Luttrell, *A Brief Historical Relation of State Affairs* (Oxford, 1857), Vol. I, p. 490; BL. Add. MS. 36296 f.8; BL. Add. MS. 36707 f.49; & *CSPD* (1687–9), p. 380.

6.   *Life*, Vol. II, p. 262; & Bohun, *History of the Desertion*, p. 100.

7.   *Berwick*, Vol. I, p. 34; *Life*, Vol. II, p. 262; & *Ailesbury*, Vol. I, p. 214.

8.   *Evelyn's Diary*, Vol. II, pp. 285–6; Childs, *The Army, James II and the Glorious Revolution*, pp. 195–6; J. Childs, *The British Army of William III, 1689–1702* (Manchester, 1987), pp. 4 & 77; J.R. Jones, *The Revolution of 1688 in England* (London, 1972, rpt. 1988), p. 309; H. & B. van der Zee, *William and Mary* (London & Basingstoke, 1973), pp. 262–3; *Burnet*, Vol. III, Book IV, pp. 799–800; & BL. Add. MS. 36707 f.48.

9.   C. Hill, 'History and the Present', *65th Conway Memorial Lecture* (St Albans, 1989), p. 21; Cavelli (ed.), *Les Derniers Stuarts*, Vol. II, p. 436; *Ailesbury*, Vol. I, p. 215; *Hyde Correspondence*, Vol. II, p. 229; R. West, *The Life and Strange, Surprising Adventures of Daniel Defoe* (London, 1997), p. 41; R. Beddard, 'The Guildhall Declaration of 11 December 1688 and the Counter-Revolution of the Loyalists', *The Historical Journal*, Vol. XI, no. 3 (1968), pp. 404, 411 & 417–20; & J. Carswell, *The Old Cause* (London, 1954), pp. 64–6, 353 & 357.

10. Childs, *The Army, James II and the Glorious Revolution*, p. 193; J. Mackintosh, *History of the Revolution in England in 1688* (London, 1834), p. 552; *Ailesbury*, Vol. I, pp. 213–16; J. Mackay, *Catherine of Braganza* (London, 1937), p. 273; Bohun, *History of the Desertion*, p. 101; R.G. Howarth (ed.), *Letters and the Second Diary of Samuel Pepys* (London, Toronto, & New York, 1932),

pp. 198–9; R. Ollard, *Pepys. A Biography* (London, 1974), pp. 307–8; A. Bryant, *Samuel Pepys. The Saviour of the Navy* (London, 1938, rpt. 1949), p. 346; Cavelli (ed.), *Les Derniers Stuarts*, Vol. II, p. 438; *Evelyn's Diary*, Vol. II, p. 286 & Vol. III, p. 288; *Burnet*, Vol. III, Book IV, pp. 799–800; & *Hyde Correspondence*, Vol. II, p. 226.

11. Bohun, *History of the Desertion*, pp. 102–3; *Evelyn's Diary*, Vol. II, p. 286 & Vol. III, p. 288; Cavelli (ed.), *Les Derniers Stuarts*, Vol. II, p. 438; & *Ailesbury*, Vol. II, p. 215.

12. Though Hopkins is right in doubting that James held a conference with Claverhouse at Rochester, sanctioning a rising in Scotland, it seems likely that the King did command both of the lords to watch over his affairs in Scotland. This, however, was an informal injunction. See: Lord Lindsay, *Lives of the Lindsays* (Wigan, 1840), Vol. II, pp. 161–2; C.S. Terry, *John Graham of Claverhouse* (London, 1905), pp. 242–3; A.H. Tayler, *John Graham of Claverhouse* (London, 1939), pp. 207–8; M. Barrington, *Grahame of Claverhouse, Viscount Dundee, 1648–1689* (London, 1911), p. 197; D. Middleton, *The Life of Charles, 2nd Earl of Middleton* (London, 1957), pp. 126–7; & P. Hopkins, *Glencoe and the End of the Highland War* (Edinburgh, 1998), pp. 122 & 162.

13. *Ailesbury*, Vol. I, p. 216; F.W. Hamilton, *The Origin and History of the First, or Grenadier Guards* (London, 1874), Vol. I, pp. 315–6 & 318; Rapin de Thoyras, *History of England*, Vol. II, p. 782; Bohun, *History of the Desertion*, p. 103; RA/M3 f.695; Luttrell, *Brief Relation*, Vol. I p. 487; Mackintosh, *History of the Revolution*, pp. 552–3; Melvin, 'Irish Troop Movements', pp. 100–2; A. Fitzroy, *Henry, Duke of Grafton, 1663–1690* (London, 1921), p. 68; & BL. Add. MS. 36707 f.51.

14. Rapin de Thoyras, *History of England*, Vol. II, p. 782; RA / M3 ff.694–5; *Burnet*, Vol. III, Book IV, p. 801; *Ailesbury*, Vol. I, p. 216; Cavelli (ed.), *Les Derniers Stuarts*, Vol. II, pp. 440–1;

Anon., *Life of William III*, p. 160; & *Hyde Correspondence*, Vol. II, p. 230.

15. *Life*, Vol. II, p. 265; & RA / M3 f.695.

16. *Ailesbury*, Vol. I, p. 217; *Berwick*, Vol. I, p. 34; *Evelyn's Diary*, Vol. II, p. 286 & Vol. III, p. 289; Bohun, *History of the Desertion*, p. 103; Cavelli (ed.), *Les Derniers Stuarts*, Vol. II, p. 441; *Burnet*, Vol. III, Book IV, p. 801; & Anon., *Life of William III*, p. 160.

17. *Ailesbury*, Vol. I, p. 217; *Life*, Vol. II, p. 266; Anon., *Life of William III*, p. 160; BL. Add. MS. 10118 f.196, & *Evelyn's Diary*, Vol. III, p. 288; *Hyde Correspondence*, Vol. II, p. 229; Bohun, *History of the Desertion*, p. 104; Browning (ed.), *Memoirs of Sir John Reresby*, p. 540; *Burnet*, Vol. III, Book IV, p. 801; Rapin de Thoyras, *History of England*, Vol. II, p. 782; Cavelli (ed.), *Les Derniers Stuarts*, Vol. II, p. 441; & RA / M3 ff.696–8.

18. *Evelyn's Diary*, Vol. II, p. 286 & Vol. III, p. 289; *CSPD* (1687–9), p. 381; *Life*, Vol. II, p. 267; Bohun, *History of the Desertion*, p. 104; Browning (ed.), *Memoirs of Sir John Reresby*, p. 541; RA / M3 ff.699–701; *Burnet*, Vol. III, Book IV, pp. 801–2; H. Belloc, *James the Second*, 2nd edn (London, 1928), pp. 230–1; Middleton, *Life of Charles, 2nd Earl of Middleton*, p. 126; *Hyde Correspondence*, Vol. II, p. 229; Luttrell, *Brief Relation*, Vol. I, p. 489; Anon., *Life of William III*, p. 161; & *Ailesbury*, Vol. I, p. 218.

19. Head was MP for the city in 1667 and March 1679, an Alderman, and the Mayor in 1683. Though identified as one of Shaftesbury's supporters and an informant during the Popish Plot, he seems to have treated the King with all due respect during his stay in Rochester. His former home subsequently became known as 'Abdication House', before being split between a private dwelling and a branch of the Capital and Counties Bank at the close of the nineteenth century. After subsequent mergers, it is now a branch of the Lloyds/TSB bank, but continues to boast a plaque which records: 'James II of England and VII of Scotland stayed at this house as the guest of Sir Richard Head before embarking for France on the 23rd December 1688, when he finally left England'. See also: *Ailesbury*, Vol. I, pp. 218–20; B.D. Henning (ed.), *The House of Commons, 1660–1690* (London, 1983), Vol. II, pp. 517–18; & S. Harrison & S. Evemy, *Rochester upon Medway, the Tale of a City* (London, n/d.), p. 29.

20. *Life*, Vol. II, p. 269; RA/M3 ff.701–2; Bohun, *History of the Desertion*, p. 105; *Burnet*, Vol. III, Book IV, pp. 803–4; & *CSPD* (1687–9), p. 382; & *Ailesbury*, Vol. I, p. 213.

21. W. Fuller (impostor), *A Plain Proof of the Father and Mother of the Pretended Prince of Wales* (London, 1700), pp. 4–8 & 10–14; A. Shield & A. Lang, *The King over the Water* (London, 1907), p. 21; *Ailesbury*, Vol. I, p. 224; & RA / M3 f.713; & *Life*, Vol. II, pp. 269–71 & 274.

22. J. Oldmixon [pub. anon.], *The History of England during the reigns of the Royal House of Stuart* (London, 1730), pp. 764–5; & F.C. Turner, *James II* (London, 1948), p. 454.

23. *Hyde Correspondence*, Vol. II, p. 231.

24. *Burnet*, Vol. III, Book IV, pp. 800 & 803–4.

25. Hewitson (ed.), *Diary of Thomas Bellingham*, p. 38; RA/M3 f.718; *Burnet*, Vol. III, Book IV, p. 802; G.H. Jones, *Charles Middleton. The Life and Times of a Restoration Politician* (Chicago & London, 1967), p. 238; & Oldmixon, *History of England*, p. 763.

26. *Life*, Vol. II, p. 270; & RA / M3 ff.714–15.

27. *Life*, Vol. II, p. 268.

28. *Life*, Vol. II, p. 271; Jones, *Charles Middleton*, p. 238; Anon., *Life of William III*, p. 169; & Oldmixon, *History of England*, p. 764.

29. *Ailesbury*, Vol. I, pp. 219–21; Oldmixon, *History of England*, p. 763; Middleton, *Life of Charles, 2nd Earl of Middleton*, p. 127; J. Miller, *Bourbon and Stuart. Kings and Kingship in France and England in the Seventeenth Century* (London, 1987), p. 238; Beddard

(ed.), *A Kingdom Without a King*,
p. 63; & Dalrymple, *Memoirs*, Vol. I,
p. 184.

30. *Hyde Correspondence*, Vol. II, pp. 232–3.

31. RA / M3 f.726; A. Fea, *James II and His Wives* (London, 1908), p. 215; Anon., *Father Peter's Policy Discovered: Or, the Prince of Wales Prov'd a Popish Perkin* (London, 1689), p. 1; Middleton, *Life of Charles, 2nd Earl of Middleton*, pp. 127–8; Miller, *Bourbon and Stuart*, p. 238; & *Ailesbury*, Vol. I, pp. 220–5.

32. Henning (ed.), *House of Commons*, Vol. II, p. 518; Oldmixon, *History of England*, p. 765; & *Ailesbury*, Vol. I, p. 233.

33. Jones, *Charles Middleton*, p. 239; Anon., *The Life of James II. Late King of England* (London, 1702), pp. 230–1; *Life*, Vol. II, pp. 274–5; RA / M3 ff.719–24; BL. Add. MS. 10118 ff.197–8; Oldmixon, *History of England*, p. 765; Bohun, *History of the Desertion*, pp. 105–7; & Rapin de Thoyras, *History of England*, Vol. II, p. 783.

34. *Life*, Vol. II, p. 274; RA / M3 f.724; Rapin de Thoyras, *History of England*, Vol. II, p. 783; D. Defoe (pub. anon.), *The Englishman's Choice and True Interest: In a Vigorous Prosecution of the War against France* (London, 1694), pp. 5, 11–12 & 17; & Anon., *Life of James II. Late King of England*, p. 231.

35. Camden Society (ed.), *The Autobiography of Sir John Bramston* (London, 1845), p. 342; Anon., *An Account of the Reasons of the Nobility and Gentry's Invitation of his Highness the Prince of Orange into England* (London, 1688), pp. 6 & 10; Bohun, *History of the Desertion*, p. 105; *Life*, Vol. II, p. 277; RA / M3 ff.726–7 & 730; Middleton, *Life of Charles, 2nd Earl of Middleton*, p. 128; Jones, *Charles Middleton*, p. 239; Browning (ed.), *Memoirs of Sir John Reresby*, p. 541; Oldmixon, *History of England*, p. 765; Burnet, Vol. III, Book IV, p. 804; Fea, *James II and his Wives*, pp. 219–20; Luttrell, *Brief Relation*, Vol. I, p. 491; Dalrymple, *Memoirs*, Vol. I, p. 185; BL. Add. MS. 36707 f.53; *Ailesbury*, Vol. I, p. 225; & *Berwick*, Vol. I, p. 37.

36. *Life*, Vol. II, pp. 277–8; & RA / M3 ff.730–1.

37. *Life*, Vol. II, p. 277; & RA / M3 ff.731–2.

38. *Life*, Vol. II, p. 278; RA / M4 f.1; RA/M3 ff.734–5; Cavelli (ed.), *Les Derniers Stuarts*, Vol. II, pp. 400 & 402; & Mackintosh, *History of the Revolution*, p. 562.

39. G.M. Musgrave, *By-Roads and Battlefields in Picardy* (London, 1861), pp. 13–14; J. Haswell, *James II. Soldier and Sailor* (London, 1972), pp. 296–7 & fn. p. 297; D. Ogg, *William III* (London, 1956), p. 41; Revd F. Sanders, *Abrégé de la Vie de Jacques II. Roy de la Grande Bretagne*, ed. P.F. Brettonneau (Paris, 1703), p. 55; & J. Dulon, *Jacques II. Stuart. Sa Famille et les Jacobites à Saint-Germain-en-Laye* (St-Germain-en-Laye, 1897), fn. p. 4; & *Berwick*, Vol. I, p. 37.

CHAPTER TWO: THE EMPTY THRONE

1. Dr Truislen, *The Difference between words esteemed Synonymous in the English Language; and the proper choice of them determined* (London, 1766), Vol. I, chp. 1, p. 3. Such is the continued passion aroused by the suggestion that James II voluntarily gave up the throne that the word 'abdication' is scored through in the British Library's open shelves copy of the *Jacobite Peerage*, and the word 'departure' boldly written in, by a modern hand. See: Marquis of Ruvigny & Raineval (ed.), *The Jacobite Peerage* (Edinburgh, 1904), p. vii.

2. *Ailesbury*, Vol. I, p. 225; Dalyrmple, *Memoirs*, Vol. I, p. 187; J. Macpherson (ed.), *Original Papers* (London, 1775), Vol. I, p. 300; Jones, *Charles Middleton*, pp. 240 & 251; & *Hyde Correspondence*, Vol. II, pp. 233–4 & 238.

3. Bohun, *History of the Desertion*, p. 132; E. Cruickshanks, *The Glorious Revolution* (Houndmills, Basingstoke, 2000), pp. 25–34 & 96–7; &

E. Cruickshanks (ed.), *By Force or by Default? The Revolution of 1688–89* (Edinburgh, 1989), pp. 28–41 & 82–103.

4. H. Ainsworth, *James the Second; or the Revolution of 1688. An Historical Romance*, 3 vols in 1 (London, 1848), pp. 92–3, 146, 156–8, & 299; T. Longueville, *The Adventures of James II of England* (London, 1904), p. 227; Dulon, *Jacques II Stuart*, pp. 20, 31 & 64; Cruickshanks (ed.), *By Force or by Default?*, pp. 8–24; M. Ashley, 'Is there a Case for James II?', *History Today*, Vol. XIII (1963), pp. 347–52; M. Ashley, *James II* (London, Toronto & Melbourne, 1977), pp. 9–14, 156, 183–98; 222, 224, 268, 290 & 293–4; J. Miller, 'The Potential for Absolutism in Later Stuart England', *History*, Vol. 69 (1984), pp. 197–9 & 201–7; M. Kishlansky, *A Monarchy Transformed, Britain 1603–1714* (London, 1996), p. 267; W.A. Speck, *James II. Profiles in Power* (London & New York, 2002), pp. 3, 28, 91–2, 124–5, & 147–53; Haswell, *James II*, pp. 133, 158–64, 167, & 180; C. Petrie, 'James the Second: A Revaluation', *Nineteenth Century*, Vol. 114 (1933), pp. 475–84.

5. So complete was the collapse of the Whig school that a flurry of correspondence in *The Times* in the summer of 2000, provoked by the expansion of the European Union, could dismiss the Bill of Rights and refashion the Glorious Revolution as no more than a foreign invasion at the behest of a handful of 'English traitors' who had sold their nation's sovereignty to the Prince of Orange. The alleged historical parallel was plain: that the rapidly expanding EU represented the same manner of insidious threat, masquerading under the promise of new freedoms, as William of Orange once had. *The Times*, 28 April, 1–2 May, & 6 May 2000. See also: Cruickshanks, *Glorious Revolution*, pp. 50 & 102; L. Pinkham, *William III and the Respectable Revolution* (Harvard, 1954, rpt. 1969), p. 236–9; C. Rose, *England in the 1690s.*

Revolution, Religion and War (Oxford, 1999), p. xiii; Ogg, *William III*, p. 7; & W.E. Brown, 'A Plea for James II', *Contemporary Review* (October, 1925), pp. 501–8.

6. Central Office of Information, 'Parliament and the Glorious Revolution' (London, 1988), p. ii; Chacksfield, *Glorious Revolution, 1688*, p. 5; D. Szechi, 'Mythistory versus History: the Fading of the Revolution of 1688', *The Historical Journal*, Vol. XXXIII (1990), pp. 143–53; G.M. Trevelyan, *The English Revolution 1688–1689* (London, Oxford, & New York, 1938, rpt. 1965), pp. 128–31; G.M. Trevelyan, *England under Queen Anne: Blenheim* (London & Glasgow, 1930, rpt. 1965), pp. 115–30; T.B. Macaulay, *The History of England. From the Accession of James the Second*, ed. C.H. Firth, 6 vols (London, 1913–15), passim; C.H. Firth, *A Commentary on Macaulay's History of England* (London, 1964), pp. 277–303; H.T. Dickinson, 'The Eighteenth Century Debate on the Glorious Revolution', *History*, Vol. LXI (1976), pp. 28–45; A. Marwick, *The Nature of History* (London & Basingstoke, 1970), pp. 43–4; & S. Taylor, '"Plus ça change?" New Perspectives on the Revolution of 1688', *The Historical Journal*, Vol. XXXVII (1994), pp. 457–70.

7. L. Schwoerer, 'Celebrating the Glorious Revolution, 1689–1989', *Albion*, Vol. XXII, no. 1 (Spring, 1990), pp. 19–20.

8. A. MacLachlan, *The Rise and Fall of Revolutionary England. An Essay on the Fabrication of Seventeenth-Century History* (Houndmills, Basingstoke, 1996), pp. 310–12; T. Benn, *The End of an Era. Diaries, 1980–1990* (London, 1994), p. 548; Cruickshanks, *Glorious Revolution*, p. 2; & Schwoerer, 'Celebrating the Glorious Revolution', pp. 3–4 & 16–19; Taylor, '"Plus ça change?", p. 457.

9. C. Hill, *Some Intellectual Consequences of the English Revolution* (London, 1980, rpt. 1997), p. 16. See also his scathing summation of the Declaration of

Rights: C. Hill, *The Century of Revolution, 1603–1714* (Edinburgh, 1961), pp. 276–7.

10. H.J. Kaye, *The British Marxist Historians* (Houndmills, Basingstoke, 1984, rpt. 1995), pp. 104–5; Beddard (ed.), *A Kingdom Without a King*, pp. 6–7; B. Fitzgerald, *Daniel Defoe. A Study in Conflict* (London, 1954), p. 68; & London District C.P.G.B, *Communist Manifesto Centenary Meeting and Pageant* (London, 1948), p. 4.

11. J.C.D. Clark, '1688 and All That', *Encounter* (Jan. 1989), p. 16; & J.C.D. Clark, 'The Glorious Revolution Debunked', *Sunday Telegraph* (24 July 1988), p. 15. These findings are echoed by Cruickshanks, *Glorious Revolution*, p. 102.

12. A.L. Morton, C. Hill & W. Thompson, '1688. How Glorious was the Revolution?', *Our History*, no. 79 (July 1988), pp. 28–31. Morton had already reduced the period to a brief overview that had far more to say about the significance of the Duke of Monmouth, than it did about William III. See: A.L. Morton, *A People's History of England*, 2nd edn (London, 1948 rpt. 1989), pp. 241–5.

13. J. Stewart, *The Great Orange Myth. The Williamite War in Ireland, 1688–92* (Dublin, *c.* 1988), pp. 2–4, 7–9, 13–19.

14. See: R.F.J. Parsons, 'The Role of Jacobitism in the Modern World', *The Royal Stuart Society*, Occasional Paper no. XXVIII (1986), pp. 2–3, 14, 18, 21, 27, 33–6, & 39. Compare this prolonged and vociferous attack upon popular democracy and modernity with the world view embodied in: C. MacKenzie, *Hunting the Fairies* (London, 1948), pp. 164 & 204–5; C. MacKenzie, *The Monarch of the Glen* (London, 1941, rpt. 2000), pp. 12, 16, 19–20, & 282–3; & J. Aiken, *The Wolves of Willoughby Chase* (Harmondsworth, Middlesex, 1962 rpt. 1968), p. 6. See also: J. Eccleshare, 'Joan Aiken, 1924–2004 – Obituary', the *Guardian* (Wednesday, 7 January 2004), p. 25.

15. E. Corp, 'James II and Toleration: The Years in Exile at Saint-Germain-en-Laye', *The Royal Stuart Society*, Occasional Paper no. LI (1997); E. Corp, 'The Jacobite Court at Saint-Germain-en-Laye: Etiquette and the use of the Royal Apartments' in E. Cruickshanks (ed.), *The Stuart Courts* (Stroud, 2000), pp. 240–55; E. Cruickshanks (ed.), *By Force or by Default?*; E. Cruickshanks & E. Corp (eds), *The Stuart Court in Exile and the Jacobites* (London & Rio Grande, Ohio, 1995); & D.G. Scott, 'Sacredness of Majesty: The English Benedictines and the Cult of King James II', *The Royal Stuart Society*, Occasional Paper no. XXIII (1984). For the finest example of this genre, see: E. Corp, with E. Gregg, H. Erskine-Hill & G. Scott, *A Court in Exile. The Stuarts in France, 1689–1718* (Cambridge, 2004). This book was published as my own work was going to press and provides an exceptionally rich – and sumptuously illustrated – account of the cultural life of the exiled court, which will be of enormous use to future generations of researchers.

16. J. Macky [pub. anon.], 'A View of the Court of St. Germain from the Year 1690 to 95. With an Account of the Entertainment Protestants meet with there. Directed to the Malecontent Protestants of England' (London, 1696), reprinted in W. Oldys & T. Park (eds), *Harleian Miscellany* (London, 1810), Vol. VI, pp. 390–7; E. Corp, 'The Exiled Court of James II and James III: A Centre of Italian Music in France, 1689–1712', *Journal of the Royal Musical Association*, Vol. 120 (1995), pp. 216–31; & Corp, 'Jacobite Court' in Cruickshanks (ed.), *The Stuart Courts*, pp. 241, 244, & 250.

17. See, respectively: S.S. Webb, *Lord Churchill's Coup. The Anglo-American Empire and the Glorious Revolution Reconsidered* (New York, 1995), p. 165; H. & B. van der Zee, *1688. Revolution in the Family* (London & New York, 1988); and the highly derivative M. Waller, *Ungrateful Daughters. The Stuart Princesses who stole their Father's*

Crown (London, 2002).

18. S.E. Prall, *The Bloodless Revolution. England, 1688* (Madison, Wisconsin & London, 1985), p. xv; & L. Stone, 'The Bourgeois Revolution of Seventeenth-Century England', *Past & Present*, no. 109 (1985), pp. 44–54.

19. A. McInnes, 'When was the English Revolution?', *History*, Vol. 67, no. 221 (Oct. 1982), pp. 380 & 387. See also: Beddard (ed.), *A Kingdom Without a King*, p. 6; & J.G.A. Pocock, 'The Fourth English Civil War: Dissolution, Desertion and Alternate Histories in the Glorious Revolution', *Government and Opposition*, Vol. XXIII (1988), pp. 150–66.

20. Cruickshanks (ed.), *By Force or by Default?*, p. ii; R. Hutton, 'The Glory of 1688', *The Royal Stuart Society*, Occasional Paper no. XLVI (1995), p. 1; J.R. Hertzler, 'Who Dubbed it "The Glorious Revolution"', *Albion*, Vol. XIX (1987), pp. 579–85; Webb, *Lord Churchill's Coup*, p. 167; & Rose, *England in the 1690s*, pp. xii–xiii.

21. Camden Society (ed.), *Autobiography of Sir John Bramston*, p. 356.

22. D.L. Jones (ed.), *A Parliamentary History of the Glorious Revolution* (London, 1988), p. 10.

23. C.C.P. Lawson, *A History of the Uniforms of the British Army*, Vol. I (London, 1940 rpt. 1962), pp. 40–1.

24. *CSPD* (1687–9), p. 383; Beddard (ed.), *A Kingdom Without a King*, pp. 165–8; Jones (ed.), *Parliamentary History*, pp. 10–12; *Evelyn's Diary*, Vol. II p. 286; J. Carswell, *The Descent on England. A Study of the English Revolution of 1688 and its European Consequences* (London, 1969), pp. 217–18; M. Ashley, *The Glorious Revolution of 1688* (London, 1966), p. 179; Jones, *Revolution of 1688 in England*, p. 311; BL. Add. MS. 36707 ff.54–5; Browning (ed.), *Memoirs of Sir John Reresby*, p. 542; *Life*, Vol. II, pp. 285–6; & Oldmixon, *History of England*, p. 767.

25. Jones (ed.), *Parliamentary History*, pp. 14 & 16; S.B. Baxter, *William III* (London, 1966), pp. 243 & 246–7; Carswell, *Old Cause*, p. 71; J. Ridley,

The Roundheads (London, 1976), p. 256; & B. Worden, *Roundhead Reputations. The English Civil Wars and the Passions of Posterity* (London, 2001), pp. 33–7.

26. Jones (ed.), *Parliamentary History*, p. 12; Carswell, *Descent on England*, p. 218; Beddard (ed.), *A Kingdom Without a King*, p. 65; Baxter, *William III*, pp. 246–7; *Burnet*, Vol. III, Book IV, p. 803; & Jones, *Revolution of 1688 in England*, p. 312.

27. Dalrymple, *Memoirs*, Vol. I, p. 187; Carswell, *Descent on England*, pp. 218–19; Jones, *Revolution of 1688 in England*, p. 312; Prall, *Bloodless Revolution*, pp. 245–7; Browning (ed.), *Memoirs of Sir John Reresby*, pp. 543–4; *Burnet*, Vol. III, Book IV, p. 803; & Jones (ed.), *Parliamentary History*, pp. 11–13.

28. Carswell, *Descent on England*, pp. 218–19; Ashley, *Glorious Revolution*, pp. 180–1; *Burnet*, Vol. III, Book IV, p. 809; Jones (ed.), *Parliamentary History*, pp. 11–13 & 16–17; Trevelyan, *English Revolution 1688–1689*, pp. 71–3; W.A. Speck, *Reluctant Revolutionaries. Englishmen and the Revolution of 1688* (Oxford & New York, 1988), pp. 92–3; Cruickshanks, *Glorious Revolution*, pp. 35–6; Howarth (ed.), *Letters and the Second Diary of Samuel Pepys*, p. 200; C. Tomalin, *Samuel Pepys. The Unequalled Self* (London, 2002), p. 350; Ollard, *Pepys*, p. 310; & Bryant, *Pepys. Saviour of the Navy*, p. 372.

29. Jones (ed.), *Parliamentary History*, p. 15; A. Strickland, *The Lives of the Seven Bishops Committed to the Tower in 1688* (London, 1866), pp. 352–3; J.R. Porter, 'The Non–Juring Bishops', *The Royal Stuart Society*, Occasional Paper no. IV (1973), pp. 3–4 & 8; *Evelyn's Diary*, Vol. II, p. 287; *Burnet*, Vol. III, Book IV, pp. 810–11; Carswell, *Descent on England*, pp. 221–2; Dalrymple, *Memoirs*, Vol. I, pp. 187 & 195; BL. Add. MS. 36707 f.35; RA / M4 f.9; & Carswell, *Old Cause*, p. 72.

30. Dalrymple, *Memoirs*, Vol. I, p. 187; Ailesbury, Vol. I, p. 233; Anon., *Life of*

James II. Late King of England,
pp. 230–5; & *Life*, Vol. II, pp. 285 &
286–90.

31. Anon., *The Debate at Large, between the
     House of Lords and House of Commons
     . . . Relating to the Word Abdicated and the
     Vacancy of the Throne* (London &
     Westminster, 1695), p. 20; *Life*, Vol. I,
     p. 291; G.L. Cherry, *The Convention
     Parliament 1689: A Biographical Study of
     its Members* (New York, 1966),
     pp. 174–5; *Burnet*, Vol. III, Book IV,
     pp. 811–12; *CSPD* (1688–9),
     pp. 408–10; Browning (ed.), *Memoirs of
     Sir John Reresby*, pp. 544–5; Anon.,
     Life of William III, p. 183; Dalrymple,
     Memoirs, Vol. I, Part I, p. 194; & Jones
     (ed.), *Parliamentary History*, pp. 25,
     109–11 & 121.

32. Anon., *Debate at Large*, pp. 21–3 & 29;
     Browning (ed.), *Memoirs of Sir John
     Reresby*, p. 546; *Evelyn's Diary*, Vol. II,
     p. 290; Dalrymple, *Memoirs*, Vol. I,
     pp. 199–200; *Burnet*, Vol. III, Book IV,
     pp. 815–16; J. Miller, '"Abdicate" and
     "Contract" in the Glorious
     Revolution', *The Historical Journal*,
     Vol. XXV (1982), pp. 541–55; RA / M4
     ff.49–50; & Jones (ed.), *Parliamentary
     History*, pp. 22–5 & 125–35.

33. Dalrymple, *Memoirs*, Vol. I,
     pp. 199–200; Jones (ed.), *Parliamentary
     History*, pp. 26–7; Jones, *Revolution of
     1688 in England*, pp. 315–16; Speck,
     Reluctant Revolutionaries, p. 102;
     Evelyn's Diary, Vol. II, p. 291; *Ailesbury*,
     Vol. I, p. 235; Wilton Rix (ed.), *Diary
     and Autobiography of Edmund Bohun*,
     p. 82; & Browning (ed.), *Memoirs of
     Sir John Reresby*, pp. 546–7; & RA / M4
     f.58.

34. *Ailesbury*, Vol. I, p. 235; R. Doebner
     (ed.), *Memoirs of Mary, Queen of
     England* (Leipzig, 1886), p. 6; Jones
     (ed.), *Parliamentary History*,
     pp. 31–3; Carswell, *Descent on England*,
     p. 224; *Burnet*, Vol. III, Book IV,
     p. 818; & Dalrymple, *Memoirs*, Vol. I,
     p. 201.

35. Cherry, *Convention Parliament 1689*,
     pp. 164–5, & 174–5; *Debate at Large*,
     op.cit. pp. 23–6; *Burnet*, Vol. III,
     Book IV, pp. 819–20; Ashley, *Glorious*

Revolution, p. 183; Dalrymple,
Memoirs, Vol. I, pp. 194, 196 & 203;
Jones, *Revolution of 1688 in England*,
p. 316; D. Green, *Queen Anne*
(London, 1970), pp. 52–3; C.
Cotteril, *The Whole Life and Glorious
Actions of Prince George of Denmark*
(London, 1708), pp. 5–7; Baxter,
William III, pp. 247–8;
J.R. Jones, *Court and Country,
England 1658–1714* (London, 1978,
rpt. 1993), p. 253; H.W. Chapman,
Mary II, Queen of England (London,
1953), p. 156; & Jones (ed.),
Parliamentary History, pp. 16, 33–7 &
162–5; Anon. (ed.), *His Highness, The
Prince of Orange, His Letter to the Lords
Spiritual and Temporal, Assembled at
Westminster in this Present Convention,
January the 22, 1689* (London, 1689),
pp. 1–2.

36. Dalrymple, *Memoirs*, Vol. I, p. 203.

37. Dalrymple, *Memoirs*, Vol. I, p. 206;
     Evelyn's Diary, Vol. II, p. 291; Jones
     (ed.), *Parliamentary History*, pp. 34–7 &
     71–2; *Burnet*, Vol. III, Book IV, pp.
     821–2; Browning (ed.), *Memoirs of Sir
     John Reresby*, pp. 551–2; *CSPD* (1687–9),
     p. 393; & RA / M4 f.72.

38. Ashley, *Glorious Revolution*, pp. 183–4 &
     206–9; G. Holmes, *The Making of a
     Great Power. Late Stuart and early
     Georgian Britain, 1660–1722* (London
     & New York, 1993), pp. 216–17;
     Chapman, *Mary II*, pp. 158–60; &
     A. Strickland, *Lives of the Queens of
     England from the Norman Conquest*,
     Vol. XIII, *Mary II* (Philadelphia, 1903),
     pp. 193–4.

39. Ashley, *Glorious Revolution*, p. 207;
     BL. Add. MS. 36707 ff.60 & 63–4; Ogg,
     William III, p. 53; & Jones (ed.),
     Parliamentary History, p. 44.

40. Doebner (ed.), *Memoirs of Mary, Queen
     of England*, p. 10; Anon., *Life of
     William III*, p. 184; Baxter, *William III*,
     p. 248; BL. Add. MS. 10118 f.206;
     Chapman, *Mary II*, pp. 164–6; *Burnet*,
     Vol. III, Book IV, p. 825 & Vol. IV,
     Book V, p. 2; Dalrymple, *Memoirs*,
     Vol. I, p. 209; & RA / M4 f.74.

41. *CSPD* (1689–90), p. 1; H. & B. van der
     Zee, *1688. Revolution in the Family*

(London, 1988), p. 237; Chapman, *Mary II*, pp. 166–7; Strickland, *Lives of the Queens of England*, Vol. XIII, pp. 200–1; Baxter, *William III*, pp. 247–8; *Evelyn's Diary*, Vol. II, p. 292; Browning (ed.), *Memoirs of Sir John Reresby*, pp. 554–5; J. Miller, *The Glorious Revolution* (London & New York, 1983), p. 22; Carswell, *Descent on England*, pp. 225–6; Trevelyan, *English Revolution*, p. 78; Jones, *Revolution of 1688 in England*, pp. 317–19; Ogg, *William III*, p. 53; Jones (ed.), *Parliamentary History*, pp. 41–6; & *Burnet*, Vol. III, Book IV, p. 825.

42. *Dangeau*, Vol. I, p. 141 & f.n. p. 141; & Cavelli (ed.), *Les Derniers Stuarts*, Vol. II, pp. 400, 402–3 & 456–8; Fea, *James II and his Wives*, p. 223; & RA / M4 f.1.

43. *Dangeau*, Vol. I, p. 143; Cavelli (ed.), *Les Derniers Stuarts*, Vol. II, pp. 428–9 & 450–1; *Berwick*, Vol. I, p. 37; *Life*, Vol. II, p. 283; & RA / M4 f.1.

44. *Dangeau*, Vol. I, p. 139; Cavelli (ed.), *Les Derniers Stuarts*, Vol. II, pp. 453–5; Haile, *Queen Mary of Modena*, pp. 222–3; P. Miller, *James [the Old Pretender]* (London, 1971), p. 24; Shield & Lang, *King over the Water*, pp. 32–3; & Hopkirk, *Queen over the Water*, p. 159; V.C.G. Zuccoli, *Maria di Modena, Regina d' Inghilterra* (Milan, 1940), p. 153; RA 1/23 f.1; & BL. Add. MS. 10118 ff.192–4.

45. *Marchioness de Sévigné*, Vol. IX, pp. 30–1 & 33; Cavelli (ed.), *Les Derniers Stuarts*, Vol. II, p. 461; C. Oman, *Mary of Modena* (Bungay, Suffolk, 1902), p. 139; BL. Add. MS. 28226 f.78; BL. Add. MS. 10118 f.194; J. Southorn, 'Mary of Modena, Queen Consort of James II and VII', *The Royal Stuart Society*, Occasional Paper no. XL (1992), pp. 6–7; & E. & M.S. Grew, *The English Court in Exile. James II at Saint-Germain* (London, 1911), pp. 51–2.

46. BL. Add. MS. 10118 ff.198 & 449; V. Cronin, *Louis XIV* (London, 1964), p. 317; *Dangeau*, Vol. I, p. 144; Fea, *James II and his Wives*,

pp. 63–4; Cavelli (ed.), *Les Derniers Stuarts*, Vol. II, pp. 462–3 & 475; Dulon, *Jacques II Stuart*, pp. 5–6; Southorn, 'Mary of Modena', p. 7; Macaulay, *History of England*, Vol. III, p. 1252; Sanders, *Abrégé de la Vie de Jacques II*, pp. 56–7; RA / M4 ff.1–2; *Life*, Vol. II, p. 285; & *Berwick*, Vol. I, pp. 37–8.

47. *Marchioness de Sévigné*, Vol. IX, p. 48; Grew, *English Court in Exile*, pp. 65–6; Cavelli (ed.), *Les Derniers Stuarts*, Vol. II, pp. 462–3; Sanders, *Abrégé de la Vie de Jacques II*, p. 57; BL. Add. MS. 10118 f.449; & RA / M4 f.2.

48. *Dangeau*, Vol. I, pp. 145–6 & 149–50; Historical Manuscripts Commission, *Calendar of the Stuart Papers belonging to His Majesty the King, preserved at Windsor Castle* (London, 1902), Vol. I, p. 35; BL. Add. MS. 10118 f.201; & Cavelli (ed.), *Les Derniers Stuarts*, Vol. II, pp. 483–6.

49. HMC, *Calendar of Stuart Papers*, Vol. I, pp. 36–7; Cavelli (ed.), *Les Derniers Stuarts*, Vol. II, pp. 488–9 & 492–4; Hopkirk, *Queen over the Water*, pp. 180–1; *Life*, Vol. II, pp. 322–4; & Haile, *Queen Mary of Modena*, pp. 237–8.

50. HMC, *Calendar of Stuart Papers*, Vol. I, p. 36; & Cavelli (ed.), *Les Derniers Stuarts*, Vol. II, pp. 486–7.

51. F. von Ludwig, *The History of the Popes*, trans. D.E. Graf (London, 1957), Vol. XXXII, pp. 513–14; Cavelli (ed.), *Les Derniers Stuarts*, Vol. II, pp. 489–90 & 514; & Ogg, *William III*, p. 38.

52. HMC, *Calendar of Stuart Papers*, Vol. I, pp. 35–7; & Cavelli (ed.), *Les Derniers Stuarts*, Vol. II, pp. 479–80, 489–90, 495–8, 502, 505 & 516–19.

53. *Life*, Vol. II, pp. 323–4; RA / M4 ff.121–7; & Cavelli (ed.), *Les Derniers Stuarts*, Vol. II, pp. 495–8 & 506.

54. J.P. Spielman, *Leopold I of Austria* (London, 1977), pp. 146–7 & 216 fn. 3; RA / M4 ff.121–7; *Life*, Vol. II, p. 324; & Cavelli (ed.), *Les Derniers Stuarts*, Vol. II, pp. 499–501.

55. *Life*, Vol. II, pp. 325–6; & Cavelli (ed.), *Les Derniers Stuarts*, Vol. II, pp. 499–501.

56. Mackintosh, *History of the Revolution*, p. 564.

57. HMC, *Calendar of Stuart Papers*, Vol. I, p. 37.

58. *CSPD* (1689–90), pp. 375–6; Cavelli (ed.), *Les Derniers Stuarts*, Vol. II, pp. 465 & 503; Hopkirk, *Queen over the Water*, pp. 170–1; BL. Add. MS. 36296 ff.14–15; & H. Hornyold, *Genealogical Memoirs of the Family of Strickland of Strickland of Sizergh* (Kendal, 1928), p. 135.

59. It would appear that James, and his secretaries, had chosen to forget his own escape from England in 1648, disguised as a young girl. See: J.P. Kenyon, *Robert Spencer, Earl of Sunderland, 1641–1702* (London, 1958), pp. 226–9 & 238–41; Cavelli (ed.), *Les Derniers Stuarts*, Vol. II, p. 506; Haile, *Queen Mary of Modena*, p. 240; Hopkirk, *Queen over the Water*, p. 169; RA / M4 ff.2–3; & *Life*, Vol. II, pp. 283–4.

60. *CSPD* (1689–90), pp. 8, 18 & 29; Grew, *English Court in Exile*, pp. 84–5; Haile, *Queen Mary of Modena*, p. 239; *Dangeau*, Vol. I, p. 155; & Oman, *Mary of Modena*, p. 160.

61. *CSPD* (1689–90), p. 13; BL. Add. MS. 18,447 f.78; & Cavelli (ed.), *Les Derniers Stuarts*, Vol. II, p. 472.

62. Haile, *Queen Mary of Modena*, p. 240; *Dangeau*, Vol. I, p. 153; *Life*, Vol. II, p. 283; & Cavelli (ed.), *Les Derniers Stuarts*, Vol. II, pp. 471, 473, 501 & 504.

63. P.K. Monod, *Jacobitism and the English People, 1688–1788* (Cambridge, 1989, rpt. 1993), pp. 96–7, 101, 111–12, 118, 120 & 153; G. Spraggs, *Outlaws and Highwaymen. The Cult of the Robber in England from the Middle Ages to the Nineteenth Century* (London, 2001), pp. 172, 181–2, 222 & 343 n. 49; Dalrymple, *Memoirs*, Vol. II, p. 188; Childs, *British Army of William III, 1698–1702*, pp. 21–2; Great Britain Parliament, *Journals of the House of Commons* (London, 1803), Vol. X, p. 50; Browning (ed.), *Memoirs of Sir John Reresby*, pp. 563–5; & C.D. Ellestad, 'The Mutinies of 1689',

Journal of the Society for Army Historical Research, Vol. LIII, no. 213 (Spring, 1975), p. 13.

64. Ellestad, 'Mutinies of 1689', p. 16; & Browning (ed.), *Memoirs of Sir John Reresby*, p. 565.

65. Ellestad, 'Mutinies of 1689', pp. 18–21; BL. Add. MS. 10118 f.213; & R.E. Scouller, 'The Mutiny Acts', *Journal of the Society for Army Historical Research*, Vol. L no. 201 (Spring, 1972), pp. 42–4.

66. Childs, *The Army, James II and the Glorious Revolution*, pp. 2, 4–5, 65–6, & 78; Browning (ed.), *Memoirs of Sir John Reresby*, pp. 566–7; Cavelli (ed.), *Les Derniers Stuarts*, Vol. II, pp. 524–5 & 532–5; *Burnet*, Vol. III, Book IV, pp. 806–8; *Evelyn's Diary*, Vol. II, p. 294; & J.G. Simms, *Jacobite Ireland, 1685–91* (Fakenham, Norfolk, 1969), pp. 33–6, & 39–42; J. Miller, 'The Earl of Tyrconnel and James II's Irish Policy, 1685–1688', *The Historical Journal*, Vol. XX (1977), pp. 804–7, 812 & 816–21; *Berwick*, Vol. I, p. 42; & C. Petrie, *The Great Tyrconnel. A Chapter in Anglo-Irish Relations* (Cork & Dublin, 1972), pp. 141, 143–4, 149, 153–4 & 156.

67. *Life*, Vol. II, pp. 320–2; Cavelli (ed.), *Les Derniers Stuarts*, Vol. II, pp. 507 & 529–30; J.T. Gilbert (ed.), *A Jacobite Narrative of the War in Ireland, 1688–1691* (Dublin, 1892), pp. 35, 39–40 & 43; Simms, *Jacobite Ireland*, pp. 49–53; & RA / M4 ff.108 & 114.

68. Simms, *Jacobite Ireland*, pp. 53–4; Cavelli (ed.), *Les Derniers Stuarts*, Vol. II, pp. 530–5; *Life*, Vol. II, p. 322; & *Burnet*, Vol. IV, Book V, p. 17.

69. *Life*, Vol. II, pp. 319–20; & RA / M4 ff.106–8.

70. *Life*, Vol. II, p. 322; Cavelli (ed.), *Les Derniers Stuarts*, Vol. II, pp. 537–41; & *Dangeau*, Vol. I, pp. 149–50 & 153–4.

71. *Marchioness de Sévigné*, Vol. IX, pp. 52, 75–6, 85 & 100; & Cavelli (ed.), *Les Derniers Stuarts*, Vol. II, pp. 504 & 528.

72. Cavelli (ed.), *Les Derniers Stuarts*, Vol. II, pp. 531 & 536; *Dangeau*, Vol. I, p. 147; & RA / M4 f.108.

73. Turner, *James II*, p. 463, fn. 1.

74. Turner, *James II*, p. 456. See also: Ashley, *James II*, pp. 278–89; Haswell, *James II*, pp. 303–7; & Miller, *James II*, pp. 234–42.

75. Hopkirk, *Queen over the Water*, p. 173; Miller, *James II*, pp. 226; Petrie, *The Great Tyrconnel*, p. 165; Haile, *Queen Mary of Modena*, pp. 229–30; Turner, *James II*, p. 456; Ashley, *James II*, pp. 9–14 & 295; Jones, *Revolution of 1688 in England*, p. 53; Lindsay, *Lives of the Lindsays*, Vol. II, p. 45; Middleton, *Life of Charles, 2nd Earl of Middleton*, pp. 74–5; & van der Zee, *William and Mary*, pp. 58–9; B. Bevan, *King James the Third of England. A Study of Kingship in Exile* (London, 1967), p. 26; A.J. Guy & J. Spencer-Smith, *1688. Glorious Revolution?* (London, 1988), p. 7; & Macaulay, *History of England*, Vol. III, pp. 1225 & 1241. See also: J. Callow, *The Making of King James II* (Stroud, 2000), pp. 17–21, 63, 151, 213–14, 237, 261, 264, 279–80 & 303–4.

76. Speck, *James II*, p. 76. It is a shame that Speck chooses not to engage with the central thesis of my earlier book, *The Making of King James II*, regarding the myth that seeks to divide consideration of James's early life from his record as King, and damns the scholarship with faint praises. This is particularly surprising as elsewhere he draws really rather heavily upon my own work. Compare: Speck, *James II* (2001), pp. 17–21, 24, 156–8, 160 & 163, with Callow, *Making of King James II* (2000), pp. 2–8, 60–8 & 143–7.

77. *Marchioness de Sévigné*, Vol. IX, p. 133; Cavelli (ed.), *Les Derniers Stuarts*, Vol. II, p. 490; & Grew, *English Court in Exile*, p. 88.

78. J.A. Lynn, *The Wars of Louis XIV, 1667–1714* (Harlow, Essex, 1999), p. 203; Cavelli (ed.), *Les Derniers Stuarts*, Vol. II, pp. 471, 501, 526, 542–3 & 550–2; & RA / M4 ff.113–14.

79. Cavelli (ed.), *Les Derniers Stuarts*, Vol. II, pp. 525, 527 & 544–50; *Marchioness de Sévigné*, Vol. IX, pp. 118 & 121; Grew, *English Court in Exile*, p. 148; J.B. Wolf, *Louis XIV* (London, 1968), pp. 310–13; Browning (ed.), *Memoirs of Sir John Reresby*, pp. 562–3; *Dangeau*, Vol. I, pp. 258–9; & Duc de Saint-Simon, *Memoirs*, trans. & ed. L. Norton, 3 vols (London, 1999–2000), Vol. III, p. 467.

80. Cavelli (ed.), *Les Derniers Stuarts*, Vol. II, pp. 527–8; & *Dangeau*, Vol. I, p. 258.

CHAPTER THREE: WHEN THE KING ENJOYS HIS OWN AGAIN

1. *Life*, Vol. II, p. 322; Cavelli (ed.), *Les Derniers Stuarts*, Vol. II, pp. 553 & 562–3; *Dangeau*, Vol. I, p. 159; & *Berwick*, Vol. I, p. 43.

2. *Marchioness de Sévigné*, p. 143; Grew, *English Court in Exile*, p. 151; *Dangeau*, Vol. I, p. 157; Cavelli (ed.), *Les Derniers Stuarts*, Vol. II, pp. 557–61, 571–2 & 574; & BL. Add. MS. 36296 f.25.

3. *Life*, Vol. II, p. 327; RA / M4 ff.130–1; Cavelli (ed.), *Les Derniers Stuarts*, Vol. II, pp. 567, 573–4 & 578; J.A. Murphy, *Justin MacCarthy, Lord Mountcashel, Commander of the First Irish Brigade in France* (Clonmel, Eire, 1959, rpt. 1999), p. 16; J.C. O'Callaghan, *History of the Irish Brigades in the Service of France* (Glasgow, 1870, rpt. Dublin, 1968), p. 11; Gilbert (ed.), *Jacobite Narrative*, pp. 43 & 46; K. Haddick-Flynn, *Orangeism. The Making of a Tradition* (Dublin, 1999), pp. 40–1; BL. Add. MS. 10118 f.221; BL. Add. MS. 36296 ff.35–41; Anon., *Life of James II. Late King of England*, pp. 263–4.

4. A. Hamilton, *The Actions of the Enniskillen-men* (London, 1690, rpt. 1849), p. xiii; Gilbert (ed.), *Jacobite Narrative*, pp. 43–5; *CSPD* (1689–90), p. 34. See also: BL. Add. MS. 36707 f.65, for a similar confusion among the English gentry as to their former sovereign's whereabouts.

5. *Life*, Vol. II, p. 328; RA / M4 f.112; T. Gray, *No Surrender! The Siege of Londonderry, 1689* (London, 1975), p. 55; I. McBride, *The Siege of Derry in Ulster Protestant Mythology* (Dublin,

1997), pp. 15 & 22; W.A. Maguire
(ed.), *Kings in Conflict* (Belfast, 1990),
p. 47; BL. Add. MS. 10118 f.398.

6.   E. Corp (ed.), *L' Autre Exil: Les Jacobites
     en France au debut du XVIIIe Siècle*
     (Languedoc, 1992), p. 25; Cavelli
     (ed.), *Les Derniers Stuarts*, Vol. II,
     pp. 578 & 587–8; Petrie, *Great
     Tyrconnel*, pp. 163–4; Grew, *English
     Court in Exile*, p. 153.

7.   Cavelli (ed.), *Les Derniers Stuarts*,
     Vol. II, pp. 575 & 585; N. Plunket,
     Derry and the Boyne, intro. B. Clifford
     (Belfast, 1990), pp. 88–9; *180 Loyal
     Songs* (London, 1685), p. 186; Anon.,
     A Gossips Feast, or Morrall Tales
     (London, 1647), p. 5; Anon.,
     A Collection of Loyal Songs, Poems, Etc.
     (n/p., 1750), pp. 24–5, 59–60 & 69–70;
     Gilbert (ed.), *Jacobite Narrative*,
     pp. 46–7; O'Callaghan, *Irish Brigades*,
     p. 11; Simms, *Jacobite Ireland*, pp. 63–4;
     Petrie, *Great Tyrconnel*, p. 164; *CSPD*
     (1689–90), p. 38; Grew, *English Court
     in Exile*, pp. 188–90; RA / M4 f.138; &
     Life, Vol. II, pp. 329–30.

8.   Anon., *The Life of James II. Late King of
     England*, pp. 266–7; BL. Add. MS.
     10118 f.221; Cavelli (ed.), *Les Derniers
     Stuarts*, Vol. II, p. 586; Plunket, *Derry
     and the Boyne*, p. 89; Petrie, *Great
     Tyrconnel*, pp. 164–5; Simms, *Jacobite
     Ireland*, pp. 63–4; Grew, *English
     Court in Exile*, pp. 190–1; RA / M4
     f.139; & *Life*, Vol. II, p. 330.

9.   Maguire (ed.), *Kings in Conflict*,
     pp. 123 & 125; Hopkirk, *Queen over the
     Water*, p. 187; BL. Add. MS. 10118
     f.221; Cavelli (ed.), *Les Derniers Stuarts*,
     Vol. II, pp. 588–9 & 591; Plunket,
     Derry and the Boyne, pp. 89 & 95;
     BL. Add. MS.36296 f.56; Gilbert
     (ed.), *Jacobite Narrative*, pp. 48–9
     & 54; Philostelus (pseud.), *Letter
     Right Honourable Sir Ralph Gore . . .
     Concerning a lately Published Proposal
     for a Voluntary Subscription to Erect a
     Trophy in Memory of the Deliverance
     of this Kingdom, by the Glorious Victory at
     the Boyne* (Dublin, 1732), p. 12; S.
     Mulloy, 'French Engineers with the
     Jacobite Army in Ireland, 1689–91',
     The Irish Sword, Vol. XV (1983),

p. 222; RA / M4 f.140; & *Life*, Vol. II,
p. 328.

10. Herbert to the Earl of Nottingham,
     quoted in E.B. Powley, *The Naval Side
     of King William's War* (London, 1972),
     p. 135.

11. P. Aubrey, *The Defeat of James Stuart's
     Armada, 1692* (Leicester, 1979), p. 35;
     Dalrymple, *Memoirs*, Vol. I, p. 332;
     Powley, *Naval Side of King William's
     War*, pp. 138–42; Gilbert (ed.), *Jacobite
     Narrative*, pp. 70–1; *Life*, Vol. II,
     pp. 370–1; & Simms, *Jacobite Ireland*,
     p. 68.

12. W. Doran, 'Bishop Thomas Nicolson:
     First Vicar-Apostolic, 1695–1718',
     The Innes Review, Vol. XXXIX, no. 2
     (1988), pp. 116–19; R.P. Barnes,
     'Scotland and the Glorious Revolution
     of 1688', *Albion*, Vol. III, (1971),
     pp. 123–5; R.P. Barnes, 'James VII's
     forfeiture of the Scottish Throne',
     Albion, Vol. V (1973), pp. 299–304;
     S.H.F. Johnston, *The History of the
     Cameronians (Scottish Rifles)* (London,
     1947),Vol. I, pp. 22–3; T. Carter,
     *Historical Record of the Twenty-Sixth, or
     Cameronian Regiment* (London, 1867),
     pp. 2–6; J.K. Hewison, *The Covenanters*
     (Glasgow, 1908), Vol. II, pp. 515–17 &
     521–3; *Life*, Vol. II, pp. 342–3;
     Cruickshanks (ed.), *By Force or by
     Default?*, pp. 75–6; Rose, *England in the
     1690s*, p. 14; Ailesbury, Vol. I, p. 250;
     CSPD (1689–90), p. 38; RA / M4
     ff.176–80; & *Life*, Vol. II, pp. 336–44.

13. Barnes, 'James VII's forfeiture',
     pp. 305–13; Hopkins, *Glencoe and the
     End of the Highland War*, p. 140;
     Johnston, *History of the Cameronians*,
     Vol. I, pp. 23–5; Hewison, *Covenanters*,
     Vol. II, pp. 522 & 524–5; Cruickshanks
     (ed.), *By Force or by Default?*, pp. 76–7;
     CSPD (1687–9), p. 392; RA / M4
     ff.180–1 & 192–3; *Life*, Vol. II,
     pp. 345–8; G. Smythe (ed.), *Letters of
     John Grahame of Claverhouse, Viscount
     Dundee with Illustrative Documents*,
     pp. 35–7, 39 & 43; H. Mackay, *Memoirs
     of the War carried on in Scotland and
     Ireland, 1689–1691*, eds. J.M. Hog,
     P.F. Tytler, & A. Urquhart (Edinburgh,
     1833), pp. 5–7 & 12–13.

14. A.M. Scott, *Bonnie Dundee. John Graham of Claverhouse* (Edinburgh, 1989, rpt. 2000), p. 170; Smythe (ed.), *Letters of . . . Claverhouse*, pp. 46, 52, 63, 68–9 & 78–9; Mackay, *Memoirs of the War*, pp. 46–7; Hewison, *Covenanters*, Vol. II, pp. 525–6; *Life*, Vol. II, p. 349; RA / M4 ff.196–8; J. Prebble, *Glencoe. The Story of the Massacre* (London, 1966), pp. 73 & 75–6; Petrie, C., *The Jacobite Movement. The First Phase, 1688–1716* (London, 1948), p. 82; Hopkins, *Glencoe and the End of the Highland War*, pp. 127–30, 133, 138–40, 146 & 149.

15. D. McBane, *The Expert Swordsman's Companion* (Glasgow, 1728), pp. 78–9; BL. Add. MS. 10118 f.232; Smythe (ed.), *Letters of . . . Claverhouse*, pp. 47 & 54–6; Barrington, *Grahame of Claverhouse*, pp. 351–2; Tayler, *John Graham of Claverhouse*, pp. 266 & 268–70; Terry, *John Graham of Claverhouse*, pp. 336–41; S. Reid, 'Killiecrankie, 1689' (Leigh-on-Sea, 1989), pp. 19–21; Mackay, *Memoirs of the War*, pp. 50–6; Petrie, *Jacobite Movement. The First Phase*, p. 83; Hewison, *Covenanters*, Vol. II, pp. 526–8; Prebble, *Glencoe*, p. 76; *Life*, Vol. II pp. 350–1; RA / M4 ff.201–2; & Hopkins, *Glencoe and the End of the Highland War*, pp. 157–9.

16. BL. Add. MS. 10118 f.236; BL. Add. MS. 36707 f.68; Barrington, *Grahame of Claverhouse*, pp. 353–5; Tayler, *John Graham of Claverhouse*, pp. 271–2 & 274–9; Terry, *John Graham of Claverhouse*, pp. 342–3 & 350–4; Reid, 'Killiecrankie', pp. 28–9; Prebble, *Glencoe*, p. 77; Mackay, *Memoirs of the War*, pp. 57–8; Hopkins, *Glencoe and the End of the Highland War*, pp. 159–60 & 176–7; Hewison, *Covenanters*, Vol. II, pp. 528–30; *Life*, Vol. II, pp. 351–3; RA / M4 f.203; Scott, *Bonnie Dundee*, pp. 224–5.

17. P. Walker, *Biographia Presbyteriana* (Edinburgh, 1827), Vol. I, p. 208; Johnston, *History of the Cameronians*, Vol. I, pp. 25–36; Anon., *The Exact Narrative of the Conflict at Dunkeld* (London, 1689), pp. 1–3; Mackay, *Memoirs of the War*, pp. 70–1; Carter, *Historical Record*, pp. 7–8; Hewison, *Covenanters*, Vol. II, p. 531; Hopkins, *Glencoe and the End of the Highland War*, p. 183; *Life*, Vol. II, pp. 353–4; & RA / M4 ff.206 & 208.

18. Walker, *Biographia Presbyteriana*, Vol. I, p. 209; BL. Add. MS. 10118 f.235; Anon., *Exact Narrative of the Conflict at Dunkeld*, pp. 4–7; Johnston, *History of the Cameronians*, pp. 36–7; Carter, *Historical Record*, pp. 8–9; Hewison, *Covenanters*, Vol. II, p. 531; Prebble, *Glencoe*, p. 78; Hopkins, *Glencoe and the End of the Highland War*, pp. 186–7; & *Life*, Vol. II, p. 354.

19. Anon., *Exact Narrative of the Conflict at Dunkeld*, pp. 6–7; Johnston, *History of the Cameronians*, pp. 37–8; Carter, *Historical Record*, pp. 14–16; Hopkins, *Glencoe and the End of the Highland War*, pp. 188–9; Hewison, *Covenanters*, Vol. II, p. 532; Prebble, *Glencoe*, pp. 79–81; *Berwick*, Vol. I, pp. 44–5; Gray, *No Surrender!*, pp. 72–9 & 83; Gilbert (ed.), *Jacobite Narrative*, pp. 64–5; Simms, *Jacobite Ireland*, pp. 96–8; RA / M4 f.141; & *Life*, Vol. II, p. 331.

20. *Berwick*, Vol. I, p. 46; Plunket, *Derry and the Boyne*, p. 95; Gray, *No Surrender!*, pp. 83–4 & 88–90; Simms, *Jacobite Ireland*, p. 99; Grew, *English Court in Exile*, pp. 214–15 RA / M4 ff.143–6; & *Life*, Vol. II, p. 332.

21. There is much confusion among the sources as to whether the distance stipulated under the terms of the truce was 5, 4, or 2 miles from the city walls. Unsurprisingly, Jacobite writers claimed the longer distance, while Derry's defenders claimed the shorter. Gilbert (ed.), *Jacobite Narrative*, p. 62; Plunket, *Derry and the Boyne*, p. 95; BL. Add. MS. 36296 f.57; Gray, *No Surrender!*, p. 92; Simms, *Jacobite Ireland*, pp. 99–100; Petrie, *Great Tyrconnel*, pp. 171–2; RA / M4 ff.147–8; & *Life*, Vol. II, p. 333.

22. BL. Add. MS. 36296 f.57; Plunket, *Derry and the Boyne*, pp. 95–6; P. McCartney, 'The Siege of Derry – 1689' (Derry, 1988, rpt. 1993), pp. 10–11; Gray, *No Surrender!*,

pp. 92–3 & 105–9; Gilbert (ed.), *Jacobite Narrative*, pp. 62–4; R. Doherty, *The Williamite War in Ireland, 1688–1691* (Dublin, 1998), p. 53; RA / M4 ff.148 & 151; Simms, *Jacobite Ireland*, pp. 99–101; *Life*, Vol. II, pp. 333–4; & *Berwick*, Vol. I, p. 47.

23. Gray, *No Surrender!*, pp. 96–7; Gilbert (ed.), *Jacobite Narrative*, p. 65; McBride, *Siege of Derry*, pp. 16–17; & *Life*, Vol. II, p. 334.

24. Hamilton, *Actions of the Enniskillen-Men*, pp. 22–3; F. Madan (ed.), *Stuart Papers relating chiefly to Queen Mary of Modena and the Exiled Court of James II* (London, 1889), Vol. I, p. 5; Gray, *No Surrender!*, pp. 105–8; & Gilbert (ed.), *Jacobite Narrative*, p. 65.

25. Gilbert (ed.), *Jacobite Narrative*, p. 63; Cavelli (ed.), *Les Derniers Stuarts*, Vol. II, p. 591; & Grew, *English Court in Exile*, p. 218.

26. *Life*, Vol. II, p. 322.

27. Plunket, *Derry and the Boyne*, pp. 96–9; Gray, *No Surrender!*, pp. 113 & 116–18; Gilbert (ed.), *Jacobite Narrative*, pp. 63–4 & 67–8; J.G. Simms, 'The Siege of Derry', *The Irish Sword*, Vol. VI, (1963–4), pp. 222–4; Maguire (ed.), *Kings in Conflict*, p. 67; Doherty, *Williamite War*, pp. 60–1; RA / M4 ff.151 & 240; Grew, *English Court in Exile*, p. 170; Simms, *Jacobite Ireland*, pp. 103–4; *Life*, Vol. II, pp. 334–5; & *Berwick*, Vol. I, pp. 48–52.

28. Though in Dublin there was, in fact, one contested seat. See the seminal account: J.G. Simms, *The Jacobite Parliament of 1689* (Dundalk, 1974), p. 5, BL. Add. MS. 38145 ff.15–16; Madan (ed.), *Stuart Papers*, Vol. I, p. 4; Gilbert (ed.), *Jacobite Narrative*, pp. 63–4 & 69; Haswell, *James II*, p. 300; *Life*, Vol. II, p. 355; RA / M4 f.241; Petrie, *Great Tyrconnel*, pp. 173–4 &177; Simms, *Jacobite Ireland*, pp. 74–5 & Grew, *English Court in Exile*, pp. 205–7 & 209–10.

29. Anon., *The Life of James II. Late King of England*, pp. 281–2; *Life*, Vol. II, p. 355; Plunket, *Derry and the Boyne*, p. 100; Gilbert (ed.), *Jacobite Narrative*, pp. 241–5; RA / M4 ff.210–15; Simms,

Jacobite Ireland, pp. 75–6 & 86–7; Grew, *English Court in Exile*, p. 217; *Devotions*, p. 3; & Trinity College, MS. 3529 f.3.

30. Anon., *The Life of James II. Late King of England*, p. 282; *Life*, Vol. II, pp. 355–6; Gilbert (ed.), *Jacobite Narrative*, pp. 61–2 & 69–70; RA / M4 ff.210–15; Simms, *Jacobite Ireland*, p. 81; & Grew, *English Court in Exile*, pp. 217–19.

31. Corp (ed.), *L' Autre Exil*, pp. 30–1; Plunket, *Derry and the Boyne*, p. 101; Gilbert (ed.), *Jacobite Narrative*, p. 58; RA / M4 f.215; & *Life*, Vol. II, p. 356.

32. Anon., *The Life of James II. Late King of England*, pp. 286–93; BL. Add. MS. 10118 f.223; Plunket, *Derry and the Boyne*, p. 101; Gilbert (ed.), *Jacobite Narrative*, pp. 57–8 & 61; Ailesbury, Vol. I, p. 253; Simms, *Jacobite Ireland*, pp. 82; & *Life*, Vol. II, pp. 356–8.

33. Anon., *The Life of James II. Late King of England*, p. 308; RA / M4 f.229; *Life*, Vol. II, p. 358; Simms, *Jacobite Ireland*, pp. 81–3; & Petrie, *Great Tyrconnel*, pp. 178–9.

34. Grew, *English Court in Exile*, p. 218; Gilbert (ed.), *Jacobite Narrative*, pp. 247–50; & Simms, *Jacobite Parliament*, p. 10.

35. *Life*, Vol. II, pp. 358–61; Simms, *Jacobite Parliament*, p. 11; & Simms, *Jacobite Ireland*, p. 83.

36. Corp (ed.), *L' Autre Exil*, pp. 29–30; Haswell, *James II*, p. 300; Simms, *Jacobite Parliament*, pp. 12–14; Simms, *Jacobite Ireland*, pp. 79–81 & 84–5; Grew, *English Court in Exile*, pp. 219–20; *Life*, Vol. II, p. 361; & Petrie, *Great Tyrconnel*, p. 179.

37. Macpherson, *Original Papers*, Vol. I, p. 303; Cavelli (ed.), *Les Derniers Stuarts*, Vol. II, p. 592; Simms, *Jacobite Parliament*, pp. 17–18; Simms, *Jacobite Parliament*, pp. 79, 81 & 93–4; Petrie, *Great Tyrconnel*, p. 170; & *Life*, Vol. II, pp. 361–5.

38. HMC, *Calendar of Stuart Papers*, Vol. I, p. 46; Miller, 'Tyrconnel and James II's Irish Policy', pp. 809–10; D.C. Boulger, *The Battle of the Boyne* (London, 1911), p. 147; BL. Add. MS. 38145 f.7; RA / M4 ff.231–40; Simms, *Jacobite Ireland*, pp. 65–6; &

Grew, *English Court in Exile*, pp. 222–4.

39. HMC, *Calendar of Stuart Papers*, Vol. I, p. 44; Simms, *Jacobite Ireland*, p. 92; & Grew, *English Court in Exile*, pp. 198, 207 & 211.

40. Maguire (ed.), *Kings in Conflict*, pp. 127–8 & 130–2; BL. Add. MS. 38145 ff.7 & 9; Simms, *Jacobite Parliament*, p. 91; *Life*, Vol. II, pp. 369–70; & Grew, *English Court in Exile*, pp. 197, 199–200 & 202.

41. BL. Add. MS. 10118 f.237; BL. Add. MS. 38145 f.3; Gilbert (ed.), *Jacobite Narrative*, pp. 267–72; Mulloy, 'French Engineers', p. 222; D. & H. Murtagh, 'The Irish Jacobite Army, 1689–91', *The Irish Sword*, Vol. XVIII (1990), p. 33; RA / M4 f.253; Simms, *Jacobite Ireland*, pp. 70–1; Grew, *English Court in Exile*, pp. 169 & 184–5; Petrie, *Great Tyrconnel*, p. 173; & *Life*, Vol. II, pp. 327–8.

42. Corp (ed.), *L'Autre Exil*, pp. 36–7; & BL. Add. MS. 10118 ff.214–15.

43. Hamilton, *Actions of the Enniskillen-men*, pp. 40 & 81–2; Plunket, *Derry and the Boyne*, pp. 112–13; & *Berwick*, Vol. I, pp. 53–4.

44. Simms, 'Siege of Derry', p. 229; McBride, *Siege of Derry*, p. 19; BL. Add. MS. 10118 f.219; Plunket, *Derry and the Boyne*, pp. 110–11; BL. Add. MS. 36707 f.67; Powley, *Naval Side of King William's War*, pp. 220–6; Gray, *No Surrender!*, pp. 143–8 & 160–4; Gilbert (ed.), *Jacobite Narrative*, pp. 78–81; Anon., *Life of William III*, p. 238; RA / M4 ff.243–4; *Life*, Vol. II, pp. 365–7; Simms, *Jacobite Ireland*, pp. 106–8;

45. Mulloy, 'French Engineers', pp. 223–4; J.G. Simms (ed.), 'James II and the Siege of Derry', *The Irish Sword*, Vol. III, (1957–8), p. 287; & A.L. Sells (ed. & trans.), *The Memoirs of James II. His Campaigns as Duke of York, 1652–1660* (London, 1962), pp. 146–7; BL. Add. MS. 10118 f.222; RA / M4 ff.242.

46. HMC, *Calendar of Stuart Papers*, p. 44; Gray, *No Surrender!*, pp. 176–9; & RA / M4 f.257.

47. BL. Add. MS. 10118 f.230; BL. Add. MS. 38145 f.4; BL. 36707 f.63; Powley, *Naval Side of King William's War*, pp. 229–30 & 239; Plunket, *Derry and the Boyne*, pp. 113–15; Gray, *No Surrender!*, pp. 189–90; Simms, 'Siege of Derry', pp. 226 & 230–2; Maguire (ed.), *Kings in Conflict*, p. 70; RA / M4 ff.260–1; & Simms, *Jacobite Ireland*, pp. 109–10.

48. Gilbert (ed.), *Jacobite Narrative*, p. 84; Plunket, *Derry and the Boyne*, pp. 113–14; Powley, *Naval Side of King William's War*, pp. 249–50 & 254–5; Gray, *No Surrender!*, pp. 193–6; *Life*, Vol. II, p. 368; McBride, *Siege of Derry*, p. 19; Anon., *Life of William III*, pp. 238–9; RA / M4 f.246; Simms, *Jacobite Ireland*, pp. 111–12; & *Berwick*, Vol. I, p. 55. The heroism shown by both sides at Derry does, indeed, lend truth to the view that fact can often be far more dramatic and moving than any form of fiction. This was not lost upon Derry's modern day 'Apprentice Boys' when, in the late 1990s, they tried to pitch the idea of a movie centring about the siege of Derry to the film producers of Hollywood. The unfortunate Colonel Lundy was to have been played by Alan Rickman, while Gene Hackman was considered ideal for the fiery Revd Walker. Unsurprisingly, the movie was never made, and as one resident of the Bogside was heard to comment: 'They're asking us to celebrate the siege as if it was Rorke's Drift. They're forgetting we were the Zulus'. See: R. Carroll, 'Bravehearts of Derry look to Hollywood', the *Guardian* (8 August 1998), p. 3.

49. Murphy, *Justin MacCarthy*, pp. 21–4; Plunket, *Derry and the Boyne*, p. 112; Simms, *Jacobite Ireland*, pp. 116–19; Powley, *Naval Side of King William's War*, pp. 252–3; Gray, *No Surrender!*, pp. 196–7; & Gilbert (ed.), *Jacobite Narrative*, pp. 81–2 & 85; Anon., *Life of William III*, p. 239; O'Callaghan, *Irish Brigades*, pp. 12–21; Mulloy, 'French Engineers', p. 223; RA / M4 ff.247 & 249; & *Life*, Vol. II, pp. 368–9.

50. Powley, *Naval Side of King William's War*, pp. 259–61; BL. Add. MS. 10118 f.235; Plunket, *Derry and the Boyne*, p. 115; Gilbert (ed.), *Jacobite Narrative*, p. 87; Anon., *Life of William III*, p. 240; O'Callaghan, *Irish Brigades*, p. 22; Ailesbury, Vol. I, p. 251; G. Moir, *The Suffolk Regiment* (London, 1969), pp. 8–9; J. Childs, 'A Patriot for Whom? Marshal Schomberg – for God and for Honour', *History Today*, Vol. XXXVIII (1988), p. 48; J.G. Simms, 'Schomberg at Dundalk, 1689', *The Irish Sword*, Vol. X (1971–2), pp. 14–16; Simms, *Jacobite Ireland*, p. 123; *Life*, Vol. II, pp. 372–3 & 374–5; & *Berwick*, Vol. I, p. 56.

51. Hewitson (ed.), *Diary of Thomas Bellingham*, p. 82; BL. Add. MS. 37660 ff.1–9 & 23; BL. Add. MS. 38145 f.1; Anon., *Life of William III*, pp. 240–1; Childs, 'Marshal Schomberg', p. 48; Simms, 'Schomberg at Dundalk', pp. 17–19; RA / M4 ff.263, 267 & 271; Simms, *Jacobite Ireland*, pp. 126–7; Grew, *English Court in Exile*, pp. 216, 222 & 226; & *Berwick*, Vol. I, pp. 57 & 78–9.

52. Corp (ed.), *L' Autre Exil*, p. 37; BL. Add. MS. 36296 f.61; BL. Add. MS. 38145 f1–2; Plunket, *Derry and the Boyne*, pp. 115 & 117; Gilbert (ed.), *Jacobite Narrative*, pp. 87–9; Ogg, *William III*, p. 50; Anon., *Life of William III*, pp. 240–1; Simms, 'Schomberg at Dundalk', pp. 19–23; *CSPD* (1689–90), p. 272; RA / M4 ff.276, 279 & 286–7; *Berwick*, Vol. I, pp. 57–8; & *Life*, Vol. II, pp. 373, 376–82 & 384.

53. Rapin de Thoyras, *History of England*, Vol. III, p. 133; Madan (ed.), *Stuart Papers*, Vol. I, p. 5; BL. Add. MS. 10118 f.244; Childs, 'Marshal Schomberg', p. 48; Plunket, *Derry and the Boyne*, p. 117; Anon., *Life of William III*, pp. 245 & 265; Ailesbury, Vol. I, p. 253; Simms, 'Schomberg at Dundalk', pp. 23–5; RA / M4 ff.271, 291–2 & 296; & *Life*, Vol. II, pp. 382–3.

54. *Life*, Vol. II, p. 384.

CHAPTER FOUR: THE BANKS OF THE BOYNE

1. M.E. Grew, *William Bentinck and William III* (London, 1924), p. 168; Doebner (ed.), *Memoirs of Mary, Queen of England*, pp. 21–2; BL. Add. MS. 10118 f.258.

2. *Marchioness de Sévigné*, Vol. IX, p. 157; & *Burnet*, Vol. IV, Book V, p. 47.

3. BL. Add. MS. 10118 f.249; BL. Add. MS. 38145 f.16; Plunket, *Derry and the Boyne*, p. 123; Simms, *Jacobite Ireland*, pp. 141–2; *Burnet*, Vol. IV, Book V, p. 47; & *Life*, Vol. II, pp. 390 & 392.

4. HMC, *Calendar of Stuart Papers*, Vol. I, pp. 41–4; BL. Add. MS. 38145 ff.3, 5, 7, 11 & 13; *Letters of Madame*, Vol. I, p. 97; C.M. Howard, *Reminiscences for My Children* (Carlisle, 1837), Vol. II, p. 196.

5. Aubrey, *Defeat of James Stuart's Armada*, p. 46; & Rapin de Thoyras, *History of England*, Vol. III, p. 134.

6. R. Hall, *Flags and Uniforms of the French Infantry under Louis XIV, 1688–1714*, 2nd edn (Farnham, Surrey, 2002), plates 58–9; & Murphy, *Justin MacCarthy*, pp. 31–3; BL. Add. MS. 38145 ff.3–5; Gilbert (ed.), *Jacobite Narrative*, p. 89; O'Callaghan, *Irish Brigades*, pp. 8–9; Simms, *Jacobite Ireland*, p. 138; M.G. McLaughlin & C. Warner, *The Wild Geese* (London, 1980), p. 5; *Life*, Vol. II, p. 387; & *Berwick*, Vol. I, p. 60.

7. Surprisingly, neither d'Avaux nor von Rosen had their careers damaged by their conduct in Ireland. The Ambassador had proved himself to be a faithful servant of the King of France and later had a successful diplomatic career as the French representative to Sweden and Holland. The General was promoted to Marshal of France in 1703, but was not actively employed and retired to his estate in Alsace. He died in 1714, at the venerable age of 87. BL. Add. MS. 38145 ff.9 & 13; RA / M4 f.306; Simms, *Jacobite Ireland*, p. 139; & *Berwick*, Vol. I, pp. 58–60.

8. Turner, *James II*, p. 493; Gilbert (ed.), *Jacobite Narrative*, p. 92; Rose, *England*

in the 1690s, p. 13; *Ailesbury*, Vol. I, pp. 270–1; S. Mulloy, 'French eye-witnesses of the Boyne', *The Irish Sword*, Vol. XV (1982–3), pp. 105 & 107; Saint-Simon, *Memoirs*, Vol. III, p. 467; RA / M4 ff.306–7; *Life*, Vol. II, p. 387; Simms, *Jacobite Ireland*, p. 140; & Petrie, *Jacobite Movement. The First Phase*, p. 94. See also Tyrconnel's equally pessimistic assessments of the Jacobite army's fighting potential: BL. Add. MS. 38145 ff.5–7, 13, 15 & 17; O'Callaghan, *Irish Brigades*, p. 8.

9.   Gilbert (ed.), *Jacobite Narrative*, pp. 92–4; Plunket, *Derry and the Boyne*, p. 123; BL. Add. MS. 36296 ff.128–30; Anon., *Life of William III*, p. 266; RA / M4 ff.294 & 299–300; *Life*, Vol. II, pp. 385–6; & *Berwick*, Vol. I, pp. 61–2.

10.   Anon., *The Life of James II. Late King of England*, pp. 337–8; BL. Add. MS. 38145 ff.19 & 28–9; Anon. (ed.), *Derriana: or, A Collection of Papers Relative to the Siege of Londonderry* (Londonderry, 1794), p. 129; J.M. Maguire, *The Battle of the Boyne* (London, 1894), p. 5; RA / M4 ff.250–1; Simms, *Jacobite Ireland*, p. 143; & *Berwick*, Vol. I, p. 63.

11.   Belloc, *James the Second*, pp. 253–68; Haswell, *James II*, p. 302; BL. Add. MS. 36296 f.79; BL. Add. MS. 38145 ff.4 & 11; BL. Add. MS. 38145 ff.12, 20, 22 & 25; Plunket, *Derry and the Boyne*, pp. 124; Gilbert (ed.), *Jacobite Narrative*, p. 95; Anon., *Life of William III*, p. 267; Anon. (ed.), *Derriana*, pp. 129–30; Maguire, *Battle of the Boyne*, p. 5; M.V. Ronan, *The Boyne Valley and its Antiquities* (Dublin, Belfast, Cork, & Waterford, *c.* 1936), pp. 8 & 31–3; Mulloy, 'French eye-witnesses', pp. 107–8; J.G. Simms, 'Eye-Witnesses of the Boyne', *The Irish Sword*, Vol. VI, (1963), p. 17; Maguire (ed.), *Kings in Conflict*, pp. 51–7; RA / M4 ff.320 & 325–6; & *Life*, Vol. II, pp. 392–4. Tyrconnel had no doubt that there could only be one outcome to the battle and had feared James's desire for an engagement. In June, he had attempted to persuade Mary of Modena to exert pressure on her husband not to fight. He warned that: 'if you venture the Battle and lose it, you are . . . lost to all intents, England, France and all the world will desert and dispise you, and you will bee blamed for your conduct bee it never soo good, whereas if you can preserve the small army from being beaten, you have a hundred chances for you . . . I am not for venturing the loss of all to preserve a place which you must loose as soon as the Battle is lost, and which I think is not of the consequence to us'. BL. Add. MS. 38145 ff.28–9.

12.   *Berwick*, Vol. I, pp. 68–9; BL. Add. MS. 36296 ff.79–80; Plunket, *Derry and the Boyne*, pp. 124–5; Gilbert (ed.), *Jacobite Narrative*, pp. 95–9; Anon., *Life of William III*, p. 268; *Dangeau*, Vol. I, p. 197; Anon. (ed.), *Derriana*, p. 131; J. Kinross, *The Boyne and Aughrim. The War of the Two Kings* (Moreton-in-Marsh, 1997), p. 45; Doherty, *Williamite War*, pp. 109–10; RA / M4 ff.327–8; & *Life*, Vol. II, pp. 394–5; & Simms, *Jacobite Ireland*, p. 147.

13.   BL. Add. MS. 36296 f.80; BL. Add. MS. 38145 ff.23, 25 & 28; P.W. Sergeant, *Little Jennings and Fighting Dick Talbot. A Life of the Duke and Duchess of Tyrconnel* (London, 1913), Vol. II, p. 658; Gilbert (ed.), *Jacobite Narrative*, pp. 98–100; Moir, *Suffolk Regiment*, p. 11; Anon., *Life of William III*, pp. 268–9; Anon. (ed.), *Derriana*, pp. 131–2; Simms, 'Eye-Witnesses of the Boyne', p. 18; & Simms, *Jacobite Ireland*, pp. 147–8.

14.   Sergeant, *Little Jennings*, Vol. II, p. 495; Plunket, *Derry and the Boyne*, p. 126; BL. Add. MS. 36296 f.80; Gilbert (ed.), *Jacobite Narrative*, p. 100; P. Beresford Ellis, *The Boyne Water. The Battle of the Boyne, 1690* (London, 1976), pp. 79–80; Maguire, *Battle of the Boyne*, p. 6; Simms, 'Eye-Witnesses of the Boyne', pp. 19–20; Simms, *Jacobite Ireland*, p. 148; Doherty, *Williamite War*, pp. 113–14; Belloc, *James the Second*, pp. 263–4; P. Lenihan, *1690. Battle of the Boyne* (Stroud, 2003), pp. 135–6; Petrie, *Great Tyrconnel*, p. 205; Anon., *Life of William III*,

p. 268; & *Life*, Vol. II, pp. 395–6; & RA / M4 ff.329–31.

15. Gilbert (ed.), *Jacobite Narrative*, p. 101; Sergeant, *Little Jennings*, Vol. II, pp. 496–8; Plunket, *Derry and the Boyne*, p. 126; BL. Add. MS. 36296 f.80; A.T. Mahan, *The Influence of Sea Power upon History, 1660–1783* (Boston, 1890, rpt. London, 1965), pp. 182 & 183–5; Haswell, *James II*, p. 303; Beresford Ellis, *Boyne Water*, pp. 87–90; Anon. (ed.), *Derriana*, pp. 133–4; Belloc, *James the Second*, pp. 265–6; Simms, 'Eye-Witnesses of the Boyne', p. 21; Anon., *Life of William III*, pp. 269–70; RA / M4 ff.332–3 & 339–41; *Life*, Vol. II, pp. 396–9; & *Berwick*, Vol. I, pp. 64–5.

16. BL. Add. MS. 10118 f.259; Beresford Ellis, *Boyne Water*, pp. 91 & 93–5; Anon. (ed.), *Derriana*, p. 135; Maguire, *Battle of the Boyne*, p. 7; Simms, 'Eye-Witnesses of the Boyne', p. 23; Doherty, *Williamite War*, p. 116; Anon., *Life of William III*, p. 270; Belloc, *James the Second*, pp. 265–6; Simms, *Jacobite Ireland*, p. 149; P. Wauchope, *Patrick Sarsfield and the Williamite War* (Dublin, 1992), p. 107; & *Life*, Vol. II, pp. 399–400.

17. Beresford Ellis, *Boyne Water*, p. 99; BL. Add. MS. 10118 f.259; Plunket, *Derry and the Boyne*, p. 127; Gilbert (ed.), *Jacobite Narrative*, p. 102; Childs, 'Marshal Schomberg', p. 46; Anon. (ed.), *Derriana*, p. 136; Anon., *Life of William III*, pp. 270–1; Wauchope, *Patrick Sarsfield*, p. 107; RA / M4 f.344; *Life*, Vol. II, p. 400; & *Berwick*, Vol. I, pp. 65–6 & 68.

18. BL. Add. MS. 36296 ff.80–2; Sergeant, *Little Jennings*, Vol. II, p. 658; Beresford Ellis, *Boyne Water*, pp. 97–9; Anon. (ed.), *Derriana*, pp. 136–7; Maguire, *Battle of the Boyne*, p. 9; Maguire (ed.), *Kings in Conflict*, pp. 77–8; Anon., *Life of William III*, pp. 271–2; RA / M4 ff.341, 343 & 345–7; & *Life*, Vol. II, pp. 400–1.

19. Mulloy, 'French eye-witnesses', p. 108; Beresford Ellis, *Boyne Water*, pp. 103–4, 106–10 & 114; & Simms, 'Eye-Witnesses of the Boyne', p. 24.

20. BL. Add. MS. 36296 ff.81–2; L. von Ranke, *A History of England*, 6 vols (Oxford, 1875), Vol. VI, p. 143; Sergeant, *Little Jennings*, Vol. II, p. 659; Beresford Ellis, *Boyne Water*, p. 114; Simms, 'Eye-Witnesses of the Boyne', pp. 24–5; & Anon., *Life of William III*, p. 272.

21. BL. Add. MS. 10118 f.259; Cavelli (ed.), *Les Derniers Stuarts*, Vol. II, pp. 576–7; Gilbert (ed.), *Jacobite Narrative*, p. 103; Beresford Ellis, *Boyne Water*, p. 119; Simms, 'Schomberg at Dundalk', p. 25; Simms, *Jacobite Ireland*, p. 151; Ronan, *Boyne Valley*, p. 33; Anon., *Life of William III*, p. 272; *Life*, Vol. II, p. 400; & *Berwick*, Vol. I, pp. 65–6 & 68. See also: the Latin inscription on Schomberg's memorial, St Patrick's Cathedral, Dublin.

22. *Life*, Vol. II, pp. 399–401; Plunket, *Derry and the Boyne*, p. 127; Gilbert (ed.), *Jacobite Narrative*, pp. 102–4; Beresford Ellis, *Boyne Water*, p. 132; Ronan, *Boyne Valley*, p. 33; Simms, 'Eye-Witnesses of the Boyne', p. 25; Simms, *Jacobite Ireland*, p. 151; Anon., *Life of William III*, p. 272; & *Berwick*, Vol. I, p. 68.

23. *Life*, Vol. II, pp. 401–2; & RA / M4 ff.347–8.

24. Anon., *The Life of James II. Late King of England*, p. 353; BL. Add. MS. 36296 f.82; BL. Add. MS. 36707 f.85; Anon., *Life of William III*, p. 274; RA / M4 f.349; *Berwick*, Vol. I, p. 66; & *Life*, Vol. II, p. 401.

25. In compiling his notes for an unpublished biography of James II, Prior Johnston of the English Benedictines notes that, on leaving Ireland, James was assailed by 'a great Dog, ugly to look at, [which] would needs follow his Majesty and the Seamen not suffering him to enter the ship, he cast himself into the Sea, and swam after the King, at which his Majesty was so moved that he caused the Dog to be taken up, who presently making his Adresse to the King as long as his Majesty lived he always kept close about him and was very jealous of all that came neare his Royal Master'. Though Johnston added that

'I have heard seriously related for a certain truth by severall who do not see what it could import to lye in such a matter' it would seem a pity that neither the King or his hagiographers showed a similar concern for the fate of the Irish soldiers whom James had just abandoned without a second thought. See: BL. Add. MS. 10118 f.259. See also: Plunket, *Derry and the Boyne*, p. 128; Beresford Ellis, *Boyne Water*, p. 130; R. Morgan, 'Fort Duncannon, County Wexford', *Arquebusier*, Vol. XXVII, no. 6 (Spring, 2004), p. 17; Anon. (ed.), *Derriana*, p. 137; RA / M4 ff.351–9; *Life*, Vol. II, pp. 402–6; & *Berwick*, Vol. I, pp. 66–7.

26. *Berwick*, Vol. I, pp. 70–3 & 95; BL. Add. MS. 37662 ff.2–3; Gilbert (ed.), *Jacobite Narrative*, pp. 113–17 & 260–7; Maguire (ed.), *Kings in Conflict*, p. 80; Beresford Ellis, *Boyne Water*, p. 148; O'Hara family (pseudonym for J. Banim), *The Boyne Water* (Dublin, 1865), p. 484; D. Stevenson, *Highland Warrior. Alasdair MacColla and the Civil Wars* (Edinburgh, 1980, rpt. 1994), pp. 296–8; RA / M4 ff.382–95; Simms, *Jacobite Ireland*, pp. 158, 160 & 165–71; *Life*, Vol. II, pp. 415–18; & Wauchope, *Patrick Sarsfield*, pp. 127, 129, 131–6 & 138–9.

27. *Life*, Vol. II, pp. 636–8; *For My Son the Prince of Wales, 1692*, Royal Library, ff.102–14; & *Ailesbury*, Vol. I, p. 267.

28. Sells (ed.), *Memoirs of James II*, p. 68; BL. Portland Papers MS. 70522 ff.15–29; Haswell, *James II*, p. 302; Lawson, *History of the Uniforms of the British Army*, Vol. I, p. 38; Beresford Ellis, *Boyne Water*, pp. 144–9; O'Hara family (pseud.), *Boyne Water*, pp. xii, 481–2 & 484; *Ailesbury*, Vol. I, pp. 266–7; Anon. (ed.), *Derriana*, p. 138; Simms, 'Eye-Witnesses of the Boyne', p. 26; RA / M4 ff.360–1; & *Life*, Vol. II, p. 406.

CHAPTER FIVE: THE TEMPER OF THE TIMES

1. W. Kennet, *History of England* (London, 1706), Vol. III, p. 604; *Letters of Madame*, Vol. I, pp. 95–6; *Ailesbury*, Vol. I, p. 258; BL. Add. MS. 10118 f.259; RA / M4 f.359; & Turner, *James II*, pp. 493–4.

2. Turner, *James II*, p. 493; BL. Add. MS. 10118 f.259; RA / M4 ff.366–7 & 374; & *Life*, Vol. II, pp. 411–13.

3. *Life*, Vol. II, p. 413; RA / M4 ff.368–72 & 379; BL. Add. MS. 37662 f.6; Mahan, *Influence of Sea Power*, pp. 184–6; Mr. le Gendre, *The History of the Reign of Lewis the Great* (London, 1699), pp. 218–23; & Dalrymple, *Memoirs*, Vol. I, p. 444.

4. *Letters of Madame*, Vol. I, p. 97.

5. Dalrymple, *Memoirs*, Vol. I, p. 444; *Life*, Vol. II, p. 413; & BL. Add. MS. 37660 ff.15–18 & 24.

6. RA / M4 ff.419 & 435–6; & D. McKie, 'James, Duke of York, F.R.S.', *Notes and Records of the Royal Society of London*, Vol. XIII (1958), pp. 8–15.

7. Porter, 'Non-Juring Bishops', pp. 2 & 8; Strickland, *Lives of the Seven Bishops*, pp. 79–82; Browning (ed.), *Memoirs of Sir John Reresby*, pp. 562 & 570–2; BL. Add. MS. 37660 ff.15–18, 24, 34 & 38; BL. Add. MS. 37662 f.2; NA. SP. 32/1 f.127; *CSPD* (1689–90), pp. 111–12, 115 & 117.

8. Anon., *The Abdicated Prince* (London, 1690), p. 60; & Anon., *A Dialogue Between K.W. and Benting* (no place or date, probably London, 1694–5), pp. 3 & 6–7.

9. BL. Add. MS. 39923 ff5–6; Monod, *Jacobitism and the English People*, pp. 98–9, 221 & 264–5; Porter, 'Non-Juring Bishops', p. 8; Strickland, *Lives of the Seven Bishops*, pp. 195 & 198–201; J. Callow, 'Richard Graham, Viscount Preston', *Oxford Dictionary of National Biography* (forthcoming); C.F. Mullett, 'Religion, Politics, and Oaths in the Glorious Revolution', *Review of Politics*, Vol. X (1948), pp. 463–7 & 470; RA / M4 f.471; *Life*, Vol. II, p. 441; & Burnet, Vol. IV, Book V, p. 69.

10. Callow, 'Richard Graham' (forthcoming); RA / M4 f.475; *Life*, Vol. II, pp. 441–3; & Burnet, Vol. IV, Book V, pp. 69–70.

11. Southorn, 'Mary of Modena', p. 7; Strickland, *Lives of the Seven Bishops*,

pp. 202–3, 209–12, 215; Ogg, *William III*, pp. 43–4; *Ailesbury*, Vol. I, p. 278; Luttrell, *Brief Relation*, Vol. II, p. 271; E. Cruickshanks & J. Black (eds), *The Jacobite Challenge* (Edinburgh, 1988), p. 64; T.B. Howell (ed.), *A Complete Collection of State Trials* (London, 1812), Vol. XII, pp. 646–71 & 671–747; RA / M4 ff.476–9; J. Garrett, *Triumphs of Providence, The Assassination Plot, 1696* (Cambridge, 1980), p. 15; *Life*, Vol. II, pp. 443–4; & *Burnet*, Vol. IV, Book V, pp. 70–1.

12. *Burnet*, Vol. IV, Book V, p. 70; Strickland, *Lives of the Seven Bishops*, pp. 217–19; Porter, 'Non-Juring Bishops', pp. 7–9; & *Life*, Vol. II, pp. 410–11 & 473.

13. Lord Acton (ed.), 'Letters of James the Second to the Abbot of La Trappe', *Miscellanies of the Philobiblion Society*, Vol. XIV (London, 1872–6), p. 9; Le Gendre, *History of the Reign of Lewis the Great*, pp. 226–7; Anon. (ed.), *Memoirs of the Duke de Villars* (London, 1735), pp. 176–7; *Dangeau*, Vol. I, p. 211; & *Life*, Vol. II, pp. 412–13.

14. Le Gendre, *History of the Reign of Lewis the Great*, p. 228; *Dangeau*, Vol. I, p. 213; HMC, *Calendar of Stuart Papers*, Vol. I, p. 64; A.J. Krailsheimer (ed.), *The Letters of Armand-Jean de Rancé* (Kalamazoo, Michigan, 1984), Vol. II, p. 167; & BL. Add. MS. 37662 f.4.

15. J.G. Simms, 'Marlborough's Siege of Cork, 1690', *The Irish Sword*, Vol. IX (1969–70), pp. 113–23; Simms, *Jacobite Ireland*, pp. 178 & 180–1; W.S. Churchill, *Marlborough. His Life and Times* (London, 1933, rpt. Chicago, 2002), Vol. I, p. 291; BL. Add. MS. 37662 f.7; Gilbert (ed.), *Jacobite Narrative*, pp. 117–19; H. Murtagh, 'Galway and the Jacobite War', *The Irish Sword*, Vol. XII (1975–6), p. 4; RA / M4 ff.396–400; *Life*, Vol. II, p. 419; Wauchope, *Patrick Sarsfield*, pp. 165–8; C. Petrie, *The Marshal Duke of Berwick* (London, 1953), pp. 80–1; *Berwick*, Vol. I, pp. 73 & 77–82.

16. *Berwick*, Vol. I, pp. 81–2; Gilbert (ed.), *Jacobite Narrative*, pp. 111 & 127; Simms, *Jacobite Ireland*, pp. 189–91 &

195–7; Petrie, *Great Tyrconnel*, pp. 229 & 243–4; RA / M4 ff.408–17; & *Life*, Vol. II, pp. 420–4.

17. *Berwick*, Vol. I, p. 83; Gilbert (ed.), *Jacobite Narrative*, p. 128; Petrie, *Great Tyrconnel*, p. 248; RA / M4 f.444; *Life*, Vol. II, pp. 424–5 & 433–4; & Wauchope, *Patrick Sarsfield*, pp. 176, 189 & 193.

18. Gilbert (ed.), *Jacobite Narrative*, p. 129; Simms, *Jacobite Ireland*, pp. 203–4; Petrie, *Great Tyrconnel*, p. 249; RA / M4 ff.444–8, 451 & 455; Wauchope, *Patrick Sarsfield*, pp. 198–9; Petrie, *Marshal Duke*, p. 89; *Life*, Vol. II, pp. 451–2; & *Berwick*, Vol. I, p. 83.

19. Gilbert (ed.), *Jacobite Narrative*, p. 133; Simms, *Jacobite Ireland*, pp. 204–5; Murtagh, 'Galway and the Jacobite War', pp. 5–6 & 8; RA / M4 ff.401, 408 & 499–501; *Life*, Vol. II, p. 456; & Wauchope, *Patrick Sarsfield*, pp. 208–9 & 214.

20. *DNB*, Vol. XXII, p. 308; Gilbert (ed.), *Jacobite Narrative*, pp. 134–6; Simms, *Jacobite Ireland*, pp. 206–11; Wauchope, *Patrick Sarsfield*, pp. 210–12; RA / M4 ff.506–12; & *Life*, Vol. II, pp. 453–5.

21. Gilbert (ed.), *Jacobite Narrative*, pp. 139–40; Maguire (ed.), *Kings in Conflict*, pp. 85–6; Kinross, *Boyne and Aughrim*, pp. 83 & 84; *Life*, Vol. II, pp. 456–7; Doherty, *Williamite War*, p. 170; Simms, *Jacobite Ireland*, pp. 217 & 219; & Wauchope, *Patrick Sarsfield*, pp. 219–21.

22. Gilbert (ed.), *Jacobite Narrative*, pp. 140–4, 146–8 & 274; Maguire (ed.), *Kings in Conflict*, pp. 86 & 88–9; Kinross, *Boyne and Aughrim*, pp. 85–9; Doherty, *Williamite War*, pp. 172 & 174–83; Petrie, *Great Tyrconnel*, pp. 251–3; Wauchope, *Patrick Sarsfield*, pp. 223–4 & 226–33; RA / M4 ff.517–23; Simms, *Jacobite Ireland*, pp. 220–8; *Berwick*, Vol. I, pp. 89–92; & *Life*, Vol. II, p. 458.

23. BL. Add. MS. 38145 f.4; Gilbert (ed.), *Jacobite Narrative*, pp. 155, 157 & 282; Anon. (ed.), *Memoirs of the Duke de Villars*, pp. 194–5; Murtagh, 'Galway and the Jacobite War', pp. 10–12; Murtagh, 'Irish Jacobite Army',

pp. 32–3; *Life*, Vol. II, pp. 459–62; RA / M4 ff.524–5 & 535–6; National Army Museum, *1688. Glorious Revolution?*, p. 51; Wauchope, *Patrick Sarsfield*, p. 250; Simms, *Jacobite War*, p. 242; *Berwick*, Vol. I, pp. 93 & 95; & Petrie, *Great Tyrconnel*, pp. 253–4.

24. Gilbert (ed.), *Jacobite Narrative*, pp. 167–8, 170, 174–81 & 298–308; O'Callaghan, *Irish Brigades*, pp. 28–9 & 32; Murtagh, 'Galway and the Jacobite War', pp. 13–14; Simms, *Jacobite Ireland*, p. 250; *Life*, Vol. II, pp. 465–6; Wauchope, *Patrick Sarsfield*, pp. 258–62; & McLaughlin & Warner, *Wild Geese*, p. 5.

25. BL. Add. MS. 37662 ff.1 & 12; Gilbert (ed.), *Jacobite Narrative*, pp. 185–7 & 191; Ogg, *William III*, p. 51; Maguire (ed.), *Kings in Conflict*, pp. 144–8, 154–6, 161–4 & 172; RA / M4 ff.528 & 531; & Simms, *Jacobite Ireland*, pp. 262–4

26. BL. Add. MS. 37662 ff.1–2 & 14; Baxter, *William III*, p. 273; Prebble, *Glencoe*, pp. 19, 151–2, 160, 171, 198 & 201–2; Brown, *Kingdom or Province? Scotland and the Regal Union, 1603–1715* (New York, 1992), p. 172; *Life*, Vol. II, pp. 430–1; & Hopkins, *Glencoe and the End of the Highland War*, pp. 310–11 & 315–16.

27. HMC, *Calendar of Stuart Papers*, Vol. I, p. 66; RA / M4 ff.551–2; Prebble, *Glencoe*, pp. 171, 231 & 235; & Hopkins, *Glencoe and the End of the Highland War*, pp. 317–18 & 321.

28. Hopkins, *Glencoe and the End of the Highland War*, p. 325; & Prebble, *Glencoe*, pp. 176, 201 & 224.

29. Prebble, *Glencoe*, p. 252; Brown, *Kingdom or Province?*, p. 172; RA / M4 f.557; & Hopkins, *Glencoe and the End of the Highland War*, pp. 331–2 & 334–7.

30. HMC, *Calendar of Stuart Papers*, Vol. I, p. 74; Petrie, *Jacobite Movement. The First Phase*, p. 110; Shield & Lang, *King over the Water*, p. 39; B. St. John, *La Cour de Jacques II à Saint-Germain-en-Laye* (Paris, 1913), pp. 22–4; & S.V. Grancsay, 'A Stocking Knife Associated with James II of England',

in S.V. Granscay, *Arms and Armour* (New York, 1986), pp. 82–3.

31. Shield & Lang, *King over the Water*, p. 39; & St John, *La Cour de Jacques II*, p. 24.

32. Cronin, *Louis XIV*, p. 262; RA / M4 ff.461 & 563; & Aubrey, *Defeat of James Stuart's Armada*, p. 78.

33. *Life*, Vol. II, p. 477; & BL. Add. MS. 37662 ff.16–17.

34. Macpherson, *Original Papers*, Vol. I, pp. 408–9; & BL. Add. MS. 37662 ff.10 & 12.

35. BL. Add. MS. 37662 f.10; Haile, *Queen Mary of Modena*, p. 284; Aubrey, *Defeat of James Stuart's Armada*, p. 74; & *Life*, Vol. II, p. 474.

36. HMC, *Calendar of Stuart Papers*, Vol. I, p. 68; Gilbert (ed.) *Jacobite Narrative*, pp. 302 & 306; O'Callaghan, *Irish Brigades*, pp. 28–9; RA / M4 ff.544 & 548–9; *Life*, Vol. II, pp. 467 & 478–9; & Simms, *Jacobite Ireland*, pp. 251, 259–61.

37. HMC, *Calendar of Stuart Papers*, Vol. I, pp. 66–7; G. Rowlands, 'An Army in Exile: Louis XIV and the Irish Forces of James II in France, 1691–1698', *The Royal Stuart Society*, Occasional Paper no. LX (2001), pp. 5–6; Wauchope, *Patrick Sarsfield*, p. 284; O'Callaghan, *Irish Brigades*, pp. 29–31; McLaughlin & Warner, *Wild Geese*, pp. 5 & 34; & *Berwick*, Vol. I, pp. 97–8.

38. HMC, *Calendar of Stuart Papers*, Vol. I, pp. 66–70; *Life*, Vol. II, pp. 478–9; *Berwick*, Vol. I, pp. 97–8; O'Callaghan, *Irish Brigades*, pp. 30–1; Macpherson, *Original Papers*, Vol. I, p. 39; & *Dangeau*, Vol. I, p. 229.

40. Macpherson, *Original Papers*, Vol. I, p. 397; Aubrey, *Defeat of James Stuart's Armada*, p. 79; RA / M4 ff.580–2; *CSPD* (1700–2), pp. 161–4; *Berwick*, Vol. I, pp. 97–8; & HMC, *Calendar of Stuart Papers*, Vol. I, p. 72.

41. Dalrymple, *Memoirs*, Vol. I, p. 494; Aubrey, *Defeat of James Stuart's Armada*, p. 79; Haile, *Queen Mary of Modena*, p. 285; E. Gregg, 'Was Queen Anne a Jacobite?', *History*, Vol. 57, no. 191 (Oct. 1972), p. 365; Anon., *Life of William III*, p. 331; RA / M4 f.583; &

J.R. Jones, *Marlborough* (Cambridge, 1993), pp. 49–50.

42. BL. Add. MS. 10118 ff.299–303 & 312; BL. Add. MS. 37661 ff.3, 5–6 & 10; Anon., *Life of William III*, pp. 330–1; RA / M4 ff.584–615; & *Life*, Vol. II, pp. 479–88.

43. BL. Add. MS. 10118 f.298; Anon., *Life of William III*, p. 330; RA / M4 ff.615–17 & 627; & *Life*, Vol. II, pp. 488–9 & 492.

44. HMC, *Calendar of Stuart Papers*, Vol. I, p. 71; *Life*, Vol. II, pp. 491–2; Macpherson, *Original Papers*, Vol. I, pp. 414–15; Aubrey, *Defeat of James Stuart's Armada*, pp. 79–80; BL. Add. MS. 37661 f.11; BL. Add. MS. 39923 f.9; Mahan, *Influence of Sea Power*, pp. 187–8; Anon., *A Narrative of the Victory Obtained by the English and Dutch Fleet . . . Over that of France, Near La Hogue* (London, 1744), pp. 7–8; Saint-Simon, *Memoirs*, Vol. I, p. 9; RA / M4 ff.577 & 628; & *Berwick*, Vol. I, pp. 98–9.

45. *Berwick*, Vol. I, p. 100; Mahan, *Influence of Sea Power*, pp. 189–90; Aubrey, *Defeat of James Stuart's Armada*, pp. 89–92; Anon., *Narrative of the Victory Obtained*, p. 25; Saint-Simon, *Memoirs*, Vol. I, p. 9; RA / M4 ff.622–3 & 629; & *Life*, Vol. II, p. 493.

46. Aubrey, *Defeat of James Stuart's Armada*, p. 114; Mahan, *Influence of Sea Power*, p. 190; Anon., *Narrative of the Victory Obtained*, pp. 25–9, 33–6 & 54–6; RA / M4 ff.629–30; *Life*, Vol. II, p. 494; BL. Add. MS. 37661 f.11; & *Berwick*, Vol. I, pp. 100–1.

47. Aubrey, *Defeat of James Stuart's Armada*, pp. 116–20; Anon., *Narrative of the Victory Obtained*, pp. 30–1 & 38; RA / M4 ff.630, 632–3 & 638; & *Life*, Vol. II, pp. 494 & 496.

48. Dalrymple, *Memoirs*, Vol. I, p. 508; Aubrey, *Defeat of James Stuart's Armada*, p. 121; Anon., *Narrative of the Victory Obtained*, pp. 31–2, 38 & 40; Saint-Simon, *Memoirs*, Vol. I, p. 9; & BL. Add. MS. 10118 f.449.

49. *Ailesbury*, Vol. I, p. 360; Macpherson, *Original Papers*, Vol. I, p. 419; HMC, *Calendar of Stuart Papers*, p. 73; Mahan, *Influence of Sea Power*, pp. 190–1;

M. Ragazzi, *Maria Beatrice d' Este, Regina d' Inghilterra* (Assisi, 1942), pp. 245 & 247; G. Barany, *The Anglo-Russian Entente Cordiale of 1697–1698. Peter I and William III at Utrecht* (New York, 1986), pp. 19–20; Garrett, *Triumphs of Providence*, p. 53; Howell (ed.), *State Trials*, Vol. XII, pp. 1051, 1053 & 1056; RA / M4 ff.638–9 & 642; *Life*, Vol. II, p. 495; & *Berwick*, Vol. I, pp. 101–2.

50. Acton (ed.), 'Letters of James II', p. 15; Krailsheimer (ed.), *Letters of de Rancé*, pp. 191–2 & 195; Hopkirk, *Queen over the Water*, p. 211; Oman, *Mary of Modena*, p. 171; BL. Add. MS. 37661 f.3; Aubrey, *Defeat of James Stuart's Armada*, p. 127; Anon., *Life of William III*, p. 334; RA / M4 ff.634 & 636–7; *Life*, Vol. II, pp. 494–5; & Haile, *Queen Mary of Modena*, pp. 289–90.

51. BL. Add. MS. 10118 f.312; *Dangeau*, Vol. I, p. 229; Haswell, *James II*, p. 304; S. Cole, 'Princess Over the Water: A Memoir of Louise Marie Stuart, 1692–1712', *The Royal Stuart Society*, Occasional Paper no. XVIII (1981), p. 1; RA / M4 f.640.

52. *DNB*, Vol. XXXV, p. 126; Ogg, *William III*, p. 91; Lawson, *History of the Uniforms of the British Army*, Vol. I, pp. 62–3; BL. Add. MS. 37661 ff.3–4; BL. Stowe MS. 444 f.4; *Life*, Vol. II, p. 496; & *Letters of Madame*, Vol. I, p. 108.

CHAPTER SIX: THE SHADOW COURT

1. Saint-Germain-en-Laye Musée des Antiquities Nationales, *Le Domaine Royal: Ses Châteaux, Ses Jardins* (Paris, 1997), pp. 1, 3, 5, & 14–5; Oman, *Mary of Modena*, pp. 156–7; Grew, *English Court in Exile*, pp. 58–61; Cruickshanks (ed.), *Stuart Courts*, pp. 242–3; F. Maxwell Stuart, *Lady Nithsdale and the Jacobites* (Traquair House, Peebleshire, 1995), p. 21; BL. Add. MS. 36296 f.22; & E. Corp & J. Sanson (eds), *La Cour des Stuarts à Saint-*

Germain-en-Laye au temps de Louis XIV
(Paris, 1992), pp. 94–5.

2. Oman, *Mary of Modena*, p. 157; Sizergh
    Castle Collection, SIZ C 100–2 & SIZ T
    101; *Ailesbury*, Vol. I, p. 323;
    Cruickshanks & Corp (eds), *Stuart
    Court in Exile*, pp. 19 & 22; Corp &
    Sanson (eds), *La Cour des Stuarts*,
    pp. 209–10; A. Hamilton, 'Zeneyde' in
    Oeuvres Diverses (London, 1776),
    pp. 238–40; P.F. Riley, *A Lust for Virtue.
    Louis XIV's Attack on Sin in Seventeenth-
    Century France* (Westport, Connecticut,
    2001), pp. 116 & 145; C.E. Lart (ed.),
    *The Parochial Registers of Saint Germain-
    en-Laye* (London, 1910), Vol. I, p. viii;
    & O'Callaghan, *Irish Brigades*, fn. 2
    p. 190. The most authoritative
    accounts of life at the Jacobite court
    are the following series of articles:
    E. Corp, 'La ville de Saint-Germain-en-
    Laye a l'epoque des jacobites' in Corp
    & Sanson (eds), *La Cour des Stuarts*
    (Paris, 1992), pp. 209–10; the
    'Introduction' to Cruickshanks & Corp
    (eds), *Stuart Court in Exile*,
    pp. xii–xxiii; N. Genet-Rouffiac,
    'Jacobites in Paris and Saint Germain-
    en-Laye' in *Stuart Court in Exile*,
    pp. 15–38; and the new collection of
    essays: Corp *et al.*, *Court in Exile*.

3. Sadly, the series of grottoes, with their
    statues of Classical deities such as
    Orpheus, Hercules, and Perseus and
    Andromeda, which showcased
    complicated fountains fed by state-of-
    the-art hydraulic pumps, was
    abandoned from 1655 to 1660, and
    had been long demolished by the time
    that James II came to St Germain.
    Anthony Hamilton provided a graphic
    account of the palace's 'vast
    promenade' and beautiful parks being
    overrun, on a feast day, by the
    'bourgeois [of the town] . . . with their
    muddy dogs, [and] their evil little
    children'. *Devotions*, pp. 79–80; Corp &
    Sanson (eds), *La Cour des Stuarts*,
    p. 131; A. Goujon, *Histoire de la Ville et
    du Château de St. Germain-en-Laye*
    (St-Germain-en-Laye, 1829), p. 402;
    A. Zega & B.H. Dams, *Palaces of the Sun
    King* (London, 2002), pp. 34 & 147;

    Oman, *Mary of Modena*, p. 158; BL.
    Add. MS. 36296 ff.22–3; St Germain,
    Le Domaine Royal, p. 19; Hamilton,
    Oeuvres Diverses, p. 244; RA. 1/66
    ff.1–3; BL. Add. MS. 37662 f.5; &
    Dangeau, Vol. I, p. 210.

4. *Life*, Vol. II, pp. 619–21; *Devotions*,
    p. 34; Bevan, *King James the Third*,
    p. 30; Hornyold, *Genealogical Memoirs*,
    pp. 135 & 142–4; HMC, *Calendar of
    Stuart Papers*, Vol. I, p. 114–15;
    Hamilton, *Oeuvres Diverses*, p. 239;
    Madan (ed.), *Stuart Papers*, Vol. I,
    p. 26; PRO. SP.32.238; D.G. Scott,
    'John Betham et l' Education du
    Prince de Galles', *Revue de la
    Bibliotheque Nationale*, no. 46 (1992),
    pp. 31–3; & Corp *et al.*, *Court in Exile*,
    pp. 265–8.

5. *Devotions*, pp. 3–4; Trinity College,
    MS.3529 ff.3–4; & *Life*, Vol. II, p. 622.

6. It would appear that James had begun
    to outline his guide for his son while
    he was in Dublin in 1690, but, as with
    all his writings, he took some time to
    hone his prose and properly marshal
    his thoughts. Consequently, it was only
    in 1692 – as his projects for the
    invasion of England waxed and then
    waned – that he returned to complete
    his set of fragmentary instructions.
    Life, Vol. II, pp. 618–42; *For My Son the
    Prince of Wales, 1692*, Royal Library,
    ff.1–138; & HMC, *Calendar of Stuart
    Papers*, Vol. I, pp. 114–17.

7. W. Fuller, *A Brief Discovery* (London,
    1696), p. 19; Bevan, *King James the
    Third*, p. 28; & Oman, *Mary of Modena*,
    p. 176.

8. An explicit link was drawn by Jacobite
    propagandists between the premature
    death of the Princess and the example
    of her father's sacrifice. Thus, Louise
    Marie: 'died expressing the warmest
    sentiments of piety, and the most
    perfect resignation, uttering often her
    Royal Father's dying words and
    ejaculations, as inheritrix of his piety'.
    Dangeau, Vol. I, p. 372 & Vol. II,
    pp. 81–2; Hamilton, *Oeuvres Diverses*,
    p. 239; Cole, 'Princess Over the
    Water', pp. 2–3, 9, 12, 15–16; Bevan,
    King James the Third, pp. 31–2; Haile,

Queen Mary of Modena, p. 429;
R. Hatton, *Charles XII* (London, 1974),
p. 17; Hopkirk, *Queen over the Water*,
p. 262; Miller, *James*, pp. 137–8; Oman,
Mary of Modena, pp. 224–5; Lart (ed.),
Parochial Registers of Saint Germain,
Vol. I, p. 129; Sanders, *Abrégé de la Vie
de Jacques II*, p. 101; Anon., *Memoirs of
the Chevalier de St. George: With some
Private Passages of the Life of the Late
James II, Never Before Published*
(London, 1712), p. 78; Madan (ed.),
Stuart Papers, Vol. II, p. 377; Saint-
Simon, *Memoirs*, Vol. I, p. 348; Scott,
'John Betham', pp. 33–7; & Corp *et al.*,
Court in Exile, pp. 269–75.

9. Macaulay, *History of England*, Vol. V,
    pp. 2330–2; Miller, *James II*, p. 235;
    Macky, 'View of the Court', Vol. VI,
    pp. 390–3; & Hamilton, *Oeuvres
    Diverses*, pp. 237–47.

10. Hamilton, *Oeuvres Diverses*, pp. 239–40;
    Devotions, p. 6; Trinity College,
    MS. 3529 f.6; & Hopkirk, *Queen over the
    Water*, p. 219.

11. *Life*, Vol. II, pp. 621–2; *For My Son the
    Prince of Wales, 1692*, Royal Library,
    ff.10 & 13–14; Ainsworth, *James the
    Second*, pp. 92–3, 156–8 & 299; &
    Kishlansky, *Monarchy Transformed*,
    p. 267.

12. HMC, *Calendar of Stuart Papers*, Vol. I,
    p. 61; *Devotions*, p. 90; Trinity College,
    MS.3529 f.90; *Life*, Vol. II, p. 605; &
    Hopkirk, *Queen over the Water*, p. 234.

13. BL. Add. MS. 15904 ff.167–71; Macky,
    'View of the Court', pp. 393–4;
    Hamilton, *Oeuvres Diverses*, pp. 237–46;
    Grew, *English Court in Exile*, p. 281; &
    Life, Vol. II, p. 473.

14. HMC, *Calendar of Stuart Papers*, Vol. I,
    pp. 77 & 79; *Life*, Vol. II, pp. 471–2;
    BL. Add. MS. 36296 f.23; Ruvigny
    (ed.), *Jacobite Peerage*, pp. 216–17;
    Hamilton, *Oeuvres Diverses*, p. 238; &
    Dulon, *Jacques II Stuart*, p. 43.

15. One anonymous French wit penned
    the following lines about the exiled
    Court at St Germain:

        It is here that James
        the Second
        Without minister or

        mistress,
        Went in the
        morning to Mass
        And in the evening
        went for a Sermon.

    Dulon, *Jacques II Stuart*, p. 43; Hopkirk,
    Queen over the Water, p. 229; Lart (ed.),
    Parochial Registers of Saint Germain,
    Vol. I, p. 153; *Devotions*, pp. 99–100;
    O'Callaghan, *Irish Brigades*, pp. 148–9;
    Petrie, *Marshal Duke*, pp. 101–2,
    109–10 & 116; Wauchope, *Patrick
    Sarsfield*, pp. 296 & 299–300; BL. Add.
    MS. 10118 f.381; *Dangeau*, Vol. I,
    pp. 278–9; Trinity College, MS.3529
    ff.99–100; & *Devotions*, pp. 99–100.

16. It was also rumoured that Tyrconnel's
    son was the father of Henrietta's little
    girl. See; Petrie, *Marshal Duke*,
    pp. 116–17, 188 & 333–4; J. Callow,
    'Arabella Churchill', *Oxford Dictionary
    of National Biography* (forthcoming);
    Churchill, *Marlborough*, Vol. I,
    pp. 47–8; Fea, *James II and his Wives*,
    pp. 302–3; Grew, *English Court in Exile*,
    pp. 350–1; O'Callaghan, *Irish Brigades*,
    pp. 149–50; Oman, *Mary of Modena*,
    p. 182; *Dangeau*, Vol. I, pp. 292–3; &
    Saint-Simon, *Memoirs*, Vol. II, p. 87.

17. HMC, *Calendar of Stuart Papers*, Vol. I,
    pp. 81–2, 85, 89, 95–7, 100, 104–5,
    107–9, 114, 117, 121, 124–8, 130,
    132–4, & 137; & Madan (ed.), *Stuart
    Papers*, Vol. I, pp. 16–17, 35–6 & 41–2.

18. HMC, *Calendar of Stuart Papers*, Vol. I,
    pp. 64, 82, 126, & 129; RA / 1 / 78 f.1;
    Maxwell Stuart, *Lady Nithsdale*, p. 19; &
    Hornyold, *Genealogical Memoirs*, p. 150.

19. HMC, *Calendar of Stuart Papers*, Vol. I,
    p. 86; Ruvigny (ed.), *Jacobite Peerage*,
    p. 217; & *State Trials*, Vol. XII,
    pp. 1051–6.

20. HMC, *Calendar of Stuart Papers*, Vol. I,
    pp. 81–2; RA / 1 / 73 f.1; RA / 1 / 75
    ff.1–2; RA / 1 / 76–7; & RA / 1 / 82–3.

21. *Ailesbury*, Vol. I, pp. 272 & 324;
    Cruickshanks & Corps (eds), *Stuart
    Court in Exile*, pp. 26–9; Middleton,
    Charles, 2nd Earl of Middleton,
    pp. 148–9; Jones, *Charles Middleton*,
    p. 268; Hopkirk, *Queen over the Water*,
    p. 234; Macpherson (ed.), *Original*

Papers, Vol. I, pp. 417–19; Monod, *Jacobitism and the English People*, p. 103; Cavelli (ed.), *Les Derniers Stuarts*, Vol. II, pp. 576–7; H. Douglas, *Jacobite Spy Wars. Moles, Rogues and Treachery* (Stroud, 1999), p. 7; & BL. Add. MS. 37661 ff.3, 9 12 & 14.

22. *Dangeau*, Vol. I, pp. 210 & 270–1; P. McLynn, 'Factionalism among the Exiles in France: The Case of Chevalier Ramsay and Bishop Atterbury', *The Royal Stuart Society*, Occasional Paper no. XXXIII (1989), p. 1; & BL. Add. MS. 10118 f.226.

23. HMC, *Calendar of Stuart Papers*, Vol. I, pp. 87, 106–7, 120, 122, & 140.

24. Ruvigny (ed.), *Jacobite Peerage*, pp. xv–xviii; & *Ailesbury*, Vol. I, p. 360.

25. HMC, *Calendar of Stuart Papers*, Vol. I, pp. 77–8; 109–10; Corp *et al.*, *Court in Exile*, p. 186; E. Hawkins, *Medallic Inscriptions of the History of Great Britain and Ireland* (Portsmouth, 1885), Vol. II, pp. 215–17; *CSPD* (1700–1702), p. 136; & Monod, *Jacobitism and the English People*, pp. 74–5.

26. Hamilton thought that though the 'view is truly enchanting, the walks are marvellous and the air is so inviting that you could eat four meals a day' the palace swarmed with priests and impoverished widows. Only a handful of the women followed 'the most up-to-date fashion', or were particularly beautiful, while the vast majority of the men were dull or venal. James's courtiers were, he declared, a bunch of hypocrites, 'men of a quite despicable character', soured by their experiences and making a mere display of their piety. Cruickshanks & Corp (eds), *Stuart Court in Exile*, pp. xiv–xvi & xviii; Jones, *Charles Middleton*, p. 265; Macky, 'View of the Court', pp. 391–7; & Hamilton, *Oeuvres Diverses*, pp. 237–47.

27. Hornyold, *Genealogical Memoirs*, p. 145; Corp *et al.*, *Court in Exile*, pp. 183 & 187–9; Corp & Sanson (eds), *La Cour des Stuarts*, pp. 107 & 117–18.

28. A grim little rhyme accompanied the print of 'James the Evicted King', proclaiming that:

I have made a hash of the whole of England: Because I am in such a hurry.
I would have my fame refilled in all the world; But an Orange has spoiled everything.

See Plate 9.
See also: Defoe, *Englishman's Choice*, pp. 17, 19, 22 & 30; *Dangeau*, Vol. I, pp. 267 & 282; Corp & Sanson (eds), *La Cour des Stuarts*, pp. 109–12.

29. *Devotions*, pp. 31, 35, 54, 61, 64, 68, 83–4, 88–9 & 97–101; Trinity College, MS. 3529 ff.31, 35, 54, 61, 64, 68, 83–4, 88–9 & 97–101; Corp & Sanson (eds), *La Cour des Stuarts*, pp. 106–7; & Corp *et al.*, *Court in Exile*, pp. 184 & 187.

30. Corp *et al.*, *Court in Exile*, pp. 183, 186 & 190–1; Corp & Sanson (eds), *La Cour des Stuarts*, p. 118; & Monod, *Jacobitism and the English People*, pp. 73–6.

31. *Devotions*, pp. 73, 79 & 98; Trinity College, MS. 3529 ff.73, 79 & 98; Haile, *Queen Mary of Modena*, pp. 517–20; & Corp & Sanson (eds), *La Cour des Stuarts*, pp. 112 & 128.

32. BL. Add. MS. 10118 f.226; Corp *et al.*, *Court in Exile*, pp. 182, 184–5 & 198–200; & Corp & Sanson (eds), *La Cour des Stuarts*, pp. 106, 136 & 141.

33. Hamilton, *Oeuvres Diverses*, pp. 237–46; Hornyold, *Genealogical Memoirs*, pp. 136, 145–6, 150–1, & 160; & BL. Add. MS. 37662 f.5.

CHAPTER SEVEN: ECLIPSE AT RYSWICK

1. W. Jerdan (ed.), *Letters from James Earl of Perth . . . to his Sister, the Countess of Erroll* (London & New York, 1845, rpt. 1968), pp. 27–9; *Berwick*, Vol. I, pp. 111–13; Baxter, *William III*, pp. 312–15; Churchill, *Marlborough*, Vol. I, pp. 365–7; *Life*, Vol. II, p. 516; Lynn, *Wars of Louis XIV*, pp. 233–40; Ogg, *William III*, p. 92; Anon.,

*A Particular Relation of the Battel fought
on the 29th of July 1693* (London,
1693), p. 6; & Anon., *The Paris Relation
of the Battel of Landen, July 29th 1693*
(London, 1693), p. 21.

2. Jerdan (ed.), *Letters from James Earl of
Perth*, p. 28; O'Callaghan, *Irish
Brigades*, pp. 171–6; Wauchope, *Patrick
Sarsfield*, pp. 297–8; *Berwick*, Vol. I,
pp. 113–14; Petrie, *Marshal Duke*,
pp. 99–100; Le Gendre, *History of the
Reign of Lewis the Great*, pp. 239–41 &
248–51; Anon., *Life of William III*,
p. 368; National Army Museum, *1688.
Glorious Revolution?*, pp. 7 & 61–3;
BL. Stowe MS. 444 f.14; BL. Add. MS.
37661 ff.3–4, 15–17 & 32; RA / M4
f.700; *Berwick*, Vol. I, pp. 113–14

3. O'Callaghan, *Irish Brigades*, pp. 33 &
176–8; Murphy, *Justin MacCarthy*, p. 42;
W. Jerdan (ed.), *Letters from James Earl
of Perth, Lord Chancellor of Scotland, to
his Sister, the Countess of Erroll* (London,
1845, rpt. London & New York, 1968);
Howell (ed.), *State Trials*, Vol. XII,
pp. 1269–70 & 1280; *Berwick*, Vol. I,
pp. 116–17; & HMC, *Calendar of Stuart
Papers*.

4. RA / M4 ff.650–2; *Life*, Vol. II,
pp. 502–3; & *Ailesbury*, Vol. I,
pp. 330–1.

5. *Life*, Vol. II, pp. 502–5; Anon., *Life of
James II, Late King of England*,
pp. 399–401; Anon., *His Majesties Most
Gratious Declaration to all his Loving
Subjects* (St-Germain-en-Laye, 1693),
pp. 1–3; BL. Add. MS. 39923 f.11;
Porter, 'Non-Juring Bishops', p. 9; &
RA / M4 ff.658–66.

6. *Life*, Vol. II, pp. 505–10; E.E. Reynolds,
Bossuet (New York, 1963), p. 204;
Turner, *James II*, p. 496; Macaulay,
History of England, Vol. V, p. 2342;
BL. Add. MS. 10118 ff.319–21; Anon.,
His Majesties Most Gratious Declaration,
pp. 1–3; & RA / M4 ff.678, 681 &
695–7.

7. It is notable that an extract from this
letter survives only in Clarke's *Life*, its
contents noted down by the King's
later editors from an original that is
not included in the main collections
of James's correspondence with the

abbé de La Trappe. The kernel of
James's argument is cribbed, almost
directly, from Bossuet's judgement
upon his Declaration, and reinforces
both the King's desire for constant
self-justification and his frankly
unoriginal turn of mind. See: *Life*,
Vol. II, p. 510; Acton (ed.), 'Letters of
James the Second', pp. 21–4;
Krailsheimer (ed.), *Letters of de Rancé*,
Vol. II, pp. 219–20; RA / M4 ff.683–4;
HMC, *Calendar of Stuart Papers*, Vol. I,
pp. 94–5; & Reynolds, *Bossuet*, p. 204.

8. *Life*, Vol. II, pp. 505–6; & RA / M4
ff.684–5 & 689.

9. *Life*, Vol. II, pp. 511, & 514–16; Jones,
Charles Middleton, p. 256; & Porter,
'Non-Juring Bishops', p. 6.

10. HMC, *Calendar of Stuart Papers*, Vol. I,
pp. 85–6; Petrie, *Jacobite Movement.
The First Phase*, Vol. I, p. 84; *Life*,
Vol. II, pp. 471–2; RA / M4 ff.559–62;
Hopkirk, *Queen over the Water*, pp. 206
& 218–19; Grew, *English Court in Exile*,
p. 350; & *Dangeau*, Vol. I, pp. 270–1.

11. Macpherson (ed.), *Original Papers*,
Vol. I, pp. 459–64; *Life*, Vol. II,
pp. 522–3; RA / M4 ff.714–16; &
Churchill, *Marlborough*, Vol. I,
pp. 368–9, 372–6, 381–2, 383–6, &
393–4.

12. Jerdan (ed.), *Letters from James Earl of
Perth*, pp. 32–3; Jones, *Charles
Middleton*, p. 261; *Dangeau*, Vol. I,
p. 268; Haile, *Queen Mary of Modena*,
pp. 291, 308 & 311–13; Hopkirk, *Queen
over the Water*, p. 220; & Oman, *Mary of
Modena*, p. 184.

13. BL. Add. MS. 10118 f.336; RA / M4
ff.721–4; Chapman, *Mary II*, pp. 250–4;
Haile, *Queen Mary of Modena*, p. 310;
Life, Vol. II, p. 525; & Burnet, Vol. IV,
Book V, pp. 136–8.

14. *Letters of Madame*, Vol. I, p. 119;
BL. Add. MS. 10118 f.343; Rose,
England in the 1690s, p. 42; Le Gendre,
History of the Reign of Lewis the Great,
p. 263; *Dangeau*, Vol. I, p. 276; RA /
M4 ff.725–6; *Burnet*, Vol. IV, Book V,
pp. 138–9; & Acton (ed.), 'Letters of
James the Second', pp. 26–8. It is
notable that the editors of the King's
official biography chose to edit the

text of this letter to the abbé de La Trappe and to put a rather more humane gloss upon events, see: *Life*, Vol. II, pp. 526–7.

15. Chapman, *Mary II*, pp. 255–6 & 258–9; H. de Castries (ed.), *Moulay Ismail et Jacques II* (Paris, 1903), pp. 46–7; Burnet, Vol. IV, Book V, p. 138; van der Zee, *William and Mary*, pp. 388–9; *Evelyn's Diary*, Vol. II, p. 333; & *Letters of Madame*, Vol. I, p. 119.

16. Acton (ed.), 'Letters of James the Second', pp. 32, 38; *Devotions*, pp. 2–4 & 61; Trinity College, MS. 3529 ff.2–4 & 61; Krailsheimer (ed.), *Letters of de Rancé*, Vol. II, p. 239; RA / M4 ff.728 & 730; & *Life*, Vol. II, p. 527.

17. Sells (ed. & trans.), *Memoirs of James II*, pp. 39–40 & 52.

18. Sells (ed. & trans.), *Memoirs of James II*, pp. 53, 74, 90, 94, 96, 124, 126, 168 & 279.

19. Sells (ed. & trans.), *Memoirs of James II*, pp. 144–50, 159–60, 166, 180 & 265–7.

20. Sells (ed. & trans.), *Memoirs of James II*, pp. 51–3; *Devotions*, p. 18, Trinity College, MS. 3529 f.18; Acton (ed.), 'Letters of James the Second', pp. 9, 29; & Krailsheimer (ed.), *Letters of de Rancé*, Vol. II, pp. 245–6.

21. BL. Add. MS. 10118 f.355; Jones, *Charles Middleton*, p. 264; Ailesbury, Vol. I, p. 363; RA / M4 ff.734–5 & 760–2; *Life*, Vol. II, pp. 530–1; Garrett, *Triumphs of Providence*, pp. 98–101; Burnet, Vol. IV, Book V, p. 164; Haile, *Queen Mary of Modena*, pp. 320–1; *Life*, Vol. II, pp. 540–1; & *Berwick*, Vol. I, pp. 132–3.

22. Howell (ed.), *State Trials*, Vol. XII, pp. 1311; RA / M4 ff.750, 753–4, 759 & 769–770; Garrett, *Triumphs of Providence*, pp. 28–34, 49–50, 111–14 & 120–2; Burnet, Vol. IV, Book V, pp. 165–7; *Life*, Vol. II, pp. 543–52; & *Berwick*, Vol. I, pp. 134–5.

23. BL. Add. MS. 28224 ff.7, 9 & 13; Anon., *Life of William III*, p. 447; RA / M4 ff.748–9; *Life*, Vol. II, pp. 538–40 & 542–3; *Letters of Madame*, Vol. I, p. 130; & *Berwick*, Vol. I, p. 133.

24. BL. Add. MS. 10118 f.372; Macpherson, *Original Papers*, Vol. I,

pp. 561–2; NA. SP. 32/12 ff.131–2; Ailesbury, Vol. II, p. 367; *Letters of Madame*, Vol. I, p. 133; Anon., *Life of William III*, p. 447; Howell (ed.), *State Trials*, Vol. XII, p. 1311; & *Life*, Vol. II, pp. 540 & 545–6. See also: BL. Add. MS. 37661 ff.33–4.

25. Garrett, *Triumphs of Providence*, pp. 88–9 & 109–10; Jones, *Marlborough*, p. 52; BL. Add. MS. 10118 ff.441–2; RA / M4 ff.753–4; & *Life*, Vol. II, pp. 540 & 546–50.

26. *Berwick*, Vol. I, p. 133; RA / M4 ff.749, 771–3; Garrett, *Triumphs of Providence*, p. 101; & *Life*, Vol. II, pp. 543–4.

27. *Dangeau*, Vol. I, p. 298; Macpherson, *Original Papers*, Vol. I, pp. 555–6; BL. Add. MS. 39923 f.15; BL. Add. MS. 28224 ff.7 & 13; BL. Add. MS. 10118 ff.355 & 361; Churchill, *Marlborough*, Vol. I, pp. 400–7; Carswell, *Old Cause*, p. 84; Ailesbury, Vol. II, p. 412; Anon., *Life of William III*, pp. 448–53; RA / M4 ff.803–4 & 811–12; *Life*, Vol. II, pp. 553–5; Garrett, *Triumphs of Providence*, pp. 135–9, 155–7, 167–9, 190–4 & 250–3; *Berwick*, Vol. I, pp. 135–6; Burnet, Vol. VI, Book V, pp. 167–9.

28. BL. Add. MS. 10118 f.371; Carswell, *Old Cause*, pp. 84–6; Anon., *Life of William III*, pp. 457–60; RA / M4 ff.808–11; *Life*, Vol. II, pp. 555–7; Burnet, Vol. IV, Book V, pp. 171–4, 181–5 & 189–93; & Garrett, *Triumphs of Providence*, pp. 186–202, 250–1 & 254–5.

29. BL. Add. MS. 10118 f.361; Garrett, *Triumphs of Providence*, pp. 148, 154 & 261; Barany, *Anglo-Russian Entente*, p. 19; Jones, *Charles Middleton*, p. 265; Ogg, *William III*, pp. 95–6; Carswell, *Old Cause*, p. 75; *Letters of Madame*, Vol. I, pp. 133 & 135; Ailesbury, Vol. II, p. 367; RA / M4 ff.779–85; *Berwick*, Vol. I, p. 137; & *Life*, Vol. II, pp. 546–52.

30. Acton (ed.), 'Letters of James the Second', pp. 47–8; Ogg, *William III*, pp. 94–5; BL. Add. MS. 28224 ff.15 & 19; Ailesbury, Vol. II, p. 365; RA / M4 ff.813–14; & *Life*, Vol. II, p. 559.

31. *Devotions*, p. 57; & Trinity College, MS. 3529 f.57.

32. Acton (ed.), 'Letters of James the Second', pp. 57–8; Dulon, *Jacques II Stuart*, p. 22; Haswell, *James II*, p. 304; Barany, *Anglo-Russian Entente*, pp. 21, 26 & 29; Madan (ed.), *Stuart Papers*, Vol. I, pp. 25–6; Anon. (ed.), *Memoirs of the Duke de Villars*, pp. 261–2 & 282–5; Le Gendre, *History of the Reign of Lewis the Great*, pp. 295–300; RA / M4 ff.819–20; Petrie, *Jacobite Movement. The First Phase*, p. 112; & *Life*, Vol. II, p. 561.

33. Van der Zee, *William and Mary*, pp. 408–9 & 460–1; H.W. Chapman, *Queen Anne's Son. A Memoir of William Henry, Duke of Gloucester, 1689–1700* (London, 1954), pp. 64–8 & 77; Hopkirk, *Queen over the Water*, p. 232; Petrie, *Marshal Duke*, p. 107; Haile, *Queen Mary of Modena*, pp. 324–5; Cole, 'Princess Over the Water', p. 4; & Bevan, *King James the Third*, p. 34.

34. BL. Add. MS. 28224 f.23; Macpherson (ed.), *Original Papers*, Vol. I, pp. 561–4; Acton (ed.), 'Letters of James the Second', pp. 53–4; *Life*, Vol. II, p. 563; Ogg, *William III*, p. 94; RA / M4 f.847; & Grew, *English Court in Exile*, pp. 372–3.

35. *Life*, Vol. II, pp. 564–5 & RA / M4 ff.827 & 830–3.

36. *Life*, Vol. II, pp. 562 & 566–71; RA / M4 f.834; Acton (ed.), 'Letters of James the Second', pp. 63–4; Baxter, *William III*, pp. 352–4; Le Gendre, *History of the Reign of Lewis the Great*, pp. 286–8; & Grew, *William Bentinck*, pp. 274–6.

37. *Life*, Vol. II, pp. 572–4; RA / M4 ff.850–1; Grew, *William Bentinck*, p. 274; & BL. Add. MS. 28224 f.25.

38. Grew, *William Bentinck*, fn. 1 p. 288; Acton (ed.), 'Letters of James the Second', pp. 68–9; Baxter, *William III*, pp. 356–7; Ogg, *William III*, p. 96; Wolf, *Louis XIV*, pp. 485–6; Churchill, *Marlborough*, Vol. I, pp. 425–6; Le Gendre, *History of the Reign of Lewis the Great*, pp. 287–93 & 304–5; BL. Add. MS. 28224 f.23; *Burnet*, Vol. IV, Book V, pp. 199–202; & *Life*, Vol. II, pp. 574–5.

39. Grew, *William Bentinck*, p. 290.

40. Lynn, *Wars of Louis XIV*, pp. 262–3; Wolf, *Louis XIV*, pp. 486–7; Churchill, *Marlborough*, Vol. I, pp. 424–6; Ogg, *William III*, p. 96; Le Gendre, *History of the Reign of Lewis the Great*, pp. 308–10; Ragazzi, *Maria Beatrice d' Este*, pp. 271–2; Madan (ed.), *Stuart Papers*, Vol. I, pp. 29–30; *Burnet*, Vol. IV, Book V, pp. 202–3; & BL. Add. MS. 10118 f.380.

41. Acton (ed.), 'Letters of James the Second', pp. 68–70; *Life*, Vol. II, pp. 575–6; RA / M4 ff.862–3; & Saint-Simon, *Memoirs*, Vol. I, p. 93.

42. Shield & Lang, *King over the Water*, p. 46; RA / M4 ff.848–9 & 858–61; *Life*, Vol. II, p. 575; Hopkirk, *Queen over the Water*, p. 232; & Haile, *Queen Mary of Modena*, pp. 330–1.

43. Macpherson (ed.), *Original Papers*, Vol. I, pp. 568–9; Haile, *Queen Mary of Modena*, p. 328; Hopkirk, *Queen over the Water*, pp. 232–3; Middleton, *Charles, 2nd Earl of Middleton*, pp. 162–3; Oman, *Mary of Modena*, pp. 187–8; & HMC, *Calendar of Stuart Papers*, Vol. III, pp. 522–5.

44. Grew, *English Court in Exile*, pp. 378–9; Macpherson (ed.), *Original Papers*, Vol. I, pp. 569–71; Haile, *Queen Mary of Modena*, p. 330; & *Life*, Vol. II, pp. 572–4. Mary of Modena's injunction to the Mother Superior to 'pray burn my letter', as in the case of many other individuals who have held public office, appears to have been, in fact, the surest way to ensure the survival of a document.

45. Rowlands, 'Army in Exile', pp. 17–18; Hall, *Flags and Uniforms*, p. 91 & plate 070A; Murtagh, 'Irish Jacobite Army', p. 32; McLaughlin & Warner, *Wild Geese*, p. 7; & *Berwick*, Vol. I, p. 139.

46. O'Callaghan, *Irish Brigades*, pp. 189–91.

CHAPTER EIGHT: THE ROYAL PENITENT

1. Chateaubriand, *Vie de Rancé*, 2nd edn (Brussels, n.d.), pp. 260–2; Grew,

English Court in Exile, pp. 343–4;
A.J. Luddy, *The Real de Rancé. Illustrious Penitent and Reformer of Notre Dame de la Trappe* (London, New York & Toronto, 1931), p. 253; & BL. Add. MS. 10118 ff.273–4. Chateaubriand neatly, and prosaically, characterised James after the failure of his Irish campaign as 'a seabird which the storm has thrown up onto the shore'.

2. H. Bremond, *The Thundering Abbot. Armand de Rancé, Reformer of La Trappe*, trans. F.J. Sheed (London, 1930), pp. 100, 115, 117; Krailsheimer (ed.), *Letters of de Rancé*, Vol. II, pp. 134 & 161; A.J. Krailsheimer, *Armand-Jean de Rancé, Abbot of La Trappe* (Oxford, 1974), pp. 83–5 & 256; E.K. Sanders, *Jacques Benigne Bossuet* (London, 1921), pp. 73; T. Merton, *The Waters of Siloe* (Garden City, New York, 1951), pp. 36–7 & 48; Luddy, *Real de Rancé*, pp. 82–3, 87–8, 230–2, 235 & 258; & Saint-Simon, *Memoirs*, Vol. I, pp. 85–6.

3. Bremond, *Thundering Abbot*, pp. 99, 111, 113; *Life*, Vol. II, pp. 528–9; Merton, *Waters of Siloe*, pp. 37 & 40–7; Luddy, *Real de Rancé*, pp. 155–7, 177–8 & 194; & Krailsheimer, *Armand-Jean de Rancé*, pp. 88–92 & 94–8.

4. *Devotions*, pp. 1–3, 62–3 & 145; Trinity College, MS. 3529 ff.1–3, 62–3 & 145; & Sells (ed. & trans.), *Memoirs of James II*, pp. 291–2.

5. *Life*, Vol. II, pp. 8–9; *Devotions*, pp. xxvii, 1–5, 23–5, & Appendix I; Corp & Sanson (eds), *La Cour des Stuarts*, p. 48; Anon. (ed.), *The Writings of the Late King of Great Britain* (Paris, 1690); A. Hyde, *A Copy of a Paper Written by the late Dutchess of York* (London, n/d), pp. 1–2; Acton (ed.), 'Letters of James the Second', p. 100; M. Ashley, *Charles II* (London, 1971), p. 320; R. Hutton, *Charles II. King of England, Scotland & Ireland* (Oxford & New York, 1991), pp. 455–7; & J. Miller, *Charles II* (London, 1991), p. 382; Acton (ed.), 'Letters of James the Second', p. 7; Madan (ed.), *Stuart Papers*, Vol. I, pp. 254–61 & Vol. II, pp. 279–83 & 287–8; BL. Add. MS. 10118 f.395; & RA 1 / 17 ff.1–3.

6. Ironically, at the time Evelyn expressed his approval of James's 'free and ingenuous profession of what his own religion is', compared to Charles II's 'concealment upon . . . politic accounts', and concluded that the new King possessed 'a most sincere and honest nature'. *Evelyn's Diary*, Vol. II, pp. 237–9.

7. *State Tracts* (London, 1693), Part II, p. 273; Acton (ed.), 'Letters of James the Second', p. 7; *Devotions*, Appendix I, pp. 174–5; & Madan (ed.), *Stuart Papers*, Vol. I, p. 78 & Vol. II, pp. 279–88. James appeared to admit the fragmentary nature of Charles II's jottings in January 1691, when he wrote to the abbé de Rancé that his own copy of the paper 'is more a paraphrase than a translation, because he [i.e. Charles II] wrote in few words of great power'.

8. Acton (ed.), 'Letters of James the Second', pp. 73–4; *Dangeau*, Vol. I, p. 151; Oman, *Mary of Modena*, p. 152; & Dulon, *Jacques II Stuart*, p. 43.

9. On occasion, James's impromptu visits to monastic houses could produce unforeseen results. Thus, 'one rainy day coming wrapp'd up in his cloke out of his coach' he went unrecognised by the aged and half-blind porter at St Edmund's monastery in Paris. While the porter went to seek out the Prior to enquire whether the stranger should be granted leave to enter, several of the monks were startled to come upon the exiled King as he strolled through their cloister. See: BL. Add. MS. 10118 f.367. Also: *Life*, Vol. II, p. 583; Cavelli (ed.), *Les Derniers Stuarts*, Vol. II, pp. 481–2, 525 & 528; & *Dangeau*, Vol. I, pp. 157–8.

10. Corp & Sanson (eds), *La Cour des Stuarts*, p. 210; A. Plowden, *Henrietta Maria* (Stroud, 2001), p. 258; Hopkirk, *Queen over the Water*, pp. 186, 229, 244, 249, 261, & 295–7; Haile, *Queen Mary of Modena*, pp. 272–4; Oman, *Mary of Modena*, pp. 160–2; Southorn, 'Mary of Modena', p. 7; Grew, *English Court in Exile*, pp. 116–19; Madan (ed.), *Stuart*

Papers, Vol. I, pp. xii, 1, 4, 6, 81 & 89;
& *Dangeau*, Vol. I, pp. 157–8.

11. Anon., *Memoirs of King James II*, pp. 3–5
& 22–3; *Life*, Vol. II, pp. 583–4;
BL. Add. MS. 28224 f.21; Madan (ed.),
Stuart Papers, Vol. I, pp. 6–8, 35 & 75;
& RA / M4 ff.884–6.

12. Bishop J.B. Bossuet, *Letters of Spiritual
Direction*, trans. G. Webb & A. Walker
(London, 1958), pp. 35–9;
Krailsheimer (ed.), *Letters of de Rancé*,
pp. 278–9; & Krailsheimer, *Armand-
Jean de Rancé*, pp. 256–8.

13. BL. Add. MS. 10118 ff.272–3; *Life*,
Vol. II, pp. 528–9; Merton, *Waters of
Siloe*, p. 48; Luddy, *Real de Rancé*,
pp. 13–18, 21–3 & 252; Krailsheimer,
Armand-Jean de Rancé, pp. 7, 9 & 266;
M. d'Exauville, *Histoire de L' Abbé de
Rancé: Reformateur de la Trappe* (Paris,
1842), pp. 284–5; & RA / M4 f.881.

14. Psalm 118.7–18.

15. Krailsheimer (ed.), *Letters of de Rancé*,
Vol. II, p. 162; Luddy, *Real de Rancé*,
pp. 253–4; RA. 1/66 ff.1–3; & Grew,
English Court in Exile, p. 343.

16. Grew, *English Court in Exile*, pp. 340–1;
Luddy, *Real de Rancé*, pp. 255–7;
Krailsheimer, *Armand-Jean de Rancé*,
p. 267; d'Exauville, *Histoire de L' Abbé de
Rancé*, pp. 284–5; RA 1 / 9; RA 1 / 21;
RA 1 / 68; & RA 1 / 70. See also:
Callow, *Making of James II*, pp. 148–50.

17. Krailsheimer (ed.), *Letters of de Rancé*,
Vol. II, pp. 161–3; Luddy, *Real de
Rancé*, pp. 255–6; Krailsheimer,
Armand-Jean de Rancé, p. 98; Haswell,
James II, p. 305; Acton (ed.), 'Letters of
James the Second', pp. 3–5; *Devotions*,
pp. 67–8; Trinity College, MS. 3529
ff.67–8; & *Life*, Vol. II, pp. 528–9.

18. Macaulay, *History of England*, Vol. I,
pp. 151, 168, 190, 195, 462, 468 &
505–6; Vol. II, pp. 708–9; H.M.
Gwatkin, *Church and State in England to
the Death of Queen Anne* (London,
1917), p. 367; & A. Carrel, *History of the
Counter-Reformation in England for the
Re-establishment of Popery under Charles II
and James II* (London, 1846), pp. 97,
144 & 346–8.

19. Krailsheimer (ed.), *Letters of de Rancé*,
Vol. II, p. 167; Luddy, *Real de Rancé*,

pp. 262–4; Krailsheimer, *Armand-Jean
de Rancé*, pp. 268–9; & Acton (ed.),
'Letters of James the Second', pp. 3–4.

20. Acton (ed.), 'Letters of James the
Second', pp. 14 & 51.

21. *Devotions*, pp. 3–4, 61–2, 68, 71, 108,
138, 140 & 164; Trinity College, MS.
3529 ff.3–4, 61–2, 68, 71, 108, 138, 140
& 164; *Life*, Vol. II, pp. 527–8; & Acton
(ed.), 'Letters of James the Second',
p. 13.

22. *Devotions*, pp. 71–2; Trinity College,
MS. 3529 ff.71–2; RA. 1/66 ff.1–3; &
RA / M4 ff.879–81.

23. *Devotions*, pp. 15, 64, 73 & 80; & Trinity
College, MS. 3529 ff.15, 64, 73 & 80.

24. *Life*, Vol. II, pp. 585–6; Krailsheimer
(ed.), *Letters of de Rancé*, Vol. II,
pp. 164–5; *Ailesbury*, Vol. II, p. 496;
F. Sanders, *An Abridgement of the Life of
James II*, ed. Fr. F. Brettonneau
(London, 1704), pp. 45 & 57; & RA /
M4 ff.891–2.

25. Krailsheimer (ed.), *Letters of de Rancé*,
Vol. II, pp. 178 & 182; Acton (ed.),
'Letters of James the Second', p. 11;
RA 1/64 ff.1–4; RA 1/65 ff.1–4; & RA
1/66 ff.1–3.

26. Acton (ed.), 'Letters of James the
Second', p. 4; Trinity College, MS.
3529 f.111 & *Devotions*, p. 111.

27. Macpherson (ed.), *Original Papers*,
Vol. I, p. 537.

28. Acton (ed.), 'Letters of James the
Second', pp. 70–1 & 88; &
Krailsheimer (ed.), *Letters of de Rancé*,
Vol. II, pp. 243 & 246; Krailsheimer,
Armand-Jean de Rancé, p. 268; & A.J. de
Rancé, Abbé de La Trappe, *Conduite
Chretienne Adressée a S.A.R. Mme.* (n/p.
1697).

29. *Dangeau*, Vol. I, pp. 283–4; Acton
(ed.), 'Letters of James the Second',
p. 50; Luddy, *Real de Rancé*, pp. 264–5;
Krailsheimer, *Armand-Jean de Rancé*,
pp. 54–5 & 269–70; & Krailsheimer
(ed.), *Letters of de Rancé*, Vol. II,
pp. 237 & 240.

30. Luddy, *Real de Rancé*, pp. 275–9 &
284–5; Krailsheimer, *Armand-Jean de
Rancé*, pp. 53 & 55–7; & Bremmond,
Thundering Abbot, pp. 244, 250–4, 260,
262–4, 270 & 275–7.

31. Krailsheimer (ed.), *Letters of de Rancé*, Vol. II, pp. 249–53; Luddy, *Real de Rancé*, pp. 280–3; Krailsheimer, *Armand-Jean de Rancé*, pp. 56–7; RA / M4 f.893; Bremmond, *Thundering Abbot*, pp. 277–80, & Acton (ed.), 'Letters of James the Second', pp. 79 & 82–3.

32. Acton (ed.), 'Letters of James the Second', p. 99.

33. F. Skeet, "The Eighth Duchess of Norfolk", Part I, *The Stonyhurst Magazine*, no. 257 (June, 1925), pp. 73–4; J. Callow, "The Last of the Shireburnes: The Art of Death and Life in Recusant Lancashire, 1660–1754", *Recusant History*, Vol. XXVI, no. 4 (October, 2003), p. 596; H. Barnes, *On Touching for the King's Evil* (Kendal, 1895), pp. 344–5, 348, 351–2, 354 & 356–8; M. Bloch, *The Royal Touch. Monarchy and Miracles in France and England*, trans. J.E. Anderson (New York, 1961, rpt. 1989), p. 219; W. Beckett, *A Free and Impartial Enquiry into the Antiquity and Efficacy of Touching for the Cure of the King's Evil* (London, 1722), pp. 7–9, 26–7, 31, 33; Anon., *His Grace the Duke of Monmouth honoured in his Progress in the West of England in an account of an Extraordinary Cure of the King's Evil* (London, 1680), pp. 1–2; & Corp & Sanson (eds), *La Cour des Stuarts*, p. 160.

34. Beckett, *Free and Impartial Enquiry*, pp. 26–9; W. Beckett, "Account of Three Long-Lived Persons", in *Register Book of the Royal Society*, Vol. XI (November, 1722), ff.230–1; W. Beckett, "Some Remarks upon the Observation mentioned in the Revd Mr. Wasses Letter", in *Register Book of the Royal Society*, Vol. XII (June, 1724), f.482; M. Tobin, *A True Account of Mr. Timothy Beaghan . . . Famous for Curing the Kings-Evil* (London, 1697), pp. 3–7; Bloch, *Royal Touch*, pp. 203–4; Corp (ed.), *L'Autre Exil*, p. 87; Barnes, *On Touching for the King's Evil*, p. 348; Skeet, "Eighth Duchess", p. 73; Callow, "Last of the Shireburnes", pp. 596–7; & J. Gerard, *Stonyhurst College*

35. (London, New York, & Sydney, 1894), p. 77.
Letters of Madame, Vol. I, pp. 97 & 99; BL. Add. MS. 10118 f.34; B. Neveu (ed.), *Jacques II Mediateur Entre Louis XIV et Innocent XI* (Paris, 1967), p. 748; & J. Swarbrick, *Dolls in Religious Dress* (unpublished manuscript, 2001), pp. 1–5. I am grateful to Judith Swarbrick for making her wholly original, and extremely interesting, research available to me.

36. *Devotions*, pp. 14, 34–6 & 38; & Trinity College, MS. 3529 ff.14, 34–6 & 38.

37. *Devotions*, pp. 35–7 & 55; Trinity College, MS. 3529 ff.35–7 & 55.

38. Acton (ed.), 'Letters of James the Second', pp. 77 & 81–2; Grew, *English Court in Exile*, p. 396; Madan (ed.), *Stuart Papers*, Vol. I, p. 82; Trinity College, MS. 3529 f.125; & *Devotions*, p. 125.

39. *Devotions*, pp. 125–6; & Trinity College, MS. 3529 ff.125–6.

40. Corp (ed.), *L'Autre Exil*, p. 89; Anon., *Memoirs of King James II*, pp. 27–8; *Devotions*, pp. 77, 132 & 139; Trinity College, MS. 3529 ff.77, 132 & 139; Sanders, *Abridgement of the Life of James II*, p. 45; & Acton (ed.), 'Letters of James the Second', pp. 5, 25, 31–2, 37, 39, 45, 47, 54–5, 66, 70, 72 & 75–6.

41. Anon., *Memoirs of King James II*, p. 15; Luddy, *Real de Rancé*, pp. 205–6; & D. Ogg, *Europe in the Seventeenth Century* (London, 1948), pp. 328–9.

42. *Devotions*, pp. 61–4; & Trinity College, MS. 3529 ff.61–4.

43. *Devotions*, pp. 83 & 87–8; Trinity College, MS. 3529 ff.83 & 87–8; & Madan (ed.), *Stuart Papers*, Vol. I, p. 83.

44. *Life*, Vol. II, pp. 590–1; & RA / M4 ff.906–8.

45. J.P. Lallemant, *The Holy Desires of Death: or, a Collection of Some Thoughts of the Fathers of the Church, to Shew How Christians Ought to Despise Life, and to Desire Death*, trans. T.V.F. Sadler (London, 1678); J.E. Nieremberg, *Bilancia del Tempo, O Sia La Differenza Fra il Temporale e l'Eterno* (Venice, 1731); J.E. Nieremberg, *Contemplations*

on the State of Man in this Life, and in that which is to Come, trans., ed., & reworked by J. Taylor, Bishop of Down and Connor, and of Dromore (London, 1684); BL. Add. MS. 10118 ff.407–8; Trinity College, MS. 3529 f.97; & *Devotions*, p. 97.

46. Anon., *Memoirs of King James II*, p. 23; & *Ailesbury*, Vol. II, p. 496.

47. Sanders, *Abridgement of the Life of James II*, pp. 58 & 102; Acton (ed.), 'Letters of James the Second', pp. 104–5; BL. Add. MS. 10118 ff.407–8; Trinity College, MS. 3529 ff.162–3; & *Devotions*, pp. 162–3.

CHAPTER NINE: THE DEATH OF A KING

1. Cavelli (ed.), *Les Derniers Stuarts*, Vol. II, pp. 414–15; BL. Add. MS. 10118 ff.430–1; & Castries (ed.), *Moulay Ismail et Jacques II*, pp. 66–8; & 102.

2. Castries (ed.), *Moulay Ismail et Jacques II*, pp. 63–5, 69–72, 96, 98, & 103; & BL. Add. MS. 10118 ff.430–1.

3. Castries (ed.), *Moulay Ismail et Jacques II*, pp. 97–8, & 100.

4. Castries (ed.), *Moulay Ismail et Jacques II*, pp. 49 fn. 1 & 52.

5. Saint-Simon, *Memoirs*, Vol. I, p. 98; Le Gendre, *History of the Reign of Lewis the Great*, p. 284; BL. Add. MS. 10118 f.380; *Letters of Madame*, Vol. I, p. 159; & *Dangeau*, Vol. I, pp. 329–30; 335–7 & 339.

6. HMC, *Calendar of Stuart Papers*, Vol. I, pp. 124 & 130; Madan (ed.), *Stuart Papers*, Vol. I, pp. 31 & 41–2; Carswell, *Old Cause*, p. 88; RA / M4 f.877; & *Life*, Vol. II, pp. 580–1.

7. *CSPD* (1698), pp. 20, 28 & 42; Anon. (ed.), *Memoirs of the Duke de Villars*, p. 260; RA / M4 ff.871–3; *Life*, Vol. II, p. 579; Grew, *English Court in Exile*, pp. 388–9; & N.A. Robb, *William of Orange* (London, 1966), Vol. II, p. 425.

8. Grew, *William Bentinck*, pp. 302–6; F. McLynn, *The Jacobites* (London & New York, 1985, rpt. 1988), pp. 176–7;

Dangeau, Vol. I, p. 335; Robb, *William of Orange*, pp. 426–7; & Grew, *English Court in Exile*, pp. 389–90.

9. *Life*, Vol. II, pp. 577–88; *Dangeau*, Vol. I, p. 344; & *CSPD* (1698), pp. 72 & 110.

10. *CSPD* (1698), pp. 74–5; *Dangeau*, Vol. I, pp. 333 & 357; & Grew, *English Court in Exile*, pp. 390–2.

11. Robb, *William of Orange*, p. 428; Grew, *English Court in Exile*, pp. 391–2; & Grew, *William Bentinck*, pp. 277, 279 309–14 & 328.

12. *CSPD* (1698), pp. 86, 110, 138 & 210–11; & *Dangeau*, Vol. I, pp. 344 & 350–1.

13. *CSPD* (1698), pp. 211, 270 & 275; Grew, *English Court in Exile*, pp. 392–3; Grew, *William Bentinck*, p. 344; *Life*, Vol. II, fn. pp. 577–8; & Dalrymple, *Memoirs*, Vol. III, p. 87.

14. Haile, *Queen Mary of Modena*, pp. 331 & 334; Hopkirk, *Queen over the Water*, pp. 232–3; *Dangeau*, Vol. I, pp. 316, 343, & 350; McLynn, *Jacobites*, p. 176; Grew, *William Bentinck*, pp. 332 & 352; S. Thurley, *The Lost Palace of Whitehall* (London, 1998), pp. 56–7; Beddard (ed.), *A Kingdom Without a King. The Journal of the Provisional Government in the Revolution of 1688* (Oxford, 1988), pp. 69 & 90; Jones, *Marlborough*, p. 53; Kenyon, *Sunderland*, pp. 302–3; *DNB*, Vol. XIII, pp. 47–8; Churchill, *Marlborough*, Vol. I, pp. 431–2; S. Jenkins (ed.), 'The King's Apartments. Hampton Court Palace', *Apollo Magazine*, Vol. CXL (1994), p. 13; Carswell, *Old Cause*, p. 93; Saint-Simon, *Memoirs*, Vol. II, p. 87; & BL. Add. MS.10118 f.371.

15. *CSPD* (1698), pp. 85–6; Churchill, *Marlborough*, Vol. I, pp. 452–3 & 455; Baxter, *William III*, pp. 366–9; Grew, *William Bentinck*, pp. 350–1; Barany, *Anglo-Russian Entente*, p. 54; & Anon. (ed.), *Memoirs of the Duke de Villars*, pp. 353–6, 359, 363–70, & 375.

16. Acton (ed.), 'Letters of James the Second', p. 77.

17. Acton (ed.), 'Letters of James the Second', p. 75; Hopkirk, *Queen over the Water*, pp. 232–3; Haile, *Queen Mary of*

Modena, pp. 334 & 337; & Oman, *Mary of Modena*, pp. 187.

18. *Dangeau*, Vol. I, p. 360; & *Life*, Vol. II, p. 588.

19. Saint-Simon, *Memoirs*, Vol. I, pp. 111–14; *Life*, Vol. II, p. 588; RA / M4 ff.897–9; Acton (ed.), 'Letters of James II', pp. 80–1; Trinity College, MS. 3529 f.53; & *Devotions*, p. 53.

20. Cole, 'Princess Over the Water', pp. 3–4 & 6; Grew, *English Court in Exile*, pp. 396–7; Miller, *James*, pp. 44–6; Bevan, *King James the Third*, p. 31; Shield & Lang, *King over the Water*, pp. 45, & 48–9; Madan (ed.), *Stuart Papers*, Vol. I, pp. 34 & 38; & BL. Add. MS. 10118 f.379.

21. H. Kamen, *Philip V of Spain. The King who Reigned Twice* (New Haven & London, 2001), pp. 3–5; Churchill, *Marlborough*, Vol. I, pp. 455 & 457–8; Cronin, *Louis XIV*, pp. 333–6; Saint-Simon, *Memoirs*, Vol. I, pp. 139–41, *Dangeau*, Vol. I, pp. 435, 439 & 445–9; Dulon, *Jacques II Stuart*, p. 25; Ogg, *William III*, p. 101; Madan (ed.), *Stuart Papers*, Vol. I, p. 46; Anon. (ed.), *Memoirs of the Duke de Villars*, pp. 376–8, 380–1, 383, 399 & 404–6; & Wolf, *Louis XIV*, pp. 502–8.

22. Haile, *Queen Mary of Modena*, p. 348; Haswell, *James II*, p. 304; HMC, *Calendar of Stuart Papers*, pp. 138 & 144; BL. Add. MS. 10118 f.396.

23. Brown, *Kingdom or Province?*, p. 179; BL. Add. MS. 10118 f.396; & Grew, *English Court in Exile*, pp. 404–5.

24. Corp & Sanson (eds), *La Cour des Stuarts*, p. 139; Reynolds, *Bossuet*, pp. 253–4; *Dangeau*, Vol. I, p. 388; Acton (ed.), 'Letters of James the Second', pp. 86–7; Grew, *English Court in Exile*, p. 400; Cole, 'Princess Over the Water', p. 9; Southorn, 'Mary of Modena', p. 7; BL. Add. MS. 28224 ff.27, 31 & 33; Madan (ed.), *Stuart Papers*, Vol. I, pp. 9 & 33.

25. Haile, *Queen Mary of Modena*, pp. 342 & 346–7; Hopkirk, *Queen over the Water*, p. 237; Chateaubriand, *Vie de Rancé*, pp. 273–5; Bremond, *Thundering Abbot*, pp. 282–3; Krailsheimer (ed.), *Letters of de Rancé*, Vol. II, p. 254; Merton, *Waters of Siloe*, p. 49; Luddy, *Real de Rancé*, pp. 293–9 & 306–9; Krailsheimer, *Armand-Jean de Rancé*, pp. 57–8; HMC, *Calendar of Stuart Papers*, Vol. I, p. 155; C. Petrie (ed.), *The Duke of Berwick and His Son* (London, 1951), pp. 26–7; & Madan (ed.), *Stuart Papers*, Vol. I, pp. 42 & 85–6.

26. Petrie, *Duke of Berwick and His Son*, pp. 26–7; Chapman, *Queen Anne's Son*, pp. 139–41; Green, *Queen Anne*, pp. 79–80 & 335; Ogg, *William III*, p. 53; Haile, *Queen Mary of Modena*, p. 343; Acton (ed.), 'Letters of James the Second', pp. 99–100; Miller, *James*, p. 57; Anon. (ed.), *Memoirs of the Duke de Villars*, p. 550; Madan (ed.), *Stuart Papers*, Vol. I, p. 42; & BL. Add. MS. 28224 f.34.

27. *Dangeau*, Vol. I, p. 428; Macpherson, *Original Papers*, Vol. I, pp. 616–17; Grew, *English Court in Exile*, pp. 413–14; & *CSPD* (1700–2), p. 136.

28. M. Kroll, *Sophie Electress of Hanover* (London, 1973), pp. 194 & 226–7; J.R. Jones, *Country and Court* (London, 1983), p. 310; & Shield & Lang, *King over the Water*, pp. 50–1.

29. *Letters of Madame*, Vol. I, pp. 197; Anon., *Life of William III*, p. 619; & 200; & *Dangeau*, Vol. II, p. 4.

30. *Life*, Vol. II, p. 591 & p. 591 fn.; *Dangeau*, Vol. II, p. 5; Anon., *Life of James II. Late King of England*, p. 412; Saint-Simon, *Memoirs*, Vol. I, p. 152; RA / M4 f.909; *Lamentations*, 5: 1–2.

31. *Lamentations*, 5: 15–16.

32. *Dangeau*, Vol. II, p. 8; *Life*, Vol. II, pp. 591–2; Anon., *The Memoirs of King James II* (London & Westminster, 1702), p. 28; Grew, *English Court in Exile*, pp. 417–18; Saint-Simon, *Memoirs*, Vol. I, p. 152; Dulon, *Jacques II Stuart*, p. 33; & Madan (ed.), *Stuart Papers*, Vol. I, p. 49 & Vol. II, p. 338.

33. BL. Add. MS. 10118 f.397; BL. Add. MS. 28224 f.35; Madan (ed.), *Stuart Papers*, Vol. II, p. 299; Ailesbury, Vol. II, p. 496; *Dangeau*, Vol. II, p. 11; *Berwick*, Vol. I, pp. 149–52; Petrie, *Duke of Berwick and His Son*, pp. 26–7; RA / M4

ff.909–10; *Life*, Vol. II, p. 592; & Petrie, *Marshal Duke*, pp. 120–3.

34. *Dangeau*, Vol. II, p. 10; Acton (ed.), 'Letters of James the Second', p. 94; Grew, *English Court in Exile*, pp. 417–23; Ragazzi, *Maria Beatrice d'Este*, p. 297; Oman, *Mary of Modena*, pp. 191–2; HMC, *Calendar of Stuart Papers*, Vol. I, p. 159, Sizergh Castle, SIZ Misc. 4; Sanders, *Abrégé de la Vie de Jacques II*, p. 135; BL. Add. MS. 28224 ff.35–7; Madan (ed.), *Stuart Papers*, Vol. I, pp. 49–50 & Vol. II, pp. 299 & 304; & RA / M4 f.910.

35. BL. Add. MS. 28224 ff.36–7; Madan (ed.), *Stuart Papers*, Vol. I, pp. 51–2; & *Berwick*, Vol. I, p. 153.

36. Madan (ed.), *Stuart Papers*, Vol. II, pp. 318 & 322; Saint-Simon, *Memoirs*, Vol. I, pp. 154–5; *Dangeau*, Vol. II, p. 16; BL. Add. MS. 10118 f.398; BL. Add. MS. 15904 f.115; & N.N. Barker, *Brother to the Sun King, Philippe, Duke of Orléans* (Baltimore & London, 1989), pp. 230–1.

37. *Dangeau*, Vol. II, p. 22; Anon., *Memoirs of the Chevalier de St. George*, pp. 24–6; *Ailesbury*, Vol. II, p. 496; RA / M4 ff.910–13; & *Life*, Vol. II, pp. 592–4.

38. *Letters of Madame*, Vol. I, p. 214; Anon., *King James the Second. His Last Expressions and Dying-Words* (London, 1702), p. 1; Sanders, *Abrégé de la Vie de Jacques II*, pp. 142–3; RA / M4 ff.912–13; & *Life*, Vol. II, pp. 593–4.

39. Anon., *King James the Second. His Last Expressions and Dying-Words*, p. 1; & *Life*, Vol. II, p. 594.

40. Anon., *King James the Second. His Last Expressions and Dying-Words*, p. 1; Sanders, *Abrégé de la Vie de Jacques II*, pp. 142–3; RA / M4 ff.914–15; & *Life*, Vol. II, pp. 594–5.

41. Anon., *King James the Second. His Last Expressions and Dying-Words*, p. 1; *Letters of Madame*, Vol. I, p. 214; HMC, *Calendar of Stuart Papers*, Vol. II, pp. 516–18; *Dangeau*, Vol. II, p. 23; BL. Add. MS. 10118 ff.403–4; RA / M4 ff.916–17 & 933; & *Life*, Vol. II, pp. 595–6.

42. Saint-Simon, *Memoirs*, Vol. I, p. 168; Cronin, *Louis XIV*, pp. 339–40; Wolf,

Louis XIV, p. 515; Corp & Sanson (eds), *La Cour des Stuarts*, p. 82; Sanders, *Abrégé de la Vie de Jacques II*, p. 139; *Dangeau*, Vol. II, p. 26; & *Life*, Vol. II, p. 597.

43. Saint-Simon, *Memoirs*, Vol. I, p. 168; *Life*, Vol. II, p. 597; *Berwick*, Vol. I, pp. 154–5; Haile, *Queen Mary of Modena*, p. 353; Dalrymple, *Memoirs*, Vol. II, p. 166; BL. Add. MS. 10118 f.403; RA / M4 ff.918–19; & *Life*, Vol. II, p. 597.

44. *Dangeau*, Vol. II, pp. 22–4; Cronin, *Louis XIV*, p. 340; Corp & Sanson (eds), *La Cour des Stuarts*, p. 146; Dalrymple, *Memoirs*, Vol. II, p. 166; Madan (ed.), *Stuart Papers*, Vol. II, p. 344; BL. Add. MS. 10118 f.438; Anon, *Life of William III*, p. 629; RA / M4 ff.922–4 & 926; & *Life*, Vol. II, pp. 597–8.

45. BL. Add. MS. 10118 ff.401 & 403; Dalrymple, *Memoirs*, Vol. II, p. 166; Ragazzi, *Maria Beatrice d'Este*, pp. 302–3; *Dangeau*, Vol. II, p. 22, RA /M4 f.927; & *Life*, Vol. II, pp. 597–8.

46. *Life*, Vol. II, pp. 619–42; *For My Son the Prince of Wales, 1692*, Royal Library, ff.1–138; W. Fuller (impostor), *Plain Proof*, pp. 4–7 & 10–14; Miller, *James*, pp. 202–3; A.J. Youngson, *The Prince and the Pretender* (London, 1985), p. 81; Ogg, *William III*, p. 102; PRO. SP.32.13 no. 5; Dalrymple, *Memoirs*, Vol. II, p. 166; Saint-Simon, *Memoirs*, Vol. I, p. 169; & BL. Add. MS. 15904 ff.30, 34–5 & 37.

47. BL. Add. MS. 28224 f.40; BL. Add. MS. 10118 ff.400 & 403; Shield & Lang, *King over the Water*, pp. 74, 113 & 123–4; & Miller, *James*, pp. 106–7 & 115.

48. *Life*, Vol. II, p. 599; Anon., *The Life of James II. Late King of England*, p. 411; Saint-Simon, *Memoirs*, Vol. I, p. 169; *Berwick*, Vol. I, pp. 156 & 432–3; BL. Add. MS. 10118 ff.34, 38, 41, 394, 400–1, 404–7 & 419; Dulon, *Jacques II Stuart*, p. 35; Ragazzi, *Maria Beatrice d'Este*, pp. 300–4; Anon., *Life of William III*, p. 628; Anon., *Memoirs of the Chevalier de St. George*, pp. 35–6; Madan (ed.), *Stuart Papers*, Vol. II, p. 348;

Dangeau, Vol. II, pp. 25–6; & RA / M4 ff.930–2 & 935.

49. Fea, *James II and his Wives*, p. 288; *Life*, Vol. II, pp. 602–3; Anon., *The Life of James II. Late King of England*, p. 411; Southorn, 'Mary of Modena', p. 8; Saint-Simon, *Memoirs*, Vol. I, p. 168; Scott, 'Sacredness of Majesty', p. 1; BL. Add. MS. 10118 f.402; BL. Add. MS. 20311 ff.4–6; *Dangeau*, Vol. II, pp. 25–6; & RA / M4 ff.939–40.

50. *Life*, Vol. II, p. 603; Sizergh Castle, SIZ T 87; Corp & Sanson (eds), *La Cour des Stuarts*, p. 151; Corp (ed.), *L'Autre Exil*, p. 85; J.G. Alger, 'The Posthumous Vicissitudes of James II', *Nineteenth Century and After*, Vol. XXV (Jan. 1889), p. 104; Fea, *James II and his Wives*, p. 288; BL. Add. MS. 28224 f.39; BL. Add. MS. 10118 ff.400, 402–5 & 434; Madan (ed.), *Stuart Papers*, Vol. II, p. 350; & RA / M4 ff.939–40.

51. Despite all their precautions the Queen insisted on 'kissing the urn through the black crape which covered it' before fainting, which caused the nuns present 'to fear for her life'. Corp & Sanson (eds), *La Cour des Stuarts*, pp. 141 & 148; Scott, 'Sacredness of Majesty', p. 2; Fea, *James II and his Wives*, pp. 292 & 297; Haile, *Queen Mary of Modena*, p. 355; Ragazzi, *Maria Beatrice d'Este*, p. 305; Madan (ed.), *Stuart Papers*, Vol. II, p. 352; BL. Add. MS 10118 ff.402; RA / M4 ff.935–6 & 940–3; & *Life*, Vol. II, p. 601.

52. BL. Add. MS. 10118 ff.400 & 410; Scott, 'Sacredness of Majesty', p. 2; Sanson & Corp (eds), *La Cour des Stuarts*, p. 147; & Madan (ed.), *Stuart Papers*, Vol. II, p. 359.

53. HMC, *Calendar of Stuart Papers*, Vol. I, pp. 160–1, 168–9, 171–2, 175, & 178; Madan (ed.), *Stuart Papers*, Vol. I, pp. 89–90; *Letters of Madame*, Vol. I, p. 214; Southorn, 'Mary of Modena', p. 11; & Sanders, *Abrégé de la Vie de Jacques II*, pp. 164–6.

54. P. de Sainte Catherine, *Oraison Funèbre de Jacques II* (Bordeaux, 1701), pp. 3–4, 6–7, 13–14, 16, 20, 20–1, & 23.

55. HMC, *Calendar of Stuart Papers*, Vol. I, pp. 171–3; C. de Aquino, *Sacra Exequialia in Funere Jacobi II* (Rome, 1702), pp. 31–43; Sanders, *Abrégé de la Vie de Jacques II*, pp. 169–70; Scott, 'Sacredness of Majesty', pp. 1 & 3; & H.E. de Roquette, *Oraison Funebre de . . . Prince Jacques II, Roi de la Grande Bretagne* (Paris, 1702), pp. 3–4, 5, 15–16, 18–19, 24, 27–8, 32, 35–6, 40, 44–6, 49, 51–2, & 55–6. See also: Dulon, *Jacques II Stuart*, pp. 41–2.

56. It is significant, here, to note that there were no depositions taken from the inhabitants of St Germain concerning the healing powers of the King. HMC, *Calendar of Stuart Papers*, Vol. I, p. 188; Oman, *Mary of Modena*, p. 195; Dulon, *Jacques II Stuart*, pp. 41–2; Madan (ed.), *Stuart Papers*, Vol. II, pp. 514–35; BL. Add. MS.10118 ff.408 & 419–20; RA / M4 f.978; *Life*, Vol. II, pp. 615–16; & St John, *La Cour de Jacques II*, p. 47.

57. BL. Add. MS. 10118 ff.41, 419 & 436–7; Macpherson (ed.), *Original Papers*, Vol. I, pp. 597–9 fn.; Scott, 'Sacredness of Majesty', pp. 3–4; BL. Add. MS. 20311 ff.9–12; St John, *La Cour de Jacques II*, p. 48; & Madan (ed.), *Stuart Papers*, Vol. II, p. 517. As the practical and political efficacy of Jacobitism declined, belief in the role of the late King as an intermediary with God, who could bring about counter-revolutionary change, grew exponentially. Thus, in November 1707, Meriel Priest, of St Suplice's Seminary in Montreal, Quebec, testified that in August 1685 he had sat next to a mysterious 'stranger' during his stay in Paris, who had predicted that King James would lose his throne within four years, but that his son would one day be restored through the help of the Pope and the cardinals. See: BL. Add. MS. 10118 f.34.

58. P. Burke, 'How to be a Counter-Reformation Saint' in K. von Greyerz (ed.), *Religion and Society in Early Modern Europe, 1500–1800* (London, 1984), pp. 48 & 50; Scott, 'Sacredness

of Majesty', pp. 4 & 8; Corp (ed.),
L'Autre Exil, p. 97; Corp & Sanson
(eds), *La Cour des Stuarts*, p. 151;
BL. Add. MS. 10118 ff.436–7; BL. Add.
MS. 20311 ff.10–15; & Madan (ed.),
Stuart Papers, Vol. II, pp. 518–35.

59.   *Letters of Madame*, Vol. I, p. 216.

60.   *Dangeau*, Vol. II, pp. 233 & 236; Petrie,
Marshal Duke, pp. 111–12; *Berwick*,
Vol. I, p. 142; J. Berenger, *Turenne*
(Paris, 1987), p. 492; & Sells (ed. &
trans.), *Memoirs of James II*, p. 53.
A second copy of James's military
memoirs was copied for another of the
Bouillon clan, Bishop Henri-Oswald
de la Tour d'Auvergne, in 1704, by
command of Mary of Modena. See
BL. Portland Papers 70522
frontispiece & f.401.

61.   E. Gregg, 'New Light on the
Authorship of the "Life of James II"',
English Historical Review, Vol. CVIII
(1993), pp. 953–4. This seminal
article, the product of meticulous
archival research, has succeeded in
clarifying many of the issues
surrounding the composition of the
King's memoirs, and will be of
enormous use to future generations of
scholars in evaluating James's writings.
See also: Callow, *Making of James II*,
pp. 1–7.

62.   D.G. Scott, 'The Collector: A Look at
Benedictine Archives through the Eyes
of Bro. Benet Weldon, 1674–1713',
Catholic Archives, Vol. VI (1986),
pp. 26–7; Anon., *An Elegy on the Death
of the late King James* (London, 1701),
p. 1; Anon. ('By a Lady'), *On the Death
of King James* (London, *c.* 1701),
pp. 1–2, 4–5, 7–8, 11, & 13–14; &
BL. Add. MS. 20311 ff.30–5.

63.   HMC, *Calendar of Stuart Papers*,
Vol. IV, pp. 3–4; Miller, *James*,

pp. 69–70; Shield & Lang, *King over the
Water*, pp. 56–7; Macaulay, *History of
England*, Vol. VI, p. 2990; Jones, *Charles
Middleton*, p. 268; Bevan, *King James the
Third*, p. 39; Saint-Simon, *Memoirs*,
Vol. I, pp. 169 & 346; *CSPD* (1700–2),
pp. 422 & 424–5.

64.   Macpherson (ed.), *Original Papers*,
Vol. I, p. 600; Haile, *Queen Mary of
Modena*, pp. 358–9 & 362–3; Oman,
Mary of Modena, pp. 197–8; Miller,
James, p. 68; & Hopkirk, *Queen over the
Water*, pp. 244–5.

65.   *Dangeau*, Vol. II, p. 135 fn.; & Haile,
Queen Mary of Modena, p. 499. Though
the Papal Court had done nothing to
advance James's progress on the road
to beatification in the early 1700s, the
Old Pretender was prepared to
finance a fresh campaign in 1734.
Aged witnesses once again swore
statements about the nature of the
miraculous cures wrought by his
intercession, and a dossier was passed
to Rome for a second time in January
1735. However, though James's cause
was still being promoted in 1740, the
lack of funds and the apparent
hopelessness of his case finally
compelled his son to abandon the
venture. See: Scott, 'Sacredness of
Majesty', pp. 9–10.

66.   Alger, 'Posthumous Vicissitudes',
p. 105; Corp & Sanson (eds), *La Cour
des Stuarts*, p. 151; *Berwick*, Vol. I,
pp. 203–4; & Vol. II, pp. 320–1; Petrie,
Marshal Duke, pp. 161, 188, 210–15,
247 & 302–3; Haile, *Queen Mary of
Modena*, p. 499; *Dangeau*, Vol. II, p. 135
fn.; Dulon, *Jacques II Stuart*, p. 160;
Scott, 'Sacredness of Majesty', p. 9; &
Voltaire, *The Age of Louis XIV*, trans.
M.P. Pollack (London, 1751 & 1753,
rpt. 1961), p. 146.

Bibliography

MANUSCRIPT SOURCES

The Royal Archives, Windsor Castle
RA / M1-4: *The Life of James the Second, King of England etc. Collected out of Memoirs Writ of his own hand.* Transcribed by Etienne Monnot
RA / MS 1: Stuart Papers
For My Son the Prince of Wales, 1692: James II's manuscript, The Royal Library

The British Library
Add. MS. 828: Lansdowne Papers, Captain John Stevens' 'Monasticon Continuation'
Add. MS. 10118: 'A Course and Rough First Draught of ye History of England's Late Most Holy and Most Glorious Royal Confessor and Defender of ye True Faith King James II' by J. Johnston
Add. MS. 15904: 'Lettres de Madame Maintenon'
Add. MS. 20311: Papers of Cardinal F.A. Gualterio
Add. MS. 28224: Letters of James II and his Queen to Lord Caryll, 1692–1710
Add. MS. 28226: Correspondence of Lord Caryll, 1648–1711
Add. MS. 36296: Lieutenant John Stevens' Journal in Ireland, 1689–1691
Add. MS. 36707: Correspondence of James Harrington, 1669–93
Add. MS. 37660: Letter Book of Lord Melfort, December 1689–March 1690
Add. MS. 37661: Letter Book of Lord Melfort, June–December 1692
Add. MS. 37662: Letter Book of Henry Brown, St Germain, 1690–1
Add. MS. 38145: Letter Book of Lord Tyrconnel to Mary of Modena, 1689–90
Add. MS. 39923: Jacobite and other letters
Add. MS. 61270: Blenheim Papers, Correspondence of the Duke of Berwick, ff.1–53
Add. MS. 70293: Portland Manuscripts, Letter from Prince William of Orange to Lords Halifax, Shrewsbury, and Delamere, 17 December 1688 (O.S.)
Harleian MS. 6852 ff.402–403: 'A True Account of the Taking of the King at Ness Point, December 11, 1688'
Portland Papers MS. 70522: 'Memoires de Jacques Second, Roy de la Grande Bretagne, de Glorieuse Memoire'
Stowe MS. 444: 'Colonel J. Richard's Campaign of 1692–1693'

Trinity College Library, Dublin
MS. 3529: James II's Devotional Papers

Stonyhurst College, Clitheroe, Lancashire
James II's Holy Week Book, *L'Office de la Semaine Sainte Connadnent du Roy* (Paris, privately printed and bound, *c.* 1690s)
Princess Louise Marie Stuart's Prayer Book, *Missale Romanum* (Paris, privately printed and bound, *c.* 1690s)

PRIMARY PRINTED SOURCES

Acton, Lord (ed.), 'Letters of James the Second to the Abbot of La Trappe' in *Miscellanies of the Philobiblion Society*, Vol. XIV (London, 1872–6), pp. i–xv & 1–101

Anon., *The Abdicated Prince* (London, 1690)

Anon., *An Account of the Reasons of the Nobility and Gentry's Invitation of his Highness the Prince of Orange into England* (London, 1688)

Anon., *An Act Against Corresponding with the late King James and his Adherents* (London, 1697)

Anon., *Advice before it be too Late: or, a Breviate for the Convention* (London, 1689)

Anon., *The Anatomy of an Arbitrary Prince; or King James the II* (London, 1689)

Anon., *La Cour de St. Germain, ou les Intrigues Galantes du Roy et de la Reine d' Angleterre* (St-Germain-en-Laye, 1695)

Anon., *A Dialogue Between K.W. and Benting, Occasioned by his Going into Flanders after the Death of the Queen* (n.p., c. 1695–6)

Anon., *The Debate at Large, between the House of Lords and House of Commons . . . Relating to the Word Abdicated and the Vacancy of the Throne* (London & Westminster, 1695)

Anon., *The Declaration of the Lords Spiritual and Temporal in and about the Cities of London and Westminster, Assembled at Guildhall, 11 December 1688* (London, 1688)

Anon., *An Elegy on the Death of the late King James* (London, 1701)

Anon., *The Exact Narrative of the Conflict at Dunkeld* (London, 1689)

Anon., *His Majesties Most Gratious Declaration to all his Loving Subjects* (St-Germain-en-Laye, 1693)

Anon., *The Life of James II. Late King of England* (London, 1702)

Anon., *The Life of William III, Late King of England and Prince of Orange* (London, 1703)

Anon., *The Memoirs of King James II. Containing an account of the Transactions of the last twelve years of his Life: with the circumstances of his death* (London & Westminster, 1702)

Anon., *Memoirs of the Chevalier de St. George: with some Private Passages of the Life of the Late James II, Never Before Published* (London, 1712)

Anon., *King James the Second. His Last Expressions and Dying-Words* (London, 1702)

Anon. ('By a Lady'), *On the Death of King James* (London, c. 1701)

Anon., *The Paris Relation of the Battel of Landen, July 29th 1693* (London, 1693)

Anon., *A Particular Relation of the Battel fought on the 29th of July 1693* (London, 1693)

Anon., *A Remonstrance and Protestation of all the Good Protestants of this Kingdom, Against Deposing their Lawful Sovereign K. James* (London, 1689)

Anon., *A Short and True Relation of Intrigues transacted both Home and Abroad to Restore the Late King James* (London, 1694)

Anon., *The True and Genuine Explanation of One King James's Declaration* (London, 1692)

Anon. (ed.), *Derriana: or, A Collection of Papers Relative to the Siege of Londonderry* (London & Derry, 1794)

Anon. (ed.), *His Highness, the Prince of Orange, His Letter to the Lords Spiritual and Temporal, Assembled at Westminster in this Present Convention, January the 22, 1689* (London, 1689)

Anon. (ed.), *Memoirs of the Duke de Villars, Marshal-General of the Armies of his Most Christian Majesty* (London, 1735)

Aquino, C. de, *Sacra Exequialia in Funere Jacobi II* (Rome, 1702)

Bathurst, B. (ed.), *Letters of Two Queens* [Mary II & Anne] (London, 1924)

Beddard, R. (ed.), *A Kingdom Without a King. The Journal of the Provisional Government in the Revolution of 1688* (Oxford, 1988)

Bentham, J., *A Brief Treatise* (Paris, 1693)

Bohun, E. (pub. anon.), *The History of the Desertion, or An Account of all the Publick Affairs in England, From the Beginning of September 1688 to the Twelfth of February Following* (London, 1689)

Boulhillier, C. de, Bishop de Troyes, *Harangue fate a la Reine d'Angleterre* (Paris, 1700)

Bray, W. (ed.), *Diary and Correspondence of John Evelyn*, 4 vols (London, 1850–2)

Browning, A. (ed.), *Memoirs of Sir John Reresby*, 2nd edition, preface by M.K. Geiter & W.A. Speck (London, 1991)

Bruce, T., Earl of Ailesbury, *Memoirs of Thomas, Earl of Ailesbury*, 2 vols (Westminster, 1890)

Camden Society (ed.), *The Autobiography of Sir John Bramston* (London, 1845)

Castries, H. de (ed.), *Moulay Ismail et Jacques II. Une apologie de l' Islam par un Sultan du Maroc* (Paris, 1903)

Cavelli, C. de (ed.), *Les Derniers Stuarts à Saint-Germain-en-Laye*, 2 vols (Paris, London & Edinburgh, 1871)

Clarke, J.S. (ed.), *The Life of James the Second, King of England, Memoirs Collected out of Writ of his Own Hand, together with the King's Advice to his Son, and His Majesty's Will*, 2 vols (London, 1816)

Cotteril, C., *The Whole Life and Glorious Actions of Prince George of Denmark* (London, 1708)

Dalrymple, J., *Memoirs of Great Britain and Ireland*, 3 vols (Edinburgh, 1771 & 1788)

Davenport, J. (ed. & trans.), *Memoirs of the Court of France . . . From the Diary of the Marquis de Dangeau*, 2 vols (London, 1825)

Davies, G. (ed.), *Papers of Devotion of James II* (Oxford, 1925)

Davis, T., *The Patriot Parliament of 1689*, ed. G. Duffy (London, 1893)

Defoe, D. (pub. anon.), *The Englishman's Choice and True Interest: In a Vigorous Prosecution of the War against France* (London, 1694)

Doebner, R. (ed.), *Memoirs of Mary, Queen of England (1689–1693), together with her Letters and those of Kings James II and William III to the Electress Sophia of Hanover* (Leipzig, 1886)

Duclaux, A.M.F. (ed. & trans.), *Letters of the Marchioness de Sévigné*, 10 vols (London, 1927)

Fuller, W. (impostor), *A Plain Proof of the Father and Mother of the Pretended Prince of Wales* (London, 1700)

Gendre, Mr le, *The History of the Reign of Lewis the Great, Till the General Peace concluded at Reswick, in the year, 1697* (London, 1699)

Gilbert, J.T. (ed.), *A Jacobite Narrative of the War in Ireland, 1688–1691* (Dublin, 1892)

Grew, M.E., *William Bentinck and William III (Prince of Orange). The Life of Bentinck Earl of Portland from the Welbeck Correspondence* (London, 1924)

Hamilton, A. *The Actions of the Enniskillen-men* (London, 1690, rpt. 1849)

Hamilton, A., 'Zeneyde' in *Oeuvres Diverses* (London, 1776), pp. 237–383

Hawke, M., *Killing is Murder, and No Murder: or, An Excertation concerning a Scurrilous Pamphlet of one William Allen, a Jesuistical Impostor Intituled Killing No Murder* (London, 1657)

Historical Manuscripts Commission, *Twelfth Report, Appendix, Part VII. The Manuscripts of S.H. le Fleming Esq. of Rydal Hall* (London, 1890)

Historical Manuscripts Commission, *Calendar of the Stuart Papers belonging to His Majesty the King, preserved at Windsor Castle*, Vols I–II & VII (London, 1902, 1904 & 1923)

Horwitz, H. (ed.), *The Parliamentary Diary of Narcissus Luttrell, 1691–1693* (Oxford, 1972)

Howarth, R.G. (ed.), *Letters and the Second Diary of Samuel Pepys* (London, Toronto & New York, 1932)

Howell, T.B. (ed.), *A Complete Collection of State Trials*, Vols XII–XIII (London, 1812)

Hyde, H., *The State Letters of Henry Earl of Clarendon*, 2 vols (Oxford, 1763)

Jerdan, W. (ed.), *Letters from James Earl of Perth, Lord Chancellor of Scotland, to his sister, the Countess of Erroll* (London, 1845, rpt. London & New York, 1968)

Jones, D.L. (ed.), *A Parliamentary History of the Glorious Revolution* (London, 1988)

King, W., *The State of the Protestants of Ireland under the late King James's Government* (London, 1691)

Krailsheimer, A.J. (ed.), *The Letters of Armand-Jean de Rancé, Abbot and Reformer of la Trappe* (Kalamazoo, Michigan, 1984)

Lallemant, J.P., *The Holy Desires of Death: or, a Collection of Some Thoughts of the Fathers of the Church, to Shew How Christians Ought to Despise Life, and to Desire Death*, trans. T.V.F. Sadler (London, 1678)

Lart, C.E. (ed.), *The Parochial Registers of Saint Germain-En-Laye. Jacobite extracts of births, marriages and deaths*, 2 vols (London, 1910 & 1912)

Louis XIV, *Memoires for the Instruction of the Dauphin*, ed. & trans. P. Sonnino (New York & London, 1970)

Luttrell, N., *A Brief Historical Relation of State Affairs*, 6 vols (Oxford, 1857)

Mackay, H., *Memoirs of the War carried on in Scotland and Ireland, 1689–1691*, ed. J.M. Hog, P.F. Tytler & A. Urquhart (Edinburgh, 1833)

Macky, J. (pub. anon.), 'A View of the Court of St. Germain from the Year 1690 to 95. With an Account of the Entertainment the Protestants meet with there', in *Harleian Miscellany* (London, 1810), Vol. VI pp. 390–7

Macpherson, J. (ed.), *Original Papers; Containing the Secret History of Great Britain . . . To Which are Prefixed Extracts from the Life of James II*, 2 vols (London, 1775)

McCarmick, W., *A Farther Impartial Account of the Actions of the Inniskilling-men* (London, 1691)

Madan, F. (ed.), *Stuart Papers relating chiefly to Queen Mary of Modena and the Exiled Court of King James II*, 2 vols (London, 1889)

Neveu, B. (ed.), *Jacques II Mediateur Entre Louis XIV et Innocent XI* (Paris, 1967)

Nieremberg, J.E., *Contemplations on the State of Man in this Life, and in that which is to Come*, trans., ed., & reworked by J. Taylor, Bishop of Down and Connor, and of Dromore (London, 1684)

Nieremberg, J.E., *Bilancia del Tempo, O Sia la Differenza Fra il Temporale e l'Eterno* (Venice, 1731)

Oates, T., *Eikon Basike, or the Picture of the Late King James Drawn to Life*, 2 parts (London, 1696)

Oldmixon, J. [pub. anon.], *The History of England during the reigns of the Royal House of Stuart* (London, 1730)

Oldys, W., & Park, T. (eds), '*The Harleian Miscellany: A Collection of . . . Pamphlets and Tracts . . . Selected from the Library of Edward Harley, Second Earl of Oxford*, 10 vols (London, 1808–13)

Petrie, C. (ed.), *The Duke of Berwick and his Son, some unpublished Letters and Papers* (London, 1951)

Philostelus (pseud.), *Letter to the Right Honourable Sir Ralph Gore . . . Concerning a lately Published Proposal for a Voluntary Subscription to Erect a Trophy in Memory of the Deliverance of this Kingdom, by the Glorious Victory at the Boyne* (Dublin, 1732)

Plunket, N., *Derry and the Boyne. A Contemporary Catholic Account of the Siege of Derry, the Battle of the Boyne, and the General Condition of Ireland in the Jacobite War*, intro. B. Clifford (Belfast, 1990)

Rapin de Thoyras, P., *The History of England*, trans. N. Tindal, 2nd edition, 5 vols (1732–47)

Ruvigny & Raineval, Marquis of (ed.), *The Jacobite Peerage* (Edinburgh, 1904)

Saint-Simon, Duc de, *Memoirs*, trans. & ed. L. Norton, 3 vols (London, 1999–2000)

Sanders, Revd F, *An Abridgement of the Life of James II*, ed. Fr F. Brettonneau S.J. (London, 1704)

Sells, A.L. (ed. & trans.), *The Memoirs of James II. His Campaigns as Duke of York, 1652–1660*, intro. by A. Bryant (London, 1962)

Sexby, E., & Titus, S. (pub. anon.), *Killing No Murder: Briefly Discoursed in Three Questions* (London, rpt. 1689)

Smythe, G. (ed.), *Letters of John Grahame of Claverhouse, Viscount Dundee with Illustrative Documents* (Edinburgh, 1826)

Stevenson, G.S. (ed. & trans.), *The Letters of Madame. The Correspondence of Elizabeth-Charlotte of Bavaria, Princess Palatine, Duchess of Orléans*, 2 vols (London, 1924)

Tayler, A. & H. (eds), *The Stuart Papers at Windsor* (London, 1939)

Trenchard, J., & Moyle, W. [pub. anon.], *An Argument shewing that a Standing Army is Inconsistent with a Free Government* (London, 1697)

Weller Singer, S. (ed.), *The Correspondence of Henry Hyde, Earl of Clarendon and of his brother Laurence Hyde, Earl of Rochester*, 2 vols (London, 1828)

Wilton Rix, S. (ed.), *The Diary and Autobiography of Edmund Bohun* (Beccles, 1853)

SECONDARY SOURCES

Adamson, J. (ed.), *The Princely Courts of Europe, 1500–1750* (London, 2000)

Ashley, M., *The Glorious Revolution of 1688* (London, 1966)

Ashley, M., *James II* (London, Toronto & Melbourne, 1977)

Aubrey, P., *The Defeat of James Stuart's Armada, 1692* (Leicester, 1979)

Bagwell, R., *Ireland under the Stuarts*, 3 vols (London, 1906–16)

Barker, N.N., *Brother to the Sun King, Philippe, Duke of Orléans* (Baltimore & London, 1989)

Baxter, S.B., *King William III* (London, 1966)

Belloc, H., *James the Second*, 2nd edition (London, 1928)

Berenger, J., *Turenne* (Paris, 1987)

Beresford Ellis, P., *The Boyne Water. The Battle of the Boyne, 1690* (London, 1976)

Bevan, B., *I was James the Second's Queen* (London, 1963)

Bevan, B., *King James the Third of England. A Study of Kingship in Exile* (London, 1967)

Bloch, M., *The Royal Touch. Monarchy and Miracles in France and England*, trans. J.E. Anderson (New York, 1961, rpt. 1989)

Boulger, D.C., *The Battle of the Boyne* (London, 1911)

Bouron, M., Briere, J., & Veyssiere-Pomot, C., *La Domaine Royal: ses Châteaux, ses Jardins* (St-Germain-en-Laye & Paris, 1997)

Bremond, H., *The Thundering Abbot. Armand de Rancé, Reformer of La Trappe*, trans. F.J. Sheed (London, 1930)

Callow, J., *The Making of King James II. The Formative Years of a Fallen King* (Stroud, 2000)

Capefigue, M., *Jacques II à Saint-Germain*, 2 vols (Paris, 1833)

Carrel, A., *History of the Counter-Revolution in England for the Re-establishment of Popery under Charles II and James II* (London, 1846)

Carswell, J., *The Old Cause* (London, 1954)

Carswell, J., *The Descent on England. A Study of the English Revolution of 1688 and its European Consequences* (London, 1969)

Chapman, H.W., *Mary II, Queen of England* (London, 1953)

Chateaubriand, *Vie de Rancé* (Paris, 1844, rpt. Brussels, n/d)

Cherry, G.L., *The Convention Parliament 1689: A Biographical Study of its Members* (New York, 1966)

Childs, J., *The Army, James II and the Glorious Revolution* (Manchester, 1980)

Childs, J. *The British Army of William III, 1689–1702* (Manchester, 1987)

Churchill, W.S., *Marlborough. His Life and Times*, Vol. 1 (London, 1933, rpt. Chicago, 2002)

City of Rochester Society, *Rochester, the Past 2000 Years* (Rochester, 1999)

Corp, E. (ed.), *L'Autre Exil: Les Jacobites en France au debut du XVIIIe Siècle* (Languedoc, 1992)

Corp, E., & Sanson, J. (eds), *La Cour des Stuarts à Saint-Germain-en-Laye au temps de Louis XIV* (Paris, 1992)

Corp, E. with Gregg, E., Erskine-Hill, H., & Scott, G., *A Court in Exile. The Stuarts in France, 1689–1718* (Cambridge, 2004)

Cruickshanks, E. (ed.), *By Force or by Default? The Revolution of 1688–89* (Edinburgh, 1989)

Cruickshanks, E., *The Glorious Revolution* (Houndmills, Basingstoke, 2000)

Cruickshanks, E. (ed.), *The Stuart Courts* (Stroud, 2000)

Cruickshanks, E., & Black, J. (eds), *The Jacobite Challenge* (Edinburgh, 1988)

Cruickshanks, E., & Corp, E. (eds), *The Stuart Court in Exile and the Jacobites* (London & Rio Grande, Ohio, 1995)

Dalton, J., *Illustrations . . . of King James's Irish Army* (Dublin, 1855)

Danaher, K., & Simms, J.G., *The Danish Force in Ireland* (Dublin, 1962)

Doherty, R., *The Williamite War in Ireland, 1688–1691* (Dublin, 1998)

Douglas, H., *Jacobite Spy Wars. Moles, Rogues and Treachery* (Stroud, 1999)

Earle, P., *The Life and Times of James II* (London, 1972)

Exauville, M. d', *Histoire de L'Abbé de Rancé: Reformateur de la Trappe* (Paris, 1842)

Fea, A., *James II and his Wives* (London, 1908)

Firth, C.H., *A Commentary on Macaulay's History of England* (London, 1938, rpt. 1964)

Fitzroy, A., *Henry, Duke of Grafton, 1663–1690* (London, 1921)

Garrett, J., *The Triumphs of Providence. The Assassination Plot, 1696* (Cambridge, 1980)

Goubert, P., *Louis XIV and Twenty Million Frenchmen*, trans. A. Carter (New York, 1970)

Goujon, A., *Histoire de la Ville et du Château de St. Germain-en-Laye* (St-Germain-en-Laye, 1829)

Gray, T., *No Surrender! The Siege of Londonderry, 1689* (London, 1975)
Green, D., *Queen Anne* (London, 1970)
Gregg, E., *Jacobitism* (London, 1988)
Grew, E. & M.S., *The Court of William III* (London, 1910)
Grew, E. & M.S., *The English Court in Exile. James II at Saint-Germain* (London, 1911)
Grew, M.E., *William Bentinck and William III* (London, 1924)
Greyerz, K. von (ed.), *Religion and Society in Early Modern Europe, 1500–1800* (London, 1984)
Guy, A.J., & Spencer-Smith, J. (eds), *1688. Glorious Revolution?* (London, 1988)
Haddick-Flynn, K, *Orangeism. The Making of a Tradition* (Dublin, 1999)
Haile, M., *Queen Mary of Modena* (London & New York, 1905)
Hall, R., *Flags and Uniforms of the French Infantry under Louis XIV, 1688–1714*, 2nd edition (Farnham, Surrey, 2002)
Harrison, S., & Evemy, S, *Rochester upon Medway, the Tale of a City* (London, 1996)
Haswell, J., *James II. Soldier and Sailor* (London, 1972)
Hay, M.V., *The Enigma of James II* (London & Glasgow, 1938)
Hayes, R., *Biographical Dictionary of Irishmen in France* (Dublin, 1949)
Higham, F.M.G., *King James the Second* (London, 1934)
Hill, C., *Some Intellectual Consequences of the English Revolution* (London, 1980, rpt. 1997)
Hopkins, P., *Glencoe and the End of the Highland War* (Edinburgh, 1998)
Hopkirk, M., *The Queen over the Water* (London, 1953)
Johnston, S.H.F., *The History of the Cameronians (Scottish Rifles)*, Vol. I 1689–1910 (London, 1947)
Jones, G.H., *Charles Middleton. The Life and Times of a Restoration Politician* (Chicago & London, 1967)
Jones, J.R., *The Revolution of 1688 in England* (London, 1972, rpt. 1988)
Jones, J.R. (ed.), *Liberty Secured? Britain before and after 1688* (Stanford, California, 1992)
Jones, J.R., *Marlborough* (Cambridge, 1993)
Kamen, H., *Philip V of Spain. The King who Reigned Twice* (New Haven & London, 2001)
Kantorowicz, E.H., *The King's Two Bodies. A Study in Medieval Political Theology* (Princeton, New Jersey, 1957)
Kenyon, J.P., *Robert Spencer, Earl of Sunderland, 1641–1702* (London, 1958)
Kinross, J., *The Boyne and Aughrim. The War of the Two Kings* (Moreton-in-Marsh, 1997)
Krailsheimer, A.J., *Armand-Jean de Rancé, Abbot of La Trappe* (Oxford, 1974)
Lane, J. [pub. anon.], *The Adventures of King James II of England* (London, New York & Bombay, 1904)
Lenihan, P., *1690. Battle of the Boyne* (Stroud, 2003)
Longueville, T., *The Adventures of James II of England* (London, 1904)
Luddy, A.J., *The Real de Rancé. Illustrious Penitent and Reformer of Notre Dame de la Trappe* (London, New York, & Toronto, 1931)
Ludwig, F. von, *The History of the Popes*, trans. D.E. Graf, Vol. XXXII (London, 1957)
Lynn, J.A., *The Wars of Louis XIV, 1667–1714* (Harlow, Essex, 1999)
Macaulay, T.B., *The History of England. From the Accession of James the Second*, ed. C.H. Firth, 6 vols (London, 1913–15)
McCartney, P., *The Siege of Derry – 1689* (Derry, 1988, rpt. 1993)
Maccubin, R.P., & Hamilton-Phillips, M. (eds), *The Age of William III and Mary II. Power, Politics and Patronage, 1688–1702* (Williamsburg & New York, 1989)
Mackintosh, J., *History of the Revolution in England in 1688* (London, 1834)
MacLachlan, A., *The Rise and Fall of Revolutionary England. An Essay on the Fabrication of Seventeeth-Century History* (Houndmills, Basingstoke, 1996)
McBride, I., *The Siege of Derry in Ulster Protestant Mythology* (Dublin, 1997)
Maguire, J.M., *The Battle of the Boyne* (London, 1894)
Maguire, W.A. (ed.), *Kings in Conflict. The Revolutionary War in Ireland and its Aftermath, 1689–1750* (Belfast, 1990)
Merton, T., *The Waters of Siloe* (Garden City, New York, 1951)
Middleton, D., *The Life of Charles, 2nd Earl of Middleton* (London, 1957)

Miller, J., *The Life and Times of William and Mary* (London, 1974)

Miller, J., *The Glorious Revolution* (London & New York, 1983)

Miller, J., *Bourbon and Stuart. Kings and Kingship in France and England in the Seventeenth Century* (London, 1987)

Miller, J., *James II* (New Haven & London, 1978, rpt. 2000)

Miller, J., *The Stuarts* (London & New York, 2004)

Miller, P., *James* [the Old Pretender] (London, 1971)

Monod, P.K., *Jacobitism and the English People, 1688–1788* (Cambridge, 1989, rpt. 1993)

Monod, P.K., *The Power of Kings. Monarchy and Religion in Europe, 1589–1715* (New Haven & London, 1999)

Mullett, M., *James II and English Politics, 1678–1688* ((London, 1994)

Murphy, J.A., *Justin MacCarthy, Lord Mountcashel, Commander of the First Irish Brigade in France*, 2nd edition (Clonmel, Eire, 1959, rpt. 1999)

O'Callaghan, J.C., *History of the Irish Brigades in the service of France* (Glasgow, 1870, rpt. Dublin, 1968)

O'Conor, M., *The Irish Brigades* (Dublin, 1855)

O'Donnell, E., *The Irish Abroad* (London, 1915)

Ogg, D., *William III* (London, 1956)

Oman, C., *Mary of Modena* (Bungay, Suffolk, 1962)

Oyly, G. d', *The Life of William Sancroft, Archbishop of Canterbury*, 2nd edition (London, 1890)

Petrie, C., *The Jacobite Movement. The First Phase, 1688–1716* (London, 1948)

Petrie, C., *The Marshal Duke of Berwick* (London, 1953)

Petrie, C., *The Great Tyrconnel. A Chapter in Anglo-Irish Relations* (Cork & Dublin, 1972)

Pinkham, L., *William III and the Respectable Revolution. The Part Played by William of Orange in the Revolution of 1688* (Harvard, 1954, rpt. 1969)

Pittock, M.G.H., *Jacobitism* (Houndmills, Basingstoke, 1998)

Powley, E.B., *The Naval Side of King William's War* (London, 1972)

Prall, S.E., *The Bloodless Revolution. England, 1688* (Madison, Wisconsin & London, 1985)

Prebble, J., *Glencoe. The Story of the Massacre* (London, 1966)

Prebble, J., *The Darien Disaster* (London, 1968)

Ragazzi, M., *Maria Beatrice d'Este, Regina d'Inghilterra* (Assisi, 1942)

Ranke, L. von, *A History of England principally in the Seventeenth Century*, 6 vols (Oxford, 1875)

Reynolds, E.E., *Bossuet* (New York, 1963)

Robb, N.A., *William of Orange. A Personal Portrait*, Vol. II (London, 1966)

Ronan, M.V., *The Boyne Valley and its Antiquities* (Dublin, Belfast, Cork & Waterford, n.d., c. 1936)

Rose, C., *England in the 1690s. Revolution, Religion and War* (Oxford, 1999)

St John, B., *La Cour de Jacques II à Saint-Germain-en-Laye* (Paris, 1913)

Scott, A.M., *Bonnie Dundee. John Graham of Claverhouse* (Edinburgh, 1989, rpt. 2000)

Sergeant, P.W., *Little Jennings and Fighting Dick Talbot. A Life of the Duke and Duchess of Tyrconnel*, Vol. II (London, 1913)

Shield, A. & Lang, A., *The King over the Water* (London, 1907)

Simms, J.G., *The Jacobite Parliament of 1689* (Dundalk, 1974)

Speck, W.A., *Reluctant Revolutionaries. Englishmen and the Revolution of 1688* (Oxford & New York, 1988)

Speck, W.A., *James II. Profiles in Power* (London & New York, 2002)

Spielman, J.P., *Leopold I of Austria* (London, 1977)

Stevenson, D., *Highland Warrior. Alasdair MacColla and the Civil Wars* (Edinburgh, 1980, rpt. 1994)

Strickland, A., *The Lives of the Seven Bishops Committed to the Tower in 1688* (London, 1866)

Strickland, A., *Lives of the Queens of England after the Norman Conquest*, Vol. XIII, *Mary II* (Philadephia, 1903)

Szechi, D., *The Jacobites. Britain and Europe, 1688–1788* (Manchester & New York, 1994)

Tomalin, C., *Samuel Pepys. The Unequalled Self* (London, 2002)

Townsend, W.C., *History of the House of Commons from the Convention Parliament of 1688–9 to the Passing of the Reform Bill in 1832*, 2 vols (London, 1843–4)

Treasure, G., *Louis XIV* (London, 2001)

Trevelyan, G.M., *The English Revolution, 1688–1689* (London, Oxford & New York, 1938, rpt. 1965)

Voltaire, *The Age of Louis XIV*, trans. M.P. Pollack (London, 1751 & 1753, rpt. 1961)

Waller, M., *Ungrateful Daughters. The Stuart Princesses who stole their Father's Crown* (London, 2002)

Wauchope, P., *Patrick Sarsfield and the Williamite War* (Dublin, 1992)

Webb, S.S., *Lord Churchill's Coup. The Anglo-American Empire and the Glorious Revolution Reconsidered* (New York, 1995)

Weber, H.M., *Paper Bullets. Print and Kingship under Charles II* (Lexington, Kentucky, 1996)

Zee, H. & B. van der, *William and Mary* (London & Basingstoke, 1973)

Zee, H. & B. van der, *1688. Revolution in the Family* (London & New York, 1988)

Zuccoli, V.C.G., *Maria di Modena, Regina d'Inghilterra* (Milan, 1940)

SECONDARY ARTICLES AND PAMPHLETS

Alger, J.G., 'The Posthumous Vicissitudes of James II', *Nineteenth Century and After*, Vol. XXV (1889), pp. 104–9

Barnes, R.P., 'Scotland and the Glorious Revolution of 1688', *Albion*, Vol. III (1971), pp. 116–27

Barnes, R.P., 'James VII's forfeiture of the Scottish Throne', *Albion*, Vol. V (1973), pp. 299–313

Beddard, R., 'The Guildhall Declaration of 11 December 1688 and the Counter-Revolution of the Loyalists', *The Historical Journal*, Vol. XI, no. 3 (1968), pp. 403–20

Blackmore, H.L., & Blair, C., 'King James II's Harquebus Armours and Richard Holden of London', Vol. XIII (1991), pp. 316–34

Brown, W.E., 'A Plea for James II', *Contemporary Review* (October, 1925), pp. 501–8

Callow, J., 'The Last of the Shireburnes: the Art of Death and Life in Recusant Lancashire, 1660–1754', *Recusant History*, Vol. XXVI, no. 4 (October, 2003), pp. 589–615

Cherry, G.L., 'The Legal and Philosophical Position of the Jacobites, 1688–1689', *Journal of Modern History*, Vol. XXII, no. 4 (1950), pp. 309–21

Childs, J., 'A Patriot for Whom? Marshal Schomberg – for God and for Honour', *History Today*, Vol. XXXVIII (1988), pp. 46–52

Clark, J.C.D., 'The Glorious Revolution Debunked', *Sunday Telegraph* (24 July 1988), p. 15

Clark, J.C.D., '1688 and All That – "The English Revolution"', *Encounter* (Jan. 1989), pp. 14–17

Cole, S., 'Princess Over the Water: A Memoir of Louise Marie Stuart, 1692–1712', *The Royal Stuart Society*, Occasional Paper no. XVIII (1981)

Corp, E., 'The Exiled Court of James II and James III: A Centre of Italian Music in France, 1689–1712', *Journal of the Royal Musical Association*, Vol. 120 (1995), pp. 216–31

Corp, E., 'James II and Toleration: The Years in Exile at Saint-Germain-en-Laye', *The Royal Stuart Society*, Occasional Paper no. LI (1997)

Corp, E., 'The Last Years of James II, 1690–1701', *History Today*, Vol. LI (Sept. 2001), pp. 19–25

Daly, J., 'The Idea of Absolute Monarchy in 17th Century England', *The Historical Journal*, Vol. XXI, no. 2 (1978), pp. 227–50

Dickinson, H.T., 'The Eighteenth Century Debate on the Glorious Revolution', *History*, Vol. 61, no. 201 (Feb. 1976), pp. 28–45

Doran, W., 'Bishop Thomas Nicolson: First Vicar-Apostolic, 1695–1718', *The Innes Review*, Vol. XXXIX, no. 2 (Autumn, 1988), pp. 109–32

Ellestad, C.D., 'The Mutinies of 1689', *Journal of the Society for Army Historical Research*, Vol. LIII, no. 213 (Spring, 1975), pp. 4–21

Farquhar, H., 'Royal Charities. Part III. Continuation of Touchpieces for the King's Evil: James II to William III', *British Numismatic Journal*, Vol. XV, no. 4 New Series (1920), pp. 89–120

Ferguson, K., 'The Organisation of King William's Army in Ireland, 1689–92', *The Irish Sword*, Vol. XVIII, no. 70 (Winter, 1990), pp. 62–79

Fevre, P. Le, 'The Battle of Bantry Bay, 1 May 1689', *The Irish Sword*, Vol. XVIII, no. 70 (Winter, 1990), pp. 1–16

Fitts, J., 'Newcastle's Mob', *Albion*, Vol. V, no. 1 (1973), pp. 41–9

Gain, M.F., 'The Stuart Papers at Windsor', *The Royal Stuart Society*, Occasional Paper no. XVII (1981)

Goldie, M., 'The Roots of True Whiggism, 1688–1694', *History of Political Thought*, Vol. I, no. 2 (1980), pp. 195–236

Grancsay, S.V., 'A Stocking Knife Associated with James II of England', in Grancsay, S.V., *Arms and Armour. Essays . . . from the Metropolitan Museum of Art Bulletin, 1920–1964* (New York, 1986), pp. 82–3

Gregg, E., 'Was Queen Anne a Jacobite?', *History*, Vol. 57, no. 191 (Oct. 1972), pp. 358–75

Gregg, E., 'New Light on the Authorship of the "Life of James II"', *English Historical Review*, Vol. CVIII (October, 1993), pp. 947–65

Harrington, P., 'Images of the Boyne', *The Irish Sword*, Vol. XVIII, no. 70 (Winter, 1990), pp. 57–61

Hertzler, J.R., 'Who Dubbed it "The Glorious Revolution"', *Albion*, Vol. XIX (1987), pp. 579–85

Hutton, R., 'The Glory of 1688', *The Royal Stuart Society*, Occasional Paper no. XLVI (1995)

Jones, J.R., 'James II's Whig Collaborators', *Historical Journal*, Vol. III, no. 1 (1960), pp. 65–73

McInnes, A., 'When was the English Revolution?', *History*, Vol. 67, no. 221 (Oct. 1982), pp. 377–92

McKie, D., 'James Duke of York, F.R.S.', *Notes and Records of the Royal Society of London*, Vol. XIII (1958), pp. 6–18

McLynn, P., 'Factionalism among the Exiles in France: The Case of Chevalier Ramsay and Bishop Atterbury', *The Royal Stuart Society*, Occasional Paper no. XXXIII (1989)

Melvin, P., 'Irish Troop Movements and James II's Army in 1688', *The Irish Sword*, Vol. X (1982), pp. 87–105

Melvin, P., 'Irish Soldiers and Plotters in Williamite England', *The Irish Sword*, Vol. XIII (1985), pp. 256–67, & Vol. XIV, pp. 271–86

Miller, J., '"Abdicate" and "Contract" in the Glorious Revolution', *The Historical Journal*, Vol. XXV (1982), pp. 541–55

Miller, J., 'The potential for Absolutism in Later Stuart England', *History*, Vol. 69, no. 226 (June, 1984), pp. 187–207

Mitchell, A.A., 'The Revolution of 1688 and the Flight of James II', *History Today*, Vol. XV (1965), pp. 496–504

Mullett, C.F., 'A Case of Allegiance: William Sherlock and the Revolution of 1688', *Huntington Library Quarterly*, Vol. 10 (Nov. 1946), pp. 83–104

Mullett, C.F., 'Religion, Politics, and Oaths in the Glorious Revolution', *Review of Politics*, Vol. X (Oct. 1948), pp. 462–74

Mulloy, S., 'French eye-witnesses of the Boyne', *The Irish Sword*, Vol. XV (1982–3), pp. 105–11

Mulloy, S., 'French Engineers with the Jacobite Army in Ireland, 1689–91', *The Irish Sword*, Vol. XV (1983), pp. 222–32

Mulloy, S., 'The French and the Jacobite War in Ireland, 1689–91', *The Irish Sword*, Vol. XVIII, no. 70 (Winter, 1990), pp. 17–31

Murtagh, H., 'Galway and the Jacobite War', *The Irish Sword*, Vol. XII (1975–6), pp. 1–14

Murtagh, D. & H., 'The Irish Jacobite Army, 1689–91', *The Irish Sword*, Vol. XVIII (1990), pp. 30–48

Nenner, H., 'The Traces of Shame in England's Glorious Revolution', *History*, Vol. LXXIII (1988), pp. 238–47

O'Carroll, D., 'An Indifferent Good Post: The Battlefield of the Boyne', *The Irish Sword*, Vol. XVIII, no. 70 (Winter, 1990), pp. 49–56

Parsons, R.F.J., 'The Role of Jacobitism in the Modern World', *The Royal Stuart Society*, Occasional Paper no. XXVIII (1986)

Petrie, C., 'James the Second. A Revaluation', *Nineteenth Century*, Vol. 114 (October, 1933), pp. 475–84

Plumb, J.H., & Simpson, A., 'A Letter of William, Prince of Orange, to Danby on the Flight of James II', *Cambridge Historical Journal*, Vol. V, no. 1 (1935), pp. 107–8

Pocock, J.G.A., 'The Fourth English Civil War: Dissolution, Desertion and Alternative Histories in the Glorious Revolution', *Government and Opposition*, Vol. XXIII (1988), pp. 151–66

Porteous, T.C., 'New Light on the Lancashire Jacobite Plot, 1692–1694', *Transactions of the Lancashire and Cheshire Antiquarian Society*, Vol. L (1934–5), pp. 1–64

Porter, J.R., 'The Non-Juring Bishops', *The Royal Stuart Society*, Occasional Paper no. IV (1973)

Reid, S., 'Killiecrankie, 1689', *Partizan Press* pamphlet (Leigh-on-Sea, 1989)

Sachse, W.L., 'The Mob in the Revolution of 1688', *Journal of British Studies*, Vol. IV (1964), pp. 23–40

Scott, D.G., 'Sacredness of Majesty: The English Benedictines and the Cult of King James II', *The Royal Stuart Society*, Occasional Paper no. XXIII (1984)

Scott, D.G., 'The Collector: A Look at Benedictine Archives through the Eyes of Bro. Benet Weldon, 1674–1713', *Catholic Archives*, Vol. VI (1986), pp. 25–42 & 53

Scott, D.G., 'John Betham et l'Education du Prince de Galles', *Revue de la Bibliotheque Nationale*, no. 46 (1992), pp. 31–8

Schwoerer, L., 'Women and the Glorious Revolution', *Albion*, Vol. XVIII (1986), pp. 197–218

Schwoerer, L., 'Celebrating the Glorious Revolution, 1689–1989', *Albion*, Vol. XXII, no. 1 (1990), pp. 1–20

Scouller, R.E., 'The Mutiny Acts', *Journal of the Society for Army Historical Research*, Vol. L, no. 201 (Spring, 1972), pp. 42–5

Simms, J.G., 'Eye-Witnesses of the Boyne', *The Irish Sword*, Vol. VI (1963), pp. 15–27

Simms, J.G., 'Marlborough's Siege of Cork, 1690', *The Irish Sword*, Vol. IX (1969–70), pp. 113–23

Simms, J.G., 'James II and the Siege of Derry', *The Irish Sword*, Vol. III (1957–8), pp. 286–7

Simms, J.G., 'The Siege of Derry', *The Irish Sword*, Vol. VI (1963–4), pp. 221–33

Simms, J.G., 'Schomberg at Dundalk, 1689', *The Irish Sword*, Vol. X (1971–2), pp. 14–25

Southorn, J., 'Mary of Modena, Queen Consort of James II and VII', *The Royal Stuart Society*, Occasional Paper no. XL (1992)

Steele, I., 'Governors or Generals?: A Note on Martial Law and the Revolution of 1689 in English America', *William and Mary Quarterly*, Vol. XLVI (1989), pp. 304–14

Stewart, J., 'The Great Orange Myth. The Williamite War in Ireland, 1688–1692', *Communist Party of Ireland* pamphlet (Dublin, 1990)

Szechi, D., 'Mythistory versus History: The Fading of the Revolution of 1688', *The Historical Journal*, Vol. XXXIII (1990), pp. 143–53

Taylor, S., '"Plus ca change?" . . . New Perspectives on the Revolution of 1688', *The Historical Journal*, Vol. XXXVII, no. 2 (1994), pp. 457–70

Zon, B., 'Jacobitism and Liturgy in the Eighteenth Century English Catholic Church: An Unlikely Marriage', *The Royal Stuart Society*, Occasional Paper no. XLI (1992)

Index